Migration und Globalisierung
in Zeiten des Umbruchs

Friedrich Altenburg, Anna Faustmann,
Thomas Pfeffer, Isabella Skrivanek
(Hrsg.)

Migration und Globalisierung in Zeiten des Umbruchs

Festschrift für
Gudrun Biffl

Bibliographische Information der Deutschen Nationalbibliothek: Die Deutsche Nationalbibliothek verzeichnet diese Publikation in der Deutschen Nationalbibliografie; detaillierte bibliografische Daten sind im Internet über http://dnb.d-nb.de abrufbar.

© 2017

Dieses Werk ist lizensiert unter der Creative Commons Lizenz Namensnennung 4.0 International (https://creativecommons.org/licenses/by/4.0/)

Die in der Publikation geäußerten Ansichten liegen in der Verantwortung der Autor/inn/en und geben nicht notwendigerweise die Meinung der Donau-Universität Krems wieder.

Verlag: Edition Donau-Universität Krems
Herstellung: tredition GmbH, Hamburg
ISBN Taschenbuch: 978-3-903150-21-8
ISBN e-Book: 978-3-903150-23-2

Kontakt:
Department für Migration und Globalisierung
Donau-Universität Krems
www.donau-uni.ac.at/mig
migration@donau-uni.ac.at

Coverfoto: Cem Firat
Satz: Thomas Pfeffer
Umschlaggestaltung: Michael Zehndorfer, Marion Lanser

Zitiervorschlag: Friedrich Altenburg, Anna Faustmann, Thomas Pfeffer, Isabella Skrivanek (Hg.) (2017) Migration und Globalisierung in Zeiten des Umbruchs. Festschrift für Gudrun Biffl. Krems (Edition Donau-Universität Krems).

Inhaltsverzeichnis

ZUM GELEIT

Friedrich Faulhammer
Gudrun Biffl und die Donau-Universität Krems 11

Heinz Fassmann
Gudrun Biffl und die Schnittstelle Wissenschaft und Politik 13

Jean-Christophe Dumont, Thomas Liebig
Gudrun Biffl and the OECD 15

Friedrich Altenburg, Anna Faustmann, Thomas Pfeffer, Isabella Skrivanek
**Migration und Globalisierung
in Zeiten des Umbruchs. Zur Einleitung** 17

TEIL 1:
KONZEPTIONELLE ÜBERLEGUNGEN ZUR MIGRATIONSFORSCHUNG

Rainer Bauböck
**Perspektivische Verschiebungen:
Migration und Mobilität im Zeitalter der Globalisierung** 29

Martin Ruhs
**Making linkages in migration research:
"Migrants" and "mobile citizens" in the European Union** 37

Thomas Pfeffer
**Migration in der Weltgesellschaft:
Welche Forschungsgegenstände beobachtet die Soziologie?** 47

TEIL 2:
INTERNATIONALE ÖKONOMISCHE UND POLITISCHE PERSPEKTIVEN

Philip Martin
**Managing Migration:
Recruiters and low-skill Migrants** 65

Matthias Czaika
„Global Competition for Talent":
eine migrationspolitische Herausforderung 83

Daniela Bobeva
Migrant remittances and
macroeconomic developments in the source countries 101

Joe Isaac
Inter-Cultural and other Forces in the Transfer of
Human Resource Management and
Industrial Relations Practices under Globalization 115

Bernhard Perchinig
The Challenge of Migration for Crisis and Disaster Management:
Key concepts and recommendations 135

Ewald Walterskirchen
Europa am Scheideweg
zwischen Integration und Re-Nationalisierung? 155

Teil 3:
Auswirkungen der Fluchtmigration

Johannes Berger, Ludwig Strohner
Ökonomische und fiskalische Auswirkungen
der Fluchtmigration in Österreich 169

Friedrich Heckmann
Lebensverläufe unbegleiteter minderjähriger
Flüchtlinge in Deutschland 191

Vedran Dzihic, Cengiz Günay
Die Rückkehr der Grenzen:
Globale Trends, regionale Spiegelungen 209

Teil 4:
Migration und Arbeitsmarkt

Peter Huber, Thomas Horvath, Julia Bock-Schappelwein
Integration von Migrant/inn/en in Österreich:
Wo steht Österreich im internationalen Vergleich? 219

Stephan Marik-Lebeck, Josef Kytir
**Längsschnittanalyse der Erwerbsverläufe der
Migrationskohorten 2010, 2011 und 2012** 237

August Gächter
**Qualifikationen aus dem Ausland und die Schwierigkeit,
sie adäquat in Beschäftigung zu bringen** 253

TEIL 5:
MIGRATION UND BILDUNG

Lorenz Lassnigg, Mario Steiner
**Wer zu spät kommt? Zuwanderung als ‚blinder Fleck'
in der österreichischen Bildungspolitik** 277

Gülay Ateş, Christoph Reinprecht
**Reziproke Lerneffekte:
Einsichten aus einem europäischen Projekt der Erwachsenenbildung
mit ethnischen Minderheiten und MigrantInnen** 301

Manfred Zentner
Young people's participation in the globalised world 315

TEIL 6:
MIGRATION UND SOZIALE UNGLEICHHEIT

Karin Heitzmann
**Armut und Ausgrenzung von Migrant/inn/en in Österreich:
Aktuelle Situation und Entwicklungen zwischen 2010 und 2016** 333

Thomas Leoni
**Migrationspolitik als Prüfstein
des sozialinvestiven Wohlfahrtsstaats** 349

Hedwig Lutz, Christine Mayrhuber
Bedingungslose Grundeinkommen und Globalisierung 365

Johann Bacher
**Polarisierungstendenzen in Österreich?
Ergebnisse einer latenten Klassenanalyse
der Einstellungen zur Immigration** 379

Tania Berger
Sozialraum, Wohnen und Migration 397

TEIL 7:
INTER- UND TRANSDISZIPLINÄRE BEITRÄGE ZUM THEMA MIGRATION

Gerald Steiner
**Agriculture-dominated Societies, Climate Change and Migration:
a Case for Transdisciplinarity** 411

Peter Parycek, Margarita Fourer, Shefali Virkar, Dino Pitoski,
Gabriela Viale Pereira, Thomas J. Lampoltshammer
**Impact of Information and Communication Technologies and their
Application to Challenges of Migration** 417

İnci Dirim
**‚Jemand hat Migrationshintergrund' oder
‚Jemand hat *einen* Migrationshintergrund'?
Eine zuschreibungskritisch-linguistische Reflexion** 435

Aga Trnka-Kwiecinski
**Wenn die Hüllen fallen - Ein Essay zum Verhältnis von
Geschlecht und Macht in Orient und Okzident** 441

Autorinnen und Autoren 457

Gudrun Biffl: Lebenslauf und Publikationen 465

ZUM GELEIT

Gudrun Biffl und die Donau-Universität Krems

Seit nun 22 Jahren besteht die Donau-Universität Krems als öffentliche Universität für Weiterbildung; die letzten 13 Jahre davon hat Universitäts-Professorin Doktorin Gudrun Biffl die Arbeit unserer Universität wesentlich geprägt, zunächst als Universitätsrätin (2004 bis 2007), dann als Professorin, Dekanin und Departmentleiterin.

Als wir vor zwei Jahren, 2015, unser 20-jähriges Bestehen als Universität begangen haben, suchten zeitgleich rund eine Million Flüchtlinge den Weg nach Europa – eine Entwicklung, die noch heute zu den zentralen Herausforderungen unserer Zeit gilt. Als Universität für Weiterbildung arbeitet die Donau-Universität Krems mit ihrer Expertise in Lehre und Forschung an der Bewältigung solcher aktuellen sowie zukünftiger gesellschaftlicher Herausforderungen. Auf Basis dessen kann man Gudrun Biffls zentrale Themen Migration und Integration als beispielgebend für die Positionierung unseres Hauses sehen. So begreift die Donau-Universität Krems den demographischen Wandel, der sich in einer veränderten Altersstruktur und in einer durch Migrationen beförderten Vielfalt ausdrückt, als Herausforderung und Chance gleichermaßen und sieht dabei ihre gesellschaftspolitische Aufgabe in der Förderung der Diversität und sozialen Inklusion.

Als Donau-Universität Krems sind wir stolz darauf, als erste österreichische Universität einen spezifischen Lehrstuhl für Migration, Integration und Sicherheit eingerichtet zu haben. In diesem Kontext sehen wir es auch als besondere Verantwortung, eine hohe soziale Durchlässigkeit in der Lehre zu ermöglichen, sowie Themen zur Gleichbehandlung und Antidiskriminierung in Lehre und Forschung einzubinden. Gerade die Lehrgänge am Department für Migration und Globalisierung sind in ihrer Studierendenstruktur Ausdruck gesellschaftlicher Diversität in unserem Land. Gudrun Biffl hat dabei in Lehre und Forschung einen Bogen von der Wirtschaft bis zur Religion gespannt und dafür Sorge getragen, das Thema Migration interdisziplinär und aus vielen Perspektiven heraus zu betrachten.

In ihrer Eigenschaft als Dekanin und Forscherin hatte Gudrun Biffl wesentlichen Anteil an dem Aufgreifen dieser gesellschaftlichen Herausforderungen in universitären Prozessen und in ihren vielfältigen Kontakten zu den wesentlichen gesellschaftlichen und politischen Stakeholdern. Die wissenschaftliche Befassung mit Migration und Integration ist für sie dabei nicht isoliert und losgelöst, sondern steht in einer konstanten Wechselbeziehung zur Gesellschaft. Gudrun Biffl war die gesellschaftliche Wirksamkeit der Arbeit des Departments immer ein großes Anliegen und verstand dies auch als bewusstes Engagement ihrer selbst, wie auch ihrer Mitarbeiterinnen und Mitarbeiter. Das von ihr ins Leben gerufene Dialogforum Migration und Integration ist beispielsweise eine der vielzähligen Initiativen des Departments und versteht sich als Ort der Vernetzung und des Austausches zwischen Wissenschaft, Politik, Verwaltung und zivilgesellschaftlicher Praxis.

Gudrun Biffls mediale Präsenz unterstreicht diese gesellschaftliche Anbindung und machte sie zu einer sichtbaren Botschafterin unseres Hauses.

Ihr Status als OECD Berichterstatterin, als Mitglied des ExpertInnenrates für Integration und Vorsitzende des Statistikrates sind ebenso Belege für ihre breite Anerkennung wie die ihr verliehenen Auszeichnungen. Hervorzuheben sind insbesondere das Goldene Ehrenzeichen der Republik Österreich und der Käthe Leichter Staatspreis für Frauenforschung, Geschlechterforschung und Gleichstellung in der Arbeitswelt, die sie beide 2009 erhielt.

Weniger öffentlich wahrnehmbar, aber von ebenso großer Bedeutung für die Donau Universität Krems war Gudrun Biffls Wirken nach innen: Als Mitglied des Senats, Vorsitzende des Ehrungsausschusses und stellvertretende Vorsitzende des Arbeitskreises für Gleichbehandlungsfragen hat Gudrun Biffl ihre Standpunkte stets eingebracht und zu fruchtbaren Diskursen über Departmentgrenzen hinweg beigetragen. Nicht zuletzt das PhD Programm Migration Studies ist besonderer Ausdruck eines über Fächergrenzen blickenden Zugangs. Des Weiteren war sie als eine der ersten Professorinnen an der Donau-Universität Krems eine wesentliche Wegbereiterin hin zum näher rückenden Ziel eines ausgewogenen Frauenanteils in Führungspositionen, dessen Erreichung jedoch nach wie vor kontinuierlicher Förderungsschritte bedarf.

Als Rektor der Donau-Universität begrüße ich diese Festschrift als eine ausdrückliche Würdigung für Gudrun Biffl durch die wissenschaftliche Community. Ich danke Gudrun Biffl für ihr prägendes Wirken, die vielen Diskurse sowie für die geordnete Übergabe ihres Departments an ihren Nachfolger, Univ.-Prof. Dr. Mathias Czaika, und hoffe, dass die Verbindung zu unserem Haus weiter wirkt im Sinne des gesellschaftlichen Wandels, der uns insgesamt begleiten wird.

Mit den besten Wünschen für Gudrun Biffls weitere Wege,

Friedrich Faulhammer
Rektor der Donau-Universität Krems

Gudrun Biffl und die Schnittstelle Wissenschaft und Politik

Auf der Homepage der Donau-Universität Krems wurde im Personenverzeichnis beim Eintrag „Gudrun Biffl" der Zusatz „in Ruhe seit 30. September 2017" hinzugefügt. Dieser Zusatz bezieht sich auf die dienstrechtliche Stellung, keine Frage, denn eine aktuelle Beschreibung des tatsächlichen Tuns und Handelns von Gudrun Biffl kann es wohl nicht sein und eine normative Aufforderung des Rektorats, sich in den Zustand der Ruhe zu begeben, schließe ich aus. Gudrun Biffl ist aus dem aktiven Dienst als §98-Professorin ausgeschieden, in den Ruhestand wird sie sich in absehbarer Zeit noch nicht begeben und soll sie auch nicht. Sie hat eine beachtliche Breite an Wissen und Kompetenz aufgebaut, die für eine gelernte Ökonomin fast schon untypisch ist und diese Breite ist weiterhin gefragt. Erfolgreiche Ökonomen – männlich und weiblich – wissen unglaublich viel über einen vergleichsweise engen Ausschnitt der wirtschaftlichen und gesellschaftlichen Realität, Gudrun Biffl blieb dagegen immer thematisch breit und kann Fragen zum Arbeitsmarkt, zu Migration und Integration, zu Bildung und Ausbildung ebenso bearbeiten wie jene aus der Familien- und Genderforschung.

Anfang der 1990er-Jahre traf ich erstmals Gudrun Biffl. Ich war damals am Institut für Demographie der Österreichischen Akademie der Wissenschaften tätig und habe mit Rainer Münz viel über Migration gearbeitet. Das war damals – eigentlich wie heute – ein wichtiges und politisch umkämpftes Thema. Die FPÖ lancierte das Volksbegehren „Österreich zuerst" und die Zivilgesellschaft reagierte mit dem Lichtermeer auf die wachsende Skepsis der Bevölkerung gegenüber Zuwanderung. Rainer Münz und ich waren als Wissenschaftler herausgefordert, faktenbasierte Informationen bereitzustellen, auch um das Gefühl „Österreich wird überflutet" relativieren zu können. Bei einem Mittagessen in einem brasilianischen Restaurant – warum dieser Ort ausgewählt wurde, entzieht sich meiner Erinnerung – traf ich erstmals Gudrun Biffl und wir besprachen die Datensituation in Österreich und diskutierten die Möglichkeiten der Verbesserung. Informationen über Migration waren in den 1990er-Jahren mehr Schätzung als valide Ergebnisse einer Statistik. Die Situation hat sich seit damals deutlich verbessert und Österreich kann heute auf eine zuverlässige Migrationsstatistik zurückgreifen, und dennoch ist Gudrun Biffl auch heute noch, 25 Jahre nach unserer ersten Begegnung, an der Verbesserung der Datensituation interessiert und kann dies inzwischen als Vorsitzende des Statistikrates der Statistik Austria auch aktiv fördern.

In den folgenden Jahren und Jahrzehnten traf ich Gudrun Biffl immer wieder bei unterschiedlichen Gelegenheiten und in unterschiedlichen Funktionen. Unsere wissenschaftlichen Interessen haben einen großen Überlappungsbereich und so ist es selbstverständlich, dass man sich in dem kleinen Land Österreich immer wieder über den Weg läuft. Die Begegnungen waren immer durch Freundlichkeit und gegenseitige Sympathie gekennzeichnet und unsere wissenschaftlichen Diskussionen blieben immer sachlich und zielorientiert. Regelmäßig traf ich Gudrun Biffl schließlich im 2009 gegründeten Expertenrat für Integration, der zuerst im Innen- und später im Außenministerium angesiedelt war. Gudrun Biffl ist – gemeinsam mit Thomas Oliva – für das Handlungsfeld „Arbeit und Beruf" zuständig. Sie entwickelten Pläne und Instrumente, um die arbeitsmarktbezogene Integration der Zugewanderten zu verbessern. Das System der dualen Ausbildung nahm dabei immer einen besonderen Stellenwert ein, weil es eine gelungene Brücke zwischen einer schulischen und berufspraktischen Ausbildung herstellt und junge Menschen mit Migrationshintergrund gleichsam automatisch in das Erwerbsleben integriert. Gudrun Biffl betonte darüber hinaus beispielsweise die Bedeutung der Produktionsschulen, der zeitlich begrenzten Förderung des Einstiegs von jugendlichen Langzeitarbeitslosen in den Arbeitsmarkt und den Ausbau flexibler Kinderbetreuung, um die niedrige Erwerbsquote der zugewanderten Frauen zu heben. Sie blieb mit ihren Plänen und Vorschlägen immer realistisch und hatte ein gutes Gefühl für das politisch Machbare. Sie forderte nicht die Weltverbesserung in einem Zuge und mit einer Maßnahme, sondern setzte sich für Ideen ein, mit deren Hilfe, schrittweise umgesetzt, die Vision einer offenen, liberalen und dennoch vom Leistungsgedanken getragenen Gesellschaft verwirklicht werden könnte. Dieser Realismus auf der einen Seite und das Streben nach einer übergeordneten Idee auf der anderen Seite waren die Basis unserer guten Zusammenarbeit, denn auch ich verfolge die Vision der offenen und liberalen Gesellschaft, in der Leistung zählt und die durch die gemeinsame Idee von Freiheit, Rechtsstaatlichkeit und Gleichberechtigung getragen wird.

Ich danke Gudrun Biffl für die produktive Zusammenarbeit im Expertenrat für Integration, aber auch für die Zusammenarbeit und Begegnung in anderen Gremien und für den von uns getragenen wissenschaftlichen Diskurs. Überraschenderweise gibt es trotz der inhaltlichen Überlappungsbereiche keine gemeinsame Publikation oder ein gemeinsam durchgeführtes Forschungsprojekt. Wäre nicht jetzt eine Gelegenheit dafür, wenn die unmittelbaren Lehraufgaben und institutionellen Verpflichtungen an der Donau-Universität weggefallen sind? Ad multos annos wünsche ich und auf ein gemeinsames Projekt oder Publikation freue ich mich!

Heinz Fassmann
Vorsitzender des Expertenrats für Integration

Gudrun Biffl and the OECD

Gudrun Biffl has been Austrian National Expert in the OECD's Expert Group on Migration for a full 40 years. The Expert group - known under its French acronym, SOPEMI, from *Système d'observation permanente des migrations* - was established in 1973. The core of SOPEMI has always been a group of widely-renowned national experts (correspondents) who prepare annual reports on the migration development in their countries. The original membership of SOPEMI consisted of eleven OECD member countries. In the following years, several more joined the group, and Austria joined in 1977. Gudrun was thus one of the first members of the group. She is also one of the longest-serving experts, together with UK correspondent John Salt. Upon the occasion of her 30th anniversary as correspondent for Austria, a small ceremony took place at the OECD in presence of the Austrian Ambassador.

The role of the Expert group has been to provide the OECD member countries with a mechanism for the timely sharing of information on international migration, the collection of migration statistics as well as the improvement of their comparability, and to serve the basis for the publication OECD annual report on international migration. Over time, the SOPEMI group has developed into a key source of up-to-date and first-hand information on past, current and emerging developments regarding migration. This domain has been a key priority area for the OECD ever since the organisation's establishment more than 50 years ago, as the membership of the OECD included both key sending and receiving countries of migration.

The core of Gudrun's work for the OECD was always to be one of the leading members of the expert group, which collected systematically information on migration trends and policies in the OECD member countries in order to identify emerging problems in international co-operation. The type of information that might be included in the report has been steadily refined over the years. In an attempt to enhance the comparability of national reports, during the 1980s the OECD Secretariat prepared a ‚grid' outlining the main topics deserving attention. Gudrun was always very reactive in responding to this, and also proposed new and emerging issues to the Secretariat. Gudrun certainly had her ‚pet topics' – irregular migration, free mobility, posted workers, gender issues, etc., but the list of topics of specific expertise is a long one.

As the process of international migration evolved and more countries joined SOPEMI, the scope of the annual report broadened. Today the network is a unique institution, global in scope. The basis for the annual SOPEMI report has always been its standard statistical tables on immigration, emigration and labour stocks and flows. Since the beginning, Gudrun has provided and co-ordinated the data collection for Austria. Her vast network in Austria was particularly useful in this context. Who would have managed to collect and get sense of the Austrian statistics if not Gudrun? Gradually a wider range of data have been collected and presented and major attempts made to improve comparability between countries. The inclusion of the four settlement countries (Australia, Canada, New Zealand and the United States) in the 1980s raised issues of comparability, especially in relation to the conceptual distinctions of migration movements (foreign-born/foreigners; permanent/temporary migration; family reunification/accompanying family) between participating countries and the set of statistical tables compiled. Although from the outset there were attempts to generalise, the preponderance of the case by case descriptive presentation continued. The growing number of countries within SOPEMI and the convergence of migration interests between countries required improvement of migration statistics as well as of their comparability. Gudrun has always been a supporter of this approach, and her help in obtaining comparability for the Austrian data was crucial.

Austria is a country in Central Europe, and few Austrians represent its position and history better than Gudrun, who has always been up-to-date not only of the developments in Austria, but also on the countries in Central and Eastern Europe. Not surprisingly, perhaps, she became friends with the SOPEMI experts from these countries, whose ‚integration' into the group has been close to her heart ever since the fall of the Iron Curtain. But Gudrun integrated virtually everybody. She did this with great joy and ease. Not only because her ‚culture generale' is very impressive, but also her linguistic skills – Russian, Hungarian, Spanish – not to mention her native German, English, and French *bien sûr*!

Gudrun Biffl was also during several years Austrian representative to the Working Party on Migration, one of the longest-standing working parties in the OECD. This is not surprising: Gudrun was ‚Ms Migration in Austria' in many positions, both nationally and internationally. She contributed to the organisation of a number seminars co-organised by the OECD, for example on immigrants and the labour market, on the labour market integration of immigrant women, on the link between migration and trade, and on migration in Central and Eastern Europe. All of this culminated in the joint organisation by the OECD and Gudrun in the Austrian Chancellery on „Migration, free trade and regional integration in Eastern Europe". What a fitting topic for Gudrun!

In addition to her contributions to the Expert group, Gudrun also provided her rich expertise for a number of reports, for example the 2013 evaluation of the Austrian labour migration system. And in her work, she always values the work of the OECD. Gudrun is a great Ambassador, both for Austria and for the OECD work on migration.

Jean-Christophe Dumont
Head of the OECD's International Migration Division

Thomas Liebig
Senior Migration Expert in the OECD's International Migration Division

Migration und Globalisierung in Zeiten des Umbruchs. Zur Einleitung

Friedrich Altenburg, Anna Faustmann, Thomas Pfeffer, Isabella Skrivanek

Wir leben in Zeiten des Umbruchs, was in vielfacher Hinsicht als Folge von Migration und Globalisierung beschrieben werden kann. Doch gleichzeitig sind diese beiden Phänomene auch selbst von Veränderungen betroffen.

Versteht man unter Globalisierung die Entwicklung eines Systems von multilateralen Institutionen, Regeln und Allianzen, das den Wiederaufbau von Europa nach dem zweiten Weltkrieg, die Abwicklung des Kommunismus sowjetischer Prägung und die Anbindung Chinas an die Weltwirtschaft als historisch erfolgreichstes Projekt zur Armutsbekämpfung, aber eben auch eine Zunahme von sozialer Ungleichheit und von regionalen Unterschieden im globalen Vergleich ermöglichte, dann ist diese Entwicklung multilateraler politischer Kooperationen mit dem Brexit, der Wahl Donald Trumps zum US-Präsidenten und einem internationalen Trend zur Re-Nationalisierung ins Stocken geraten. Man kann diese Veränderung der politischen Großwetterlage auch als ein Kippen der paradigmatischen Konfliktlinie im politischen Diskurs interpretieren, wodurch ein ‚new political divide' zwischen international offenen und national geschlossenen Gesellschaftskonzeptionen die traditionelle Dichotomie zwischen linken und rechten Positionen überlagert, einer Bruchlinie, die sich durch die meisten politischen Lager und Parteien zieht (economist, 2016). Gleichzeitig lässt sich – einer anderen Definition von Globalisierung folgend – behaupten, dass dieser Trend zur Re-Nationalisierung unter den Bedingungen sich intensivierender, weltweiter Kommunikations- und Beobachtungszusammenhänge in den meisten gesellschaftlichen Funktionsbereichen (z.B. Politik, Wirtschaft, Wissenschaft, Bildung, Sport, Kunst, etc.) erfolgt, also unter den Bedingungen einer kommunikativen Globalisierung, die Weltgesellschaft konstituiert.

Auch die Charakteristik von Migration und ihre Wahrnehmung in der Öffentlichkeit haben sich verändert. Gerade Österreich erlebte in den letzten Jahrzehnten mehrere Migrationsbewegungen (Ungarn-Krise 1956, Gastarbeiteranwerbung in den 1960er und 1970er Jahren, Transitmigration von politischen Flüchtlingen im Kalten Krieg, der Fall des Eisernen Vorhangs und die gewaltsame Auflösung Jugoslawiens in den 1990ern, Freizügigkeit innerhalb der EU v.a. seit der Osterweiterung 2004 und zuletzt Fluchtmigration, zugespitzt aufgrund der Syrienkrise). Aus dieser historischen Perspektive überrascht nicht mehr das Eintreten größerer Migrationsereignisse selbst, sondern nur mehr die Überraschung darüber. Trotzdem können auch Veränderung in der öffentlichen Wahrnehmung von Migration in Österreich und anderen (OECD)-Ländern konstatiert werden, die von der Solidarität mit (v.a. europäischen) Flüchtlingen, über die Erwartung wirtschaftlicher Belebung durch erhoffte Beseitigung von Arbeitskräftemangel bis hin zur Akzeptanz der Personenfreizügigkeit als Voraussetzung und Nebeneffekt der EU-Mitgliedschaft reichen. Aber erst der relativ rasche Anstieg der Fluchtmigration (bzw. einem ‚mixed flow' aus außereuropäischen Ländern) der letzten Jahre, besonders in Zusammenhang mit der Syrienkrise, und der von manchen Akteuren verbreitete Eindruck eines Verlusts kultureller Identität und staatlicher Kontrolle machte Migration zu einem bestimmenden Thema in der politischen Auseinandersetzung, das Wahlen entscheiden und den Zusammenhalt der Europäischen Union gefährden kann. So weist eine Eurobarometer Umfrage für 2015 Migration als das bei weitem größte wahrgenommene Problem aus, weit vor Terrorismus oder den Sorgen um die Entwicklung der Wirtschaft (TNS Opinion & Social, 2015).

„Der gesellschaftspolitische Stellenwert des Gegenstandes und die enorme öffentliche Nachfrage nach Antworten" (Kalter, 2008, S. 12) bestimmte auch die Entwicklung der Migrationsforschung. Aufbauend auf US-amerikanischen Vorarbeiten lässt sich die Entstehung der Migrationsforschung im deutschsprachigen Raum in den 1970er Jahren verorten. Vor allem in ihren Anfängen orientierte sie sich stark an nationalstaatlichen Problemfeldern und Handlungserfordernissen, sowie an tagespolitischen Ereignissen, und versuchte, sehr praxisorientierte Antworten und Lösungsvorschläge zu entwickeln (Kalter, 2008, S. 11f). Dabei ging es häufig um Kosten-/Nutzenerwägungen in Bezug auf ArbeitsmigrantInnen, um Fragen der sozialen Ungleichheit und der kulturellen Differenz, v.a. in Hinblick auf Integration in nationale Wohlfahrtsstaaten. Erst mit der Zeit verschob sich der Blick zu internationalen Vergleichen und zu transnationalen Betrachtungsweisen. (Bommes, 2003, S. 42 f). War die Migrationsforschung in ihren Anfängen noch überwiegend *„angewandt-praktisch"* orientiert, so hat sich in der Zwischenzeit *„das Potential einer grundlagenorientierten und theoriegeleiteten empirischen Migrationsforschung enorm vergrößert"* (Kalter, 2008, S. 12). Gerade in Zeiten des Umbruchs, in denen die Gesellschaftsrelevanz von Migrationsforschung immer offensichtlicher wird, aber andererseits auch die Stellung von Wissenschaft unter Druck kommt (Stichwort: ‚post-truth politics'), gewinnt Grundlagenorientierung und Theorie besondere Bedeutung. Beides ist essentiell, sowohl für die Profilierung der Migrationsforschung in der interdisziplinären Zusammenarbeit, als auch in transdisziplinären Projekten für die Aufrechterhaltung einer eigenständigen Position gegenüber den Interessen involvierter Akteure der Praxis. Grundlagenorientierung und Theorie sind wesentliche Voraussetzung dafür, um die Wissenschaftlichkeit und die Faktenorientierung von Migrationsforschung auch in diesem in der Öffentlichkeit oft heißumkämpften Bereich aufrechterhalten zu können.

Für uns HerausgeberInnen gibt es aber noch einen weiteren Umbruch, der für die Erstellung dieses Sammelbandes konstituierend ist: Gudrun Biffl, Pionierin der österreichischen Migrationsforschung und Gründerin des Departments für Migration und Globalisierung, übergab im September 2017 die Leitung des Departments und emeritierte als Professorin. Als MitarbeiterInnen am Department bietet uns die vorliegende Festschrift nicht nur die Gelegenheit, unsere Chefin, Mentorin und Freundin zu ehren, sondern auch einen Anlass, um über die Fundamente unserer Arbeit nachzudenken, die von Gudrun Biffl gelegt wurden. Gudrun Biffl war als Ökonomin mit den Schwerpunkten Arbeitsmarkt, Bildungs- und Sozialpolitik schon früh von der besonderen Bedeutung von Migration überzeugt. Sie erkannte den Facettenreichtum des Themas und die Weitläufigkeit des Forschungsfeldes und reagierte folgerichtig mit dem Aufbau vielfältiger interdisziplinärer Kooperationen. In ihrem unbändigen Gestaltungswillen entwickelte sie zahlreiche transdisziplinäre Projekte mit Akteuren der Politik, der öffentlichen Verwaltung und der Zivilgesellschaft. Nicht zuletzt das von Gudrun Biffl ins Leben gerufene Dialogforum Migration – Integration[1] ist Ausdruck ihrer Bemühungen, den intensiven Austausch zwischen den genannten Bereichen zu ermöglichen. Und bei aller lokalen Verankerung im österreichischen Kontext hat sie immer in globalen Zusammenhängen gedacht und die internationale Vernetzung gesucht, was zu ihrer langjährigen Kooperation mit der OECD und zu vielen internationalen Forschungsaufenthalten führte.

Wir haben versucht, möglichst viele dieser zahlreichen Kontakte aus Gudrun Biffls Forschungskarriere anzusprechen, um auf diese Weise eine Annäherung an ihre reichhaltigen Forschungsinteressen und Netzwerke zu bekommen. Der Erfolg unserer Anfrage an Gudruns Netzwerke spricht für sich: 48 AutorInnen haben auf 482 Seiten insgesamt 28 Beiträge und drei Geleitworte verfasst. Die Beiträge dieser Festschrift gliedern sich in sieben Kapitel und werden durch ein Verzeichnis der AutorInnen, sowie dem wissenschaftlichen Werdegang und die Publikationsliste Gudrun Biffls ergänzt.

Teil 1: Konzeptionelle Überlegungen zur Migrationsforschung

Den ersten Teil dieses Sammelbandes bilden Beiträge, die sich unterschiedlichen spezifischen konzeptionellen Fragen der Migrationsforschung widmen.

Rainer Bauböck geht in seinem Beitrag von der Feststellung aus, dass die Migrationsforschung in weiten Teilen von einem starken Fokus auf die Perspektive der Aufnahmestaaten gekennzeichnet ist, und argumentiert eine Verlagerung dieser Betrachtungsweise hin in Richtung auf einen reflektierten Wechsel zwischen einer transnationalen Makroperspektive und einer biographischen Mikroperspektive.

Martin Ruhs plädiert im nächsten Beitrag für eine stärkere Verknüpfung von Theorie und Empirie sowie eine Verbindung disziplinärer und themenspezifischer Zugänge in der Migrationsforschung. Er sieht darin einen wichtigen Weg, um innovative Analyse hervorzubringen, die sowohl zur wissenschaftlichen Auseinandersetzung als auch zur evidenzbasierten Debatte und Politikgestaltung rund um Fragen der Migration beitragen. Seine Überlegungen führt er am Beispiel einer

---

[1] http://www.dialogforum-integration.at/

konzeptionellen Verbindung von Mobilität von EU-BürgerInnen und Migration von Drittstaatsangehörigen aus.

Der Beitrag von *Thomas Pfeffer* beschäftigt sich schließlich mit der Einbettung von Migration in das systemtheoretische Konzept der Weltgesellschaft. Diese Betrachtung führt einen theoretischen Analyserahmen für Migrationsphänomene ein, der auch sozialstrukturellen Voraussetzungen und Folgen internationaler Migration stärker Rechnung trägt, als die vorrangige Betrachtung der Lebenswelten von MigrantInnen.

Teil 2: Internationale ökonomische und politische Perspektiven

Der zweite Teil des vorliegenden Sammelbandes befasst sich mit internationalen Perspektiven auf Migration und Globalisierung, wobei ökonomische und politische Aspekte im Vordergrund stehen.

Philip Martin beschäftigt sich in seinem Beitrag mit internationaler Arbeitsmigration im niedrigen Qualifikationssegment und beleuchtet die Rolle von ArbeitsvermittlerInnen und Anwerbern (*recruiters*) als Intermediäre zwischen ArbeiterInnen in einem Land und Arbeitsplätzen in einem anderen. Seine Betrachtungen zeigen auf, dass gerade niedrig qualifizierte ArbeitsmigrantInnen oftmals bereit sind, deutlich höhere Kosten für internationale Arbeitsvermittlung als gesetzlich festgelegt zu entrichten. Um die Migrationskosten insbesondere im niedrig qualifizierten Bereich entsprechend gering zu halten, spielen staatliche Anreizmodelle für internationale Arbeitsvermittlungen eine wichtige Rolle.

Der Beitrag von *Mathias Czaika* widmet sich der Migration hochqualifizierter Arbeitskräfte und veranschaulicht insbesondere die Bedeutung dieser Form der Migration für beteiligte Ökonomien. Ein Überblick über migrationspolitische Maßnahmen zur Anwerbung hochqualifizierter ArbeitsmigrantInnen zeigt die Intensivierung dieser Aktivitäten vor allem in den letzten beiden Dekaden und den damit verbundenen internationalen Wettbewerb um Talente auf. Der Beitrag schließt mit grundlegenden migrationspolitischen Empfehlungen zur Erhöhung der Effizienz des globalen Arbeitsmarktes für Hochqualifizierte.

Daniela Bobeva analysiert aktuelle Entwicklungen der Geldtransfers durch MigrantInnen. Im Vordergrund steht dabei die Rolle der Aufnahmeländer. Anhand einer Analyse verschiedener makroökonomischer Indikatoren kann gezeigt werden, dass Inflation, Arbeitslosigkeit und Lohnniveau in den Aufnahmeländern der MigrantInnen einen signifikanten Einfluss auf die Rücküberweisungen von MigrantInnen in ihre Herkunftsländer haben.

Inwiefern Globalisierungsprozesse unterschiedliche Managementansätze und -techniken beeinflussen, ist Inhalt des Beitrags von *Joe Isaac*. Er identifiziert drei wesentliche Faktoren, die Transfer und Konvergenz von Managementprinzipien im Kontext der Globalisierung fördern, nämlich der steigende internationale Wettbewerb, technologische Innovationen sowie Übertragung von Personalmanagementprinzipien von multinationalen Unternehmen auch auf ihre Niederlassungen.

Gleichzeitig zeigt der Beitrag auf, dass kulturelle Unterschiede der Konvergenz von Managementprinzipien entgegenwirken können.

Bernhard Perchinig behandelt in seinem Artikel die Herausforderungen für Krisen- und Katastrophenmanagement, die in Zusammenhang mit Migration entstehen. Er betont die Bedeutung der Sensibilisierung und Inklusion von MigrantInnen in Bereitschaftsplanung und Katastrophenvorsorge und identifiziert den Zugang von MigrantInnen zu allgemeinen und mobilitätsbezogenen Leistungen und Zivilschutz als wichtigste Handlungsfelder.

Ewald Walterskirchen befasst sich mit der Frage der Weiterentwicklung der Europäischen Union und verdeutlicht die Polarisierung in Bezug auf die europäische Integration. Er behandelt die Frage, ob sich die Europäische Union hin zu einer politischen Union entwickeln, oder ob es eher zu einer Rückkehr zu wirtschaftlicher Zusammenarbeit kommen wird und welche Rolle dabei die innereuropäische Personenfreizügigkeit spielt.

Teil 3: Auswirkungen der Fluchtmigration

Im Zentrum des dritten Teils steht die Fluchtmigration mit ihren Auswirkungen auf Wohlfahrtsstaaten, zwischenstaatliche Politik und Lebensoptionen von geflüchteten Individuen.

Johannes Berger und *Ludwig Strohner* untersuchen die ökonomischen und fiskalischen Effekte dieser Migration für Österreich. Auf Basis von Modellberechnungen treffen sie Aussagen zu Beschäftigung und Arbeitslosenquote bis 2020: Demnach steigen sowohl Beschäftigung wie auch Arbeitslosigkeit, wobei sich Wirtschaft und Staatshaushalt nach einem negativen Netto-Effekt in den Folgejahren wieder erholen.

Mit den individuellen Auswirkungen traumatischer Fluchtmigration befasst sich *Friedrich Heckmann* am Beispiel von unbegleiteten minderjährigen Flüchtlingen in Deutschland. Trotz traumatisierender Erfahrungen und schwieriger Rahmenbedingungen kann Integration, gemessen an persönlicher Stabilität und schulischem Erfolg, unter der Voraussetzung einer intensiven Begleitung gelingen.

Auf die wiederbelebte „harte Grenze" um Europa, die definiert, wer „in" und wer „out" ist, nehmen *Vedran Dzihic* und *Cengiz Günay* in ihrem Beitrag Bezug. Sie konstatieren eine Abwertung des Internationalismus und einen schrittweisen Rückzug zum Nationalstaat, festgemacht an den Entwicklungen an der und um die sogenannte Westbalkanroute im Jahr 2015.

Teil 4: Migration und Arbeitsmarkt

Den Zusammenhängen von Migration und Arbeitsmarkt, denen insbesondere aus ökonomischer Perspektive eine wichtige Bedeutung zukommt, widmet sich das dritte Kapitel.

Im ersten Beitrag zum Arbeitsmarkt verorten *Peter Huber, Thomas Horvath* und *Julia Bock-Schappelwein* Österreich im internationalen Vergleich anhand der

Zaragoza-Indikatoren. Sie zeigen auf, dass Österreich bei der Integration von MigrantInnen in keiner der analysierten Dimensionen zu den internationalen Best-Practice-Beispielen zählt. Allerdings relativiert sich dieser Befund für die Arbeitsmarktintegration, wenn nur Länder mit ähnlicher Zuwanderungsstruktur wie Österreich berücksichtigt werden.

Stephan Marik-Lebeck und *Josef Kytir* nutzen die Möglichkeit der neu aufgebauten statistischen Register und führen eine Kohortenanalyse der Erwerbsverläufe der Neuzugezogenen der Jahre 2010-12 durch. Sie veranschaulichen, dass nur etwa die Hälfte der Neuzugezogenen länger als fünf Jahre in Österreich verbleibt. Die Erwerbsbeteiligung schließt innerhalb der ersten fünf Jahre auf das Niveau der jeweiligen Staatsangehörigkeitsgruppe auf, allerdings bei EU-Staatsangehörigen schneller als bei Drittstaatsangehörigen, sowie bei Männern schneller als bei Frauen.

Die Rolle ausländischer Qualifikationen im österreichischen Arbeitsmarktkontext behandelt *August Gächter* in seinem Beitrag basierend auf Volkszählungs- und Mikrozensusdaten. Er findet deutliche Hinweise, dass die Herkunft der Ausbildung und die Herkunft der Eltern Risikofaktoren für die adäquate Nutzung am österreichischen Arbeitsmarkt bleiben, auch wenn andere beschäftigungsrelevante Merkmale berücksichtigt werden.

Teil 5: Migration und Bildung

Das fünfte Kapitel befasst sich mit den Herausforderungen für Bildungsinstitutionen und die Struktur von Bildungsangeboten durch Migration.

Die Perspektiven auf Bildung im Kontext von Migration eröffnet der Beitrag von *Lorenz Lassnigg* und *Mario Steiner*. Im Mittelpunkt steht die Frage der Zuwanderung im Kontext der allgemeineren Strukturen und Praktiken der österreichischen Bildungspolitik. Die Autoren argumentieren, dass von den direkt in diesem Politikfeld engagierten AkteurInnen seit Jahrzehnten eine integrative Ausrichtung verfolgt wird, diese jedoch vor dem Hintergrund der allgemeinen politischen Verdrängung von Fragen der Zuwanderung nicht den nötigen Nachdruck bekommen hat.

Gülay Ateş und *Christoph Reinprecht* untersuchen basierend auf der wissenschaftlichen Begleitforschung zu Kursen der Persönlichkeits- und Allgemeinbildung für Angehörige migrantischer und ethnischer Minderheiten die Voraussetzungen und Rahmenbedingungen von (Erwachsenen-)Bildungsangeboten für nicht traditionelle TeilnehmerInnengruppen. Sie zeigen auf, dass niederschwellige und lebensnahe Lerninhalte sowohl Lernende als auch Lehrende in ihren Aktivitäten stärken und bereichern können. Allerdings besteht dabei großer Handlungsbedarf seitens der Kursanbieter für vertrauensbildendende Maßnahmen und für die Adaption von Lernzielen und -zwecken an die Gegebenheiten und Lernwelten der „neuen" Zielgruppen.

Eine außerschulische Bildungsperspektive nimmt der Beitrag von *Manfred Zentner* ein, in dem er der Frage nachgeht, wie die Beteiligungsmöglichkeiten von

Jugendlichen in einem von Globalisierung und Digitalisierung veränderten Rahmen erhöht werden können. Er argumentiert, dass die Digitalisierung neue Formen der Beteiligung und des Kontakts ermöglicht und die Globalisierungsprozesse veränderte, ortsunabhängige Zugehörigkeitsgefühle eröffnen. Allerdings benötigten diese neuen Möglichkeitsräume Verbesserungen im Bereich der Medien- und politischen Bildung.

Teil 6: Migration und soziale Ungleichheit

An verschiedene Aspekte der Ungleichheit, die sich aus den Analysen zur Integrationsfähigkeit des Arbeitsmarktes und des Bildungsbereichs in Kapitel vier und fünf ergeben, schließt das sechste Kapitel dieses Bandes an, das soziale Ungleichheit im Kontext von Migration aus verschiedenen Perspektiven betrachtet.

Karin Heitzmann untersucht die deutlich höhere Armuts- und Ausgrenzungsgefährdung von MigrantInnen in Österreich und skizziert Ursachenzusammenhänge für diese Benachteiligung. Sie zeigt auf, dass nicht allein bezahlte Erwerbsarbeit und die Erwerbsintensität im Haushalt wichtige Präventionsfaktoren gegen Armut sind, sondern generell die Qualität der Erwerbsarbeit (insbesondere die Höhe des Erwerbseinkommens).

Daran anknüpfend geht der Beitrag von *Thomas Leoni* der Frage nach, wie eine stärkere präventive, sozialinvestive Ausrichtung des Wohlfahrtsstaates im Kontext internationaler Migration erfolgen kann. Als zentrale Hebel nennt er Investitionen in Bildung und Humankapital, Unterstützung bei der Aktivierung und Integration am Arbeitsmarkt in allen Lebenslagen, sowie die Förderung von Chancengerechtigkeit bereits in frühen Lebensphasen.

Mit einem spezifischen Modell sozialpolitischer Absicherung, dem Bedingungslosen Grundeinkommen (BGE) im Kontext der Globalisierung, beschäftigen sich *Hedwig Lutz* und *Christine Mayrhuber*. Sie gehen der Frage nach, ob und inwieweit dieses als Instrument geeignet ist, gestiegene Einkommensungleichheiten und Unsicherheiten für ein Erwerbseinkommen abzufedern.

Ein Phänomen, das wie *Johann Bacher* in seinem Beitrag aufzeigt, auch im Kontext sozialer Ungleichheit zu verorten ist, sind Polarisierungstendenzen auf der Ebene der Einstellungen zur Immigration. Er untersucht die bei der letzten Bundespräsidentenwahl feststellbaren Polarisierungstendenzen mit Hilfe einer latenten Klassenanalyse und zeigt auf, dass schwache Polarisierungstendenzen bereits 2003 auffindbar sind und 2014/15 zugenommen haben. Seine Ergebnisse verdeutlichen, dass GegnerInnen von Zuwanderung häufiger unter angespannten finanziellen Verhältnissen leben und öfters von Arbeitslosigkeit betroffen sind.

Einen weiteren Aspekt sozialer Ungleichheit in Österreich, die Benachteiligung von MigrantInnen am Wohnungsmarkt, behandelt *Tania Berger* in ihrem Beitrag. Sie geht der Frage nach, wie Segregation von ethnischen Gruppen in räumlichen abgegrenzten Wohnbereichen entsteht und wie einkommensschwache Familien mit Migrationshintergrund mit leistbarem Wohnraum versorgt werden können.

Als Handlungsfelder nennt sie dabei u.a. den Ausbau von Beratung, Konfliktmanagement sowie Quartiersarbeit.

Teil 7: Inter- und transdisziplinäre Beiträge zum Thema Migration

Spezifische inter- und transdisziplinäre Perspektiven auf das komplexe Phänomen Migration werden in Kapitel sieben eingenommen.

Gerald Steiner nimmt in seinem Beitrag Bezug auf den Klima Wandel als einen der möglichen Treiber von krisenhafter Migration und begreift diesen als systemische Störung in einem komplexen Mensch-Umwelt System. Er argumentiert, dass Störungen dieser Art einer spezifischen transdisziplinären Zusammenarbeit von Wissenschaft, Wirtschaft und Gesellschaft bedürfen, um innovative Lösungen zu finden, mit denen man Herausforderungen dieser Dimension begegnen kann.

Auch *Peter Parycek, Margarita Fourer, Shefali Virkar, Dino Pitoski, Gabriela Viale Pereira,* und *Thomas J. Lampoltshammer* nehmen die Komplexität moderner Migrationsbewegungen als Ausgangspunkt für Ihre Überlegungen: Sozioökonomische und kulturelle Integration stellen für sie ebenso Herausforderungen dar wie die Menge an Daten, die moderne Gesellschaften generieren. Informations- und Kommunikationstechnologien wird bei der Bewältigung dieser Herausforderungen eine besondere Rolle zugewiesen.

In zwei weiteren Beiträgen setzen sich die Autorinnen mit dem Platz bzw. der Rolle auseinander, die bestimmten Gruppen durch symbolische Handlungen zugewiesen wird – in einem Fall durch die Sprache, in anderem Fall durch die Kleidung.

Aus einer linguistischen Perspektive geht *Inci Dirim* der Frage nach, welchen feinen Unterschied die Formulierung macht, ob jemand *einen* Migrationshintergrund oder einfach nur Migrationshintergrund hat, und hinterfragt damit zugleich die Konstruktion dieser in der Migrationsforschung derzeit gängigen Definition.

Aga Trnka-Kwiecinski greift die, auch durch die jüngste Gesetzesänderung aktuelle, Debatte um das Kopftuch auf und kommt in ihrem Beitrag zum Schluss, dass nicht nur das Kopftuch, sondern auch die zugleich stattfindende Refolklorisierung der Autochthonen Ausdruck nach wie vor bestehender ungleich verteilter Machtverhältnisse zwischen den Geschlechtern sind.

Die hier vorliegenden Beiträge geben einen ersten Eindruck von der großen Bandbreite von Gudrun Biffls Forschungsinteressen und Kooperationsbeziehungen, ohne sie auch nur annähernd vollständig abbilden zu können[2]. Deutlich wird etwa das große Gewicht auf ökonomische und politische Fragen der Migration, auf Fragen der Integration in Bildung und Arbeitsmarkt, aber auch auf Fragen der sozialen Ungleichheit. Unbeleuchtet blieb in diesem Band der Aspekt der kulturel-

---

[2] Eine etwas genauere Annäherung bietet etwa Gudrun Biffls Publikationsliste am Ende dieses Bandes.

len und religiösen Diversität, dem sich Gudrun Biffl schon lange mit großer Aufmerksamkeit widmet.

Die skizzierte Übersicht über die Fülle von Gudrun Biffls Forschungsinteressen und Netzwerke ermöglicht es uns auch, einige Entwicklungsfelder zu identifizieren, mit denen wir uns künftig verstärkt auseinandersetzen wollen, etwa dem internationalen Vergleich, der Perspektive der Herkunftsländer, aber auch der Untersuchung von Migration als transnationales Phänomen entlang von Wanderungsströmen, Netzwerken und Wertschöpfungsketten. Im klaren Bewusstsein der Fundamente, die Gudrun Biffl gelegt hat, werden wir uns diesen Herausforderungen in Zeiten des Umbruchs widmen.

Literatur

Bommes, M. (2003). Migration in der modernen Gesellschaft. *geographische revue, 5/2003*(2), 41–58.

economist. (2016, Juli). Globalisation and politics. The new political divide. *The Economist*. Abgerufen von https://www.economist.com/news/leaders/21702750-farewell-left-versus-right-contest-matters-now-open-against-closed-new

Kalter, F. (2008). Stand, Herausforderungen und Perspektiven der empirischen Migrationsforschung. *Kölner Zeitschrift für Soziologie und Sozialpsychologie, Sonderheft 48/2008 Migration und Integration*, 11–36.

TNS Opinion & Social. (2015). *Die öffentliche Meinung in der Europäischen Union. Standard-Eurobarometer 84, Herbst 2015*. Europäische Kommission, DG COMM. Abgerufen von http://ec.europa.eu/commfrontoffice/publicopinion/index.cfm/ResultDoc/download/DocumentKy/70151

TEIL 1:
KONZEPTIONELLE ÜBERLEGUNGEN ZUR MIGRATIONSFORSCHUNG

Perspektivische Verschiebungen: Migration und Mobilität im Zeitalter der Globalisierung

Rainer Bauböck

Zusammenfassung

Internationale Migration ist per Definition ein grenzüberschreitendes Phänomen. Dennoch betrachtet die Migrationsforschung dieses Phänomen überwiegend aus der Perspektive der Aufnahmestaaten. Ich argumentiere in diesem kurzen Beitrag für eine Erweiterung des Blicks auf Migration durch kontrollierten Sichtwechsel zwischen einer transnationalen Makroperspektive einerseits und biographischen Mikroperspektive andererseits.

Migration und Staat

Das systematische sozialwissenschaftliche Studium der Migration beginnt Ende des 19. Jahrhunderts mit einem Papier des deutsch-britischen Geographen Ernst Georg Ravenstein im Auftrag der Royal Statistical Society. Ravenstein's „Gesetze der Migration" befassen sich mit allgemeinen Mustern menschlicher Wanderungsbewegungen, wie etwa, dass der Umfang von Migration mit der Entfernung zwischen Ursprungs- und Zielort abnimmt oder dass Migrationen in der Regel Gegenbewegungen vom Ziel- zum Ursprungsort auslösen (Ravenstein 1885). Interessant ist, dass in dieser Betrachtung Staaten und deren Grenzen keine Rolle spielen. Migration unterscheidet sich in dieser Sichtweise von allgemeiner geographischer Mobilität lediglich durch den längerfristigen Aufenthalt am Zielort. Binnenmigration vom Land in die Stadt und internationale Migration folgen denselben sozialen Gesetzmäßigkeiten und können in den Dimensionen Raum und Zeit mit denselben Methoden gemessen und beschrieben werden wie der tägliche Weg vom Wohnsitz zum Arbeitsort.[1]

Ökonomische Theorien der Migration betrachten diese in erster Linie als rationales nutzenoptimierendes Verhalten von Individuen oder Haushalten im Kontext von geographisch differenzierten Arbeitsmärkten (Todaro 1969, Stark 1991). Auch diese Modelle sind auf Binnenwanderung ebenso anwendbar wie auf internationale Migration. Der Staat spielt eine gewisse Rolle in der Erklärung von Migration, weil politische Regulierung Disparitäten zwischen regionalen oder

---

[1] Siehe dazu Torsten Hägerstrand's Raum-Zeit-Geographie (Hägerstrand 1975).

gesamtstaatlichen Arbeitsmärkten oder Sozialsystemen erzeugt und aufrechterhält, aber der Staat wird in erster Linie als Adressat von Empfehlungen gesehen, wie durch freie oder regulierte Migration die Effizienz der Allokation von Arbeitskraft gesteigert werden könnte.

Im Gegensatz zu dieser Betrachtung des Staates als Verursacher ökonomischer Disparitäten und wirtschaftspolitischen Akteur interessieren sich die Politikwissenschaften primär für staatliche Migrationskontrolle. In historisch vergleichender Sicht ist es bemerkenswert, dass diese ein relativ junges Phänomen ist. Bis zur allgemeinen Einführung von Reisepässen im Gefolge des Ersten Weltkriegs (Torpey 2000) hatten europäische Staaten wenig administrative Kapazitäten und technische Mittel zur Erfassung und Regulierung von Personenbewegungen über ihre Grenzen. Auch war die Konstellation staatlicher Interessen fundamental anders als heute: während die Überseekolonien in erster Linie daran interessiert waren, das Land mit europäischen Einwanderern zu besiedeln, waren die europäischen Staaten bemüht, Auswanderung zu beschränken (Green and Weil 2007). Die Menschenrechte auf freie Binnenmigration und Auswanderung (nach Artikel 13 der Allgemeinen Erklärung der Menschenrechte) und das Recht von Staaten auf Kontrolle der Einwanderung ausländischer Staatsangehöriger haben sich erst in der zweiten Hälfte des 20. Jahrhunderts als allgemeine Normen des Völkerrechts durchgesetzt.

Für Historiker und Politikwissenschaftler ist es wichtig, die Entwicklung und Zielsetzung staatlicher Migrationskontrolle zu verstehen und zu erklären. Deren Effektivität wird in der soziologischen Migrationsforschung jedoch vielfach angezweifelt (Massey 1993). Migrationsströme werden in dieser Sicht von ökonomischen Disparitäten ausgelöst und durch Kettenwanderung in familiären und ethnischen Netzwerken pfadabhängig verstärkt. Staatliche Kontrolle kann bestenfalls Migranten und Migrantinnen[2] in rechtliche Kategorien einteilen, aber den Umfang und Verlauf von Migrationsflüssen kaum beeinflussen. Diese Sicht unterschätzt den Einfluss des Staates jedoch in zweierlei Hinsicht. Erstens ist der Zerfall oder Zusammenbruch staatlicher Ordnung mindestens ebenso wichtig als Auslöser internationaler Migrationsbewegungen wie anhaltende ökonomische Ungleichheit zwischen Staaten. Zweitens hat die Effektivität (wenn auch nicht unbedingt die Effizienz) staatlicher Migrationskontrolle in wirtschaftlich entwickelten Zielländern deutlich zugenommen, wie sich etwa am dramatischen Rückgang der irregulären Migration von Mexiko in die USA seit dem 11. September 2001 zeigt.

Den Staat lediglich als Regierungsgewalt zu betrachten, die Migration verursacht oder steuert, greift jedoch noch immer zu kurz. In der Rechtstheorie werden Staaten drei Grundmerkmale zugeschrieben: Territorium, Bevölkerung und Regierungsinstitutionen (Jellinek 1929). Die ersten beiden dieser Merkmale sind von grundlegender Bedeutung für unser Verständnis von Migration. Die Unterteilung

---

[2] Im Folgenden wird aus stilistischen Gründen der Begriff „Migrant" geschlechtsneutral verwendet. Es sind immer Migrantinnen und Migranten gemeint.

der Welt in staatliche Territorien und Staatsbevölkerungen bildet jene Hintergrundstruktur, die Migration überhaupt erst als soziales Phänomen sichtbar macht. Politische Grenzen sind konstitutiv für Migration, weil sie diese von Mobilität unterscheiden. Mit anderen Worten: Mobilität verwandelt sich in Migration, wenn sie durch eine politische Grenze strukturiert wird.

Die Bevölkerungsabteilung der Vereinten Nationen definiert internationale Migration für ihre Statistiken als einen Aufenthalt von mindestens zwölf Monaten außerhalb des Geburtslandes. Der Anteil der so definierten Migranten an der Weltbevölkerung beträgt heute etwas mehr als drei Prozent. Das ist nicht viel, aber die Größe dieser Zahl hängt nicht nur von den Mustern raum-zeitlicher Mobilität ab, sondern auch davon, welche Art der Mobilität statistisch als Migration erfasst wird. Die Zahl würde sich dramatisch erhöhen, wenn wir die Aufenthaltszeit auf sechs Monate verkürzten oder als Bezugseinheit nicht Staaten, sondern deren Provinzen oder Gemeinden heranzögen, ohne dass sich damit etwas an den zugrundeliegenden Mustern geographischer Mobilität geändert hätte. Auch der Bezug der Definition auf das Geburtsland beeinflusst die Kategorisierung von Migration, weil Rückwanderungen in dieses Land, welche ja auch eine Art der grenzüberschreitenden Mobilität sind, die globale Zahl der Migranten reduzieren, statt sie zu erhöhen.

Daraus lassen sich einige „Gesetze der Migration" ableiten, die in der öffentlichen Wahrnehmung meist ignoriert werden: Bei konstanter geographischer Mobilität ist der Anteil der Migranten an der Wohnbevölkerung umso größer, je kleiner das Territorium ist. Unter den europäischen Flächenstaaten hat Luxemburg den höchsten Anteil von internationalen Migranten an der Bevölkerung – nicht deshalb, weil Luxemburg als Zielland so viel attraktiver ist als seine Nachbarn, sondern weil seine engen Grenzen auch Mobilität über kurze Distanzen in internationale Migration verwandeln.

Ein zweites „Gesetz der Migration" ist, dass Verschiebungen staatlicher Grenzen die Zahl internationaler Migranten in Proportion zum Umfang der früheren Binnenzuwanderung im Territorium des Nachfolgestaats erhöhen. Als zu Beginn der 1990er Jahre die Sowjetunion, Jugoslawien und die Tschechoslowakei zerfielen erhöhte sich dadurch schlagartig der Anteil von Personen, die sich auf Dauer in einem anderen Staat als in ihrem Geburtsland aufhielten ohne dass die Betroffenen einen Ortswechsel vollzogen hatten. Dieses Paradox erhellt, wie sehr unsere Wahrnehmung von Migration nicht nur von der Existenz politischer Grenzen abhängt, sondern auch von deren Stabilität.

Die transnationale Perspektive

All das sind triftige Gründe, dem modernen Staat eine zentrale Rolle in der Analyse von Migration einzuräumen: als regulierendem Akteur, als Arena der politischen Auseinandersetzungen, in der die Grenze zwischen Einheimischen und

Migranten gezogen wird, und als Hintergrundstruktur, welche Migration überhaupt erst konstituiert und sichtbar macht.

Keiner dieser Gründe rechtfertigt jedoch eine *einzelstaatliche* Perspektive, in der Migration immer nur unter dem Gesichtspunkt betrachtet wird, wie sie die Ökonomie, Kultur und Gesellschaft eines bestimmten Staates betrifft. Der Mainstream der Migrationsforschung war stets von der Frage geleitet, welche Wirkungen Migration auf Aufnahmegesellschaften hat. Spätestens seit der Chicago Schule der Soziologie der 1920er und 30er Jahre werden auch die Erfahrungen der Einwanderer selbst und deren Integrations- und Assimilationsprozesse ausgiebig untersucht. Was in dieser Betrachtung kaum eine Rolle spielte, waren die Auswirkungen der Emigration auf die Herkunftsstaaten und die Bindungen der Migranten an diese. In den Siedlerstaaten Amerikas und Ozeaniens waren diese blinden Flecken auch dadurch bedingt, dass europäische Einwanderung als Instrument des Nationenbaus diente. So wurde die Tatsache, dass viele der Arbeitsmigranten um 1900 saisonal zwischen Nord- und Südamerika pendelten ebenso aus dem kollektiven Gedächtnis verbannt wie jene, dass bis zu einem Drittel der Einwanderer in den USA in dieser Epoche wieder nach Europa zurückkehrten. Im Europa der Gegenwart führt ein konträrer politischer Impuls paradoxer Weise zu einer ähnlichen Wahrnehmungsverzerrung. Als Folge der ungewollten postkolonialen Zuwanderung und Niederlassung der Gastarbeiter nach dem Zweiten Weltkrieg und als Symptom der Globalisierungsängste der Gegenwart werden Migranten stets als Zuwanderer wahrgenommen, deren Zahl es zu begrenzen gilt und deren Integration staatlicher Aufsicht bedarf, und nicht als Emigranten oder transnational mobile Bevölkerung.

Diese grobe Skizze beschreibt den Mainstream der Migrationsforschung, der stets von Imperativen des Nationenbaus in den politisch und wirtschaftlich dominanten Zuwanderungsländern beeinflusst wurde. Daneben interessierten sich vor allem Geographen und Anthropologen immer schon auch für den Auswanderungskontext. Gegen Ende des 20. Jahrhunderts wurde von Entwicklungsökonomen der Weltbank der Nexus zwischen ökonomischer Entwicklung und Auswanderung neu thematisiert. Monetäre Rücküberweisungen der Emigranten in die Herkunftsländer wurden als Quelle der Entwicklung erkannt, deren Umfang jene der offiziellen Entwicklungshilfe beträchtlich übertraf. Negative Folgen der Abwanderung wurden unter dem Schlagwort „brain drain" thematisiert.[3] Auswanderungsforschung bildet einen zunehmend stärkeren Kontrapunkt zur dominanten Einwanderungsforschung, aber sie wird wie diese primär aus einzelstaatlicher Perspektive betrieben. Es gibt kaum Versuche einer Synthese, welche die Einwanderungs- mit der Auswanderungsperspektive verbindet.

Das ist insofern erstaunlich, als Immigranten und Emigranten ja identische Personen sind, die nur aus der Sicht von Staaten unterschiedlich kategorisiert werden. Anfang der 1990er Jahre wurde von einer Gruppe von Anthropologinnen rund um

---

[3] Zu diesem Thema liefern Gillian Brock und Michael Blake eine interessante Kontroverse aus der Perspektive der politischen Theorie (2015).

Nina Glick-Schiller eine transnationale Perspektive in die amerikanische Migrationsforschung eingeführt, welche die Bindungen und Aktivitäten lateinamerikanischer Migranten in den USA gegenüber ihren Herkunftsländern in den Vordergrund rückte (Glick Schiller 1994). Diese „transnationale Wende" war auf die Mikroperspektive der Migranten fokussiert und analysierte ihrer sozialen Netzwerke und lokalen Communities im Einwanderungs- und Herkunftsland. Die akademischen Protagonistinnen verknüpften dies jedoch etwas vorschnell mit einer postnationalen Programmatik des Niedergangs traditioneller Nationalstaaten.

Zur selben Zeit analysierte der schwedische Politikwissenschaftler Tomas Hammar die Transformation der Staatsbürgerschaft und der mit ihr assoziierten Rechte im Kontext der Einwanderung in west- und nordeuropäischen Staaten (Hammar 1990). Hammar diagnostizierte die Zunahme mehrfacher Staatsbürgerschaften und die Herausbildung eines neuen Status der *denizenship* (Wohnbürgerschaft). In einem viel beachteten Buch beschrieb Yasemin Soysal diese Entwicklungen als Bedeutungsverlust der Staatsbürgerschaft in einem postnationalen Zeitalter der allgemeinen Menschenrechte (Soysal 1994). Der bescheidene Beitrag des Autors dieser Zeilen bestand darin, die Entwicklung der Staatsbürgerschaft und der damit verknüpften Rechte als transnational und nicht postnational zu begreifen (Bauböck 1994, Bauböck 2003). Das bedeutet erstens, dass nicht nur die Aktivitäten und sozialen Netzwerke von Migranten transnational sind, sondern die Institutionen der Aufnahme- und Herkunftsstaaten darauf reagieren, indem sie transnationale Rechte für Nichtstaatsbürger im Inland und Staatsbürger im Ausland stärken. Zweitens entstehen damit neue Konstellationen, in denen Staatsbürgerschaften und Bürgerrechte nicht mehr ausschließlich von einzelnen Staaten bestimmt werden. Die Rechtspositionen von Migranten als Ausländer und Auslandsbürger oder auch als Doppelstaatsbürger werden von zumindest zwei Staaten unabhängig voneinander festgelegt, aber nur ihre gemeinsame Betrachtung erlaubt es zu verstehen, wie ihre Kombination die Handlungsoptionen von Migranten erweitert oder beschränkt (Bauböck 2012).

Eine transnationale Perspektive war in der Migrationsforschung natürlich immer schon präsent, wenn es um die Erklärung von internationalen Migrationsströmen ging. Die simpelsten Push und Pull Modelle kombinieren zwangsläufig Bedingungen im Herkunftsland mit jenen im Aufnahmeland. Auch die Idee, dass Gruppen von Staaten dauerhafte Konstellationen bilden, in denen Migration immer auch Rückwanderungen zur Folge haben, ist in Analysen von „migration systems" präsent. Neu ist lediglich die Idee, dass auch Fragen der Integration und politischen Teilhabe von Migranten nicht im geschlossenen einzelstaatlichen Rahmen zureichend beantwortet werden können.

Eine transnationale Perspektive wirft auch ein neues Licht auf die Debatte in der normativen politischen Theorie über die Legitimität staatlicher Migrationskontrolle. Joseph Carens, der bekannteste Befürworter offener Grenzen, argumentiert, dass die weltweite Zuschreibung extrem ungleicher Chancen aufgrund des Zufalls der Geburt als Staatsbürger eines Landes aus liberaler Sicht nicht gerechtfertigt werden kann. Neben dem Argument der globalen sozialen Gerechtigkeit führt er auch ein individuelles Freiheitsargument ins Treffen, wonach all jene Gründe, aus denen Staaten Freizügigkeit in ihrem Territorium nicht behindern dürfen, auch auf internationale Migranten anwendbar sind, die ihre Lebenschancen verbessern, mit Partnern zusammenleben oder einfach nur ihr sozio-kulturelles Milieu wechseln wollen (Carens 2013). Befürworter eines staatlichen Rechts auf Zuwanderungskontrolle sehen diese dagegen als Ausdruck demokratischer Selbstbestimmung und Bedingung für die Aufrechterhaltung nationaler Identitäten und sozialer Solidarität als Grundlagen für stabile demokratische Herrschaft (Walzer 1983, Miller 2016).

Ein „realistischer" Ansatz in der normativen politischen Theorie könnte eine dritte Perspektive in dieser Kontroverse eröffnen, ausgehend von der Tatsache, dass alle Rechtsstaaten bereits zwei grundlegende Rechte auf Migration anerkennen: ein allgemeines Auswanderungsrecht und ein unbedingtes Recht auf Einwanderung für die eigenen Staatsbürger. Personenfreizügigkeit zwischen Staaten existiert in der heutigen Welt lediglich auf der Basis von Wechselseitigkeit und nur für die Staatsbürger des jeweils anderen Landes. Dies ist auch die Grundlage für Personenfreizügigkeit in der Europäischen Union. Es bedarf allerdings keiner ökonomisch und politisch integrierten Staatenunion, um die Voraussetzungen für reziproke Personenfreizügigkeit zu schaffen. Diese existiert auch unabhängig davon zwischen Australien und Neuseeland, zwischen Großbritannien und Irland und schon vor dem Beitritt zur EU in den nordischen Staaten. Die zweite Grundlage für Bewegungsfreiheit, von der schon heute eine wachsende Zahl von Menschen profitieren, ist die mehrfache Staatsbürgerschaft, welche für die Betroffenen ja ein unbedingtes Einwanderungsrecht in zwei oder mehr Staaten kombiniert.

Eine normative Theorie der Bewegungsfreiheit könnte anerkennen, dass diese auch aus demokratischen Gründen an die Staatsbürgerschaft geknüpft ist und gleichzeitig das Ziel offener Grenzen aus Gründen der sozialen Gerechtigkeit im Auge behalten. Der erste Schritt in diese Richtung wäre eine weitere Liberalisierung der Staatsbürgerschaft durch Erleichterung der Einbürgerung in den Aufnahmestaaten und Anerkennung der Doppelstaatsbürgerschaft sowohl im Einwanderungs- als auch im Herkunftsland. Damit erhielten nicht nur privilegierte EU-Bürger Personenfreizügigkeit, sondern auch jene Migranten aus Drittstaaten, die wegen ihrer transnationalen Bindungen das stärkste Interesse an dieser haben. Der zweite Schritt wäre eine Erweiterung der Auswanderungsfreiheit um eine staatliche Pflicht, die Aufnahmechancen der eigenen Bürger in anderen Staaten durch wechselseitige Abkommen (vom Visaverzicht bis zu Niederlassungsfreiheit und Arbeitsmarktzugang) auf immer mehr Staaten auszudehnen. Um die Voraussetzungen für demokratische Bürgerrechte im Inneren aufrechtzuerhalten, ist wechselseitige Freizügigkeit jedoch nur denkbar, wenn alle beteiligten Staaten demokratisch verfasst sind und das wirtschafts- und sozialpolitische Gefälle zwischen ihnen nicht so groß ist, dass Bewegungsfreiheit Massenmigration auslösen würde, welche sowohl im Auswanderungs- als auch im Einwanderungsland die soziale und politische Stabilität untergraben würde.

Als Antwort auf die global ungerechte Verteilung von Lebenschancen durch das Geburtsrecht auf Staatsbürgerschaft taugt in dieser Sicht nur eine Politik der globalen Umverteilung von Ressourcen statt Menschen, der Förderung der demokratischen und wirtschaftlichen Entwicklung in den am meisten benachteiligten Ländern, der Aufnahme von Flüchtlingen und eine kontrollierte Zuwanderungspolitik für ökonomisch motivierte Migranten, welche die Interessen des Aufnahmestaates, des Herkunftslandes und der Migranten selbst berücksichtigt.

Schlussfolgerungen

Das von mir zuletzt skizzierte Szenario verweist auf internationale Bewegungsfreiheit als eine dritte Option zwischen Mobilität und Migration. Die politischen Binnengrenzen bleiben konstitutiv auch für Personenfreizügigkeit innerhalb der EU. Es ist die Staatsbürgerschaft in einem Mitgliedsland, welches EU-Bürgern das Recht gibt, sich in anderen Mitgliedsstaaten niederzulassen, dort zu arbeiten und nicht aufgrund der Nationalität diskriminiert zu werden. Und es sind grenzüberschreitende Tätigkeiten und Bindungen, welche die besonderen Rechte der Unionsbürgerschaft aktivieren. Gleichzeitig verlieren die politischen Binnengrenzen in diesem Raum der Bewegungsfreiheit aber an Bedeutung, weil die EU-Binnenwanderer an ihnen keiner Einwanderungskontrolle mehr unterliegen und sie nach deren Überquerung rechtlich kaum noch von Einheimischen unterschieden werden. Gleiches gilt auch für die bilaterale Freizügigkeit von Doppelstaatsbürgern. Aus normativer Sicht spricht viel für eine Globalisierung dieser Zwitterform zwischen Migration und Mobilität als Alternative zu „no borders" Utopien einerseits und zur Bekräftigung nationalstaatlicher Selbstbestimmungsrechte in Fragen der Migration und Staatsbürgerschaft andererseits.

Eine zweite Schlussfolgerung aus den Überlegungen dieses Aufsatzes richtet sich an die empirische Migrationsforschung. Ein transnationaler Ansatz muss nicht nur die Perspektiven der Sende- und Aufnahmeländer kombinieren, sondern auch die Makroperspektive der Institutionen dieser Staaten mit der Mikroperspektive der Migranten. Aus der Sicht von Staaten verlassen Auswanderer eine Gesellschaft und integrieren sich Einwanderer in eine andere. Aus der Sicht von Migranten ist es die Anwesenheit und Abwesenheit in diesen Gesellschaften, die ihre Biographien strukturiert und ihre Lebenschancen erweitert oder einschränkt. Diese Perspektiven der Transformation staatlicher Institutionen durch Migration und der Transformation migrantischer Lebensläufe durch staatliche Regulierung systematisch miteinander zu verbinden, ist eine Herausforderung, der sich die akademische Forschung noch nicht gestellt hat. Vielleicht ist eine schlüssige Synthese aus transnationalen Makro- und Mikroperspektiven auch gar nicht möglich, sondern nur ein gut reflektierter Wechsel zwischen diesen Sichtweisen.

Das von Gudrun Biffl aufgebaute und geleitete Department Migration und Globalisierung an der Donau-Universität Krems hat sich große Verdienste um die Migrationsforschung in Österreich und darüber hinaus erworben. Es steht zu hoffen, dass der Blick über den nationalstaatlichen Tellerrand hinaus, den Gudrun Biffl mit ihren vergleichenden Arbeiten über Migration, Arbeitsmarkt, Sozial- und Bildungssysteme und als Expertin für das Sopemi Netzwerk der OECD entwickelt hat, auch weiterhin in Krems gefördert wird. Migration im Kontext der Globalisierung zu verstehen, bedeutet sich auf perspektivische Verschiebungen einzulassen, die herkömmliche statische und staatliche Sichtweisen in Frage stellen.

Literatur

Bauböck, Rainer (1994) Transnational Citizenship. Membership and Rights in International Migration (Edward Elgar, Aldershot)
Bauböck, Rainer (2012) Constellations and Transitions: Combining Macro and Micro Perspectives on Migration and Citizenship. In: Schröder, Renée/ Wodak, Ruth (Ed.) Migrations. Interdisciplinary Perspectives, (Springer) 3-14.
Bauböck, Rainer (2003) Towards a Political Theory of Migrant Transnationalism. In: International Migration Review 37 (3), 700-723.
Blake, Michael/ Brock, Gillian (2015) Debating Brain Drain. May Governments Restrict Emigration? (Oxford University Press, Oxford).
Carens, Joseph H. (2013) The Ethics of Immigration. (Oxford University Press, Oxford).
Glick-Schiller, Nina/ Basch, Linda/ Szanton Blanc, Cristina (1994). Nations Unbound. Transnational Projects, Postcolonial Predicaments and Deterritorialized Nation-States. (Gordon and Breach Publishers, Amsterdam).
Green, Nancy L./ Weil, François (2007) Citizenship and Those Who Leave. The Politics of Emigration and Expatriation. (University of Illinois Press, Urbana and Chicago).
Hägerstrand, Torsten (1975) 'Space, Time and Human Conditions'. In: Karlqvist, A. (Ed.) Dynamic Allocation of Urban Space, (Farnborough).
Hammar, Tomas (1990) Democracy and the Nation State. Aliens, Denizens and Citizens in a World of International Migration. (Avebury, Aldershot).
Jellinek, Georg (1929) Allgemeine Staatslehre. 5. Auflage, (Springer.
Massey, Douglas/ Arango, Joaquín/ Graeme, Hugo/ Kouaouci, Ali/ Pellegrino, Adela/ Taylor, Edward (1993) 'Theories of International Migration: A Review and Appraisal'. In: Population and Development Review 19 (3), 431-466.
Miller, David (2016) Strangers in Our Midst. The Political Philosophy of Immigration. (Harvard University Press, Cambridge).
Ravenstein, E.G. (1885) The Laws of Migration. In: Journal of the Royal Statistical Society 48 (2), 167-235.
Soysal, Yasemin (1994) Limits of Citizenship. Migrants and Postnational Membership in Europe. (University of Chicago Press, Chicago).
Stark, Oded (1991) The Migration of Labour. (Blackwell, Oxford).
Todaro, Michael P. (1969) A Model of Labor Migration and Urban Unemployment in Less Developed Countries. In: The American Economic Review 59 (1), 138-148.
Torpey, John (2000) The Invention of the Passport: Surveillance, Citizenship, and the State. Cambridge, (Cambridge University Press, Cambridge).
Walzer, Michael (1983) Spheres of Justice. A Defense of Pluralism and Equality, (Basic Books, New York).

Making linkages in migration research: "Migrants" and "mobile citizens" in the European Union

Martin Ruhs

Abstract

This chapter makes the case for more research on international migration that – as Gudrun Biffl's work has done – links the theories and insights of different academic disciplines, connects migration with other relevant public policy issues, and takes account of the realities of public debates and policy-making. I argue that making these linkages – across disciplines, issue areas, and the theory/practice divide – can be an effective way of generating innovative analyses that contribute to academic research as well as inform migration debates and policies. To give an example from the European context, I suggest that we need much more analyses and debates that connect the "mobility" of EU citizens with the "migration" of people from outside the EU, two important policy issues that are often discussed in isolation from each other.

Introduction

I am delighted and honoured to be given the opportunity to contribute to this *Festschrift* for Gudrun Biffl. Gudrun has developed a global reputation as one of Austria's foremost experts on international migration and migration policies. She is also an excellent example of an international comparative migration researcher who has managed to connect her academic research to public debates and policy-making in and beyond Austria. Gudrun's approach to migration research provides valuable lessons for researchers interested in making their work "impact" on debates and policy-making processes beyond academia.

This chapter makes the case for more research on international migration that – as Gudrun's work has done – links the theories and insights of different academic disciplines, connects migration with other relevant public policy issues, and takes account of realities of public debate and policy-making. I argue that making these linkages – across disciplines, issue areas, and theory/practice – can be an effective way of generating innovative analyses that contribute to academic research and knowledge as well as inform migration debates and policy-making.

The chapter is structured as follows. I begin with a brief discussion of what the wide-spread, and possibly growing, scepticism about the "use" of researchers and experts in public policy debates might mean for migration research and researchers. Next, I explain why and how making links across academic disciplines, issue areas, and the common divide between "theory" and "practices" of policy-making can help advance academic research as well as inform public debates and policy-making. The fourth section then looks at a specific issue that Gudrun has analysed extensively over many years, namely, the effects and regulation of "mobility" (of EU workers) and "migration" (of "third-country nationals") in the European Union (EU).

As an example of the importance of "making linkages" in research and policy debates, I argue that we need much more analyses and debates that connect the "free movement" of EU citizens with "immigration policies" toward people from outside Europe. This is exactly the opposite approach to the one traditionally taken and advocated by the European Commission and many other European policymakers who have insisted on a clear distinction between the "mobility" of EU citizens on the one hand, and the "immigration" of third-country nationals on the other.

Migration research, researchers and "post-truth politics"

Social science research on the processes, determinants, and effects of international migration and migration policies has grown rapidly over the past few decades as evidenced, for example, by the rapidly rising numbers of academic publications on this topic (see, for example, IOM 2017). Economists, political scientists, sociologists, anthropologists, geographers, historians, legal scholars and others have all made important contributions to what we know – and, equally importantly, highlighted what we don't know – about international migration, integration and the associated policy challenges for high- and lower-income countries. In recent years some of this growing academic research on migration has become much more accessible to people outside academia (without easy access to academic journal articles). As a result, the "evidence-base" available to politicians, policymakers, civil society, journalists and others working on migration and integration has vastly improved in most high-income countries.

More and better research does not mean, of course, that public debates and policy-making have generally become more "evidence-based". The links between research, public debates and policy-making on migration and integration can be highly politicised (e.g. Boswell 2012), shaped by institutional structures (such as the characteristics of policy-making processes, e.g. Scholten et al 2015), and variable both across countries and over time (e.g. Ruhs, Palme & Tamas 2018). Furthermore, we know from existing research that public opinion on migration and refugees can be shaped by a range of different factors that have little to do with "facts", "data" and "evidence" (e.g. Blinder 2011; OECD 2010). Similarly, policy-making on migration can be influenced by a wide range of interests, institutions and ideas which may or may not be based on the realities of the scale, processes, causes and effects of migration (e.g. Hampshire 2013; Boswell et al 2011). Given these complex inter-relationships and multiple determinants of public opinion and public policies, the much lamented "disconnect" between migration policy debates and migration "realities" is neither new nor particularly surprising.

What *is* relatively new and perhaps more surprising is the apparent increase in scepticism about evidence and "experts" in public policy debates, at least in some countries. The two most prominent examples are the debates around the UK's referendum to leave the European Union in June 2016 and the presidential elections in the United States in Nov 2016. Immigration was a key issue in the run-up to both events. In the UK, high profile figures of the campaign to leave the European Union ("Vote Leave") openly and explicitly rejected the role and usefulness of "experts" in public policy debates and policy-making. In early June 2016, Michael Gove, a Conservative Cabinet Minister at the time, declared that *"people in this country have had enough of experts"* (Gove later clarified that he specifically meant economists) and Gisela Stuart, a Labour MP and Vote Leave campaigner, argued that *"there is only one expert that matters, and that's you, the voter."* (Deacon 2016). At the same time, the rise of Donald Trump in the US was accompanied by an apparent increase of a similar scepticism about the role, motivations and usefulness of so-called "experts" in public debates and policy-making. *The Economist* (2016) recently called Trump a *"leading exponent of 'post-truth' politics – a reliance on assertions that 'feel true' but have no basis in fact."*

How should social scientists who work on migration and want their research to inform public policy debates respond to these developments? Part of the answer is to study and try to understand better the dynamics and processes of public debates and policy-making, the politicisation and (mis)use of "facts" and "evidence", and the economic, social, political and other drivers of the apparent rise of "post-truth politics". Continuing efforts to make the findings and insights of existing research more accessible to the wider public and policy-makers is obviously also important. However, I argue that a large part of the response should also include critical (self-)reflection and analysis of the characteristics of the rapidly growing academic research on migration and integration, especially with regard to its ability to capture and analyse real world policy challenges. Of course, there is an important role for research that has no immediate practical "use" or policy-relevance whatsoever (see, for example, Bakewell's 2008 discussion of the importance of policy-irrelevant research into forced migration). At the same time, if one of the goals of the research is to inform migration debates and policies outside academia, it is critically important to think carefully about the multiple ways in which the design and characteristics of different types of research projects are likely to relate to their wider societal impacts. In particular, it is of critical importance to avoid disciplinary and analytical silos that prevent us from identifying and analysing important inter-linkages that, in my view, are of fundamental importance to a comprehensive analysis of public policies.

Making linkages in research on international migration and public policies

Much of Gudrun's work on international labour migration and labour immigration policies is characterised by three key analytical "linkages" which are of fundamental importance to efforts to make social science research relevant to wider public and policy debates. The first of these linkages relates to connections *across social science disciplines*. To state the obvious, international migration is an inherently multi-disciplinary issue that cannot be analysed comprehensively from the perspective and within the boundaries of one discipline alone. Disciplinary contributions are clearly important – indeed they are often the pre-condition for multi-disciplinary work – but public policy analysis requires awareness and, ideally, integration of insights from various relevant disciplines. Most of Gudrun's work is based on economics but it frequently engages with theories and insights of other disciplines such as politics and law (e.g. Biffl 2011; and Biffl & Rössl 2011).

A second key linkage that is characteristic of Gudrun's work relates to the *connections between migration and a wide range of other public policy issues*. For example, in the sphere of labour immigration, it is clear that employer demand for migrant labour is critically influenced by the institutional and regulatory framework of the labour market as well as wider public policies such as education and training policies, welfare policies, housing policies, etc. (Anderson & Ruhs 2010). This is why the economics and politics of specific labour immigration policies cannot be fully understood, and should not be analysed, without considering the connections with other public policies. By making these linkages, Gudrun' work on labour migration (e.g. Biffl & Skrivanek 2016) is an example of what is now an active and growing research literature on the relationships between immigration, immigration policies and a range of national institutions and wider public policies (see e.g. Afonso & Devitt, 2016; Menz 2009).

A third important linkage relates to the connection between migration research and "policy practices". It is hard to analyse real world policy processes without an understanding and at least some direct experience (at least as an observer) of how these processes (including the numerous and multifaceted pressures and constraints on policy-makers) play out in practice. In addition to her role as a university professor and researcher, Gudrun has engaged extensively with policy debates and policy-making processes (e.g. in her long-standing role as Austria's migration correspondent at the OECD; and, most recently as a member of Austria's new "Migration Commission" which advises the government on immigration policies).

These three analytical connections – across disciplines, issue areas and theory/practice) – are, in my view, of critical importance in migration research that aims to be relevant to public debates and policy-making. There is no doubt that making these connections can be hard in practice, for a range of reasons including: the demands of keeping up with the research literature in more than one discipline; the difficulties with staying on top of policy developments across different issue areas; and, last but not least, the variable degrees of (in)accessibility of policy-making processes to researchers, especially more junior researchers. In some countries, the incentive structures for academic researchers are (still) stacked against working across disciplines and engaging with policy-making processes. These are all real obstacles that need to be addressed by providing public policy researchers with an academic environment that clearly values inter-disciplinary research, facilitates engagement with public policies and, more generally, encourages research on migration and integration that considers the "bigger picture".

Linking "migrants" and "mobile citizens" in the European Union

The remainder of this chapter discusses research and policy debates on "migration" and "mobility" in the European Union. The EU has in recent years faced a number of major policy challenges, including on issues related to migration and mobility, that have led to highly divisive political debates among EU Member States. For example, Member States have been debating how to respond to the mass inflows of refugees and other migrants in recent years, whether and how to reform the rules for the free movement of workers within the EU as demanded by some EU countries (including but not only the UK before its referendum vote to leave the EU), and how to reform the rules for "posting workers" as part of the trade in services across EU member states (see Jongerius & Morin-Chartier 2017).

A key feature of these policy debates is the strict distinction that many people make between the effects and regulations of the mobility of EU workers (i.e. intra-EU labour mobility) and the immigration of third-country nationals. I argue that we need to connect debates about the "free movement" of EU citizens with discussions about "immigration policies" toward people from outside Europe.[1] To develop my argument, I first outline some of the key differences between how "migrants" and "mobile EU citizens" are debated and regulated in the European Union. This is followed by a brief explanation of why I think the current distinctions are problematic from moral, political, and research perspectives.

"Migrants"

There are very large differences between how EU member states currently treat "migrants" from outside Europe and "mobile EU citizens" from within Europe, in terms of both regulating their admission and rights after entry. In all countries, immigration is restricted through a range and often complex set of national admission policies that regulate the scale and selection of migrants. National immigration policies typically distinguish between high-skilled migrants (who face fewer

---

[1] The discussion in this section draws on my recent blog post for the "European Union Democracy Observatory on Citizenship" at the European University Institute (EUI): "'Migrants', 'mobile citizens' and the borders of exclusion in the European Union" (Ruhs 2017b).

restrictions on admission), lower-skilled migrants (relatively more restrictions) as well as different rules for admitting family migrants, students, asylum seekers and refugees.

National immigration policies also place considerable restrictions on the rights of migrants after admission including their access to the labour market, welfare state, family reunion, permanent residence and citizenship. As it is the case with admission policies, rights restrictions typically vary between high- and low-skilled migrant workers (with the rights of lower-skilled migrant workers significantly more restricted) and across family migrants, students asylum seekers and refugees. As I have shown in my recent research (Ruhs 2013; Ruhs 2017), European and other high-income countries' immigration policies are often characterised by trade-offs between "openness" and some "migrant rights", that is, labour immigration programmes that are more open to admitting migrant workers are also more restrictive with regard to specific rights (especially social rights).

Public debates and policy-making on immigration vary across countries but they are typically framed in highly consequentialist terms, i.e. based on the (perceived and/or real) costs and benefits of particular admission policies and restrictions of migrants' rights for the host economy and society. This cost-benefit approach to policy-making has been a long-standing feature of labour immigration policies. Arguably, it is also becoming an important factor, and in some European countries *the* most important consideration, when it comes to polices towards asylum seekers and refugees (compare Bauböck & Tripkovic 2017). Some European countries' recent policies toward refugees and migrants fleeing conflicts and violence in Syria and other places are primarily shaped by the perceived impacts on the national interest of the host country rather than by humanitarian considerations, protection needs or respect for international refugee conventions.

A central feature of national migration policy debates in European and other high-income countries is the idea of "control" i.e. the idea that immigration and the rights of migrants can be controlled and regulated, at least to a considerable degree, based on the perceived costs and benefits for the existing residents of the host country. Of course, states' control over immigration is never complete and subject to a number of constraints but the idea of control is still at the heart of national immigration debates and policy-making. Arguably, the perceived "loss of control" over immigration has been a major driver of the rise of Donald Trump in the United States, Britain's referendum vote to leave the European Union, and the growing support for right-wing parties across various European countries (see e.g. Goodwin & Milazzo 2017).

"Mobile citizens"

The policy framework for regulating the movement of EU citizens across member states, and their rights when residing in a member state other than their own, is very different from the restrictions imposed on people from outside the EU (or the European Economic Area [EEA], to be exact). The current rules for free movement give citizens of EU countries the right to move freely and take up employment in any other EU country and – as long as they are "workers" – the right to full and equal access to the host country's welfare state. This combination of unrestricted intra-EU mobility and equal access to national welfare states for EU workers is an important exception to the trade-off between immigration and access to social rights that characterises the labour immigration policies of many high-income countries. Free movement thus challenges long-standing theories and claims about the alleged incompatibility of open borders and inclusive welfare states (see, for example, Freeman 1986). Critically, while the idea of "control" is a central feature of debates and policies on the immigration of people from outside the EU, EU member states have effectively no direct control over the scale and characteristics of the inflows of EU workers. From the perspective of the EU, the overall aim has been to encourage rather than limit and control the mobility of EU citizens between different member states.

In terms of the European institutional framework, *free movement* is kept completely separate from the immigration of third-country nationals. While free movement is part of the remit of the "DG Employment, Social Affairs and Inclusion" and "DG Justice", policies for regulating immigration from outside Europe are largely dealt with by the "DG Migration and Home Affairs". One of the consequences of this division has been that EU debates and policy aimed at the integration of migrants have been heavily focused on migrants from outside the EU.

A third distinction relates to the terminology used to describe and discuss the cross-border movement of EU citizens and non-EU citizens. Many European policy-makers insist that EU citizens moving from one member state to another are not "migrants" but "mobile EU citizens". (Although I am critical of this distinction, for the sake of clarity I have stuck with this terminology in this chapter.) This distinction is not just a reflection of differences in policy approaches but also serves the purpose of framing public debates in a way that suggests that mobile EU citizens are very "different" from the (non-EU) outsiders whose migration needs to be carefully regulated and controlled.

Linking "migration" and "mobility"

The distinctions made in the public debates and policies on "immigration" and "mobile EU citizens" raise a number of important ethical, political and research questions. First, insisting on near-equality of rights for mobile EU citizens while at the same time tolerating what are sometimes severe restrictions of the rights of migrants from outside the EU is, in my view, morally problematic. On the one hand, current policy insists on equality of rights for EU workers including, for example, equal access to non-contributory welfare benefits, i.e. benefits that are paid regardless of whether the beneficiary has made prior contributions or not. On the other hand, many EU member states are unwilling to admit and protect large numbers of refugees who are fleeing violence and conflict and/or grant them full access to the national welfare state. While a preference for protecting the interests and rights of "insiders" can of course be defended on moral grounds, I suggest that the magnitude of the discrepancy between how EU member states treat each other's citizens vs some migrants from outside the EU should give us pause for critical reflection. I consider this an important area for research and analysis by, for example, political philosophers and theorists.

The disconnect between "mobile EU citizens" and "migrants" may also be politically problematic, in the sense that it potentially endangers (rather than protects, as is commonly argued) the future sustainability of the free movement of EU workers within the European Union as well as public support for immigration more generally. The inflow of "mobile EU citizens" in a particular member state has very similar types of effects, and raises very similar economic issues and tensions, as the immigration of migrants from outside the EU. As it is the case with "migrants", "mobile EU citizens" affect the labour markets and welfare states of host countries in one way or another, creating costs and benefits for different groups. Insisting that "mobile citizens" are not "migrants" runs the danger of obscuring these impacts that mobile EU citizens have on the economies and societies of their host countries. This may, in turn, prevent, or at last discourage, important debates at European level about the consequences of free movement for EU citizens who do not move, and ultimately result in a decline in political support for the free movement of labour within the EU and perhaps also for immigration more generally.

A related third question relates to the potential inter-relationships between EU member states' policies on immigration and mobility. How are our policies for the inclusion/exclusion of EU citizens related to our policies for the inclusion/exclusion of people from outside the EU? We know that past EU enlargements have in many member states led to more restrictive labour immigration policies for non EU-nationals, especially lower-skilled workers (see, for example, Zelano 2012). This may be a perfectly justifiable response within the sphere of labour immigration. The picture gets more complicated and problematic, however, if we consider the potential relationships between the free movement and equal treatment of EU *workers* and the highly regulated admission and restricted rights of *asylum seekers* and *refugees* from outside Europe. How, if at all, do the current policies for the inclusion of mobile EU citizens affect our policies for excluding/excluding asylum seekers, refugees and other migrants from outside Europe – and vice versa? These are open and important issues for future empirical research. Debates and research on migration and mobility in the European Union should engage explicitly with these wider questions and inter-relationships.

Conclusion

Gudrun Biffl's work is an excellent example of how academic research can inform public debates and policy-making on migration and integration. Successful engagement with public debates and policy-making requires an understanding of how and why research is (mis)used in public policy debates, and of when and how research conclusions get politicised. There are clearly complex inter-relationships between research, public debates and policy-making processes. As evidenced by the impact of her research outside academia, Gudrun has clearly thought a lot about these issues and inter-relationships. Current and future scholars of migration and integration can learn a lot from Gudrun's work, not only in terms of its substantive conclusions but also in terms of *how* her public policy research was approached and conducted.

Specifically, I have argued that making linkages – as Gudrun has frequently done in her work – across disciplines, issue areas, and the common divide between migration theory and policy practices should be an important strategy for future research on migration and integration, especially for research that explicitly aims to inform public debates and policy-making. To give an example from the European context, I have suggested that the interrelationships between "migrants" (from outside the EU) and "mobile workers" (from within the EU) should become a much more important question for migration research and policy debates than is currently the case. I don't know if Gudrun agrees with this particular argument about linking migration and mobility in the EU but I hope to have identified correctly some of the key features of Gudrun's applied research on international migration and integration. Current and future migration and public policy scholars have much to learn from it.

References

Afonso, A. and C. Devitt. (2016). "Comparative Political Economy and International Migration". *Socio-Economic Review* 14 (3): 591-613

Anderson, B. and M. Ruhs (2010) "Migrant workers: Who needs them? A framework for the analysis of shortages, immigration, and public policy" In: Ruhs M and Anderson B (eds) Who Needs Migrant Workers? Labour Shortages, Immigration and Public Policy, Oxford: Oxford University Press, pp. 15-56

Bauböck, R. and M. Tripkovic (2017) The integration of migrants and refugees: an EUI forum on migration, citizenship and demography, Florence: European University Institute, Robert Schuman Centre for Advanced Studies

Bakewell, O. (2008) "Research Beyond the Categories: The Importance of Policy Irrelevant Research into Forced Migration", Journal of Refugee Studies 21(4): 432-453

Biffl, G. and I. Skrivanek (2016) "The Distinction Between Temporary Labour Migration and Posted Workers in Austria: Labour Law vs Trade Law", in Howe, J. and R. Owens ed. (2016) Temporary Labour Migration in the Global Era, Hart Publishing, Oxford and Portland, Oregon.

Biffl, G. (2011) Satisfying Labour Demand through Migration in Austria, Vienna: International Organisation for Migration (IOM).

Biffl, G. and L. Rössl, ed. (2011) Migration und Integration: Dialog zwischen Politik, Wissenschaft und Praxis, Bad Vöslau: Omninum.

Boswell, C., Geddes, A. and P. Scholten (2011) "The Role of Narratives in Migration Policy-Making: A Research Framework", The British Journal of Politics and International Relations 13: 1-11

Blinder, S. (2011) "UK public opinion toward migration: Determinants of attitudes", Migration Observatory Briefing, University of Oxford

Blinder, S. and Allen, W. L. (2015) 'Constructing Immigrants: Portrayals of Migrant Groups in British National Newspapers, 2010-2012', *International Migration Review*

Boswell, C. (2012) The Political Uses of Expert Knowledge, Cambridge University Press

Deacon, M. (2016). Michael Gove's guide to Britain's greatest enemy... the experts. The Telegraph - Online Edition, June 10 2016.. Retrieved from http://www.telegraph.co.uk/news/2016/06/10/michael-goves-guide-to-britains-greatest-enemy-the-experts/

Devitt, C. (2011) Varieties of Capitalism, Variation in Labor Immigration. Journal of Ethnic and Migration Studies 37 (4): 579–96

Freeman, G. (1986) "Migration and the Political Economy of the Welfare State", Annals of the American Academy of Political and Social Science 485: 51-63

Goodwin, M. and Milazzo, C. (2017). Taking back control? Investigating the role of immigration in the 2016 vote for Brexit. The British Journal of Politics and International Relations [Online]: Available at: https://doi.org/10.1177/1369148117710799

Hampshire, J. (2013) The Politics of Immigration: Contradictions of the Liberal State, Cambridge: Polity Press

IOM (2017) World Migration Report 2018, International Organization for Migration, Geneva.

Jongerius, A., & Morin-Chartier, E. (2017). Revision of the directive on the posting of workers - Labour Mobility Package. Blogpost in: Legislative Train Schedule. Deeper and fairer internal market with a strengthened industrial base / Labour. Retrieved from http://www.europarl.europa.eu/legislative-train/theme-deeper-and-fairer-internal-market-with-a-strengthened-industrial-base-labour/file-revision-of-the-directive-on-the-posting-of-workers-labour-mobility-package

Menz, G. (2009) The Political Economy of Managed Migration: The Role of Unions, Employers, and Non-Governmental Organizations in a Europeanized Policy Domain. Oxford: Oxford University Press

Organisation for Economic Co-operation and Development, OECD (2010) *Public Opinions and Immigration: Individual Attitudes, Interest Groups and the Media*, Paris

Ruhs, M. (2017) "Labour immigration policies in high-income countries: Variations across political regimes and varieties of capitalism", *Journal of Legal Studies*, forthcoming

Ruhs, M. (2017b). Freedom of movement under attack: Is it worth defending as the core of EU citizenship? - "Migrants", "mobile citizens" and the borders of exclusion in the European Union. Blogpost in: European Union Democracy Observatory on Citizenship, European University Institute. Retrieved from http://eudo-citizenship.eu/commentaries/citizenship-forum/citizenship-forum-cat/1586-freedom-of-movement-under-attack-is-it-worth-defending-as-the-core-of-eu-citizenship?showall=&start=13

Ruhs, M. (2013) The Price of Rights: Regulating International Labor Migration. Princeton and Oxford: Princeton University Press

Ruhs, M., Palme, J. & K. Tamas (Eds.) (2018) Bridging the gaps: Linking research to public debates and policy-making on migration and integration, Delmi, Stockholm. [forthcoming]

Scholten, P., Entzinger, H., Penninx, R. and Verbeek, S. (Eds.) (2015) Integrating Immigrants in Europe: Research-Policy Dialogues, Springer.

The Economist. (2016). Art of the lie. Politicians have always lied. Does it matter if they leave the truth behind entirely? The Economist, 10 September 2016. Retrieved from https://www.economist.com/news/leaders/21706525-politicians-have-always-lied-does-it-matter-if-they-leave-truth-behind-entirely-art

Zelano, K. ed. (2012) *Labour Migration: What's in it for us? Experiences from Sweden, the UK and Poland*, FORES, Stockholm

Migration in der Weltgesellschaft: Welche Forschungsgegenstände beobachtet die Soziologie?

> *„Information ist Information, weder Materie noch Energie.*
> *Kein Materialismus, der dies nicht berücksichtigt, kann heute überleben."*
> Norbert Wiener

> *„Information ist [...] immer Information eines Systems. [...]*
> *Information ist nur im System [...] möglich."*
> Niklas Luhmann

Thomas Pfeffer[1]

Zusammenfassung

Der vorliegende Text unternimmt den Versuch, den auf MigrantInnen und ihre Lebensverhältnisse fokussierten Blick zu erweitern und zusätzliche Gegenstände für die Migrationsforschung zu identifizieren. Zu diesem Zweck werden zuerst unterschiedliche soziologische Vorstellungen von sozialen Einheiten miteinander verglichen, um dann in das systemtheoretische Konzept der Weltgesellschaft einzuführen und in einem weiteren Schritt die Eigenstrukturen von Weltgesellschaft als mögliche Forschungsgegenstände der Migrationsforschung vorzuschlagen.

Einleitung

Die Frage nach den Forschungsgegenständen der Migrationsforschung, die wir hier aus einer systemtheoretisch informierten, soziologischen Perspektive untersuchen wollen, ist sowohl theoretisch, als auch methodologisch hochgradig relevant. Nur wenn man weiß, wonach man sucht, kann man auch die dafür geeigneten Methoden wählen. Mit Popper kann man sagen, dass *„Erkenntnis [...] nicht mit Wahrnehmung oder der Sammlung von Daten oder Tatsachen"* beginnt, sondern *„mit Problemen"*, bzw. der *„Spannung zwischen Wissen und Nichtwissen"* (Popper, 1972, S. 104). Migrationsforschung beginnt daher im Idealfall nicht mit dem Auftreten von MigrantInnen, die – weil sie nun schon einmal da sind – untersucht werden, sondern mit einem – nach Möglichkeit: wissenschaftlich relevanten –

---

[1] Ich danke meinen Kolleginnen Anna Faustmann und Isabella Skrivanek für wertvolle Anregungen und Korrekturen zum vorliegenden Text.

Problem. Denn gerade dann, wenn Migration – zumindest scheinbar – verstärkt auftritt[2] und daher nicht mehr als gesellschaftliches Randproblem, sondern als zentrale gesellschaftliche Herausforderung dargestellt werden muss, stellt sich die Frage nach der Gesellschaft, in der Migration stattfindet. Welches Verständnis von sozialen Strukturen, von Gesellschaft und von gesellschaftlicher Realität haben wir vor Augen, wenn wir Migration beobachten?

Es wäre für die Migrationsforschung problematisch, hier die Gesellschaftskonzepte von Praktikern (z.B. MigrantInnen, staatlichen Institutionen, NGO's) ungeprüft zu übernehmen. Aber sowohl technokratische, als auch kritische Ansätze der Migrationsforschung bewegen sich nahe an der Praxis, und beschäftigen sich eher mit Menschen als mit sozialen Strukturen, eher mit MigrantInnen, als mit Migration:

„Die Migrationsforschung tendiert dazu, den Bezugsrahmen ihrer Forschung stark einzuschränken. Sie fokussiert weniger die sozialstrukturellen Voraussetzungen und Folgen von internationaler Migration auf den verschiedenen Ebenen der modernen Gesellschaft, sondern Migranten und ihre Lebensverhältnisse in den für bedeutsam erachteten sozialen Kontexten, wie sie aus den Bedingungen der Integration und den Strukturen sozialer Ungleichheit resultieren. Grundlage dafür ist ein eingeschränkter Begriff der Sozialstruktur, in dem im Wesentlichen die sozialen Verteilungs- und Ungleichheitsverhältnisse gefasst sind." (Bommes, 2003, S. 41)

Die starke Fokussierung auf die Untersuchung von Menschengruppen, ihren Unterschieden und Verhältnissen zueinander birgt auch die Gefahr ethnisierender Vorstellungen von Migration und Gesellschaft:

„Viele migrationssoziologische Studien setzen ethnische Gruppen als selbstverständliche Beobachtungseinheiten voraus und nehmen an, dass sich diese durch Gemeinschaftssolidarität und kulturelle Differenz auszeichnen. Diese Annahmen werden von den unterschiedlichsten Ansätzen geteilt, von der Assimilationstheorie bis zum Paradigma der transnationalen Gemeinschaften, die ansonsten wenig gemein haben. Sie alle implizieren eine Herder'sche Perspektive, welche die Unterteilung der Welt in verschiedene ‚Völker' naturalisiert." (Wimmer, 2008, S. 57)

Eine mögliche Folge dieser Beschäftigung mit MigrantInnen und ihren Lebensverhältnisse ist auch die große Nähe zu handlungstheoretischen Konzepten und Realitätsvorstellungen. Wir wollen sie im nächsten Abschnitt mit systemtheoretischen Zugängen vergleichen, bevor wir im letzten Abschnitt auf Überlegungen zu Weltgesellschaft als sozialstruktureller Rahmen für internationale Migration eingehen.

---

[2] Zweifel an einer generellen Zunahme der globalen Migration äußern etwa Czaika & de Haas (2014, S. 283): *"Although it is commonly believed that the volume, diversity, geographical scope, and overall complexity of international migration have increased as part of globalization processes, this idea has remained largely untested"*.

Handlungstheoretische vs. systemtheoretische Zugänge

Migration ist unleugbar ein Phänomen, das mit der Bewegung von Menschen im Raum zu tun hat. Wenn man einen solchen physikalischen Ausgangspunk für die Beobachtung von Migration einnimmt, dann stellt sich aus sozialwissenschaftlicher Sicht die Grundsatzfrage, in wieweit Migration als Teil einer

„außersozialen Realität – verstanden im weitesten Sinne, etwa als natürliche Umwelt, als physischer Raum, als Materialität der Welt, als Körperlichkeit des Menschen – objektiv gegeben und dem Sozialen vorgängig ist, oder ob sie als ›sozial konstruiert‹ und damit als Moment des Sozialen selbst verstanden werden muss." (Kaldewey, 2011, S. 277)

Seit den 1970ern gab es Bestrebungen, diese Frage auf die Unterscheidung zwischen Realismus und Konstruktivismus engzuführen, eine Engführung, die auch mit dem ursprünglichen Versuch zu tun hat, naturalistische Erklärungen sozialen Geschehens durch genuin sozialwissenschaftliche Erklärungen zu ersetzen. Dies führte aber zu einer Gleichsetzung der Unterscheidung von Realismus und Konstruktivismus mit der Unterscheidung von Natur- und Sozialwissenschaften, sowie zu dem Problem, nicht erklären zu können, was man unter diesen Voraussetzungen als ‚soziale Realität' zu verstehen hätte und wie man sie von einer ‚außersozialen Realität' unterscheiden müsste (Kaldewey, 2011, S. 282f).

Um dieses Realitätsproblem der Sozialwissenschaft zu analysieren, sollte daher eine andere Unterscheidung verwendet werden, nämlich die zwischen Handlungstheorie und Systemtheorie, um zu untersuchen, wie unterschiedlich diese beiden Ansätze mit sozialen und außer-sozialen Realitäten umgehen.

Vorstellungen sozialer Einheit(en) in Handlungstheorie und Systemtheorie: Teil/Ganzes vs. System/Umwelt

Da die Handlungstheorie das menschliche Individuum ins Zentrum seiner Überlegungen stellt, beruht sie auch auf traditionellen Vorstellungen von sozialen Einheiten (oder Systemen), die die Unterscheidung von Teilen und Ganzem verwenden. Auf dieser Grundlage beruht die Annahme, dass soziale Einheiten, wie etwa Organisationen oder Gesellschaften *„aus individuellen Menschen besteht wie ein Ganzes aus Teilen"* (Luhmann, 1984, S. 20). Mit dieser Grundkonzeption von sozialen Einheiten entsteht aber eine Reihe von Folgeproblemen:

1. Menschen werden in der Handlungstheorie auch physisch und psychisch als Teil von sozialen Einheiten gedacht. Die Beschreibung des Sozialen als Realitätsebene sui generis wird damit erschwert, es entsteht die Tendenz zu ‚naturalistischen' und/oder ‚psychologisierenden' Erklärungen.
2. Soziale Einheiten werden als physisch begrenzt gedacht, einerseits durch die Summe der zugehörigen Menschen und andererseits durch deren Verteilung im Raum. Im wechselseitigen Verhältnis zwischen sozialen Einheiten sind aufgrund dieser räumlichen Konzeption auch nur segmentäre (gleichartig nebenei-

nander) oder stratifikatorische Ordnungsmodelle (hierarchische Über-/ Unterordnung) vorstellbar.³
3. Eine auf der Ansammlung von Menschen abstellende Definition sozialer Einheiten setzt die für Zugehörigkeit in Frage kommenden Menschen unter erheblichen Homogenisierungsdruck, da die *„Teile im Verhältnis zum Ganzen homogen sein müßten"* (Luhmann, 1984, S. 23). Dies trifft vor allem dann zu, wenn eine einzige Form der Realteilung zwischen Menschen oder Menschengruppen (etwa: Inländer/MigrantInnen, Proletarier/KapitalistInnen, etc.) als dominant gesetzt wird.
4. Mit Blick auf Migration und Migrationsforschung könnte man formulieren, dass der Begriff der ‚Integration' eine handlungstheoretische Vorstellung von der Herstellung ‚gesamthafter' Zugehörigkeit von Menschen zu sozialen Einheiten transportiert.

Im Gegensatz dazu geht die soziologische Systemtheorie in der Tradition Niklas Luhmann's von der Vorstellung selbstreferentieller Systeme aus, also von Systemen, die sich durch ihre jeweils eigenen Operationen selbst erzeugen. Die elementaren Operationen von sozialen Systemen sind dabei Kommunikationen (und Handlungen).

Um systemintern an eigene Operationen anschließen und daraus Information gewinnen zu können, müssen selbstreferentielle Systeme die Unterscheidung von System und Umwelt verwenden. (Luhmann, 1984, S. 25) Doch Umwelt im hier verwendeten Sinn ist nicht absolut gesetzt, sondern nur in Relation zum jeweiligen System zu verstehen. *„Die Umwelt erhält ihre Einheit erst durch das System und nur relativ zum System. [...] Sie ist für jedes System eine andere, da jedes System nur sich selbst aus seiner Umwelt ausnimmt."* (Luhmann, 1984, S. 36) In einen mathematischen Formalismus gebracht *„erscheint ein System als Funktion seiner selbst und seiner Umwelt: $S=f(S, U)$."* (Vogd, 2007, S. 300)

1. *Strukturell*, auf der Ebene der basalen Operationen (Kommunikationen) sind Menschen (ihre Körper, ihr Bewusstsein) damit eindeutig in der Umwelt sozialer Systeme angesiedelt. *Semantisch* können Menschen dagegen auch Teil dieser Systeme werden, wenn und soweit sie kommunikativ von den jeweiligen Systemen thematisiert und behandelt werden.
2. Soziale Systeme grenzen sich nicht räumlich, sondern operativ von ihren jeweiligen Umwelten, aber auch voneinander ab. Im räumlichen Verhältnis zueinander sind daher auch Überlagerungen denkbar. Neben segmentären und stratifi-

---

³ Gut erkennbar ist eine solche räumlich-hierarchische Vorstellung etwa am Beispiel von Immanuel Wallerstein's Konzept eines ‚kapitalistischen Weltsystems' (Wallerstein, 1974), das den Systembegriff im Sinne einer eher handlungstheoretischen Tradition verwendet, jedenfalls aber deutlich anders als die soziologische Systemtheorie in der Tradition Luhmann's. Für die Migrationsforschung ist dies insofern problematisch, als in diesem Forschungsfeld manche Autoren Wallerstein als Systemtheoretiker missverstehen (vgl. z.B. Han, 2006), wodurch der Blick auf originär systemtheoretische Beiträge (etwa von Bommes oder Stichweh) verstellt wird.

katorischen werden damit auch funktionale Differenzierungen möglich. Die Systemtheorie unterscheidet drei Typen sozialer Systeme: Interaktionssysteme, Organisationen und Funktionssysteme (thematisch spezialisierte Kommunikationssysteme von universellem/globalem Geltungsanspruch, wie Recht, Wirtschaft, Politik, Bildung, etc.).
3. Die Zugehörigkeit von Menschen zu sozialen Systemen als Themen und/oder Adressen für Kommunikation ist abhängig vom jeweiligen Kommunikationssystem, das Menschen mit unterschiedlichen Rollenangeboten adressiert, und etwa nach Mitglieder/KlientInnen in Organisationen, oder nach Leistungsrollen/Publikumsrollen in Funktionszusammenhängen unterscheidet. (Stichweh, 2007a).
4. Mit Blick auf Migration und Migrationsforschung könnte man formulieren, dass die Systemtheorie von ‚Inklusion/Exklusion' einzelner sozialer Systeme nach den jeweils eigenen Systemrationalitäten ausgeht. Die Untersuchung von Inklusionsbedingungen erfordert daher die genauere Angabe des jeweils in den Blick genommenen Systems und seiner Beobachtungslogiken. MigrantInnen werden von sozialen System in der Regel nicht als ‚ganze Menschen' betrachtet, sondern nach den je eigenen Beobachtungslogiken, etwa im Fall von Sicherheitsbehörden unter dem Fokus ‚Aufenthaltstitel', von NGO's unter dem Blickwinkel spezifischer Formen der ‚Bedürftigkeit', vom Bildungssystem unter dem Gesichtspunkt der ‚Schulpflichtigkeit', etc.

Der Realitätsbezug von Handlungstheorie und Systemtheorie

Vereinfacht gesprochen gehen handlungstheoretische Ansätze von einer Spaltung der Welt in drei Teile aus: der physikalischen Objektwelt, dem Subjekt und einem objektivierbaren, gesellschaftlichen System von Regeln und Institutionen (Vogd, 2007, S. 300). Unterstellt wird dabei ein ‚Realitätskontinuum', dass die drei Teile in ein vertikal aufeinander aufbauendes, hierarchische Verhältnis zueinander setzt, etwa im klassischen Basis/Überbau-Theorem des Marxismus, in dem etwa Produktivkräfte als Basis fungieren, während etwa Politik oder Religion als bloße Überbauphänome beschrieben werden (Kaldewey, 2011, S. 298).

Von einer handlungstheoretischen Position aus stehen sich menschliches Individuum und Gesellschaft gegenüber wie Körper und Geist. *„Das Soziale, so könnte man diese Position auch paraphrasieren, ist die Einheit der Unterscheidung des Individuellen und des Kollektiven."* (Kaldewey, 2011, S. 298) Im Zentrum der Handlungstheorie steht dabei das menschliche Individuum als Akteur, dessen Handlungsspielraum durch materielle Zwänge, Sanktionen anderer Individuen oder durch gesellschaftliche Zwänge eingeschränkt und strukturiert werden kann. Diese Vorstellung von *„Handlungen oder Praktiken, die das Soziale, das Psychische, das Körperliche und das Physisch-Materielle ›ganzheitlich‹ umgreifen"*, macht aber die begriffliche Unterscheidung von *„genuin sozialen Formen von Strukturierung"* (Kaldewey, 2011, S. 303) äußerst schwierig. Es wird von einer einzigen, objektiv gegebenen, beobachterunabhängigen Realität ausgegangen, während der Strukturbegriff polyvalent angelegt ist.

Auch die Systemtheorie ist eine *„empirische Theorie, die sich auf die ›wirkliche Welt‹ bezieht"* (Vogd, 2007, S. 300) und die den Anspruch erhebt, dass sich ihre Aussagen in der Wirklichkeit bewähren (Luhmann, 1984, S. 30). Auch die Systemtheorie unterscheidet unterschiedliche Ebenen der Realität, aber nicht in einem essentialistischen Sinn, wie die Handlungstheorie, sondern in einem operativen Sinn, wie es das Konzept der selbstreferentiellen Systeme vorschlägt. Luhmann wendet diese Hypothese auf lebende Systeme (Organismen), psychische Systeme (Bewusstseinssysteme) und soziale Systeme (Kommunikationssysteme) an (Luhmann, 1984, S. 16), die sich auf Basis ihrer basalen Operationen unterscheiden: lebende Systeme auf Basis ihrer je eigenen Stoffwechselprozesse, psychische Systeme auf Basis ihrer je eigenen Gedanken, soziale Systeme auf Basis ihrer je eigenen Kommunikationen. Obwohl für das Zustandekommen sozialer Systeme das Vorhandensein von Organismen und Bewusstseinssystemen vorausgesetzt wird und sie möglicherweise auch strukturell gekoppelt sind, gibt es aber kein ‚Realitätskontinuum' zwischen ihnen. *„Es gibt keinen direkten Zugang physikalischer, chemischer, biologischer Vorgänge auf die Kommunikation – es sei denn im Sinne von Destruktion."* (Luhmann, 1997, S. 114)

Grundlage für selbstreferentielle Systeme, also auch für soziale Kommunikationssysteme, ist die selbsterzeugte und selbst aufrechterhaltene Unterscheidung von System und Umwelt. *„Die Umwelt ist also nicht ›Grund‹ des Systems, sondern operiert auf derselben Realitätsebene, ja sie ›existiert‹ nur für das System."* (Kaldewey, 2011, S. 285) Auf einer *operativen* Ebene erzeugt sich jedes System durch seine eigenen Operationen selbst. Auf einer *semantischen* Ebene erzeugt jedes System damit seine eigenen Beobachtungen von sich selbst und von seiner Umwelt. Die Welt ist daher nicht einfach objektiv gegeben, sondern kann nur aus beobachterabhängigen Perspektiven beschrieben werden. Systemtheorie muss daher von *„polyzentrischen und polykontexturalen Verhältnissen"* (Vogd, 2007, S. 305) ausgehen und mit systematischen Perspektivenwechseln arbeiten.

Weltgesellschaft und die regionalen Kulturen der Welt

„Migration und Migranten sind auf verblüffende Weise Phänomene geblieben, welche die Gesellschaft wie von außen zu betreffen scheinen." (Bommes, 2008, S. 20).

Diese Sichtweise scheint auf ‚methodologischem Nationalismus' (ein Begriff, der von Martins (1974) geprägt wurde) zu beruhen, also auf der konzeptionellen Gleichsetzung von Nationalstaat und Gesellschaft, die in der Migrationsforschung dazu führen kann, Migration und Integration bevorzugt aus der Problemsicht von Nationalstaaten zu beschreiben bzw. weltweit von einer Vielzahl an nationalstaatlich begrenzten Gesellschaften auszugehen. Doch Phänomene, wie internationale

Migration, globale Ungleichheit, die Europäische Union oder die olympischen Spiele können nicht auf einzelne Nationalstaaten zurückgeführt werden. Vielmehr müssen sie als Phänomene von Weltgesellschaft betrachtet werden. Der prominenteste Kandidat für eine soziologische Theorie der Weltgesellschaft ist die Systemtheorie in der Tradition Niklas' Luhmanns[4].

Die Entstehung von Weltgesellschaft durch Migration und Kommunikation

Schon die erstmalige Besiedlung des Erdballs durch die menschliche Spezies kann als Migrationsvorgang bezeichnet werden, der insgesamt rund 50.000 Jahre dauerte. Dieser Vorgang alleine hat jedoch noch nicht zur Entstehung von Weltgesellschaft geführt, da die verschiedenen Regionen und Teilpopulationen den Kontakt untereinander verloren, wodurch die Entstehung autarker, voneinander unabhängigen Gesellschaften möglich wurde. (Stichweh, 2008, S. 158)

„Weltgesellschaft erscheint als globaler Zusammenhang der Vernetzung und Unterbrechung von kommunikativ mitgeteilter Informationen" (Stichweh, 2008, S. 150). Ein solch globaler Kommunikationszusammenhang entsteht historisch gesehen erst in den letzten rund 500-600 Jahren, aufgrund der kolonialen Expansion der europäischen Gesellschaft durch die Mobilität von Entdeckern und Eroberern und der damit verbundenen *„Vollentdeckung des Erdballs"* (Stichweh, 2008, S. 151) Zentrales Charakteristikum von Weltgesellschaft ist aber nicht die Vereinheitlichung des Verhaltens oder die Durchsetzung zentralisierter Kontrolle (die beide nicht realisiert sind), sondern die Herstellung eines globalen Kommunikationszusammenhangs, der die vormalige *„Pluralität der vielen Gesellschaften in die Unizität eines einzigen weltweiten Gesellschaftssystems transformiert hat."* (Stichweh, 2008, S. 150) Die Vielzahl früherer Gesellschaften wurde von einem globalen Kommunikationszusammenhang absorbiert, der es unmöglich macht, kleinere Gemeinschaften vollständig vom Rest der Welt zu isolieren. Diese Entwicklung führt jedoch weder zu einer reinen Vereinheitlichung von kulturellen Differenzen (im Sinne einer McDonaldisierung), noch zu einer unveränderten Kontinuität bestehender regionaler Kulturen und ihrer Diversität. Vielmehr kommt es zu einem kumulativen Modell sozialer Strukturen, das von pluralen Ebenen der Strukturbildung ausgeht, und in dem die Eigenstrukturen der Weltgesellschaft ältere Strukturen überlagern und verändern. (Stichweh, 2007b, S. 135f).

Zwei zentrale Tendenzen sind für die Entstehung dieses globalen Kommunikationszusammenhangs von entscheidender Bedeutung: Migration und (technolo-

---

[4] Ein – im angelsächsischen Raum bekannteres – soziologisches Konkurrenzangebot zur Analyse von Weltgesellschaft ist der Neo-Institutionalismus in der Tradition von John F. Meyer (vgl. z.B. Krücken & Drori, 2010), der in vielen Punkten (z.B. konstruktivistische Wurzeln, Ablehnung methodologischen Individualismus, etc.) Parallelen zur Systemtheorie aufweist. Meyer ist vor allem an der Durchsetzung von globalen Modellen, Mustern oder Regelungsvorstellungen und den dadurch entstehenden Phänomenen von Konvergenz und Isomorphismus interessiert. Zu einem Vergleich von Neo-Institutionalismus und Systemtheorie siehe etwa Stichweh (2015).

gisch unterstützte) Kommunikation. Migration hat immer schon zu einer Verbreitung von Information, von Wissen, Konzepten und Werten beigetragen. Die Entwicklung und Durchsetzung von Kommunikationstechnologien (Schrift, Buchdruck, audio-visuelle Medien, digitale Medien) ermöglicht die über lokale Arrangements hinausgehende Verbreitung von Kommunikation und Information und damit die Entstehung von über das Lokale hinausgehende, gesellschaftlich relevanter Kommunikationszusammenhänge zunehmend auch unabhängig von Migration. Andererseits werden in diesen neuen Kommunikationszusammenhängen auch verstärkt Informationen über Lebens- und Erwerbsmöglichkeiten transportiert, was wiederum zu Migration beiträgt. Migration und Kommunikation sind daher parallel existierende Mechanismen zur Entwicklung, Aufrechterhaltung und Transformation von Weltgesellschaft.

Die Ausbreitung von Weltgesellschaft wird zusätzlich von sozialen Strukturen befördert, die vor der Entstehung von Weltgesellschaft nicht oder nur rudimentär vorhanden waren, und die Stichweh (2007b) als Eigenstrukturen von Weltgesellschaft bezeichnet (Stichweh, 2007b). Die meisten dieser Eigenstrukturen haben auch Bezüge zum Phänomen der Migration, wie wir in den folgenden Abschnitten sehen werden.

Globale Funktionssysteme:
Wirtschaft, Politik, Recht, Erziehung, Wissenschaft, etc.

Der wohl wichtigste Kandidat für Eigenstrukturen von Weltgesellschaft ist die Entstehung von thematisch spezialisierten Kommunikationszusammenhängen von globalem Geltungsanspruch, die so genannten kommunikativen Funktionssysteme. Funktionssysteme entstehen durch die Verknüpfung von thematisch ähnlichen Kommunikationen. So entsteht die Politik durch die am Thema Macht orientierte Kommunikation, Wirtschaft als Kommunikation über Besitz und Geld, Recht als Kommunikation über die Konformität oder Abweichung von Gesetzen, Bildung als systematischer Diskurs über den Wissensstand von Individuen, Wissenschaft als Diskurs über den Wahrheitsgehalt von Tatsachenbehauptungen, etc.

Als Beispiel dafür, wie Funktionssysteme auch noch die unterschiedlichsten regionalen Wertemuster in einen globalen Kommunikationszusammenhang bringen können, beschreibt Stichweh (2007b) die Integration der islamischen Wirtschaft in die Weltwirtschaft: Obwohl viele westliche Wirtschaftspraktiken (Verkauf von Alkohol und Tabak, konventionelle Finanzdienstleistungen, Unterhaltungsindustrie, etc.) prinzipiell inkompatibel mit islamischem Recht sind, werden doch Möglichkeiten geschaffen, auch die islamische Wirtschaft an die Weltwirtschaft anzukoppeln. Ein Instrument dafür ist etwa die Bündelung ausgewählter Investitionsmöglichkeiten, die mit islamischen Standards kompatibel sind, oder die Entwicklung von Instrumenten, die solche Investments vergleichbar und global erreichbar machen. (Stichweh, 2007b, S. 137f)

Funktionssysteme entwickeln auch ihre eigenen Semantiken, also eigene Begriffe, Modelle und Unterscheidungsmöglichkeiten, an deren Verbreitungsgeschichte man auch die Entwicklungsgeschichte der einzelnen Funktionssysteme nachzeichnen kann. Ein Beispiel dafür ist etwa das globale Bildungssystem und seine semantischen Formen, wie formale Bildungsinstitutionen, sequentiell gestufte, nationale Bildungssysteme, oder formale Bildungsabschlüsse und Qualifikationen. Schofer und Meyer (2005) konnten etwa zeigen, dass die Partizipation von signifikanten Teilen der Weltbevölkerung in primären, sekundären und tertiären Bildungseinrichtungen erst im 20. Jahrhundert auftrat. Diese drei Wellen sind in aufeinanderfolgenden, exponentiellen Kurven darstellbar (Schofer & Meyer (2005), zitiert in Baker (2014)).

Funktionssysteme unterscheiden sich auch deutlich in Hinblick darauf, wie sehr sie selbst Migration voraussetzen oder bewirken. Schon im Mittelalter basierte etwa höhere Bildung zu großen Teilen auf der temporären Migration von Studierenden und in weiten Teilen auch auf einem über das Lokale hinausgehenden Austausch der Lehrenden. Beide Tendenzen haben sich bis heute gehalten, etwa in der zunehmend internationalen Suche nach den attraktivsten Hochschulstudien oder zumindest in der Forderung nach Auslandsaufenthalten selbst bei regional besuchten Studienangeboten, sowie in der Geringschätzung von Hausberufungen bei Stellenbesetzungen an Universitäten.

Andere Muster der Migration sind etwa im Profi-Fußball zu beobachten, wo Nachwuchstalente für den Europäischen Spitzenfußball besonders stark in Afrika und Lateinamerika rekrutiert werden, während europäische Altstars in finanzstarke fußballerische Entwicklungsgebiete (China, USA, arabischer Raum) exportiert werden. Als interessanter Effekt dieser globalen Wertschöpfungskette im Fußballsport kann es zu einer Veränderung der Männlichkeitsvorstellungen in den Herkunftsländern kommen. So wurde etwa beobachtet, dass die Orientierung an den Berufsvorstellungen eines internationalen Fußballprofis unter Jugendlichen in Kamerun nicht zur Entwicklung sehr prahlerischer, machoider Männlichkeitsbilder führte, wie dies ursprünglich erwartet wurde, sondern im Gegenteil zu eher zurückhaltenden, bescheidenen Identitätsentwürfen, die im internationalen Fußball als leichter vermittelbar erscheinen (derStandard.at, 2017).

Formale Organisationen

Die Entstehung formaler Organisationen als Einheiten, die sich durch die entscheidungsorientierte Kommunikation ihrer Mitglieder konstituieren, hängt historisch eng mit der Entstehung von Funktionssystemen zusammen. Vorläufer waren im Mittelalter funktional spezifizierte Kooperationen, wie Ordensgemeinschaften, Universitäten, freie (selbstverwaltete) Städte, Handelsgesellschaften oder Handwerksgilden. Ein besonders bemerkenswertes Beispiel ist der Jesuitenorden, der aufgrund der geringen familiären Bindungen seiner Mitglieder über sehr mobiles Personal verfügte, wodurch es dem Orden möglich wurde, in wenigen Jahrzehnten ein globales Netzwerk an Bildungseinrichtungen zu etablieren. (Stichweh, 2007b, S. 137f)

Stichweh (2007b) weist noch auf drei weitere Charakteristika formaler Organisationen hin, die für die Migrations- und Integrationsforschung hochgradig relevant sein können: 1) Organisationen sind sehr effektiv im internen Transfer ihres Personals. Dabei gelingt es ihnen zum Teil sogar, politische Grenzen zu neutralisieren, die für MigrantInnen ohne Mitgliedschaft in internationalen Unternehmen viel schwerer zu überwinden sind. 2) Organisationen sind effiziente Mechanismen für den internen (und damit oft auch internationalen) Wissenstransfer. 3) Organisationen können oft ihre globale Vernetzung mit lokaler Verankerung verbinden und dadurch eine Verbindung zwischen Globalität und Lokalität herstellen. (Stichweh, 2007b, S. 137f)

Organisationen sind auch die einzigen sozialen Systeme, denen Akteursstatus zugeschrieben werden kann. Als solches sind sie besonders wichtig für die Inklusion/Integration von MigrantInnen und für den Umgang mit Diversität. So stellt sich etwa die Frage, ob und wie weit Organisationen offen sind für den Umgang mit Personen, die unterschiedliche Voraussetzungen und Bedürfnisse mitbringen. Dieser Umgang kann sich sowohl auf Publikumsrollen (etwa KundInnen, KlientInnen) beziehen, als auch auf Leistungsrollen (etwa MitarbeiterInnen, ManagerInnen). Dabei ist zu beachten, dass die Organisation eine eigene strukturelle Ebene des Umgangs mit Diversität darstellt und über eigene Inklusionsmechanismen verfügt, und dass die Organisation andererseits auch über eigene Opportunitätsstrukturen im Umgang mit Diversität verfügt. (Vgl. Biffl, et al., 2013; Imdorf, 2010).

Nationalstaaten

Gerade weil Nationalstaaten in der Praxis so häufig mit lokalen Gesellschaften (und scheinbar homogenen ethnischen Gruppen) gleichgesetzt werden, ist es notwendig, einen wissenschaftlich fundierten Begriff von Nationalstaaten zu definieren und sie als Eigenstrukturen der Weltgesellschaft zu untersuchen.

Historisch betrachtet handelt es sich bei Nationalstaaten um relativ junge Phänomene. Die ersten Nationalstaaten entstanden 1648 in Folge des Westfälischen Friedens, der den dreißigjährigen Krieg beendete. Das Konzept des Nationalstaates basiert auf der Kombination von zwei Ideen, einerseits der Idee des Selbstbestimmungsrechts von Nationen (also von Kollektiven mit gemeinsamen kulturellen Eigenschaften), und andererseits der Idee des politisch souveränen Staates. Erst im 20. Jahrhundert setzte sich die nationalstaatliche Form der politischen Kontrolle von Territorien auf globaler Ebene gegenüber stratifizierenden Alternativen, wie etwa den Großreichen oder den Kolonialstaaten, durch und ersetzten sie durch eine segmentäre Struktur formell gleicher Staaten (Stichweh, 2010, S. 305). Besonders rasant erfolgte die Verbreitung dieses Konzepts nach dem zweiten Weltkrieg, was zur Etablierung von rund 130 neuen Nationalstaaten zwischen 1945 und der Jahrtausendwende führte (Meyer, et al., 1997, S. 158). Dieser globale Prozess ist immer noch nicht vollständig abgeschlossen (siehe etwa Katalonien, Schottland), obwohl es gleichzeitig auch schon in verschiedenen Weltregionen zu

Entwicklungen kommt, um mehrere Nationalstaaten in größeren Zusammenhängen zu koordinieren.

Es ist eine wichtige Hypothese der Systemtheorie, dass es sich bei Nationalstaaten nicht um kommunikativ autarke Gesellschaften handelt, sondern um interne Differenzierungen des globalen Funktionssystems Politik. Schon im Westfälischen Frieden gründeten sich Nationalstaaten nicht autark für sich selbst, sondern in Abgrenzung voneinander. Als politische Einheiten haben Nationalstaaten die vorrangige Aufgabe, kollektiv bindende Entscheidungen zu organisieren und auf diese Weise ihre Mitglieder in das globale politische System zu inkludieren. Gemeinsam mit der Etablierung von politischer Kontrolle von Nationalstaaten über Territorien erfolgt auch die Aufteilung der Weltbevölkerung in Staatsbevölkerungen. Gerade die politische Neugründung von Nationalstaaten ist daher oft auch ein Anlass zur Umsortierung von Bevölkerungsgruppen und damit Auslöser von Migrationsereignissen. Beobachtbar ist gegenwärtig auch der Einsatz von Migration als Instrument der internationalen Politik, um die Europäische Union unter Druck zu setzen.

Dort, wo Nationalstaaten als Wohlfahrtsstaaten ausgeprägt sind, fällt ihnen noch eine zweite Aufgabe zu, nämlich die Moderation des Zugangs ihrer Mitglieder zu weiteren globalen Funktionssystemen (Wirtschaft, Recht, Bildung, etc.), ohne diese Systeme selbst kontrollieren zu können (Stichweh, 2010, S. 305).

Nationalstaaten sind nicht nur Subsysteme des globalen Funktionssystems Politik, sie weisen auch in mehrfacher Hinsicht Eigenschaften von Organisationen auf:

1. Nationalstaaten produzieren kollektiv bindende Entscheidungen und kommunizieren diese nach innen und nach außen.
2. Nationalstaaten unterscheiden zwischen Mitgliedern (BürgerInnen) und Nicht-Mitgliedern (TouristInnen, AusländerInnen mit Bleiberecht, etc.). Erst die politisch-administrative Entscheidung von Nationalstaaten über Mitgliedschaft verwandelt lebensweltlich wahrgenommene ‚Ortswechsel', ‚Mobilität' oder ‚Wanderschaft' in ‚Migration', meist in Zusammenhang mit der Zuweisung längerfristiger Aufenthaltsrechte an Nicht-Mitglieder auf dem jeweiligen staatlichen Territorium. Diese Unterscheidung zwischen der ‚Kernpopulation' und ‚Residualpopulation' (Bommes, 2003, *S. 50*), oder zwischen StaatsbürgerInnen und anderen EinwohnerInnen (Personen ohne Staatsbürgerschaft mit unterschiedlichen Berechtigungen) eines Wohlfahrtsstaates ist folgenreich:
„Der Staat als Wohlfahrtsstaat, d.h. als sozialer Ausgleichsmechanismus nach innen errichtet eine Ungleichheitsschwelle nach außen, die durch Migranten überschritten wird. [...] Internationale Migration ist nicht nur Ausdruck der erfolgreichen Überwindung der wohlfahrtsstaatlichen Ungleichheitsschwellen durch Migranten. Sie ist zugleich Teil einer inneren Umstrukturierung der Verteilungs- und Ungleichheitsverhältnisse in Wohlfahrtsstaaten selbst." (Bommes, 2003, S. 50)
3. Nationalstaaten verfügen auch über hoheits- oder wohlfahrtsstaatliche Administration, die in Organisationen strukturiert ist. Nur noch in seltenen Fällen

zielen Nationalstaaten auf rigide Vollinklusion ihrer administrativen Subsysteme in eine einzige, zentrale Organisation. Die üblichere Variante ist eher ein Arrangement unterschiedlicher, funktional differenzierter Organisationen und Steuerungsmechanismen, die von staatlicher Bürokratie über öffentlich-rechtliche Institutionen bis hin zu privaten Organisationen bzw. von direkter Intervention über indirekte Rahmenvorgaben bis hin zu wettbewerblich vergebener Ko-Finanzierung reichen können.

Dieses Arrangement an unterschiedlichen Organisationen bedeutet auch heterogene, je eigene organisatorische Rationalitäten, Perspektiven und Strategien im Umgang mit Migration und Integration. Auffallend sind in diesem Zusammenhang etwa unterschiedliche Zuständigkeiten für eigentlich verwandte Politikbereiche, z.b. für Aufenthaltsrechte bei Sicherheitsbehörden vs. für Integrationsagenden bei Arbeitsmarkt- und Sozialbehörden. Bemerkenswert ist auch der Umstand, dass wohlfahrtsstaatliche Institutionen von Migration in unterschiedlichem Ausmaß und zu unterschiedlichen Zeiten herausgefordert werden. So sind etwa im Kontext von Fluchtmigration Sicherheitsbehörden und Sozialbehörden früher und anders betroffen, als Bildungs- und Gesundheitseinrichtungen.

Aufschlussreich ist auch die wenig überraschende Erkenntnis, dass die Inklusionsangebote in wohlfahrtsstaatlichen Institutionen häufig auf sesshaften Karriereverläufen aufbauen und auf bestimmte Lebensphasen abgestellt sind. Das kann zu dem Problem führen, dass MigrantInnen zu spät kommen, etwa um ausreichend Sozialversicherungszeiten erwerben zu können, oder um unter die Schulpflicht zu fallen, wodurch sie zumindest von traditionellen Bildungseinrichtungen nicht mehr adressiert werden.

Andere, weitere Eigenstrukturen von Weltgesellschaft

Neben den schon genannten können in Anlehnung an Stichweh (2007b) noch einige weitere Eigenstrukturen von Weltgesellschaft in Stichworten angeführt werden:

1. *De-Lokalisierte Netzwerke*
   Netzwerke bedürfen geringerer Voraussetzungen als Organisationen und können daher sehr heterogene Entitäten miteinander verbinden können. Während in der Vergangenheit Netzwerke vor allem lokal existierten, können sie durch Kommunikationstechnologien immer weitere Distanzen überwinden und immer mehr Knotenpunkte einbinden. Aus migrationsforscherischer Sicht sind Netzwerkphänomene etwa in Zusammenhang mit internationalen Wertschöpfungsketten, mit Kettenmigration, aber auch mit Formen transnationaler Sozialkontakte und Wechselbeziehungen interessant. (Stichweh, 2007b, S. 138)
2. *Epistemic Communities und die Globalisierung von Wissen*
   Epistemische Communities basieren auf starken kognitiven und normativen Selbstverpflichtungen, nicht auf formeller Mitgliedschaft, wie in Organisationen, oder auf losen Kontakten, wie in Netzwerken. Professionelle, wissen-

schaftliche, oder disziplinäre Communities sind Beispiele für diese Strukturform. Zentral für epistemische Communities ist auch das Vorhandensein je spezifischer Wissensbestände, die weiterentwickelt und global verbreitet werden. (Stichweh, 2007b, S. 141)

3. *Welt-Ereignisse als räumlich-zeitliche Repräsentation von Weltgesellschaft*
Welt-Ereignisse ermöglichen die reflexive Bezugnahme auf Weltgesellschaft, indem sie weltweit dazu zwingen, sich als Darsteller oder Beobachter zu verhalten. Welt-Ereignisse kommen in den unterschiedlichsten Funktionsbereichen vor, etwa im Sport (Olympische Spiele), in der Unterhaltungsindustrie (Welttourneen), in der Bildung (globale Universitäts-Rankings), etc. Auch große Terroranschläge, wie der 11. September 2001, fallen in diese Kategorie von Ereignissen, die zwar lokal stattfinden, aber global die Aufmerksamkeit bündeln. (Stichweh, 2007b, S. 143)

4. *Märkte als selbst-ähnliche soziale Strukturen*
In einer soziologischen Definition können Märkte als Struktur betrachtet werden, in der sich alle TeilnehmerInnen wechselseitig wahrnehmen und daraus operative Konsequenzen ziehen. Dieses Prinzip funktioniert ungeachtet der Größe von Märkten, weshalb es einzelnen Akteuren relativ leicht möglich ist, zwischen lokalen und globalen Ebenen und Märkten hin und her zu wechseln. (Stichweh, 2007b, S. 145)

Angesichts dieser großen Bandbreite an Eigenstrukturen der Weltgesellschaft lässt sich auch konstatieren, dass Diversität nicht mehr alleine durch räumliche Unterschiede lokaler Kulturen, sondern in zunehmendem Maße auch durch die delokalisierten Strukturen der Weltgesellschaft, die sich darüberlegen, entsteht. (Stichweh, 2007b, S. 147) Aufgrund der dadurch beförderten Pluralität der Kulturen bleiben Situationen der Interkulturalität keine Ausnahmefälle, sondern werden im Gegenteil zur Alltagserfahrung in der Weltgesellschaft. (Stichweh, 2010b) Menschen sind zunehmend dazu aufgefordert, sich an den unterschiedlichsten sozialen Kontexten zu beteiligen und zwischen ihnen zu wechseln. Dass dies nicht immer als angenehm empfunden wird, zeigen gerade in der jüngsten politische Auseinandersetzungen, wie der Brexit oder die amerikanische Präsidentenwahl, in denen *vor dem Hintergrund von Weltgesellschaft* wieder verstärkt lokale Bezüge gesucht werden.

Schlussfolgerungen

Der vorliegende Text nahm die Kritik an der soziologischen Migrationsforschung zum Anlass, um über etablierte, vor allem aber über alternative, zusätzliche Forschungsgegenstände der Migrationsforschung nachzudenken.

Mit dem bisher sehr erfolgreichen und produktiven Fokus auf MigrantInnen hat sich die traditionelle Migrationsforschung vor allem auf MigrantInnen und ihren Lebenswelten, auf demographische Entwicklungen und quantitativen Beschreibungen von Bevölkerungsgruppen, auf soziale Ungleichheit und Abweichung migrantischer Gruppen, auf Input/Output-Relationen zwischen Territorien (Nationalstaaten oder Weltregionen) in Hinblick auf Bevölkerungsverschiebungen, Remittances oder Handelsströme, aber auch auf politisch-administrative Maßnahmen in Hinblick auf Migration und Integration fokussiert.

Da es sich bei internationaler Migration um ein globales Phänomen handelt, eröffnet das systemtheoretische Konzept der Weltgesellschaft eine große Fülle an weiteren Forschungsgegenständen für die Migrationsforschung, die es erlauben, die sozialstrukturellen Voraussetzungen und Folgen internationaler Migration noch stärker in den Blick zu nehmen und durch zusätzliche Perspektiven zu ergänzen. Diese möglichen Forschungsgegenstände reichen etwa von den Semantiken, die in den verschiedenen Funktionssystemen verwendet werden, um Migration zu beobachten und zu bearbeiten, über Inklusions- und Exklusionsmechanismen von Organisationen und wohlfahrtsstaatlichen Einrichtungen bis hin zur Bedeutung von MigrantInnen für die Aufrechterhaltung und Veränderung internationaler Wertschöpfungsketten, Netzwerke und Märkte. Spannende Fragestellungen wären auch die Suche nach soziostrukturellen Gründen für die unterschiedliche Mobilität von Menschen, Waren, Geld und Zertifikaten, oder dem Zusammenhang zwischen der sozialen Kontrolle des Raums und der räumlichen Kontrolle sozialer Sachverhalte.

Es ist in jedem Fall ein vielversprechendes Unterfangen, Migration nicht als isoliertes Phänomen zu betrachten, sondern die Untersuchung von Migration als analytisches Instrument zu verwenden, um Phänomene der Weltgesellschaft zu verstehen. Ich danke Gudrun Biffl ganz herzlich dafür, dass sie mir Zugang zu diesen Möglichkeiten geschaffen hat.

Literatur

Baker, D. P. (2014). *The Schooled Society. The Educational Transformation of Global Culture*. Stanford: Stanford University Press.
Biffl, G., Pfeffer, T., & Altenburg, F. (2013). *Diskriminierung in Rekrutierungsprozessen verstehen und überwinden*. Schriftenreihe Migration und Globalisierung, Krems: Edition Donau-Universität Krems.
Bommes, M. (2003). Migration in der modernen Gesellschaft. *Geographische Revue, 5/2003*(2), 41–58.
Bommes, M. (2008). Migration und die Veränderung der Gesellschaft. *Aus Politik Und Zeitgeschichte - APuZ, 35–36/2008*, 20–25.
Czaika, M., & de Haas, H. (2014). The globalization of migration. Has the world become more migratory? *International Migration Review, 48*(2), 283–323.
derStandard.at. (2017). 'Der Hyper-Macho wird es hier nicht schaffen.' Interview mit Niko Besnier. *DerStandard.at (Online-Ausgabe)*. Retrieved from http://derstandard.at/2000054578609/Der-Hyper-Macho-wird-es-hier-nicht-schaffen
Han, P. (2006). *Theorien zur internationalen Migration: Ausgewählte interdisziplinäre Migrationstheorien und deren zentrale Aussagen* (1st ed.). Stuttgart: UTB GmbH.

Imdorf, C. (2010). Die Diskriminierung ‚ausländischer' Jugendlicher bei der Lehrlingsauswahl. In U. Hormel & A. Scherr (Eds.), *Diskriminierung* (pp. 197–219). VS Verlag für Sozialwissenschaften.

Kaldewey, D. (2011). Das Realitätsproblem der Sozialwissenschaften: Anmerkungen zur Beobachtung des Außersozialen. *Soziale Systeme: Zeitschrift Für Soziologische Theorie, 17 (2011)*(2), 277–307.

Krucken, G., & Drori, G. S. (Eds.). (2010). *World Society: The Writings of John W. Meyer.* Oxford: Oxford University Press, U.S.A.

Luhmann, N. (1984). *Soziale Systeme: Grundriß einer allgemeinen Theorie.* Frankfurt am Main: Suhrkamp.

Luhmann, N. (1997). *Die Gesellschaft der Gesellschaft* (Vols 1–2). Frankfurt am Main: Suhrkamp.

Martins, H. (1974). Time and Theory in Sociology. In J. Rex (Ed.), *Approaches to Sociology* (pp. 246–294). London: Routledge and Kegan Paul.

Meyer, J. W., Boli, J., Thomas, G. M., & Ramirez, F. O. (1997). World Society and the Nation State. *American Journal of Sociology, 103,* 144–181.

Popper, K. R. (1972). Die Logik der Sozialwissenschaften. In T. W. Adorno (Ed.), *Der Positivismusstreit in der deutschen Soziologie* (pp. 103–124). Darmstadt: Luchterhand.

Schofer, E., & Meyer, J. W. (2005). The Worldwide Expansion of Higher Education in the Twentieth Century. *American Sociological Review, 70,* 898–920.

Stichweh, R. (2007a). Inklusion und Exklusion in der Weltgesellschaft - Am Beispiel der Schule und des Erziehungssystems. In J. Aderhold & O. Kranz (Eds.), *Intention und Funktion. Probleme der Vermittlung psychischer und sozialer Systeme* (pp. 113–120). Wiesbaden: VS Verlag für Sozialwissenschaften.

Stichweh, R. (2007b). Structure Formation in World Society. The Eigenstructures of World Society and the Regional Cultures of the World. In I. Rossi (Ed.), *Frontiers of Globalization Research:: Theoretical and Methodological Approaches* (pp. 133–150). New York: Springer Science & Business Media.

Stichweh, R. (2008). Kontrolle und Organisation des Raums durch Funktionssysteme der Weltgesellschaft. In J. Döring & T. Thielmann (Eds.), *Spatial Turn* (pp. 149–164). Bielefeld: transcript Verlag.

Stichweh, R. (2010a). Funktionale Differenzierung der Weltgesellschaft. In G. Albert & S. Sigmund (Eds.), *Soziologische Theorie kontrovers. Sonderheft 50/2010 der Kölner Zeitschrift für Soziologie und Sozialpsychologie* (Vol. 50, pp. 299–306).

Stichweh, R. (2010b). Interkulturelle Kommunikation in der Weltgesellschaft. Zur politischen Soziologie der Integration und Assimilation. In R. Stichweh (Ed.), *Der Fremde. Studien zu Soziologie und Sozialgeschichte.* Berlin: Suhrkamp.

Stichweh, R. (2015). Comparing Systems Theory and Sociological Neo-Institutionalism: Explaining Functional Differentiation. In B. Holzer, F. Kastner, & T. Werron (Eds.), *From Globalization to World Society: Neo-Institutional and Systems-Theoretical Perspectives.* New York: Routledge.

Vogd, W. (2007). Empirie oder Theorie? Systemtheoretische Forschung jenseits einer vermeintlichen Forschung. *Soziale Welt, Sonderheft 'Soziologische Systemtheorie und empirische Forschung',* 295–321.

Wallerstein, I. (1974). *The Modern World-System: Capitalist Agriculture and the Origins of the European World-Economy in the Sixteenth Century* (Reprint edition). Berkeley: University of California Press.

Wimmer, A. (2008). Ethnische Grenzziehungen in der Immigrationsgesellschaft. Jenseits des Herder'schen Commonsense. *Kölner Zeitschrift Für Soziologie Und Sozialpsychologie., Sonderheft 48/2008 Migration und Integration.,* 57–80.

TEIL 2:
INTERNATIONALE ÖKONOMISCHE UND POLITISCHE PERSPEKTIVEN

Managing Migration:
Recruiters and low-skill Migrants

Philip Martin

Abstract

International migrants are people who cross national borders, changing themselves, the places they leave, and the places to which they move. It is a pleasure to acknowledge the contributions of Gudrun Biffl, an empirical labor economist who emphasizes the analysis of data on migrants and their real-world impacts rather than building models based on assumptions. Biffl's careful analysis of the impacts of especially low-skilled migrants, and the implications of their presence for the lifelong training and learning of all workers, combine with her pioneering role in fostering migration studies to create solid shoulders on which her collaborators and students can build. Biffl is a giant in migration research.

About 60 percent of the world's international migrants are in the labor force of the country to which they moved. International labor migrants are an average 10 percent of the 687 million workers in the 58 high-income or industrial countries (ILO, 2015, Annex A)[1], and the migrant share of workers is expected to rise because of persisting demographic and economic inequalities as revolutions in communication, transportation, and rights make it easier to learn about opportunities abroad, move to take advantage of them, and stay abroad. Labor markets have three major functions, viz, recruitment, remuneration, and retention, and the recruitment of especially low-skilled migrant workers illustrates the frequent clash between markets and rights that are mediated by governments. Efforts to keep recruiter fees below market levels to protect migrants often fail, since workers are willing to pay for higher wage jobs.

Introduction

Almost half of the world's residents are economically active, meaning there were 3.5 billion workers among the 7.3 billion people in the world in 2015, including over four percent who were working outside the country in which they were born (ILO, 2015).[2] Most workers never leave the country in which they were born, but

---

[1] The ILO's 58 rich countries include most of the OECD member countries except Mexico and Turkey, the GCC countries, Russia, and places such as Hong Kong, Macau, Puerto Rico, and Réunion.
[2] The ILO estimated world employment at 3.3 billion in 2015, plus 200 million unemployed.

150 million migrant workers employed in another country in 2013, usually one that offers higher wages than can be earned at home.

If the world is divided into the 30 richer industrial countries with almost 700 million workers and the 170 poorer countries with 2.9 billion workers, the 60 million migrant workers in richer countries are an average 10 percent of industrial country workers. The migrant worker share of the labor force ranges from less than five percent in Korea and Japan to over 25 percent in Australia and Switzerland. The share of migrants among all workers in poorer countries is less than two percent, but the range is wide, from less than one percent in China and India to over 90 percent in some Gulf oil-exporting states.

Most people never cross a national border for any reason; international migration for work is the exception, not the rule. However, international labor migration is increasing, making the recruiters who move low-skilled workers over borders ever more important. A low-skilled migrant with less than a secondary school education rarely strikes out on her own for a job in another country because she does not know how to navigate the process of obtaining a contract with a foreign employer, securing a passport and visa, and departing for the job.

Recruiters or merchants of labor are the key intermediaries that connect workers in one country with jobs in another; they are the glue of the international labor market. Migration involves two countries, so recruiters must learn about the needs of foreign employers, government regulations in both migrant-sending and – receiving countries, and the skills and desires of local workers who are seeking jobs abroad. In many countries, recruiters are more familiar with local government regulations than with employer and worker needs, and some use this knowledge to extract money from employers, workers, or both.

International Labor Migration

The UN defines international migrants as persons outside their country of birth for a year or more, regardless of the reason for being abroad, legal status, or plans to settle or return (UN DESA, 2015). This inclusive definition encompasses naturalized citizens, immigrants joining family members who have settled in the destination country, temporary students and workers, and unauthorized foreigners, refugees and asylum seekers, and anyone else abroad at least one year.

The UN estimated 244 million international migrants in 2015, or 3.3 percent of the world's 7.3 billion people. The World Bank (2015b), which uses a slightly different methodology, reported 249 million migrants. Both organizations distribute migrants similarly across the four major migration corridors: south-south, south-north, north-north, and north-south. Most migrants are in industrial[3] or

---

[3] The World Bank considers 32 of the OECD countries to be high income (not Mexico and Turkey), plus 47 non-OECD countries and places, from Hong Kong and Macao to the Gulf oil exporters to Argentina, Russia, Singapore, and Venezuela.

northern countries, 56 percent, but the largest group moved from south to south, or from one developing country to another, 38 percent. Almost a quarter of international migrants moved from north to north or from one industrial country to another, and six percent moved from north to south or from an industrial to a developing country.

Each international migrant is unique, and each migration corridor has unique features. The largest stock of migrants, 95 million or 38 percent in 2015, moved from one developing country to another, as from the Indonesia to Malaysia or Nicaragua to Costa Rica (Table 1). The second-largest stock, 84 million or 34 percent, moved from a developing to an industrial country, as from Morocco to Spain, Mexico to the US, or the Philippines to South Korea, that is, a third of international migration involves south-north movement. Some 56 million people or 22 percent of international migrants moved north to north or from one industrial country to another, as from Canada to the US. Finally, over 14 million people or six percent of migrants were north to south migrants who moved from industrial to developing countries, as with Japanese who work or retire in Thailand.

Some 140 million migrants are in industrial countries, making migrants over 10 percent of the 1.2 billion residents of industrial countries. There are 109 million migrants in developing countries, where they are less than two percent of developing country residents and workers. These migrants may be barely noticeable in population giants such as China and Indonesia.

	Destination Industrial	Destination Developing	Total
Origin (absolute, in million)			
Industrial	56	14	70
Developing	84	95	179
Total	140	109	249
Origin (in %)			
Industrial	22%	6%	28%
Developing	34%	38%	72%
Total	56%	44%	100%

Table 1 International Migrants in 2015

Source: World Bank Migration and Remittances Fact Book, 2015, p 28.

Most of the world's countries participate in the international migration system as countries of origin, transit, or destination, and often all three. This is a change from the past, when most countries were either sources of or destinations for migrants. Mexico today sends migrants to the US, receives migrants from Guatemala, and is a transit country for Central Americans moving to the US.

Europe is *the* continent of international migration, with a tenth of the world's people and a third of the world's international migrants, some 76 million. Asia is second to Europe, with 75 million international migrants. Both Asia and Europe have a quarter of the world's 200 countries, but Asia has 60 percent of the world's people and large-scale internal migration in population giants such as China and

India. Europe, by contrast, is a region with many national borders and fewer people; many European nations were created or had their borders adjusted after wars to ensure that the "right people" were in the "right countries". Over half of European countries are members of the EU, which promotes freedom of movement of EU citizens, so that EU citizens may move to another EU country and live and work on an equal basis with citizens of that country.

North America had 54 million international migrants in 2015, almost a quarter of the world's total, including 47 million in the US and seven million in Canada. Africa had 21 million migrants, including over three million in South Africa and two million in Ivory Coast. Latin America and the Caribbean have over nine million migrants, led by two million in Argentina and over a million each in Venezuela and Mexico. Oceania had eight million migrants, including almost seven million in Australia and a million in New Zealand.

Two-thirds of international migrants live in 20 countries. The US had 47 million or almost 20 percent of the world's migrants in 2015, followed by 12 million each in Germany and Russia; 10 million in Saudi Arabia; nine million in the UK; and eight million each in the UAE, Canada and France. The major sources of migrants were India, with 16 million born-in-India persons abroad; Mexico 12 million; Russia 11 million; China 10 million; Bangladesh seven million; and Pakistan and Ukraine, six million each. The Philippines, Syria, UK and Afghanistan each have at least five million persons abroad.

Migrants from some countries are concentrated in one foreign country, while other diasporas are scattered widely. Almost all Mexican migrants are in the US, while only 20 percent of Indians are in the UAE, the country hosting the most Indians. Similarly, the Filipino diaspora is widely dispersed: a third of the Filipinos who are abroad in the US, followed by almost a quarter in the Gulf oil exporters.

Most migrants are young and of working age. The ILO estimated that 150 million or 65 percent of all international migrants were in the labor forces of the countries to which they moved in 2013.[4] Some 73 percent of migrants 15 and older were employed or seeking jobs, compared with 64 percent of non-migrants (ILO, 2015). Both male and female migrants have higher labor force participation rates than non-migrants, 78 percent for migrant men compared to 77 percent for native men and 67 percent for migrant women compared to 51 percent for native women. Much of this difference in labor force participation reflects age: migrants are more likely to be of working age than natives.

A third of migrant workers were in Europe, a quarter in North America, and most of the rest in Asia; three fourths of all migrant workers were in what the ILO considers to be high-income countries (ILO, 2015a, pxii). Over 70 percent of all migrant workers were employed in services (including domestic workers), 18

---

[4] The ILO applied ILO estimates of labor force participation to DESA estimates of migrants 15 and older to estimate migrant labor forces. The ILO acknowledges that its migrant labor force estimates may or may not include temporary residents who are permitted to work, such as foreign students, and irregular migrants.

percent in industry (construction and manufacturing), and 11 percent in agriculture.

About eight percent of international migrant workers, some 11.5 million, were domestic workers employed in private homes. Three-fourths of migrant domestic workers are women, 80 percent are in high-income countries, and two-thirds of female migrant workers are in south east Asia, Europe, and the Arab states. Most of the world's 67 million domestic workers are not migrants, but migrants are over 80 percent of all domestic workers in the Arab states and in North America.

The highest shares of migrants among all workers are in the Gulf oil-exporting countries, where 90 percent or more of private sector workers are migrants in some countries. Overall, the ILO estimated that 36 percent of all workers in the Arab states were migrants in 2013, followed by 20 percent in North America and 16 percent in Europe (ILO, 2015, p16).

Inequalities and Revolutions

The major drivers of international migration are persisting demographic and economic inequalities between countries as globalization makes it easier to learn about opportunities abroad and cheaper to travel and take advantage of them (Martin, Abella, Kuptsch, 2006). Many demand-pull factors in receiving countries and supply-push factors in sending countries motivate people to cross national borders, from recruitment by some employers to environmental changes that make traditional ways of earning a living less viable.

There are also more international migrants because there are more countries and more national borders to cross. The number of generally recognized nation-states rose from 43 in 1900 to 193 in 2000, and more national borders means more international migrants.[5]

The demographic inequality motivating international migration is straightforward. The world's population reached an historic milestone on October 31, 2011 when, for the first time, there were seven billion people on earth, up from six billion in 1998.[6] The world's population was 7.3 billion in 2015, and is projected to continue increasing by 80 million a year to reach 9.6 billion in 2050.

Almost all of the additional 2.3 billion people are expected to be born in the world's 170 poorer countries, where the total population is projected to surpass eight billion. The most populous countries in 2050 are projected to be India with 1.6 billion people, China with 1.4 billion, and the US and Nigeria, each with 400 million.[7] The population of the 30 wealthier countries is expected to remain stable

---

[5] The number of generally recognized states doubled from 90 to 180 between the mid-1960s and the mid-1990s (Held et al, 1999).
[6] See: www.un.org/apps/news/story.asp?NewsID=40257&Cr=population&Cr1#.WFW7XijYI04
[7] Nigeria had 182 million people in 2015, while the US had 321 million. The total fertility rate, or the average number of children per woman, was 5.5 in Nigeria and 1.9 in the US. Nigeria

at 1.2 billion over the next 35 years, reflecting growth in Canada and the US and shrinking populations in many European countries and Japan.

The world adds the equivalent of a Germany a year in developing countries. This means that there is a youth bulge in many African and Asian countries while workforces in Europe and Japan are shrinking, suggesting that youthful migrants could stabilize the populations and workforces of aging societies.

Since richer countries can attract migrants because of their higher wages, the decision about whether to stabilize populations via immigration is a policy choice. There are many possibilities, from industrial countries accepting immigrants to settle and integrating them and their families, opening doors to migrant caregivers and other guest workers but encouraging them to depart after a few years, or encouraging rich-country retirees to move to lower-cost countries, shifting people from higher to lower income countries rather than moving workers from poorer to richer countries.

Alternatively, some developing countries may get rich quickly, so that their workers are reluctant to seek foreign jobs. Several countries have made the transition from emigration country to migrant destination within a generation, including Italy and Spain, but many others, particularly in Africa and South Asia, are likely to have more workers than jobs for the foreseeable future. If countries in Europe and Japan have more jobs than workers, while African and Asian countries have more workers than jobs, demographic inequality may set the stage for compensating migration flows from faster-growing developing countries to shrinking industrial countries.

The second inequality motivating international migration is economic. The 30 high-income countries had a sixth of the world's 7.3 billion people in 2015 but two-thirds of the world's $78 trillion of economic output, an average $42,000 per person per year, nine times more than the $4,500 average in the poorer 170 countries (World Bank, 2017, p14).[8] Especially young people are motivated to migrate from poorer to richer countries for nine times higher earnings, even if higher living costs in richer countries mean that the actual income gain is less. Globalization and disaporas make potential migrants today far more aware of opportunities in richer country than were European migrants considering a move to the Americas in the 19th century.

The very poorest people often lack the resources to move to another country. However, economic development in poorer countries can increase desires for better jobs and incomes faster than the economy delivers them, so that migration

---

will grow despite emigration, while the US will grow with immigration, but nonetheless, Nigeria's population is projected to be larger than the US population in 35 years (PRB, 2015).

[8] The World Bank reported 1.2 billion people in high-income countries in 2015 with a combined Gross National Income (GNI) of $50 trillion or an average $42,000 per person (Atlas method of computing GNI). The combined population of low (638 million), lower-middle income (2.9 billion), and upper-middle income (2.6 billion) was 6.2 billion, and their combined GNI was $28 trillion or $4,500 per person. The per capita GNI of sub-Saharan Africa, $1,600, was a sixth of the $24,000 of Europe and Central Asia.

may rise with economic growth, the paradox of the migration hump. This is what happened in Mexico, where discussion of the economic take off expected with NAFTA in 1994 was followed quickly by a deep recession and devaluation in 1995 that contributed to an upsurge in Mexico-US migration during the late 1990s, when there was a US jobs boom (Martin, 1998-99). Apprehensions of unauthorized foreigners just inside the US peaked at 1.8 million in 2000, and of over 4,900 a day or over 200 an hour.

There is a second dimension to economic differences between countries that encourages internal and international migration. Agriculture is the world's number one employer, engaging 30 percent of the world's 3.5 billion workers as farmers or hired workers (ILO, 2015). In rich countries, where agriculture employs less than five percent of workers, farmers have higher average incomes and more wealth than urban residents, and their incomes and wealth are often bolstered by government subsidies (Martin, 2009) In poor countries, where agriculture employs over half of workers, farmers are poorer than urban residents, and governments often tax them by allowing monopoly input suppliers to charge high prices for seeds and fertilizers or monopoly output buyers to offer low prices for cotton, cocoa, and other commodities.

Rural youth quickly realize that they will not get rich farming as their parents and grandparents did. For many, economic mobility requires occupational and geographic mobility, getting away from farming and moving to cities. Once in urban areas, rural youth find it easier to learn about opportunities abroad and access the recruiters, travel agents, and other parts of the migration infrastructure that can help them to cross national borders for better opportunities. In this way, movement out of agriculture in developing countries increases both urbanization and international migration.

Demographic and economic inequalities are like the plus and minus poles on a battery; they provide the potential for action but await a spark or link to induce migration. Three revolutions of the past half century, in communications, transportation, and rights, make it easier for potential migrants to learn about opportunities abroad, cross borders, and stay abroad. Adjusting the rights of migrants to manage migration is often the first instinct of policy makers grappling with migration crises, engendering conflict with the UN's rights-based approach to migrant workers that emphasizes the need for governments to treat migrants equally.

The communications revolution shrinks the world and makes it easier for people in one country to learn about opportunities in another. During the age of mass migration in the 19th century, pioneering migrants typically wrote letters to friends and family describing opportunities abroad, a slow means of communication in an era of limited literacy and slow transport (Martin and Midgley, 2010). Letters from the American midwest to Scandinavia took four to six weeks to reach recipients in the 1850s. After they arrived, a literate person had to read the letter and respond, so that a year could elapse between an invitation to move and migration.[9]

Communication is much faster today via cell phones and the internet. With diasporas from countries around the world settled in most high-income countries, migrants abroad can quickly inform friends and relatives at home about opportunities abroad, finance the travel of newcomers, and help them after arrival. Mobile phones and Skype were not developed to facilitate international migration, but they make it easy and cheap for people in one country to learn about opportunities in another. Similarly, movies and TV shows are made for entertainment, not to encourage youth in developing countries to dream of sharing in the riches of the other countries, but the American TV shows Dallas and Dynasty about oil barons persuade some youth dreaming of opportunities abroad to believe the promises of recruiters that there would be riches in other countries (Martin, S, 2014).

The second revolution involves transportation. Many Europeans migrating to the North American colonies in the 18th century could not pay for one-way transportation, so they indentured themselves for four to six years to whomever met the ship in New York or Philadelphia and paid the transportation costs. Most of the poorer British and Germans who indentured themselves worked for farmers after arrival, learning how to farm in the New World while living with the farm family for whom they were obliged to work.

Transportation today is much more accessible and cheaper, usually available in all countries and costing less than $2,500 to go anywhere in the world. Even Chinese migrants who pay smugglers $20,000 to $30,000 to reach the US typically repay their migration costs from higher earnings within two years, far less time than indentured servants labored to repay their transportation costs in the 1700s. Rapid repayment helps to explain why some Chinese in Fujian and other relatively prosperous Chinese coastal provinces continue to pay high fees to smugglers to move to industrial countries, although legal student migration has largely replaced unauthorized smuggling of Chinese laborers (Kwong, 1998).

The third revolution involves the rights of individuals vis-à-vis governments. Dictatorships and world wars early in the 20th century led to the creation of the United Nations in 1945 and an emphasis on protecting the human rights of individuals that was encapsulated in the Universal Declaration of Human Rights (United Nations, 1948). Many national constitutions written after World War II in post-war Europe, and in newly independent former colonies in Africa and Asia, include extensive human rights guarantees.

Governments granted individuals rights and promised them benefits to cover unemployment, old age, and ill health. There was relatively little international migration when European governments developed social welfare systems in the 1950s and as many former colonies became independent in the 1960s, so these systems often granted benefits to all qualifying residents and workers rather than

---

[9] In 1870, an estimated 25 percent of the world's adults were literate. Literacy rose to 50 percent by 1950, and to 80 percent by 2000 (Kenny, 2012, Chapter 5).

drawing distinctions between citizens and non-citizens. One reason for universal social welfare systems was to eliminate distinctions between peoples that in the past had led to conflict.

Human and social rights guarantees make it difficult for governments to remove foreigners who want to stay. Once inside a richer country, migrants can use administrative proceedings and courts to argue that they should be allowed to remain because they have developed roots in the country or would face persecution at home. Governments have found it very difficult to draw a sharp distinction between refugees and economic migrants, even though many migrants have mixed motives for migration, that is, both economic and non-economic motives for moving. In such cases, governments must determine whether a particular person is a refugee entitled to protection who should be allowed to stay or an economic migrant seeking better opportunities who should be returned.[10]

Migration and Labor Markets

Work is the exchange of effort for reward. Work involves employees giving up control over some of their time to employers in exchange for monetary wages and work-related benefits. Unlike many other market transactions, such as a customer buying an item in a store and never shopping there again, work is unusual because it requires a continuous relationship between employer and employee in the workplace, as supervisors assess employee performance and workers consider their satisfaction with the job. Employers may terminate unsatisfactory workers, and dissatisfied workers may quit their jobs.

There is a second important dimension of labor markets that make them unique. Goods that are purchased do not care who buys or consumes them, but workers care about their supervisors and fellow workers and the society in which they live. Workers are not clothing or tools in other ways as well. Workers are multidimensional, with lives outside the workplace that include raising families, participating in leisure activities, and voting for politicians who collect taxes and allocate resources while setting the rules of the society and economy.

Mobility is the key to labor market adjustments; mobility ensures that the "best" workers are in the "best" jobs. Employers try to recruit the best workers, develop remuneration packages to encourage them to perform, and offer promotions to retain them, since experience is usually associated with higher productivity. Workers may quit one job and move to another to achieve higher wages, better benefits, or more opportunities. The movement of workers between jobs is considered a normal component of well-functioning labor markets.

International borders and limits on migrant worker mobility between employers while abroad complicate labor market adjustments. Instead of advertising for local

---

[10] UNHCR recognizes the reality of mixed migration flows, and developed a 10-point plan in 2006 to provide advice to governments: http://www.unhcr.org/en-us/mixed-migration.html

workers under non-discrimination laws, employers may specify that they will hire only male or female guest workers. Once in another country, migrant workers are usually prohibited from switching jobs unless they obtain the approval of both the old and new employer and a government agency. Migrant workers must generally leave the country when their contracts expire or if they are terminated by their employers, preventing wages and benefits from rising with experience and productivity.

Labor markets have three major functions, viz, recruitment, remuneration, and retention. Recruitment matches workers with jobs, remuneration or the wage and benefit system motivates workers to perform their jobs, and retention systems assess workers to identify and retain the best. Most workplaces have human resources departments to manage these three labor market Rs to ensure that the firm has productive and satisfied employees.

National borders complicate the three Rs. When jobs are in one country and workers in another, language differences and variance in education and training standards and certificates can make it hard to match workers in one country with jobs in another efficiently. Employers seeking workers in other countries often turn to private recruiters in their own country or abroad to find workers to fill jobs, and these intermediary recruiters can make job-matching more efficient or simply add to the cost of matching workers with jobs. Governments often regulate recruiter-worker transactions, and this regulation can improve protections for workers and reduce migration costs or add to complications and worker-paid migration costs.

The other two R-labor market functions may also be complicated by national borders. ILO conventions and many national laws call for equal pay for equal work, so that all workers doing the same job receive the same wage regardless of their citizenship or work-permit status. It can be hard to ensure equality in the workplace. Even if migrant and local workers receive the same wages, migrants may be cheaper than local workers because employers do not have to pay work-related taxes on migrant earnings, especially if migrants will not be in the country long enough to receive benefits. For example, the US exempts employers from paying federal social security and unemployment insurance (UI) taxes on the earnings of many guest workers, which can save employers up to 15 percent on payroll taxes (Martin, 2014c).[11]

In addition to payroll tax savings, migrants may work harder than local workers because their right to be in the country depends on satisfying their employer. The superior work performance of migrants is lauded by employers who emphasize that migrants are abroad in order to work and send money home to their families, making them eager to please the employer and volunteer for overtime work. Many US employers of low-skilled H-2A and H-2B guest workers cite their "reliability and loyalty", emphasizing that they are in the US to work and that they cannot

---

[11] The H-2A program allows US farmers anticipating labor shortages to receive certification to employ guest workers, generally up to 10 months.

easily switch employers (Martin, 2014c). British employers similarly praise the work ethic of Poles and other Eastern European workers, saying that soft skills such as being willing to work unsocial hours and reliably coming to work are more important than English (Ruhs and Anderson, 2010).

The final labor market function, retention, is also complicated by national borders. Most studies find that more experienced workers have higher productivity. However, guest worker programs that require workers to depart after two or three years can mean the loss of experienced workers and their replacement with new hires who must be trained. Some governments allow seasonal workers to return year-after-year, and some permit employers to sponsor migrant workers for permanent resident status, but most guest worker programs require migrants to depart when contracts end, forcing experienced workers to leave.

Recruitment, remuneration, and retention are challenging for native employers and workers, and these 3 Rs are more complicated when jobs are in one country and workers in another. The fact that workers must be matched with jobs across borders adds to costs, especially during recruitment.[12]

Matching workers with jobs has costs that are usually borne by employers seeking workers and individuals seeking jobs. Employers advertise for workers, request that current employees inform their friends and relatives about vacancies, and notify public and private employment services that they are seeking workers. Workers seeking jobs contact employers directly, ask their social networks about job openings, and turn to public and private agencies that specialize in helping workers to find jobs.

The major cost for both employers and workers in job search is opportunity cost, the cost of not having a job filled for employers and the cost of not working while engaged in job search for workers. The financial costs of advertising for workers in newspapers or paying recruiters, and worker costs to visit employers and public and private agencies, are usually small relative to these opportunity costs, which explains why most jobs are filled quickly and why most jobless workers find jobs within a few months.

International migration can slow worker-job matches. There are four major phases in the international labor migration process, and each can generate migration costs that are paid by workers. Employers set the migration process in motion by developing job descriptions, obtaining government approval to fill jobs with migrant workers (usually after seeking and failing to find local workers), and contacting workers in another country directly or via a recruiter to fill the job. If the employer utilizes a local recruiter, that recruiter may incur costs to contact workers in another country directly or via a recruiter in worker countries of origin.

Migrant workers appear in the second phase, when they learn about foreign job opportunities, obtain contracts to fill foreign jobs, apply for passports and undergo

---

[12] Many authors attack international labor markets because governments favor high-skilled over low-skilled migrants and often distinguish between legal and desired versus illegal and dangerous migrants.

health, criminal and other checks before receiving visas, and have their documents and contracts approved before departure. Some migrant workers receive weeks or months of language, skills or other training before departure and, even if the training is free, there are opportunity costs as migrants study rather than work. Most worker payments to recruiters and government agencies are made during this second phase of the migration cycle, and many workers take out loans to cover these costs.

The third phase involves migrant workers employed abroad, typically for two or three years. As the end of their contracts approaches, migrants may seek to have their contracts renewed and remain abroad or return to their country of origin to rest before going abroad again. If migrants return to stay, they can invest savings from employment abroad to start a business or to find a wage job. Some migrants are entitled to end-of-service bonuses, reimbursement of some expenses, and refunds of social security contributions upon completion of their contracts.

The fourth phase involves re-integration at home or preparation to go abroad again. The re-integration process is not well understood, so there is little reliable data on the share of migrants who return to stay versus those who cycle between work abroad, rest at home, and going abroad again. Farm employers say that workers admitted under guest worker programs that permit eight or ten months of employment abroad often return year-after-year for several decades. There are also many reports of so-called serial migrants who work two or three years abroad, return for a year or two, and then go abroad again as their savings diminish (Parrenas, 2015).

Workers incur several types of costs in each of the four migration phases, including monetary and opportunity costs. For example, the opportunity costs of not working may be higher than the travel costs paid by rural workers who must go to capital cities to sign contracts and receive pre-departure training. Migrants may also incur costs if they receive substandard wages and benefits abroad or if they work abroad in jobs that do not utilize their skills. In some migration corridors, maximum migration costs and their division between employers, workers, recruiters, and government agencies are specified in bilateral agreements or program rules. In others, only some or none of worker-paid migration costs are regulated.

Recruiters and Migrants

Recruiters are the merchants of labor who match workers in one country with jobs in another. Recruiters are paid for their services, and governments more often aim to regulate the fees recruiters charge *workers* rather than the fees they charge *employers*. Most governments allow markets to determine employer-paid fees to recruiters.

Many governments set maximum worker-paid fees at less than what workers are willing to pay for higher-wage foreign jobs. As a result, alternative allocative mechanisms often determine who goes abroad, including the willingness of workers to pay recruiters and their agents. The "unfairness" of low-wage workers paying high upfront fees for 3-D jobs (dangerous, difficult and dirty) abroad, and often borrowing money at high interest rates to pay recruitment costs, makes recruiters convenient villains. Migrant workers arrive abroad in debt and are vulnerable because they do not want to lose their jobs and return to recruitment debts at home that were incurred in anticipation of high foreign wages.

Recruiters, as with information brokers in other markets where prices are not always transparent, can charge different prices for similar services. Such differential pricing is an example of price-discriminating monopoly. If a recruiter controls access to workers that the employer wants to hire, employers who are "desperate" for workers will pay more to recruiters than employers who can wait to fill jobs. Price discrimination may also work in reverse. If employers "sell" jobs to recruiters, they can effectively auction their job offers to the recruiter willing to pay the most.

Recruiters who place workers in jobs abroad can charge workers different prices for their services if they can determine how much workers are willing to pay. The key to determining what workers will pay are agents and subagents who live in or visit villages with low-skilled workers. These agents get to know potential migrants, can determine what workers are willing to pay, and inform the recruiter, who often collects from the worker and reimburses the agent.

Recruiters who place low-skilled workers in foreign jobs are often agents rather than partners. Agents often bring parties together for a one-time transaction, which gives them less incentive to learn about employer and worker needs. In low-skilled occupations such as domestic service and construction laborer, where there are more workers seeking foreign jobs than there are jobs available, agent-recruiters can charge workers to move up the queue of those waiting to go abroad. Even if low-skilled workers know they are paying higher-than-government-set maximum fees for foreign jobs, they may not complain if they get what they want, a foreign job that offers a higher wage.

The distinctions between agents and partners can be clarified by examining the nature and frequency of three types of transactions, viz, real estate, recruitment, and remittances. Real estate and recruitment are similar in the sense that each transaction is unique, reflecting the needs of particular buyers and the attributes of each house, just as worker traits and job characteristics are unique. Housing and recruitment transactions occur rarely, sometimes only once a lifetime, and often require navigating several markets, such as both the labor market and the credit market.

Sending remittances, by contrast, involves a standard commodity and is a transaction repeated frequently. The consequences of bad decisions are also different. Home buyers and migrant workers are often "locked in" by the loans taken to buy a house and find a job abroad, while a poor remittance transaction usually results in the loss of only a portion of worker earnings.

There are other similarities between real estate and recruitment transactions. Even though many homes and condos are similar or identical, heterogeneity allows agents to charge high commissions because each buyer is unique. Agents may invest time to learn buyer needs and priorities in terms of space, neighborhood, price and other factors, so that "finding exactly the right house" works against transparency and competition, minimizing the cost-reductions expected with more transactions. Similarly, recruiters may offer similar or identical jobs abroad to low-skill workers, but justify charging differential fees by saying that they invest to learn which foreign job is best for a particular worker. Making what appear to be homogeneous transactions to outsiders heterogeneous to participants helps recruiters to extract money from employers and workers.

Real estate transactions are similar to low-skilled workers going abroad in their frequent reliance on credit. Many home buyers rely on credit to purchase homes, just as many migrant workers take out loans to pay recruitment fees. In both cases, people are forced to negotiate two unfamiliar markets, for housing or foreign jobs and for credit to complete the transaction. Home buyers seeking credit can do so in a fairly transparent market because of regulation and the security of the house being purchased, but migrants seeking credit must usually navigate a less transparent credit market that offers less security to lenders, since the foreign work contract may not generate expected earnings to repay the loan.

There are other similarities between buying real estate and working abroad. Housing has both investment and consumption benefits, just as moving abroad to work generates income, may lead to new skills or settlement abroad, and can help rural youth to escape conservative rural villages. There is usually mobility in both real estate and migration transactions, as people move over local borders to new homes just as migrants move over national borders to jobs.

How should recruiters of low-skilled workers be regulated to improve worker protections? The straightforward regulatory solution is for governments to set maximum worker-paid fees and enforce them. However, this does not work in practice because there may be 100 workers seeking 10 higher-wage jobs abroad, allowing recruiters to auction scarce foreign jobs among workers seeking them.

One way to strengthen migrant worker protections is to provide incentives for recruiters to comply with protective labor laws. These incentives can be symbolic, such as awarding recruiters who agree to abide by a code of conduct and have no adjudicated complaints against them a seal of approval that they can use to attract foreign employers or local workers. Alternatively, economically significant compliance incentives, such as lower fees for government services, preferred access to foreign job offers or local workers seeking jobs, and allowing A-rated recruiters to certify that they have followed government regulations, can persuade recruiters to abide by worker protection laws.

There are two types of economic incentives that could improve recruiter behavior, micro and macro. Micro incentives affect individual recruiters, while macro incentives affect the recruitment industry. Micro incentives to influence recruiter behavior fall into three major categories, viz, costs, taxes, and publicity. Good or A-rated recruiters could pay lower fees and or receive faster government processing of the paperwork required to send workers abroad, A-rated recruiters can be granted tax exemptions and tax credits, and A-rated recruiters can receive awards that generate more business. If such government incentives raise revenues more than costs, recruiters have incentives to maintain compliant or A-ratings.

Macro incentives and policies can reshape the recruitment industry and its relationships with employers and workers by favoring larger over smaller recruiters, permitting foreign employers to recruit workers directly, and encouraging long-term partner relationships between employers and recruiters rather than short-term agent transactions. Larger recruiters can achieve economies of scale that lower their costs per worker deployed and develop market power to avoid destructive competition that allows foreign employers to charge recruiters for jobs. Larger recruiters can become comprehensive one-stop shops for employers and migrants, offering everything from training for foreign jobs and skills certification to placement in foreign jobs and handling travel arrangements.

There are other advantages to fewer and larger recruiters, who can develop standard procedures for preparing workers for departure and maintain contact with them while they are employed abroad. As workers abroad near the end of their contracts, recruiters can remind them of end-of-contract and other benefits they have earned and certify any skills acquired abroad for future local or foreign employers. Fewer and larger recruiters are easier for regulatory agencies to monitor.

Conclusions

Recruiters or merchants of labor are the glue of international labor markets, the intermediaries between workers in one country and jobs in another. They have long been considered necessary evils to fill less-desirable jobs. Private recruiters today are involved in the movement of most of the 10 million workers who cross national borders each year, generating revenues of $10 billion to $20 billion a year for the international recruitment industry.

Worker-paid migration costs are a concern for three reasons. First, they are high, absorbing from low-skilled workers one to 10 months foreign earnings and diverting money that could go to migrants and their families into the pockets of better off recruiters and others in the migration infrastructure. Survey data show that recruiters often add little value to worker-job matches, that is, they do not ensure employers that workers have needed skills nor put workers in the job best suited to their skills.

Second is the regressive nature of recruitment costs, with lower-skill and lower-wage workers paying more in migration costs than high-skilled migrants because the supply of low-skilled workers exceeds the demand for them. Highly skilled workers invest in earning degrees and obtaining certification of their skills. The fact that demand often exceeds supply for highly skilled workers, and that the costs of poor worker-job matches rise with the level of skills, means that employers are willing to invest more to recruit high-skilled workers and to pay their migration costs.

Third is the lack of transparency about recruitment costs. No one knows exactly how much low-skilled workers pay for foreign jobs. Media reports suggest that many workers pay far more than one month's foreign earnings to get contracts for jobs abroad, and exposés of workers who arrive abroad in debt can leave the impression that most workers pay a significant fraction of their foreign earners to recruiters and others. Data from workers returning from Gulf oil-exporting countries in 2015 and 2016 do not agree with this conventional wisdom, as low-skilled workers reported relatively modest migration costs (Martin, 2017).

Matching workers with jobs is a core function of labor markets and subject to extensive government regulation. Governments enact laws that lay out minimum standards, from wages and benefits to safe working conditions, and rely on workers to complain in order to enforce these regulations. This same approach is used to regulate recruiters, who are generally required to identify themselves by obtaining licenses, and to pass tests and post bonds to do business. Workers are educated about recruiter regulations, and their complaints prompt investigations of suspect recruiters.

Recruiting is an economic business, and licensed recruiters try to maximize profits. The current regulatory model aims to protect workers by penalizing recruiters who violate protective laws. If recruiter-worker interactions are akin to victimless crimes in the sense that some workers willingly pay recruiters more than legal maximums in order to ensure that they are selected to fill foreign jobs, relying on worker complaints to ensure compliance is unlikely to be effective.

An alternative to the stick of enforcement is the carrot of government incentives that increase the revenue of good recruiters. Governments can offer three major economic incentives to induce better recruiter behaviour: lower processing costs, tax breaks, and awards and introductions. Good or A-rated recruiters can be exempted from some or all fees, providing recruiters with some of the revenue that would otherwise come from migrant workers. The justification for lower fees is that governments need to spend less to check on good recruiters and the workers they send abroad.

Similarly, good recruiters can be exempted from VAT and other taxes that consume 15 percent to 25 percent of their revenues. The justification for giving good recruiters tax breaks is the same as that for offering incentives to foreign investors. Just as foreign investment can bring new technologies and create jobs, so sending workers abroad can speed development at home, justifying tax exemptions and subsidies for good recruiters. Awards and the opportunity to accompany political leaders abroad can help good recruiters to expand their business, giving them a leg up in the competition with other recruiters.

Offering incentives to recruiters is an example of the empirical approach to labor markets associated with Gudrun Biffl. Instead of building models of how the recruitment industry should work, or of how government-to-government agreements could eliminate recruiters, the empiricism of Biffl focuses on how employers, recruiters and workers actually behave, opening the door to incentives to reinforce penalties and effectuate lasting changes in the labor market.

References

International Labor Organization. 2015. ILO Global Estimates of Migrant Workers. December 15. www.ilo.org/global/topics/labour-migration/publications/WCMS_436343/lang--en/index.htm

Held, David, Anthony McGrew, David Goldblatt, and Jonathan Perraton. 1999. Global Transformations: Politics, Economics, and Culture. Stanford. http://www.sup.org/books/title/?id=1565

Kwong, Peter. 1998. Forbidden Workers Illegal Chinese Immigrants and American Labor. New Press. http://thenewpress.com/books/forbidden-workers

Martin, Philip. 2017. Merchants of Labor: Recruiters and International Labor Migration. Oxford University Press. https://global.oup.com/academic/product/merchants-of-labor-9780198808022?cc=us&lang=en&

Martin, Philip, 2014a. The United States: The Continuing Immigration Debate in Hollifield, James, Philip Martin and Pia Orrenius. Eds. 2014. Controlling Immigration. A Global Perspective. Stanford University Press. www.sup.org/book.cgi?id=22520

Martin, Philip, 2014b. Germany: Managing Migration in the 21st Century in Hollifield, James, Philip Martin and Pia Orrenius. Eds. 2014. Controlling Immigration. A Global Perspective. Stanford University Press. www.sup.org/book.cgi?id=22520

Martin, Philip, 2014c. The H-2A Program; Evolution, Impacts, and Outlook. Pp 33-62. Chapter 2 in David Griffith, Ed. (Mis)managing Migration. Guestworkers' Experiences with North American Labor Market. SAR Press. http://sarweb.org/index.php?sar_press_mismanaging_migration

Martin, Philip and Elizabeth Midgley. 2010. Immigration in America. Population Reference Bureau. June. www.prb.org/Publications/PopulationBulletins/2010/immigrationupdate1.aspx

Martin, Philip, Manolo Abella and Christiane Kuptsch. 2006. Managing Labor Migration in the Twenty-First Century. Yale University Press. http://yalepress.yale.edu/yupbooks/book.asp?isbn=0300109040

Martin, Susan. 2014. International Migration Evolving Trends from the Early Twentieth Century to the Present. Cambridge. www.cambridge.org/us/academic/subjects/politics-international-relations/international-relations-and-international-organisations/international-migration-evolving-trends-early-twentieth-century-present

Parrenas, Rhacel. 2015. Servants of Globalization: Migration and Domestic Work. Stanford University Press. http://www.sup.org/books/title/?id=21323

Ruhs, Martin and Bridget Anderson. Eds. 2010. Who Needs Immigrant Workers? Labour Shortages, Immigration, and Public Policy. Oxford University Press. https://global.oup.com/academic/product/who-needs-migrant-workers-9780199580590?cc=us&lang=en&

UN DESA Department of Economic and Social Affairs. 2015. International Migration Report 2015. http://www.un.org/en/development/desa/population/migration/index.shtml

United Nations. 1948. The Universal Declaration of Human Rights. New York: United Nations. http://www.un.org/en/documents/udhr/index.shtml

World Bank. 2017. World Development Indicators. http://data.worldbank.org/products/wdi

„Global Competition for Talent":
Eine migrationspolitische Herausforderung

Mathias Czaika

Zusammenfassung

Zahlreiche empirische Studien haben gezeigt, dass die Zuwanderung hochqualifizierter Arbeitskräfte einen wesentlichen Beitrag zum Wirtschaftswachstum, den öffentlichen Finanzen, sowie der allgemeinen Wettbewerbs- und Innovationsfähigkeit der aufnehmenden Volkswirtschaft leisten kann. Im Kontext allgemeiner Bedenken hinsichtlich der nationalen Identität und des soziokulturellen Wandels als Folge zunehmender ethnisch-religiöser Vielfalt ist die Bedeutung qualifizierter Zuwanderung zur Sicherung wirtschaftlicher Nachhaltigkeit derzeit eher nachrangig. Dies ist fatal, da die Intensität des globalen Wettbewerbs um die besten „Hände und Köpfe" kontinuierlich zunimmt. Nur jene Gesellschaften und Volkswirtschaften, welche in der Lage sind, ein offenes, konfliktfreies Umfeld für zuwandernde *Menschen*, attraktive berufliche Bedingungen und Möglichkeiten für die *Arbeitnehmer,* sowie ein positives wirtschaftliches Klima für die *Arbeitgeber* zu schaffen, werden in einem sich intensivierenden globalen Wettbewerb um hochqualifizierte Arbeit nicht das Nachsehen haben.

Einleitung

Europäische Zuwanderung ist zunehmend durch eine Ambivalenz zwischen relativ liberaler, wenn auch selektiven Zuwanderungsregelungen gegenüber hochqualifizierten ausländischen Arbeitskräften aus Drittstaaten und eher restriktiven Maßnahmen in Bezug auf gering qualifizierte Migration gekennzeichnet. Die Einwanderung von gering qualifizierten Migranten und Arbeitskräften, insbesondere wenn sie aus ärmeren, ethnisch und kulturell distanzierteren außereuropäischen Ländern stammen, wird zunehmend als ein Problem wahrgenommen, welches der massiven Beschränkung bedarf, wohingegen hochqualifizierte Menschen und Zuwanderer in den meisten politischen und gesellschaftlichen Zirkeln weitestgehend positive Resonanz und Unterstützung finden. Es wird politisch anerkannt, dass „wissensbasierte" Volkswirtschaften unter einem sich verstärkendem internationalem Druck stehen, Strategien zu entwickeln, welche zur Gewinnung, Auswahl und Bindung hochqualifizierter Arbeitskräfte geeignet sind (Doomernik et al., 2009, OECD, 2008). Gleichzeitig erwarten aber auch weite Teile der Gesellschaft, dass ausländische Arbeitskräfte lediglich für jene Vakanzen rekrutiert werden sollen, die von inländischen Arbeitskräften nicht dauerhaft besetzt werden können und dass sie zusätzlich auch einen nachhaltigen (Netto-)Beitrag zur Finanzierung der öffentlichen Haushalte leisten.

Die internationale Migration von hochqualifizierten Arbeitskräften ist natürlich kein neues Phänomen, auch wenn sie immer stärker durch semi-permanente Mobilität gekennzeichnet ist. Die Migration von Hochqualifizierten ist hierbei ein Korrelat von Restrukturierungsprozessen in segmentierten und international sich immer mehr integrierenden Arbeitsmärkten und Wertschöpfungsketten, die zu einer zunehmenden internationalen Arbeitsteilung im Kontext sich globalisierender, weltwirtschaftlicher Strukturen führt (Czaika 2018).

In diesem Kontext ist die internationale Anwerbung und Rekrutierung von Arbeitskräften mit teilweise hochspezialisiertem Wissen und Fähigkeiten für viele Länder ein wichtiger Bestandteil einer nachhaltigen Wirtschafts- und Zuwanderungspolitik zur langfristigen Förderung des wirtschaftlichen Wachstums- und Entwicklungsprozesses geworden. Dabei sind es jedoch nicht nur industrialisierte bzw. post-industrialisierte Volkswirtschaften, welche eine steigende Nachfrage nach knappem spezialisiertem Humankapital entwickelt haben und sich daher verstärkt auf dem internationalen Arbeitsmarkt qualifizierter Arbeitskräfte „zu bedienen" versuchen. Auch die sich dynamisch entwickelnden Länder mittleren Einkommens (sog. Schwellenländer), aber auch jene mit einem noch relativ geringen Einkommensniveau, versuchen verstärkt ihre meist knappen „Talente" im Land zu behalten sowie ihre qualifizierten Fachkräfte aus dem Ausland zurückzugewinnen (Cerna und Czaika 2018).

In den vergangenen beiden Jahrzehnten haben immer mehr Länder damit begonnen, Maßnahmen zu ergreifen, um qualifizierte Zuwanderer wie beispielsweise Akademiker und Wissenschaftler, medizinisches Personal, Ingenieure, IT-Spezialisten und andere hochqualifizierte Fachkräfte anzuwerben. Jüngste Erhebungen zeigen, dass in den 2000er Jahren die Mehrheit der OECD-Länder sowie eine wachsende Zahl von Nicht-OECD-Ländern selektive Einwanderungspolitiken entwickelten, die speziell darauf abzielen, hochqualifizierte Arbeitskräfte anzuziehen oder zumindest im Land zu halten (Abbildung 1).

Eine wachsende Zahl von Industrie- und Entwicklungsländern arbeitet daran, ihre Einwanderungssysteme neu zu gestalten und dabei unterschiedlichste Instrumente zur Anwerbung, Auswahl und Integration von (hoch-)qualifizierten Arbeitskräften einzusetzen. Dieser Prozess hat zu einer weltweiten Verbreitung von verschiedensten, teilweise innovativen migrationspolitischen Instrumenten geführt. Im Jahr 2015 verfolgten fast die Hälfte der 172 UN-Mitgliedsstaaten das Ziel, das Niveau hochqualifizierter Zuwanderung zu erhöhen, indem ausländische Arbeitskräfte angezogen und einheimische Talente zum Bleiben angeregt werden sollen. Dieser Anteil hat sich seit 2005 verdoppelt, als noch 22 Prozent aller UN-Mitgliedstaaten zusätzlichen Bedarf an hochqualifizierten Arbeitskräften zum Ausdruck brachten und entsprechende Maßnahmen implementiert hatten (Abbildung 1). Hochentwickelte, zumeist sich im Übergang zu post-industrialisierten Wissensökonomien befindende westliche Volkswirtschaften, sind Vorreiter dieses globalen Trends. Zwei Drittel der OECD-Staaten haben eine Politik umgesetzt, die speziell auf das Anwerben und Auswählen von hochqualifizierten Zuwanderern

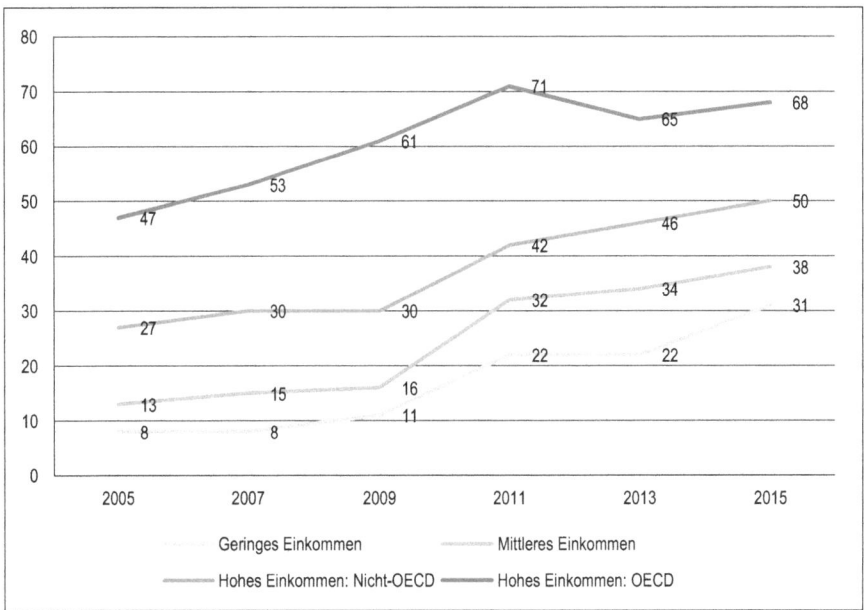

Abbildung 1 Der globale Wettbewerb um Talente, Anteil der Länder nach Einkommenskategorie

Quelle: Czaika und Parsons (2017) basierend auf World Population Policies database[1].

abzielt (Czaika und Parsons, 2017). Infolgedessen intensiviert sich der „globale Wettbewerb" um hochqualifizierte Arbeitskräfte immer weiter und eine kontinuierlich zunehmende Zahl von Staaten, Unternehmen und anderen Akteuren treten in diesen Wettbewerb um die besten „Hände und Köpfe" ein (Boeri et al., 2012, Kapur und McHale, 2005).

Dieses internationale Engagement scheint angesichts der rapiden Bevölkerungsalterung und des zunehmenden Fachkräftemangels in fast allen hochentwickelten Ländern, aber zunehmend auch in nachstrebenden Wirtschaftsmächten, wie Brasilien, Russland, Indien, China (sog. BRIC-Staaten) oder auch der Türkei, Südafrika, Malaysia, und den Golfstaaten, als plausible Politikoption zu gelten (Cerna und Czaika, 2018). Demographischer, ökonomischer und technologischer Wandel in Kombination mit international operierenden Akteuren und Unternehmungen sowie die Angleichung von Bildungssystemen haben die Voraussetzungen für die Entstehung eines internationalen Arbeitsmarkts für hochqualifizierte Arbeit geschaffen. Dieser sich dynamisch globalisierende Arbeitsmarkt zeichnet sich durch einen wechselseitigen Auswahlprozess zwischen dem „knappen" Angebot an qualifizierten Fachkräften und den rekrutierenden Staaten und Unternehmen mit Nachfrage nach Fachkräften mit Spezialwissen und -kompetenzen aus (Chiswick, 2011).

---

[1] https://esa.un.org/poppolicy/wpp_datasets.aspx

Hochqualifizierte Arbeitnehmer und gut ausgebildete Menschen spielen aufgrund ihrer Kenntnisse, Erfahrungen und Expertise in fast allen privaten und öffentlichen Sektoren eine Schlüsselrolle. Sie werden dabei häufig als „Wissensarbeiter" (DTI, 2002) bezeichnet, deren Berufsalltag von kreativem Denken und Entwickeln geprägt ist (Davenport, 2005). Eine einheitliche Definition eines hochqualifizierten Migranten ist jedoch noch nicht etabliert, weshalb allgemein zumeist der Bildungsstand, die Einkommenshöhe oder die Art der Beschäftigung zur Definition herangezogen werden. Hochqualifizierte Arbeitskräfte werden in jedem Fall als wertvoller Beitrag für jede Volkswirtschaft angesehen. Insbesondere in den innovationsgetriebenen Wissensökonomien des 21. Jahrhunderts gelten „Kopfarbeiter" als wesentlicher Bestandteil oder sogar als Voraussetzung für langfristiges Wirtschaftswachstum und Wohlstandssicherung.

Der Markt für hochqualifizierte Arbeit

Im vergangenen halben Jahrhundert hat eine weltweite Bildungsrevolution stattgefunden, wodurch sich in fast allen Ländern der Erde das durchschnittliche Bildungsniveau rapide erhöht hat. Dies ist insbesondere auf den stetig abnehmenden Anteil an Menschen ohne Primarschulbildung sowie den steilen Anstieg der Sekundar- und Tertiärbildung zurückzuführen (Czaika 2018). Zwischen 1950 und 2010 ist der Anteil der Weltbevölkerung (im Alter über 25 Jahre) ohne Primarbildung auf deutlich unter 20 Prozent gesunken, und eine Fortschreibung des langfristigen Trends lässt in den nächsten zwei Jahrzehnten einen uneingeschränkten Zugang der Weltbevölkerung zu Primarschulbildung erwarten (Czaika 2018). Der in naher Zukunft realisierte, allgemeine Zugang zu Primarschulbildung wird jedoch die globale Bildungsexpansion nicht verlangsamen, sondern vielmehr die Notwendigkeit und Dynamik zur Qualifizierung und den Erwerb von weiterführenden akademischen sowie fachlichen Kompetenzen beschleunigen.

Der Anstieg dieses weltweiten Angebots an qualifizierten Arbeitskräften ist nachfrageseitig auf ein steigendes Bildungsinteresse und angebotsseitig auf massive private und öffentliche Investitionen in Primar-, Sekundar- und Tertiärbildungskapazitäten zurückzuführen. Bildung nährt den „Hunger" nach mehr und besserer Bildung und schafft somit eine kontinuierlich wachsende Zahl an Menschen, die nach mehr, besserer und ausdifferenzierterer Bildung und Qualifikationen streben. Der „Return on Investment" in Form von erhöhter Produktivität und entsprechender Entlohnung ist eine wichtige Triebkraft dieser Entwicklung.

Eine Folge des steigenden Bildungsniveaus ist das Bedürfnis sowie die Notwendigkeit von qualifizierten und hochspezialisierten Arbeitskräften nach internationaler Mobilität. Bildung nährt sowohl den Wunsch nach einem „besseren Leben" als auch die Kenntnis, wie und insbesondere wo dieses bessere (Arbeits-)Leben zu erreichen ist. Die wachsende Zahl mobiler, qualifizierter Arbeitskräfte ist Ausdruck eines sich selbst verstärkenden Prozesses. Danach fördert die allgemeine Zunahme des Humankapitals und die damit zusammenhängende Ausweitung der beruflichen und privaten Ansprüche an das „gute Leben" in Kombination mit einer geographischen Konzentration hochwertiger Beschäftigungsmöglichkeiten - vor allem in einigen Wirtschaftsmetropolen der „OECD-Welt" - die internationale Mobilität von hochqualifizierten Menschen. Tertiär ausgebildete Menschen haben eine etwa dreimal höhere Wanderungsneigung als weniger formal ausgebildete Menschen. Insbesondere die sogenannte Mobilitätslücke zwischen tertiär und sekundär ausgebildeten Menschen scheint sich tendenziell eher zu vergrößern (Czaika 2018). Diese Mobilitätslücke ist Ausdruck und Folge von Unterschieden in den Bestrebungen und Möglichkeiten zwischen hoch qualifizierten und ausgebildeten Menschen und jenen, die weniger formale Ausbildung genossen haben.

Insgesamt dürfte das weltweit steigende Angebot an qualifizierten und hochqualifizierten Arbeitskräften die Zahl der international mobilen Fachkräfte weiter ankurbeln. Die zunehmende Spezialisierung und der Erwerb von Wissen und Fähigkeiten sowie räumlich konzentrierte Beschäftigungsmöglichkeiten machen es erforderlich, dass Fachkräfte mobiler werden, um ihre erworbenen spezifischen Fähigkeiten adäquat einzusetzen. Diese Mobilitätsnotwendigkeit bezieht sich nicht nur auf interne Bewegungen in Richtung nationaler Ballungsgebiete, sondern findet zunehmend grenzüberschreitend in Richtung „global cities" (Sassen 1998) statt. Gleichzeitig können sich hochqualifizierte Fachkräfte in weiten Teilen der Welt relativ ungehindert zwischen internationalen Destinationen bewegen. Durch die kontinuierliche Beseitigung institutionell-rechtlicher Hindernisse sowie migrationspolitischen Maßnahmen, welche proaktiv die barrierefreie transnationale Migration von Hochqualifizierten ermöglichen sollen, sind heutige Humankapitalbewegungen tendenziell temporärer und zirkulärer, als die eher traditionelle (permanente) Migration. Die Akkumulation von Bildung und Humankapital dürfte daher in Zukunft sowohl die internationale Migration als auch die eher kurzfristige Mobilität weiter ankurbeln.

Auf der anderen Seite dieses globalen Marktes für hochqualifizierte Arbeit beobachten wir eine wachsende Nachfrage nach spezialisierten Wissen, Kompetenzen und Expertise. Die meisten entwickelten und aufstrebenden Volkswirtschaften erleben hierbei eine Nachfragelücke in bestimmten Sektoren und Berufen, die durch das heimische Angebot an hochqualifizierten Arbeitskräften nicht ausreichend befriedigt werden kann. Diese strukturellen Engpässe werden sich in Zukunft aufgrund einer weiteren Ausdifferenzierung von Qualifikationsanforderungen möglicherweise sogar noch vergrößern, weshalb qualifikationsspezifische Einwanderung immer häufig als Mittel zur Überwindung dieser Engpässe angesehen wird. International steigt die Nachfrage nach Fachkräften seit Jahrzehnten kontinuierlich an, sodass in vielen OECD Staaten hochqualifizierte, tertiär ausgebildete Arbeitskräfte in naher Zukunft die Mehrheit unter den Zuwanderern darstellen werden (Czaika 2018). Die Transformation zu wissensbasierten Volkswirtschaften verstärkt die Nachfrage von Unternehmen nach einer spezialisierten und diversifizierten Qualifikationsstruktur des Arbeitsangebots, welches sich in vielen OECD Staaten zumindest kurzfristig nicht im erforderlichen Umfang reproduzieren lässt. Dieser Makrotrend dürfte somit den internationalen Wettbewerb um die knappe Ressource Humankapital weiter intensivieren.

Die internationale Mobilität hochqualifizierter Arbeitskräfte spiegelt auch die zunehmenden Anstrengungen von Unternehmen und anderen Rekrutierungsakteuren wider, temporäre oder strukturelle Arbeits- und Qualifikationsengpässe in stark nachgefragten Berufen mit internationalen Arbeitskräften zu besetzen. Dabei können hochqualifizierte Arbeitskräfte in ihren Beschäftigungsentscheidungen immer häufiger zwischen mehreren Jobangeboten auswählen: Sollte die Attraktivität einer bestimmten Stelle, eines Unternehmens oder einer Stadt, Region oder Landes als unzureichend wahrgenommen werden, können sich viele Fachkräfte für attraktivere Alternativangebote entscheiden. Diese Flexibilität internationale mobiler, hochqualifizierter Arbeitskräfte sowie die sich rasant verändernde Qualifikationsbedarfe fordern die „konkurrierenden" Länder und Unternehmen heraus, ihre Rekrutierungsstrategien und -angebote kontinuierlich den Bedarfen anzupassen, um die Fähigkeit zur Gewinnung und Bindung hochqualifizierter Arbeitskräfte zu erhöhen.

Während sich in den globalisierenden Arbeitsmärkten die Migrations- und Beschäftigungsmöglichkeiten für hochqualifizierte Arbeitskräfte stark erweitert hat, könnte die Zahl der potenziellen Herkunftsländer, aus denen diese Arbeitskräfte rekrutiert werden können, trotz des globalen Anstiegs des Humankapitalniveaus, eher abnehmen. Eine wachsende Zahl aufstrebender Staaten im globalen Süden, welches bislang eher Nettoexporteure von Humankapital waren, sieht sich zunehmend einem ähnlichen Fachkräftemangel ausgesetzt sieht wie große Teile der „OECD Welt". Sie versuchen deshalb, ihre qualifizierten Arbeitskräfte vom Bleiben zu überzeugen, beziehungsweise Abgewanderte aus dem Ausland zurück zu locken.

Anwerbung und Auswahl hoch qualifizierter Arbeitskräfte

In den vergangenen beiden Dekaden haben die OECD und in geringerem Maße Nicht-OECD-Regierungen Maßnahmen ergriffen, die darauf abzielen, hochqualifizierte Zuwanderer anzuwerben und auszuwählen, um sowohl den kurzfristigen, oftmals konjunkturbedingten Mangel an qualifizierten Arbeitskräften abzufedern, als auch strukturelle Angebotslücken in bestimmten Sektoren, wie dem Gesundheitsbereich, IKT oder den so genannten MINT-Bereichen, auszugleichen.

Grundsätzlich kann hier zwischen nachfrageseitigen und angebotsseitigen Strategien unterschieden werden. Erstere setzen normalerweise ein Arbeitsangebot vor dem Erhalt einer Arbeits- und Aufenthaltserlaubnis voraus, wohingegen bei einer angebotsseitigen Anwerbe- und Auswahlpolitik dies nicht grundsätzlich notwendig ist. Hier wird der Arbeitsmarktzugang vielmehr durch eine Prüfung individueller Qualifikationen und anderer persönlicher Charakteristiken, die oftmals im Rahmen eines Punkteverfahrens festgestellt werden, erteilt. Viele Staaten setzen jedoch auch Misch- oder Hybridformen ein, welche mit unterschiedlicher Priorisierung und Intensität sowohl kurz-, mittel- als auch langfristige Strategien beinhalten, um internationales Know-how, Wissen und Humankapital anzuwerben (vgl. Abella, 2006, Czaika und Parsons 2017).

Nachfrageseitige Politikstrategien

Eine unmittelbar von der aktuellen Arbeitsmarktsituation bestimmte Nachfragepolitik ist eher kurzfristig angelegt und wird von entsprechenden Konjunktur- und Beschäftigungszyklen beeinflusst. Der Bedarf der Arbeitgeber ist dabei die treibende Kraft, da es bei diesem Politikansatz zuvorderst um die rasche Schließung einer zumeist sehr spezifischen Angebotslücke geht. Ein Grundprinzip für die Zulassung ausländischer Arbeitnehmer ist hierbei die Beschäftigungsfähigkeit des Migranten, welcher durch ein von Arbeitgeberseite betriebenes „Sponsoring" sichergestellt werden soll. In diesem nachfrageseitigen, von Unternehmen initiierten Anwerbe- und Auswahlprozess, nehmen Arbeitgeber in der Regel eine aktive Rolle bei der Rekrutierung und Förderung der ausländischen Fachkraft ein, damit sich diese für befristete oder unbefristete Arbeits- und Aufenthaltsgenehmigungen qualifizieren. Dieses „Job-Contingency"-Prinzip soll hierbei die Beschäftigungsfähigkeit („employability") ausländischer Arbeitnehmer auf dem einheimischen Arbeitsmarkt gewährleisten. Natürlich kann, trotz der relativ effektiven Auswahl ausländischer Arbeitskräfte zur Behebung von Arbeitsmarktengpässen, das Erfordernis eines Jobangebots und einer Arbeitsmarktprüfung auch hochqualifizierte Zuwanderung abschrecken. Dies insbesondere dann, wenn trotz hoher Qualifikation des potentiellen Zuwanderers keine unmittelbaren Arbeitsmarktengpässe in dem entsprechenden Sektor (Stichwort „Mangelberuf") bestehen (Czaika und Parsons, 2017). Die meisten europäischen Einwanderungssysteme (einschließlich der Blauen Karte der EU und der österreichischen Rot-Weiß-Rot Karte), als auch die befristeten US-Arbeitsvisa (H1B) basieren auf dem Prinzip des Jobangebots.

Häufig setzt die arbeitgeberseitig beantragte Gewährung einer Arbeitserlaubnis eine regionale, nationale oder sogar europaweite Arbeitsmarktprüfung voraus, bei der fallspezifisch sichergestellt werden soll, dass keine „gleichwertigen" inländischen Arbeitskräfte verfügbar sind. Die bürokratische Belastung durch entsprechende Arbeitsmarktüberprüfungen kann jedoch beachtlich sein. Viele Länder betreiben daher sogenannte sektorspezifische Arbeitskräftemangellisten, welche für entsprechend qualifizierte Bewerber normalerweise eine individuelle Arbeitsmarktprüfung ersetzen. Mangellisten beschleunigen die Rekrutierung, insbesondere wenn ganze Berufssparten von einem hohen Arbeitskräftebedarf betroffen sind. Die z.T. zweifelhafte Stringenz der zugrundeliegenden Analyse zur Ermittlung eines Mangelberufs und des entsprechenden Arbeitskräftebedarfs wird jedoch häufig kritisiert (Sumption 2013).

Staaten rekrutieren qualifizierte Arbeitskräfte zuweilen auch auf der Grundlage bilateraler oder multilateraler Abkommen und stellen hierfür zumeist temporäre, oftmals aber auch dauerhafte Arbeits- und Aufenthaltsrechte zur Verfügung. Andere Politikstrategien verfolgen oftmals das Ziel, internationale Investoren und Unternehmungen anzuziehen. Diese eher indirekte Rekrutierungsstrategie ermöglicht qualifizierten Arbeitskräften eine Arbeits- und Aufenthaltserlaubnis auf Basis einer innerbetriebliche Entsendung von qualifiziertem Personal („Expatriates").

Angebotsseitige Politikstrategien

Eine noch kleine aber wachsende Zahl von Staaten verfolgt einen eher langfristigen Ansatz, bei welchem versucht wird, Humankapital unabhängig von einem unmittelbar konjunkturellen Fachkräftebedarf zu akkumulieren, um dadurch die langfristigen Kapazitäten für Wissensproduktion und Innovation zu stärken. Die hoch mobile Gruppe von „top end" Wissens- und Facharbeitern erhalten hierbei oft unmittelbaren oder zumindest zügigen Zugang zu unbefristeten Aufenthaltsrechten und auch zur Staatsbürgerschaft.

In diesen eher langfristig angelegten migrationspolitischen Strategien wird Humankapital auf individueller Basis durch sogenannte Punktsysteme bewertet, in denen ausländische Bewerber anhand ihrer Qualifikationen, ihres Alters, ihrer Berufserfahrung, ihrer Sprachkenntnisse und ihres Verdienstpotentials Punkte ansammeln. Arbeitsangebote sind hierbei in der Regel nicht erforderlich, obwohl Bewerber, die sich bereits vor der Einreise eine Arbeitsstelle gesichert haben, oftmals zusätzliche Punkte hierfür erhalten. Kanada (seit 1967) und Australien (seit 1989) sind Vorreiter dieser Punktesysteme, welche grundsätzlich als relativ effektiv gelten, hochqualifizierte Migranten anzuwerben (Facchini und Lodigiani, 2014, Czaika und Parsons, 2017). In jüngerer Zeit haben diese Systeme jedoch auch gezeigt, dass sie teilweise Bewerber auswählen, die nicht unmittelbar bestehende Arbeitsmarktengpässe adressieren und oftmals für längere Zeit, trotz hoher Qualifikationen, auf dem Arbeitsmarkt nicht vermittelbar sind, bzw. nur unter- oder nicht qualifikationsadäquat beschäftigt werden (Aydemir, 2013). Die meisten Länder, welche inzwischen Punkte-basierte Systeme implementiert haben, zielen daher zunehmend darauf ab, angebots- und nachfrageseitige Elemente in sogenannten Hybridsystemen zu kombinieren, um die Ziele Humankapitalakkumulation und Beschäftigungsfähigkeit zu gewährleisten.

Die eher langfristig angelegte Humankapitalstrategie umfasst insbesondere auch Maßnahmen, die sich an ausländische Studierende und Absolventen postgradualer Ausbildung richten, welche oftmals als „halbfertiges" Humankapital beschrieben werden (Khadria, 2001). Dieser Politikansatz zielt auf die dauerhafte Anwerbung und Integration dieser teilweise oder vollständig im Inland ausgebildeten Arbeitskräften, welche nicht nur professionell, sondern auch soziokulturell gebildet und somit als sozial und ökonomisch gut integrierbar gelten. Die meisten westlichen Länder bieten daher inzwischen Arbeitssuche-Visa an, die es Hochschulabsolventen ermöglichen soll, innerhalb eines gewissen Zeitraums eine adäquate Beschäftigung zu finden. Innerhalb dieses Zeitraums (normalerweise zwischen 6 und 24 Monaten) soll ausländischen Absolventen die Möglichkeit geboten werden, die Kriterien für reguläre hochqualifizierte Beschäftigung zu erfüllen.

Grundsätzlich ist die verfolgte migrationspolitische Strategie und die entsprechende Ausgestaltung des Zuwanderungsregimes von den wirtschaftlichen Zielen und dem Gewicht oftmals konkurrierender politischer Akteure und Interessengruppen beeinflusst. Migrationspolitik wird immer mehr in einem komplexen politisch-ökonomischen Kontext ausgehandelt und gestaltet, in welchem die Interessen und Präferenzen von Politikern und Wählern, Arbeitgebern, Gewerkschaften und anderen politisch aktiven Gruppen miteinander konkurrieren. Dieser

Wettbewerb resultiert in länderspezifischen Regelungen, Vorschriften und Maßnahmen, die zunehmend durch einen hohen Grad an Komplexität gekennzeichnet sind (Czaika und de Haas 2013).

Der Wettbewerb um die effektivsten politischen Maßnahmen im Bereich der Migration Hochqualifizierter hat jedoch erst begonnen. Der migrationspolitische Wettbewerb, welcher sich in Zukunft noch verstärken dürfte, hat in den letzten Jahren einige innovative Politikinstrumente und Maßnahmen hervorgebracht, die als Teil eines „Einwanderungspakets" (Papademetriou et al., 2008) verstanden werden können, welches länderspezifische Regelungen von Einwanderungs- und Aufenthaltsbestimmungen umfasst. Es ist erwiesenermaßen unwahrscheinlich, dass eine einzelne migrationspolitische Maßnahme per se dazu führt, dass ein Land für hochqualifizierte Migranten mehr oder weniger attraktiv wird. Das Konzept des Einwanderungspakets verdeutlicht vielmehr die Bedeutung des gesamten migrations- und integrationspolitischen Instrumentariums in Kombination mit der Bereitstellung von anderen öffentlichen Gütern und Versorgungsleistungen (Papademetriou et al., 2008, Papademetriou und Sumption, 2013).

Es wird darüber hinaus immer mehr erkannt, dass der Zustrom von Fachkräften zu signifikanten positiven Externalitäten führen kann, indem ergänzende Expertise und Kompetenzen rekrutiert werden, welche die Produktivität aller Arbeitnehmer (und auch des eingesetzten Kapitals) erhöhen und infolgedessen weitere qualifizierte ausländische Arbeitskräfte anziehen können (Peri und Sparber, 2009). Eine hochqualifizierte Zuwanderung führt somit zu sogenannten positiven Externalitäten, die sowohl innerhalb als auch zwischen einzelnen Berufsgruppen und beruflichen Netzwerken eine Migrationsdynamik auslösen können (Beine et al., 2011). Qualifikationsrekrutierende Migrationsstrategien, welche lediglich auf existierende Nachfragelücken reagieren, können daher zumindest kurzfristig weitgehend ineffektiv sein, wenn (i) entsprechende Komplementaritäten zwischen Berufsgruppen und (ii) langfristige Karriere- und Bleibeperspektiven für diese international hoch mobile Gruppe an Hochqualifizierten unberücksichtigt bleiben.

Die Migration hochqualifizierter Arbeitskräfte ist sowohl pfadabhängig, als auch ein sich selbst verstärkender Prozess, welcher ein attraktives professionelles und soziokulturelles Umfeld voraussetzt, aber auch selbst schafft (Czaika und Toma 2017). Metropolen fungieren hier normalerweise als Knotenpunkte eines global vernetzten Humankapitalsystems. An diesen Knotenpunkten wird wissenschaftliche, technische oder Management-Expertise produziert und reproduziert (Florida 2003). Städtische Metropolen sind in diesem System wichtige Gravitationszentren, in denen professionelle und kulturelle Vielfalt einen fruchtbaren Boden für soziale, wirtschaftliche und technische Innovationen hervorbringen kann. Dadurch werden Metropolen selbst zu wichtigen Determinanten für die internationale Mobilität von Hochqualifizierten (Ozgen et al. 2014).

Die Entwicklung und Wirksamkeit migrationspolitischer Maßnahmen

Eine kürzlich abgeschlossene Untersuchung durch Czaika und Parsons (2017) hinsichtlich migrationspolitischer Entwicklungen in 19 OECD-Staaten im Zeitraum von 2000 bis 2012 verdeutlicht die relative Verbreitung der oben genannten Politikstrategien und -instrumente. Beispielsweise setzen drei Viertel dieser 19 hochentwickelten Länder „Job-Continency"-Systeme ein, während etwa die Hälfte zusätzlich bedarfsorientierte Politikeinstrumente, wie Mangellisten und Arbeitsmarkttests, nutzen. Zehn Länder verwenden hierbei auch numerische Obergrenzen (Quoten). Punktbasierte Systeme werden in sechs Ländern verwendet. Das am schnellsten sich verbreitende Politikinstrument ist das Visum für postgraduale Arbeitssuche. Im Jahr 2000 hatte noch keines der 19 untersuchten Länder ein solches Instrument eingesetzt, während zehn Jahre später fast die Hälfte der beobachteten Staaten entsprechende Maßnahmen, die ausländischen Absolventen eine Bleibemöglichkeit einräumen sollen, eingeführt hatte.

Neben den genannten Auswahlinstrumenten enthalten Einwanderungspakete in der Regel zusätzliche Elemente, welche die Attraktivität der anwerbenden Länder erhöhen sollen. Beispielsweise stellt die Aussicht auf ein dauerhaftes Aufenthaltsrecht, welches zur langfristigen (Karriere-)Planung notwendig ist, einen wichtigen Zuwanderungsanreiz für potenzielle ausländische Arbeitskräfte dar. Hochqualifizierten Migranten wird daher unmittelbar oder nach einer gewissen Frist eine dauerhafte Aufenthaltserlaubnis angeboten. Dieses Recht wird normalerweise auch Familienangehörigen von qualifizierten Arbeitsmigranten zugestanden, auch wenn einzelne Länder dies nur nach einer bestimmten Zeitspanne erlauben (z. B. Korea oder Rumänien). Für die meisten hochqualifizierten Migranten ist das sofortige Recht auf Familiennachzug eine unabdingbare Voraussetzung für den Zuzug, deren Abwesenheit sich immens negativ auf die Attraktivität eines Standortes auswirkt. Mehr als 80 Prozent der 19 untersuchten OECD Staaten bieten daher sofortige Familienzusammenführungsrechte an. In ähnlicher Weise gilt die Bereitstellung einer Arbeitserlaubnis für Familienangehörige als ein wichtiger Faktor bei der erfolgreichen Anwerbung hochqualifizierter Migranten. Solche attraktivitätsfördernden Bestimmungen für Familienangehörige von hochqualifizierten Zuwanderern haben in den letzten Jahren stark an Popularität gewonnen. Des Weiteren nutzen immer mehr Staaten finanzielle Anreize, wie beispielsweise Steuerbefreiungen und finanzielle Zulagen, um international hochqualifizierte Arbeitskräfte anzuwerben oder zum Verbleiben anzuhalten. In der vergangenen Dekade hat die Zahl der Länder, die solche finanziellen Anreizsysteme implementiert haben, deutlich zugenommen (Czaika und Parsons 2017).

Interessanterweise hat sich die jüngste globale Wirtschaftskrise (seit 2007/08), welche in zahlreichen Ländern auch noch nicht überwunden ist, trotz im Allgemeinen negativen Auswirkungen auf den Gesamtzustand der jeweiligen Arbeitsmärkte nur unerheblich auf die Nachfrage nach hochqualifizierten Arbeitskräften und die entsprechenden internationalen Wanderungsbewegungen ausgewirkt. Migrationsströme hochqualifizierte Arbeitskräfte, ebenso wie entsprechende migrationspolitische Strategien scheinen relativ unabhängig von wirtschaftlichen Schwankungen zu sein. Zumindest zeigt sich diese Resilienz entsprechender Politikgrößen im Kontext der globalen Wirtschaft- und Finanzkrise nach 2007 (Czaika and Parsons 2018). Trotz einiger Nachjustierungen und geringer Anpassungen, wie beispielsweise bei Arbeitskräftemangellisten oder einzelnen Neubewertungen in punktebasierten Zuwanderungssystem, haben sich in den meisten Ländern keine wesentlichen Politikumkehrungen ergeben. Die Nachfrage nach hochqualifizierten Arbeitskräften hat sich in einer wachsenden Anzahl von Berufssparten eher noch verstärkt, und sowohl Staaten, als auch Städte und Unternehmen werden zu immer aktiveren nachfrageseitigen Akteuren auf dem globalisierten Markt für Humankapital.

Die Maßnahmen nachfrageseitiger Akteure richten sich zunehmend auch an ausländische Studierende und Hochschulabsolventen. Investitionen in sogenanntes „halbfertiges" Humankapital gelten oft als wirksame politische Option für die langfristige Akkumulation von Humankapital. Das karrieremäßig frühzeitige Anwerben von „high potentials" wird als eine effiziente Strategie gesehen, da bei dieser Gruppe relativ niedrige Integrations- und Absorptionskosten anfallen, insbesondere, wenn sie im Inland ausgebildet wurden, und deshalb normalerweise auf dem Arbeitsmarkt die besten Ergebnisse unter allen Zuwanderern erzielen (OECD 2008). Infolgedessen haben viele Länder anerkannt, dass eine großzügigere Bereitstellung von Visa für Studium und Arbeitssuche eine nützliche und tragfähige politische Strategie ist, auch in wirtschaftlichen Krisenzeiten.

Viele Staaten haben auch bilaterale und multilaterale Abkommen unterzeichnet, welche die soziale Absicherung, die Doppelbesteuerung sowie die Anerkennung ausländischer Abschlüsse und Diplome regeln sollen. Diese Abkommen sollen den Übergang und die Integration hochqualifizierter Migranten in den Arbeitsmarkt erleichtern. Hierbei haben Abkommen, welche die Anerkennung ausländischer Qualifikationen regeln, in den vergangenen zehn Jahren die größte politische Aufmerksamkeit erlangt. In der Regel zielen diese Vereinbarungen auf bestimmte Berufe und/oder Fachbereiche ab und regeln, oft durch Berufsverbände initiiert, die Qualität und Vergleichbarkeit von Lehrinhalten und Studiengängen, um die Gleichwertigkeit mit inländischen Studiengängen zu gewährleisten. Empirische Untersuchungen zeigen, dass solche Abkommen die Mobilität sowohl von qualifizierten als auch von nicht qualifizierten Arbeitskräften wirksam fördern können (Czaika und Parsons, 2017). Des Weiteren zielen internationale Steuerabkommen unter anderem darauf ab, die Doppelbesteuerung von Lohn- und Kapitaleinkünften zu vermeiden. Auch wenn allgemein davon ausgegangen wird, dass solche Abkommen mobilitätsfördernd wirken, legen empirische Befunde nahe, dass solche Vereinbarungen nur sehr begrenzte Wirkung haben (Czaika und Parsons, 2017). Schließlich zielen Abkommen zur Regelung sozialer Absicherung darauf ab, die Rechte in Bezug auf die Gleichbehandlung von Auslandsbezügen zu regeln, beispielsweise was die Transferierbarkeit von Rentenbezügen, Leistungen bei Invalidität, Zahlungen an verwitwete oder pflegende Angehörige oder Leistungen bei Arbeitslosigkeit betrifft. Diese hochkomplexen Rechtssachverhalte werden zunehmend international abgestimmt und wirken sich tendenziell positiv auf die Migrationsbereitschaft aus.

Die Effektivität diverser migrationspolitischer Instrumente auf die Migrationsströme von hochqualifizierten Zuwanderern in 10 OECD-Staaten wird von Czaika und Parsons (2017) statistisch untersucht. Wir stellen dabei fest, dass angebotsseitige Punkte-Systeme in der Regel effektiver bei der Anwerbung und Auswahl hochqualifizierter Migranten sind im Vergleich zu eher nachfrageseitigen Systemen, wo das Zuwanderungsverfahren durch das Arbeitgeber-„Sponsoring" initiiert und durch einen Arbeitsmarkttest oder eine „Qualifikationsmangelliste" ergänzt wird. Andere, eher finanzielle Anreizinstrumente, wie Steuererleichterungen oder -zulagen, führen oftmals zu besseren Wirkungen. Des Weiteren sind Angebote, welche einen sofortigen dauerhaften Aufenthaltsstatus gewähren, für hochqualifizierte Arbeitskräfte sehr attraktiv, und damit effektiv.

Insgesamt ist jedoch die Frage, ob und unter welchen Bedingungen bestimmte migrationspolitischen Instrumente ihre intendierten Wirkungen erzielen nur vorläufig zu beantworten und erfordert weitere, großangelegte empirischen Untersuchungen. Da sich in den letzten Jahren die wissenschaftliche als auch öffentliche Debatte hinsichtlich der „richtigen" Migrationspolitik stark auf die Zuwanderung gering qualifizierter Arbeitskräfte sowie von Asylsuchenden oder irregulär Migrierende konzentriert hat, wurde viel weniger Forschung und öffentliche Aufmerksamkeit der Migration von Hochqualifizierten und deren Anwerbung gewidmet. Diese Wirksamkeit von Anwerbe- und Selektionsinstrumenten, für welche eine systematische Untersuchung gerade erst beginnt, kann auf Grundlage der bisherigen Datenlage als recht ambivalent bezeichnet werden. Das Design wirksamer, d.h. zielführender Politikmaßnahmen bedarf eines besonderen Verständnisses für die Eigenheiten dieses spezifischen, global sich integrierenden Arbeitsmarktes. Solide Kenntnis der grundlegenden und spezifischen Treiber und Dynamiken der internationalen Fachkräftemigration ist daher eine wesentliche Voraussetzung für die Entwicklung einer realistischen und effektiven Migrationspolitik, welche darauf abzielen soll, das Mobilitäts- und Migrationsverhalten dieser Zielgruppe in einer beabsichtigten Richtung zu beeinflussen (Czaika und de Haas 2013). Simple Annahmen wie jene, dass hochqualifizierte Menschen primär auf der Suche nach höheren Löhnen sind und deshalb durch eine liberale („open door") Zuwanderungspolitik, in Kombination beispielsweise mit Steuererleichterungen, angeworben werden können, sind nicht notwendigerweise erfolgreich. Die in zahlreichen Ländern inzwischen praktizierten Rekrutierungsbemühungen in Form einer quasi- „open door" bzw. „red carpet" Zuwanderungsregulierung für Hochqualifizierte haben hierbei nicht grundsätzlich die gewünschten Ergebnisse erbracht, da die Wirksamkeit dieser Programme doch oft als recht uneinheitlich eingeschätzt wird.

Migrationsentscheidungen sind weit davon entfernt, deterministisch zu sein. Sie hängen vielmehr von einem komplexen, sich über die Zeit veränderndem Mix an Präferenzen und Ideen über „das gute Leben" und beruflichen Zielen und Bestrebungen ab. Eine effektive Migrationspolitik, welche darauf abzielt, die „besten Hände und Köpfe" anzuziehen, basiert auf einer umfassenden Kenntnis der oft vielfältigen, vom Beschäftigungssektor und Lebenssituation abhängenden Migrationsmotiven ab. Eine gut konzipierte Migrationspolitik fördert Migrationsoptionen, das heißt sie bietet Menschen mit gesuchten Fähigkeiten und Qualifikationen, Berufen, Alter, Erfahrung, Ausbildung, und manchmal auch sozialer und kultureller Hintergründen die notwendigen Möglichkeiten, sowohl temporär, zirkulär als auch permanent migrieren zu können. Stark nachgefragte, hoch qualifizierte und oftmals hoch mobile Arbeitskräfte nehmen Zuwanderungsbestimmungen und -offerten als Anreizstrukturen wahr und entscheiden sich meist für das attraktivste „Gesamtpaket".

Diese Gesamtpakete beinhalten natürlich mehr als nur etwaige Einreise- und Aufenthaltsbestimmungen (Papadimitriou und Sumption 2013). Empirische Befunde deuten darauf hin, dass migrationspolitische Maßnahmen zwar Migrationsprozesse beeinflussen, die Größenordnung dieser Effekte jedoch im Vergleich zu anderen Politikmaßnahmen und strukturellen Determinanten begrenzt ist. So sind Arbeitsmarktregulierungen, Bestimmungen im Wohnungswesen, in der Bildung, bei der Besteuerung oder bei der sozialen Sicherheit – das heißt Maßnahmen, die nicht primär auf Migration an sich fokussiert sind – Teil eines viel umfassenderen Einwanderungspakets. Infolgedessen erfordert das Design wirksamer und effizienter Migrations- und Anwerbestrategien eine umfassende und integrierte Bewertung und Abstimmung aller migrationsrelevanten Politiken. Das betrifft auch Politiken, deren Hauptzweck nicht die Anwerbung und Selektion hochqualifizierter Migranten darstellt.

Aus politischer Sicht besteht das Problem mangelnder Effektivität von einzelnen Politikmaßnahmen daher oftmals darin, dass die entsprechende Migrationspolitik oftmals eher eng definiert und konzipiert ist und andere wirtschaftliche, soziale und kulturelle Politikfelder unberücksichtigt bleiben. Um die Wirksamkeit von Rekrutierungsstrategien zu erhöhen, müssen kohärente, „whole-of-government"-Zuwanderungsstrategien entwickelt werden, welche in die wirtschaftlichen, sozialen und politischen Strukturen und Transformationen des Landes und den allgemeinen Kontext internationaler Migrationsprozesse und -dynamiken eingebettet sind. In einer Welt, in der immer mehr Länder und Unternehmen um hochqualifizierte Arbeitskräfte konkurrieren, müssen politische Maßnahmenpakete, welche darauf abzielen, die *allgemeine* Attraktivität eines Standorts zu erhöhen, Chancen für hochqualifizierte Arbeitsmigranten im Hinblick auf eine gute Beschäftigung sowie sichere, angenehme Lebensbedingungen bereitstellen.

Zusammenfassung und Schlussbemerkungen

Die Migration Hochqualifizierter ist inzwischen zu einem globalen Phänomen geworden und von zentralem Interesse für die beteiligten Ökonomien. Dementsprechend versuchen immer mehr Staaten in den verschiedensten Teilen der Welt Maßnahmen zu entwickeln, um dringend benötigtes Humankapital international anzuwerben oder eigene „Talente" im Land zu halten. Dieser Beitrag sollte einen Überblick über dieses noch wenig beforschte Gebiet der Migration hochqualifizierter Arbeitskräfte geben und insbesondere auf die migrationspolitischen Maßnahmen eingehen, welche Staaten zur Anwerbung und Auswahl von Arbeitsmigranten derzeit zur Verfügung stehen. Die Übersicht hat verdeutlicht, dass insbesondere in den beiden vergangenen Dekaden eine Intensivierung dieser migrationspolitischen Aktivitäten stattgefunden hat und sich entsprechende Instrumente und „Best practices" zur Rekrutierung und zur Auswahl von hochqualifizierten Arbeitskräften etabliert wurden. Auch wenn die allgemeine Nachfrage nach hochqualifizierten Arbeits- und Fachkräften unvermindert anhält, bleibt in vielen Teilen der Welt das Thema Zuwanderung ein höchst umstrittenes. Jedoch haben sich trotz zunehmend restriktiver werdenden Politikmaßnahmen und ausländerfeindlichen öffentlichen Debatten gegenüber „unerwünschten" Geringqualifizierten eher liberalere Ansichten und Politikansätze hinsichtlich der Zuwanderung dringend benötigtem Humankapital verfestigt. Trotz einiger Kontroversen in der öffentlichen Debatte haben sich die meisten westlichen, aber auch zahlreiche nichtwestliche Länder, verstärkt darum bemüht, internationale Talente zu rekrutieren und an den heimischen Arbeitsmarkt zu binden.

Die übergeordneten Ziele dieser Rekrutierungsanstrengungen sind vielfältig und nicht immer uneingeschränkt vereinbar. Hierzu zählen beispielsweise die Befriedigung ganz spezifischer und oftmals kurzfristiger Arbeitsmarktengpässe, die Akquise von hochqualifiziertem Humankapital als Stimulus für nationale Innovationssysteme, oder die Abfederung des demografischen Übergangs und der damit verbundenen Sicherstellung der Nachhaltigkeit der Sozialsysteme bis zur möglichen Intention der Schwächung internationaler Wettbewerber auf dem globalen Markt für Hochqualifizierte. Es ist absehbar, dass sich diese Gründe für die Implementierung attraktiver migrationspolitischer Maßnahmenpakete im Laufe des nächsten Jahrzehnts eher noch verstärken werden, da aufgrund der steigenden strukturellen Nachfrage nach hochqualifizierter Arbeit in den meisten Ländern dieser Welt eine Umkehrungen dieses Trends unwahrscheinlich erscheint. Diese „Krisenfestigkeit" hochqualifizierter Migrationsströme und –migrationspolitischer Strategien ist teilweise auch mit einem Trend hin zu „hybriden" Zuwanderungssystemen verbunden, welche sowohl nachfrage- als auch angebotsseitige Maßnahmen kombinieren, um die Vielfalt, und teilweise Gegensätzlichkeit in den migrationspolitischen Zielen hinsichtlich der quantitativen als auch qualitativen Zusammensetzung der zuwandernden Arbeitsbevölkerung auszubalancieren.

Abschließend möchte ich einige grundlegende Empfehlungen anbieten, welche sowohl die Effizienz des globalen Arbeitsmarktes für Hochqualifizierte erhöhen, als auch die Wettbewerbsfähigkeit bei der internationalen Rekrutierung verbessern sollen.

Internationale Standardisierung von Abschlüssen und Zeugnissen: Auch wenn der Bologna- sowie der Kopenhagen-Prozess, aber auch die Etablierung des Europäischen Qualifikationsrahmens auf eine Homogenisierung der Qualifikationsarchitekturen abzielen, steht die Entwicklung von einheitlichen internationalen Qualitätsstandards noch aus (Biffl/Pfeffer 2013). Es gibt erhebliche Unterschiede in der Qualität der jeweiligen Bildungssysteme, und die inhaltlich zugrunde liegenden Standards von Abschlüssen und Zeugnissen sind oftmals nur auf dem Papier ähnlich, geschweige denn gleichwertig. Dies kann zu einer Über- oder Unterschätzung des Qualifikationsniveaus und des Humankapitals von Personen führen, die mit entsprechenden negativen Konsequenzen hinsichtlich Beschäftigungs- und Einstufungsniveau rechnen müssen, da sie in Bereichen und für Aufgaben eingesetzt werden, die oftmals nicht ihrer Qualifikation entsprechen. Die Vereinheitlichung und Vereinfachung der Anerkennungsverfahren für ausländische Qualifikationen kann das Risiko einer solchen unangemessenen Beschäftigung reduzieren. Die internationale Koordination und Standardisierung von Regelungen zur Anerkennung von Qualifikationen ausländischer Arbeitskräfte sowie die Transparenz über Arbeitsbedingungen und -standards können die Effizenz des globalen Arbeitsmarktes für Hochqualifizierte erhöhen.

Vereinfachte Einwanderungssysteme und Zulassungsregelungen: Viele Zuwanderungssysteme, insbesondere solche mit einer längeren Tradition, haben über die Zeit multiple Partikularinteressen berücksichtigt und haben dadurch übermäßig komplexe Regelungen und Vorschriften zu Zulassungs- und Integrationsverfahren entwickelt. Diese komplexen Regelungssysteme sind oft nicht nur inkohärent und ineffizient, sondern auch für interessierte ausländische Fachkräfte oft ohne professionelle Unterstützung nicht nachvollziehbar. Gesetzliche, verfahrenstechnische und praktische Komplexitäten schaffen Unsicherheiten und Kosten für potentiell zuwanderungswillige Arbeitskräfte und rekrutierende Unternehmen, beispielsweise in Form von notwendigen (Rechts-)Beratungsdiensten. Klare, einfache rechtliche und berufliche Zugänge und Perspektiven für dauerhafte oder langfristige Einwanderung und Beschäftigung bilden den Kern eines wirksamen migrationspolitischen Pakets.

Internationale Mobilitätsvisa: Auch wenn langfristige Möglichkeiten oder Wege zur dauerhaften Einwanderung starke Migrationsanreize von hoch qualifizierten Arbeitskräften schaffen, erfordert eine ressourceneffiziente internationale Allokation von Humankapital und Wissensverbreitung eine nicht nur trans-, sondern multinationale Mobilität zwischen oftmals mehreren internationalen Beschäftigungs- und Lebensstandorten. Die Etablierung und großzügige Bereitstellung von langfristigen und dauerhaften Visa- und Arbeitsgenehmigungen, die in mehreren Ländern und Arbeitsmärkten gleichzeitig gültig sind, dürfte die allgemeine Mobilitätsdynamik bzw. „Umlaufgeschwindigkeit" des Humankapitals und dadurch der Verbreitung von Wissen erhöhen.

Internationale Arbeitsagentur: Hochqualifizierte Arbeitskräfte werden nicht nur von großen, multinationalen Unternehmen mit gut ausgestatteten Personalmanagement- und Rekrutierungskapazitäten angeworben, sondern auch kleinere und mittlere Unternehmen (KMU) sind verstärkt auf dem internationalen Arbeitsmarkt für qualifizierte und hochqualifizierte Arbeit aktiv. Diese Unternehmen benötigen Unterstützung bei ihren Rekrutierungsbemühungen, da ihnen oft die notwendigen Kapazitäten und Erfahrung fehlen, um eine aktivere Rolle auf dem entsprechenden internationalen Arbeitsmarkt zu spielen. Eine internationale Arbeitsvermittlungsagentur kann das internationale „Matching-making" zwischen Unternehmen und ausländischen Arbeitskräften verschiedenster Qualifikationsniveaus und Berufsprofile erleichtern. Denkbar wären (i) Systeme gegenseitiger Interessenbekundungen, (ii) die Erfassung und Bereitstellung von (Online-)Informationen über nationale und regionale Qualifikationslücken, (iii) Hilfe und Unterstützung für Unternehmen und Zuwanderungswilligen bei der Übersetzung und Anerkennung von Qualifikationen und der Bereitstellung von Rechtsberatung, (iv) Bereitstellung von Information bezüglich Rekrutierungs- und Arbeitsprogrammen, oder über Möglichkeiten für berufliche Ausbildungen, Stipendien, Lehrlingsausbildungen, Traineeprogramme und Hochschulabschlüsse, Jobmessen usw.

Migrationsmonitoringsysteme: Migrationspolitische Maßnahmen, die darauf abzielen, die internationale Rekrutierung von hochqualifizierten Arbeitskräften wirksam zu steuern, müssen integraler Bestandteil eines internationalen Monitoring- und Analysesystems von Arbeitsangebot und -nachfrage auf allen Qualifikationsniveaus sein. Die politischen Entscheidungsträger sollten zu jedem Zeitpunkt in der Lage sein zu wissen, wie viel und welche Arten von Humankapital und Qualifikationen sowohl lokal, national als auch international produziert und verfügbar sind, als auch nachgefragt werden. Internationale, zentralisierte Migrationsinformations- und Datensammlungseinheiten müssen auf nationale Datenerfassungs- und Informationssysteme zugreifen können. Schließlich müssen grundsätzlich die Ressourcen und Kapazitäten für angewandte Migrationsforschung erweitert werden, um ein umfangreiches, evidenzbasiertes Fachwissen und Einschätzungen zur internationalen Arbeitsmarktdynamik auf Basis methodisch modernster Migrationsdiagnosemöglichkeiten bereitzustellen.

Literatur

Abella, M. (2006) Global competition for skilled workers and consequences. In: Kuptsch, C. and Pang, E. F. (eds.) *Competing for global talent*. Geneva: International Labour Office-International Institute for Labour Studies and Singapore Management University.

Aydemir, A. (2013) Skill-based immigrant selection and labor market outcomes by visa category. In: Constant, A. F. & Zimmermann, K. F. (eds.) *International Handbook on the Economics of Migration* (Chapter 23): 432-452. Cheltenham: Edward Elgar.

Beine, M., Docquier, F. & Özden, C. (2011) Diasporas. *Journal of Development Economics*. 95 (1), 30–41.

Biffl, G. & Pfeffer, T. (2013) Recognition of qualifications of citizens of another EU Member State. In: FEANI News. The European Engineers Publication, Issue 11, June 2013, pp 19-26

Boeri, T. (2012) Introduction. In: Boeri, T., Brücker, H., Docquier, F. & Rapoport, H. (eds.) *Brain Drain and Brain Gain: The Global Competition to Attract High-skilled Migrants*. Oxford: Oxford University Press.

Cerna, L. & Czaika, M. (2015) European Policies to Attract Talent: The Crisis and Highly Skilled Migration Policy Changes. In: Triandafyllidou, A., Isaakyan, I. & Schiavone, G. (eds.) *High Skill Migration and Recession: Gendered Perspectives*. Basingstoke: Palgrave Macmillan.

Cerna, L., & Czaika, M. (2018) Rising Stars in the Global Race for Skill? A Comparative Analysis of Brazil, India and Malaysia, forthcoming *Journal of Ethnic and Migration Studies*

Chiswick, B. R. (2011) *High-skilled Immigration in a Global Labor Market*. Washington, D.C.: American Enterprise Institute Press.

Czaika, M. (2018) High-Skilled Migration: Introduction and Synopsis, in: Czaika, M. (ed) High-Skilled Migration: Drivers and Policies, Oxford University Press

Czaika, M. & de Haas, H. (2013) The Effectiveness of Immigration Policies. *Population and Development Review*. 39 (3), 487–508.

Czaika, M. & Parsons, C. (2017) The gravity of high-skilled migration policies. *Demography*. 54 (2), 603–630.

Czaika, M. & Toma, S. (2017) International academic mobility across space and time. The case of Indian academics. Forthcoming *Population Space and Place*.

Davenport, T. H. (2005) *Thinking For A Living: How to Get Better Performance and Results From Knowledge Workers*. Boston: Harvard Business School Press.

Doomernik, J., Koslowski, R. & Thränhardt, D. (2009) The Battle for the Brains: Why Immigration Policy Is Not Enough to Attract the Highly Skilled. Brussels Forum Paper Series. Washington, D.C.: German Marshall Fund of the United States.

DTI (2002) Knowledge Migrants: The Motivations and Experiences of Professionals in the UK on Work Permits. London: Department of Trade and Industry.

Facchini, G. & Lodigiani, E. (2014) Attracting Skilled Immigrants: An Overview of Recent Policy Developments in Advanced Countries. *National Institute Economic Review*. 229 (1), R3–R21.

Florida, R. (2003) Cities and the creative class. *City & Community*. 2 (1), 3–19.

Kapur, D. & McHale, J. (2005) Give us your best and brightest: the global hunt for talent and its impact on the developing world. Washington, D.C.: Center for Global Development.

Khadria, B. (2001) Shifting Paradigms of Globalization: the Twenty First Century Transition towards Generics in Skilled Labour Migration from India. *International Migration*. 39 (5), 45–71.

OECD (2008) A Profile of Immigrant Populations in the 21st Century: Data from OECD Countries. Paris: OECD.

Ozgen, C., Peters, C., Niebuhr, A., Nijkamp, P. & Poot, J. (2014) Does Cultural Diversity of Migrant Employees Affect Innovation? *International Migration Review*. 48, 377–416.

Papademetriou, D. G., Somerville, W. & Tanaka, H. (2008) *Talent in the 21st-Century Economy*. Washington, D.C.: Migration Policy Institute.

Papademetriou, D. G. & Sumption, M. (2013) Attracting and Selecting from the Global Talent Pool – Policy Challenges. Washington, D.C.: Migration Policy Institute.

Peri, G. & Sparber, C. (2009) Task Specialization, Immigration, and Wages. *American Economic Journal: Applied Economics*. 1 (3), 135–169.

Sumption, M. (2013) The Elusive Idea of Labor-Market 'Shortages' and the U.S. Approach to Employment-Based Immigration Policy. In: Fix, M., Papademetriou, D. G. & Sumption, M. (eds.) Immigrants in a Changing Labor Market. Washington, DC: Migration Policy Institute.

Migrant remittances and macroeconomic developments in the source countries

Daniela Bobeva

Abstract

Decades of studies on migrant remittances make one think that everything has been already said, but the recent dynamics of remittances challenge the accumulated knowledge. The economic downturn in the remittance source countries led to a decline in the outflows and a further stagnation while the inflows to these countries sharply increased. The role of the source countries in remittances dynamics needs more attention. This article empirically examines the role of a set of macroeconomic indicators on the outflows of remittances in seven of the top ten source countries of remittances. Particular attention is given to the fluctuations in remittance outflows over the international business cycles and more specifically during the recent global crisis. The constructed model found a significant impact of inflation, unemployment and wages in the source countries on the outflow of remittances, while the economic growth has no significant direct impact.

Introduction

Remittances have enjoyed a great academic interest for many years. The recent crisis dynamited remittances and the factors that shape up their directions and scope. Such a deep crisis that affected mainly developed countries provokes the academic curiosity to verify whether the conventional theory on remittances works. Although the theory suggests that remittances are more stable than other financial flows during the different phases of the cycle, crisis increases macroeconomic volatility and thus may have profound effects on remittance flows. While most of the literature is dedicated to the impact of remittances mainly on the home and to certain extend on the host country of migrants, the factors that drive those bilateral flows had not been on the top of the research agenda. In most of the cases the remittances simply have no significant impact on the sending country, since the studies are rather small compared to the size of developed economies. The other reason is that remittances are studied mainly in the area of development economics and the researchers are focused on assessing the remittances as a benefit from the extensive emigration from developing countries and as a compensation of the loss of population, labour and skills. As Elbadawi and Rocha (1992) point out, demographic portfolio and macroeconomic factors, together with special incentive policies, determine official remittances. The complexity of migrant remittances is associated with the variety of factors of personal and macro nature that impact them. Also, the factors related with the migrant home and host countries and their particular role attract the attention of the researchers. Several studies try to measure macroeconomic factors on the remittance outflows, such as GDP growth, real exchange rates, consumption, financial developments and income distribution. The selection of indicators and econometric approaches feeds the great differences in the outcome of the empirical examinations.

In this paper, the recent changes in remittances outflows from seven top remittance countries[1] are studied and also the impact of their macroeconomic framework on remittance outflows. First, the literature is reviewed in seeking for consensus results as to what are the most significant macroeconomic indicators that impact remittances outflows, as well as the econometric models applied. Studying macroeconomic factors from the remittance source country prospective is not sufficiently covered in migration literature although some authors confirm that source country factors better explain the remittance outflow. Moreover, the recent crisis hit more the economies of source than recipient countries of remittances, which could be expected to increase the role of migrant host country factors. A qualitative analysis is conducted aiming at defining the developments of each of the selected macroeconomic indicators and their relevance and limitations to the remittances outflows. Based on that qualitative analysis a balanced panel data model is constructed and applied.

Theory about the role of source country macroeconomy for remittances

There is no consensus about the role of macroeconomic factors in the migrant host country on the scope of outflow of remittances. Also, the authors choose different macroeconomic indicators and techniques in their studies. Cooray and Mallick (2013) test a dynamic panel data model using the system-GMM method over the period 1970-2007. They argue that remittance inflows increase with the volatility in migrant host countries, especially for middle-income countries. Lower interest rates in migrant host countries lead to larger remittance outflows. Another study (Alkhathlan 2013) empirically examines the relationship between economic growth and outflows of workers' remittances in Saudi Arabia from 1970 to 2010. The results show that there is a negative but statistically insignificant relationship between outflows of workers' remittances and economic growth in the long term and a negative and statistically significant relationship between workers' remittances and economic growth in the short term. Huang and Vargas-Silva (2005)

---

[1] We use the terms host country and source country with the same meaning as the country, from which the remittances are transferred, and as the country, from which the migrants make the money transfers.

examine whether the migrant host and/or home country macroeconomic conditions are the ones affecting remittances. They find that migrant host country economic conditions are most important factors driving remittances, and that the home country economic conditions have no significant effect on remittances. In a study of Egypt, El-Sakka and Mcnabb (1999) find that the black market premium and interest rate differentials are important variables explaining remittances.

Elbadawi and Rocha (1992) use fixed effects panel estimation techniques and came to the results that macroeconomic factors together with special incentive programmes determine official remittances. Also using fixed effect panel estimation techniques, Higgins et al. (2004) make a conclusion (not supported by other authors) that unemployment in the host country and the exchange rate are significant determinants of remittances. The authors use different quantitative approaches in assessing the macroeconomic determinants for the outflow of remittances. The techniques used include least squares, fixed effect panel estimation and seemingly unrelated regressions (SUR) models. Some authors use vector error correction models (VECM) to study the relationship between remittances and other macroeconomic variables. They find some advantages in using VECM models since they can solve the endogeneity problem between remittances and other macroeconomic variables. Other authors use variance decompositions, impulse response functions and Granger causality tests derived from VECM. Also, some authors apply autoregressive distributed lag (ARDL) and the error correction model (ECM) (Alkhathlan 2013).

Capitalising on the research conducted so far, we apply both qualitative and quantitative approach. We use balanced panel data model, which consists of the following variables: dependent ones (remittances[2]) and independent ones (real GDP growth, unemployment rate, inflation rate[3] and gross average wage[4]). We test the data for the period 1999-2016 in seven countries – France, Germany, Italy, Russian Federation, Spain, United Kingdom and United States. The selection of countries is based on the significance of remittance outflows in the world. They are among the top ten remittance source countries and constitute for about 25% of the entire world remittances outflows. They are also members of the OECD, except Russian Federation, which is also included as a country with a large outflow of remittances ranking tenth in the world.

In order to assess the dependence between variables under consideration, we use the pooled OLS model that specifies constant coefficients. It is a usual assumption for cross-sectional analysis, and the logarithmic analytical form is the following:

$$logR_{it}=\alpha+\beta_1 logGDP_{it}+\beta_2 logUnem_{it}+\beta_3 logInfl_{it}+\beta_4 logWage_{it}+u_{it}$$

---

[2] World Bank migration and remittances data, https://tinyurl.com/migration-remittances-data.
[3] Data for real GDP growth, unemployment rate and inflation rate are from IMF database, World economic outlook, https://tinyurl.com/world-economic-outlook-data.
[4] Gross Average Monthly Wages, UNECE, https://tinyurl.com/average-monthly-wages-data.

where:

R_{it} — dependent variable remittances with a cross-sectional dimension for each country i and a time dimension t;
GDP_{it} — dependent variable real GDP growth;
$Unem_{it}$ — unemployment rate;
$Infl_{it}$ — inflation rate;
$Wage_{it}$ — gross average wage in a country i and a period t.

Migration and remittances

It is logical to expect that the remittances depend mostly on the stock of migrant population. The recent crisis impacted both the flows and the stock of foreign population in the OECD countries including those under consideration here. The number of migrants decreases in all countries during 2009 and 2010 and then stagnates till 2013, when the refugee crisis in Europe forms a large immigration, while in the USA the economic recovery stimulates gradual increase of both seasonal and permanent migrants. The sharpest decline of immigration inflows occurs in Spain, which could be associated with the economic recession. Russian Federation immigration follows the general pattern, while the inflow in France is rather stable during the entire period. The inflow of foreign population in Germany has constantly increased in the last ten years, and most sharply after 2013, mainly due to the refugee crisis. The German economy performs well during the global economic downturn, which supports this trend.

The relation between immigration and remittances is determined by many factors, mainly by type of migration (seasonal or permanent), duration of migration, gender, age, skills, etc. Some groups of migrants remit more, some less. The economic crisis, though, has impacted all the groups and the data below confirm that scope of remittances.

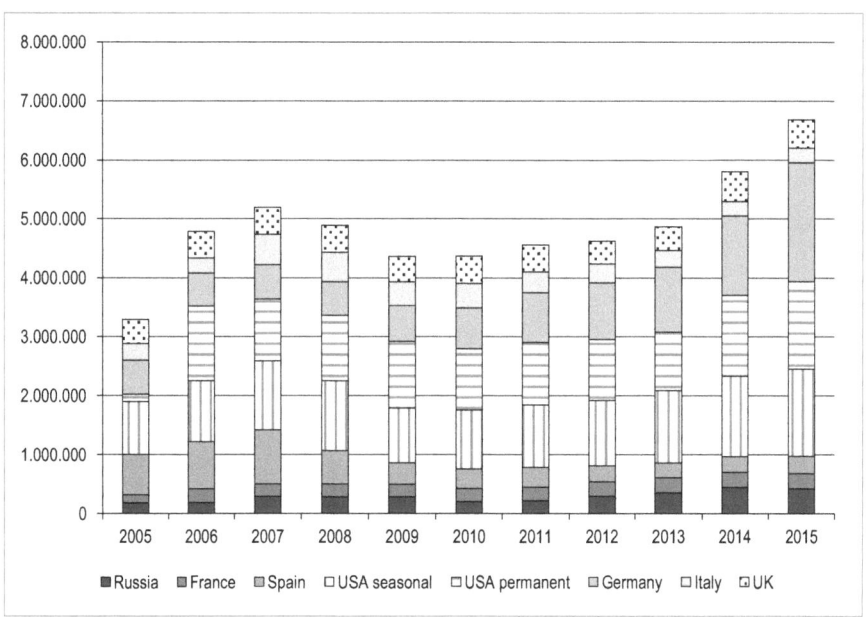

Figure 1 Inflows of foreign population

Source: OECD (2017) International Migration Outlook, p. 250.

Migrant remittances and the crisis

There are studies (Cooray & Mallick 2013) that empirically assess the impact of macroeconomic volatility of both migrant host and home country on the remittances. They conclude that remittance inflows decrease with economic uncertainty in home countries of migrants but increase with economic uncertainty in host countries for migrants, i.e. remittance inflows are pro-cyclical to migrants' home country volatility but counter-cyclical to the volatility in host countries for migrants. These results are hard to explain if data for the outflow of remittances is reviewed.

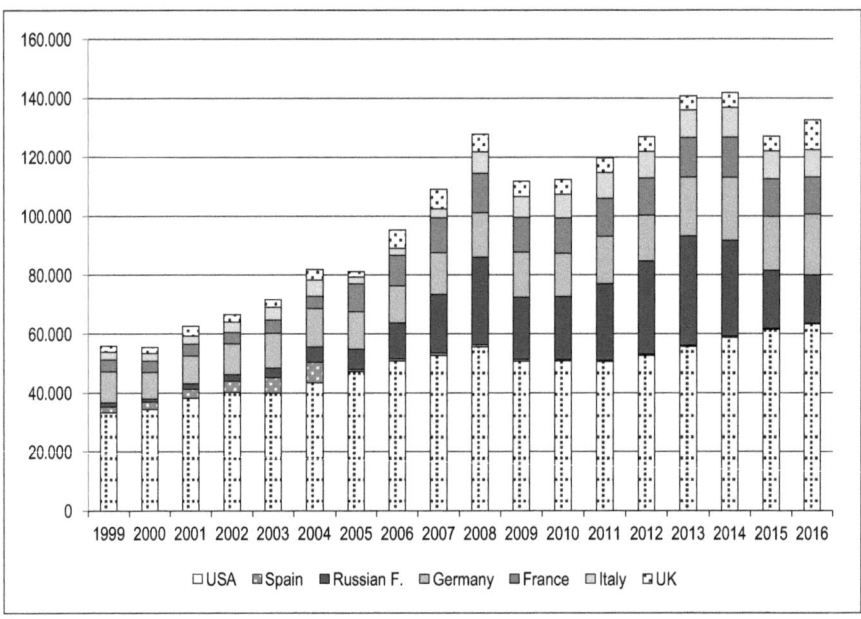

Figure 2 Migrant remittance outflows, 1999-2016 (USD million)

Source: Data from World Bank migration and remittances database.

Before the crisis, remittances experience smooth growth. The downturn in the developed economies during the recent crisis leads to a decline in the remittances and makes them very volatile. Remittances' sustainable growth is interrupted by the crisis, when they drop down for two consecutive years (2009 and 2010) and then start slowly to increase. Within this general dynamics, country specifics widen. The outflow of migrant remittances from the USA, which is the main source country, stagnates for three years and then starts to recover, but slower than in the pre-crisis period. The outflow from Germany and France seems more stable, while the one from Russian Federation is the most volatile.

Every country is both recipient and source of remittances. The inflow of remittances to the developed countries has not yet gained academic interest, since it has no significant role for their economies. The sustainable growth of inflow of remittances to these countries deserves some attention. Last ten years mark a slight change in the balance between the outflows and inflows of remittances. High income countries almost triple the inflow of remittances from USD 46.556 billion in 2005 to USD 140.545 billion in 2015. In the EU the outflows in personal remittances stagnate below EUR 40 billion between 2009 and 2013. The inflows though dramatically increased since 2007 with a growing importance of income flows, generated by EU citizens working abroad topping up from EUR 25 billion in 2007 to EUR 43.6 billion in 2015.[5] The remittances inflow to the OECD coun-

---

[5] Eurostat, Personal remittances statistics, https://tinyurl.com/remittances-data

tries also increases from USD 64.908 to 154.289 billion for the same period. As compared to the huge GDPs of high income countries, the inflow of remittances is marginal for those countries, but fast growing. Received remittances to GDP ratio for euro area increase from 0.41% in 2004 to 0.65% in 2015. The size of remittances to the low income countries is small, compared to the inflows received by high income and middle income countries. The factors that explain the inflows of remittances to the high income countries may be different from those to the developing countries and need further analysis, which is not subject of this study.

Assessing the macroeconomic factors for the outflow of remittances

Most of the theoretical work on remittances has been devoted to the answer of the question why migrants remit. Some remit simply from altruism (supporting families at home), some invest the saved money, or save for further security and risk diversification, or compensate family for past expenditure, etc. Remittance is a personal choice but it is made in a changing environment that strongly impacts both the ability and the decision to remit. Migrant remittance is about personal and family economics and finance that are driven by micro factors, but they are a reflection of the macro factors, and among those – of the economic ones. While the decision to remit is a combination of economic and non-economic factors, the one about how much to remit is motivated mainly by economic factors. What are the factors that impact the scope of the remitted amounts? We test the significance of four factors – GDP growth, unemployment, inflation, and wages. All estimations are made in the R Studio and results can be summarized as follows:

$$logR_{it} = \frac{-9.65854}{(0.033563)} - \frac{1.04401}{(0.103996)}logGDP_{it} - \frac{1.76455}{(0.024730)}logUnem_{it}$$
$$+ \frac{4.47715}{(0.009718)}logInfl_{it} + \frac{1.22139}{(0.010960)}logWage_{it} + u_{it}$$

R-squared=0.78117   p-value=0.037308
The econometric results are supported by the following tests:

We apply the Breusch-Pagan Lagrange multiplier (LM) test to decide between a random effects regression and a simple OLS regression. The null hypothesis in the LM test is that variances across countries are zero and there is no panel effect across countries.

Lagrange Multiplier Test – (Breusch-Pagan) for balanced panels
data: log(Y) ~ log(X)
chisq = 51.855, df = 1, p-value = 5.974e-13
alternative hypothesis: significant effects

The p-value less than 0.05 shows that we can accept the null hypothesis as a valid one, which means that the classical regression model is appropriate for these data.

We also use the Breusch-Pagan test for heteroscedasticity in a linear regression model. It tests whether the variance of the errors from a regression is dependent on the values of the independent variables. In that case, heteroscedasticity is present.

studentized Breusch-Pagan test
data: $\log(Y) \sim \log(X)$
$BP = 9.575$, $df = 4$, p-value $= 0.05823$
There is no presence of heteroskedasticity.

According to the estimations, the real GDP growth is statistically insignificant explanatory variable when econometrically testing the remittances drivers in host developed countries. Most of the studies examine the impact of remittances on the GDP growth mainly to the recipient countries. The assumption that the downturn will have a direct impact on the remittances has been not confirmed, although the studied economies follow similar economic growth pattern.

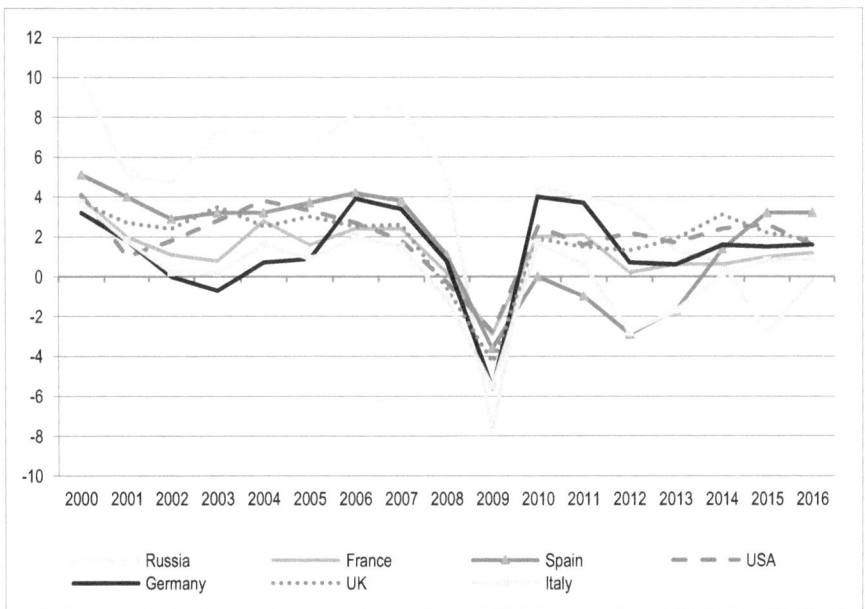

Figure 3 GDP growth (annual %)

Source: IMF (2017) World economic outlook.

Economic growth does not have direct visible impact on the abilities of migrants to remit, since this indicator forms the general framework. Remittances are much more dependent on unemployment, inflation and wages than on the overall macroeconomic performance, framed by the GDP growth.

The model results show that the remittances from the seven developed countries are strongly dependent on the inflation in those countries. An inflation increase of 1% leads to 4.5% increase in remittances. The inflation is also related to the purchasing power of the source country currency. The purchasing power of currency, in which the income is received, plays an important role for migrant's abilities to remit. If the currency in the host country of migrants devaluates against the currency in the home country, the incentive to emigrate and remit diminishes. In such situation, in order to transfer home the amount that would have the same purchasing power, the migrant needs to remit more. The exchange rates' dynamics of four currencies (EUR, USD, GBP and RUB) follow very different patterns. Although during the crisis they slightly devaluate shortly against some currencies of home countries of migrants, in a long run they appreciate. Substantial part of remittances, particularly in the EU, is between the countries that use EUR or fixed to EUR and its impact is neutral. That is why this indicator is not included in the model.

The results indicate a negative relationship between remittances and unemployment in the migrant host country. If unemployment rate goes up with 1%, remittances will fall down by 1.8%. The employment plays an important role, since most of migrants' incomes are from employment. The economic crisis strongly impacts employment and unemployment of migrants. Migrants in the OECD countries, included in the sample, have experienced immediate impact of the downturn of employment with more intensity than the native population.[6] So, we could assume even stronger impact of this indicator on the outflow of remittances, if the unemployment of migrants is used in the model. Unfortunately, such comparable data for the 17-year period are not available.

The overall unemployment in all the remittance source countries has increased during crisis. The highest increase of unemployment occurs during the crisis in Spain, accompanied also with a sharp shrinking of remittance outflow. This is also the case of Italy. The USA unemployment rates drop down shortly after the crisis, while unemployment in Germany has been rather low and stable in the entire period.

---

[6] OECD (2017) International Migration Outlook. p. 64-68.

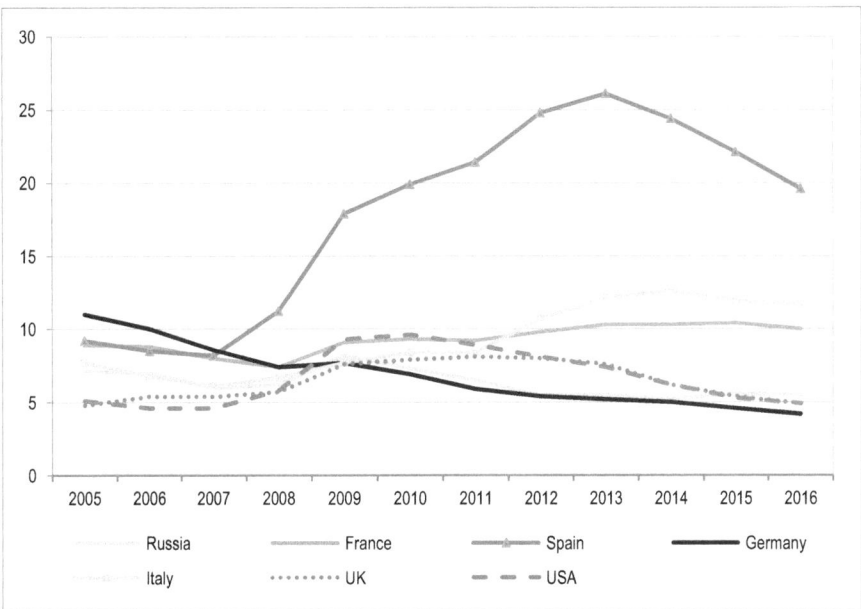

Figure 4 Unemployment rate (%)

Source: IMF (2017) World economic outlook.

It is well proved (Straubhaar 1986) in plenty of studies that an important factor for migrant remittances is the income level of migrant host country. In the model we test the significance of Gross Average Monthly Wages on the dynamics of remittance outflow. In all studied countries the economic crisis has induced decrease or/and stagnation of wages. The negative impact is more pronounced in Spain and Italy, while the USA wages are not affected by the crisis and keep increasing.

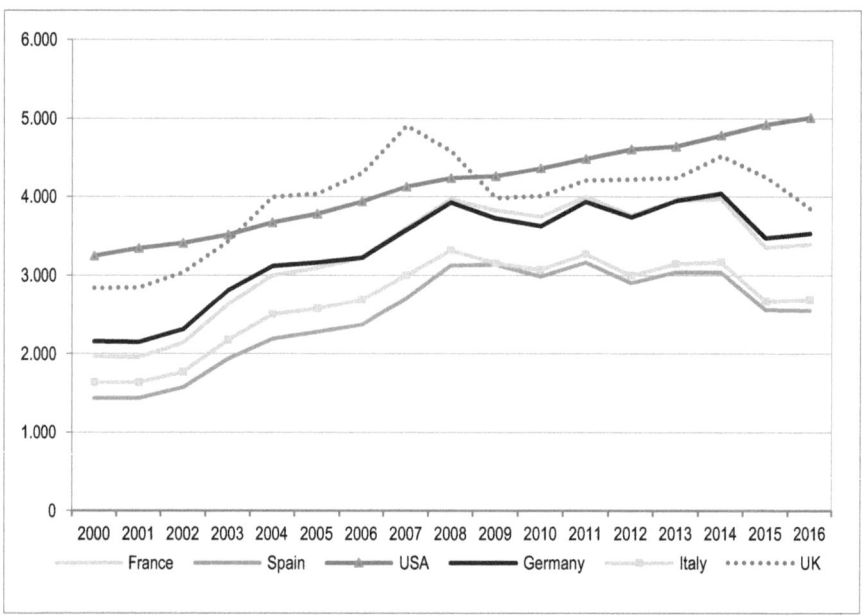

Figure 5 Gross average monthly wage (USD)

Source: UNECE, https://tinyurl.com/average-monthly-wages-data

The model results show that 1% increase in the gross average monthly wages leads to 1.22% increase of remittances outflow. Having in mind that the income levels of migrants in general are lower than the average ones in the host country of migrants, the impact of host country wages on remittances may be even stronger.

Conclusions

The recent crisis has challenged the academic research, which ignores the role of the host country of migrants and focuses only on the home country factors that determine the remittances. The remittances' sustainable growth is interrupted by the crisis, since the economies of the main source countries have been hit hard. The overall tendency is that outflow drops down for two consecutive years (2009 and 2010) and then starts caching up again, but slower than in the pre-crisis period. Although these tendencies are common within the group of studied countries, the outflow of remittances contracts more sharply in the countries hit harder by the crisis. Another interesting tendency is that high income countries start receiving much more remittances, and this tendency is hard to explain with the conventional development theory. The flows of remittances between the high income countries also accelerate significantly.

The remittances outflow does not immediately respond to the worsening economic situation in the host country for migrants. This confirms the theory that suggests that this flow is most stable, compared to the other financial flows.

Testing the four main macroeconomic factors that the literature suggests of having an impact on remittances, we find a significant impact of three of them. Inflation, unemployment and incomes in the source countries impact the outflow of remittances. We could imagine, though, a much stronger impact of unemployment and wages in the source countries, if in the model we would include the unemployment and wages of migrants instead the overall macro data.

References

Alkhathlan, K. (2013) The nexus between remittance outflows and growth: A study of Saudi Arabia. *Economic Modelling*, 2013, vol. 33, issue C, pages 695-700

Bimal, G. (2006) Migrants' Remittances and Development: Myths, Rhetoric and Realities. International Organization for Migration.

Cooray, A. V. / Mallick, D. (2013) International business cycles and remittance flows. The BE Journal of Macroeconomics, 13 (1), p. 515-547.

El Mouhoub, M. / Oudinet, J. / Unan, E. (2008) Macroeconomic Determinants of Migrants' Remittances in the Southern and Eastern Mediterranean Countries. CEPN Working paper, February 2008.

Elbadawi, I. / de Rezende Rocha, R. (1992). Determinants of expatriate workers' remittances in North Africa and Europe. Policy Research working papers, N WPS 1038. Transition and macro – adjustment. Washington, DC: World Bank. http://documents.worldbank.org/curated/en/623711468741892408/Determinants-of-expatriate-workers-remittances-in-North-Africa-and-Europe.

Huang, P. / Vargas-Silva, C. (2005) Macroeconomic Determinants of Workers' Remittances: Host vs. Home Country's Economic Conditions. EconPapers: International Finance, 2005 – econwpa.wustl.edu.

Khalid, A. A. (2013) The nexus between remittance outflows and growth: A study of Saudi Arabia. *Economic Modelling*, Vol. 33, July 2013, p. 695-700.

Naufal, G. (2017) Impact of Remittance Outflows on Sending Economies: The Case of the Russian Federation. United Nations Economic and Social Commission for Asia and the Pacific 2017 Moscow, Russia.

Straubhaar, T. (1986) The Determinants of Workers' Remittances: The Case of Turkey. Weltwirtschaftliches Archiv, 122, pp. 728-740.

World Bank Group. (2016). Migration and Remittances Factbook 2016. Third Edition. Washington, DC: World Bank. https://openknowledge.worldbank.org/handle/10986/23743

Inter-Cultural and other Forces in the Transfer of Human Resource Management and Industrial Relations Practices under Globalization

Joe Isaac[1]

Abstract

The paper highlights major forces promoting the transfer and convergence of management philosophy and techniques in a globalising world, namely increased international competition, technological innovations and the transfer of HRM principles by Multinational Enterprises to their subsidiaries. The paper also identifies factors which are responsible for resistance against convergence, which are largely cultural in nature. The diverging forces lead to structural and technological convergence of organisations internationally and culturally-bound national work related practices and worker preferences. Special attention is given to one major source of inter-cultural difference between countries, in particular between the USA and the EU, i.e., collective bargaining and unionism. Further, the paper focusses on cultural differences between EU-Member States, spanning from tax laws over social welfare philosophy and practices, to priorities of protection against risks and sources of funding. The paper suggests that the forces of globalisation, in the EU epitomized by the pressure of the monetary and fiscal discipline of a common currency, may tilt the balance of European social market economies away from the social towards the market with trade and migration paving the way. The paper is largely based on a review of pertinent literature.

Introduction

Globalisation is a new word for an old phenomenon. At the end of the 19th Century, goods and services, money in the form of silver and gold, ideas, practices and people moved across state boundaries freely throughout most of the world. In recent years we have come something close to that world, except that the move-

---

[1] Because of my advanced age and physical disabilities, I have not been in a position to write a new paper for inclusion in this Festschrift. However, I am pleased to have been allowed to include in this volume an abridged version of a Working Paper published by the Austrian Institute of Economic Research (Isaac 2003) as an expression of my great admiration for Gudrun's academic standing and my long association with her. I am indebted to Gudrun Biffl, Bill Harley, Anne-Wil Harzing, Willem Noe and Graham Sewell for helpful advice on this paper.

ment of people is now restricted, and that technology, especially in the speed of travel and communications, has created a completely new dimension to the economic, social and cultural integration of the modern world we now term 'globalisation'. On a regional basis, the EU is perhaps the closest replica of the circumstances prevailing at the close of the 19th Century, like an extended version of the Habsburg Empire but with greater complications, especially with EU enlargement.[2]

Many aspects of globalisation have attracted the attention of scholars apart from economic issues such as trade, labour practices, the emergent dominance of the service sector, migration, and the reduction of state authority in economic and social policy. Barriers have been lowered and blinds have been raised on fashions in art, music, films, clothing, cuisine, which have spread globally at an astonishing speed on the wings of media advertising, multinational enterprises and mass marketing techniques induced by the economies of scale. In this process, considerable convergence and even homogenisation of these various elements have taken place. Driving these developments is the greatly increased pressure of competition, forcing efficiency on organisations. And it is in this context that management plays a critical role.

The management of people is one of the most complex and, at the same time, the most important task of any organization. Complex, because managing people is to manage a factor of production with embedded attitudes and values – a culture – which may or may not respond to particular managerial practices; important, because the growth or survival of an organization depends on effective management. This is not a new problem. It goes back to the industrial revolution; but the philosophical, ideological and economic underpinnings of management principles have evolved over time under the pressure of competition in a changing environment of products, materials and technology.

My task is to review recent ideas on management philosophy and techniques in the context of globalisation, and to consider the forces leading to the transfer and convergence of these ideas and practices globally, as well as to the persistence of differences through cultural and other forces. Although the paper will focus on the EU as at present constituted, it will also try to consider the implications of EU enlargement on the convergence issue.

In recent years, the efficiency of Taylorism[3] with its emphasis on de-skilled operations and narrow job classifications, a management concept in vogue for most of the 20th Century to deal with mass production, has been questioned in the face of two reinforcing pressures – on the one hand, the emergent post-industrial information and knowledge-based society, affected by fundamental changes in technology brought about particularly by the electronic revolution; and, on the other

---

[2] Visions of a united Europe go back to Roman times with the crowning of Charlemagne as Emperor of the Holy Roman Empire in 800. For a brief historical background, see Noe, 2002.

[3] Named after the American Frederick Taylor whose writings on management issues were very influential in the first half of the 20th Century.

hand, increased international competition arising from greater global economic integration involving the dismantling of trade protection and liberalisation of capital movements. In this competitive environment, productivity growth and other elements of economic efficiency such as reliability of quality and delivery, are critical factors in the survival of enterprises and the prosperity of countries. To meet this challenge, attention has been focused on a more effective use of labour, and it is in this context that the human resource management (HRM) concept has been widely promoted as a basis for more efficient management.

Meaning and significance of HRM and IR

First, a brief explanation of the meaning and significance of HRM and industrial relations (IR). Perhaps it is easier to start with the older concept, IR.

Broadly, IR refers to the relationship between employers and workers, the issues that arise in the employment relationship – pay, working conditions and other terms of employment – and the processes for resolving these issues. The determination of these issues may take place on an individual worker basis, as they were in the early days of industrialization, or, more commonly these days, on a collective basis with workers being represented by unions – a process providing a better balance of power between employer and employee. The right to collective bargaining and its associated right to strike, are social rights enshrined in two of the ILO's Labour Standards under Conventions 87 and 98[4], and many countries have enacted laws to give effect to these Conventions. Resort to collective bargaining obviously encroaches on the employer's right to manage; and the extent of encroachment depends on the interests of the parties and the price they are prepared to pay as to where the line is drawn

HRM is a comparative newcomer in the lexicon of management, sometimes referred to as a 'new way of managing employees' (Storey, 2001: 4), developed in the US in the 1960s and 1970s. Obviously, any organisation where people are employed, involves the management of 'human resources', a somewhat pretentious term for 'labour'. But there are explicit and implicit overtones to the meaning and practice attached to HRM on which there is still a lively debate (Storey, 2001). Its immediate antecedent is personnel management (PM), also a US inspired development, which, it is said, lacks the analytical sophistication and strategic approach of HRM and is largely prescriptive. Others have argued that the downgrading of PM, largely by business consultants and academics, is unjustified and that the essential elements of HRM are inherent in a proper application of PM and that coherence with the overall strategy of the organization is not necessarily excluded in such application. *'HRM is not a magic recipe making everything that preceded*

---

[4] Forming part of the 1998 ILO Declaration on Fundamental Rights which are also set out in United Nations International Bill on Human Rights.

its announcement redundant' (Torrington, 1998: 36; Grant, and Oswick, 1998; see also Sisson, 2001).

It is not fruitful for our purposes to engage in a 'largely abstract debate on definition' *(Torrington,* 1998: 27). HRM is the new name of the game. Storey's (p. 6) broad definition is useful.

> *"Human resource management is a distinctive approach to employment management which seeks to achieve competitive advantage through strategic deployment of a highly committed and capable workforce using an array of cultural, structural and personnel techniques."*

Elaborating on this definition and drawing out certain generic principles from it, the widely accepted view of HRM is that it places primary emphasis on human resources as the most important factor in efficient enterprise performance. This emphasis must be seen in the context of technological developments which have displaced the de-skilled processes assumed by Taylorism and call for the application of the scarcer higher skills. Importantly, HRM seeks to develop a culture of 'high commitment' to the organization from employees. It applies a strategic, proactive and integrated approach consistent with the strategy of the organization in its various sectional functions – finance, investment, production, marketing etc[5]. Further, it puts responsibility for the formulation and evaluation of the HRM policy on line management and not, as in PM, on the personnel department.

Drawing on the teachings of organizational behaviour and psychology, the processes associated with such policy are in the method of selection, training, career development, communication, performance appraisal, and reward systems. To give workers a sense of participation and empowerment, responsibility is devolved lower down the line. The management structure is less hierarchical, jobs are designed and workers are trained to facilitate semi-autonomous work groups, multi-skilling and flexibility in the use of labour[6]. This is of course an idealized academic constructed picture of HRM, based on the beliefs and assumptions of 'leading edge' practitioners, which has been presented by John Storey (2001: 7) in a classified form.

Studies of applied HRM (or something substantially like it) in the US and UK appear to indicate that they have generally produced positive profit and productivity outcomes not only short term but also long term (Huselid, et al., 1997; Guest, 1997: 263; Collins, and Porras, 1998) although the reliability of such conclusions are not without doubters (Storey, 2001: 14). Moreover, the effect on the well-being of employees may be negative. There is evidence of increased stress

---

[5] 'Strategy' more simply means the plan by which certain integrated objectives of the organisation are to be achieved. For a fuller treatment of the meaning of 'strategy', see Purcell, (2001: 65-66).

[6] A convenient classification of the main elements of HRM is provided by Story (2001: 7, Figure 1.1) Another classification – commitment, flexibility, quality and strategic integration – is suggested by Guest (1991).

among workers (Woodall and Winstanley, 2001: 39) but it is not clear that this is necessarily due to the application of HRM techniques as such.

Transfers and the forces of convergence

The acceptance internationally of the main HRM practices, if not its philosophy, as a tool of efficient use of labour, is reflected in their promotion and application world-wide, but with significant variations. The transfer from the US of the concept and their application in part or in whole, was propelled by a number of interlinked forces.

First, increased international competition unleashed by globalisation in the last two decades, made improved organisational efficiency a condition for the survival of business enterprises, the economic growth of countries and rising living standards. In these circumstances, not surprisingly, managerial efficiency became a prime target for review, and HRM became the focus of special interest. It is to be expected also that international mobility of capital may provide pressure on workers and unions, threatened with closure or shrinkage of employment opportunities, to accede to HRM practices seen by their employers as providing them with a competitive edge.

Second, the application of technological innovations is an essential means of securing competitive advantage. In recent years, the innovations which have spread internationally in manufacturing and service industries, have generated new products and new forms of work and work patterns, heralding a *'new industrial revolution ... and the fragmentation of mass markets'* (Piore and Sabel, 1984). This called for new approaches to management and industrial relations (Morley et al, 2000: 202), providing the impetus for the application of HRM principles.

Third and perhaps the most explicit manifestation of HRM transfer mechanism, has come from MNEs (Multi-National Enterprises) which, partly because of their size and managerial resources, have the incentive to carry their HRM principles and their senior personnel to their subsidiaries in other countries, subject, of course, to any legal requirements in the host country. Some of these practices of the MNEs could be expected to spread to local organisations in the host country.

Finally, a veritable explosion of academic and professional publications, HRM courses in business schools, international conferences, management consultants, improved communications and publicity mechanisms generally – all of these, bearing the message of increased efficiency, have assisted the spread of HRM processes. The EC (European Commission 2001) and OECD (1998) have added to the flow of advice on efficient management of labour practices.

Persistence of differences

However, the persistent differences and resistance, at least in part, to the forces of convergence, come from several sources.

First, it should not be assumed that, even in the US where the concept was developed, the HRM principles are widely adopted – *'where rhetoric has so far outstrip[ped] reality'* (Kochan and Dyer, 2001: 273). Writing of the UK, Guest (2001) contends that perhaps in the majority of organizations in the private sector, there is a low level of HRM and no union presence, where managers 'may behave as tyrants or may display benevolent paternalism' (p. 111).

Second, because American literature dominates the subject and many of the early applications of HRM were in non-union firms, it should not be assumed that there is a 'universal' or 'best practice' HRM model, often assumed to be the US model, which can be applied everywhere. While general or generic principles may be drawn from the text book exposition of HRM for application in an organization, they should obviously be tailored to the features and requirements of the particular workplace or industry under consideration, as well as to the level of economic development in the country concerned, to the availability of managerial capacity, the type of ownership, the resources of the organization, and to the supply of appropriate skills[7]. Recent UK surveys show a low but increasing level of application of HRM practices (Guest, 2001: 110).

Moreover, the relevance of many of the practices prescribed by HRM principles may be questioned for SMEs, which form the substantial majority of enterprises. A distinction needs to be made between policy and practice, rhetoric and reality (Legge, 1995). Not every element of HRM policy is capable of application even if so desired by management. Nor does it follow that wherever HRM policy is in place, workers do become fully committed to the organization (Storey, 2001: 6). Thus, more commonly, the application of a number of parts of the total range of HRM practices, with modifications whenever necessary or expedient, may be a more common feature of its manifestation (Sisson, 2001: 86). Or, as it has been put in other words (Adler et al, 1986), organisations are becoming more similar internationally in terms of their structure and technology while existing work related practices and worker preferences continue to be culturally-bound nationally[8].

Third, cultural differences provide the most important source of resistance to HRM models drawn from other countries[9]. Thus one authority (Communal and Brewster, 2003: 5) has said:

---

[7] For a fuller list, see Salamon (1997).

[8] This view has been criticised by McGaughey and De Cieri (1999) on the (theoretical) grounds that it unduly simplifies the complex dynamics of the convergence process.

[9] While we are concerned in this paper largely with transference matters in US and Europe, it is interesting to note that traditional culture in shaping HRM practices is particularly important in developing countries. Jackson, (2003). Zhu and Warner (2003), point out that despite the pressure for greater managerial flexibility following the Asian financial crisis, tradi-

"People cannot be managed in a vacuum; they are managed within a context (e.g., cultural, social, educational, religious, geographical, legal, historical) The process of HRM is therefore not neutral; it is surrounded by cultural, social and other norms characteristic of human behaviour."

Culture is of course an imprecise term embodying a number of elements reflecting the attitude and values of people on particular issues. One suggested broad definition (Tylor, 1913, quoted in Petit, et al, 1994: 169) is in the following terms:

"Culture is a complex ensemble which includes the knowledge, beliefs, art, morals, laws, customs, and all of the other capacities and habits acquired by man as a member of society."

Others may prefer to specify some of the elements separately, for example, legal requirements, for particular emphasis.

Industrial Relations

In the area of management, the role of industrial relations and in particular, of collective bargaining and unionism is perhaps the most important source of intercultural difference especially between the US and EU countries. US management generally has had a longstanding philosophical objection to unionism and collective bargaining as an unwarranted encroachment on its 'right to manage'[10]; and in the years after the 1970s, it reverted to the pre-1930s anti-union stance (Barbash, 1985; Phelps Brown, 1983). Despite the 'New Deal' inspired legislation providing for collective bargaining and the right to strike, procedural tactics possible under the legislation, have tended to marginalize union power.

HRM developed in the US, and it came from personnel managers and consultants who were anti-union or ignored the relevance of unions in the design of HRM (Beaumont, 1991: 300; Kochan et al, 1986: 62). The early studies of HRM were generally conducted in non-union workplaces, for example, Hewlett Packard and IBM. The US Department of Labor (1993) lists HRM characteristics suggestive of a kind of 'best practice' statement, which does not include unions in the various management processes (Brewster, 2002: 257).

The 'high commitment' concept which is at the heart of US HRM doctrine, assumes that the inherent interests of the worker and the employer are in complete harmony or can be made to be so – the 'unitarist' view (Storey, 2001: 12); whereas IR assumes that, despite a wide degree of common interest and cooperation between them, there is a residual conflict on pay and conditions to be resolved from

---

tional cultural characteristics (such as collectivism, harmony, loyalty, hierarchy, paternalism) are still a strong force in HRM in Japan and Taiwan.

[10] The advice of the international firm of management consultants, Arthur Anderson included: *'Managers must be free to manage'* (Brewster, 2002).

time to time as a natural rather than a pathological feature of employment relations – the 'pluralist' view.

Consistent with the unitarist assumption, HRM work practices are designed to strengthen the identification of the worker with the organisation and improve their performance in the interest of both sides[11]. Cases can be quoted of the success of such an approach[12]. On the other hand, there are US cases which show that workers and unions can be involved in strategic decision making, thereby increasing mutual trust with benefit to economic performance (Kochan et al, 1986: 145). Thus, in such matters of training, performance evaluation, and reward systems, it is arguable that the participation of union officials may be an effective way of ensuring trust in these practices. There is also evidence that increased commitment to the organisation need not necessarily mean reduced commitment to the union and to collective bargaining (Deery et al., 1994). Nor does it follow that union participation is inconsistent with higher productivity performance, (Alterburg et al., 1998; Katz, 1986; Krueger, and Summers, 1988). A plea for bringing unions and public policy makers in the US into HRM processes as a means of raising productivity growth has been made by American academic writers (Kochan and Dyer, 2001: 273).

Thus, it is arguable that conceptually and on practical efficiency grounds, there is no reason to suppose that HRM is incompatible with collective bargaining. It could even be said that HRM and IR may be *'different perspectives on the same process'* (Morley et al, 2000: 207). Moreover, even the Harvard HRM model (Beer et al., 1984) includes unions among the stakeholders in the production process[13].

All this may sound strange to EU ears, for whom it will be evident that the task of management goes beyond finding efficient methods of production. The stakeholders[14] in business activity are not only the owners of capital – the shareholders – but also those who supply labour services to the enterprise – the employees – as well as those who buy the products, and, where health, safety, welfare and environmental concerns are involved, the community at large. On this view, the task of management is to strive for a balance between economic efficiency, equity

---

[11] Guest (1990) goes as far as to say that the philosophy of HRM is either to deny the existence of separate worker interests, or to subordinate them to the employer's interest.

[12] In Australia, a large mining firm with a long tradition of collective bargaining, recently decided to embrace HRM philosophy by persuading most of its workers, under the inducement of better pay, to accept individual contracts, a form encouraged by a change in Australian labour law. The company was subsequently able to rationalise its workforce by downsizing and so increase productivity (Mackinnon Hearn, 2003).

[13] A useful reconciliation of HRM and IR is suggested by Gospel, (1992) by incorporating effectively within HRM, three elements - work relations, employment relations and industrial relations. Such an approach is also reflected in the European Commission's approach (European Commission, Final Report, 2002).

[14] The stakeholder approach was first advanced by Freeman (1984). It is essentially a normative concept connected to the 'property rights' of labour. It may also be considered to have an instrumental element for greater efficiency (Donaldson and Preston, 1995).

and the public interest. It follows that all three – HRM, IR and legislation – are relevant considerations (see Kochan and Dyer, 2001: 274). This stakeholder approach is still well embedded in the EU social culture and provides a sharp contrast to that of the US. And it is increasingly argued that *'long term, sustained, competitive advantage is only feasible'* (Storey, 2001: 12) when the needs of the various stakeholders are taken into account.

The contrast between US attitude to unions and that of the EU countries (excluding the UK) has an important bearing on how HRM processes may be expected to work in the EU countries. This can best be appreciated against the backdrop of the effects of globalisation on the EU states. Global competition has affected member states differently. The EU itself is a more complete form of economic integration on a regional basis than it is with the rest of the world, inter-member trade making up close to 90% of its GDP. In the circumstances, there is strong incentive, through pressure for harmonising economic and social policies as far as possible, to ensure that the openness of trade and labour mobility does not result in social dumping. To give effect to such a policy and to avoid undesirable social outcomes, corporatist and neo-corporatist processes, calling for dialogue and collaboration between governments, employers and unions, has been necessary; something far from any contemplation in the US.

Thus, subject to the adjustment problems which may emerge from EU Enlargement, it is reasonable to suppose that in the foreseeable future, industrial relations in the EU countries will continue to embody the concept of 'social partnership' involving social dialogue on economic and social issues and 'collective rights'[15]. In this process, national trade union bodies have remained powerful institutions and have maintained their authority to speak for workers and to be listened to by the employers and governments. Further, there is no challenge to the right of collective bargaining and its associated right to strike.

Moreover, it is important to note that the standing of unions and the commitment to social partnership at the national level, is reinforced at the EU level. The EU Charter on Fundamental Rights issued following the Nice Summit of December 2000 (European Union, 2001) committed member states to observe a whole range of rights – civil, social, political and economic. A number of social rights, including equal opportunity, have been incorporated into the laws of the member states and are enforceable in the European Court of Justice and the Court of Human Rights. Although the right of collective bargaining and to strike have so far not been incorporated and are subject solely to the rights of the states under the principle of subsidiarity, there is reason to believe that breach of such rights by a member state could invite a legal threat to its membership of the EU (Biffl and Isaac, 2002). Thus the ethos of the EU, backed by the law, imposes obligations on member states to ensure that union bargaining rights are respected.

---

[15] The European Union (2001), while advocating the HRM approach to work practices, goes out of its way to emphasise the importance of maintaining the role of unions and social partnership.

But more than this. The institutional framework at the European level has been greatly strengthened by the 1997 Amsterdam Treaty (Sisson, 2003: fig. 1) which requires, *inter alia*, for the Commission to consult the social partners on socio-economic policy matters before bringing down legislation. Further, this point is reinforced by the EC social model (Szyszczak, 2000: 164), based on a set of social values – including individual rights, democracy, free collective bargaining, social welfare, social solidarity and market economies – as stated in the White Paper on Social Policy (European Union, 1994). In addition, the mechanism for ensuring dialogue between the social partners on this issue is sustained by the requirement under the EC Treaty (Art. 138(1)) that the Commission *'shall take any relevant measure'* to facilitate social dialogue between the partners *'by ensuring balanced support for the parties'*. The importance of such dialogue should not be underestimated as a device to bring recalcitrant States into line (Mosely, Keller & Speckesser, 1998). Furthermore, by an EU directive, successively smaller organisations are required to establish works councils across Europe (Communal and Brewster, 2003: 8).

A further important development has been the establishment of European Works Councils covering some 650 MNCs (Multi-National Corporations) agreeing to establish a transnational machinery for information and consultation (Sisson, 2003: 6). While this does not mean that the concept of a 'European industrial relations system' is a likely prospect in the foreseeable future, a platform exists at the European level for the European Trade Union Confederation to engage in dialogue with employers on industrial relations issues, providing the opportunity of at least resisting any dilution of the existing social rights principles[16]. But there are sceptics who regard the social dialogue at this level as a time-wasting, ritualistic process, a *'matter of form rather than substance'* (Hyman, 2001: 290). Differences in industrial relations practices between EU states may be expected to persist, but the commitment to union collective bargaining and associated rights, sharply distinguishes the operation of HRM in EU states, from that in the US and a number of Anglo-Saxon countries (Biffl and Isaac, 2002) where the social partnership ethos is lacking[17]. Moreover, the States coming in under the European enlargement process will be expected to abide by the Copenhagen conditions which require the newly admitted States to adopt *inter alia* 'the common rules, standards and policies that make up the body of EU law'.

---

[16] The European Commission (2002b: 32) has argued that, to cope with a more competitive knowledge economy, the role of industrial relations at local, regional or national level can be enhanced by developments at the European level particularly on those issues with a European dimension. The Report envisages substantial changes in work practices but insists that such changes should be brought about with the *'strong involvement of the social partners at all levels'*.

[17] The dependence of Ireland on US private direct investment in developing the electronic industry, has led the Government to allow these companies to be absolved from honouring the social partnership concept, thus excluding the unions from their HRM policies (Green, 2003).

Summing up the main differences between US and EU

Significant differences between US and EU HRM concepts have been highlighted in which cultural differences, reflected especially in the legal framework, both national and supra-national, the role of trade unions and social partnership concept provide the distinguishing features between them. It has also been suggested that the *'common philosophies, structures and practices'* in Europe, establish certain identifiable traits of management: EU is focussed on people, whereas in the US people are considered a *'resource'* (Calori et al., 1994: 32); EU takes a stakeholder rather than a shareholder approach (p. 35) and a willingness to negotiate with its internal management at different levels and employees, as well as external stakeholders (p. 36); EU appears to be more capable of managing international diversity because of greater familiarity and respect for cultural diversity (p. 38), and is less *'imperialistic'* in the export of their management models (p. 39). This is not to say that European enterprises ignore profitability, rather they believe that *'you cannot have profit without fulfilling social responsibility'* (p. 84).

Convergence within EU?

The question now arises whether the forces of economic integration and competition within the EU and the Charter on Fundamental Social Rights and various harmonising provisions of the EU, provide grounds for expecting convergence of HRM/IR practices within the EU; or whether here, as in relation to the US, cultural forces offer resistance to convergence. The answer appears to be that there is considerable diversity within the substantially common character of EU HRM, even before EU enlargement (Communal and Brewster, 2003: 4). This is despite the fact that MNEs operate with fewer restrictions within the EU and can bring about greater convergence of HRM and IR practices. Thus, some MNEs take a highly decentralised approach allowing subsidiaries to apply practices believed to be more compatible with national context for example, retail banking and electricity (Edwards, T. 2003). Even in the automotive industry, there is a significant degree of diversity in processes for determining changes in work practices within Europe[18] (Baldry, 1994). It should be noted that the OECD, ILO and the United Nations have issued guidelines for application by MNEs on labour, human rights

---

[18] In Germany and Austria, the process is separated from wage bargaining, and entirely by national negotiation, while workers are consulted continuously on design and implementation via the works council. In the UK, the process is part of wage bargaining on a quid-pro-quo basis. In Spain, the changes are treated as a matter of management prerogative in which unions have no input at all.

and environmental standards (Murray, 2001) which are substantially consistent with related elements of the EU Charter[19].

In this connection it is worth considering inter-cultural differences. The famous 1980 study by Hofstede (1980) provides an illustration. The work has been criticised as being rather broad-brush but it is nonetheless of interest in reviewing management issues – what the objectives of an organization should be, what motivates people, how they should relate to their colleagues and supervisors, and how people should be trained. Another attempt at identifying national differences in culture and institutions, affecting the philosophy and style of management in different EU countries may be cited. (Calori *et al.*, 1994) The difference between the UK and Continental EU countries, especially on the place of unions, was mentioned earlier. It is submitted that, in broad terms, in Southern Europe (covering the Latin countries), compared to Northern Europe (which includes the Nordic and Germanic countries), management is more hierarchical and less formalized, there is more state intervention, and there are more family businesses, especially in Italy. Sub-dividing the broad Northern grouping, in Germany, business has strong links with banks and a system of co-determination with workers' representation on Boards. The Nordic countries differ from the Germanic countries and Benelux in having a larger public sector. Nordic management is said to be more concerned with the quality of working life while Germanic management is more concerned with performance and status. Benelux and Switzerland have developed a blend of European and Anglo-Saxon models. And so it goes on.

Another differentiating factor: the education and training systems of managers may have a bearing on differences in management practices. (Tyson, and Wikander, 1994) It appears from a survey that 24% of German managers had a worker employment background, compared to 1% of their French counterparts. While 50% of French senior managers came from the middle and upper class, 33% did so in Germany; while 46% of French managers graduated from the prestigious 'Grandes Ecole', only 16% of German managers graduated from the equivalent schools (Calori and Seidel, 1994: 64).

The influence of HRM managers at Board of Directors level varies between EU countries, reflecting the importance placed by the Board on the HRM function. It is more prevalent in France (88%), Sweden (79%) and Spain (77%) than in the UK (49%) and Germany (46%); although in Germany, the presence of an employee director (by law) makes up to some extent for the difference. In Sweden and the Netherlands, worker representation on Boards also occurs.

There are differences in Member State labour laws[20], in the forms, structure, power and density of unions, in union ideologies and links with political parties,

---

[19] I have found no record on how closely the specified standards have been observed. For a detailed study of control mechanisms of MNEs towards their subsidiaries in other countries and the processes involved, see Harzing, A.-W. K, 1999.

[20] For example, contrary to most other EU countries, under Austrian, Belgium and UK laws, the right to strike is not explicitly allowed or restricted. Whereas in France, Italy, Spain and Portugal, the right to strike is written into the constitution. Most Member States, except

religious bodies, and collective bargaining coverage[21]. In addition important differences in tax laws, in social welfare philosophy and practices have persisted, varying in their priorities of protection against risks, composition of social expenditure, sources of funding, and the administration of welfare services. Four models have been distinguished: Anglo-Saxon (Ireland, UK), Continental European (Austria, Belgium, Germany, France, Luxembourg, Netherlands), Scandinavian (Denmark, Finland, Sweden), and Southern European (Spain, Greece, Italy, Portugal; Biffl, 2003b).

The considerable diversity in the level of training of the workforce has been analysed by the OECD (1999). Formal and continuing training is relatively low in Southern European countries (Greece, Italy, Portugal and Spain), while it is relatively high in the UK, France and most of the Nordic countries. There is also considerable variation between EU countries in the age of the trainees. In the Nordic countries (except Finland), older workers receive as much training as younger ones, while they receive less training in France, Greece, Portugal and Spain. A strong link has also been found between national levels of educational attainment and achievement on the one hand, and workforce training on the other, underlining the importance of schooling in later training.

Finally, evidence of diversity is shown in an extensive survey covering over 800 organisations, both private and public, employing more than 50 persons in 10 EU countries and 50 case studies[22]. The purpose of the study was to discover the extent to which, what it calls, *'new forms of work organisation'* are being applied and what the obstacles and its underlying causes to this form of organisation are. In substance, the study defines *'new forms of organisation'* with a strategic approach in which the various sections of an organisation are integrated and operate consistently to meet the objectives of the organisation[23]. This is referred to as the *'system'* approach.

Although the Report maintains that there is no single 'right' organisation or 'right' combination of new forms of work practices, it does argue for a 'system' approach as most likely to yield efficiency outcomes. And it refers to studies in Germany and the US to support this contention (p. 17). However, while it sees the scheme as promoting a closer relationship between management and employees, it is aware of the risk of *'potential intensification of work, and an erosion of traditional relationships between unions, workers and managers'* (p. 6). It claims that

---

UK/Ireland, draw a distinction between conflict of interest and conflict of rights disputes. On the latter, disputes are resolved by arbitration or by labour courts. The considerable divergence is regarded as a major barrier to harmonization and convergence (Szyszczak, 2000: 33).

[21] Collective bargaining coverage varies from almost 100% in Austria and Belgium, to, at the lower end, the UK at 36 percent (Carley, 2002: 6).

[22] Entitled 'New forms of work organisation: the obstacles to wider diffusion', final report, October 2002, the study was sponsored by the European Commission and carried out by Business Decisions Limited with an advisory group mainly of academics

[23] A group of inter-related and internally consistent work practices and human resource management policies' (p. 2).

there is no evidence from its study to show that it is more difficult to implement changes where employees are represented by trade unions. However, this conclusion seems to contradict the survey finding that the second most important source of resistance is from employees and their representatives (p. 45).

All in all, despite a central core of commitment, particularly on the place of unions and collective bargaining in management activity, there are significant differences in management practices among the EU countries[24]. Many of these differences have a historical basis, the lapse of time consolidating them into a cultural force. But are most of them critical to efficient management or simply alternative methods of management, a matter of 'taste'? The answer is not clear and deserves to be investigated further. It may turn out that they work reasonably well in their particular settings.

Will any of these differences persist? One view on EU convergence is that *'The idiosyncratic national institutional settings are so variable that no common model is likely to emerge for the foreseeable future'* (Brewster, 2001: 268). Another view is that *'while transfer will lead to change, it will not necessarily lead to convergence because transferred practices often go through a process of transmutation, in that they operate differently in the recipient unit from the way they had operated in the donor unit'* (Edwards, 2003). Yet another view is that there will be a slow convergence as countries take from each other what is seen as the *'best characteristics of each culture ... there will be a slow osmosis': 'The French won't change, the Germans won't change, but they will adopt good practices from their neighbours.'* And there will be a slow convergence of management systems world-wide *'especially between Europe and the United States'* (Calori and de Woot, 1994: 70-71).

Concluding observations:
the challenge to inter-cultural differences from economic and technological forces

While cultural differences can apply a brake on imported management philosophies and techniques, 'culture' is not static even if it changes slowly[25]. In this connection, while it is interesting to consider whether there will be greater convergence in such HRM practices as performance evaluation, reward systems, communications methods, etc., perhaps the most important question to ask concerns the character of industrial relations in EU countries. In particular, to what extent

---

[24] The roots of what has been called the 'European paradox' reflecting the tension arising from the co-existence of unity and diversity ('diverse but not adverse') is discussed in Noe, 2002.

[25] The experience of a number of Anglo-Saxon countries, including Australia, New Zealand, the UK and Canada, all countries with a long tradition of unionism, shows that changes in the political climate can bring down legislation less sympathetic to unionism on the pretext of the competitive pressures of globalisation.

the role of unions will be compromised by the challenges facing them in the changing environment in which they operate – declining union density and power in most countries, growing unemployment and employment insecurity in the face of downsizing, outsourcing, relocation, sub-contracting and other segmentation devices facilitated by technology and the intimidating force of capital mobility internationally.

Further, pressure on the unions to conform has come from the spread of flexible work arrangements such as casual and part-time employment, fixed-term appointments, core and peripheral employees, home-based work, teleworking and other such arrangements for which union membership appears to have little appeal (Mayne, Brewster and Morley, 2000). Many of these practices have been associated with the adoption of HRM and new technology under global competition. In the circumstances, what is the future role of European unions in dealing with HRM practices? Are they simply likely to accede passively to management demands for flexibilisation, being realistic about their loss of power *vis-à-vis* management in the competitive international economic environment? Will such 'nominal' union power result in a loss of appeal of unionism and lead to a further decline in union membership?

The spectre of the 'Americanisation' of European industrial relations, at least towards it, under the pressure of the monetary and fiscal discipline of a common currency, cannot be discounted. In this connection, one writer (Hyman, 2001: 288-89) has argued that competitive market forces *'are tilting the balance of European social market economies away from the social'*; and that the present diversity of industrial relations and the associated management practices, is the result of many decades of protectionism in which nation states had substantial power to determine economic policy. Globalisation has altered this context. And especially within EU, now with monetary union, Member States have effectively little room to manoeuvre on monetary and fiscal policy without violating the rules to which they are bound. These disciplines are *'inherently antagonistic to the principles of social protection and social partnership which underlie most European industrial relations systems'* (Hyman, 2001: 289). Can it be argued that even in the EU, the acceptance of unionism by management may be a thin veneer, held down by legislation and the present political forces which sustain it?

A further pertinent question: how will the present EU states be affected by EU Enlargement? Although productivity is generally lower in the Accession States, wages are also appreciably lower and hours longer than in the EU States. Will there be *'One Europe or Several'*[26]? The answer to these questions must be in the nature of inferences drawn from the meagre factual material, with some inconsist-

---

[26] The title of a research project sponsored by the European Foundation for the Improvement of Living and Working Condition.

encies, currently available about accessing states[27]. (Biffl, 2002; European Commission, 2002)[28].

However, on the information available[29], the following points produce a picture of contrast with the EU:

- A high proportion of people of working age appear to be either self-employed or in the informal economy which has grown following the collapse of the command economies, some of the sharp increase in unemployment having been absorbed into the informal economy. It is estimated that between 30 and 50% of GDP is derived from this sector compared to 10 to 20% in the present EU members (Biffl, 2003a: 1). On the reasonable assumption that productivity in this sector is lower than productivity in the formal economy, the proportion of persons involved in the former is higher than is indicated by GDP measures. This means that a large proportion of the working population have no legal or social protection.
- Unionism is weak, affected by political rivalry in some states, and weaker than is suggested by density figures[30] - at the upper end, Slovenia and Slovakia (40%), and at the lower end, Hungary (20%), Poland[31] and Lithuania (15%) (Carley, 2002: 2). The average rate of unemployment is twice that of EU member countries (Carley, 2002: 8). Although the right to strike (except political strikes in some states) is protected under their constitutions (Nagy, 1996: 16), many workers prefer to take multiple jobs, some in the informal economy, rather than strive to improve their positions through collective bargaining (European Commission, 2002: 98).
- In the formal economy, 50 to 60% of employees work in enterprises with less than 50 workers. In Slovakia, 97% are units with less than 50, of which 80% employ less than 10 persons. In these small establishments, management practices must be assumed to be basic with nothing like the sophistication expected of HRM. The relative low pay of Personnel Managers reflects the low status of HRM/IR. Worker training from employers is not common although compared to the EU members, a higher proportion of the population have been educated beyond lower secondary level (Carley, 2002: 8).
- Collective bargaining is generally at the enterprise level. Most SMEs do not engage in collective bargaining.

---

[27] For purposes of convenience we will refer solely to the CEECs.
[28] There are no systematic studies of trade unionism, strikes, collective agreements and other industrial relations matters (European Commission, 2000: 118).
[29] Unless otherwise indicated, the data on the accession countries presented below are drawn from European Commission, 2002a.
[30] Comparative figures should be treated with caution because of different definitions adopted, many of the unemployment figures are estimates, and the size of the informal sector would have affected the estimate of the size of the workforce.
[31] In Poland, unions have become increasingly marginalized by channels of non-union representation such as workers' councils and employee representation on supervisory boards. European Industrial Relations Observatory, on line, August 2002.

- Many foreign investors are not in favour of collective bargaining.
- Except in Slovenia and Slovakia, (Carley, 2002: 3) collective bargaining is also impaired by union rivalry while there is no tradition of employers joining associations.
- Although there are legal provisions on labour standards and collective bargaining in line with ILO Conventions, enforcement is poor (Musiolek, 2002). In Hungary, the minimum wage is determined by regular tripartite agreements; and in the Czech Republic and Slovakia, wider issues are covered (Carley, 2002: 3).

These are still early days. With the pressure of EU social principles, in time, greater convergence in the CEECs towards EU practices may be expected. However, this could take a long time. Meanwhile, the impact of trade and migration between EU and CEECs will produce changes in the structure of industry on both sides (Biffl, 2003). The relative abundance of unskilled labour in the CEECs, the relatively lower wages generally in these countries, and the opportunity afforded by technology for the export of services without emigration, will draw certain industries away from the EU and produce unemployment there, unless those affected are re-skilled and/or are relocated – often easier said than done. In addition, the flow of unskilled migrant workers into the Member States, will compound the unemployment problems in those states as well as add to the size of the informal sector.

Although the adjustment problems should not be exaggerated, since the combined GDPs of the CEECs is less than 10% of the EU's GDP (Dyker, 2000: 5), unless offset by significant trading complementarity, competition from accession countries in addition to global competition, could present a challenge to the EU's social economy, social partnership and stakeholder approach with their overtones of equity. This is particularly pertinent if the world slides into a major recession. In the circumstances, the convergence *de facto* of EU's HRM/IR towards the American philosophy, may not be altogether fanciful. This trend could be expected to take place in some states more than in others, bearing in mind the substantial autonomy of the member states on labour law. Inter-cultural forces are not static, especially when they have to contend with economic and technological imperatives.

References

Adler, N.J., Doktor, R. and Reading, S.G., 1986, 'From the Atlantic to the Pacific century: cross-cultural management reviewed', *Journal of Management*, 12,2, 295-318.

Alterburg *et al.*, 1998, 'Efficiency wage, trade unions and employment' *Oxford Economic Papers*, 50, November 1998.

Baldry, C., 1994: 103, 'Convergence in Europe: a matter of perspective?' *Industrial Relations Journal*, 5,2.

Barbash, J. 1985, 'Do we really want labor on the ropes?' *Harvard Business Review*, July-August 1985.
Beaumont, P.B., 1991, 'The US human resource management literature: a review', in G. Salaman, G. (Ed), *Human Resource Strategies*, The Open University.
Biffl, G., 2000, *Labour Statistics – Towards Enlargement*, WIFO Working Paper.
Biffl, G. and Isaac, J., 2002, 'How effective are the ILO's Labour Standards under globalisation', *WIFO Working Paper*.
Biffl, G., 2003a, 'The economic role of migrants in the production of tradeables and non-tradeables: the case of Austria'.
Biffl, G., 2003b, 'The dividing line between labour market and social policy: institutional and legal framework', unpublished paper.
Brewster, C., 2002, 'Transfer of HRM around the world', Conference on Human Resource Management across Countries: the cultural dimension, Athens University of Economics and Business.
Brewster, C. and Hegewisch, A. (Eds), 1994, *Policy and Practice in European HRM*, Routledge, London.
Calori, R. and De Woot, P. (Eds.), 1994, *A European Management Model. Beyond Diversity*, Prentice Hall, New York.
Calori and Seidel, 1994, 'The dynamics of management systems in Europe', in Calori, R. and De Woot, P. (Eds).
Carley, M., 2002, *Industrial Relations in the EU Member States and candidate countries*, European Foundation for the improvement of Living and Working Conditions.
Collins, J.C. and Porras, J.L., 1998, *'Built to Last: Successful Habits of Visionary Companies*, London, Random House).
Communal, C. and Brewster, C., 2003, 'HRM in Europe' in Harzing, A.W.K. and Van Ruysseveldt, R. (Eds.) *International Human Resource Management* (2003) London: Sage Publications (forthcoming).
Deery, S., Erwin, P and Iverson, R., 1994, *British Journal of Industrial Relations*, 32, 4, 581-97.
Donaldson, T. and Preston, L., 1995, 'The stakeholder theory of the corporation: Concepts, evidence, implications', *Academy of Management Review*, 20: 65-91.
Dyker, D., 2000, *The Dynamic Impact on the Central-East European Economies of Accession to the European Union*, Economic and Social Research Programme 'One Europe or Several', Working Paper 06/00. Website: www.one-europe.ac.uk
Edwards, T., 2003 'The transfer of employment practices across borders in multinational companies', Harzing, A.W.K. and Van Ruysseveldt, R. (Eds.) *International Human Resource Management* (2003) London: Sage Publications (forthcoming):
European Commission, 2001, *Green Paper – Partnership for a New Organisation of Work*.
European Commission, 2002a, *Industrial Relations in Europe*.
European Commission, *Final Report*, 2002b, 'New Forms of Work Organisation: the Obstacles to Wider Diffusion'.
European Commission, 2002, *The Report of the High Level Group on Industrial Relations and Change in the* European Union.
European Industrial Relations Observatory, on line, August 2002.
European Union, *Green Paper – Partnership for a new Organisation of Work* (2001).
Flood, P., 1998: 62, in Sparrow, P. and Marchington, M. (Eds.) *Human Resource Management: the New Agenda*, London, Pitman.
Gospel, G., 1992, *Markets, Firms and Management*, CUP.
Grant, D. and Oswick, C., 1998, 'Of believers atheists and agnostics: practitioners' views on HRM', *Industrial Relations Journal*. 29(3): 178-93.
Green, R., 2003, 'Where does knowledge come from in a knowledge-based economy?, Seminar at the University of Melbourne, April 6, 2003.
Guest, D.E., 1990, 'Human resource management and the American dream', *Journal of Management Studies*, 27, 4,377-97.

Guest, D.E., 1991, 'Personnel Management: the end of Orthodoxy', *British Journal of Industrial Relations*, 29,1: 75-96.
Guest, D.E., 1997: 263, 'Human resource management and performance: a review and research agenda', *International Journal of Human Resource* Management, 8(3); 263-290).
Gunnigle, P. et al., 1994, 'European industrial relations: change and continuity', in Brewster and Hegewisch, 1994.
Harzing, A.-W.K, 1999, *Managing Multi-Nationals. An International Study of Control,* Edward Elgar.
Hofstede, G.H., 1980, *Culture's Consequences: International Differences in Work and Related Values, Beverly Hills, Sage).*
Huselid, M. et al., 1997, 'Technical and strategic human resource management effectiveness as determinants of firm performance', *Academy of Management Journal*, 40(1).
Isaac, J.E. 2003. Inter-Cultural and other Forces in the Transfer of Human Resource Management and Industrial Relations Practices under Globalization. WIFO Working Papers Nr. 202.
Jackson, T., 2003, 'HRM in developing countries', Harzing, A.W.K. and Van Ruysseveldt, R. (Eds.) *International Human Resource Management* (2003) London: Sage Publications (forthcoming).
Hyman, R., 2001, 'The Europeanisation – or the erosion – of industrial relations?', *Industrial Relations Journal* 32.4.
Katz, I.F. 1986, 'Efficiency wage theories: partial evaluation' in Stanley Fischer (Ed.) NBER Macroeconomics Annual, MIT Press.
Kochan, T.A., Katz, H.C. and McKersie, R.B., 1986, *The Transformation of American Industrial Relations*, Basic Books, New York.
Kochan, T. and Dyer, I., 2001, 'HRM: an American view', in Storey, J. (Ed.) 2001.
Krueger, A.B. and Summers, L.H., 1988, 'Efficiency wages and inter-industry wage structure', *Econometrica*, 56, March.
Legge, K., 1995, *Human Resource Management: Rhetorics and Realities,* Basingstoke: Macmillan.
Mackinnon Hearn, B., 2003, 'How the West was lost? Hamersley Iron, the birthplace of a decade of de-unionisation', Paper to the Association of Industrial Relations Academics of Australia and New Zealand Conference, February 2003.
McGaughy, S.L. and De Cieri, H., 1999, 'Reassessment of convergence and divergence dynamics: implications for international HRM', *The International Journal of Human Resource Management* 10: 235-250.
Mayne, Brewster and Morley, 2000 in Brewster, C.J. et al. (Eds.) *New Challenges for European Human Resource Management.*
Morley, M., Brewster, C., Gunningle, P. and Mayrhofer, W., (Eds). 2000, *New Chalenges for European Human Resource Management,* St Martin's Press, New York.
Mosely, H., Keller, T & Speckesser, S., 1998, *The Role of the Social Partners in the Design and Implementation of Active Measures*, ILO, Geneva.
Nagy, L., 1996, *Labour Law and Industrial Relations in* Central *and Eastern Europe,* Kluwer, Deventer.
Petit, M et al., 1994, 'European cultural integration', in Calori, R. and De Woot, P., 1994.
OECD. 1998, *Technology, Productivity, and Job Creation – Best Policy Practices*, Paris.
OECD. 1999, *Employment Outlook*, Paris.
Management Today Global Salary Survey August 2001
Murray, J., 2001, 'A new phase in the regulation of multi-national enterprise: the role of the OECD', *Industrial Law Journal*, 30, 3,255-270.
Phelps Brown, H., 1983: Ch.XII, *The Origins of Trade Union Power*, Clarendon Press, Oxford).
Piore, M. and Sabel, C., 1984, *The Second Industrial Divide: Prospects for Prosperity*, Basic Books, New York.
Purcell, J. 2001, 'The meaning of strategy in human resource management', in Storey J. (Ed.), 2001:

Salamon, M., 1997, *Industrial Relations in Theory and Practice*. Prentice-Hall, London.
Sisson, K., 2001, 'Human resource management and the personnel function', in Storey, J.
Sisson J., 2003, Industrial relations in Europe: a multi-level system in the making', in Harzing, A.W.K. and Van Ruysseveldt, R. (Eds.) *International Human Resource Management* (2003) London: Sage Publications (forthcoming).
Storey, J. (Ed.), 2001, *Human Resource Management. A Critical Text*, 2nd Edition, Thomson Learning.
Storey, J., 2001, 'Human resource today: an assessment', in Storey, J., (Ed.) 2001, Ch. 1.
Szyszczak, E., 2000, *EC Labour Law,* Longman.
Torrington, D., 1998: 36, 'Crisis and opportunity in HRM: the challenge for the personnel functions' in Sparrow, P. and Marchington, M. (Eds.) *Human Resource Management: the New Agenda.*
Tylor, E., 1913, *Primitive Culture*, Murray, London.
Tyson, S. and Wikander, L., 1994, 'The education and training of human resource managers in Europe' in Brewster and Hegewisch, (Eds.), 1994, *Policy and Practice in European HRM*, Routledge, London.
Woodall and Winstanley, 2001, 'The place of ethics in HRM', in Storey, J. (Ed.), 2001.
Zhu, Y. and Warner, M., 2003, 'HRM in East Asia', in Harzing, A.W.K. and Van Ruysseveldt, R. (Eds.) *International Human Resource Management* (2003) London: Sage Publications (forthcoming).

The Challenge of Migration
for Crisis and Disaster Management:
Key concepts and recommendations

Bernhard Perchinig[1]

Abstract

The article discusses the challenges of migration for crisis and disaster management. Based on research for the international "Migrants in Countries of Crisis Initiative" (MICIC), it discusses the state of the art of disaster research with regard to the concepts of vulnerability, resilience building and migration and stakeholder inclusion in crisis preparedness planning and disaster mitigation. It highlights main areas of action for a better inclusion of migrants in crisis management with regard to access of migrants to general services and mobility support and discusses the need for civil protection in Austria to learn from the lessons of the MICIC-Initiative.

Introduction

In the actual political debate, the terms "migration" and "crisis" are often linked together – the "migration crisis" is depicted as one of the major European political challenges, whereby migration is often framed as element of a crisis instead as a normal fact of life. This paper will focus on a completely different aspect of a crisis: When a country is hit by natural disaster or political crisis, both citizens and migrants are affected, but often access to support and disaster relief is legally or practically limited to citizens. Relief and disaster mitigation efforts are often planned and implemented without considering migration: Other than refugees, who are protected by an international legal framework, the protection needs of migrants in a country experiencing a crisis are not covered by international law. The lack of reflection on the impacts of migration on crisis and disaster governance is one of the major challenges in international humanitarian aid, as it does not only hamper access of migrants to disaster relief, but also neglects the potentials of migrants for resilience building.

Further to the humanitarian dimension, the degree of inclusion of migrants' needs in disaster preparedness planning also highlights the strengths and deficien-

---

[1] The author wishes to thank Anna Faustmann and Maegan Hendow for valuable comments and suggestions on the first draft of the paper.

cies of migrants' integration into a society. Preparedness planning needs the inclusion of and cooperation with the resident population independent from nationality or place of birth, and the delivery of aid and support in an emergency will be massively hampered if resident migrants are not defined as a relevant target group by humanitarian aid and civil protection agencies and organisations. Including the perspective of migrants in crisis preparedness planning thus has to be understood as an – often neglected – element of integration policies.

The paper is organised as follows: The first part will discuss the key concepts in academic disaster research and the international governance framework of aid with regard to the challenges migration poses to traditional concepts of civil protection, humanitarian aid and crisis and disaster management. A discussion of the specific needs of migrants in crisis and disaster mitigation and the potentials of migrant involvement into disaster preparedness planning will follow. In the third section, the paper will develop suggestions for an improved involvement of migrants into crisis and disaster management based on the results of the MICIC project. The final chapter will discuss the lessons Austria can learn from the MICIC project.

The paper is based on research conducted by the author and his colleagues at the International Centre for Migration Policy Development (ICMPD) (Hendow et al. 2017, Perchinig 2016; Perchinig et al. 2017) within the framework of the EU-funded project "Migrants in Countries in Crisis: Supporting an evidence based approach"[2], which supported the "Migrants in Countries of Crisis Initiative"[3] (MICIC). The MICIC-Initiative was launched in 2014 by the Governments of the Philippines and the United States to address the impacts of crises – conflicts and natural disasters – on migrants with the goal *"to improve the ability of States and other stakeholders to better prepare for, respond to, and protect the lives, dignity, and rights of migrants caught in countries experiencing conflicts and natural disasters'"*[4]. Based on stakeholder consultations and research studies, the MICIC-Initiative has implemented a number of recommendations and a repository of good practices (available on the MICIC webpage) for improved protection of migrants in countries of crises, which have also served as background material for this paper[5].

Key concepts in disaster studies

Until today, the scientific understanding of "disaster" is largely modelled along the concept of a natural disaster, e.g. an earthquake or a tsunami. Nevertheless, the conceptual framing of "disaster" has undergone major changes in the last quarter

---

[2] See https://www.icmpd.org/our-work/migrants-in-countries-in-crisis/
[3] See https://micicinitiative.iom.int
[4] See https://micicinitiative.iom.int/about-micic/approach
[5] These documents are available at: https://micicinitiative.iom.int/resources-and-publications

of the 20th century. In the 1970s, the disaster narrative focused on the concept of "hazard", understood as an unexpected disruptive event caused by natural powers leading to severe damage to infrastructure. Remedies were focused on technical solutions aimed at a reduction of the probability of material damage, e.g. by improving the construction and quality of infrastructure. This "end of the pipe" strategy was later accompanied by a focus on risk reduction and mitigation measures. Whereas the first strategy aimed at a reduction of the likelihood of hazards, e.g. by improved monitoring of potential natural hazards, such as volcanoes, the second sought to mitigate the damage caused by a disaster. Typical examples for this strategy are e.g. the construction of polders to mitigate flood damage or the development of floodplains in order to divert impacts of floods to unsettled areas (Frerks et al. 2011, p. 105f.)[6].

In the 1990s, this technical understanding of disaster and crises gradually gave place to a more sociological definition of disaster as a process of interaction between external forces (such as natural hazards and conflicts) and the socioeconomic and political conditions in a society influencing the magnitude of impact and the potential for recovery. From this perspective, the socioeconomic and political conditions of certain groups or communities leading to inequality with regard to both their risk of becoming victims of a disaster and their coping capacity were regarded as major factors previously neglected by the technical disaster narrative (Wisner et al. 2003). In this context, the concept of vulnerability became crucial[7].

In disaster studies, vulnerability is understood as a concept to describe the differences in the degree of damage incurred from (natural) hazards that are manifested for an individual person, for a community, a city or an entire region. Vulnerability thus refers to the propensity of the exposed persons or systems to experience harm and suffer damages when impacted by hazard events, and thus relates to two aspects: a) the nature and magnitude of a hazard and b) the potential of a person, a community or a system to mobilise resources to protect against hazards and to minimize their impact.

Understanding disasters as complex interactions between the physical environment and society, the concept underscores the social construction of risk and the role of the division of power and unequal access to resources in a society. Highlighting the societal conditions, the coping capacity, the power relations and the social capital of the person or community concerned, the concept of vulnerability is strongly linked to social inequality as major influencing factor. (Fekete et al. 2014, p. 5). The understanding of vulnerability as *"the characteristics of a person or group and their situation that influence their capacity to anticipate, cope with, resist and recover from the impact of a natural hazard"* (Wisner et al 2003, p. 107) shifted the focus from technical concerns – e.g. the construction of earthquake-safe roads and housing – to the affected population. This paradigm

---

[6] This overview of the conceptual framing of crisis and disaster is based on Frerks et al. 2011.
[7] It is not possible to cover the broad academic debate on different conceptions of vulnerability (i.a. Birkman et al. 2011, Lewis and Kelman 2010, Zhou et al. 2010) in this paper; nevertheless, a short introduction into the framing of the term will be given.

shift also brought politics into disaster science. Now the effects of (poor) governance or political or military conflicts on the social production of vulnerability among specific groups or communities gained prominence in research and the political debate.

This new focusing on the interaction between the susceptibility for natural or other hazards, unsafe living conditions and limited access to resources and political power also directed the attention to the ways in which the organizational, institutional and political contexts influence vulnerability. In this vein, the "new humanitarism" stresses the need of interventions at a structural level reducing poverty and inequality of power. Although having become more influential in recent years, this position is not shared by all actors in the field of humanitarian aid (Birkman et al. 2011, p. 198).

The sociological framing greatly influenced the international debate on disaster risk reduction and disaster risk management. At the UN level, international cooperation on disaster and crisis management reaches back to 2000, when the UN General Assembly adopted the "International Strategy for Disaster Reduction"[8] and established the United Nations Office for Disaster Risk Reduction (UNISDR) as the focal point for coordination tasked to ensure synergies among the disaster reduction activities of the United Nations system.

UNISDR was the driving force behind the World Conference for Disaster Reduction, which took place in Hyogo from January 18-22, 2005. At the conference, the participants agreed to the first common system of international coordination on disaster management, the "Hyogo Framework of Action" (UNISDR 2005). The framework centred around two core concepts: a) disaster preparedness based on a set of indicators for early warning and risk reduction on the one hand, and b) fostering resilience of the population as the central element of the preparation for effective disaster response.

The Disaster Risk Index developed by the UN Development Programme in 2004 (UNDP 2004) clearly showed that disasters affected the poorest groups in society most dramatically, as they were not only most prone to be hit by a disaster, but also most often lacked the necessary means to recover and rebuild. Following this understanding, "vulnerability assessments" – based on either proximity to a place of disaster or pre-defined individual characteristics (mainly gender, age, disability or ethnic minority status) – have become major tools in decision making on priorities in humanitarian aid in the 1990s (Birkmann 2007). This shift towards vulnerability as the core category for disaster preparedness planning is also reflected in the successor of the Hyogo-Framework, the "Sendai Framework for Disaster Risk Reduction 2015-2030" (UNISDR 2015), which was adopted by the UN on March 18, 2015.

In recent years, academics and development actors have increasingly questioned the institutional delivery of aid towards "vulnerable groups" in case of a

---

[8] The current version of the Strategy can be consulted at https://www.unisdr.org/who-we-are/international-strategy-for-disaster-reduction, visited 12.8.2017

crisis as paternalistic and unsustainable (Barnett and Walker 2015). According to the critics, linking vulnerability to attributes of persons or groups – e.g. gender, age, or minority status – would contribute to victimisation and disempowerment and neglect the agency of individuals and communities. Inspired by several studies proving that local communities, and not professional aid providers, usually were the "first responders", both academics and the international aid community now shifted their attention to human agency in crisis situations (De Miliano et al. 2015, p. 23). This debate recently triggered a reframing of the concept of vulnerability. Whereas in the debate of the 1990s and 2000s specific attributes of persons or groups (e.g. women, children, the elderly) were seen as reasons for vulnerability, now the situations producing vulnerability came to the forefront of the debate. This focus-shift to vulnerability-producing situations further strengthened a socio-political understanding of crisis and disaster: If power-differentials and inequality in specific situations produce vulnerability, an analysis of the factors and the development of measures to change these conditions become a main element of action. In this understanding, the empowerment of individuals and communities to withstand vulnerable situations has to stand at the core of humanitarian action: *"Vulnerability is not a fixed criterion attached to specific categories of people, and no one is born vulnerable per se."* (European Commission – DG ECHO 2016, p. 51).

This focus on human agency and coping strategies linked well with the concept of resilience, which had been gaining prominence both in environmental system analysis and psychology since the 1990s, and now was imported into the field of disaster sciences. Originating in health psychology (Antonovsky 1987), where resilience describes the capacity of an individual to positively adapt to adverse conditions[9], the term is now widely used both in ecology and in social sciences. Here it is understood *"as the buffer capacity or the ability of a system to absorb perturbations, or the magnitude of disturbance that can be absorbed before a system changes its structure by changing the variables and processes that control its behaviour"* (Adger 2005, 249, in Djalante et al. 2011, p. 5). In this sense, "social resilience" is understood as the capacity of social groups and communities to recover from, or respond positively to a crisis and to mobilise their powers of resistance, recovery and creativity (Maguier and Hagan 2007).

Based on this understanding, resilience analysis has become the dominant approach in disaster preparedness planning today (Park et al. 2013). "Resilience building" within communities and the civil society is a main target of disaster preparedness planning and is regarded as a major element of effective crisis governance (Ahrens and Rudolph 2006, p. 217). Community based disaster management directly involves vulnerable people themselves in planning and implementation of mitigation measures. This bottom up approach has received wide acceptance because considered communities are the best judges of their own vulner-

---

[9] Fletcher and Sarkar 2013 give a good overview on the development of the concept of resilience in psychology.

ability and can make the best decisions regarding their well-being (Pandey and Okazaki 2005). The link between vulnerability and resilience has also been stressed by the United Nations International Strategy for Disaster Risk Reduction (UNISDR), which defines resilience as the ability to *'resist, absorb, accommodate to and recover from the effects of a hazard in a timely and efficient manner'* (Fekete et al. 2014, p. 6).

Fostering social and individual resilience as a means to reduce vulnerability is linked well to a needs-based approach to crisis governance (Zetter 2015). While it remains undisputed that governments have the prime responsibility for managing disasters and for assigning the roles of different stakeholders in crisis management, the dominant top-down approach describing authorities as the providers of help to "victims" has often proved insufficient and ineffective. In many cases, it failed to meet appropriate and vital human needs, in particular the needs of the poor, who in first place have limited survival resources and do not enjoy adequate infrastructure and access to social services. In this sense, resilience building has to be understood as a process of social learning and empowerment: *"We suggest that resilience is seen as the shared social capacity to anticipate, resist, absorb and recover from an adverse or disturbing event or process through adaptive and innovative processes of change, entrepreneurship, learning and increased competence"* (Frerks et al. 2011, p. 213).

Despite the embedding of disaster management in the UN framework, migration has been widely neglected in this debate. While the Sendai Framework contains some references to migrants (UNISDR 2015, 9, 17, 22), there are hardly any references to migration to be found in the relevant EU documents. Humanitarian aid and civil protection are still largely conceptualised within the framework of a "nation-state container" with a population imagined as perfectly fluent in the state language and culturally homogeneous. This framing leads to a neglect of the discussion of the needs of migrants in disaster situations.

Migration, vulnerability and resilience

As discussed above, vulnerability is a concept focusing on the effects of social inequality and power differentials on the capacity to cope with hazards. In crisis situations, different aspects of vulnerability become relevant. Further to aspects relating to social conditions and general power differentials, migration may add specific dimensions of vulnerability, but may also be a resource of resilience. Both aspects challenge the dominant concepts of crisis management, which do not consider cross-border mobility as an issue of contingency planning and disaster mitigation.

Following Bustamante´s discussion of immigrants´ vulnerability in human rights discourses, migration may add to vulnerability through the power differentials between citizens and foreigners enshrined in the very nature of a state, which may be reinforced by cultural elements justifying the lower status of immigrants as compared to nationals. In this understanding, vulnerability is not associated with personal characteristics and traits of immigrants, but with the legal and social status ascribed to migrants (Bustamante 2002, p. 340). Four specific dimensions of migration-related vulnerabilities have to be mentioned:

a) All aspects of legal discrimination based on the fact of not holding the citizenship of the country of residence, which lead to exclusion from or limited access to resources and services, e.g. legal differentiations between citizens and foreigners with regard to access to e.g. the labour market, housing and social support provision, education or health;
b) All aspects related to international border crossing and residence in another country, e.g. the restriction of mobility rights by visa regulations, or temporary or spatial limits of the right of residence. In this respect, a further differentiation between migrants holding a regular status of residence and migrants with an irregular status is necessary (Carrera and Parkin 2011, p. 25ff.; Commission for Human Rights 2007, p. 7ff.): Whereas legally resident migrants may be excluded from a broad array of citizens´ rights, access to basic services (electricity, water supply etc.) and their residence status usually will be undisputed, and their place of residence will be recorded in population databases, if existent. Irregular residents, on the contrary, often are denied access even to basic services. As irregular migrants often try to remain invisible to authorities – as to not to threaten their residency in the host country – so too will they remain invisible for the stakeholders involved in disaster mitigation and relief, i.a. due to the lack of registration in the population register. On the other hand, an irregular status will be often instrumental as ground for discrimination and exploitation, or may be tolerated by (weak) authorities to support semi-legal economic activities they may profit from due to corruption.
c) Socio-cultural factors linked to migration, in particular the lack of integration, e.g. the lack or limited knowledge of the local language(s) or communication practices, limited knowledge of the institutional framework of the country of residence, or lack of or limited access to social networks of residents, may also add to vulnerability.
d) Discrimination: Whereas the acquisition of knowledge of the local language(s) and on local ways of life may mitigate vulnerability based on socio-cultural factors, ethnic or origin-based discrimination aims at the exclusion or limitation of access to economic, social and political resources. Ethnic and origin-based discrimination may be also an issue for citizens, but is more likely to occur with regard to migrants.

On the other hand, migration may also add to resilience of a local community giving access to a broader range of resources and support by the members of migrant families abroad, or by the possibility to relocate to the country of origin, or to be evacuated from the disaster site by the state of origin. Migration status may in- or decrease vulnerability, depending on context and situation:

"Certain issues, such as displacement, could be considered a threat, vulnerability, or a capacity depending on the scenario, the population concerned and the moment in time. While being displaced is most often considered as a vulnerability, the ability to remove oneself from a threat could also be considered a capacity, and likewise the danger of displacement, including arbitrary displacement, can be a real or perceived threat before it happens or during the actual displacement." (European Commission, DG ECHO 2016, p. 11).

Migration issues in crisis management

The phases of a crisis

Crises and disasters have a complex and multifaceted development which does not easily allow for a neat separation of different phases. For analytical reasons it nevertheless makes sense to differentiate between the different phases of a crisis in order to improve crisis management. In disaster studies, the concept of a four-phase "crisis management cycle" has gained wide acceptance (Coppola 2015). According to UNSIDR (2009), these phases are defined as follows:

- Preparedness:
  "The knowledge and capacities developed by governments, professional response and recovery organizations, communities and individuals to effectively anticipate, respond to, and recover from, the impacts of likely, imminent or current hazard events or conditions." (UNISDR 2009, p. 21)
- Mitigation:
  "The lessening or limitation of the adverse impacts of hazards and related disasters." (UNISDR 2009, p. 19)
- Response:
  "The provision of emergency services and public assistance during or immediately after a disaster in order to save lives, reduce health impacts, ensure public safety and meet the basic subsistence needs of the people affected." (UNSIDR 2009, p. 28)
- Recovery:
  "The restoration, and improvement where appropriate, of facilities, livelihoods and living conditions of disaster-affected communities, including efforts to reduce disaster risk factors." (UNISDR 2009, p. 27).

The MICIC Initiative differentiates between a pre-crisis, emergency and post-crisis phase. Compared to the UNSIDR definitions, the pre-crisis phase covers preparedness-planning and mitigation, the emergency phase response, and the post-crisis phase recovery. It is important to note, that these phases should not illustrate a sequence of actions, but describe a crisis as a learning process, whereby recovery should be linked to improved preparedness and mitigation to a reduction of the impact of future disasters.

Areas of intervention

Crises and disasters do not only concern dedicated disaster response organisations. The functioning of societies hinges on a broad variety of services provided to the public by public or private companies and organisations. These "general services" include both infrastructure services e.g. local transport networks, railway or bus services, postal services, or telecommunications; as other essential services provided directly to the person, like e.g. health services, child care, long-term care or social and psychological assistance services. These services play both a preventive and a socially cohesive/inclusive role.

Depending on the institutional framework of a country, these services can be delivered by public institutions, by private companies, or by a combination of both. Further to these services, the provision of goods by private companies and shops is a main precondition for the functioning of everyday life. The functioning of these institutions is a central aspect in all phases of a crisis.

Providing mobility options to victims in order to remove them from areas affected by natural disasters or conflicts into safe areas often is a main element in crisis and disaster management. As an element of general services mobility related services play a specific role in crisis management, as removal from the crisis area often is a key element of first response. In this respect, relocation within a country, removal to a neighbouring country, and removal to the country of origin or to another country have to be distinguished. Whereas in cases of natural disasters relocation in the country or removal to another country will mainly hinge on the capacity of the state and rescue organisations to provide transportation, in cases of conflict security issues, e.g. the unavailability of law enforcement authorities, or the lack of state control of certain areas of the country, may seriously hamper mobility. These issues usually cannot be solved by rescue organisations, but need the involvement of the authorities.

Whereas removal within a country and to a neighbouring country can be provided to both citizens and migrants, migrants may also have the opportunity to move to their country of origin, which will involve also the authorities of the countries of origin of the migrants.

Crisis management

The development of a crisis management cycle with the participation of all relevant stakeholders, including migrants, is a challenge for public authorities. The quality of crisis management hinges on the inclusion of a broad variety of stakeholders, including actors from the public sector, the private sector and civil society organisations on the local and state level. Stakeholders should not only include immediate crisis response providers, general services providers and mobility providers in the country, but also go beyond borders and involve stakeholders from neighbouring states and regional dialogue networks to foster transnational mobility. To facilitate cooperation, sustainable network structures with clear lines of communication and responsibility need to be established.

Inclusive crisis management structures as described above allow the development of improved adaptation strategies in crisis-situations, but also increase transaction costs. The inclusion of stakeholders in crisis management has to be well-conceived in the pre-crisis phase in order to learn ways of successful cooperation before they are needed. Only pre-established networks of cooperation breed innovation and resilience and improve the overall quality of crisis governance.

In several countries crisis and disaster management networks have already been set up and include a broad variety of actors. As their experience has shown, mechanisms of regular exchange of information and training are necessary to improve their functioning, and they need to be connected to a high-ranking focal point within government, e.g. a ministry, to receive sufficient support and be able to fulfil coordinative functions over a broad range of levels of decision making.

In order to successfully reach out to migrants, the inclusion of migrants' organisations, migrant community leaders and interlocutors to migrant communities is crucial already during the development of these networks. Depending on the situation in the respective country, the contact to migrant organisations and the knowledge about their places of residence will differ strongly. In some countries, a registration system and well established networks of migrant organisations will exist, which provide information on the whereabouts of the migrants, whereas in other countries registration systems might be missing, or specific groups of migrants stay invisible, or fear to get into contact with the authorities.

A further channel of communication will be consulates of countries of origin with their tradition to reach out towards the citizens. As well as in the pre-crisis phase, cooperation during the crisis-phase with the authorities of the countries of origin of migrants, as well as of transit countries, is essential. In this respect, consulates can have an important role as access points for information and as providers of first financial and technical support to their citizens.

Lessons from the MICIC – project: Relevant areas of action in the pre-crisis, the emergency and the post-crisis phase

The activities of stakeholders in crisis management follow different internal logics, and different decision making procedures, depending on the task of the stakeholders and the crisis phase. The following section discusses the relevant approaches of stakeholders involved into immediate disaster response, stakeholders providing general services in a region affected by a crisis, and – due to its utmost relevance in emergencies – stakeholders providing mobility related support. It is mainly based on the analysis of reports on the regional consultations in Africa, Asia, Europe and the Americas within the MICIC-Initiative and on research on the migrants experienced in crises in Central Africa, Côte d'Ivoire, the Lebanon, Libya, South Africa and Thailand coordinated at ICMPD (Hendow et al. 2017), and the "Guidelines to Protect Migrants in Countries Experiencing Conflict or Natural Disaster" published by the MICIC-Initiative (Migrants in Countries in Crisis (MICIC) Initiative 2016).

Pre-crisis phase

As migration can be both linked with vulnerability and capacity, disaster preparedness planning and response has to be based on an accurate analysis of the effects of migration on vulnerability-producing situations and necessary mitigation measures. In this context, both the knowledge of the whereabouts of migrants and a trustful relationship between the migrant population and the institutions providing support and civil protection is crucial.

Both disaster preparedness planning and emergency response measures usually are implemented by state authorities, mainly the police or the military, with support of non-governmental organisations, like e.g. the respective Red Cross and Red Crescent societies. This combination of state authorities and NGOs – which has proven successful in most cases of emergencies – may entail a specific challenge with regard to migration: Irregularly resident migrants might shine away from seeking support from state authorities, as they might fear consequences when notifying the police about their presence. This situation most likely will lead to wrong assessments of needs for emergency response and thus impact negatively on the whole population affected by a disaster. In order to overcome this challenge, there is the need to establish a strict firewall between crisis response and migration control. Migrants should be informed clearly and in a multilingual format that rescue services operate without taking into account the migration status of victims and do not report to the migration authorities not only during a crisis, but also in pre-crisis times.

Disaster response organisations can prepare for a better inclusion of migrants mainly in the pre-crisis phase. In this respect "Know your population!" is a main imperative. A functioning and sustainable population registration system can deliver this information, if migrants are included independently of their legal status and on the same footing as citizens. In practice, population registers are often missing or lack reliability. To overcome these difficulties, administrations of population registers should communicate with migrant representatives and/or NGOs working with migrants on the ground to check and complete their information. Consular services can provide important support if they collect data on the whereabouts of their citizens. Registration of citizens at consulates in the pre-crisis phase will help to collect relevant information. In order to cover all migrants, irregular migrants should be included into registration. Rescue organisations should be informed about the migrant population and their needs and encouraged to recruit migrants among their staff.

Measures to improve the language proficiency of migrants in the main language(s) of the host country are a key strategy in disaster preparedness. Nevertheless, first aid providers should provide information in the main migrant's native languages and offer interpretation services to be accessible also to those with insufficient knowledge of the local language(s). In this respect, setting up multilingual hotlines and text (SMS) services, and informing migrants about hotline-telephone numbers and accessibility in pre-crisis time is essential. Mobile phone based and IT based multilingual information services can complete these tools. Consulates and embassies of the countries of origin of the resident migrants should be included into these efforts.

Crisis situations often lead to traumatisation of victims, who will not only need adequate medical care, but also psychological assistance. The effects of trauma on individual behaviour are influenced by cultural traditions, thus post-traumatic stress disorder (PTSD) may take different forms (Wilson 2005). First responders need to receive adequate intercultural training to be able to cope professionally with PTSD-related behaviour unknown in their cultural context.

Public and general services

The provision of public and general services is organised differently from country to country. It is essential to analyse the structure and institutional set up of providers in the pre-crisis phase, to include them into stakeholder inclusion measures and to develop clear procedures for access to basic services in and at the aftermath of a crisis.

Access to basic services has to be based on the principle of needs assessment and discrimination-free service delivery. In order to successfully reach out to migrants, providers should be encouraged to pro-actively reach out to migrant leaders, interlocutors and NGOs working with migrants to get information about and assess migrants´ needs. Also in this field, it will be helpful to prepare multilingual information material. As migrants´ vulnerabilities may lead to unequal treatment by service providers, adequate anti-discrimination policies including a revision of procedures leading to unequal access to services are necessary.

Emergency phase

Crisis and disaster response may concern activities in situ and measures to remove victims out of affected areas, and will address both local residents as migrants. Furthermore, crisis responses may be different in cases of natural disasters and civil wars. Whereas in the first case, at least immediate disaster response in many cases will be administered without legal differentiation between citizens and migrants, in cases of civil war there often will be an intentional divide between different population groups with regard to access to support and services. In the case of international migrants, the authorities of countries of origin may also step in as a specific set of actors.

Immediate emergency response

Immediate disaster response concerns immediate life-saving activities, e.g. recovery operations, first medical support, provision of shelter, and the distribution of food, water and emergency supplies. Disaster relief services are usually implemented following the principle of triage. Triage systems categorise victims in different categories regarding the gravity of damages in order to provide (medical) support to those most in need first (Robertson-Steel 2006). When on scene, rescue teams usually do not differentiate according to any other criteria, thus migrant status usually does not play a role in first response rescue operations on the spot. Triage approaches are also applied when deciding which locations to focus on first for disaster relief. In this respect, the number of people affected and the gravity of disaster impacts are the main indicators for prioritisation of disaster response.

Triage can be an effective tool for levelling systemic power dynamics, which create barriers for marginalised persons to access to emergency response services; however, there are several specific challenges with regard to migration:

a) The application of a triage-approach has to be based on a sufficient level of information about the resident population.
b) Communication between the rescuers and the victims is essential to apply triage successfully.
c) Basic trust between victims and rescuers has to be established.

In cases of a complex emergency – a major humanitarian crisis of a multi-causal nature that requires a system-wide response (Duffield 1994, 5) – immediate emergency response may be hampered by the full or partial breakdown of national institutions, the infrastructure and/or the public order. "Complex emergencies" are typically characterized by an extensive violence and loss of life, the displacements of populations, widespread damage to societies and economies, the hindrance or prevention of humanitarian assistance by political and military constraints and significant security risks for humanitarian relief workers in some areas, and need large-scale and multifaceted humanitarian assistance[10]. These emergencies usually lead to large scale mass movements of refugees and displaced persons and often overwhelm the capacities of national disaster management structures. In these cases, the involvement of International Organisations and the cooperation with other countries is necessary to deliver support to victims, which can be fostered by the development of cooperation agreements with international relief organisations in due time.

General services

In the emergency phase, reaching out to migrant communities and the provision of services irrespective of the legal status is a clear priority. Migrants should be addressed in multilingual formats, and there should be a clear message that authorities involved into rescue operations provide relief irrespective of legal status.

---

[10] See also http://www.ifrc.org/en/what-we-do/disaster-management/about-disasters/definition-of-hazard/complex-emergencies/

Furthermore, procedures granting equal access independently from migration status, national origin or citizenship should be established.

Information on available services should be given by all available means of communication. If possible, community leaders and interlocutors should be asked to spread the information. In any case, the provision of services should not be hindered by the migration status of the person concerned. Access to all services – if available – should be provided to the population concerned on a needs based paradigm, including free service provision.

Access to information and to communication facilities is a major issue in a crisis. This does not only concern the communication of authorities with migrants, and the distribution of information to migrants making use of different channels of communication including both personal and digital communication, but also migrants´ communication needs. In this respect, access to public internet terminals or free WiFi-spots, and access to a sufficient number of sockets for charging mobile phones, or the supply of cheap sim-cards for mobile phones, will help migrants to communicate with each other and with their families. As in a crisis WiFi connections might not function, mobile phone service providers should be encouraged to grant a certain number of free or cheap minutes for calls and a certain number of free or cheap megabytes of data-transfer for communication with the main source countries of immigrants.

For dissemination of information, a broad variety of channels should be used. Regarding electronic communications, text services (SMS) have proven more stable in a crisis than internet-based services.

Mobility related services

Equal access to services and access to information about mobility options, and protection against violence and exploitation during travel and transit are a central element of crisis management. Main stakeholders in this area are law enforcement authorities, public and/or private transport providers, and public and/or private providers of related infrastructure. Removal to a neighbouring country will involve the authorities of this country, which will need to grant border-crossing and (temporary) resident permits to disaster victims. Removal to the country of origin will involve both the authorities of this country and the authorities of (potential) transit countries as stakeholders.

Migrants' vulnerabilities may increase the risk of becoming victims of violence and (sexual) exploitation during travel. In particular, irregular migrants, migrants restricted in their mobility by lack of identity documents, which might have been lost or withheld by employers, or migrants not holding a visa for countries they intend to reach for protection, will be confronted with increased travel risks.

These risks can be mitigated by public authorities of the country of residence through the provision of provisional identity and travel documents, and by third countries through the granting of humanitarian entry and residence visa independently of the legal status of the migrant, and by the organisation of safe and reliable transport facilities for migrants in transit.

The consulates of the countries of origin can facilitate mobility by the smooth issuance of travel documents and by material, logistic or other support to migrants. Neighbouring countries can support mobility by granting humanitarian entry or transit visas and/or (temporary) residence permits. In case of a serious breakdown of the public order, evacuation procedures for migrants, if necessary with the support of international organisations, might become necessary.

Both (temporary) return and re-integration in the country of origin as remigration to the country of residence are options taken by migrants affected by a crisis in their country of residence. Both options link the authorities and public service providers of the countries of origin to the crisis country, in particular if the crisis leads to mass returns of citizens challenging the reintegration capacity of the country.

Post-crisis phase

Public and general services

Whereas in the post-crisis phase emergency response organisations reduce their involvement and their services are taken over by general service providers, the transfer of information about their activities and experiences, and the specific needs encountered by migrants to general providers is essential. Thus there is a need to include the issue of services for migrants into an organised hand-over to general service providers and to secure a follow-up with migrant organisations, consulates and intermediators.

The re-establishment of basic services is a main task in the post-crisis phase. When re-establishing services and rebuilding, "rebuilding better" should be the target. "Rebuilding better" does not only concern the material infrastructure, but also the empowerment of the population and social cohesion. In this respect, adequate inclusion of migrants should be secured not only by safeguarding access to adequate information, but also by the implementation of clear antidiscrimination and equality procedures which prevent the privileging of nationals over immigrants, and by pro-active inclusion of migrants into rebuilding activities.

Mobility related services

Both the migrant and the non-migrant population may have left the area of crisis and consider either return or settlement in another place. Although "rebuilding" is a guiding paradigm in disaster response, it is important to note that rebuilding does not always need to be the best solution for everyone affected by a crisis Mobility and resettlement should also be considered as a valid choice, and persons wishing to remove should also be supported.

Other than citizens, migrants may also choose to return to their country of origin or to another country, which will involve authorities of the country of origin. Return of ex-patriate citizens will often also involve the import of money, household goods, cars, or machinery or equipment used in companies owned by the citizens abroad. To foster return, many countries have implemented tax exemption for returning citizens. Financial authorities are thus to be seen as major stakeholders in the return process.

Re-integration mainly concerns housing, access to the labour market, schooling and access to health and social services. Independently from legal aspects, the authorities will have to face the challenge of providing housing, recognising training certificates obtained abroad, and integrating children, who might not be fluent in the main language(s) of the country, into the education system. Information, orientation and language classes may be required for spouses or children, or for returning adults born and raised abroad. These tasks might involve authorities, private companies and civil society organisations and will be akin to those required for the integration of immigrants.

Migrants returning to the country of origin will often stay connected to their previous country of residence. In immediate post-crisis situations, unpaid salaries or loan repayments might have to be claimed, or property rights might have to be secured. Migrant entrepreneurs might need to claim open payments of business partners, or solve situations regarding loans or the selling or re-opening of their business. All these activities will involve transnational legal and financial service providers, like attorneys or business agencies, but also trade unions or civil society organisations supporting migrants in the enforcement of their entitlements. In this respect, regional migration dialogues can be an important venue to solve issues related to transnational payment and property claims by bringing the relevant regulatory authorities of the countries concerned together under the umbrella of improved migration and mobility management.

Family members or children of migrants not holding the passport of the country of origin of the spouse or the parents of the children, but also household personnel or widowers of citizens are most often excluded from the right to travel to and take residence in the country of origin of the spouse. To mitigate this situation, it is advisable to pass legislation granting access and – at least – temporary residence to spouses and children of (deceased) nationals and to facilitate their naturalisation.

Conclusion: Lessons for Austria

Although this paper has been developed in a context related mainly to crises in non-OECD countries, the experiences of the MICIC project also can provide valuable lessons for Austria.

Whereas Austria as one of the richest countries of the world has established a well-organised civil protection and crisis management system involving public authorities, the military and a variety of voluntary organisations, like fire brigades or the local Red Cross societies[11], the framing of civil protection still follows a nation-state container model. The "Austrian Security Strategy" – the core document for crisis management planning – mentions migration several times as a potential challenge for stability and potential security risk[12]. There are only two references to the migrant population in the document. Whereas the first statement *"The relatively high proportion of individuals with migration background living in Austria entails additional expertise which can also be used in the interests of security. At the same time, it also brings about specific challenges concerning internal security"* (Federal Chancellery of the Republic of Austria 2013, p. 8) mainly links migration with security, the second highlights the potential of soldiers with migration-background for the Austrian army (Federal Chancellery of the Republic of Austria 2013, p. 10). Nowhere the document mentions activities aiming at the inclusion of migrants in crisis preparedness planning, and no reports on measures including migrants into preparedness planning can be found on the relevant webpages.

This lack of reflection on outreach to and inclusion of migrants also characterises the various brochures on civil protection issues available to the public at the webpage of the Ministry[13]. Although most brochures on fire protection, earthquake protection or radiation protection are available in German and English, none of them is available in the most relevant languages of settled migrants in Austria. The mobile-phone application "KATWARN" sending localisation-based civil protection warnings to its users, even is available only in German.

With a population of some 1,9 million migrants or children from migrant families (Statistik Austria 2016, p. 22), Austria is one of the countries with the highest proportion of migrants and persons with migrant parentage in Europe. Despite the increased focus on German language acquisition in integration policy, a certain percentage of (newly arrived) migrants will not be fluent in German (yet) also in the future, and the functioning and structure of the crisis response system in Austria will not be known to a large part of the migrant population too.

Reaching out to migrants in the field of crisis preparedness planning and preparing the main civil protection organisations for the challenges of a migration society obviously has not been perceived as a major challenge by the main actors in this policy field yet. As the results of the MICIC-project highlight, these challenges should become a priority of action for the next future in order to safeguard inclusive crisis management.

---

[11] See the overview at the homepage of the Federal Ministry of the Interior: http://www.bmi.gv.at/204/start.aspx, accessed 12.8.2017

[12] See e.g. Federal Chancellery of the Republic of Austria 2013, pp. 5, 7, 10, 11, 13, 18.

[13] See http://www.bmi.gv.at/204_english/start.aspx, accessed 12.8.2017

References

Adger, Neil W./ Hughes, Terry P./ Folke, Carl/ Carpenter, Stephen R./ Rockstrom, Johann (2005) Social-Ecological Resilience to Coastal Disasters. In: Science, Vol. 309, 1036–1039.

Ahrens, Joachim/ Rudolph. Patrick M. (2006) The Importance of Governance in Risk Reduction and Disaster Management. In: Journal of Contingencies and Crisis Management, Vol. 14/4, 207–220.

Antonovsky, Aaron (1987) Unraveling the Mystery of Health – How People Manage Stress and Stay Well, (Jossey-Bass Publishers, San Francisco).

Barnett, Michael/ Walker Peter (2015) Regime Change for Humanitarian Aid: How to Make Relief More Accountable. In: Foreign Affairs, Vol 94, 130–145.

Birkmann, Joern (2007) Risk and vulnerability indicators at different scales: Applicability, usefulness and policy implications. In: Environmental Hazards, Vol. 7/2007, 20-31.

Birkmann, Joern/ Cardona Omar D./ Tibaduiza, Martha L. C./ Welle, Torsten (2013) Framing vulnerability, risk and societal responses: the MOVE framework. In: Natural Hazards, Vol. 67/2013, 193–211.

Bustamante, Jorge A. (2002) Immigrants' Vulnerability as Subjects of Human Rights. In: International Migration Review, Vol 36/2, 333-354.

Carrera, Sergio/ Parkin, Joanna (2011) Protecting and Delivering Fundamental Rights of Irregular Migrants at Local and Regional Levels in the European Union. (Centre for European Policy Studies, Brussels).

Commission for Human Rights of the Council of Europe (2007) The Human Rights of Irregular Migrants in Europe. Issue Paper 2007/1. (Council of Europe, Strasbourg)

Coppola, Damon P. (2015) Introduction to International Disaster Management. 3rd edition. Amsterdam et al (Elsevier)

De Miliano, Cecile/ Faling, Marijn/ Clark-Ginsberg, Aaron/ Crowley, Dominic/ Gibbons, Pat (2015) Resilience: The Holy Grail or Yet Another Hype? In: Gibbons, Pat/ Heintze, Hans-Joachim (eds.): The Humanitarian Challenge. Cham (Springer Publishing), 17–30

Djalante, Riyanti/ Holley, Cameron/ Thomalla, Frank (2011) Adaptive Governance and Managing Resilience to Natural Hazards. In: International Journal for Disaster Risk Science, Vol 2/4, 1–14

Duffield, Mark (1994) Complex Emergencies and the Crisis of Developmentalism. IDS Bulletin 25.4, (Institute of Development Studies, Sussex)

European Commission - DG ECHO (2016) Humanitarian Protection. Improving protection outcomes to reduce risks for people in humanitarian crises. DG ECHO Thematic Policy Document No. 8. Brussels (European Commission). Available at: http://ec.europa.eu/echo/what/humanitarian-aid/policy-guidelines_en. Download: 3.11.2016

Federal Chancellery of the Republic of Austria (2013) Austrian Security Strategy. Security in a new Decade – Shaping Security. Vienna (Federal Chancellery of the Republic of Austria). Available at https://www.bundeskanzleramt.gv.at/sicherheitsstrategie; download 12.8.2017

Fekete, Alexander/ Hufschmidt, Gabriele/ Kruse, Sylvia (2014) Benefits and Challenges of Resilience and Vulnerability for Disaster Risk Management. In: International Journal for Disaster Risk Science, Vol. 5/2014, 3–20

Fletcher, David/ Sarkar, Mustafa (2013) Psychological Resilience. A Review of Definitions, Concepts and Theories. In: European Psychologist, Vol. 18/1, 12-23

Frerks, Georg/ Warner, Jeroen/ Wejs, Bart (2011) The Politics of Vulnerability and Resilience. In: Revista Ambiente & Sociedade, Vol. 14/2, 105–122

Hendow, Maegan/ / Bravi, Alessandra/ Kraler, Albert/ Pailey, Robtel Neajai/ Perchinig, Bernhard/ Schaur, Katharina (2017) Migrants in countries of crises. A comparative study of six crisis situations. Vienna (ICMPD), forthcoming

Lewis, James/ Kelmann, Ilan (2010) Places, people and perpetuity. Community capacities in ecologies of catastrophe. In: ACME – An International E-Journal for Critical Geographies, Vol. 9/2, 191 – 220

Migrants in Countries in Crisis (MICIC) Initiative (2016) Guidelines to Protect Migrants in Countries Experiencing Conflict or Natural Disaster. Geneva (IOM), available at https://micicinitiative.iom.int/sites/default/files/document/micic_guidelines_english_web_13_09_2016.pdf, accessed 22.7.2016

Pandey, Bishnu/ Okazaki, Kenji (2005) Community Based Disaster Management: Empowering Communities to Cope with Disaster Risks. (UN Centre for Regional Development, Tokyo).

Park, J./ Seager T.P./ Rao, P.S.C./ Convertino, M./ Linkov, I. (2013) Integrating Risk and Resilience Approaches to Catastrophe Management in Engineering Systems. In: Risk Analysis, Vol. 33/3, 356 – 367.

Perching, Bernhard/ Rasche, Lucas/ Schaur, Katharina (2017) Humanitarian aid and civil protection policies in the European Union and the MICIC Initiative. Vienna (ICMPD), forthcoming

Perchinig, Bernhard (2016) Actors and stakeholder involvement in crisis mitigation. MICIC Initiative Research Brief. Vienna (ICMPD). Available at: https://micicinitiative.iom.int/sites/default/files/resource_pub/docs/brief_actors_and_stakeholders_final.pdf, accessed 12.06.2017

Robertson-Steel, Iain (2006) Evolution of triage systems. In: Emergency Medicine Journal, Vol. 23/2, 154-1

Statistik Austria (2016) migration & integration. zahlen.daten.indikatoren 2016. Vienna (Statistik Austria)

UNDP (2004) Reducing Disaster Risk. A Challenge for Development. (UNDP/Bureau for Crisis Prevention and Recovery, New York)

UNISDR (2005) Hyogo Framework for Action 2005-2015: Building the Resilience of Nations and Communities to Disasters. New York (UNISDR). Available at https://www.unisdr.org/we/coordinate/hfa, downloaded 22.1.2016

UNISDR (2009) 2009 UNISDR Terminology on Disaster Risk Reduction. New York (UNISDR). Available at https://www.unisdr.org/we/inform/terminology, downloaded 22.1.2016

UNISDR (2015) Sendai Framework for Disaster Risk Reduction. Making the Difference for Poverty, Health and Resilience. New York (UNISDR). Available at http://www.unisdr.org/we/coordinate/sendai-framework, downloaded 22.01.2016

Wisner, Ben/ Blaikie, Piers/ Cannon, Terry/ Davis, Ian (2003) At Risk. Natural hazards, peoples' vulnerability and disaster. (Routledge, London, New York)

Zhou, Hongjian/ Wang, Jing'ai/ Wan, Jinhong/ Jia, Huicong (2010) Resilience to natural hazards: A geographic perspective. In: Natural Hazards, Vol. 53/1, 21-41

Europa am Scheideweg
zwischen Integration und Re-Nationalisierung

Ewald Walterskirchen

Zusammenfassung

Europa braucht mehr Integration, um das Projekt Wirtschafts- und Währungsunion zu einem guten Ende zu führen. Eine politische Union könnte am Ende der Währungsunion stehen. Derzeit gibt es jedoch in den Mitgliedsländern massiven Widerstand gegen eine stärkere Integration. Die einen lehnen die Zuteilung von Flüchtlingen kategorisch ab, für andere kommt eine Transferunion und ein Finanzministerium der EU überhaupt nicht in Frage. Europa steht also am Scheideweg: Politische Union in irgendeiner Form oder Rückkehr zu bloß wirtschaftlicher Zusammenarbeit. Es ist fraglich, ob die Währungsunion die zweite Alternative überleben kann.

Einleitung

Die EU-Kommission wählte für eine ihrer letzten Wirtschaftsprognosen den Titel: *„Moderates Wachstum in schwierigen Zeiten"*. Sind die Zeiten wirklich so schwierig? Der Ausbruch der Finanzkrise liegt immerhin schon 10 Jahre zurück. Mit einiger Verzögerung zeichnet sich nun auch in der Europäischen Union ein wirtschaftlicher Aufschwung ab. Die Zeiten sind heute also eher politisch als wirtschaftlich turbulent.

Die Großbaustellen Europas sind die Flüchtlings- und Migrationskrise, die schwelende Eurokrise, die hohe Jugendarbeitslosigkeit und der EU-Austritt Großbritanniens. Wie können diese Probleme gelöst werden? Die üblichen Hinweise auf den Dublin- und Lissabon-Prozess sowie auf Strukturreformen und Budgetdisziplin der Mitgliedsländer werden wohl nicht ausreichen.

Konjunktureller Rückenwind für die europäische Wirtschaft

Vor einigen Jahren stand die europäische Wirtschaft vor schier unüberwindlichen Schwierigkeiten. Die Europäische Union taumelte von einer Krise in die nächste. Kaum war die Finanzkrise einigermaßen überstanden, setzte die Eurokrise ein. Griechenland und einige andere südeuropäische Länder stürzten unerwartet in eine

Schuldenkrise. Im vergangenen Jahr gesellten sich dann noch die Flüchtlingskrise und der EU-Austritt Großbritanniens dazu.

Heute sieht zumindest die wirtschaftliche Situation wesentlich besser aus. Die Wirtschaft der EU wuchs 2015 und 2016 um rund 2% - 2016 zum ersten Mal seit Jahren nicht mehr langsamer als in den USA. Auch für die Jahre 2017 und 2018 ist mit einem Wachstum von 2% zu rechnen. Das bedeutet eine deutliche Verbesserung gegenüber den Jahren 2007-2013 Von einer wirtschaftlichen Krise kann keine Rede sein. Die entscheidenden Impulse kommen von der Erholung der Weltkonjunktur. Im Frühjahr 2016 ging von China eine deutliche Belebung der Weltkonjunktur aus, die dann auch Südamerika und Russland erfasste (Slater/Szendrei 2017). Ein Drittel der Beschleunigung des Welthandelswachstums geht unmittelbar auf die erhöhten Importe Chinas zurück.

Die fatalen Auswirkungen der Finanzkrise auf die Banken und die Staaten als Retter in letzter Not scheinen nach einem Jahrzehnt im Wesentlichen überwunden zu sein. Reinhart/Rogoff (2009) haben in einer historischen Untersuchung von Finanzkrisen gezeigt, dass es gewöhnlich viele Jahre (oft ein Jahrzehnt) dauert, bis die Volkswirtschaften nach einer Finanzkrise wieder Tritt fassen. Richard Koo (2014) fand eine plausible Erklärung dafür: Die Bilanzen der Wirtschaftsunternehmen und Banken kommen durch die erforderlichen Abschreibungen nach einer Finanzkrise derart durcheinander, dass die Unternehmen jahrelang kaum investieren, sondern ihre Gewinne zur Bilanzkonsolidierung verwenden.

In den letzten zwei Jahren gab der deutliche Wertverlust des Euro gegenüber dem Dollar den Exporten des Euro-Raums neue Impulse, und der niedrige Ölpreis ließ die Inflation gegen Null sinken. Die Realeinkommen legten zu und die Kaufstimmung der Konsumenten verbesserte sich.

Die Wirtschaftspolitik trug auch ihren Teil zur konjunkturellen Erholung bei: Die Fiskalpolitik wirkte - gemessen an der Veränderung des strukturellen Budgetsaldos - in den letzten Jahren nicht mehr restriktiv. Noch wichtiger war aber die ultra-expansive Geldpolitik der EZB. Sie drückte den Eurokurs und verbesserte die Investitionsbereitschaft. Die Europäische Zentralbank verfolgte eine Politik des „Quantitative Easing" und kaufte Staatsanleihen in großen Mengen auf. PopulistInnen in Deutschland kritisierten die damit verbundenen niedrigen Zinssätze freilich als „Enteignung" des deutschen Sparers.

Es ist immer verlockend, die Erholung der Konjunktur einer erfolgreichen Politik zuzuschreiben. Daniel Gros (2017) spricht von der verborgenen Stärke der Eurozone, die mit der „sanften Sparpolitik" zusammenhänge. Dank der Sparpolitik habe die Eurozone eine solide Basis und sei in der glücklichen Lage, den zu erwartenden Aufschwung von einer relativ niedrigen Schuldenquote aus zu starten. Die Schuldenquote liegt im Euro-Raum bei 90%, in den USA bei 107% und in Japan bei über 200%. Entscheidend ist aber nicht die Schuldenquote, sondern wieviel jedes Jahr an Zinsen für die Schulden aufgewendet werden müssen. Interessanterweise zahlt Japan, das großteils Inlandsschulden hat, nicht mehr Zinsen für seine hohe Staatsschuld als der Euro-Raum (jeweils gut 2% des BIP). Daniel Gros betont auch, dass der Aufschwung in der EU ohne fiskalische Konjunkturbelebungsmaßnahmen gelungen sei. Kein Wunder, wenn der Aufschwung von andern Weltregionen ausgeht und die EU Trittbrettfahrerin ist.

Mittelfristige Aussichten

Wie stehen die mittelfristigen Wachstumschancen? Viele Ökonomen und Ökonominnen sorgen sich um das schwache Produktivitätswachstum der letzten Jahre, das sie nicht wirklich erklären können. Dazu kommt das stagnierende inländische Arbeitskräftepotenzial in vielen europäischen Ländern.

Die hohe Arbeitslosigkeit und die prekären Jobs deuten darauf, dass noch viele ungenutzte oder unterbeschäftigte Arbeitskräfte eingegliedert werden können. Auch die hohe Teilzeitbeschäftigung bietet Spielraum zur Ausdehnung des Arbeitsvolumens. Darüber hinaus klopfen mehr MigrantInnen an unsere Türen. Weiters wird der Zustrom von Zuwanderern aus Ostmitteleuropa nach Großbritannien verebben und auf die Euro-Länder umgeleitet werden. Die Bevölkerung im erwerbsfähigen Alter wird zwar in der Eurozone im nächsten Jahrzehnt zurückgehen, aber die Eingliederung von Arbeitslosen, die Zuwanderung und die höhere Erwerbsbeteiligung von Frauen und älteren Personen könnten das mehr als ausgleichen.

Der Hauptgrund für das schwache Produktivitätswachstum ist der Überschuss an Arbeitskräften, der notgedrungen in schlechtbezahlte, wenig produktive Jobs drängt. Verstärkt wird dies noch durch eine schwache Investitionstätigkeit, welche innovative Ideen nur zögerlich in die Realität umsetzt. In Jahren der Hochkonjunktur ist es gerade umgekehrt: Dann steigt die Produktivität, weil die Investitionen boomen und die Arbeitnehmer in produktivere Jobs wechseln können. Für schlecht bezahlte Jobs finden sich dann kaum inländische Bewerber. Rein angebotsseitige Überlegungen (Technologie, Bildung, Flexibilität) bezüglich des Produktivitätswachstums führen in die Irre. Die mittelfristigen Wirtschaftsaussichten für Europa sind nicht so schlecht, wie uns Schätzungen des künftigen Produktionspotenzials weismachen wollen.

Hohe Arbeitslosigkeit:
Eines der großen Probleme der EU

Die Politiker und Politikerinnen könnten sich ja mit der wirtschaftlichen Entwicklung zufriedengeben, wären da nicht die hohen Arbeitslosenzahlen und die Staatsschulden, die durch höheres Wirtschaftswachstum abgebaut werden sollen. Der Erfolg wirtschaftspolitischer Strategien wird meist daran gemessen, wie sich die wirtschaftspolitischen Ziele - Wachstum, Vollbeschäftigung, Preisstabilität und ausgeglichenes Budget - in Relation zu anderen Staaten entwickeln.

In Bezug auf Wachstum und Beschäftigung im internationalen Vergleich machte Europa im letzten Jahrzehnt keine gute Figur. Die steigenden Beschäftigungszahlen zeichnen ein zu rosiges Bild, weil sie auf prekäre und Teilzeitjobs zurückgehen. Die Arbeitslosenquote sinkt im Euro-Raum zwar langsam, sie ist aber mit 9½% im Jahr 2017 noch sehr hoch. Das verursacht beträchtliche Kosten, Unruhen in den Vorstädten und Unmut in den alten Industriegebieten. Viele jugendliche Arbeitslose bleiben ohne Perspektiven.

Die Globalisierung und die technologischen Veränderungen tangieren nicht nur die wenig Qualifizierten, sondern auch die Mittelschichten. Das betrifft ihre Einkommenssituation ebenso wie ihre Beschäftigungschancen.

Für die Wirtschaft bringt die hohe Arbeitslosigkeit gewisse strategische Vorteile: Sie verringert die Macht der Gewerkschaften und verleiht der Forderung nach Arbeitsmarktreformen und Lohnflexibilität mehr Nachdruck. Aber auch die Wirtschaft bekommt die fehlende Kaufkraft zu spüren.

Konservative ÖkonomInnen sehen in mangelnden Strukturreformen auf dem Arbeitsmarkt die Hauptursache der hohen Arbeitslosigkeit. Der renommierte Ökonomieprofessor Charles Wyplosz gab dagegen der von Deutschland initiierten Austerity-Politik die Schuld an Millionen Arbeitslosen in der Europäischen Union. In den USA, wo keine restriktive Fiskalpolitik mitten in der Rezession verfolgt wurde, lag die Arbeitslosenquote in den letzten Jahren etwa halb so hoch wie im Euro-Raum.

Eurokrise schwelt weiter

Der Euro ist zu einer angesehenen und stabilen Währung geworden. Ein Viertel der Währungsreserven der Welt werden in Euro gehalten. Überdies sind wir alle heilfroh, dass wir nicht mehr Geld wechseln müssen, wenn wir ins benachbarte Ausland fahren.

Die Europäische Währungsunion hatte aber einen gravierenden Geburtsfehler: anhaltende Inflationsunterschiede zwischen den alten Weich- und Hartwährungsländern. Diese Unterschiede wurden zwar wesentlich kleiner, sie verschwanden aber nicht völlig. Seit dem Beginn der Währungsunion betrug die Inflationsrate in Deutschland etwa 1%, in Südeuropa 2% bis 3%.

Das hatte zwei Konsequenzen: Erstens verschlechterte sich die preisliche Wettbewerbsfähigkeit Südeuropas Jahr für Jahr. Zweitens waren die Realzinssätze in Südeuropa sehr niedrig, oft sogar negativ: Das verleitete zu hohen Krediten für Wohnungen (Spanien) oder Infrastrukturinvestitionen (Griechenland). Der alte Unterschied zwischen dem Hartwährungs- und dem Weichwährungsblock konnte also nicht völlig beseitigt werden. Das wäre aber die Voraussetzung für eine funktionierende Währungsunion gewesen (Wolf 2014).

Deutschland, das vor fast zwei Jahrzehnten noch als „the sick man of the euro" (Economist, 3.6.1999) bezeichnet wurde, hat seine kostenmäßige Wettbewerbsfähigkeit vor allem durch geringe Lohn- und Preissteigerungen sowie die Agenda 2010 massiv verbessert. In den zehn Jahren vor der Finanzkrise erhöhten sich die nominellen Lohnstückkosten in Deutschland zwischen 1998 und 2008 kumuliert um nur 4%, in Italien dagegen um 30% und in Spanien um 33%. Auf Dauer kann das innerhalb eines Währungsgebiets nicht gut gehen.

Eineinhalb Jahrzehnte lang kam es zu enormen Verschiebungen in der preislichen Wettbewerbsfähigkeit zwischen den Euroländern, die jetzt nicht mehr durch Auf- bzw. Abwertungen korrigiert werden können. Der Euro schützt Deutschland und seine „Satellitenstaaten" vor einer massiven Aufwertung, verhindert aber gleichzeitig eine Abwertung in den südeuropäischen Ländern.

In den letzten Jahren haben die südeuropäischen Länder zwar etwas Terrain gut gemacht, die Niveauunterschiede der Lohnstückkosten sind aber immer noch gewaltig. Eine europaweite Koordinierung der Lohnpolitik wäre für ein reibungsloses Funktionieren der Währungsunion wünschenswert. Das ist jedoch eine Utopie, weil die nationalen Gewerkschaften ihre Autonomie nie aufgeben werden.

Die Länder Südeuropas haben es also in der Vergangenheit nicht geschafft, die Lohn- und Preissteigerungen jenen des Euro-Raums oder gar Deutschlands anzugleichen. Die Hauptgründe sind die größere Streikbereitschaft und die höheren anfänglichen Preissteigerungen, die über inflationsorientierte Lohnforderungen immer weitergewälzt werden. Deutschland hat Südeuropa die Anpassung freilich durch extreme Lohnzurückhaltung bis vor wenigen Jahren stark erschwert.

Leistungsbilanz und Budget

Für die Entwicklung der Leistungsbilanz sind zwei Faktoren entscheidend: die preisliche und strukturelle Wettbewerbsfähigkeit der Wirtschaft sowie die Entwicklung der Inlandsnachfrage in Relation zu den Handelspartnern. Die Leistungsbilanz verbessert sich, wenn die Inlandsnachfrage langsamer als bei den Handelspartnern wächst. Aus diesem zweiten Grund ist die Leistungsbilanz kein geeigneter Gradmesser für die wirtschaftliche Leistungsfähigkeit eines Landes

In Deutschland sind extrem niedrige Lohnsteigerungen, Exporterfolge und schwache Inlandsnachfrage eine explosive Mischung, die zu sehr hohen Leistungsbilanzüberschüssen führt: +8,5% des BIP im Jahr 2016. Man spricht von einer „*internen Abwertung*" Deutschlands durch niedrige Lohnerhöhungen. Präsident Trump lauft gerade dagegen Sturm. In Südeuropa sind dagegen relativ hohe Lohnsteigerungen, Exportschwäche und kräftige Inlandsnachfrage die Garanten für massive Leistungsbilanzdefizite.

Die meisten ÖkonomInnen glaubten, dass die Leistungsbilanzen der einzelnen Euro-Länder in der Währungsunion keine Bedeutung mehr hätten. Es sei ja kein Abwertungsdruck mehr zu befürchten. Die Eurokrise hat die ÖkonomInnen jedoch eines Besseren belehrt: Es wird bei hohen Leistungsbilanz- und Budgetdefiziten nicht auf eine Abwertung, sondern auf einen Staatsbankrott spekuliert. Die Leistungsbilanz bleibt also auch im Euro-Raum höchst relevant.

Es besteht ein enger Zusammenhang zwischen Budget- und Leistungsbilanzdefiziten („twin deficits"). Jene Euro-Länder, die eine stark passive Leistungsbilanz haben, weisen besonders hohe Budgetdefizite auf. Dagegen haben Deutschland, Norwegen, Schweiz, Dänemark und Schweden hohe Leistungsbilanzüberschüsse und deshalb auch eine vergleichsweise günstigere Budgetsituation.

Die Kausalrichtung ist nicht eindeutig. Oft verläuft sie von der Leistungsbilanz zum Budget: Eine Verschlechterung der Wettbewerbsfähigkeit bremst die wirtschaftliche Entwicklung eines Landes. Durch Steuer- und Abgabenausfälle werden in der Folge hohe Budgetdefizite „erlitten".

Andererseits können aber auch exzessive Staatsausgaben (z.b. in Griechenland) die Inlandsnachfrage anheizen und zu überproportional hohen Importen (z.b. von Waffen und U-Booten) führen. Dieser Einflussfaktor ist aber innerhalb der Währungsunion meist weniger wichtig als die Wettbewerbsfähigkeit.

Man kann dieses Problem auch von der Zahlungsbilanz her sehen: Ein Exportüberschuss bedeutet definitionsgemäß, dass ein Land mehr spart als es investiert. Der Weltwirtschaft tut es gut, wenn Defizitländer mehr sparen und Überschussländer mehr investieren. Das hat auch der Internationale Währungsfonds wiederholt festgestellt.

Der Zusammenhang zwischen Leistungsbilanz- und Budgetdefiziten wurde in der Europäischen Union vernachlässigt. Budgetdefizite wurden bloß einer „liederlichen" Budgetpolitik zugeschrieben, makroökonomische Ungleichgewichte wurden lange Zeit negiert. Es besteht kein Zweifel, dass Überschüsse in der Leistungsbilanz ebenso ein Problem darstellen wie Defizite.

Die Finanzkrise hat den Bemühungen um Budgetkonsolidierung im Euro-Raum einen Strich durch die Rechnung gemacht. Die Regierungen des Euro-Raums hatten es zwischen 1997 und 2007 geschafft, die Staatsschuldenquote von 81% auf 71% des BIP zu senken und damit dem Maastricht-Ziel (60%) näher zu kommen. Die Kosten der Finanzkrise blähten jedoch die Verschuldung wieder auf: Die Staatsschuldenquote stieg im Euro-Raum um ein Drittel auf 97% des BIP im Jahr 2011.

Eurokrise: Ursachen und Folgen

Die Eurokrise brach im Jahr 2010 aus: Die finanzielle Stabilität einiger Euroländer geriet in Gefahr. Im Juli 2012 gelang es dem EZB-Präsidenten Mario Draghi, die Lage durch ein mutiges Statement zu beruhigen: Er werde alles tun („whatever it takes"), um die gemeinsame Währung zu retten. Die Finanzmärkte vertrauten seinem Wort.

Mit seltener Einmütigkeit hat sich eine große Zahl von Ökonomen verschiedener theoretischer Richtungen auf eine Ursache geeinigt (Baldwin/Giavazzi 2015). Der entscheidende Grund für die Eurokrise war ein *„Sudden Stop"* der massiven Kapitalströme vom Zentrum der EU in die Peripherie nach Südeuropa. Plötzliche Verunsicherung führte zu diesem *„Sudden Stop"* der Kapitalströme und löste die Krise aus. Der Mechanismus war somit ähnlich wie bei den Krisen in Lateinamerika und Südostasien.

Frankreich, Italien und Spanien reagierten auf die Krise mit einer verstärkten Spaltung des Arbeitsmarktes. Während die Beschäftigten bei hoher Streikbereitschaft ihre Rechte weitgehend sichern konnten, wurden den Neueintretenden überwiegend prekäre Jobs angeboten. Der Begriff „1000-Euro-Generation" macht heute in Südeuropa die Runde.

Die langfristigen Chancen für die Jugend haben sich damit massiv verschlechtert. Eine Generation mit prekären Jobs, von denen sie nicht leben und kaum Pensionsansprüche erwerben kann, wächst in Südeuropa – und nicht nur dort - heran.

Die Länder Südeuropas brauchen eine Wachstumsstrategie. Dabei geht es nicht nur um Strukturreformen, sondern auch um Exportförderung, Anreize für die Ansiedlung von Unternehmen, Importstopp für Waffenkäufe etc.

Die anhaltenden Schwierigkeiten italienischer Banken, die Diskussionen um einen Schuldenerlass für Griechenland und die hohe Jugendarbeitslosigkeit in Südeuropa erinnern uns daran, dass die Eurokrise noch nicht überwunden ist.

Neben dem kleinen Griechenland ist das große Italien ein zentrales Problem des Euroraums. Den Griechen konnte man noch drohen, sie aus dem Euroraum hinauszuwerfen. Ein Austritt Italiens würde dagegen den Euroraum destabilisieren. Die italienische Wirtschaft stagniert seit einem Jahrzehnt. Sie ist vor allem gegenüber osteuropäischen Autozulieferern und chinesischen Textilproduzenten nicht konkurrenzfähig. Trotz kräftiger Einsparungen sind die öffentlichen Finanzen in einer schwierigen Situation. Das Budgetdefizit lag 2016 bei (nur) 2½% des BIP. Die Staatsschuldenquote erreichte jedoch 133%, und der Zinsaufwand für die Staatsschuld machte 4% des BIP aus - doppelt so viel wie in der EU. Das Primärbudget (ohne Zinszahlungen) weist in Italien einen ebenso hohen Überschuss wie in Deutschland auf.

Die populistische Fünf-Sterne-Bewegung hat ein Referendum über den Verbleib Italiens im Euroraum (nicht in der EU) angekündigt. Wenn Italien für einen Austritt aus dem Euroraum stimmen sollte, dann wäre die gesamte Währungsunion in Gefahr. Denn die neue Währung würde gegenüber dem Euro stark abwerten und Italien könnte seine hohen Euro-Auslandsschulden nicht mehr zur Gänze begleichen. Das Szenario eines Austritts Italiens aus der Währungsunion ist allerdings unwahrscheinlich.

Wirtschafts- und sozialpolitische Aspekte

Insgesamt stimmt es optimistisch, dass die sozialpolitischen Errungenschaften Europas trotz der Finanzkrise, der Eurokrise und der Austeritypolitik in den meisten Ländern weitgehend erhalten werden konnten. Nur in Griechenland kam es unter dem Diktat der Troika zu einem Kahlschlag von Löhnen, Pensionen und Leistungen des Gesundheitswesens. Erinnerungen an die Argentinienkrise wurden wach. Wir können daraus folgende Lehren ziehen, welche die ostasiatischen Länder schon lange gezogen haben: Anhaltende Leistungsbilanzdefizite müssen vermieden werden, weil sie von ausländischen Kapitalgebern abhängig machen. Wenn ein Land Notkredite vom Internationalen Währungsfonds benötigt, dann werden ihm die Daumenschrauben angesetzt. Budgetdefizite sollten wie in Japan möglichst im Inland finanzierbar sein. Dann handelt es sich primär um ein Verteilungsproblem zwischen Staat und privatem Sektor.

Martin Wolf (2014), Chefkommentator der Financial Times, hielt es für einen Fehler, eine gemeinsame Währung ohne politische Union einzuführen. Der Euro sei letztlich schuld an der europäischen Krise. Die Deutschen haben davor gewarnt, aber die Franzosen und Italiener wollten die Währungsunion unbedingt.

Jetzt sind die Deutschen die Hauptprofiteure, die Italiener (neben den Griechen) die Hauptleidtragenden.

Martin Wolf argumentiert, dass die Austeritypolitik keinen Sinn macht für die Eurozone, sie kann nur für ein kleines offenes Land angewendet werden. In Deutschland werde die schwache Inlandsnachfrage durch China ausgeglichen. Das deutsche Export-Modell sei nicht auf eine kontinentale Wirtschaft anzuwenden.

Für den Euro-Raum seien gemeinsame Anleihen (Eurobonds) ein zentrales Anliegen. Man könne keine Bankenunion ohne Eurobonds haben. Wenn man eine gemeinsame Währung hat, muss man auch die Schulden teilen – meint Martin Wolf. Deshalb müsse die EU ja noch nicht ein Bundesstaat wie die USA werden, aber zumindest eine Föderation wie die Schweiz. Die Schweiz hat ein gemeinsames Schulden- und Währungssystem und eine föderale Staatskassa. Das brauche die EU auch. Deutschland sträubt sich aber vehement gegen ein gemeinsames europäisches Schuldenregime.

Deutschland will mit der Austeritypolitik sicherstellen, dass die deutschen Banken ihr Geld wieder zurückbekommen. Die Wirtschaft in Italien und Griechenland kommt damit aber nicht wirklich voran. Auch für deutsche ÖkonomInnen (Becker/Fuest 2017) hat die Kontrolle der Staatsschulden – neben der effektiven Regulierung der Banken - Vorrang, um die Eurokrise endlich zu überwinden.

Brexit und die Freizügigkeit der Arbeitskräfte

Während im Jahr 2010 die Finanzmärkte die Existenz der Währungsunion in Frage stellten, tun dies heute die Wähler (Walterskirchen 2017). Populistische Anti-Europa-Parteien, die gegen Zuwanderung hetzen, gibt es nicht nur in England, sondern auch in Frankreich, Italien und Österreich. Der klare Sieg von Macron in Frankreich scheint diesen Parteien jedoch einen Dämpfer versetzt zu haben. Die osteuropäischen Staaten sind positiv zur EU eingestellt, sie mauern jedoch gegen Flüchtlinge und AsylbewerberInnen. Polen und Ungarn weichen in ihren Rechtsvorstellungen von der EU ab.

In Großbritannien haben ältere Menschen und die Landbevölkerung für einen Austritt aus der EU gestimmt. Sie sahen offenbar ihren Lebensstil durch das Fremde, durch die massive Zuwanderung, bedroht. Die Jungen und die Londoner stimmten für einen Verbleib Großbritanniens.

Das Brexit-Votum hat große politische und wirtschaftliche Unsicherheit ausgelöst und wirkt sich schon im Vorfeld negativ auf die britische Wirtschaft aus. Der Finanzplatz London ist jedenfalls vom Brexit betroffen. Aber auch viele amerikanische und japanische Unternehmen, die Großbritannien als Einfallstor zum EU-Markt sahen, sind verunsichert.

Es ist mit schwierigen Verhandlungen zu rechnen. Harter Brexit heißt keine Teilnahme am Binnenmarkt, sondern ein eigenes Handelsabkommen mit Großbritannien. Gleichzeitig können die BritInnen die Zuwanderung aus der EU kontrollieren und Arbeitskräfte aus EU-Ländern ausweisen. Sanfter Brexit bedeutet Teilnahme am EU-Binnenmarkt oder an einer Zollunion, aber begrenzte Kontrolle der Zuwanderung aus der EU.

Der Austritt Großbritanniens aus der EU ist zweifellos ein Fehler. Der Hauptgrund für das Brexit-Votum der Briten war die freie Zuwanderung von Arbeitskräften aus der Europäischen Union, die zu jener aus dem ehemaligen Commonwealth hinzukam. Mehr als 900.000 PolInnen und 230.000 RumänInnen leben und arbeiten heute in Großbritannien.

Bis zu einem gewissen Schwellenwert bringt die Arbeitskräftemigration beiden Seiten Vorteile. Jenseits dieser Schwelle werden dagegen die Integrationsfähigkeit und -bereitschaft eines Landes durch Asylbewerber sowie Zuwanderer aus der EU überfordert. Besonders problematisch wird die Situation, wenn sich die Zuwanderung auf wenige Länder konzentriert.

Die völlige Freiheit des Binnenmarktes funktioniert auch bei den Kapitalbewegungen nicht klaglos. Typische Ausnahmefälle sind Zypern und Griechenland. Für stark konzentrierte Kapital- und Wanderungsbewegungen gilt im Grunde das Gleiche. Je früher überbordende Zahlungs- und Migrationsströme gestoppt werden, umso eher können Krisen verhindert werden.

Europäische Union am Scheideweg: Politische Einheit oder bloß wirtschaftlicher Zusammenschluss?

Die Europäische Union befindet sich in einer „Existenzkrise" (Juncker). Sie muss sich neu aufstellen, denn die Hoffnungen der Bevölkerung auf steigenden Wohlstand und innere Sicherheit haben sich nicht erfüllt. Zu den Prioritäten einer „neuen EU" sollten nicht nur Bankenunion und Zukunftsinvestitionen (Aiginger 2016), sondern auch eine neue Finanz- und Migrationspolitik gehören.

Der renommierte Ökonomieprofessor Paul de Grauwe schreibt in einem Standard-Artikel (2017, S.19): *„Der Euro hat versagt – besonders in Italien".* Wir müssen eine politische Union schaffen. Es geht nicht nur um eine einheitliche Geldpolitik der EZB, sondern auch um die Fiskalpolitik. Wir brauchen Eurobonds, d.h. eine gemeinsame Anleihe für alle Länder. Dafür brauchen wir eine Euro-Regierung. Ohne politische Union ist der Euro irgendwann Geschichte. *„Wer nun keine budgetäre Union will, sollte zurück zu seiner nationalen Währung gehen."* Auch eine gemeinsame Arbeitslosenversicherung könnte stabilisierend wirken. De Grauwe schlägt vor, dass die gemeinsamen Ausgaben der Eurozone 5 bis 10% der Wirtschaftsleistung ausmachen sollten. Derzeit hat die EU ein Budget von 1% des BIP.

Die Kommission in Brüssel mit ihren Detailvorschriften („Gurkenkrümmung") wird immer häufiger zur Zielscheibe der Frustration in der Bevölkerung. Präsident Juncker reagierte darauf mit einem Weißbuch, das fünf verschiedene Wege zur Weiterentwicklung der EU aufzeigte. Dani Rodrik (2017, S.1) kritisiert an der Position der EU-Kommission, dass sie sich um die zentrale Frage drücke: *„Either political integration catches up with economic integration or economic integration needs to be scaled back."* Auch der US-Ökonom Kenneth Rogoff (2017, S.1) schreibt *„The Eurozone Must Reform or Die [...] The status quo is probably not sustainable."*

Vertiefung der Währungsunion

Im Reflexionspapier zur weiteren Vertiefung der Währungsunion hat die European Commission (2017) eine Reihe von Reformvorschlägen unterbreitet. Sie hat auch ein Finanzministerium für die Eurozone mit eigenem Budget andiskutiert, das nicht nur die Budgetkontrolle, sondern auch die makroökonomische Stabilisierung für die Eurozone übernehmen sollte. Emmanuel Macron, der einige der besten französischen Ökonomen (Jean Pisani-Ferry, Philippe Martin) als Berater hat, ließ schon mit einem ähnlichen Vorschlag aufhorchen. *„Der vorsichtige Vorschlag eines Finanzministeriums für die Eurozone erscheint zunächst durchaus diskussionswürdig.* (Pekanov/Schratzenstaller 2017, S.4). Aus Deutschland hört man freilich bisher nur ein striktes Nein zu dieser Frage.

Pekanow/Schratzenstaller kritisieren am Papier der EU-Kommission, dass die soziale Dimension ausgespart wird. Es wird nur die europäische Säule sozialer Rechte kurz erwähnt. Buti/Pichelmann (2017) argumentieren, dass die EU bloß ein Agent der Globalisierung sei, weil sie keine Kompetenz habe, Verteilungseffekte anzusprechen.

Eine politische Union könnte die Währungsunion sicherlich stabilisieren, d.h. eine Budgetunion, Eurobonds, eine vollständige Bankenunion, eine gemeinsame Arbeitslosenversicherung usw. Deutschland ist aber - als betroffenes Land - nicht dazu bereit und wird auch in Zukunft nicht dazu bereit: Nur keine Transferunion. Generell besteht derzeit eine ablehnende Haltung der Bevölkerung in der EU gegen weitere Integrationsschritte mit Autonomieverlust an Brüssel: Ein Kampf der nationalen Massen gegen die globalen Eliten.

Die Alternative dazu könnte ein Zerfall der Währungsunion sein, d.h. konkret ein Austritt Italiens aus der Eurozone – wie Beppe Grillo fordert. Derzeit sieht es nicht danach aus. Aber in der nächsten Rezession, wenn die Finanzanleger wieder ihr Geld aus Italien und Südeuropa zurückziehen werden, könnte es so weit sein. Deutschland wird dann gemeinsam mit Brüssel noch drastischere Austerity- Programme von Italien und Griechenland fordern. Es ist nicht auszuschließen, dass die Bevölkerung dann den Populisten in die Arme läuft.

Derzeit weckt der überlegene Wahlsieg von Emmanuel Macron große Hoffnungen in Frankreich und der Europäischen Union. Frankreich könnte wieder ein gleichrangiger Partner Deutschlands in der EU werden. Dazu wäre es hilfreich, wenn Macron und sein Team mehr Budgetspielraum bekäme, um Reformen durchzuführen. Macrons Sieg hat auch die Diskussion um ein EU-Finanzministerium und Eurobonds wieder angeheizt.

Die vier Grundfreiheiten: Befristete Ausnahmen?

In der EU wird möglichst viel durch Regeln bestimmt. „Rules rather than discretion" lautet die Devise. Willkürliche Politik und Ausnahmeregelungen werden möglichst vermieden. Bei der Lösung neuer Probleme helfen jedoch die alten Regeln (z.B. Dublin-Prozess für die Flüchtlingsfrage) nichts. Es müssen politische Entscheidungen getroffen werden.

Der freie Binnenmarkt ist das Glaubensbekenntnis der Europäischen Union. Daran darf nicht gerüttelt werden. Die vier Grundfreiheiten für den Waren-, Dienstleistungs-, Kapital- und Personenverkehr gelten als unantastbar. Für die EU ist deshalb die freie Zuwanderung von Arbeitskräften aus anderen EU-Ländern nicht verhandelbar, selbst wenn sie massive Verwerfungen im Arbeitsmarkt- und Sozialbereich verursacht.

Das Problem der Arbeitsmigration innerhalb des Binnenmarktes liegt – ähnlich wie bei den AsylbewerberInnen – darin, dass sich die Zuwanderung stark auf bestimmte Länder (z.B. Großbritannien, Deutschland, Österreich, Skandinavien) konzentriert.

Die Auswanderung von Arbeitskräften aus EU-Staaten in die übrige EU (als Ganzes) sollte ungehindert bleiben. Aber einzelne EU-Staaten, die unter der Konzentration der Zuwanderung leiden, sollten das Recht erhalten, ausnahmsweise Obergrenzen einzuführen bzw. den Zustrom von Arbeitskräften auf eine befristete Zeit zu beschränken. Wenn Großbritannien vor dem Votum eine befristete Ausnahmeregelung erhalten hätte, wäre der Brexit wahrscheinlich verhindert worden.

Wenn sich die auswanderungswilligen Osteuropäer in Zukunft auf kleine europäische Länder konzentrieren, weil ihnen der Zutritt nach Großbritannien verwehrt wird, dann können sich diese Länder nicht dagegen wehren – außer durch Austritt. Die ultraliberalen Regeln der EU züchten geradezu den Nationalismus und Populismus in Europa. Die EU riskiert eher einen Zerfall als über begründete und befristete Ausnahmen von ihren Binnenmarktregeln - d.h. vom freien Zustrom von Arbeitskräften - zu verhandeln. Zu befristeten Ausnahmen von der „Grundfreiheit des Personenverkehrs" für bestimmte Einwanderungsländer sind Brüssel und die Oststaaten keinesfalls bereit.

Literatur

Aiginger, K. (2016), New Dynamics for Europe: reaping the benefits of socio-ecological transition, Brussels

Baldwin R., Giavazzi F., eds. (2015), The Eurozone Crisis: A Consensus View of the Causes and a Few Possible Solutions, CEPR e-book

Becker, J., Fuest, C. (2017), Der Odysseuskomplex. Ein pragmatischer Vorschlag zur Lösung der Eurokrise, Hanser, München

Buti, M., Pichelmann, K. (2017), European integration and populism: Addressing Dahrendorf's quandary, VOX CEPR's Policy Portal, 22 February

De Grauwe, Paul (2017), Der Euro hat versagt – besonders in Italien, DerStandard, 7. Juni

Eichengreen, B., Wyplosz, Ch. (2017) Europe's Fiscal Conundrum, in Giavazzi, F., Benassy-Quéré, A. (eds.), Europe's Political Spring: Fixing the Eurozone and Beyond, CEPR e-book

European Commission (2017), Reflection Paper on the Deepening of the European Economic and Monetary Union, Brussels

Gros, D. (2017), The Eurozone's Hidden Strength, Social Europe, 7 June

Koo, R. (2014), The Escape from Balance Sheet Recession, Wiley

Pekanov, A., Schratzenstaller, M. (2017), Mehr Pragmatismus, weniger Dogmatismus – Der schwierige, aber nötige Weg zur Vollendung der Wirtschafts- und Währungsunion. Wien. ÖGfE Policy Brief 15'2017

Reinhart, C., Rogoff, K. (2009), This Time is Different. Eight Centuries of Financial Folly, Princeton

Rodrik, D. (2017), How much Europe can Europe tolerate? Project Syndicate, 14 March

Rogoff, K. (2017), The Eurozone Must Reform or Die, Project Syndicate, 14 June

Slater,A., Szendrei V. (2017), China-commodity nexus at the heart of global upturn, Oxford Economics, Global Research-Briefing, June

Walterskirchen, E. (2017), Die wirtschaftlichen Probleme der Europäischen Union, in: Österreichisches Jahrbuch für Politik 2016, Böhlau, Wien

Wolf, M. (2014), The Shifts and the Shocks, Allen Lane, London

TEIL 3:
AUSWIRKUNGEN DER FLUCHTMIGRATION

Ökonomische und fiskalische Auswirkungen der Fluchtmigration in Österreich

Johannes Berger, Ludwig Strohner

Zusammenfassung

Österreich und Europa erlebten in den vergangenen Jahren eine starke Zuwanderung von Asylwerber/inne/n, insbesondere aus Syrien, Afghanistan und dem Irak. Neben Schweden und Deutschland ist Österreich das Land der Europäischen Union mit der stärksten Zuwanderung relativ zur Bevölkerung.

In diesem Beitrag werden die ökonomischen und fiskalischen Effekte dieser Migration für Österreich untersucht. Dabei ist festzuhalten, dass Asyl primär unter humanitären und nicht unter ökonomischen Gesichtspunkten zu sehen ist. Dennoch müssen die wirtschaftlichen und fiskalischen Effekte von Beginn an mitgedacht werden. Die Analyse erfolgt auf Basis des Makromodells PuMA von EcoAustria. Untersucht wird die Fluchtmigration der besonders zuwanderungsstarken Jahre 2013-2018, die Auswirkungen auf fiskalische und ökonomische Größen werden bis zum Jahr 2020 ermittelt. Gemäß den Modellergebnissen wird die Beschäftigung aufgrund der Fluchtmigration (der Jahre 2013 bis 2018) bis 2020 um 1% oder 40.000 Personen stärker zunehmen, als es ohne Fluchtmigration der Fall wäre. Das reicht aber nicht aus, um den deutlichen Anstieg des Arbeitskräfteangebots, insbesondere bei Geringqualifizierten, vollständig in Beschäftigung zu bringen. Insgesamt wird die Arbeitslosenquote gemäß den Analysen bis zum Jahr 2020 um 0,4 Prozentpunkte höher ausfallen als ohne Fluchtmigration. Dies trifft primär die Gruppe der Flüchtlinge selbst. Unter den Ansässigen ändert sich die durchschnittliche Arbeitslosenquote hingegen kaum. In einem gewissen Ausmaß werden allerdings geringqualifizierte Ansässige verdrängt. Die Zuwanderung von Flüchtlingen führt zu zusätzlichem privaten Konsum und Investitionen und erhöht das BIP. Da die Bevölkerung aber stärker zunimmt, dämpft die Fluchtmigration das BIP pro Kopf.

Angesichts der starken ökonomischen Effekte sind auch die fiskalischen Auswirkungen der Fluchtmigration beträchtlich. Sowohl die öffentlichen Einnahmen, als auch die öffentlichen Aufwendungen nehmen signifikant zu. Nachdem die Aufwendungen stärker zunehmen, ist der Netto-Effekt auf den Budgetsaldo in der vorgenommenen kurz- und mittelfristigen Betrachtung negativ. Die stärksten Effekte ergeben sich in den Jahren 2016-2018 mit einem negativen Saldo von jeweils 0,4-0,5% des BIP. In den Folgejahren verbessert sich der Saldo jedoch deutlich, was zum einen auf den Wegfall mancher öffentlicher Aufwendungen, zum anderen auf die schrittweise Integration in den Arbeitsmarkt zurückzuführen ist.

Die vorgelegten Befunde dürfen allerdings nicht allgemein auf Migration übertragen werden. Vielmehr zeigen eine Reihe von Untersuchungen positive Auswirkungen von Migration, insbesondere bei höherqualifizierter Zuwanderung.

Die volkswirtschaftlichen Effekte fallen positiver aus, je stärker Qualifikationsmaßnahmen greifen und je rascher die Integration in den Arbeitsmarkt gelingt. Aus diesem Grund sollten Aktivierungs- und Qualifikationsmaßnahmen für Asylberechtigte und -werber/innen mit hoher Bleibewahrscheinlichkeit früh beginnen. Durch den hohen Anteil an jungen Asylwerber/inne/n besteht die Chance, die unterdurchschnittliche Qualifikationsstruktur durch Aus- und Weiterbildung noch zu verbessern.

Einleitung und Motivation

Österreich und Europa erlebten in den vergangenen Jahren eine starke Zuwanderung von Asylwerber/inne/n. Dieses Thema nimmt in der medialen und politischen Diskussion einen sehr breiten Raum ein. Dabei macht die Migration von Flüchtlingen nur einen Teil des Zu- und Wegzugs von Personen aus.

Bei der Nettomigration nach Österreich, also der Differenz aus Zuzügen aus dem Ausland und Wegzügen ins Ausland, können für die letzten 30 Jahren drei Phasen verstärkter Nettozuwanderung nach Österreich unterschieden werden: Die erste Phase steht im Zusammenhang mit der Jugoslawien-Krise Anfang der 1990er Jahre. Im Jahr 1991 erreichte die Nettomigration mit 77.000 Personen einen ersten Höhepunkt. Die zweite Periode stärkerer Nettozuwanderung, die nach der Jahrtausendwende einsetzte, ist auf einen Anstieg bei den Asylanträgen sowie auf die verstärkte Ost-Integration der Europäischen Union zurückzuführen.

Schließlich zeigte sich in den letzten Jahren wieder ein kräftiger Anstieg der Nettozuwanderung. Dieser wurde zunächst von der Arbeitsmarktöffnung für die neuen Mitgliedstaaten der EU ausgelöst und in der Folge vom starken Zustrom von Flüchtlingen verstärkt. Dadurch ergibt sich im Jahr 2015 eine Nettozuwanderung nach Österreich im Ausmaß von 113.000 Personen. Im Jahr 2016 nahm die Nettomigration auf 65.000 Personen ab, lag aber dennoch deutlich über dem langjährigen Durchschnitt. Beachtlich ist die starke Dynamik der Wanderungsbewegungen im betrachteten Zeitraum: die Zahl der Wegzüge aus Österreich lag seit 1995 immer über 60.000 Personen jährlich und erreichte zuletzt sogar mehr als 100.000 Personen.

Ökonomische und fiskalische Auswirkungen der Fluchtmigration in Österreich 171

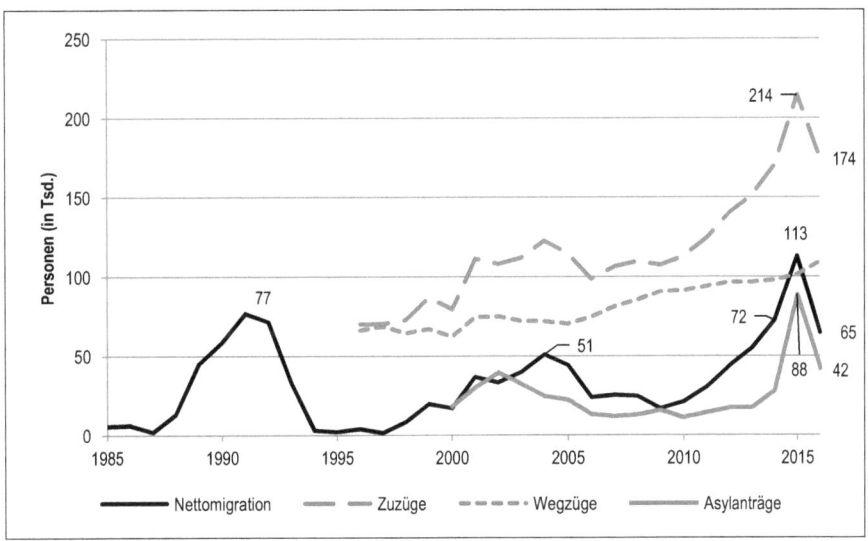

Abbildung 1 Internationale Zu- und Abwanderungen Österreichs 1985-2016
Quelle: Statistik Austria, Asylstatistik BMI.

Asylanträge waren in der Vergangenheit von geringerer Bedeutung, wie Abbildung 1 zeigt. Ab dem Jahr 2014 nahm die Zahl der Asylanträge deutlich zu und erreichte im Jahr 2015 ein Ausmaß von 88.300 Personen. Im Jahr 2016 hat sich die Situation etwas beruhigt, die Zahl der Asylanträge betrug aber immerhin noch 42.100.

In der Europäischen Union insgesamt wurden im Zeitraum 2015 bis inklusive April 2017 2,8 Millionen Asylanträge gestellt. Beinahe die Hälfte dieser Anträge (1,3 Millionen) entfielen auf Deutschland, gefolgt von Italien, Ungarn, Schweden und Frankreich mit jeweils rund 200.000 Anträgen und Österreich mit 140.000 Anträgen. Entscheidend ist insbesondere die Zahl der Asylanträge relativ zur Wohnbevölkerung. Die 2,8 Millionen Anträge entsprechen einem Anteil von 0,55% der Bevölkerung der EU. Demgegenüber stehen Ungarn, Schweden, Österreich und Deutschland mit einer deutlich höheren relativen Betroffenheit.[1] In Österreich zum Beispiel belief sich das Ausmaß auf 1,6% der Wohnbevölkerung.

Der vorliegende Beitrag untersucht die volkswirtschaftlichen und fiskalischen Auswirkungen der Fluchtmigration in Österreich. Zunächst werden Befunde zur Struktur bzw. den Eigenschaften von Asylwerber/inne/n aufbereitet. Im darauf-

---

[1] Die Zahlen für Ungarn sind hinsichtlich der Auswirkungen auf die Integration von Flüchtlingen mit Vorsicht zu interpretieren. Im Sommer 2015 wurden dort sehr viele Asylanträge gestellt, die Asylwerber/innen sind aber in der Folge zu großen Teilen nach Deutschland, Schweden und Österreich gewandert.

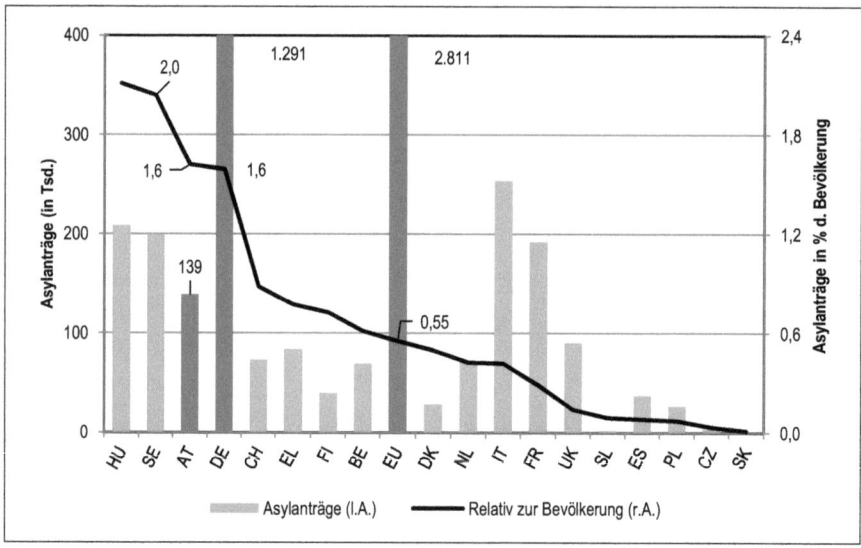

Abbildung 2 Asylanträge in Europa, 2015-April 2017

Quelle: Eurostat, eigene Berechnungen, „Skalierung" auf 400.000 Anträge zur besseren Übersichtlichkeit.

folgenden Kapitel werden die volkswirtschaftlichen Auswirkungen der Fluchtmigration in Österreich auf Basis des makroökonomischen Modells PuMA analysiert. Anschließend werden die fiskalischen Auswirkungen der Fluchtmigration untersucht. Schließlich werden arbeitsmarktpolitische Empfehlungen abgegeben.

Herkunft und Struktur der Asylwerbenden

Herkunft und Anerkennungsquoten

Von 2015 bis Juli 2017 stammen rund zwei Drittel aller Asylwerber/innen in Österreich (145.300) aus den drei Haupt-Herkunftsländern Afghanistan (39.600), Syrien (38.100) und Irak (17.300).

Die Anerkennungsquoten im Asylverfahren unterscheiden sich stark nach dem Herkunftsland. Berücksichtigt man neben positiven Asylentscheidungen auch die Gewährung von subsidiärem Schutz und humanitärem Aufenthalt als *positive Anerkennungen*, so enden mehr als 90% der Verfahren bei Personen aus Syrien mit einem Aufenthaltstitel, aber nur jeweils rund 50% bei Personen aus Afghanis-

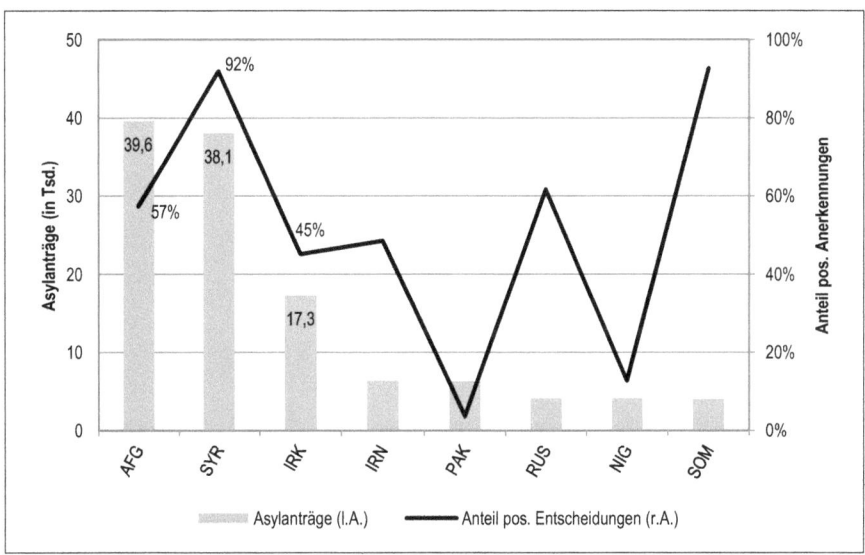

Abbildung 3 Asylanträge und Anteil positiver Entscheidungen 2015 bis Juli 2017 nach Herkunftsland, acht bedeutendste Herkunftsländer

Quelle: Asylstatistik BMI, eigene Berechnungen.

tan bzw. Irak und Iran.[2] Insgesamt wurden 2015 bis Juli 2017 64.536 *positive* Entscheidungen getroffen, der Großteil davon Asylgewährungen (49.617; außerdem 10.466 Subsidiärer Schutz und 4.453 humanitäre Aufenthaltstitel). Zu beachten ist auch die hohe Anzahl sogenannter Sonstiger Entscheidungen. Rund 24.000 Asylverfahren endeten in diesem Zeitraum mit einer sogenannten Sonstigen Entscheidung, das heißt z.B. mit einer Einstellung des Verfahrens, weil sich die Person nicht mehr in Österreich aufhält.

Altersstruktur und Geschlecht

Bemerkenswert ist die außergewöhnlich junge Altersstruktur der Asylwerber/innen in den letzten Jahren. Knapp 40% sind jünger als 18 Jahre und nur 15% sind älter als 35 Jahre. Im Vergleich dazu sind nur 17% der österreichischen Bevölkerung jünger als 18 Jahre, aber 60% älter als 35 Jahre. Zudem sind rund 70% der Asylwerber/innen männlich.

---

[2] Die in der Abbildung dargestellten Asylanträge und Entscheidungen beziehen sich jeweils auf den Zeitraum 2015 bis Juli 2017. Dadurch sind bei den Entscheidungen auch Personen berücksichtigt, die vor 2015 einen Antrag gestellt haben. Gleichzeitig liegen für viele Asylanträge aus den Jahren 2015 bis 2017 noch keine Entscheidungen vor.

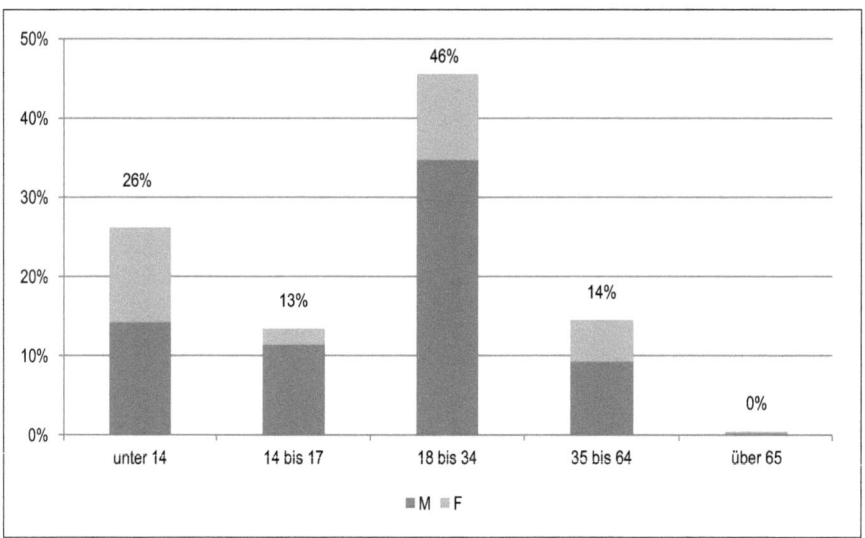

Abbildung 4 Asylanträge 2015 bis Juni 2017 in Österreich nach Alter und Geschlecht

Quelle: Eurostat.

Quelle	Gruppe	Geringe Qualifikation	Mittlere Qualifikation	Hohe Qualifikation
Central Bureau of Statistics Syria	Gesamtbevölkerung Syrien	77,9%	12,6%	9,5%
Battisti und Felbermayr (2015)	Umfrage unter Flüchtlingen in der Türkei	80,0%	11,1%	8,9%
IAB, Brücker (2015) (DE)	SV-Pflichtig Beschäftigte und Erwerbslose	71,0%	8,0%	8,0%
BAMF (2016) (DE); Gewichtung n. Anerkennung in Ö	**Befragung unter Flüchtlingen in D**	59,2%	23,0%	17,8%
AMS Kompetenzcheck (2017); Gewichtung n. Anerkennung in Ö	Kompetenzcheck alle TeilnehmerInnen	48,5%	30,4%	21,1%
AMS Kompetenzcheck (2017)	Kompetenzcheck SyrerInnen	38,0%	37,0%	25,0%
Vergleich: Wohnbevölkerung 25-64 in Österreich		**17,0%**	**62,4%**	**20,6%**

Einteilung in 3 Bildungsgruppen von den Autoren vorgenommen entsprechend ISCED (1997): Gering ISCED 0-2, Mittel ISCED 3-4, Hoch ISCED 5+. Differenzen zu 100%: keine Angaben.
Die dargestellten Untersuchungen beziehen sich überwiegend auf Volljährige, die dementsprechend ihre Ausbildung schon abgeschlossen haben. Daher wird hier der Vergleich mit der Bevölkerung zwischen 25 und 64 Jahren in Ö durchgeführt.

Tabelle 1 Befunde zur Bildungsstruktur von Asylwerber/inne/n

Quellen: diverse (siehe Spalte 1).

Bildungsstruktur

In Bezug auf die Bildungsstruktur von Asylwerber/inne/n besteht eine gewisse Unsicherheit, die sich auch in der medialen Diskussion widerspiegelt. Mehrere Quellen und Informationen, etwa die Bildungsstruktur der Bevölkerung in Syrien vor Ausbruch des Krieges, Umfragen unter Flüchtlingen oder Daten zu Beschäftigten und Erwerbslosen, legen allerdings übereinstimmend nahe, dass ein hoher Anteil von Asylwerber/inne/n nur eine geringe Schulbildung aufweist. Dies gilt insbesondere im Vergleich zur Bildungsstruktur der Bevölkerung westeuropäischer Länder wie Österreich (siehe Tabelle 1).

In der folgenden Untersuchung der ökonomischen und fiskalischen Auswirkungen der Fluchtmigration wird auf Erhebungen der Bildungsstruktur des deutschen Bundesamts für Migration und Flüchtlinge (BAMF) zurückgegriffen, weil die Stichprobengröße bei der Befragung von 420.000 Personen in den beiden verwendeten Publikationen besonders groß ist.[3] Nach dieser Erhebung sind rund 59% gering-, 23% mittel- und 18% hochqualifiziert.[4]

Durch den hohen Anteil an jungen Asylwerber/inne/n besteht jedoch eine Chance, die unterdurchschnittliche Qualifikationsstruktur durch Aus- und Weiterbildung noch zu verbessern. Deutlich positiver fallen Ergebnisse des AMS-Kompetenzchecks in Österreich aus. Diese Zahlen sind jedoch mutmaßlich durch eine verzerrte Stichprobe nicht repräsentativ.

Über das formale Bildungsniveau hinaus stellt sich die Frage, ob Bildungsabschlüsse in den Herkunftsländern der Fluchtmigration mit jenen in Europa vergleichbar sind. So zitiert Wößmann (2016) aus einer Analyse auf Basis der PISA- und der TIMSS-Studie. Er kommt zu dem Ergebnis, dass in Deutschland 16% der Jugendlichen die absoluten Grundkompetenzen nicht erreichen, bei Schüler/inne/n in Syrien sind es jedoch 65%. Demnach liegt bei Gleichaltrigen das durchschnittliche syrische Leistungsniveau in Schulen in etwa um 140 PISA-Punkte hinter dem deutschen, was einem Rückstand von vier bis fünf Schuljahren entspricht.[5]

---

[3] Einschränkend muss darauf hingewiesen werden, dass in der Erhebung nicht die höchste *abgeschlossene* Bildungseinrichtung, sondern die höchste *besuchte* Bildungseinrichtung abgefragt wird. Da Schul- bzw. Studienabbrecher so eingeordnet werden, als ob sie die Einrichtung abgeschlossen haben, überschätzt diese Vorgangsweise das tatsächliche Bildungsniveau. Zudem weist etwa die OECD (2017) darauf hin, dass bei derartigen Umfragen auch ein „Klügermachen" beobachtet werden kann, verbunden mit der Hoffnung einer höheren Anerkennungswahrscheinlichkeit. Auch das spricht in der Tendenz für eine Überschätzung des tatsächlichen Bildungsniveaus.

[4] Eine aktuelle Publikation (BAMF 2017) wird aus redaktionellen Gründen nicht mehr in den Berechnungen berücksichtigt und daher auch nicht in der Tabelle dargestellt. Die Zahlen weichen nur minimal von den hier verwendeten Zahlen ab, der Anteil der geringqualifizierten würde demnach von 59,2% auf 59,6% ansteigen.

[5] Allfällige Diskrepanzen zwischen Bildungsabschlüssen werden in der folgenden Modellanalyse berücksichtigt, weil Lohn- und Beschäftigungsunterschiede zwischen Ansässigen und Asylwerber/inne/n bei gleichem Bildungsabschluss in die Analyse einfließen, siehe dazu das nächste Unterkapitel.

Arbeitsmarktintegration

Mittel- und längerfristige Befunde über die Arbeitsmarktintegration von Flüchtlingen sind naturgemäß noch nicht verfügbar, auch deshalb, weil Migration aus den betreffenden Herkunftsregionen in Österreich in der Vergangenheit eine untergeordnete Rolle gespielt hat. Es kann aber auf Daten aus Schweden zurückgegriffen werden, das auch im letzten Jahrzehnt schon eine starke Zuwanderung aus der Region aufwies.[6]

Arbeitsmarktintegration relativ zur Ansässigen Bevölkerung	Geringe Qualifikation	Mittlere Qualifikation	Hohe Qualifikation
Differenz Arbeitslosenquote (in PP)	24,4	14,8	17,9
Erwerbsbeteiligung kurzfristig (kürzer als 5 Jahre Aufenthalt)	-17,0	-25,7	-23,9
Erwerbsbeteiligung längerfristig (mehr als 5 Jahre Aufenthalt)	-6,3	-9,2	-12,8
Lücke Stundenlohn	-0,8%	-12,6%	-22,1%

Gering ISCED 0-2, Mittel ISCED 3-4, Hoch ISCED 5+.

Tabelle 2 Arbeitsmarktintegration von anerkannten Flüchtlingen in Schweden, relativ zur ansässigen Bevölkerung

Quelle: LFS, EU-SILC Schweden, eigene Berechnungen.

Die Erfahrungen in Schweden zeigen, dass die Arbeitslosenquote von Flüchtlingen deutlich über jener der ansässigen Bevölkerung liegt, je nach Ausbildungsgruppe um 15 bis 25 Prozentpunkte. Außerdem ist die Erwerbsbeteiligung von Flüchtlingen insbesondere in den ersten Jahren deutlich niedriger als jene in der ansässigen Bevölkerung. Kurzfristig (in den ersten fünf Jahren des Aufenthalts) ist diese um rund 20 Prozentpunkte geringer, längerfristig (nach den ersten fünf Jahren) um rund 10 Prozentpunkte. Dementsprechend ist die Beschäftigungsquote von anerkannten Flüchtlingen deutlich unterdurchschnittlich. Das Lohndifferential zur ansässigen Bevölkerung ist nach Ausbildungsgruppe unterschiedlich. Während es bei der Gruppe der geringqualifizierten, auch vor dem Hintergrund des überdurchschnittlichen Anteils an Männern (und der Tatsache, dass Löhne von Männern im Schnitt höher sind als jene von Frauen), klein ist, ist es bei besser qualifizierten Personen deutlich höher.[7]

Ökonomische Auswirkungen

Aus ökonomischer Sicht stellt Zuwanderung insbesondere eine Ausweitung des Arbeitsangebots dar. Dementsprechend zeigen wissenschaftliche Analysen, dass

---

[6] Siehe etwa Ruist (2013).
[7] Die Gründe für diese Lohndifferentiale werden an dieser Stelle nicht untersucht. Gründe dafür können zum Beispiel Überqualifizierung, eine Nicht-Vergleichbarkeit oder fehlende Anrechenbarkeit von Bildungsabschlüssen, Sprachprobleme oder Diskriminierung sein.

Migration die Beschäftigung im Zielland erhöht. Dieser Beschäftigungsanstieg verstärkt Investitionsanreize und beides zusammen erhöht die Wirtschaftsleistung des Ziellandes. Die empirische und theoretische Literatur legt aber auch nahe, dass diese Angebotserhöhung kurzfristig zu einer gewissen Lohnzurückhaltung und zu Verdrängungseffekten am Arbeitsmarkt führen kann. Mittel- und langfristig passt sich aber die Volkswirtschaft an die geänderten Rahmenbedingungen an (zum Beispiel durch Ausweitung des Kapitalstocks), sodass Migration mittel- und längerfristig nur beschränkte Auswirkungen auf Lohnentwicklung und Beschäftigungswahrscheinlichkeit hat.[8,9] Dieser allgemeine Befund gilt jedoch nur dann, wenn die Struktur der Zuwandernden jener der einheimischen Bevölkerung entspricht. Wenn aber die Qualifikations- und Erwerbsstruktur, wie im vorigen Kapitel dargestellt, unterdurchschnittlich ist, sind auch längerfristig stärkere arbeitsmarktspezifische Auswirkungen von Zuwanderung zu erwarten. Weiters ist zu berücksichtigen, dass die zusätzlichen (öffentlichen) Ausgaben im Zusammenhang mit der Fluchtmigration (etwa für Grundversorgung oder Bildungsausgaben, siehe das nachfolgende Kapitel zu den fiskalischen Effekten) die Nachfrage und damit Wachstum und Beschäftigung erhöhen.

	2013	2014	2015	2016	2017	2018	2019	2020
Bevölkerungsanstieg durch Aufenthaltsanerkennungen (Jahresschnitt)	2,1	10,0	25,8	50,0	79,0	108,1	137,0	152,5

Tabelle 3 Bevölkerungsanstieg durch Aufenthaltsanerkennungen, in Tsd. Personen

Quelle: eigene Abschätzung auf Basis der dargestellten Annahmen.

Die folgende Analyse der ökonomischen Auswirkungen der Fluchtmigration in Österreich erfolgt auf Basis des makroökonomischen Modells PuMA (PUblic policy Model for Austria) von EcoAustria, das Schwerpunkte bei der Modellierung von Demographie, Arbeitsmarkt und öffentlichem Sektor hat und dementsprechend besonders gut für die Analyse geeignet ist.[10] Untersucht werden dabei die Auswirkungen der Migrationsperiode 2013-2018 mit besonders starkem Zuzug von Asylwerber/inne/n, die ökonomischen und fiskalischen Effekte werden bis zum Jahr 2020 dargestellt. In Bezug auf die Anzahl von Asylwerber/inne/n für die noch nicht realisierten Jahre 2017 und 2018 wird angenommen, dass die von der Österreichischen Bundesregierung vereinbarte Obergrenze eingehalten wird. Unter Berücksichtigung der Anzahl der Asylwerber/innen und der aktuellen Aner-

---

[8] Diese Ergebnisse finden sich in mehreren Arbeiten (etwa in Levine 1999, Barrell et al. 2006 oder Baas und Brücker 2007).
[9] Sehr plakativ ausgedrückt: Deutschlands Bevölkerung ist 10 mal so groß wie jene Österreichs, die Arbeitslosenquote ist dennoch ähnlich hoch.
[10] Die vorliegende Analyse ist eine Aktualisierung der Modellrechnungen in Berger et al. (2016a) bzw. Berger et al. (2017). Eine ähnliche Analyse erfolgte für Deutschland im Auftrag der Europäischen Kommission (Berger et al. 2016b).

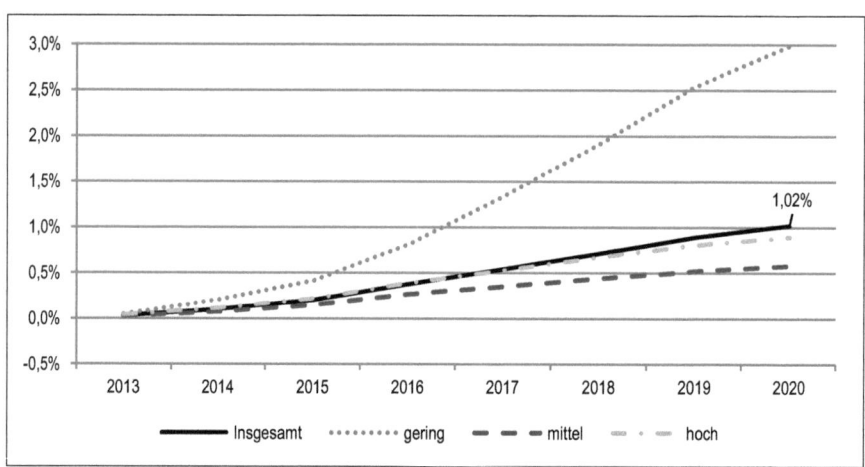

Abbildung 5 Beschäftigungseffekte der Fluchtmigration in Österreich
Quelle: Modellsimulation EcoAustria-PuMA.
Ergebnisse als Niveauunterschied zum Referenzszenario ohne Fluchtmigration. Anm.: untersucht wird Fluchtmigration der Jahre 2013-2018 und ihre ökonomischen und fiskalischen Auswirkungen 2013-2020.
Gering ISCED 0-2, Mittel ISCED 3-4, Hoch ISCED 5+.

kennungsquoten ergibt sich durch die Fluchtmigration der Jahre 2013-2018 insgesamt ein Bevölkerungsanstieg durch Aufenthaltsanerkennungen (Asylberechtigte, Gewährung von Subsidiärem Schutz und Humanitäre Aufenthaltstitel) um 152.500 Personen. Dabei ist anzumerken, dass die positiven Entscheidungen (und damit der freie Arbeitsmarktzugang) aufgrund der Dauer der Asylverfahren zeitlich verzögert sind.[11]

Auswirkungen auf die Beschäftigung

Die Modellanalyse mit PuMA verdeutlicht, dass die Fluchtmigration aufgrund des höheren Arbeitsangebots und der zusätzlichen Nachfrage die Beschäftigung signifikant erhöht, trotz der unterdurchschnittlichen Beschäftigungsquote von Flüchtlingen. Bis zum Jahr 2020 steigt die Beschäftigung im Vergleich zum Referenz-

---

[11] Diese Zahl ist deutlich höher als in der EcoAustria Policy Note vom April 2017 (Berger et al. 2017), in der rund 100.000 Berechtigungen angenommen wurden. Dies ist auf vier Gründe zurückzuführen: i) in der damaligen Policy Note wurden nur Asylwerber/innen berücksichtigt, die zusätzlich zum mehrjährigen Schnitt zugewandert sind (um die Effekte der Änderung der Migrationsmuster zu untersuchen), während in der vorliegenden Studie alle Asylwerber/innen berücksichtigt werden; ii) Der vorliegende Beitrag untersucht mit dem Zeitraum 2013-2018 eine Periode etwas höherer Zuwanderung als die Policy Note, die den Zeitraum 2015-2019 betrachtet; iii) die Anerkennungsquoten des Jahres 2017 sind höher als jene in 2015, dementsprechend werden für zukünftige Entscheidungen etwas höhere Anerkennungsquoten angenommen; iv) in den hier angegebenen Zahlen sind auch Kinder berücksichtigt, die in Österreich geboren werden.

szenario ohne Fluchtmigration um 1% (Abbildung 5). Dies entspricht einem Beschäftigungsanstieg um rund 40.000 Personen. Der Beschäftigungszuwachs fällt mit rund 3% bei den Geringqualifizierten deutlich stärker aus, was auf den vergleichsweise hohen Anteil von Personen mit höchstens Pflichtschulabschluss unter den Asylwerber/inne/n zurückzuführen ist.

Obwohl der große Teil der Fluchtmigration in den Jahren 2015 und 2016 erfolgte, findet der Beschäftigungszuwachs erst über die Zeit statt, was verschiedene Gründe hat: Erstens erhalten Flüchtlinge erst mit der Gewährung des Aufenthaltstitels vollen Zugang zum Arbeitsmarkt und Asylverfahren dauern im Schnitt einen beträchtlichen Zeitraum. Zweitens erfolgt die Arbeitsmarktintegration nicht umgehend, wie sich auch aus den schwedischen Erfahrungen zeigt. Drittens sind Flüchtlinge im Schnitt sehr jung, sodass viele von ihnen erst nach Jahren und nach absolvierter Ausbildung dem Arbeitsmarkt zur Verfügung stehen. Und schließlich benötigt auch die Volkswirtschaft selbst eine gewisse Anpassungszeit an die geänderten Rahmenbedingungen.

Auswirkungen auf die Arbeitslosenquote

Der Beschäftigungsanstieg fällt deutlich schwächer aus als die Zunahme des Arbeitskräfteangebots, weshalb die Arbeitslosigkeit deutlich ansteigt. Die Arbeitslosenquote legt wegen der Fluchtmigration (der Jahre 2013-2018) bis 2020 um 0,4 Prozentpunkte zu (siehe oberer Teil von Abbildung 6). Die Abbildung verdeutlicht, dass dieser Anstieg sehr stark auf die Gruppe der Geringqualifizierten zurückzuführen ist, deren Arbeitslosenquote mittelfristig um rund 1 ¾ Prozentpunkt zunimmt. Dieser starke Anstieg der Arbeitslosenquote konzentriert sich vor allem auf Flüchtlinge selbst. Die durchschnittliche Arbeitslosenquote in der bereits ansässigen Bevölkerung[12] ist nahezu unbeeinträchtigt, kurzfristig ergeben sich aufgrund der zusätzlichen Nachfrage sogar leicht dämpfende Effekte. Es zeigen sich allerdings gewisse Verdrängungseffekte bei der ansässigen geringqualifizierten Bevölkerung, deren Arbeitslosenquote um rund 0,2 Prozentpunkte zunimmt.

---

[12] Der Begriff der „ansässigen Bevölkerung" bezieht sich in der Folge auf die Bevölkerung ohne die zugezogenen Fluchtmigrant/inn/en.

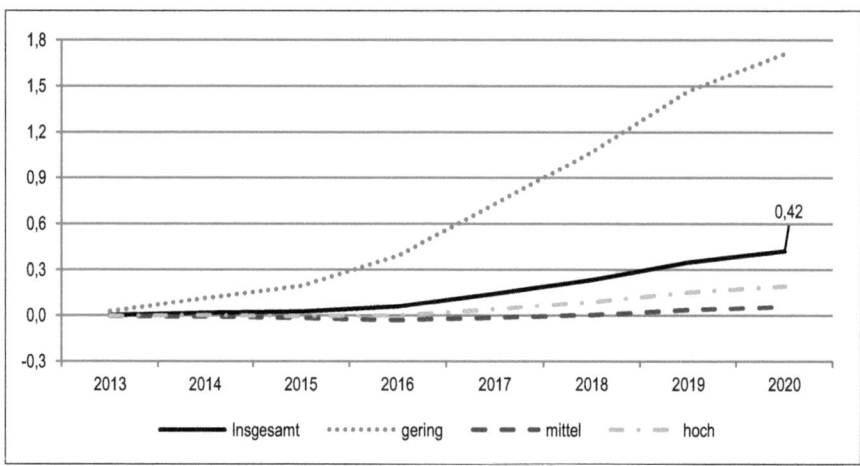

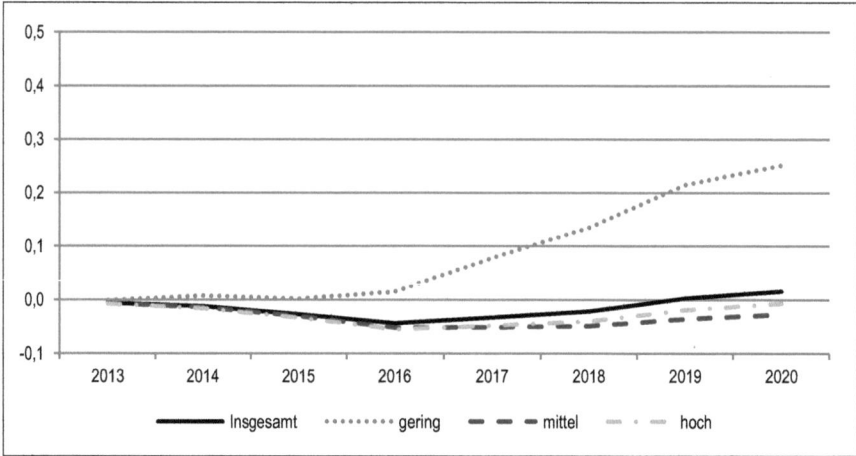

Abbildung 6 Arbeitslosigkeitseffekte der Fluchtmigration in Österreich 2013-20, Arbeitslosenquote gesamte Bevölkerung (oben) und Arbeitslosenquote Ansässige (unten)

Quelle: Modellsimulation EcoAustria-PuMA.
Ergebnisse als Niveauunterschied zum Referenzszenario ohne Fluchtmigration. Anm.: untersucht wird Fluchtmigration der Jahre 2013-2018 und ihre ökonomischen und fiskalischen Auswirkungen 2013-2020.
Gering ISCED 0-2, Mittel ISCED 3-4, Hoch ISCED 5+.

Ökonomische und fiskalische Auswirkungen der Fluchtmigration in Österreich 181

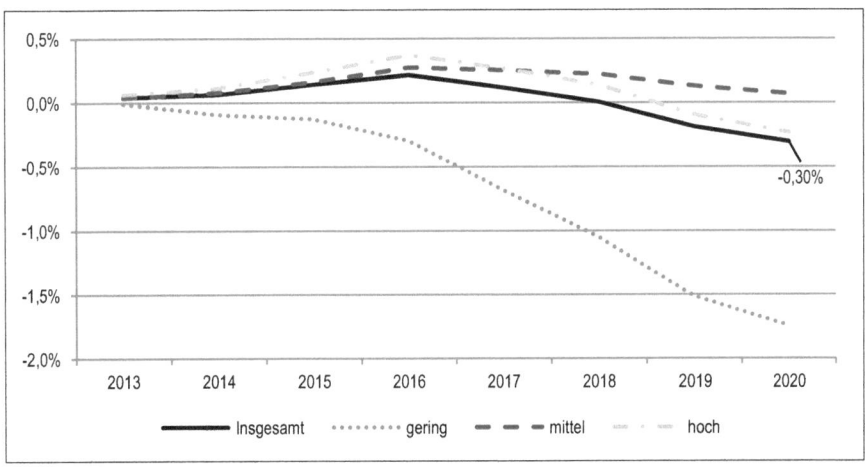

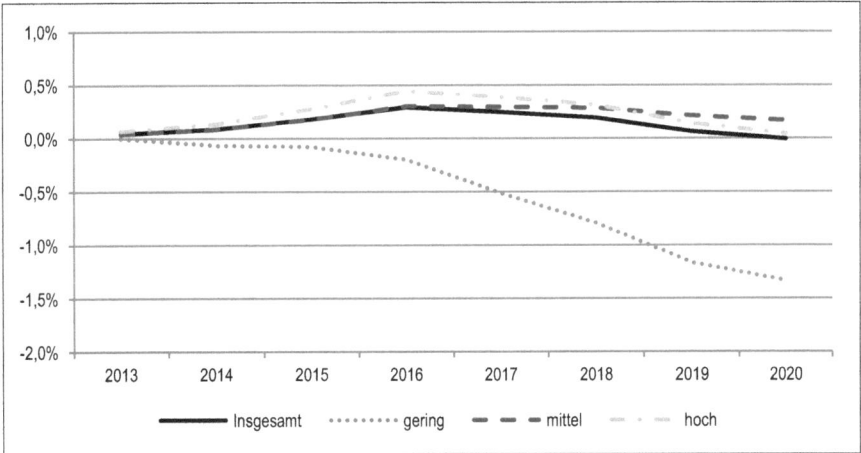

Abbildung 7 Lohneffekte gesamte Bevölkerung (oben) und ansässige Bevölkerung (unten) der Fluchtmigration in Österreich 2013-2020

Quelle: Modellsimulation EcoAustria-PuMA.
Ergebnisse als Niveauunterschied zum Referenzszenario ohne Fluchtmigration. Anm.: untersucht wird Fluchtmigration der Jahre 2013-2018 und ihre ökonomischen und fiskalischen Auswirkungen 2013-2020.
Gering ISCED 0-2, Mittel ISCED 3-4, Hoch ISCED 5+.

Auswirkungen auf die Lohnentwicklung

Da die Bildungsstruktur der Flüchtlinge unterdurchschnittlich ist bzw. diese häufig nicht ihrer beruflichen Qualifikation entsprechend eingesetzt werden, finden sie oft unterdurchschnittlich produktive und entlohnte Beschäftigung. Dies dämpft die gesamtwirtschaftliche Lohnentwicklung. Im Schnitt über alle Beschäftigten wachsen die Lohneinkommen um rund 0,3% schwächer als im Referenzszenario ohne Fluchtmigration (Abbildung 7).

Wiederum ist dieser Effekt auf Geringqualifizierte konzentriert, deren Löhne um rund 1,5% schwächer ausfallen als im Referenzszenario. Die bereits ansässige Bevölkerung ist von dieser Lohndämpfung im Schnitt nicht betroffen, der durchschnittliche Lohn ansässiger Beschäftigter ist unverändert bzw. entwickelt sich kurzfristig sogar leicht positiv. Es zeigen sich aber lohndämpfende Effekte bei geringqualifizierten Ansässigen, deren Löhne um rund 1% geringer als im Referenzszenario sind. Bezogen auf das unterste Dezil der Bruttojahreseinkommen von ganzjährig und Vollzeit unselbständig Beschäftigten (von jährlich € 23.288) entsprechen die 1,3% im Jahr 2020 einer Dämpfung um € 310.

Auswirkungen auf BIP und Konsum

Auch die makroökonomischen Größen reagieren auf die starke Zuwanderung. Der Anstieg der Beschäftigung löst zusätzliche Investitionen aus, um den Kapitaleinsatz je Arbeitnehmer/in auf das gewünschte Niveau zu bringen. Das BIP steigt infolge des Beschäftigungsanstiegs und der dadurch ausgelösten zusätzlichen Investitionen. Im Jahr 2020 erhöht die Fluchtmigration der Jahre 2013-2018 das BIP um knapp 0,7% (bezogen auf das BIP 2016 entspricht dies rund € 2,3 Mrd.). Dieser Anstieg fällt aber deutlich schwächer aus als der Beschäftigungsanstieg, das heißt die durchschnittliche Arbeitsproduktivität sinkt. Dies spiegelt sich auch

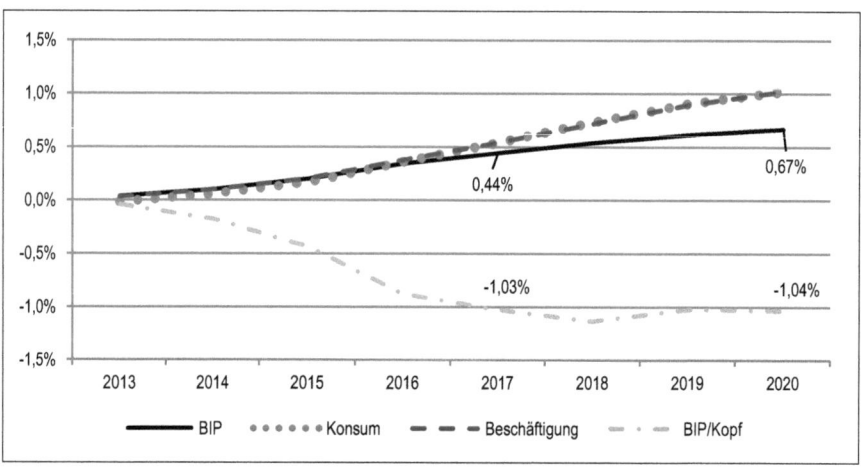

Abbildung 8 Makroökonomische Auswirkungen der Fluchtmigration in Österreich

Quelle: Modellsimulation EcoAustria-PuMA.
Ergebnisse als Niveauunterschied zum Referenzszenario ohne Fluchtmigration. Anm.: untersucht wird Fluchtmigration der Jahre 2013-2018 und ihre ökonomischen und fiskalischen Auswirkungen 2013-2020.

Makroökonomische Auswirkungen	2013	2014	2015	2016	2017	2018	2019	2020
BIP	0,04%	0,10%	0,20%	0,35%	0,44%	0,54%	0,61%	0,67%
Investitionen	0,76%	0,88%	1,06%	1,30%	1,35%	1,37%	1,28%	1,19%
Priv. Konsum	-0,02%	0,06%	0,17%	0,36%	0,54%	0,73%	0,90%	1,02%
BIP/Kopf	-0,04%	-0,18%	-0,44%	-0,88%	-1,03%	-1,13%	-1,02%	-1,04%
Arbeitsmarkt: Gesamte Bevölkerung	**2013**	**2014**	**2015**	**2016**	**2017**	**2018**	**2019**	**2020**
Bruttostundenlohn	0,04%	0,07%	0,14%	0,22%	0,12%	0,01%	-0,19%	-0,30%
- gering	-0,01%	-0,09%	-0,13%	-0,30%	-0,69%	-1,05%	-1,52%	-1,75%
- mittel	0,04%	0,08%	0,16%	0,27%	0,25%	0,22%	0,13%	0,07%
- hoch	0,06%	0,11%	0,24%	0,37%	0,27%	0,14%	-0,10%	-0,23%
Beschäftigung	0,03%	0,10%	0,20%	0,37%	0,54%	0,72%	0,89%	1,02%
- gering	0,05%	0,20%	0,41%	0,81%	1,34%	1,91%	2,54%	2,99%
- mittel	0,03%	0,07%	0,15%	0,27%	0,35%	0,44%	0,52%	0,58%
- hoch	0,04%	0,11%	0,22%	0,39%	0,53%	0,67%	0,81%	0,89%
Arbeitslosenquote (in PP)	0,00	0,02	0,03	0,06	0,14	0,23	0,35	0,42
- gering	0,02	0,11	0,19	0,39	0,73	1,07	1,47	1,71
- mittel	0,00	-0,01	-0,02	-0,03	-0,02	0,00	0,04	0,06
- hoch	0,00	0,00	-0,01	0,00	0,04	0,09	0,15	0,19
Arbeitsmarkt: Ansässige Bevölkerung	**2013**	**2014**	**2015**	**2016**	**2017**	**2018**	**2019**	**2020**
Bruttostundenlohn	0,04%	0,09%	0,18%	0,29%	0,24%	0,19%	0,06%	-0,01%
- gering	0,00%	-0,07%	-0,08%	-0,20%	-0,51%	-0,79%	-1,17%	-1,33%
- mittel	0,04%	0,09%	0,18%	0,30%	0,30%	0,28%	0,21%	0,17%
- hoch	0,07%	0,14%	0,28%	0,44%	0,39%	0,31%	0,14%	0,04%
Arbeitslosenquote (in PP)	-0,01	-0,01	-0,03	-0,04	-0,03	-0,02	0,00	0,02
- gering	0,00	0,01	0,00	0,02	0,08	0,14	0,22	0,25
- mittel	-0,01	-0,01	-0,03	-0,05	-0,05	-0,05	-0,04	-0,03
- hoch	-0,01	-0,02	-0,03	-0,05	-0,05	-0,04	-0,02	-0,01

Tabelle 4 Auswirkungen der Fluchtmigration auf Arbeitsmarkt und Wirtschaft

Quelle: Modellsimulation EcoAustria-PuMA.
Ergebnisse als Niveauunterschied zum Referenzszenario ohne Fluchtmigration. Anm.: untersucht wird Fluchtmigration der Jahre 2013-2018 und ihre ökonomischen und fiskalischen Auswirkungen 2013-2020.
Gering ISCED 0-2, Mittel ISCED 3-4, Hoch ISCED 5+, PP Prozentpunkte.

in der Entwicklung des BIP/Kopf wider. Die Fluchtmigration reduziert das BIP/Kopf um rund 1%.[13] Der private Konsum liegt im Vergleich zum Referenzszenario ohne Fluchtmigration im Jahr 2020 um 1% höher.

---

[13] Eine Analyse der längerfristigen ökonomischen und budgetären Effekte der Fluchtmigration wird im Auftrag des Fiskalrats durchgeführt (Holler und Schuster 2016). Insbesondere wenn man die in der dortigen Studie (aus methodischen Gründen) geringere Zahl von Asylberechtigten berücksichtigt, sind die Auswirkungen sehr ähnlich. Im Hauptszenario von Holler und Schuster dämpft die Fluchtmigration das BIP/Kopf um rund ¾ % im Jahr 2020.

Fiskalische Auswirkungen

Die Fluchtmigration hat signifikante Auswirkungen auf den öffentlichen Haushalt, sowohl auf die Aufwendungen, als auch auf die Einnahmen. In der vorliegenden Analyse werden auf der Einnahmenseite Konsum- und Einkommensteuern, SV- und Lohnsummenabgaben sowie Steuern auf unternehmerische Tätigkeit (z.B. KESt und KöSt) berücksichtigt. Auf der Aufwendungsseite werden die Bereiche Gesundheit, Bildung, Kinderbetreuung, Familienförderung, Arbeitsmarktpolitik, die Grundversorgung, Bedarfsorientierte Mindestsicherung sowie sonstige Aufwendungen im Zusammenhang mit der Migration von Asylwerber/inne/n (Verfahrens- und Transportkosten, Türkei-Fazilität und Grenzmanagement) betrachtet.[14] Die ökonomischen Auswirkungen von Migration auf die ansässige Bevölkerung spiegeln sich auch in den von dieser Gruppe entrichteten Abgaben und erhaltenen öffentlichen Aufwendungen wider.

Die Analyse der fiskalischen Auswirkungen basiert zum einen auf Simulationsergebnissen mit dem PuMA-Modell, zum anderen auf ‚modellexternen' Berechnungen. Insbesondere die Auswirkungen auf der Einnahmenseite sind mit dem Modell detailliert abschätzbar. So erhöht die zusätzliche Beschäftigung die Einnahmen bei Einkommensteuern und im Bereich der Sozialversicherungs- und Lohnsummenabgaben. Daneben ergeben sich aber auch Auswirkungen auf Seite der öffentlichen Aufwendungen, die nicht explizit im Modell abgebildet sind und daher auf Basis anderer Quellen separat ermittelt werden.

Öffentliche Einnahmen

In Tabelle 5 sind die Auswirkungen der Fluchtmigration auf die öffentlichen Einnahmen dargestellt. Diese Auswirkungen sind entsprechend der oben dargestellten ökonomischen Effekte durchaus signifikant. Die öffentlichen Einnahmen liegen durch die Fluchtmigration im Jahr 2020 um rund € 1,1 Mrd. bzw. knapp 0,3% des BIP höher als ohne Fluchtmigration. Der Einnahmeneffekt steigt im betrachteten Zeitraum entsprechend der schrittweisen Zunahme Asylberechtigter und der schrittweisen Arbeitsmarktintegration kontinuierlich an. Kumulativ über die Jahre 2013-2020 ergeben sich zusätzliche Einnahmen im Ausmaß von € 4,6 Mrd. oder rund 0,15% des (kumulativen) BIP. Davon entfallen € 1,6 Mrd. auf Sozialversicherungs- und Lohnsummenabgaben und € 1,5 Mrd. auf Konsumsteuern. Dazu kommen (insbesondere nachfragebedingte) Mehreinnahmen durch Abgabenleistungen der ansässigen Bevölkerung im Ausmaß von kumulativ € 0,7 Mrd.

---

[14] Aufgrund des kurzfristigen Betrachtungszeitraums bis 2020 werden allgemeine öffentliche Aufwendungen (z.B. allgemeine öffentliche Verwaltung und Infrastrukturinvestitionen) sowie öffentliche Pensionsleistungen nicht berücksichtigt.

Ein-nahmen	Konsum-steuern	Einkommens-steuer	SV- / Lohn-summen-Abgaben	Steuern auf untern. Tätigkeit	Abgaben von Ansässigen	Summe	Summe in % BIP
2013	7	2	8	-1	26	42	0,01%
2014	29	8	33	5	63	139	0,04%
2015	53	15	61	13	155	297	0,09%
2016	104	28	117	34	253	536	0,15%
2017	186	49	203	56	194	687	0,19%
2018	276	71	295	77	130	849	0,23%
2019	377	97	406	101	-15	966	0,25%
2020	448	115	487	109	-83	1.075	0,27%
Summe	1.479	385	1.610	393	723	4.591	0,16%

Tabelle 5 Auswirkungen der Fluchtmigration auf öffentliche Einnahmen

Quelle: Modellsimulation EcoAustria-PuMA.
Ergebnisse als Niveauunterschied zum Referenzszenario ohne Fluchtmigration. Anm.: untersucht wird Fluchtmigration der Jahre 2013-2018 und ihre ökonomischen und fiskalischen Auswirkungen 2013-2020.

Öffentliche Aufwendungen

In Tabelle 6 sind die zusätzlichen öffentlichen Aufwendungen dargestellt, die aus der Fluchtmigration der Jahre 2013-2018 resultieren. Kumulativ über die Jahre 2013-2020 ergeben sich dabei zusätzliche Aufwendungen im Ausmaß von € 12,7 Mrd. Dies entspricht 0,4% des (kumulierten) BIP dieser Jahre. Größte Ausgabenposten sind dabei vor allem die Grundversorgung (inkl. Sonstiger Aufwendungen) mit € 5,8 Mrd., die Bedarfsorientierte Mindestsicherung (BMS) mit € 2,4 Mrd. sowie zusätzliche Aufwendungen im Bildungs- und Gesundheitsbereich (€ 1,8 Mrd. bzw. € 1,3 Mrd.). Dabei ergeben sich auch deutliche Unterschiede im zeitlichen Verlauf. Während etwa die zusätzlichen Aufwendungen im Bereich der Grundversorgung in den Jahren 2016 bis 2018 am höchsten sind, nehmen die Ausgaben bei der BMS im Zeitverlauf deutlich zu. Durch den rückläufigen Effekt bei der Grundversorgung nehmen die zusätzlichen öffentlichen Aufwendungen insgesamt nach dem Jahr 2018 merklich ab.

Asyl-Aufwendungen	Gesundheit	Bildung	Kinderbetreuung	Familien	AMP	BMS	Grundversorgung + Sonstiges	Ansässige AMP+BMS	Summe	Summe (in % BIP)
2013	11	7	1	1	3	8	133	-4	160	0,05%
2014	40	31	3	6	13	45	321	-8	452	0,14%
2015	90	87	9	16	24	135	765	-15	1.112	0,33%
2016	175	234	21	33	45	245	1.407	-23	2.138	0,61%
2017	217	331	34	57	87	356	1.272	-18	2.335	0,65%
2018	253	379	48	83	134	467	1.102	-12	2.454	0,66%
2019	253	395	61	110	182	569	595	2	2.168	0,56%
2020	270	339	75	129	215	609	237	7	1.881	0,47%
Summe	1.309	1.804	251	435	704	2.436	5.832	-70	12.700	0,44%

Tabelle 6 Auswirkungen der Fluchtmigration auf öffentliche Aufwendungen

Quelle: Modellsimulation EcoAustria-PuMA, eigene Berechnungen.
Ergebnisse als Niveauunterschied zum Referenzszenario ohne Fluchtmigration. Anm.: untersucht wird Fluchtmigration der Jahre 2013-2018 und ihre ökonomischen und fiskalischen Auswirkungen 2013-2020.

Auswirkungen auf den Budgetsaldo

In der Nettobetrachtung der zusätzlichen öffentlichen Einnahmen und Aufwendungen sind die fiskalischen Auswirkungen der Fluchtmigration in der kurzen und mittleren Frist negativ. Kumulativ ergeben sich Mehraufwendungen im Ausmaß von € 12,7 Mrd. und Mehreinnahmen von € 4,6 Mrd., wodurch sich kumulativ ein Nettoeffekt von € 8,1 Mrd. oder knapp 0,3% des (kumulierten) BIP ergibt. Die Auswirkungen auf die Budget-Salden in den einzelnen Jahren sind in Abbildung 9 illustriert. Die stärksten Effekte ergeben sich in den Jahren 2016-2018 mit einem negativen Saldo von jeweils 0,4-0,5% des BIP. In den Folgejahren verbessert sich der fiskalische Effekt deutlich, was zum einen auf den Wegfall von öffentlichen Ausgaben (z.B. Grundversorgung und Asylverfahren) und zum anderen auf die schrittweise Integration in den Arbeitsmarkt und damit höhere öffentliche Einnahmen zurückzuführen ist.

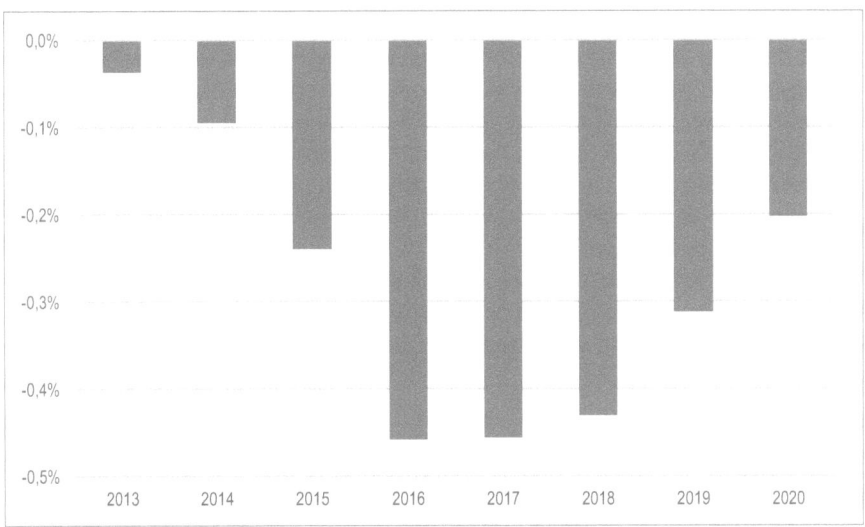

Abbildung 9 Auswirkungen der Fluchtmigration auf den Budget-Saldo, in % des BIP

Quelle: Modellsimulation EcoAustria-PuMA, eigene Berechnungen.
Ergebnisse als Niveauunterschied zum Referenzszenario ohne Fluchtmigration. Anm.: untersucht wird Fluchtmigration der Jahre 2013-2018 und ihre ökonomischen und fiskalischen Auswirkungen 2013-2020.

Arbeitsmarktpolitische Empfehlungen

Die dargestellte Analyse verdeutlicht, dass aus ökonomischer Perspektive die Herausforderungen der Fluchtmigration insbesondere bei der Arbeitsmarktintegration liegen. Je rascher und besser diese gelingt, desto positiver fallen die volkswirtschaftlichen und fiskalischen Folgewirkungen aus.

Empirische Befunde zeigen, dass es von großer Bedeutung ist, möglichst früh mit Aktivierungs- und Integrationsmaßnahmen für Asylberechtigte und Asylwerber/innen mit hoher Bleibewahrscheinlichkeit zu beginnen (siehe etwa OECD 2016 oder Bertelsmann Stiftung 2016). Diese Unterstützung sollte in einem mehrstufigen Prozess und einer effizienten Zusammenarbeit der verschiedenen Institutionen (z.B. die verschiedenen Ebenen der Gebietskörperschaften, Sozialpartner, AMS, NGOs) erfolgen. In einem ersten Schritt bedarf es einer Erfassung der Qualifikationen, Arbeitserfahrung und Fähigkeiten der Flüchtlinge. In einem zweiten Schritt geht es darum, diese Qualifikationen an die (Arbeitsmarkt-)anforderungen einer westeuropäischen Gesellschaft heranzubringen.

Der Erwerb der (deutschen) Sprache ist ein wesentlicher Schlüssel zur Integration in die Gesellschaft und den Arbeitsmarkt. Empirische Befunde legen nahe, dass dieser Spracherwerb erfolgreicher ist, wenn er gemeinsam mit Arbeitsmarkt-erfahrung gekoppelt wird (siehe etwa Lemaitre 2007 oder Aslund und Johannson 2011). Darüber hinaus ist anzudenken, den Zugang zu dem in Österreich praktizierten Modell der dualen Ausbildung auch für Asylberechtigte zu fördern, um Berufserfahrung, Ausbildung und Spracherwerb miteinander zu verbinden, gegebenenfalls auch für ältere Asylberechtigte. Empirische Untersuchungen über Schweden (Bevelander und Lundh 2007) legen nahe, dass die Integration in kleineren Städten und Gemeinden sowie in Regionen mit überdurchschnittlichem Industrieanteil besser gelingt.

Die derzeit naturgemäß nur beschränkte empirische Evidenz, welche Maßnahmen die Arbeitsmarktintegration von Flüchtlingen erfolgreich unterstützen können, verdeutlicht die Notwendigkeit einer laufenden Evaluierung der getroffenen Maßnahmen.

Literatur

AMS (2017). Arbeitsmarktintegration geflüchteter Menschen: Bilanz und Ausblick. AMS Aussendung vom 17.2.2017.

Aslund, Olof / Johansson, Per (2011). Virtues of SIN: Can increased public efforts help disadvantaged immigrants? Evaluation Review 35(4), 399-427.

Baas, Timo / Brücker, Herbert (2007). Macroeconomic consequences of migration diversion: A CGE simulation for Germany and the UK, IAB Discussion Paper 3/2008.

Barrell, Ray / Guillemineau, Catherine, Liadze, Iana (2006). Migration in Europe, National Institute Economic Review 198, 36-39.

Battisti, Michele / Felbermayr, Gabriel (2015). Migranten im deutschen Arbeitsmarkt: Löhne, Arbeitslosigkeit, Erwerbsquoten, ifo Schnelldienst 20/2015.

Berger, Johannes / Biffl, Gudrun / Graf, Nikolaus / Schuh, Ulrich / Strohner, Ludwig (2016a). Ökonomische Analyse der Zuwanderung von Flüchtlingen nach Österreich. EcoAustria und DUK Bericht im Auftrag von Wirtschaftskammer Österreich und Bundesministerium für Europa, Integration und Äußeres, DUK Schriftenreihe Migration und Globalisierung, Krems.

Berger, Johannes / Biffl, Gudrun, Schuh, Ulrich / Strohner, Ludwig (2016b). Updating of the Labour Market Model, EcoAustria und Donauuniversität Krems Research Report im Auftrag von DG EMPL der Europäischen Kommission.

Berger, Johannes / Strohner, Ludwig / Thomas, Tobias (2017). Auswirkungen der Fluchtmigration auf Wachstum und Beschäftigung in Österreich, EcoAustria Policy Note 13.

Bertelsmann Stiftung (2016). From Refugees to Workers – Mapping Labour Market Integration Support Measures for Asylum-Seekers and Refugees in EU Member States, Gütersloh.

Bevelander, Pieter / Lundh, Christer (2007). Employment Integration of Refugees: The Influence of Local Factors on Refugee Job Opportunities in Sweden, IZA Discussion Paper No. 2551.

Bundesamt für Migration und Flüchtlinge (BAMF) (2016a). Asylantragsteller in Deutschland im ersten Halbjahr 2016 – Sozialstruktur, Qualifikationsniveau und Berufstätigkeit, BAMF-Kurzanalyse 4/2016.

Bundesamt für Migration und Flüchtlinge (BAMF) (2016b). Asylantragsteller in Deutschland im Jahr 2015 – Sozialstruktur, Qualifikationsniveau und Berufstätigkeit, BAMF-Kurzanalyse 3/2016.

Bundesamt für Migration und Flüchtlinge (BAMF) (2017). Volljährige Asylerstantragsteller in Deutschland im Jahr 2016 – Sozialstruktur, Qualifikationsniveau und Berufstätigkeit, BAMF-Kurzanalyse 2/2017.

Holler, Johannes / Schuster, Philip (2016). Langfristeffekte der Flüchtlingszuwanderung 2015 bis 2019 nach Österreich, Studie im Auftrag des Fiskalrates.

Institut für Arbeitsmarkt- und Berufsforschung (IAB) (2015). Flüchtlinge und andere Migranten am deutschen Arbeitsmarkt: Der Stand im September 2015. Aktuelle Berichte, Nürnberg.

Lemaitre, Georges (2007). The integration of immigrants into the labour market: The case for Sweden, OECD Social, Employment and Migration Working Papers No. 48.

Levine, Paul (1999). The welfare economics of migration control, Journal of Population Economics 1, 23-43.

OECD (2017). Finding their way – Labour Market Integration of Refugees in Germany, OECD Publishing, Paris.

OECD (2016). Making Integration Work – Refugees and Others in Need of Protection, OECD Publishing, Paris.

Ruist, Joakim (2013). The Labor Market Impact of Refugee Immigration in Sweden 1999-2007, SULCIS Working Paper, 2013:1.

Wößmann, Ludger (2016). Bildung als Schlüssel zur Integration, ifo Schnelldienst 1/2016.

Lebensverläufe unbegleiteter minderjähriger Flüchtlinge in Deutschland

Friedrich Heckmann

Zusammenfassung

In diesem Beitrag wird der Frage nachgegangen, inwieweit im Rahmen der Jugendhilfe getätigten Maßnahmen dazu beitragen, unbegleiteten minderjährigen Flüchtlingen (UMF) in die deutsche Gesellschaft zu integrieren und sie für ein selbständiges Leben vorzubereiten und wenn ja, wie diese Ziele erreicht werden. Auf Basis der Falldokumentation von 20 UMF, die von „Wohngemeinschaft für Flüchtlingskinder Nürnberg e. V." begleitet wurden. Integration wird dabei gemessen an persönlicher Stabilität und schulischem Erfolg, basierend auf einem sicheren Aufenthaltsstatus in Deutschland. Demnach konnte in mehr als der Hälfte der explorativen Fallstudie eine erfolgte Integration nachgewiesen werden, wobei Größenordnungen unter Vorbehalt zu betrachten sind.

Einführung

Unbegleitete minderjährige Flüchtlinge – im Folgenden auch als UMF abgekürzt - sind ausländische Kinder und Jugendliche, die auf irreguläre Weise nach Deutschland einreisen und Schutz und bessere Lebenschancen als in ihren Herkunftsländern suchen. Ihre Zahlen sind in den letzten Jahren beträchtlich gestiegen, von 2.489 (2013) und 4.398 (2014) auf 14.439 (2015) und schließlich sogar auf 35.939 im Jahre 2016. Von einer eher kleinen Kategorie sind UMF zu einer beachtenswert großen Gruppe von Flüchtlingen geworden, die für die Migrations- und Integrationspolitik eine große Herausforderung darstellt.

Nach Aufgriff durch die Polizei, durch andere Behörden oder aufgrund von Selbstmeldung werden sie – in der Sprache der Jugendhilfe – „in Obhut genommen". In so genannten Clearing Stellen wird versucht, ihre Identität zu klären, werden sie gesundheitlich untersucht und werden ihnen erste Sprachkenntnisse vermittelt. Sozialrechtlich erhalten UMF den Status der Jugendhilfe, aufenthaltsrechtlich werden sie geduldet, was kein eigentlicher Aufenthaltstitel ist.

Nach der Clearingstelle werden UMF überwiegend in Wohngemeinschaften oder in anderen Formen des gemeinschaftlichen Wohnens aufgenommen und im Rahmen des Jugendhilfestatus umfassend betreut und gefördert. Sie erhalten entweder einen amtlichen oder einen privater Vormund. Ab dem 16. Lebensjahr können sie einen Asylantrag stellen, dessen Erfolgsaussichten aber stark von dem jeweiligen Herkunftsland abhängen. Mit dem Erreichen des 18. Lebensjahrs und der Volljährigkeit endet der Schutz durch die von Deutschland unterzeichnete internationale Kinderrechtskonvention und die nun Erwachsenen stehen prinzipiell unter der Drohung einer Abschiebung.

Die im Rahmen der Jugendhilfe getätigten Maßnahmen verfolgen unabhängig vom unsicheren Aufenthaltsstatus das Ziel, die Integration der Jugendlichen in die deutsche Gesellschaft zu erreichen und sie für ein selbständiges Leben vorzubereiten. Die Fragestellung der hier vorgelegten explorativen Untersuchung besteht darin zu prüfen, ob, und wenn ja, wie diese Ziele erreicht werden. Dabei werden die Lebensläufe von 20 UMF über einen Zeitraum von 10 Jahren von 2006 bis 2016 verfolgt. Umgangssprachlich könnte man fragen: Was ist aus ihnen geworden, seit sie in Deutschland sind? Während die Literatur ganz überwiegend von humanitären und rechtlichen Fragestellungen beherrscht wird, liegen die Schwerpunkte dieser Studie im Bereich der gesellschaftlichen Integration, speziell der Sozialisation der UMF in ihre neuen Lebensverhältnisse.

Im ersten Punkt dieses Berichts werden zunächst migrationssoziologische und rechtliche Bedingungen des Lebens der UMF dargestellt. Darauf folgt im zweiten eine Darstellung der sozialisationstheoretischen Konzepte für die Untersuchung. Auf dieser Grundlage wird im dritten Punkt die Fragestellung der Untersuchung präzisiert und werden die Vorgehensweise und Methoden dargestellt. Die Untersuchungsergebnisse werden in den Punkten vier bis sieben mit jeweils unterschiedlichen Schwerpunkten berichtet. Wir schließen mit einem Fazit.

In methodischer Hinsicht ist dieser Bericht auf der Basis eines begrenzten Budgets eine explorative Studie für eine Fragestellung, die bisher unerforscht ist. Es gelang, Zugang zu Akten der „Wohngemeinschaft für Flüchtlingskinder Nürnberg e. V." zu erhalten, einer Institution, die seit mehr als 25 Jahren UMF betreut und fördert.

Migrationssoziologische und rechtliche Bedingungen der Lebenssituation von UMF

Bezüglich der Ursachen und Motive des Kommens der UMF sind prinzipiell vor allem drei Komplexe möglich:

- Kinder- bzw. jugendspezifische Bedrohungslagen
- Die (ungewollte) Trennung von den Eltern während einer Flucht
- Gezieltes Senden der Kinder durch ihre Eltern.

Kinderspezifische Bedrohungslagen können z. B. bei Jungen sein, als Kindersoldat rekrutiert zu werden; bei Mädchen kann die Drohung von Zwangsverheiratung oder Genitalverstümmlung ein Motiv darstellen. Ohne bestimmte Formen der Unterstützung dürfte es für Kinder und Jugendliche aber kaum möglich sein, solchen Bedrohungslagen zu entfliehen. Dass es bei fliehenden Familien in Spannungssituationen und chaotischen Verhältnissen, wie etwa im Krieg oder bei Massenfluchten, zu ungewollten Trennungen von Kindern von ihren Familien kommen kann, ist sehr wahrscheinlich und konnte während der großen Fluchtkrise im Jahr 2015 nicht selten beobachtet werden. Zugleich bestehen unter den Bedingungen moderner Kommunikation aber viele Möglichkeiten, Kontakte und Beziehungen in der Familie wiederherzustellen, wenn nicht rechtliche Barrieren im Wege stehen.

Viele Erfahrungen und Urteile von Hilfsorganisationen, ExpertInnenen und PraktikerInnenn sprechen dafür, dass das Senden der Kinder und Jugendlichen durch ihre Eltern unter Indienstnahme von Schleusern die überwiegende Ursache und Motivform für das Phänomen der unbegleiteten Jugendlichen ist (Angenendt 2000, 136; Deutscher Caritasverband 2014, 23 f.; Heckmann 2016). Schutz der Kinder vor Gewalt und Not kann ein Motiv der Eltern sein, ein anderes und das wahrscheinlich stärkste Motiv von Eltern besteht aber darin, den Kindern Bildung, Ausbildung und Beruf in einer Form und Qualität im Ausland zu ermöglichen, die im Herkunftsland als nicht realisierbar angesehen wird. Das Erreichen einer Position in einem der entwickelten Länder durch ein Familienmitglied wird zugleich als Chance gesehen, Ressourcen für die verbliebene Familie zu gewinnen, z. B. in Form von Rücküberweisungen. In diesem Sinne hofft man, einen „Anker" im der wohlhabenden Welt zu gewinnen; dass der Anker zu einer Möglichkeit wird, selbst den Kindern nachzufolgen, ist unter den Bedingungen der Gesetzeslage zur Familienzusammenführung in Deutschland allerdings nur unter ganz restriktiven Bedingungen möglich.

Die Entscheidung für ein bestimmtes Zielland erfolgt nicht nur nach dem Bild, das man sich von diesem Land macht, sondern vor allem nach bereits bestehenden familiären oder anderen Beziehungen zu dort lebenden Personen. Durch ungeplante Ereignisse und Hindernisse für die Schleusung kann jedoch das Zielland verfehlt werden und die UMF finden sich in einem Land wieder, das keineswegs als Zielland vorgesehen war (Heckmann 2007; Scholz 2013, 102 ff. und 121 f.)

Die Lebensbedingungen der UMF stehen unter dem Primat des Rechts. *„Das Recht bestimmt den Spielraum von Institutionen und Personen, und zwar differenziert nach der Phase des Aufenthalts"* (Balluseck 2003, 9). In rechtlicher Hinsicht hat für die Lebensverhältnisse der UMF in Deutschland zunächst die Kinderrechtskonvention der Vereinten Nationen aus dem Jahr 1998 großes Gewicht, die seit 2010 uneingeschränkt gilt und den Kindern und Jugendlichen u. a. ein Recht auf Gleichbehandlung, Gesundheit, Wohlfahrt und auf persönliche Entwicklung gibt (Bundesfachverband Unbegleitete Minderjährige Flüchtlinge 2013). Die Gewährung des Status der Jugendhilfe in Deutschland mit umfassender Betreuung und Förderung ist letztlich eine Konsequenz der Anerkennung der internationalen Kinderrechtskonvention. In ihrer Wirkung wird sie jedoch z. T. relativiert durch die Unsicherheiten des Aufenthaltsstatus der UMF. „Aufgrund dieser besonderen Situation – unbegleitet, minderjährig, Ausländer – ist für ihre Lebenssituation in Deutschland das Spannungsverhältnis von Aufenthaltsrecht und Jugendhilferecht sowie dessen praktische Ausgestaltung von entscheidender Bedeutung. Während das Aufenthaltsrecht den Zuzug und die Rechtmäßigkeit des Aufenthalts von

Drittstaatsangehörigen regelt, bestimmt das Jugendhilferecht u. a. die staatlichen Aufgaben, mit denen Kinder und Jugendliche in ihrer Entwicklung zu eigenständigen Persönlichkeiten unterstützt werden sollen" (Müller 2014, 10). Bei aller Betreuung und Förderung bleibt die Rechtmäßigkeit des Aufenthalts ungeklärt und ungewiss.

Für die Kind- und Jugendphase ist allerdings zunächst über die Kinderrechtskonvention mit dem Duldungsstatus die vorläufige Sicherung des Aufenthalts gegeben. Duldung ist aber kein echter Aufenthaltstitel und beinhaltet nur den Schutz vor Abschiebung.

Um einen Aufenthaltstitel zu gewinnen ist zunächst die Antragstellung auf Asyl ein möglicher Weg und bei Anerkennung der Gründe den Antragstellern nach §25 Abs.1 AufenthG eine Aufenthaltserlaubnis zu gewähren. Ein relevanter Anteil von UMF bzw. ihrer Vormünder verzichtet jedoch auf einen Asylantrag und versucht andere Möglichkeiten der Aufenthaltsgewinnung. So gab es etwa im Jahr 2013 bei 6.584 Inobhutnahmen nur 2.486 Asylanträge (Scholz 2013, 30).

Für gut integrierte Jugendliche, die vor Vollendung des 14. Lebensjahrs eingereist sind und einen anerkannten Schul- oder Ausbildungsabschluss erreicht haben, besteht nach §25a Abs. 1 AufenthG die Möglichkeit des Erhalts eines Aufenthaltstitels. In der Literatur wird das z.T. auch als „verdienter Aufenthalt" bezeichnet. Weitere Möglichkeiten sind zusammenfassend mit den bisher genannten in der folgenden Übersicht enthalten:

- Erfolgreicher Asylantrag nach §25 Abs.1 AufenthG
- §25a Abs.1 AufenthG für gut integrierte Jugendliche
- Positive Entscheidung einer Härtefallkommission des Landtags
- Adoption durch einen deutschen Staatsbürger
- Eheschließung mit einem deutschen Staatsbürger.

Sozialisationstheoretische Konzepte der Untersuchung

Die Literatur über unbegleitete minderjährige Flüchtlinge wird durch rechtliche und humanitäre Fragestellungen und Untersuchungen beherrscht (Parusel 2009). Fragen der psychosozialen Entwicklung der Kinder und Jugendlichen in ihrer neuen Umgebung, also Aspekte ihrer Sozialisation, sind dagegen kaum zu finden. Ballusek (2003) bildet eine gewisse Ausnahme, da hier u. a. Konzepte der Sozialisationsforschung in ihrer Bedeutung für die Untersuchung der Lage von UMF diskutiert werden. Das Thema und die Untersuchung von Entwicklungsverläufen und Integrationsprozessen ist jedoch kein Schwerpunkt dieser Arbeit. Unsere Untersuchung hat sich dagegen zum Ziel gesetzt, Entwicklung und Lebensläufe von UMF in Deutschland über einen Zeitraum von 10 Jahren zu verfolgen. Das wird in Punkt 3 näher ausgeführt.

Unser allgemeines Verständnis von Sozialisation, das der Untersuchung zugrunde liegt, kann knapp wie folgt zusammengefasst werden: Sozialisation ist

Persönlichkeitsentwicklung, die in Auseinandersetzung mit und in Interaktion mit der sozialen und kulturellen Umwelt stattfindet. Sozialisation besteht zum einen aus intentionalen Prozessen, die wir Erziehung nennen, zum anderen aus nichtintentionalen Prozessen, die über Erziehung hinausgehen und die im Alltagshandeln in allen möglichen Interaktionen als Lernprozesse stattfinden. Diese sind durch Mechanismen und Prozesse wie Lernen am Modell, Belohnung und Bestrafung sowie Imitation gekennzeichnet. Das Element der „Umwelt" in der Definition von Sozialisation ist bei UMF mit besonderem Schwerpunkt die rechtliche Umwelt, da diese ganz grundlegende Bedeutung für die Lebenschancen hat. Man kann insgesamt sagen, dass Sozialisation mehr ist als:

1. Erziehung und direkte didaktische Vermittlung von kulturellen Normen, Werten und Kenntnissen
2. einfache Hereinnahme, das Eintrichtern, die Verinnerlichung von Normen, Werten und anderen kulturellen Inhalten: das Individuum reagiert nämlich auf Werteinflüsse, verarbeitet, organisiert und verändert sie auch.

Das aktive Handeln des Individuums im Sozialisationsprozess ist auch nötig, wie man am Beispiel des Wertesystems von Gesellschaften nachvollziehen kann. Das Wertesystem bzw. die Wertesysteme, wie sie gerade in einer pluralistischen Gesellschaft existieren, sind ja keineswegs einheitlich bzw. widerspruchsfrei und durch oft starke Unterschiede gekennzeichnet. Arbeitet man bei Sozialisation nur mit der Vorstellung der Hereinnahme, der Verinnerlichung oder gesellschaftlichen Prägung, dann würden Widersprüche als Widersprüche von Orientierungen einfach in die Person hineingepflanzt und konsistentes Handeln wäre nicht möglich. Die Vorstellung der Prägung oder des Eindringens von Werten übersieht die Notwendigkeit und Fähigkeit des Subjekts, handelnd, organisierend eigenständig Sozialisationseinflüsse wahrzunehmen und anzueignen, d. h. nicht nur einfach zu übernehmen.

Wir müssen also realistischerweise ein „Trichtermodell" von einem „Person-Umwelt Interaktionsmodell" der Sozialisation unterscheiden. Nach dem Interaktionsmodell eignet sich der Mensch Wissen und Werte produktiv an und wird in Entwicklungsschritten zu einem gesellschaftlich handlungsfähigen Subjekt.

Da der Lebenslauf von UMF durch drastische Veränderungen der jeweiligen Umwelten gekennzeichnet ist, sind in Anbetracht der UMF Situation besonders starke Anforderungen an die Person gestellt und kommt der Fähigkeit, mit den sehr unterschiedlichen Umwelten umzugehen und deren oft widersprüchliche Einflüsse zu organisieren, besondere Bedeutung zu. Sie ist eine Bedingung dafür, Stabilität im Lebensverlauf zu gewinnen. Unter den Rahmenbedingungen dieser Untersuchung ist es nicht möglich, durch direkte offene Interviews mit den UMF Einblick in diese Prozesse zu gewinnen. Wir wissen nur, dass es sie gibt und können aber mit unseren Mitteln der Aktenanalyse und von Experteninterviews bestimmte Ergebnisse dieser Prozesse feststellen. Das schließt ein, dass es die komplexen Anforderungen der UMF Situation nicht bewältigt werden und es zu biographischen Brüchen und Fehlentwicklungen kommt.

Unter Beachtung dieser Konzepte und unter sozialisations- und lebenslauftheoretischer Betrachtung ist es sinnvoll, folgende biographische Phasen bei UMF zu unterscheiden:

- *Sozialisation in der Herkunftsfamilie und in der Kultur des Herkunftslandes*
Bei den meisten UMF dauert diese Phase bis zum Alter von 12-14 Jahren. Diese Phase der primären Sozialisation ist außerordentlich wichtig für die Fähigkeit, mit den Anforderungen der Reise oder Flucht und den ganz neuen Bedingungen im Zielland umgehen zu können. Die Anpassungs- und Lernfähigkeit wird dabei besonders von dem kulturellen Kapital und dem Bildungsstand der Herkunftsfamilie beeinflusst (Heckmann 2015, 143ff.).
- *Reise bzw. Schleusung:*
Die Bedingungen der Reise oder Schleusung für die einzelnen UMF variieren stark, u. a. abhängig von dem Ausmaß an Geld, das die Herkunftsfamilie in das Projekt und die Schleusung investieren kann. Während es manchen möglich ist, ins Zielland zu fliegen und nicht zurückgewiesen zu werden, sind andere UMF lange Monate unter oft traumatisierenden und Leben und Gesundheit gefährdenden Bedingungen unterwegs. Der erste Kontakt mit Behörden des Ziellandes erfolgt entweder bei Aufgriff durch die Polizei oder auch durch Selbstmeldung. Es ist davon auszugehen, dass die folgende Hypothese gilt: je belastender die Flucht oder Reise, desto schwieriger der Anpassungsprozess im Zielland und umso größer die persönliche Instabilität.
- *Die erste biographische Phase im Zielland:*
Diese betrifft bei den meisten UMF das Alter von 13-15 Jahren. Sie ist gewissermaßen eine zweite Sozialisation mit der Entwicklung auch neuer Persönlichkeitsstrukturen. In der gegenwärtigen Praxis werden UMF zunächst einer so genannten Clearingstelle zugeführt, in welcher versucht wird, ihre Identität festzustellen; sie werden gesundheitlich untersucht, erhalten erste Sprachunterweisung, werden beim Ausländer- und Schulamt gemeldet und dann in einer Form des gemeinschaftlichen Wohnens untergebracht, sehr häufig in einer betreuten Wohngemeinschaft. Nach deutschem Recht wird ihnen Schutz gemäß der internationalen Kinderrechtskonvention gewährt und sozialrechtlich der Status der Jugendhilfe gegeben.

UMF erhalten in dieser Phase umfassende „rund um die Uhr" Erziehung, sozialpädagogische Betreuung und vielfältige Formen der Förderung, um einen Prozess der Integration in die deutsche Gesellschaft einzuleiten und weiter zu fördern. Unabhängig von der spezifischen Situation der UMF muss in dieser Altersgruppe beachtet werden, dass man es mit einer kritischen Phase der Identitätsbildung von Kindern zu Jugendlichen zu tun hat und Pubertätskrisen durchlaufen werden. Geht man von der These des Sendens der UMF durch Eltern aus ist auch zu vermuten, dass ein bestimmter Einfluss der Elternfamilie weiterbesteht. Da aber die privilegierte rechtliche Konstruktion der UMF von

der Annahme einer Trennung von den Eltern ausgeht, ist es ganz schwer, über deren weiteren Einfluss etwas zu erfahren. Man läuft sonst Gefahr, die besondere Förderung zu verlieren.
- *Zweite biographische Phase im Zielland:*
In Jugendhilfeplänen für UMF wird in der Altersphase von 16-18 Jahren das Ziel angestrebt, Voraussetzungen und tatsächliche Bedingungen eines selbständigen Lebens zu schaffen. Es wird angestrebt, dass die Jugendlichen aus dem gemeinschaftlichen Wohnen mit „rund um die Uhr" Betreuung in ein „außenbetreutes Wohnen" wechseln. Außenbetreutes Wohnen heißt, dass die Jugendlichen in eigenen Wohnungen leben und mit einem begrenzten Betreuungsaufwand von wenigen Stunden wöchentlich weiter betreut und kontrolliert werden, aber sich selbst nur mit einem zugeteilten Budget versorgen. Förderung, z. B. für Bildung in Form von Nachhilfestunden, ist weiter möglich, aber in eingeschränkter Form. Das Erreichen des Erwachsenenstatus bzw. bereits die Zeit davor ist für UMF in aufenthaltsrechtlicher Sicht eine Phase wachsender Unsicherheit, von Angst und Stress, da ihr Aufenthalt mit dem Wegfall der Sicherung über die internationale Kinderrechtskonvention unsicher geworden ist.
- *Erwachsenensein:*
Die nun erwachsenen Flüchtlinge, wenn sie nicht über einen erfolgreichen Asylantrag oder andere, oben genannte Möglichkeiten einen Aufenthaltstitel erwerben, haben zunächst weiter einen Duldungsstatus, aber dieser steht unter der Drohung des Vollzugs der Abschiebung. Um in Deutschland bleiben zu können, muss ein neuer Aufenthaltsstatus erreicht werden, dessen Erwerbsmöglichkeiten weiter oben beschrieben wurden. Falls Förderung in bestimmten Bereichen weiter notwendig sein sollte, kann diese nur noch stark eingeschränkt über den bisherigen Jugendhilfestatus erfolgen und muss über übliche sozialstaatliche Instrumente, wie z. B. Ausbildungshilfen oder Arbeitsmarktförderprogramme beantragt werden.

Fragestellungen und Methoden der empirischen Untersuchung

Die vorliegende empirische Untersuchung beruht auf der Auswertung der Akten und von Experteninterviews zu zwanzig UMF, die alle 2005/2006 von der „Wohngemeinschaft für Flüchtlingskinder Nürnberg e. V." in Nürnberg aufgenommen wurden und deren Lebensverläufe bis zum Jahre 2016 verfolgt werden können. Es handelt sich also nicht um eine Stichprobe, sondern die ausgewerteten Akten stehen für die Gesamtheit der im genannten Zeitraum in der Einrichtung angefallenen Fälle von UMF Aufnahme und Förderung. Über die Repräsentativität der Einrichtung für Einrichtungen in Bayern und Deutschland können wir nur die Vermutung anstellen, dass sie im Großen und Ganzen ähnlich waren. Genau wissen wir es nicht. Das Hauptinteresse für die Untersuchung dieser Fälle ist, dass man prinzipiell, wenn auch nicht mit der gleichen Genauigkeit für alle Phasen, den Lebensweg der UMF über ca. 10 Jahre rekonstruieren kann.

Die Untersuchung ist als explorativ und qualitativ zu bezeichnen, da sie sich mit bisher nicht untersuchten Fragestellungen befasst und zunächst einmal Kategorien, Beschreibungen und Grundlagen zur Hypothesenbildung über Lebenslaufprozesse bei UMF entwickelt. Es werden im Rahmen der Beschreibung nur einfache Auszählungen vorgenommen, statistische Analysen sind methodisch nicht möglich.

Die Akten, die wir auswerten konnten, beziehen sich auf das Leben der UMF in der Wohngemeinschaft, also bis etwa zum 16. Lebensjahr und bevor sie in die Phase des außenbetreuten Wohnens eintreten; oben hatten wir von der ersten biographischen Phase im Zielland gesprochen. Die Akten enthalten neben Informationen über die Arbeit der Institution mit den jeweiligen UMF u. a. Dokumente der Ausländerbehörden, des Bundesamtes für Migration und Flüchtlinge, des Jugendamtes mit Entwicklungsberichten zu den Jugendlichen, von Schulen und Ausbildungsinstitutionen sowie Dokumente zum Gesundheitszustand der WG Bewohner.

Um die Informationen in standardisierter und systematischer Weise aus den Akten zu extrahieren wurden Kategorien gebildet und für die zwanzig Personen in einer Excel-Tabelle festgehalten. Folgende Kategorien wurden entwickelt, um die Informationen aus den Akten in Stichworten zusammenzufassen. Nicht in allen Fällen konnten auch Informationen zu den Kategorien gefunden werde. Folgende Kategorien wurden verwendet:

- Identifikationsnummer, Geburtsjahr, Geschlecht, Herkunftsland
- Einreisedatum, Zeit und Dauer des WG Aufenthalts
- Entwicklung des Aufenthaltsrechtsstatus
- Fluchtgründe und Fluchtdauer
- Soziales und kulturelles Kapital der Herkunftsfamilie
- Entwicklung der Persönlichkeit und der psychischen Stabilität, der Gesundheit
- Vormundschaft (amtlich vs. privat)
- Entwicklung der kulturellen, sportlichen Interessen
- Entwicklung der sozialen Beziehungen
- Sprachliche und schulische Entwicklung, Lernmotivation, Arbeitsverhalten, Leistungen, Fördermaßnahmen
- Schlüsselereignisse während des Aufenthalts in der WG.

Um diese Informationen weiter zu verdichten, wurden auf der Basis von Sozialisations- und Integrationstheorie Integrationsbedingungen und Integrationsprozesse unterschieden. Integrationsbedingungen wurden wie folgt definiert:

- Aufenthaltsdauer in WG mit Förderung
- Kulturelles Kapital der Herkunftsfamilie
- Soziales Kapital in Deutschland
- Fluchtbedingungen
- Aufenthaltsstatus während des WG Aufenthaltes.
- Integrationsprozesse werden verstanden als:

- Sprachentwicklung
- Entwicklung der persönlichen Stabilität
- Schulische Entwicklung
- Soziale Kompetenzentwicklung
- Entwicklung kultureller, sportlicher Interessen.

Auf den einzelnen Dimensionen wurden nach Durchsicht des Materials in Hinsicht auf Entwicklung und Integrationsfortschritte auf einer Nominalskala die Werte positiv, ambivalent und negativ vergeben.

Für die Phase des außenbetreuten Wohnens entwickelten wir einen Rechercheleitfaden, mit dessen Hilfe wir die weitere Entwicklung der UMF bis zum 18. Lebensjahr, also der Phase des Erwachsenseins, verfolgen konnten. Hierzu wurden Gespräche und Recherchen mit Sozialarbeitern durchgeführt, die die Entwicklung der Jugendlichen in dieser Phase begleitet hatten, die Akten aus dem außenbetreuten Wohnen zur Verfügung hatten und Urteile über die Entwicklung in den einzelnen Dimensionen abgeben können. Diese Experten konnten auch globale Aussagen darüber machen, wie sich der weitere Weg der Jugendlichen in der Phase des Erwachsenensein gestaltet hat, da sie Kontakte zu den UMF aufrecht erhalten. Biographische Grunddaten zu den 20 UMF gibt Tabelle 1 wieder.

		männlich	weiblich
geboren	1988-1990	5	5
	1991-1994	3	7
Einreisealter	13-14	3	4
	15-16	5	7
	17		1
Herkunftsland	Vietnam	5	3
	Kambodscha	2	3
	Eritrea	1	3
	Äthiopien		3

Tabelle 1 Biographische Grunddaten der UMF

Quelle: Akten der „Wohngemeinschaft für Flüchtlingskinder Nürnberg e. V.", eigene Darstellung.

Als die 12 Mädchen und 8 Jungen einreisten bzw. eingeschleust wurden, waren sie überwiegend 15-16 Jahre (12) bzw. 13-14 Jahre (7) alt; ein Mädchen war 17 Jahre alt. Heute sind diese UMF 23-28 Jahre alt. Zumindest in groben Zügen können wir also für die große Mehrheit der untersuchten UMF für gut 10 Jahre ihren Weg verfolgen. Gegenüber den in den letzten Jahren häufigsten Herkunftsländern wie Afghanistan, Somalia, Syrien und Eritrea (Scholz 2013, 22) sind in unseren Daten ostasiatische Länder am stärksten vertreten. In der Gegenwart sind in der untersuchten Einrichtung die Herkunftsländer Eritrea, Äthiopien, Somalia, Indien, Gambia und Afghanistan am stärksten vertreten (Wohngemeinschaft für Flüchtlingskinder 2015). Mädchen sind in unseren Daten gegenüber Jungen etwas stärker vertreten.

In der Sozialisations- und Integrationsforschung erweisen sich das soziokulturelle Kapital der Herkunftsfamilie und durch diese eingeleitete Bildungsprozesse als wichtigste Größen für Entwicklungs- und Integrationsprozesse von Jugendlichen, welche gesellschaftliche Positionierung und Teilhabe im Erwachsenenalter bestimmen (Heckmann 2015, 143 ff.). Auch die Fähigkeit, eine neue Sprache zu lernen und sich in neuen gesellschaftlichen Verhältnissen zu orientieren ist stark vom mitgebrachten Bildungsstand abhängig.

Informationen über die genauere gesellschaftliche Positionierung der Herkunftsfamilien der Jugendlichen sind den Akten nicht zu entnehmen. Man ist daher auf vereinzelte Inforationen und die Interpretation von Geschichten, die die Jugendlichen erzählen, angewiesen. Aufgrund vereinzelter Angaben („Mein Vater war Fischer") und den Urteilen der betreuenden Sozialarbeiter stammt nach den Kategorien eines Schichtenmodells die große Mehrheit der Jugendlichen aus Familien der oberen Unterschicht bzw. der unteren Mittelschicht in ihren Herkunftsländern. Es bedarf gewisser Mittel, um Reise und Schleusung zu bezahlen. Arme bzw. mittellose Schichten in den Herkunftsländern verfügen nicht über solche Mittel. Wohlhabende Familien dagegen können ihre Kinder zur Ausbildung legal ins Ausland schicken.

Die vielfältigen Informationen über die UMF sollen unter den folgenden vier Fragestellungen untersucht werden:

1. Ausgehend von dem Stress der Trennung von der Familie und den Gefahren der Reise oder Schleusung soll gefragt werden, ob es gelingt, in den zwei biographischen Phasen in der Wohngemeinschaft und im außenbetreuten Wohnen eine Stabilisierung der Persönlichkeit zu erreichen und damit Grundlagen für einen Integrationsprozess zu legen.
2. Für die gesellschaftlichen Partizipationschancen und den Integrationsprozess der UMF ist die Frage der schulischen und beruflichen Kompetenzentwicklung der UMF von besonderer Bedeutung. Es soll untersucht werden: Wie verläuft die schulische und berufliche Kompetenzentwicklung? Sind UMT eine besonders integrations- und leistungsorientierte Gruppe?
3. Gelingt es den UMF, einen sicheren Aufenthaltstitel zu erreichen? Wenn ja, auf welche Weise? Wenn nein, warum nicht?
4. Abschließend und zusammenfassend soll gefragt werden, ob als Erwachsene eine Integration erreicht wurde, und wenn ja, welcher Art diese ist.

Stabilisierung der Persönlichkeit in Wohngemeinschaft und außenbetreutem Wohnen?

Der Aufenthalt in der Wohngemeinschaft in der ersten biographischen Phase und der Status der Jugendhilfe beinhalten eine Vielzahl von Bedingungen und Maßnahmen, die die Sozialisation und Integration der jungen Flüchtlinge fördern sollen. Die Wohngemeinschaft bietet sicheres und ordentliches Wohnen, gute Versorgung mit Zahlung eines Taschengeldes, medizinische und psychosoziale Betreuung, Anleitung und Mithilfe bei der Haushaltsarbeit für Jungen und Mädchen, Rekrutierung eines privaten Vormunds, Integration in das Schulsystem, Hilfe beim Deutschlernen und Organisierung fachspezifischen Nachhilfeunterrichts, gemeinsame Freizeit- und Ferienaktivitäten, Unterstützung bei Integration in Vereine und Hilfe bei aufenthaltsrechtlichen Fragen, ohne dass diese Aufzählung vollständig wäre. Diese umfassende Betreuung, Förderung und Eltern ähnliche Kontrolle ist eingebunden in die Information und Kontrolle des Jugendamtes, das im halbjährlichen Rhythmus die Erreichung der im Jugendhilfeplan festgesetzten Ziele überprüft und in Absprache mit den Jugendlichen, Sozialarbeitern und Vormund neue Verhaltensziele formuliert.

In der zweiten biographischen Phase, im außenbetreuten Wohnen, wird davon ausgegangen, dass die beschriebenen Maßnahmen zu einer bestimmten Stabilität und Kompetenz der jungen Flüchtlinge geführt haben, die es gestatten, bei Fortsetzung der finanziellen Unterstützung für Wohnung und Lebensmittel einen Großteil der Fördermaßnahmen einzustellen und nur ausgewählte, wie z.B. Nachhilfeunterricht, weiterzuführen und durch Beratung und Kontrolle weitere Sozialisations- und Integrationsfortschritte zu erzielen.

Die oben formulierte erste Fragestellung interessiert sich dafür, ob es mit den beschriebenen Maßnahmen gelingt, die durch Trennung von der Familie, den Stress der Schleusung und den Anforderungen der Situation im neuen Land entstandenen Ängste, Unsicherheiten und die Bedrohung der persönlichen Stabilität zu überwinden und neue persönliche Stabilität zu gewinnen. Das Konzept der persönlichen Stabilität bzw. Instabilität fasst Informationen zusammen, die sich u. a. auf das Vorhandensein oder Fehlen von Störungen psychosozialer Prozesse wie Verschlossenheit, starke Ängste, Schlaflosigkeit, psychische und psychosomatische Erkrankungen und die Unfähigkeit, soziale Beziehungen einzugehen, erfasst. Aussagen zur persönlichen Stabilität sind Aussagen und Urteile der betreuenden Sozialarbeiter.

	männlich	weiblich
Persönliche Stabilität	4	2
Partielle Stabilität	2	2
Fortdauernde Instabilität	2	6

Tabelle 2 Persönliche Stabilität in der ersten biographischen Phase

Quelle: Akten der „Wohngemeinschaft für Flüchtlingskinder Nürnberg e. V.", eigene Darstellung.

Zur Messung der Entwicklung persönlicher Stabilität haben wir Aussagen, Beobachtungen und Urteile in den Akten und in den Gesprächen mit den Sozialarbeitern ausgewertet und in drei Kategorien zusammengefasst. Die drei Kategorien und ihre Verteilung unter den UMF zeigt die Tabelle 2.

Von den 20 UMF, die in der Untersuchung erfasst werden, können zwei Personen nicht in die Auswertung einbezogen werden, da sie während des Aufenthalts in der WG untertauchten und vermisst gemeldet werden. Bei sechs oder einem Drittel der UMF gelingt es, in der Phase des Aufenthaltes in der Wohngemeinschaft Stabilität zu erreichen, bei vier Personen gelingt es zum Teil. Bei einem beträchtlichen Teil von acht UMF setzt sich jedoch die persönliche Instabilität fort, wobei es einen Geschlechtereffekt zu geben scheint. Zur Interpretation dieser Werte sei an die vielfältigen Stressfaktoren in der Lage der UMF gerade in der ersten biographischen Phase erinnert: Trennung von Familie und vertrauter Umgebung, Unsicherheiten und Gefahren der Reise bzw. Schleusung, Erlernen einer völlig neuen Umgebung, Sprache und Kultur, Heimweh, Unsicherheiten des Aufenthaltsstatus, Fortbestehen des Drucks elterlicher Erwartungen.

Es stellt sich nun für die zweite biografische Phase die Frage, ob es bei Fortdauer der Arbeit der Institution in Form des außenbetreuten Wohnens gelingt, persönliche Stabilität bei weiteren UMF zu erreichen. Zwar liegen die Belastungen von Familientrennung, Reise und der Stress der ersten Anpassung an die neuen Verhältnisse länger zurück, aber als neuer, potenziell Ängste produzierender Faktor kommt mit dem Erreichen der Volljährigkeit und dem Wegfall des Schutzes durch die Kinderrechtskonvention die Angst vor Abschiebung hinzu. Zudem ist die bisherige Betreuung und Förderung stark eingeschränkt und Anforderungen an Selbstorganisation und häusliche Selbstversorgung sind gestiegen.

	männlich	weiblich
Persönliche Stabilität	5	5
Partielle Stabilität	1	1
Fortdauernde Instabilität	1	3

Tabelle 3 Persönliche Stabilität in der zweiten biographischen Phase

Quelle: Akten der „Wohngemeinschaft für Flüchtlingskinder Nürnberg e. V.", eigene Darstellung.

Tabelle 3 gibt Auskunft über die Entwicklung bis zum Erreichen der Volljährigkeit. Zu beachten ist hierbei zunächst, dass sich die beobachtbare Gruppe gegenüber der ersten biographischen Phase weiter verkleinert hat. Zu den in der ersten Phase untergetauchten zwei Fällen kommt der Fall einer freiwilligen Rückreise ins Herkunftsland und der Fall einer (irregulären) Weiterreise eines Mädchens zu ihrem Freund nach England, so dass es sich in der zweiten biographischen Phase nur noch um 16 Fälle handelt. Ein positiver Trend zeigt sich darin, dass sich die Zahl der persönlichen Stabilisierungen vergrößert hat; mehr als die Hälfte der erfassten Fälle hat persönliche Stabilität erreicht, zwei weitere partielle Stabilität und vier Fälle bleiben instabil.

Zu den Personen, denen es nicht gelingt, sich zu stabilisieren, gehört UMF 2. Sie steht für die Wirkung der Unsicherheit und Angst vor dem Verlust des Aufenthalts-status. Die Jugendliche ist in der ersten Phase noch persönlich instabil, macht aber bei Sprachentwicklung, schulischen Leistungen und der Entwicklung kultureller Interessen durchgängig positive Entwicklungsschritte. Das setzt sich zunächst fort, aber mit Annäherung an die Volljährigkeit führt die lähmende Angst vor einer Ab-schiebung schließlich zu einer starken Verschlechterung der schulischen Leistungen, so dass es ihr nicht gelingt, einen Abschluss zu erreichen und eine Berufsausbildung zu beginnen. Über die Eheschließung mit einem Landsmann mit deutscher Staatsangehörigkeit erlangt sie schließlich einen Aufenthaltsstatus und wird über soziale Integration in die ethnische Community in Nürnberg weiter stabilisiert.

Kompetenzentwicklung in Schule und Ausbildung

Ein wesentliches Ziel der Betreuung und Förderung während des Aufenthaltes in der Wohngemeinschaft und während des betreuten Wohnens besteht darin, die Jugendlichen über Schule und Ausbildung für gesellschaftliche Partizipation und Teilhabe zu qualifizieren. Tabelle 4 zeigt zunächst die Entwicklung schulischer Leistungen in der ersten biographischen Phase.

	männlich	weiblich
Positive Entwicklung	7	6
Partielle Leistungsprobleme	2	2
Leistungsprobleme		1

Tabelle 4 Entwicklung der schulischen Leistungen in der ersten biographischen Phase

Quelle: Akten der „Wohngemeinschaft für Flüchtlingskinder Nürnberg e. V.", eigene Darstellung.

13 der 18 UMF zeigen an Hand von Zeugnissen und Aussagen von Lehrern eine positive Entwicklung der schulischen Leistungen. Angesichts des Fehlens jeglicher Kenntnisse der deutschen Sprache bei der Einreise nach Deutschland und ihrer schwierigen Lebenssituation spiegelt das zum einen die Qualität der Arbeit in der Wohngemeinschaft, zum anderen aber auch die selbstorganisierenden Fähigkeiten der UMF in ihrem zweiten Sozialisationsprozess.

	männlich	weiblich
Schulabschluss (Hauptschule/Quali)	6	5
Kein Schulabschluss	2	2
Keine Information über Schulabschluss		1
Abschluss Ausbildung	3	3
Ausbildung ohne Abschluss	1	
Keine Ausbildung	3	4
Keine Information zur Ausbildung	2	

Tabelle 5 Kompetenzentwicklung 2005/6 -2016

Quelle: Akten der „Wohngemeinschaft für Flüchtlingskinder Nürnberg e. V.", eigene Darstellung.

Betrachtet man allerdings über einen längeren Zeitraum die gesamte Kompetenzentwicklung in Schule und Ausbildung (Tabelle 5) relativiert sich das Bild in gewisser Weise: Fast alle UMF, die einen Schulabschluss machen, erreichen nur den Hauptschulabschluss, z. T. den so genannten qualifizierten Hauptschulabschluss („Quali"). Ein einziger Schüler erreicht den Realschulabschluss, ist auf der Fachoberschule und wird voraussichtlich im Jahr 2017 sein Fachabitur machen.

In Bezug auf den Eintritt und den Abschluss einer Berufsausbildung sieht die Bilanz noch nüchterner aus: nur etwas mehr als ein Drittel der erfassten UMF erreicht einen Abschluss; bei den Frauen sind das fast nur einfache Abschlüsse wie Hauswirtschaftlerin; einer einzigen gelingt es, einen Abschluss als Krankenschwester zu machen.

Erreichen eines sicheren Aufenthaltsstatus in Deutschland?

Es ist die von Deutschland unterzeichnete internationale Kinderrechtskonvention, die den UMF zunächst bis zur Volljährigkeit Versorgung, Schutz und über den Duldungsstatus temporäre Aufenthaltssicherheit gibt. Duldung ist aber kein eigentlicher Aufenthaltstitel, sondern nur eine zeitweise Aussetzung einer Abschiebung. Es kommt also für die UMF, sofern sie in Deutschland leben wollen, darauf an, möglichst frühzeitig einen legalen und mit Aussicht auf Dauerhaftigkeit versehenen Aufenthaltstitel zu erreichen. Man kann davon ausgehen, dass fast alle den Wunsch haben, in Deutschland bleiben zu können. Es würde den Rahmen dieser Studie sprengen, die Verläufe des Bemühens um Aufenthaltstitel bei den einzelnen Personen und in den einzelnen Schritten zu verfolgen; wir können aber zeigen, welche Ergebnisse sich im Verlauf von ca. 10 Jahren im Jahre 2016 eingestellt haben (Tabelle 6).

Aufenthalt auf der Grundlage von		Kein Aufenthalt wegen	
Asylgewährung	5	Abschiebung	3
Verdienter Aufenthalt §25a AufenthG	2	Untertauchen	2
Eheschließung mit deutschem Staatsbürger	1	Rückreise	1
Adoption durch deutsche Staatsangehörige	1	Weiterreise	1
Geburt und Vater des Kin-des mit Aufenthaltstitel	2		
Insgesamt	11		7
Keine Information	2		

Tabelle 6 Aufenthaltsstatus der UMF in Deutschland 2016

Quelle: Akten der „Wohngemeinschaft für Flüchtlingskinder Nürnberg e. V.", eigene Darstellung.

Zunächst ist festzustellen, dass es einer Mehrheit der UMF im Verlauf von 10 Jahren gelungen ist, einen legalen Aufenthaltstitel zu erreichen, in einem Fall sogar die deutsche Staatsbürgerschaft zu erlangen. Überraschend ist die Vielfalt der Wege, die dorthin beschritten wurden. Es sind insgesamt 5 verschiedene Wege, auf denen es den ja prinzipiell unter Abschiebedrohung stehenden UMF gelungen ist, einen legalen Aufenthaltstitel zu bekommen. Hierbei ist die erfolgreiche Antragstellung für Asyl am häufigsten vertreten. Unter „verdientem Aufenthalt"(zwei Fälle) ist nach dem Aufenthaltsgesetz u. a. zu verstehen, dass „es gewährleistet erscheint, dass er (der Flüchtling, FH) sich auf Grund seiner bisherigen Ausbildungs- und Lebensverhältnisse in die Lebensverhältnisse der Bundesrepublik Deutschland einfügen kann" (§25aAufenth.G). Zwei weiblichen UMF ist es gelungen, über den Schutz für ein geborenes Kind in Verbindung mit der Vaterschaft eines Mannes mit einem legalen Aufenthaltstitel einen Aufenthaltstitel zu erreichen. Eheschließung mit einem deutschen Staatsbürger und Adoption waren weitere Wege für einen legalen Aufenthalt in der untersuchten Gruppe.

Einem beträchtlichen Teil von zumindest sieben Personen gelingt es aber nicht, einen Aufenthaltsstatus zu erreichen. Abschiebung ist mit drei Fällen vertreten. In einem der drei Fälle wurde das Jugendamt informiert, dass sämtliche Angaben des betreffenden Jugendlichen falsch seien. Da dies zutraf, wurde er zunächst verklagt, die bisherigen Kosten seiner Betreuung und Versorgung von 50.000 € zu zahlen; da dies jedoch nicht möglich war, wurde er abgeschoben. In einem zweiten Fall tauchte ein UMF zunächst unter, wurde aber später in Norddeutschland aufgegriffen und anschließend abgeschoben. Der dritte Fall einer Abschiebung hing nach Aussagen der Betreuer damit zusammen, dass sich der Betroffene in sorgloser Weise um nichts gekümmert habe und erst aktiv wurde, als es schon zu spät war.

Der Fall einer Rückreise hing laut Betreuern mit dem starken Heimweh der Person zusammen. Wahrscheinlich wegen geringer Aussichten auf einen Status tauchten zwei UMF unter und es ist nicht bekannt, wo sie sich aufhalten und wie es ihnen geht. Der Fall einer Weiterreise sieht zunächst auch wie ein Untertauchen aus, aber die Person meldete sich nach illegaler Einreise in Großbritannien, wo ihr Freund lebt.

Integrationsprozesse

Legaler und sicherer Aufenthalt ist für jeden Einwanderer eine Grundvoraussetzung für Integration. Integration als umfassender gesellschaftlicher Mitgliedschaftserwerb mit den Dimensionen struktureller, kultureller, sozialer und identifikativer Integration ist ein langwieriger Prozess, der häufig über drei Generationen verläuft (Heckmann 2015, 82). Trotz eines sicheren Aufenthalts ist also nach 10 Jahren Leben in Deutschland noch keine „vollständige" Integration zu erwarten. Es werden sich aber unterschiedliche Typen von Integration herausbilden.

Für die Typenbildung konnten drei integrationsrelevante Variablen erhoben werden: Eingliederung in den Arbeitsprozess, Familienstatus und soziale Verkehrskreise. Eingliederung in den Arbeitsprozess ist der Kern aller Integration, Familiengründung verstärkt die Bindung an das Einwanderungsland und soziale Verkehrskreise indizieren Mitgliedschaft in privaten und informellen sozialen Beziehungen. Beziehungen zu Mehrheit und Minderheit werden als stärkere Form der Integration als soziale Beziehungen nur zur Minderheit angesehen.

Merkmalskombination	
Typ A: • berufstätig • Familiengründung • Soziale Beziehungen zu Mehrheit und Minderheit	4
Typ B: • berufstätig • ledig • Soziale Beziehungen zu Mehrheit und Minderheit	4
Typ C: • berufstätig • Familiengründung • Soziale Beziehungen zu Minderheit	1
Typ D: • Hausfrau • Familiengründung • Soziale Beziehungen zu Minderheit	1
Typ E: • Schüler • Ledig • Soziale Beziehungen zu Mehrheit und Minderheit	1

Tabelle 7 Typen der Integration von UMF 2016

Quelle: Akten der „Wohngemeinschaft für Flüchtlingskinder Nürnberg e. V.", eigene Darstellung.

Typ A mit Berufstätigkeit, Familiengründung und sozialen Beziehungen zu Mehrheit und Minderheit ist in diesem Sinne die stärkste und mit vier Fällen vertretene Form der Integration. Typ B mit ebenfalls vier Fällen und dem Merkmal „ledig" ist vielleicht in Vorbereitung, Typ A zu werden; das trifft auch mit Verzögerung auch auf Typ E zu. Typ C und D sind schwächere Formen der Integration, da sie zum einen soziale Beziehungen nur in der Minderheit, also ihrer jeweiligen Ethnie haben, und bei Typ B die Einbindung in Berufsarbeit fehlt.

Insgesamt gesehen haben also in der von uns erfassten Gruppe von 20 UMF 11 einen Status unterschiedlichen Grades von Integration in Deutschland erreicht. Diese Relation spiegelt die zu einem bestimmten Zeitpunkt an einem bestimmten Ort rekonstruierten Entwicklungen; aufwendige repräsentative Studien könnten klären, ob diese Daten repräsentativ sind.

Fazit

Unbegleitete minderjährige Flüchtlinge sind in der Gegenwart von einer eher wenig beachteten Randgruppe der Migration zu einer mit über 35.000 Zugängen im Jahre 2016 beachtenswert großen Gruppe geworden. Neben den Auswirkungen der gegenwärtigen allgemeinen Migrationskrise spiegelt diese Entwicklung auch die Attraktivität des Jugendhilfestatus, der den Kindern und Jugendlichen gewährt wird. Man kann diesen sicherlich als Pull Faktor für Migration bezeichnen.

Im Spiegel der Literatur und öffentlicher Diskurse besteht das Besondere dieser explorativen Studie darin, dass sie versucht hat, die Lebensverläufe von UMF über 10 Jahre zu verfolgen. Es hat sich dabei gezeigt, dass es nicht für alle Jugendlichen an Hand der erfassbaren Daten möglich ist, die gesamten 10 Jahre zu verfolgen, z. B. weil sie in ihre Heimatländer zurückkehrten oder abgeschoben wurden.

Der Stress der Trennung von der Familie, der Reise bzw. Schleusung mit ihren Gefahren und Unsicherheiten, die Anforderungen des neuen Landes und der neuen Situation mit einer ganz neuen Sozialisation bewirken zunächst eine bestimmte Destabilisierung der Persönlichkeit in der Ankunftsphase; es gelingt in der Wohngemeinschaftssituation und im betreuten Wohnen eine Mehrheit zu stabilisieren, aber es bleiben Unsicherheiten bei etwa einem Drittel der UMF. Es gelingt in der Wohngemeinschaftsphase auch, gemessen an ihren Voraussetzungen, positive Schulleistungen der UMF zu erreichen, allerdings kommen die UMF mit einer Ausnahme nicht über Hauptschulabschlüsse hinaus. Die Ausbildungsbilanz entspricht mit einem Drittel abgeschlossener Ausbildung auch nicht dem manchmal anzutreffenden öffentlichen Bild, dass es sich bei den UMF um eine besonders leistungsstarke Gruppe handele. Ihre überwiegende Herkunft aus der oberen Unterschicht oder unteren Mittelschicht mit einem eher geringen mitgebrachten Bildungskapital erschwert einen Bildungsaufstieg. Mehr als die Hälfte der Gruppe kann am Ende der beobachteten 10 Jahre als integriert bezeichnet werden.

Alle Aussagen über Größen und Relationen, die in dieser Studie und in den Tabellen dargestellt werden, fallen unter den Vorbehalt einer explorativen Studie. Erst in einer repräsentativen und wesentlich aufwändigeren Studie könnte man repräsentative Daten ermitteln. Die explorative Studie kann dabei als Hypothesengrundlage dienen und hat den Möglichkeitsraum für Ausprägungen von Daten geöffnet. Eine Ausweitung der Studie in Hinsicht auf eine qualitative Methodologie mit dem Schwerpunkt einer Rekonstruktion der Innenwelten von UMF, die mit dem Spannungsverhältnis von Willkommen und unsicherem Aufenthalt und vielen Stressfaktoren umgehen müssen, müsste UMF oder ehemalige UMF für offene Interviews und Gespräche gewinnen.

Literatur

Angenendt, Steffen 2000: Kinder auf der Flucht. Studie im Auftrag des Deutschen Komitees für UNICEF. Opladen
Ballusek, Hilde von (Hrsg.) 2003: Minderjährige Flüchtlinge. Sozialisationsbedingungen, Akkulturationsstrategien und Unterstützungssysteme. Opladen: Leske und Buderich
Balluseck, Hilde von 2003: Vorwort zu Balluseck 2003, 9-12
Bundesfachverband Unbegleitete Minderjährige Flüchtlinge 2013: Kinder zweiter Klasse. Bericht zur Lebenssituation Junger Flüchtlinge in Deutschland an die Vereinten Nationen zum Übereinkommen über die Rechte des Kindes. Berlin und München
Deutscher Caritasverband 2014: Unbegleitete minderjährige Flüchtlinge in Deutschland. Rechtliche Vorgaben und deren Umsetzung. Freiburg: Lambertus

Heckmann, Friedrich 2007: Towards a Better Understandig of Human Smuggling. www.ssoar.info/ssoar/bitstream/handle/document/35288/ssoar-2007-heckmann-Towards_a_better_understanding_of.pdf?sequence=1

Heckmann, Friedrich 2016: Experteninterviews mit Vertretern des UNHCR beim Bundesamt für Migration und Flüchtlinge und mit der Leitung und den Sozialarbeitern der „Wohngemeinschaft für Flüchtlingskinder Nürnberg e. V."

Müller, Andreas 2014: Unbegleitete Minderjährige in Deutschland 2014. Working Paper 60. Bundesamt für Migration und Flüchtlinge. Nürnberg

Parusel, Bernd 2009: Unbegleitete minderjährige Migranten in Deutschland. Nürnberg: Working Paper 26 des Bundesamtes für Migration und Flüchtlinge

Scholz, Antonia 2013: Warum Deutschland? Einflussfaktoren bei der Zielstaats-suche von Asylbewerbern. Ergebnisse einer Expertenbefragung. Nürnberg: Bundesamt für Migration und Flüchtlinge

Wohngemeinschaft für Flüchtlingskinder Nürnberg e. V. 2015: Vereinsnachrichten 20. Jahrgang Dezember 2015

Die Rückkehr der Grenzen:
Globale Trends, regionale Spiegelungen

Vedran Dzihic, Cengiz Günay

Zusammenfassung

Die Bilder vom Höhepunkt der Fluchtbewegung im Sommer 2015 haben die öffentlichen und politischen Debatten der letzten beiden Jahre massiv geprägt. Die große Flüchtlingsbewegung machte klar, dass die Grenzen bei großen Fluchtbewegungen kaum zu schützen oder zu kontrollieren sind. Intensive Kontrollen an Grenzübergängen sowie neu errichtete Grenzzäune und -wälle prägen inzwischen sogar die nationalen Grenzen zwischen einzelnen Schengen-Staaten. Die Rückkehr der „harten Grenze", die nicht nur auf Europa beschränkt ist, steht in einem krassen Gegensatz zur Idee einer weitgehend grenzenlosen Welt, die seit dem Sommer 2015 bei vielen Angst und Verunsicherung erzeugt. Es vollzieht sich, auch in einer globalen Perspektive, eine Abwertung des Internationalismus und ein schrittweiser Rückzug zum Nationalstaat. Die Rückkehr der Grenze global und in Europa wird im folgenden Artikel anhand aktueller Trends diskutiert. Mit einem Blick auf die Entwicklungen an der und um die sogenannte Westbalkanroute im Jahr 2015 illustrieren wir die Virulenz der Grenze und die Aktualität des Nationalismus.

Einleitung

Die Bilder aus dem Sommer 2015 als tausende von Flüchtlingen über die sogenannte Balkanroute in Richtung Zentraleuropa und Deutschland zogen, haben die öffentlichen und politischen Debatten der letzten beiden Jahre massiv geprägt. Die große Flüchtlingsbewegung verdeutlichte vielen europäischen Gesellschaften nicht nur anschaulich die große Zahl an Menschen, die vor den Toren Europas meist auf der Flucht vor Krieg, wirtschaftlicher Not und/oder politischer Verfolgung gestrandet sind, es machte auch klar, dass die Grenzen bei großen Fluchtbewegungen kaum zu schützen oder zu kontrollieren sind. Die Zunahme terroristischer Vorfälle und die Verbindung, die immer wieder zwischen diesen und der Fluchtbewegung und Migration hergestellt wird, beförderte die Versicherheitlichung („Securitization") der Debatte, sowie massive Investitionen in den Grenzschutz, Kontrolle und Überwachung.

Der französische Wissenschaftler Didier Bigo (2002, 65) erinnert in diesem Zusammenhang daran, dass Versicherheitlichung nicht nur eine Antwort auf ein Gefühl der Verunsicherung, oft ausgelöst durch Kriminalität, Terrorismus oder die negativen Auswirkungen der Globalisierung ist, sondern dass der Nexus zwischen diesen Gefahren und der Migration, also die Versicherheitlichung der Migration eine „Wahrheit" produziert, die wiederum von verschiedenen Institutionen bewusst als ein politisches Instrument eingesetzt und als eine Form der Gouvernementalität gebraucht und missbraucht wird.

Intensive Kontrollen an Grenzübergängen sowie neu errichtete Grenzzäune und -wälle prägen inzwischen sogar die nationalen Grenzen zwischen einzelnen Schengen-Staaten. Die Rückkehr der „harten Grenze" mit strengen Kontrollen, Grenzzäunen, -mauern, Kameras, und weiteren Restriktionen, die den Zu- und Ausgang zum und vom Territorium regulieren und vor allem kontrollieren sollen, beschränkt sich aber nicht nur auf Europa. „Die Mauer" an der Grenze zu Mexiko war ein zentrales Wahlversprechen von Präsident Trump, die Türkei errichtete einen Zaun an der syrischen Grenze und baut eine Mauer zum Iran, und Ägypten sichert inzwischen seine Südgrenze zum Sudan hermetisch ab, um nur einige der vielen globalen Beispiele zu nennen.

Grenzen und die Aktualität des Nationalstaatskonzepts

Diese Entwicklungen stehen in einem krassen Gegensatz zu der Idee einer weitgehend grenzenlosen Welt, von der seit dem Ende des Kalten Krieges und dem Fall der Berliner Mauer und des Eisernen Vorhangs lange geträumt wurde (Ohmae 1995 Shapiro and Alker 1996). Während das Niederreißen der Grenzzäune, der Abzug von Soldaten und Grenzbeamten und der grenzenlose Personenverkehr bis vor kurzem als wichtige Errungenschaften galten, erzeugen diese liberalen Ideen und Maßnahmen seit dem Sommer 2015 bei vielen Angst und Verunsicherung. Es vollzieht sich, auch in einer globalen Perspektive, eine Abwertung des Internationalismus und ein schrittweiser Rückzug zum Nationalstaat.

Die Idee eines Staates, der auf einer (konstruierten) – als ethnisch, kulturell und auch religiös weitgehend einheitlichen – Nation aufbaut, hat sich, trotz Globalisierung, internationaler Vernetzung, kulturellem Pluralismus bzw. einem wachsenden Individualismus als erstaunlich stark verwurzelt erwiesen. Wachsende Verunsicherung und eine Tendenz zur Abschottung gehen meist mit einer neuen Ausverhandlung dessen einher, was als partikulare nationale kulturelle Identität verstanden werden kann und soll. Dabei stehen sich in den meisten Fällen zwei unterschiedliche Ansätze gegenüber, die in den Debatten allerdings immer wieder vermischt und verknüpft werden; ein eher exklusiver Ansatz, in dem kulturelle Zugehörigkeit und Identität vor allem durch nationale Narrative, Symbole, Sprache und andere erkennbare Kennzeichen geprägt ist sowie ein eher inklusiver, der Identität vor allem durch Werte und Eigenschaften geprägt sieht, die jenseits kultureller Barrieren bestehen. In beiden Fällen gilt die Abgrenzung gegenüber dem Anderen als Grundvoraussetzung für die Entwicklung einer eigenen Identität. Die ständige Redefinierung von Unterschieden und Einzigartigkeit ist wichtiger Bestandteil dieses Prozesses.

Grenzen spielen in diesem Zusammenhang eine wesentliche Rolle. Sie begrenzen und ermöglichen nicht nur den politischen und rechtlichen Wirkungsbereich und die Macht, ordnen den Raum und spielen eine wesentliche Rolle in der Regelung des Handels, sondern sie kontrollieren eben auch den Zugang zu der Gesellschaft und definieren damit auch die imaginierte Gemeinschaft der Nation und prägen die Sozialisierung und die Sichtweise des Individuums, seine nationale Identität (Günay und Witjes, 2017).

Grenzen, Souveränität und Identität

In aktuellen Diskursen wird der Verlust über die Kontrolle der Grenze und damit über den Zugang zur Gemeinschaft oft mit dem Verlust der nationalen Souveränität gleichgesetzt. Demnach unterminiert ungeregelte Migration die Souveränität der Nation, die im Falle Europas und der USA als klar weiß definiert ist. Die Sorge um die Unterminierung der nationalen Souveränität spielte im Referendum über den Ausstieg Großbritanniens aus der EU eine wesentliche Rolle. Dies kam vor allem durch den Slogan der pre-Brexit Campagne „taking back control" zum Ausdruck. Wieder die Kontrolle zurück erlangen galt nicht nur als eine Kampfansage an die Vorgaben durch die EU, sondern auch gegen Migration aus anderen EU Staaten. Die Kampagne suggerierte, dass die Dinge außer Kontrolle geraten sind und dass eine Mitgliedschaft zur Europäischen Gemeinschaft die britische Nation daran hindern würde, zu kontrollieren und zu bestimmen, wer in das Land darf und wer nicht. Begleitet wurde das Brexit Referendum von einem neuen Nationalismus, der sich gegen Migration und MigrantInnen im Allgemeinen richtete. Das Referendum stand im Schatten der Bilder vom Sommer 2015.

Debatten um kulturelle Identitäten prägen nicht erst seit der sogenannten Flüchtlingskrise die politische Auseinandersetzung, vielmehr haben sie durch diese ein neues Momentum erfahren. Fragen der Identität und der „eigenen Nation" spielen spätestens seit dem Ende des Kalten Krieges in den meisten Gesellschaften eine große Rolle. Das Ende des ideologischen Zeitalters und der Traum von einer grenzenlosen Welt waren begleitet von einem Anstieg der Identitätspolitiken. Identitätspolitik musste dabei oft die fehlenden ideologischen Ansätze ersetzen. In seinem umstrittenen im Jahr 1993 erschienenen Buch „Kampf der Kulturen" sagte Samuel Huntington voraus, dass die großen Konflikte der Weltpolitik nicht mehr ideologischer oder wirtschaftlicher, sondern vielmehr kultureller Natur sein würden. Auch wenn Huntingtons Definition von Kultur und Zivilisation für die Erklärung von geopolitischen Konflikten zu kurz greift, erkannte er dennoch zu einem frühen Zeitpunkt die politische Bedeutung, die kulturelle Identitäten gewinnen würden. Anders als von vielen ModernisierungstheoretikerInnen angenommen spielte in der Zeit nach dem Kalten Krieg Religion als ein wichtiges

Element der Identität wieder eine wichtigere Rolle. Die Kriege auf dem Balkan sind dramatische Beispiele für die Heftigkeit, in der die Ausverhandlung der Grenzen nationaler, oft religiös definierter Identitäten, zum Teil stattfand.

Westbalkanroute:
Konjunktur der Grenze und des Nationalismus

In der aktuellen europäischen Debatte über Flüchtlinge und Grenze spielte die am Beginn des Artikels erwähnte Balkanroute eine ganz wichtige Rolle. Aber auch am Balkan selbst ergaben sich rund um die Flüchtlingsbewegung große Veränderungen: auch hier feierte die Idee der Grenze und der Begrenzung vom Anderen wieder eine Konjunktur, die von Nationalismus und neuer Identitätspolitik begleitet wurde. Im Folgenden diskutieren wir Entwicklungen am Balkan am Höhepunkt der Flüchtlingsbewegung im Jahr 2015 und illustrieren damit die Virulenz der Grenze und die Aktualität des Nationalismus.

Die „Flüchtlingskrise" im Jahr 2015 hat die Region des Westbalkans wieder in die internationalen Schlagzeilen gebracht. Die Balkanroute war über Monate hinweg eine zentrale Fluchtroute für Flüchtlinge auf dem Weg zu europäischen Ländern wie Deutschland, Schweden oder Österreich. Die Fluchtbewegung führte in den ohnehin instabilen Staaten des Region zu neuen Demarkations- und Identitätskonfliktlinien als auch zu neuen Nationalismen Die jüngste Grenzkrise am Balkan wurde durch einen Zaun ausgelöst. Im Juli 2015 begann Ungarn entlang seiner 110 Kilometer langen Grenze mit Serbien einen Zaun zu errichten. Als Ungarn seine Türen für Zehntausende von Flüchtlingen nach Norden schloss, kam es teilweise zu gewalttätigen Auseinandersetzungen am serbisch-ungarischen Grenzübergang Horgos. Der Zaunbau in Ungarn verursachte einen Dominoeffekt in der gesamten Region des Balkans. Die Flüchtlinge suchten nun einen anderen Weg in den Westen und wählten fortan den Weg von Mazedonien über Serbien und weiter nach Norden nach Kroatien, Slowenien und schließlich nach Österreich und Deutschland. Als Serbien anfing, Flüchtlinge nach Kroatien umzuleiten, wurde die serbisch-kroatische Grenze zum Ort der neuen Konflikte.

Zoran Milanovic, der damalige kroatische Premierminister, forderte in einer ersten Reaktion Serbien ultimativ auf, die Flüchtlinge nach Ungarn oder Rumänien zu schicken. Kroatien, so Milanovic, wird es nicht zulassen, von Serbien lächerlich gemacht zu werden.

Der Flüchtlingsstreit zwischen Serbien und Kroatien eskalierte schnell und führte zu einem regelrechten Handelskrieg. Belgrad schloss den Hauptgrenzübergang Bajakovo-Batrovci für alle Lastwägen mit kroatischen Kennzeichen und entschied sich, die Zufuhr der kroatischen Waren nach Serbien zu stoppen. Als Vergeltung und Druckmittel entschied sich Kroatien, den Grenzübergang gleich für alle Kraftfahrzeuge mit serbischen Kennzeichen zu sperren. (Balkan Insight 24.9.2015) Auf beiden Seiten wurde parallel zu diesen Grenzsperren die nationalistische Rhetorik verstärkt. Man begann mit gegenseitigen Schuldzuweisungen, charakterisierte die Handlungen der jeweils anderen Seite mal als „erbärmlich" mal als eine „Schande". Daran beteiligten sich vor allem auch die politischen Spitzenvertreter der beiden Staaten. Der mittlerweile berühmt-berüchtigte Austausch zwischen dem damaligen serbischen Premierminister Vucic und dem kroatischen Premierminister Zoran Milanovic ist eines der anschaulichsten Beispiele. Die Debatte wurde vom damaligen serbischen Sozialminister und heutigen Verteidigungsminister Aleksandar Vulin ausgelöst, der nach der Schließung der Grenzübergange zwischen Kroatien und Serbien durch die kroatischen Behörden meinte: *„Es tut mir leid, dass die kroatische Menschlichkeit und Solidarität nur zwei Tage angedauert hatten."* Der kroatische Premierminister Milanovic reagierte durchaus aus der Position der Stärke (Kroatien ist als EU-Mitgliedland von zentraler Bedeutung für den Fortschritt Serbiens im EU-Integrationsprozess) scharf und verglich die serbische Staatsmacht mit einer kleinen und nichtigen Fliege. Und er fügte hinzu: *„Ein Adler jagt keine Fliegen. Kroatien ist ein Adler."* (B92.net, 18.9.2015) Die serbische Antwort ließ nicht lange auf sich warten. Der serbische Außenminister Ivica Dacic reagierte mit dem Zitat aus einem sehr berühmten ehemaligen jugoslawischen Film *„Der Spion vom Balkan"* (Balkanski spijun) – *„Der Adler wurde abgeschossen."* Der Premierminister Vucic betonte, dass er sich nicht provozieren lassen wolle, schickte aber zugleich die Botschaft Richtung Zagreb, dass Serbien alles tun würde, um seine Interessen zu schützen. Indirekt konnte dies nur als eine militärische Warnung verstanden werden.

In diesem Grenzkonflikt, der schnell vom Charakter und dem Diskurs her an die zahlreichen geschichtlichen Konflikte zwischen Serbien und Kroatien erinnerte, spielte die Vergangenheit eine zentrale Rolle. So gab es zum Beispiel im September 2015 einen Protestbrief des serbischen Außenministeriums an die kroatische Botschaft in Belgrad, in der das Reiseverbot für die serbischen PassinhaberInnen als eine Maßnahme bezeichnet wurde, die der „zivilisierten Welt" nicht würdig sei. In der Erklärung des Ministeriums hieß es dann in einem direkten Verweis auf das verbrecherische kroatische Ustasa-Regime im Zweiten Weltkrieg: *„Durch ihren diskriminierenden Charakter können solche Maßnahmen nur mit den Maßnahmen verglichen werden, die in der Vergangenheit zur Zeit des faschistischen unabhängigen kroatischen Staates unternommen wurden."* (B92.net, 24.9.2015) Während Serbien die Erinnerung an den kroatischen Staat und seine Verbrechen im Zweiten Weltkrieg evozierte und auf die militärische Operation „Sturm" der kroatischen Armee gegen serbische Stellungen vom Sommer 1995 erinnerte, thematisierte die kroatische Seite den Krieg der 1990er Jahre und verwies auf die serbische Aggression gegen Kroatien und Verbrechen, die in der ostkroatischen Stadt Vukovar im Jahr 1991 seitens der serbischen Kampfverbände und Freischärler begangen wurde.

Dieser heftige Schlagabtausch geschah vor dem Hintergrund einer ohnehin krisenhaften Beziehung zwischen Serbien und Kroatien, die voller Ressentiments ist. (Gagnon 2004). Der zentrale Streitpunkt zwischen diesen beiden ehemaligen Kriegsgegners besteht in den diametral entgegengesetzten Interpretationen des Krieges der 1990er Jahre. Während im kroatischen Narrativ KroatInnen als Sieger in einem rechtmäßigen Krieg betrachtet werden, die nur ihre Souveränität geschützt haben, sind im serbischen Narrativ die SerbInnen Opfer der von KroatInnen durchgeführten ethnischen Säuberungen und der Politik des „faschistischen" Kroatiens. (Jovic 2012) Nationalistische Kräfte auf beiden Seiten halten diese sich gegenseitig ausschließenden Narrative hoch auf der Agenda und nutzen jede Gelegenheit, um die andere Seite als das absolute „Andere" zu definieren, von dem man sich abgrenzen soll. Diese narrative Grenze zwischen den beiden nationalen Narrativen wurde während der Ereignisse im Jahr 2015 im Zusammenhang mit der Flüchtlingskrise entlang der echten Grenze wieder aufgebaut und verstärkt. Die Grenze wurde somit zum Kristallisationspunkt für einen neuen nationalistischen Diskurs auf beiden Seiten.

Die Feindseligkeit zwischen Kroatien und Serbien in den Jahren 2015 und 2016 wurden sowohl in Zagreb als auch in Belgrad von innenpolitischen Erwägungen und Machtdynamiken geprägt. In Kroatien wurden im Februar 2016 Wahlen abgehalten. Die kroatische Wirtschaft befindet sich seit sechs Jahren in einer Rezession und zeigt erst jetzt kleine Anzeichen des Wachstums. Aus dieser Perspektive bot sich der Grenzkonflikt als ein willkommener Moment für die politischen VertreterInnen Kroatiens, alte nationalistische Rhetorik wiederzubeleben und damit von innenpolitischen Problemen abzulenken. Auf der anderen Seite befand sich der serbische Premierminister Vucic in einer Situation, in der sowohl in seiner Partei SNS als auch von rechten politischen Bewegungen ein starker Druck auf ihn ausgeübt wurde, scharf auf die als Aggression und Demütigung empfundene Haltung Kroatiens zu reagieren. So setzte man auch in den Monaten nach dem Höhepunkt des Grenzkonflikts die harsche Rhetorik fort. In Serbien fand sogar eine Debatte darüber statt, ob man neue offensive Waffensysteme anschaffen sollte, um auf einen möglichen kroatischen Angriff entsprechend reagieren zu können.

Zusammenfassend lässt sich sagen, dass die oben beschriebenen Konflikte rund um die Grenze noch einmal daran erinnerten, wie eine von außen herbeigeführte Krise (Flüchtlingskrise in diesem Fall) alte Konfliktlinien schnell verstärken kann. Wie der kroatisch-serbische Konflikt seit Herbst 2015 zeigt, bleibt die nationalistische Grenz- bzw. Begrenzungspolitik ein dominantes Muster am Balkan.

Eine solche rasant sich vollziehende Wiederbelebung der ethnonationalistischen Diskurse wie zwischen Serbien und Kroatien verweist noch einmal auf einen generellen Trend, den man auch im größeren europäischen und internationalen Kontext vorfindet. Dieser Trend lässt sich mit dem Stichwort der „Rückkehr der Grenze" und der Rückkehr der überwunden geglaubten exklusiven ethnischen Nationalstaatskonzepte umschreiben. Bereits der Begriff „ethnisch" ist in den Theorien zur Ethnizität und zum Nationalismus als derjenige bestimmt worden, der die Grenzen zwischen ethnischen Gruppen markiert und auf der selbstdefinierten „ethnischen" Unterscheidungskraft und Exklusivität beruht. (Volkan 1999) Ethnische und nationale Grenzen sind meist *„das Ergebnis eines reflexiven Selektionsprozesses; sie kommen nur im Gegensatz zu anderen, ähnlich strukturierten Gruppen vor"*. (Orywal und Hackstein 1993: 600) Ein solcher Prozess führt letztlich dazu, Grenzen und Abgrenzungslinien (sowohl in Bezug auf diskursive als auch territoriale/materielle Grenzen) in den Vordergrund zu stellen. Die binäre Logik der Unterscheidung zwischen „uns" (ethnisch homogenen) und den „anderen" verstärkt die Bedeutung von realen und konstruierten Grenzen. (Anderson 1988) Im Kern dieses Narratives der Begrenzung steht stets die eigene ethnische Gruppe, die als bessere, stärkere, widerstandsfähigere und überlegenere „Wir"-Gruppe angesehen wird, und die uns am besten gegen die „anderen" Gruppen, die allgemein als Bedrohung wahrgenommen und konstruiert werden, schützen kann. Die jüngste Flüchtlingsbewegung kann als Paradebeispiel für eine solche Konstruktion von „Andersartigkeit" (vgl. Dzihic/Nadjivan/Paic/Stachowitsch 2006) entlang der realen oder diskursiv geschaffenen Grenzen herangezogen werden.

Literatur

Anderson, B. (1988) Die Erfindung der Nation. Frankfurt am Main/New York: Suhrkamp.
Balkan Insight (24.9.2015), abrufbar unter http://www.balkaninsight.com/en/article/serbia-croatia-start-trade-war-09-24-2015.
B92.net. (18.09.2015), abrufbar unter http://www.b92.net/eng/news/politics.php?yyyy=2015&mm=09&dd=18&nav_id=95483,
B92.net. (24.09.2015), abrufbar unter http://www.b92.net/eng/news/politics.php?yyyy=2015&mm=09&dd=24&nav_id=95545.
Bigo, D. (2002) Security and Immigration: Toward a Critique of the Governmentality of Unease. Alternatives 27 Special Issue, 63–92
Dzihic, V., Nadjivan, S.,. Paic, H., Stachowitsch, S. (2006) Europa - Verflucht Begehrt. Europavorstellungen im Kontext sich wandelnder Staatlichkeit in Bosnien-Herzegowina, Kroatien und Serbien, Wien: Braumüller-Verlag.
Gagnon, V.P. (2004) The Myth of Ethnic War: Serbia and Croatia in the 1990s. Ithaca: Cornell University Press.
Günay, C. und Witjes, N. (Hrsg.) (2017) Border Politics: Defining Spaces of Governance and Forms of Transgressions, Yearbook of the Austrian Institute for International Affairs, Springer.
Huntington, S. (1993) Kampf der Kulturen: Die Neugestaltung der Weltpolitik im 21. Jahrhundert, Goldmann.
Jović, D. (2015) Fighting Old Wars Against New Enemies, New Eastern Europe, 2: 126-34
Ohmae, K. (1995) The End of the Nation-State. New York: Free Press.
Orywal, E., Hackstein K. (1993) Ethnizität: Die Konstruktion ethnischer Wirklichkeiten. In Handbuch der Ethnologie. Ed. Schweizer, Thomas, Margarete Schweizer, Waltraud Kokot. 593-609. Berlin: Dietrich Reimer Verlag.
Shapiro, M. und Alker, H. (Hrsg.) (1996) Challenging Boundaries: Global Flows, Territorial Identities. Minneapolis: University of Minnesota Press.
Volkan, V. (1999) Blutsgrenzen. Die historischen Wurzeln und die psychologischen Mechanismen ethnischer Konflikte und ihre Bedeutung bei Friedensverhandlungen, Bern/München/Wien: Scherz Verlag.

Teil 4:
Migration und Arbeitsmarkt

Integration von Migrant/inn/en in Österreich: Wo steht Österreich im internationalen Vergleich?[1]

Peter Huber, Thomas Horvath, Julia Bock-Schappelwein

Zusammenfassung

In einem internationalen Vergleich der wirtschaftlichen und sozialen Integration von Migrant/inn/en im Vergleich zur im Inland geborenen Bevölkerung erweist sich Österreich in keiner der analysierten Dimensionen als internationales Best-Practice-Beispiel. Bezieht man in den Vergleich allerdings nur Länder mit ähnlicher Zuwanderungsstruktur wie Österreich ein, relativiert sich dieser Befund hinsichtlich der Arbeitsmarktintegration, weil Migrant/inn/en in Österreich gleich gut oder besser in den Arbeitsmarkt integriert sind als Migrant/inn/en in den Vergleichsländern. Allerdings verbleiben auch hier in einigen Bereichen geringere Integrationsausmaße von Migrant/inn/en, die durch die Struktur der Zuwanderung nicht erklärbar sind. Dies betrifft die schlechte Bildungsintegration von Migrant/inn/en, aber auch ihre Benachteiligung am Wohnungsmarkt.

Einleitung

In den meisten Ländern weisen Migrant/inn/en der ersten und der zweiten Generation eine höhere Arbeitslosenquote und eine geringere Erwerbsquote auf als im Inland geborene Personen. Sie arbeiten zudem häufiger überqualifiziert, auf Arbeitsplätzen mit geringen Anforderungen an formale Qualifikationen und Kompetenzen, verdienen weniger und leben in kleineren aber oftmals teureren Wohnungen. Ferner haben sie häufig schlechtere Bildungschancen, einen schlechteren Zugang zum Gesundheitssystem und zum Wohnungsmarkt und werden auch öfter Opfer von Diskriminierung und Gewalttaten als im Inland Geborene (Battu und Sloane 2004, Bosswick et al. 2007, Chiswick und Miller 2007, Münz 2007, Algan et al. 2010, Cangiano 2012, Altorjai 2013, Cattaneo und Wolter 2015). Allerdings unterscheidet sich das Ausmaß der Benachteiligung von Migrant/inn/en in all diesen Belangen auch zwischen Zielländern. Einerseits entsteht dies, weil die Integrationschancen von Migrant/inn/en in Abhängigkeit von personenbezogenen Merkmalen wie Alter, Geschlecht, Familienstand und Bildungsniveau sowie nach Herkunftsland, Aufenthaltsdauer und Aufenthaltsgrund im Zielland variieren und Staaten eine unterschiedliche Zusammensetzung der Gruppe der Migrant/inn/en

---

[1] Dieser Beitrag basiert in weiten Teilen auf einer rezenten WIFO-Studie von Huber et al. (2017), die in dieser Publikation in wesentlichen Aspekten ergänzt und aktualisiert wurde.

aufweisen. Andererseits entstehen diese Länderunterschiede aber auch, weil sich die Zielländer in Bezug auf integrationsrelevante Institutionen, Traditionen und Kulturen sowie in ihrer Geschichte unterscheiden (Belot und Hatton 2012, Boogaart und Emmer 1986).

Die vorliegende Arbeit vergleicht das Ausmaß der Integration von Migrant/inn/en in Österreich anhand einer Vielzahl von Indikatoren mit anderen Ländern. Dadurch soll zum einen festgestellt werden, in welchen Teildimensionen in Österreich potenzieller Handlungsbedarf besteht und in welchen Bereichen Österreich besonders erfolgreich ist. Zum anderen sollen dadurch aber auch beispielhaft die vielfältigen Herausforderungen (aus methodischer Sicht wie auch auf Datenebene), denen sich ein solcher Vergleich gegenüber gestellt sieht, illustriert werden. Dazu wird eine bereits in Huber et al. (2017) verwendete Datensammlung der OECD und der Europäischen Union (OECD und EU 2015) genutzt und diese um zusätzliche Indikatoren und rezentere Daten von EUROSTAT ergänzt.

Daten und Methoden

Diese Daten orientieren sich dabei weitgehend an den sogenannten „Zaragoza-Indikatoren" zur Beurteilung der Integrationslage von Migrant/inn/en (siehe Übersicht 1).[2] Die OECD und EU (2015) erhoben in ihrer Publikation "Indicators of Immigrant Integration" 29 der 46 vorgeschlagenen Indikatoren für 41 OECD- und EU-Länder, die sich auf das Jahr 2012 beziehen. Diese Daten werden, sofern dies rezentere oder zusätzliche Informationen liefert, um EUROSTAT Daten[3] zur Integration von Migrant/inn/en ergänzt. Überdies wird in jenen Bereichen, in denen beide Datenquellen, einerseits OECD und EU und andererseits EUROSTAT, Informationen liefern, auf Unterschiede bzw. Gemeinsamkeiten in den Resultaten zwischen diesen beiden hingewiesen.

Beiden Datenquellen ist gemeinsam, dass sie nur sehr eingeschränkte Möglichkeiten bieten, um für Unterschiede in der Struktur der Migrant/inn/en (hinsichtlich ihrer Ausbildung, Aufenthaltsdauer, Herkunft und Migrationsmotive) zwischen den Ländern zu kontrollieren. Allerdings hat diese unterschiedliche Struktur wichtige Implikationen für den gemessenen Integrationserfolg von Migrant/inn/en in verschiedenen Zielländern, da beispielsweise nach den Ergebnissen vieler Studien

---

[2] Bei ihrem Treffen in Zaragoza im Jahr 2010 beschlossen die für die Integration von Migrant/inn/en zuständigen Minister/innen der EU-Staaten 21 dieser Indikatoren. DG Home Affairs (2013) schlägt in einer rezenten Evaluierung 25 zusätzliche Indikatoren vor. Insgesamt umfassen die erweiterten Zaragoza Indikatoren somit 46 Indikatoren, die in fünf integrationsrelevante Dimensionen gebündelt werden können.

[3] Diese liefern – wie aus Übersicht 1 ersichtlich – 19 Indikatoren, die allerdings nur für die EU-Länder erhoben wurden.

Integration von Migrant/inn/en: Wo steht Österreich im internationalen Vergleich?

Beschäftigung	Bildung	Soziale Inklusion	Aktive Staatsbürgerschaft	Gesellschaftliche Integration
21 Zaragoza-Indikatoren				
Beschäftigungsrate	Höchste abgeschlossene Ausbildung	Armutsrisiko	Naturalisierungsrate	Gefühlte Diskriminierung
Arbeitslosenquote	Tertiäre Ausbildung	Einkommen	Anteil Langzeitaufenthalt	Vertrauen in öffentliche Institutionen
Erwerbsquote	Schulabbruch	Subjektiver Gesundheitszustand	Anteil gewählter Repräsentanten	Zugehörigkeitsgefühl
Selbständigenquote	low (school-)performers	Wohneigentumsrate	Wahlbeteiligung	
Überqualifikation	Sprachkenntnisse			
25 zusätzliche Indikatoren				
Öffentliche Beschäftigung	Frühkindliche Erziehung	Kinderarmut	Teilnahme in Freiwilligenorganisationen	Öffentliche Wahrnehmung ethnischer Konflikte
Befristete Beschäftigung	Teilnahme Lebenslanges Lernen (LLL)	Unbehandelte Gesundheitsprobleme	Mitgliedschaft in Gewerkschaften	Öffentliche Einstellung zu Minderheiten
Teilzeitbeschäftigung	NEET	Lebenserwartung	Parteimitgliedschaften	
Langzeitarbeitslosigkeit	Resiliente Schüler/inn/en	Gesunde Lebensjahre	Politische Aktivität	
Anerkannte ausländische Diplome	Konzentration in unterdurchschnittlichen Schulen	Housing cost overburden (SILC)**		
Verbleib internationaler Student/inn/en		Beengte Wohnverhältnisse		
		Armut in Arbeit		
		Persistente Armutsgefährdung		

Hellgrau unterlegte Felder bezeichnen Indikatoren, für die Daten der OECD vorhanden sind.
Schwarz unterlegte Felder bezeichnen Indikatoren, für die Daten der EU vorhanden sind.
Dunkelgau unterlegte Felder beziehen sich auf Indikatoren, für die Daten beider Organisationen vorhanden sind
NEET: Not in Education, Employment or Training.

Übersicht 1 Liste der Zaragoza-Indikatoren und der vorgeschlagenen zusätzliche Indikatoren
Quelle: DG Home Affairs (2013).

– unabhängig vom Zielland – höher qualifizierte Migrant/inn/en mit einer längeren Aufenthaltsdauer besser integriert sind als Geringqualifizierte mit kurzer Aufenthaltsdauer (z.B. Chiswick und DebBurman 2004). Abgesehen davon wird die Struktur der Zuwanderung von migrationspolitischen Entscheidungen und den wirtschaftlichen und sozialen Gegebenheiten in den Zielländern mitentschieden. Beispiele dafür sind qualifikationsselektive Zuwanderungsregeln (z.B. in Österreich mit der Rot-Weiß-Rot-Karte, siehe Biffl et al. 2010, Biffl 2006, Biffl 2011), historische Migrationserfahrungen (z.B. die Gastarbeiterzuwanderung der 1960er- und frühen 1990er-Jahre in Österreich, siehe Biffl 2002, 2011a, Biffl und Bock-Schappelwein 2013), Arbeitsmarktsegmentierungen (z.B. Green 2011) oder auch die Selbstselektion von Migrant/inn/en (z.B. Longhi und Rokicka 2012).

Vergleiche zwischen Ländern mit sehr unterschiedlicher Zuwanderungsstruktur oder auch unterschiedlichen Migrationsregimen sind daher potentiell verzerrt und entsprechend eingeschränkt in ihrer Aussagekraft. Deshalb erstellten OECD und EU (2015) eine Ländertypologie, die auf die unterschiedliche Struktur der Zuwanderung in verschiedenen Ländern abstellt. Dies ermöglicht zumindest ansatzweise eine Kontrolle für verschiedene Muster der Zuwanderung auf Länderebene. Insbesondere teilen OECD und EU (2015) die 41 berücksichtigten Länder in 8 Gruppen ein (siehe auch Huber et al. 2017 für eine Charakterisierung dieser Zuwanderungsländergruppen):

1. *Ansiedlungsländer* – Australien, Kanada, Israel, Neuseeland
2. *Traditionelle Zuwanderungsländer (TZWL) mit hoch qualifizierter Migration* – Luxemburg, Schweiz, Großbritannien, USA
3. *Traditionelle Zuwanderungsländer (TZWL) mit niedrig qualifizierter Migration* – Österreich, Belgien, Frankreich, Deutschland, Niederlande
4. *Zuwanderungsländer mit erheblicher Asylzuwanderung* – Dänemark, Finnland, Norwegen, Schweden
5. *Neue Zielländer (NZWL) mit niedrig qualifizierter Zuwanderung* – Griechenland, Spanien, Italien, Portugal
6. *Neue Zielländer (NZWL) mit hoch qualifizierter Zuwanderung* – Zypern, Island, Irland, Malta
7. *Länder mit einer durch Gebietsveränderungen oder Minderheiten geprägten ausländischen Bevölkerung* – Kroatien, Tschechien, Estland, Ungarn, Lettland, Litauen, Polen, Slowakei, Slowenien.
8. *Neu aufkommende Zielländer mit geringem Migrant/inn/enanteil* – Bulgarien, Chile, Japan, Korea, Mexiko, Rumänien, Türkei

Gerade in den drei letztgenannten Ziellandgruppen ist die Datenlage zur Situation der im Ausland geborenen Bevölkerungsgruppen nur unzureichend. Oft werden Indikatoren nicht erhoben und in anderen Fällen sind die Gruppengrößen bei Stichprobenerhebungen zu klein, um aussagekräftige Ergebnisse zu erhalten. Überdies handelt es sich bei den klassischen Ansiedlungsländern durchwegs um außereuropäische Länder, zu denen EUROSTAT keine Daten erhebt. Daher werden in dieser Arbeit nur die unter den Ziffern 2) bis 5) genannten Ländergruppen verglichen. Dementsprechend wird Österreich im Nachfolgenden entlang der in Übersicht 1 dargestellten Dimensionen (mit Ausnahme der Dimensionen aktive Staatsbürgerschaft und gesellschaftlichen Integration[4]) zum einen mit Staaten, die traditionelle Zuwanderungsländer mit niedrig qualifizierter Migration darstellen (Belgien, Frankreich, Deutschland, Niederlande), verglichen, um so einen Vergleich zwischen Ländern mit einer möglichst ähnlichen Zuwanderungsstruktur herzustellen. Andererseits wird Österreich auch mit dem Durchschnitt der EU 28-Länder, sowie den ungewichteten Gruppenmittelwerten der anderen (unter Punkt 2 bis 5 genannten) Ländergruppen verglichen. Der Vergleich mit dem EU-Durchschnitt ist vor allem für Debatten um europäische Migrations- und Integrationspolitiken relevant. Der Vergleich mit anderen Ländergruppen unterstreicht hingegen die Bedeutung der Struktur der Zuwanderung als Bestimmungsfaktor für die integrationspolitischen Herausforderungen, denen sich Österreich gegenüber gestellt sieht. Durchgängig wird dabei der Prozentpunkteunterschied in den jeweiligen Quoten und Anteilen zwischen Migrant/inn/en (also im Ausland geborenen Personen) und den im Inland geborenen Personen dargestellt. Ein positiver Wert zeigt daher jeweils eine höhere Quote für Migrant/inn/en als für im Inland Geborene. Ein negativer Wert signalisiert demgegenüber eine niedrigere Quote für Migrant/inn/en als für im Inland Geborene.

Beschäftigung

Übersicht 2 zeigt die Ergebnisse dieses Vergleichs für verschiedene Indikatoren zur Arbeitsmarktintegration. Im Vergleich mit den anderen traditionellen Zuwanderungsländern mit niedrig qualifizierter Migration ist Österreich hinsichtlich der Arbeitsmarktintegration relativ erfolgreich. So ist die Beschäftigungsquote unter Migrant/inn/en in Österreich im Jahr 2015 laut EUROSTAT (trotz der um 2,9 Prozentpunkte niedrigeren Beschäftigungsquote unter im Ausland Geborenen Frauen als unter im Inland geborenen Frauen) nur um 0,8 Prozentpunkte niedriger als unter im Inland Geborenen, während sie in den anderen Ländern dieser Gruppe um 4,6 bis 8,3 Prozentpunkte niedriger liegt, wobei auch hier im Ausland geborene Frauen gegenüber im Inland geborenen Frauen stärker benachteiligt sind. Die Arbeitslosenquote ist in Österreich unter Migrant/inn/en (bei relativ geringen Geschlechterunterschieden) um 6,1 Prozentpunkte höher als unter im Inland Geborenen. Innerhalb der Ländergruppe bedeutet dies hinter Deutschland und den Niederlanden die dritte Stelle.[5] Der Abstand in der Erwerbsquote, in der Unterschiede in der Beschäftigung und Arbeitslosigkeit zusammengefasst werden, be-

---

[4] Die wenigen verfügbaren Indikatoren zu diesen Dimensionen wurden bereits in Huber et al. (2017) diskutiert.
[5] Dies wird auch durch die Kennzahlen laut OECD und EU (2015) bestätigt (Huber et al. 2017).

läuft sich auf 3,1 Prozentpunkte. In allen übrigen Vergleichsländern (mit Ausnahme von Belgien) ist dieser Abstand negativ. Diese vergleichsweise gute Position bei den Erwerbsquotenunterschieden, ist dabei vor allem einer im Vergleich zu im Inland Geborenen deutlich höheren Erwerbsquote der im Ausland geborenen Männer geschuldet, obwohl auch die Unterschiede bei den Frauen im internationalen Vergleich ähnlich positiv ausfallen.

Zudem ist der Anteil der überqualifiziert Beschäftigten an der Gesamtbeschäftigung unter Migrant/inn/en höher als unter im Inland Geborenen, während die Selbständigenquote unter Migrant/inn/en niedriger ist. Mit +9,2 bzw. -0,7 Prozentpunkten liegen diese Unterschiede aber ebenfalls unter dem Durchschnitt der traditionellen Zuwanderungsländer mit niedriger Qualifikation (von +10,2 bzw. -1,3 Prozentpunkten).

Allerdings weisen die traditionellen Zuwanderungsländer mit niedrig qualifizierter Zuwanderung – im Vergleich zu anderen Ländergruppen – auch eine besonders starke Schlechterstellung der Migrant/inn/en gegenüber den im Inland Geborenen bei Beschäftigungs-, Erwerbs- und auch Arbeitslosenquoten auf, die bei den Beschäftigungs- und Erwerbsquoten auch auf besonders hohe Geschlechterunterschiede zurück zu führen sind. Die durchschnittlichen Beschäftigungs- und Erwerbsquotenunterschiede fallen in dieser Ländergruppe am höchsten aus, während bei den Arbeitslosenquotenunterschieden nur die Länder mit überwiegend humanitärer Zuwanderung noch schlechter abschneiden. Obwohl der Vergleich bei der Selbständigenquote und auch bei der Überqualifizierungsrate etwas besser ausfällt, dürfte der Grund für dieses Hinterherhinken im Vergleich zu anderen Ländergruppen vor allem in der Qualifikationsstruktur der Zuwanderung dieser Länder liegen. Insbesondere weisen traditionelle Zuwanderungsländer mit hochqualifizierter Migration bei fast allen in Übersichten 2 dargestellten Indikatoren auch die besten Werte auf.

Abgesehen von Unterschieden in der Erwerbsbeteiligung ist auch die Ausgestaltung der von Arbeitskräften ausgeübten Tätigkeiten für die Bewertung ihrer Arbeitsmarktintegration von Bedeutung. So liegt der Anteil der unfreiwillig Teilzeitbeschäftigten (Übersicht 2) in Österreich unter Migrant/inn/en (insbesondere Frauen) höher als unter den im Inland Geborenen. Damit unterscheidet sich Österreich allerdings kaum von den anderen traditionellen Zuwanderungsländern mit niedrig qualifizierter Migration. Beim Anteil der befristet Beschäftigten rangiert Österreich hingegen, wohl auch aufgrund der geringen Bedeutung dieser Beschäftigungsform in Österreich (mit Ausnahme der Lehrausbildung), deutlich besser als alle anderen traditionellen Zuwanderungsländer mit niedrig qualifizierter Migration, unter dem EU-Durchschnitt und auch unter dem Durchschnitt aller anderen Ländergruppen.

Auch die Unterschiede im Anteil der Beschäftigten im öffentlichen Sektor zwischen Migrant/inn/en und im Inland Geborenen werden von OECD und EU (2015) zur Beurteilung der Arbeitsmarktlage von Migrant/inn/en herangezogen.

Integration von Migrant/inn/en: Wo steht Österreich im internationalen Vergleich?

	Arbeitslosenquote[1]			Erwerbsquote[2]			Beschäftigungsquote[2]		
	Frauen	Männer	Gesamt	Frauen	Männer	Gesamt	Frauen	Männer	Gesamt
	EUROSTAT (2015)			EUROSTAT (2015)			EUROSTAT (2015)		
Österreich	6,0	6,1	6,1	0,4	6,5	3,1	-2,9	1,8	-0,8
Belgien	9,8	10,5	10,2	-2,4	5,1	0,9	-6,7	-1,8	-4,7
Deutschland	3,6	3,5	3,6	-6,2	1,1	-2,6	-7,7	-1,2	-4,6
Frankreich	7,8	8,0	7,8	-6,6	-2,4	-4,6	-9,5	-6,7	-8,3
Niederlande	6,8	5,2	5,9	-5,1	1,9	-2,3	-8,5	-1,8	-5,8
TZWL - niedrigqualifiziert	6,8	6,7	6,7	-4,0	2,4	-1,1	-7,1	-1,9	-4,8
TZWL - hochqualifiziert	4,3	2,6	3,4	6,2	11,3	8,7	3,3	8,8	6,0
Humanitäre Zuwanderung	9,0	7,5	8,2	2,2	7,0	4,4	-3,7	0,9	-1,6
NZWL – niedrigqualifiziert	4,6	6,6	5,7	17,6	20,7	18,7	11,3	11,8	11,2
EU-28	5,3	4,7	5,0	3,6	7,4	5,2	0,4	3,4	1,6

	Befristete Verträge[1]			Langzeitarbeitslosigkeit[2]			Unfreiwillig teilzeitbeschäftigt[3]		
	Frauen	Männer	Gesamt	Frauen	Männer	Gesamt	Frauen	Männer	Gesamt
	EUROSTAT (2015)			EUROSTAT (2015)			OECD und EU (2012)		
Österreich	-0,8	-0,9	-0,9	7,8	1,3	4,1	5,2	2,5	-
Belgien	6,5	6,9	6,6	11,9	6,7	8,9	4,2	3,1	-
Deutschland	1,8	1,3	1,6	0,5	0,1	0,3	4,8	1,7	-
Frankreich	5,8	3,6	4,6	9,0	6,3	7,5	3,8	3,3	-
Niederlande	1,6	5,0	3,4	12,2	6,9	9,4	1,5	3,2	-
TZWL - niedrigqualifiziert	3,0	3,2	3,1	8,3	4,3	6,0	3,9	2,8	-
TZWL - hochqualifiziert	0,7	1,3	1,1	3,9	6,8	5,1	2,5	1,3	-
Humanitäre Zuwanderung	5,0	4,8	4,9	12,8	10,5	11,5	3,1	2,4	-
NZWL – niedrigqualifiziert	3,9	8,2	6,1	-3,6	-3,8	-3,7	8,3	4,5	-
EU-28	2,5	3,4	3,0	-0,1	-1,0	-0,6	5,8	3,5	-

	Selbständigenquote[1),4)]	Überqualifizierung[5]	Beschäftigung im Öffentlichen Sektor[6]	
			<10 Jahre	>10 Jahre
	OECD und EU (2012)			
Österreich	0,7	9,2	-12,6	-9,2
Belgien	1,8	11,5	-17,7	-8,0
Deutschland	2,0	7,3	-16,7	-7,2
Frankreich	0,8	14,6	-12,2	-10,1
Niederlande	1,1	8,4	-18,3	-3,9
TZWL - niedrigqualifiziert	1,3	10,2	-15,5	-7,7
TZWL - hochqualifiziert	1,2	2,6	-19,3	-10,9
Humanitäre Zuwanderung	1,4	16,6	-6,3	1,3
NZWL – niedrigqualifiziert	-6,0	25,2	-24,4	-15,1
EU-28	0,2	13,5	-14,4	-7,0

[1] Grundgesamtheit = Bevölkerung im erwerbsfähigen Alter (15 bis 64 Jahre alt),
[2] Grundgesamtheit = Bevölkerung Alter von 15 oder mehr Jahren,
[3] Anteil der 15- bis 64-jährigen unselbständig Beschäftigten in unfreiwilliger Teilzeitbeschäftigung (arbeiten Teilzeit, weil kein Vollzeitarbeitsplatz verfügbar ist);
[4] Anteil selbständig Beschäftigten (exklusive Landwirtschaft)
[5] Anteil der unselbständig Beschäftigten mit tertiärem Bildungsabschluss in niedrig- oder mittelqualifizierten Berufen laut ISCO.
[6] Anteil der unselbständig Beschäftigten im öffentlichen Sektor (= öffentliche Verwaltung, Gesundheits- und Bildungswesen).
Weitere Anmerkungen: Positive Werte signalisieren höhere Quoten (Anteile) unter im Ausland Geborenen als unter im Inland Geborenen, negative niedrigere Quoten (Anteile) unter im Ausland Geborenen als unter im Inland Geborenen. – TZWL – niedrigqualifiziert: Traditionelle Zuwanderungsländer mit niedrig qualifizierter Migration, TZWL – hochqualifiziert: Traditionelle Zuwanderungsländer mit hoch qualifizierter Migration, Humanitäre Zuwanderung: Zuwanderungsländer mit erheblicher Asylzuwanderung NZWL – niedrigqualifiziert: Neue Zielländer mit niedrig qualifizierter Zuwanderung (siehe auch Abschnitt: Daten und Methoden).

Übersicht 2 Arbeitsmarktindikatoren: Differenz zur Quote (zum Anteil) der im Inland Geborenen in Prozentpunkten

Quelle: OECD und EU (2015), EUROSTAT, WIFO-Berechnungen.

Der Grund hierfür ist, dass der öffentliche Sektor in vielen Ländern ein Arbeitgeber mit besonders hoher Arbeitsplatzsicherheit und auch hohen Löhnen ist. Überdies erzielen laut OECD und EU (2015) Länder, in denen Zugewanderte einen hohen Beschäftigungsanteil in diesem Sektor aufweisen, zumeist auch gute Arbeitsmarktergebnisse innerhalb der zugewanderten Bevölkerung. In einigen Ländern ist eine Beschäftigung im öffentlichen Sektor (oder in spezifischen Teilbereichen desselben) aber an den Erwerb der Staatsbürgerschaft gebunden.[6] Diese wiederum kann zumeist erst nach einer entsprechenden Aufenthaltsdauer erworben werden. Dementsprechend differenzieren die OECD und EU (2015) beim Beschäftigtenanteil des öffentlichen Sektors zwischen im Ausland Geborenen, die erst weniger als 10 Jahre im Zielland wohnen, und jenen, die bereits 10 Jahre oder länger im Zielland leben (Übersicht 2).

Unter den Migrant/inn/en mit einer kurzen (weniger als 10-jährigen) Aufenthaltsdauer liegt der Anteil der im öffentlichen Sektor Beschäftigten in Österreich – wie in annähernd allen betrachteten Aufnahmeländern – deutlich unter dem Anteil der in Österreich Geborenen. Diese Unterschiede fallen aber (mit einer Differenz zu im Inland Geborenen von -12,6 Prozentpunkten) geringer als in den Vergleichsländern derselben Staatengruppe und auch geringer als im EU-Durchschnitt aus. Für Zugewanderte mit langer Aufenthaltsdauer fallen sie demgegenüber höher als in den Vergleichsländern aus und liegen auch über dem EU-Durchschnitt. Österreich fällt somit durch einen im Vergleich zu anderen Zuwanderungsländern mit niedrig qualifizierter Migration geringen Beschäftigungsanteil der bereits länger im Land befindlichen Migrant/inn/en im öffentlichen Sektor auf.

Bildung

Auch hinsichtlich ihrer Integration in das Aus- und Weiterbildungssystem weisen Migrant/inn/en in den meisten Aufnahmeländern eine Schlechterstellung gegenüber im Inland Geborenen auf (siehe dazu z.B. Granato und Ulrich 2009, Lassnigg 2011). Um das Ausmaß der Integration im Bildungsbereich zu messen, stellen die Zaragoza-Indikatoren vor allem auf verschiedene Maßzahlen zum Schulerfolg jugendlicher Migrant/inn/en ab. Hierbei wird zwischen als Kinder Zugewanderten und Angehörigen der zweiten Generation (deren beiden Elternteile im Ausland geboren sind) sowie im Inland geborenen Kindern aus gemischten Haushalten differenziert. Diese Indikatoren zur Integration der verschiedenen Gruppen von Jugendlichen mit Migrationshintergrund weisen – im Einklang mit bisherigen Ergebnissen (z.B. Biffl und Bock-Schappelwein 2003, Biffl 2004) – auf einen

---

[6] In Österreich steht die Bewerbung um die Aufnahme in den Bundesdienst und um Funktionen und Arbeitsplätze beim Bund auch allen Zugewanderten mit unbeschränktem Zugang zum österreichischen Arbeitsmarkt offen. Nur Verwendungen, die ein Verhältnis besonderer Verbundenheit zu Österreich voraussetzen, die nur von Personen mit österreichischer Staatsbürgerschaft erwartet werden kann, sind Beamte und Beamtinnen bzw. Vertragsbedienstete mit österreichischer Staatsbürgerschaft zuzuweisen.

enttäuschenden Bildungserfolg der im Ausland geborenen Jugendlichen und auch der Angehörigen der zweiten Generation in Österreich hin (Übersicht 3).

Insbesondere erweisen sich hier die Unterschiede in den Anteilen der 15- bis 24-Jährigen mit höchstens Pflichtschulabschluss, die keiner weiteren Ausbildung nachgehen (frühzeitige Schul- und Ausbildungsabgänger/innen) zwischen Migrant/inn/en und im Inland Geborenen (bzw. Angehörigen der zweiten Generation im Vergleich zu Personen mit zwei im Inland Geborenen Elternteilen) als sehr hoch. So ist der Anteil der frühzeitigen Schul- und Ausbildungsabgänger/inn/en unter den Migrant/inn/en um 11,5 Prozentpunkte höher als unter den im Inland Geborenen, deren beiden Elternteile in Österreich geboren wurden. Unter den Angehörigen der zweiten Generation liegt dieser Unterschied bei 10,4 Prozentpunkten und unter Personen aus gemischtem Elternhaus immerhin noch bei 4,7 Prozentpunkten. Damit sind diese Unterschiede bei allen drei genannten Gruppen in Österreich die höchsten unter den traditionellen Zuwanderungsländern mit niedrig qualifizierter Migration und auch deutlich höher als der EU-Durchschnitt sowie der Durchschnitt aller anderen Zuwanderungsländergruppen.[7]

Ähnlich hoch ist in Österreich auch der Unterschied im Anteil der Jugendlichen, die weder in Beschäftigung noch Ausbildung stehen (NEETs), zwischen Personen mit und ohne Migrationshintergrund (siehe auch Tamesberger und Bacher 2014): Unter den traditionellen Zuwanderungsländern mit niedrig qualifizierter Zuwanderung weist Österreich den zweitgrößten Unterschied zwischen Migrant/inn/en und im Inland Geborenen mit zwei im Inland geborenen Eltern auf. Dieser Unterschied liegt mit 11,4 Prozentpunkten deutlich höher als der EU-Durchschnitt und auch deutlich höher als in den einzelnen Gruppen von Zuwanderungsländern. Unter den Angehörigen der zweiten Generation liegt der Unterschied bei 14,9 Prozentpunkten und ist nur in Belgien noch höher. Einzig bei den Jugendlichen mit nur einem im Ausland geborenen Elternteil ist der Unterschied mit 6,7 Prozentpunkten etwas geringer, was jedoch der höchste Wert in der Vergleichsländergruppe ist und auch deutlich höher liegt als im Durchschnitt jeder der übrigen Gruppen von Zuwanderungsländern.

Beim Anteil der 15-jährigen leseschwachen Schüler/inn/en (laut PISA-Ergebnissen) ist die relative Position Österreichs nur marginal besser. Unter den im Ausland geborenen Jugendlichen ist deren Anteil um 20,6 Prozentpunkte höher als unter den Jugendlichen mit zwei im Inland geborenen Elternteilen, und liegt damit – ebenso wie der Unterschied bei Kindern aus einem gemischten Elternhaus

---

[7] Rezentere Daten von EUROSTAT, die sich allerdings nur auf die im Ausland Geborenen beziehen, bestätigen diesen Befund. Hier liegen die Differenzen zwischen im Aus- und im Inland Geborenen bei den frühzeitige Schul- und Ausbildungsabgänger/inn/en 2015 in Österreich bei 13,5 Prozentpunkten (14,1 Frauen, 13,0 Männer) und sind damit höher als in allen Ländern der Vergleichsgruppe, allen anderen Ländergruppen und auch im EU-Durchschnitt. Ähnlich hoch sind in diesem Vergleich in Österreich die Unterschiede der NEET-Raten zwischen im In- und im Ausland Geborenen. Sie lagen 2015 bei insgesamt 12,2 Prozentpunkten (16,8 bei Frauen, 7,0 bei Männern) und waren damit ebenfalls deutlich höher als in allen anderen Ländergruppen und dem EU-Durchschnitt, rangierten aber im Mittelfeld der traditionellen Zuwanderungsländer mit niedrig qualifizierter Migration.

– etwas besser als im Durchschnitt der traditionellen Zuwanderungsländer mit niedrig qualifizierter Zuwanderung. Unter den Angehörigen der zweiten Generation liegt dieser Unterschied bei 16,3 Prozentpunkten und ist damit etwas höher als im Durchschnitt der traditionellen Zuwanderungsländer mit niedrig qualifizierter Zuwanderung und deutlich höher als der EU-Durchschnitt und der Durchschnitt aller anderen Ländergruppen.

Die Schlechterstellung der Migrant/inn/en in der Teilnahme an lebensbegleitendem Lernen (Übersicht 3, siehe dazu z.B. Sprung 2011) ist demgegenüber in Österreich etwas schwächer ausgeprägt, obwohl auch hier sowohl im Ausland geborene Männer als auch Frauen jeweils eine um 5,1 Prozentpunkte niedrigere Weiterbildungsbeteiligung aufweisen als im Inland Geborene desselben Geschlechts. Bei beiden Geschlechtern ist dieser Unterschied stärker ausgeprägt als im EU-Durchschnitt (Übersicht 3). Dieser Indikator ist ein Abbild der nationalen Ausgestaltung von aktiver Arbeitsmarkpolitik, der Qualifikationsstruktur der Zugewanderten und des Zugangs zu Weiterbildung. Dementsprechend ist der Unterschied in der Beteiligungsquote zwischen Migrant/inn/en und im Inland Geborenen zum Beispiel unter den Zuwanderungsländern mit überwiegend humanitärer Zuwanderung, die auch über eine gut ausgebaute aktive Arbeitsmarktpolitik verfügen, am niedrigsten, während er in den traditionellen Zuwanderungsländern mit hoher Qualifikation – aufgrund des geringeren Weiterbildungsbedarfs – am höchsten ist.

Ähnlich starke nationale Unterschiede bestehen hinsichtlich der Integration in die frühkindliche Bildung (siehe dazu z.B. Stamm et al. 2011). Diese hängen stark von der institutionellen Ausgestaltung der frühkindlichen Bildung im nationalen Bildungssystem und vom durchschnittlichen Bildungsniveau der Migrant/inn/en ab. In Ländern mit einem kostenlosen Zugang zur frühkindlichen Bildung und einem hohen Qualifikationsniveau der Migrant/inn/en bzw. mit einem hohen Bewusstsein gegenüber der Bedeutung von Ausbildung sind die Unterschiede zwischen Migrant/inn/en und im Inland Geborenen tendenziell geringer als in Ländern mit einer kostenpflichtigen frühkindlichen Bildung und vergleichsweise geringer qualifizierten Migrant/inn/en. Dementsprechend sind die Unterschiede in den neuen Zuwanderungsländern mit niedrig qualifizierter Migration am höchsten, während sie unter den traditionellen Zuwanderungsländern mit hoch qualifizierter Migration am niedrigsten ausfallen (Übersicht 3). In Österreich liegen diese Unterschiede (mit einem um 4,3 Prozentpunkte niedrigeren Anteil unter den Migrant/inn/en), trotz der Verfügbarkeit von Gratiskindergartenplätzen, über dem Durchschnitt der EU und auch der traditionellen Zuwanderungsländer mit niedrig qualifizierter Migration.

Integration von Migrant/inn/en: Wo steht Österreich im internationalen Vergleich? 229

	Frühzeitige Schul- und Ausbildungsabgänger [1]			Leseschwache SchülerInnen [2]			NEETs [3]		
	2. Gen.	Gem. Hintergr.	Unter 15 Zugew.	2. Gen.	Gem. Hintergr.	Unter 15 Zugew.	2. Gen.	Gem. Hintergr.	Unter 15 Zugew.
	OECD und EU (2012)								
Österreich	10,4	4,7	11,5	16,3	2,9	20,6	14,9	6,7	11,4
Belgien	0,0	0,0	6,6	17,2	5,5	19,7	18,2	6,6	14,5
Frankreich	5,3	1,1	6,8	14,0	2,0	27,1	9,1	1,8	9,4
Deutschland	4,4	-1,4	8,0	9,2	4,9	22,3	3,3	-3,8	5,5
Niederlande	1,6	-0,6	0,5	16,7	3,4	14,2	8,0	-0,3	11,3
TZWL – niedrigqualifiziert	4,3	0,8	6,7	14,7	3,7	20,8	10,7	2,2	10,4
TZWL – hochqualifiziert	0,6	-0,9	1,2	5,7	-1,9	9,9	1,9	1,2	2,0
Humanitäre Zuwanderung	5,3	2,8	9,0	13,9	2,5	20,3	7,7	3,6	9,2
NZWL – niedrigqualifiziert	-2,0	-3,1	9,8	10,0	-0,9	18,5	2,0	0,0	2,1
EU-28	1,6	0,1	7,2	0,2	-2,9	9,7	4,2	0,3	5,2

	Beteiligung am Lebensbegleitenden Lernen [4]					Resiliente SchülerInnen [5]	Früh- kindliche Bildung [6]
	EU-28 Länder	Extra-EU-28 Länder	Männer	Frauen	Gesamt		
	EUROSTAT (2015)					OECD und EU (2012)	
Österreich	-1,0	-5,8	-5,1	-5,1	-5,1	-8,5	-4,3
Belgien	-1,4	-0,1	-1,3	-1,6	-1,4	-8,8	2,3
Deutschland	.	.	-5,0	-5,6	-5,3	-9,9	0,1
Frankreich	-7,4	-7,5	-10,1	-7,0	-8,5	-11,0	-7,3
Niederlande	-2,0	-3,6	-3,5	-4,2	-3,8	-2,2	-2,2
TZWL - niedrigqualifiziert	-3,0	-4,3	-5,0	-4,7	-4,8	-8,1	-2,3
TZWL - hochqualifiziert	-6,2	-4,2	-5,7	-6,6	-6,1	-6,8	-0,8
Humanitäre Zuwanderung	0,7	2,0	-3,2	-0,6	-1,7	-11,1	-4,7
NZWL – niedrigqualifiziert	-4,3	-3,1	-3,9	-4,2	-4,0	-4,7	-7,5
EU-28	-3,1	-2,8	-4,6	-4,2	-4,3	-5,5	-2,8

[1] *Anteil der 15- bis 24-Jährigen mit höchstens Pflichtschulabschluss, die weder in Aus- noch in Weiterbildung stehen;*
[2] *Anteil der 15-jährigen Schüler und Schülerinnen mit PISA-Lesetest-Ergebnissen vom maximal Niveau 1;*
[3] *Anteil der 15- bis 34-Jährigen ohne Aus- und Weiterbildung und ohne Beschäftigung.*
[4] *Anteil der 18- bis 64-Jährigen mit zumindest einer berufsbezogenen Weiterbildung in den letzten 12 Monaten.*
[5] *Anteil der Schüler/innen aus einem sozial benachteiligten Haushalt mit gutem Schulerfolg laut PISA.*
[6] *Anteil der 3- bis 6-Jährigen in vorschulischen Einrichtungen. Gem. Hintergr.= Im Inland Geborene mit nur einem im Inland geborenen Elternteil. Unter 15 Zugew.= im Ausland Geborene, die im Alter von unter 15 Jahren zuwanderten.*
Weitere Anmerkungen siehe Übersicht 2 und Abschnitt: Daten und Methoden.

Übersicht 3 Bildungsintegration: Differenz zum Anteil der im Inland Geborenen in Prozentpunkten

Quelle: OECD und EU (2015), EUROSTAT, WIFO-Berechnungen.

Die internationalen Vergleiche des Anteils der resilienten Schüler/inn/en (d.h. des Anteils der Schüler/inn/en aus einem sozial benachteiligten Haushalt mit gutem Schulerfolg laut PISA) unterstreicht hingegen den unterdurchschnittlichen Erfolg der traditionellen Zuwanderungsländer mit niedrig qualifizierter Migration hinsichtlich der Bildungsintegration der Migrant/inn/en im Vergleich zu anderen Ländergruppen. Nur unter den Ländern mit substanzieller humanitärer Zuwanderung ist hier die Benachteiligung der Migrant/inn/en noch höher. Innerhalb der traditionellen Zuwanderungsländer mit niedrig qualifizierter Migration liegt Österreich bei diesem Indikator (mit einem um 8,5 Prozentpunkte geringeren Anteil an im Ausland Geborenen resilienten Schüler/inn/en) allerdings im Mittelfeld und nur leicht unter dem Durchschnitt der Ländergruppe.

Soziale Inklusion

Deutlich differenzierter stellt sich die Einkommenssituation der Migrant/inn/en im Vergleich zu den im Inland geborenen Personen in Österreich dar. So vergleichen etwa Huber et al. (2017) die Indikatoren zur sozialen Integration anhand der Datensammlung der OECD und EU (2015), die auf den Anteil der armutsgefährdeten Haushalte und das durchschnittliche Haushaltseinkommen abstellt. Nach diesen Ergebnissen rangiert Österreich, obwohl es im internationalen Vergleich einen nur geringen Anteil an Hocheinkommenshaushalten unter Migrant/inn/en aufweist, beim Anteil der durch Armut bedrohten Haushalte sogar etwas besser als der Durchschnitt der traditionellen Zuwanderungsländer mit niedrig qualifizierter Zuwanderung und nur unwesentlich über dem Durchschnitt der EU-28. Beim Unterschied in der Kinderarmut schneidet nur Deutschland vergleichsweise besser ab. Ähnlich liegt auch die relative Armutsrate fast im EU-Durchschnitt (siehe hierzu Huber et al. 2017).

Diese Ergebnisse werden allerdings durch eine Betrachtung der Indikatoren der EUROSTAT Datenbank, welche im Gegensatz zur EU und OECD (2015) auf Personen abstellt, deutlich relativiert (Übersicht 4). Laut diesen EUROSTAT-Daten lagen (auf der Personenebene) die Medianeinkommen von im Ausland geborenen Frauen in Österreich um 25% und von im Ausland geborenen Männern um 32% unter dem Niveau der im Inland Geborenen. Im internationalen Vergleich sind dies hohe Werte, die deutlich über dem EU-Durchschnitt und auch über dem Durchschnitt aller anderen Ländergruppen liegen.

Diese hohen Einkommensunterschiede auf Personenebene spiegeln sich auch in merklichen Unterschieden in den Armutsindikatoren zwischen Migrant/inn/en und im Inland Geborenen in Österreich. Der Unterschied im Anteil der von sozialer Ausgrenzung Betroffenen (19,0 Prozentpunkte bei den Frauen und 24,2 bei den Männern), im Anteil der Armutsgefährdeten (16,9 bzw. 22,3 Prozentpunkte), im Anteil der von Armut betroffenen Arbeitenden (9,5 bzw. 17,6 Prozentpunkte) sowie bei der Kinderarmut (26,2 Prozentpunkte) zwischen Migrant/inn/en und im Inland Geborenen auf Basis von EUROSTAT-Daten ist im internationalen Vergleich sehr hoch. Nur bei der materiellen Deprivation liegt Österreich unter dem Durchschnitt der traditionellen Zuwanderungsländer mit niedrig qualifizierter Migration.

Der Vergleich der Resultate der beiden Datenquellen (EUROSTAT in dieser Arbeit und OECD und EU (2015) in Huber et al. 2017) zeigt daher, wie wichtig es für eine vollständige Bewertung der relativen Einkommenssituation und Armutsgefährdung von Migrant/inn/en und im Inland Geborenen ist, sowohl Auswertungen auf Haushalts- als auch auf Personenebene heranzuziehen. Insbesondere

Integration von Migrant/inn/en: Wo steht Österreich im internationalen Vergleich?

	Medianlohnunterschied[1]			Materielle Deprivation[2]			Soziale Ausgrenzung[3]		
	Frauen	Männer	Gesamt	Frauen	Männer	Gesamt	Frauen	Männer	Gesamt
	EUROSTAT (2015)			EUROSTAT (2015)			EUROSTAT (2015)		
Österreich	-25,1	-32,4	-28,4	4,6	7,7	6,0	19,0	24,2	21,4
Belgien	-27,5	-25,6	-26,3	10,4	9,8	10,2	23,9	21,4	22,7
Deutschland	-6,2	-12,2	-9,3	0,0	2,9	1,4	0,6	4,2	2,4
Frankreich	-15,8	-19,1	-17,2	7,0	6,4	6,7	15,9	14,2	15,1
Niederlande	-17,9	-18,1	-18,2	10,2	6,0	8,3	19,9	13,7	17,0
TZWL - niedrigqualifiziert	-18,5	-21,5	-19,9	6,4	6,6	6,5	15,9	15,5	15,7
TZWL - hochqualifiziert	-13,4	-17,8	-15,7	2,0	2,0	2,0	9,3	10,9	10,2
Humanitäre Zuwanderung	-13,4	-18,1	-15,6	4,7	3,6	4,2	14,8	17,0	15,9
NZWL – niedrigqualifiziert	-24,9	-27,6	-26,2	14,1	17,7	15,8	19,1	22,5	20,7
EU-28	-12,6	-13,6	-13,2	5,1	4,2	4,8	11,3	10,2	11,0

	Armutsgefährdung[4]			Arbeitende Arme[5]			Kinderarmut[6]	Gute Gesundheit[7]	Unbeh. Krankheit[8]
	Frauen	Männer	Gesamt	Frauen	Männer	Gesamt			
	EUROSTAT (2015)			EUROSTAT (2015)			OECD und EU (2012)		
Österreich	16,9	22,3	19,4	9,5	17,6	13,8	26,2	-3,4	-2,3
Belgien	21,9	18,5	20,3	6,0	7,0	6,5	21,1	-0,7	0,3
Deutschland	0,9	4,4	2,6	4,4	9,0	6,8	6,5	-3,7	0,8
Frankreich	13,3	13,4	13,4	7,5	13,0	10,5	24,4	-0,8	-1,5
Niederlande	11,2	12,4	11,8	3,4	5,9	4,8	8,4	0,5	0,0
TZWL - niedrigqualifiziert	12,8	14,2	13,5	6,2	10,5	8,5	17,3	-1,6	-0,6
TZWL - hochqualifiziert	8,8	9,8	9,3	5,7	10,3	8,2	13,1	3,5	0,0
Humanitäre Zuwanderung	11,1	14,3	12,7	6,6	11,2	9,0	19,0	7,2	-4,4
NZWL – niedrigqualifiziert	16,4	18,4	17,4	16,1	14,2	15,1	18,4	16,2	-2,2
EU-28	8,9	8,7	9,0	6,9	8,1	7,2	12,4	5,2	-5,0

1) Unterschied zum jährlichen Medianeinkommen der im Inland Geborenen (in %);
2) Anteil der Personen im Alter von 18 oder mehr Jahren, die unfähig sind, für unerwartete Ausgaben, einen einwöchigen Jahresurlaub an einem anderen Ort, jeden zweiten Tag eine Fleisch-, Geflügel- oder Fischmahlzeit, angemessene Beheizung der Wohnung, langlebige Gebrauchsgüter wie Waschmaschine, Farbfernseher, Telefon oder Auto, Schulden, Rechnungen für Versorgungsleistungen aufzukommen;
3) Armutsgefährdete Personen, Personen mit Materieller Deprivation sowie Personen in Haushalten mit sehr geringer Erwerbstätigkeit (über 17 Jahre);
4) Anteil der über 18-Jährigen mit einem Einkommen von nur 60% des Medians des Äquivalenzeinkommens;
5) Anteil der über 18-Jährigen mit mindestens 7 Monaten Beschäftigung im letzten Jahr mit einem Einkommen von nur 60% des Medians des Äquivalenzeinkommen;
6) Anteil der Kinder in Haushalten mit weniger als 60% des Medians des Äquivalenzeinkommens;
7) Anteil an Personen ohne chronische Leiden, keinen gesundheitlichen Einschränkungen und (laut Eigenangabe) in guter gesundheitlicher Verfassung;
8) Personen mit einer unbehandelten Erkrankung in den letzten 12 Monaten.
Weitere Anmerkungen: siehe Übersicht 2 und Abschnitt: Daten und Methoden

Übersicht 4 Einkommen, Armut, Gesundheit: Differenz zu im Inland Geborenen in Prozentpunkten

Quelle: OECD und EU (2015), EUROSTAT, WIFO-Berechnungen.

dürfte hier, aufgrund der größeren Haushaltsgrößen von migrantischen Haushalten oder aufgrund spezifischer Sozialleistungen auf Haushaltsebene, eine Betrachtung auf Haushaltsebene zu einem besseren Bild führen als eine Betrachtung auf Personenebene.

In vielen Ländern geben Migrant/inn/en häufiger als im Inland Geborene an, einen guten Gesundheitszustand aufzuweisen und auch an keinen chronischen Erkrankungen zu leiden (Übersicht 4). Zum Teil erklärt sich dies aus einer Selbstselektion aufgrund des Healthy-Migrant-Effektes (siehe z.B. McDonald und Kennedy 2004). Dieser entsteht, weil die Migrationsneigung unter Kranken deutlich geringer ist als unter Gesunden und Migrant/inn/en im Durchschnitt meistens jünger (und daher gesünder) sind als im Inland Geborene. Dennoch sind Migrant/inn/en bei ihrer gesundheitlichen Betreuung in anderen Dimensionen oftmals benachteiligt. Insbesondere haben Migrant/inn/en laut einigen Untersuchungen (siehe Ku und Jewers 2013, Stanciole und Huber 2009) im Allgemeinen einen schlechteren Zugang zum Gesundheitssystem und Amesberger et al. (2003) verweisen auf die Heterogenität von Migrant/inn/en und auf die aufgrund ihrer sozialen Lage spezifischen Gesundheitsrisiken. Aus diesem Grund nutzen OECD und EU (2015) auch einen Indikator, der den Zugang zum Gesundheitssystem misst, indem er auf den Anteil der Personen mit einer unbehandelten Krankheit im letzten Jahr abstellt.

In Österreich ist der Anteil der Personen mit einer unbehandelten Krankheit im letzten Jahr unter den Migrant/inn/en um 2,3 Prozentpunkte niedriger als unter den im Inland Geborenen, während der Anteil der Personen mit gutem Gesundheitszustand unter den Migrant/inn/en (um 3,4 Prozentpunkte) niedriger ausfällt als unter den im Inland Geborenen. Damit fällt der Abstand in Österreich bei den unbehandelten Krankheiten etwas geringer als im EU-Durchschnitt aus.

Eine durchwegs deutlich schlechtere relative Stellung der Migrant/inn/en gegenüber den im Inland Geborenen ergibt sich hingegen bei der Wohnsituation (siehe dazu z.B. Kohlbacher und Reeger 2003, Berger et al 2014, Fassmann und Kohlbacher 2008, Fassmann und Kohlbacher 2009). In den allermeisten OECD-Ländern sind Migrant/inn/en bedingt durch ihr vergleichsweise geringeres Einkommen, ihr höheres Arbeitslosigkeitsrisiko und den damit verbundenen Zugangsbeschränkungen zu Finanzierungsmöglichkeiten seltener als im Inland Geborene Eigentümer ihrer Wohnung, leben häufiger in beengten Wohnverhältnissen und geben auch häufiger mehr als 60% ihres verfügbaren Einkommens für Wohnungskosten aus.

In Österreich war der Anteil der Wohnungseigentümer laut EUROSTAT-Daten im Jahr 2015 unter den Migrant/inn/en um 33,8 Prozentpunkte niedriger als unter den im Inland Geborenen. Zudem leben Migrant/inn/en um 9,5 Prozentpunkte häufiger in beengten Wohnverhältnissen und verzeichnen um 25,3 Prozentpunkte öfter belastende Wohnkosten als im Inland Geborene (Übersicht 5). Insbesondere hinsichtlich der belastenden Wohnkosten ist die Situation unter Migrant/inn/en relativ zu den im Inland Geborenen im Vergleich mit allen anderen traditionellen Zuwanderungsländern mit niedrig qualifizierter Migration und mit dem EU-Durchschnitt merklich angespannter.

	Wohnungsbesitzquote[1]			Beengte Wohnverhältnisse[2]			Belastende Wohkosten[3]		
	Frauen	Männer	Gesamt	Frauen	Männer	Gesamt	Frauen	Männer	Gesamt
	EUROSTAT (2015)								
Österreich	-29,9	-38,3	-33,8	8,7	10,5	9,5	22,9	28,4	25,3
Belgien	-25,5	-29,3	-27,3	11,7	9,3	10,6	1,8	4,2	2,8
Deutschland	-6,3	-7,4	-6,9	1,6	2,2	2,0	4,1	6,0	5,1
Frankreich	-10,4	-15,8	-13,0	2,4	4,0	3,2	6,7	7,2	7,0
Niederlande	-16,0	-26,2	-20,8	8,1	4,9	6,6	4,2	2,2	3,3
TZWL - niedrigqualifiziert	-17,6	-23,4	-20,4	6,5	6,2	6,4	7,9	9,6	8,7
TZWL - hochqualifiziert	-23,9	-28,5	-26,1	6,9	7,8	7,3	9,3	10,7	10,0
Humanitäre Zuwanderung	-20,4	-26,5	-23,4	3,7	6,1	4,8	9,0	11,5	10,2
NZWL – niedrigqualifiziert	-34,5	-39,4	-36,8	17,9	21,2	19,5	15,6	17,2	16,3
EU-28	-18,0	-22,1	-20,0	6,7	8,0	7,4	5,7	7,9	6,7

[1] Anteil der Haushalte mit zumindest einem über 16-jährigen Mitglied, die ihre Wohnung besitzen;
[2] Personen älter als 15 Jahre, die in einer Wohnung leben, in der weniger als ein gemeinsamer Raum, ein Raum für das für den Haushalt verantwortliche Paar, ein Raum für jeden weiteren Erwachsenen sowie ein Raum für 2 Kinder zur Verfügung stehen;
[3] Anteil der Miethaushalte mit Mietkosten von 60% oder mehr des Einkommens.
Weitere Anmerkungen: siehe Übersicht 2 und Abschnitt: Daten und Methoden

Übersicht 5 Wohnsituation, Differenz zu im Inland Geborenen in Prozentpunkten

Quelle: EUROSTAT, WIFO-Berechnungen.

Schlussfolgerungen

Insgesamt lässt ein internationaler Vergleich der wirtschaftlichen und sozialen Integration von Migrant/inn/en somit erkennen, dass Österreich in keiner der analysierten Dimensionen zu den internationalen Best-Practice-Beispielen gehört. Bezieht man in den Vergleich allerdings nur Länder mit ähnlicher Zuwanderungsstruktur wie Österreich ein, dann relativiert sich dieser Befund hinsichtlich der Arbeitsmarktintegration, weil Migrant/inn/en in Österreich anders als in den Vergleichsländern gleich gut oder besser in den Arbeitsmarkt integriert sind. Somit dürfte zumindest ein Teil der für Österreich im internationalen Vergleich ausgewiesenen schlechteren Arbeitsmarktintegration auf die Struktur der Zuwanderung in der Vergangenheit zurückzuführen sein.

In einigen anderen Bereichen bestehen aber geringere Integrationsausmaße von Migrant/inn/en, die durch die Struktur der Zuwanderung alleine nicht erklärbar sind, und bei denen somit in zukünftigen Arbeiten zu überprüfen wäre, inwieweit nationale Institutionen, Regelungen und Traditionen hier zu einer strukturellen Benachteiligung führen. So ist zum Beispiel die Bildungsintegration der im Ausland geborenen Jugendlichen und der zweiten Generation in Österreich gemäß der Mehrzahl der Indikatoren selbst im Vergleich zur Gruppe der traditionellen Zuwanderungsländer mit niedrig qualifizierter Migration deutlich unterdurchschnittlich. Insbesondere nimmt Österreich hier bei einigen zentralen Indikatoren, wie etwa beim Anteil der Personen, die frühzeitig das Bildungssystem verlassen, einen der schlechtesten Plätze unter allen EU-Ländern ein. Dies deutet auf besondere Probleme Österreichs bei der schulischen Integration von Migrant/inn/en hin.

Abgesehen davon zeigen sich auch deutliche Benachteiligungen bei der Wohnsituation der Migrant/inn/en in Österreich. Insbesondere sind Migrant/inn/en in Österreich hinsichtlich Wohnungseigentums und belastenden Wohnkosten auch im internationalen Vergleich deutlich schlechter gestellt als im Inland Geborene. Diese belegbare Benachteiligung fand in der öffentlichen Diskussion bisher deutlich weniger Beachtung als jene im Bildungsbereich, ihre Ursachen und Konsequenzen sollten allerdings in der zukünftigen Forschung noch weiter erforscht werden.

Etwas gemischter sind hingegen die Ergebnisse hinsichtlich Armutsbedrohung und Einkommenssituation. Während die Vergleiche von EUROSTAT, die auf der Personenebene ansetzen, auf einen sehr enttäuschenden Integrationstand hindeuten, indizieren die OECD-Zahlen, die sich auf die Haushaltebene beziehen, dagegen einen deutlich weniger auffälligen Unterschied zwischen Migrant/inn/en und im Inland Geborenen. Diese variierenden Ergebnisse illustrieren somit die Notwendigkeit weiterer internationaler Bemühungen zu Datenerfassung und Indikatorenbildung, die spezifische Auswertungen nach verschiedenen Dimensionen zulassen, um ein detailliertes Bild über Integrationserfolge und -hemmnisse sowie über spezifische Problemlagen für verschiedene Gruppen von Migrant/inn/en zu erhalten.

Literatur

Algan Y., Dustmann, C., Glitz, A., Manning, A. (2010) The Economic Situation of First and Second-Generation Immigrants in France, Germany and the United Kingdom. Economic Journal, 120(542), S. F4-F30.

Altorjai, S. (2013) Over-qualification of immigrants in the UK. ISER Working Paper Series No 2013-11, Essex. https://www.iser.essex.ac.uk/research/publications/working-papers/iser/2013-11.pdf (download am 3.8.2017)

Amesberger, H., Halbmayr, B., Liegl, B. (2003) Gesundheit und medizinische Versorgung von ImmigrantInnen. In: Fassmann, H., Stacher, I. (ed.), Österreichischer Migrations- und Integrationsbericht: demographische Entwicklungen, sozioökonomische Strukturen, rechtliche Rahmenbedingungen. Klagenfurt, S. 171-194.

Battu, H., Sloane, P. J. (2004) Over-education and ethnic minorities in Britain. The Manchester School, University of Manchester, 72 (4), S. 535-559.

Belot, M., Hatton, T. (2012) Immigrant Selection in the OECD, Scandinavian Journal of Economics, 114(4), S. 1105-1128.

Berger, T, Czerny, M., Faustmann, A., Perl, C. (2014) Sozialraumanalyse: Konzepte und Empfehlungen zur Umsetzung von Integration in Niederösterreich. Erstellt vom Department für Migration und Globalisierung der Donau-Universität Krems im Auftrag des Amts der Niederösterreichischen Landesregierung. Schriftenreihe Migration und Globalisierung, Krems (Edition Donau-Universität Krems).

Biffl., G. (2002) Ausländische Arbeitskräfte auf dem österreichischen Arbeitsmarkt. WIFO-Monatsberichte 75(8), S. 537-550.

Biffl, G. (2004) Chancen von jugendlichen Gastarbeiterkindern in Österreich. WISO 27(2), S.37-55.

Biffl, G. (2006) Towards a common migration policy: potential impact on the EU economy. Zeitschrift für Arbeitsmarktforschung / Journal of Labour Market Research, IAB-Nürnberg, ZAF 1/2006, S. 1-17.
Biffl, G. (2011) Migrationsmodelle und ihre Steuerbarkeit. In: Biffl, G., Dimmel, N. (Hrsg), Migrationsmanagement. Grundzüge des Management von Migration und Integration, Omninum Verlag, S. 51-66.
Biffl, G. (2011a) Entwicklung der Migrationen in Österreich aus historischer Sicht. In: Biffl, G., Dimmel, N. (Hrsg), Migrationsmanagement. Grundzüge des Management von Migration und Integration. Omninum Verlag, S. 33-50.
Biffl, G., Bock-Schappelwein, J. (2003) Soziale Mobilität durch Bildung? — Das Bildungsverhalten von MigrantInnen. In: Fassmann, H., Stacher, I. (Hrsg.), Österreichischer Migrations- und Integrationsbericht: demographische Entwicklungen, sozioökonomische Strukturen, rechtliche Rahmenbedingungen. Klagenfurt, S. 120-130.
Biffl, G., Bock-Schappelwein J. (2013) Zur Niederlassung von Ausländern in Österreich. Studie im Auftrag des BMI, WIFO-Gutachtenserie, Wien.
Biffl, G., Skrivanek, I., Berger, J., Hofer, H., Schuh, U., Strohner, L. (2010) Potentielle Auswirkungen einer Änderung der österreichischen Migrationspolitik in Richtung qualifizierte Zuwanderung auf das mittel- bis langfristige Wirtschaftswachstum (Prognosehorizont 2050). Krems, Studie im Auftrag der WKÖ und der IV.
Bosswick, W., Lüken-Klaßen, D., Heckmann, F. (2007) Housing and integration of migrants in Europe. European Foundation for the Improvement of Living and Working Conditions und Council of Europe, Dublin.
Cangiano, A. (2012) Immigration policy and migrant labour market outcomes in the European Union: New evidence from the EU Labour Force Survey. manuscript, School of Economics, University of the South Pacific, LAB-MIG-GOV project.
Cattaneo, M., Wolter S. (2015) Better migrants, better PISA results: Findings from a natural experiment. IZA Journal of Migration, 4(1), S. 1-19.
Chiswick, B.R, DebBurman, N. (2004) Educational attainment: analysis by immigrant generation, Economics of Education Review, 23(4). S. 361-379.
Chiswick, B. R., Miller, P. W. (2007) The International Transferability of Immigrants' Human Capital Skills. IZA Discussion Paper, No. 2670.
Europäische Kommission – DG Home Affairs (2013) Using EU Indicators of Immigrant Integration. Europäische Kommission, Brüssel.
Fassmann, H., Kohlbacher, J. (2008) Staatsbürgerschaftsbonus beim Wohnen? Eine empirische Analyse der Unterschiede zwischen eingebürgerten und nichteingebürgerten Zuwanderern/-innen hinsichtlich ihrer Wohnsituation in Wien, ISR-Forschungsbericht 35, Verlag der ÖAW, Wien.
Fassmann, H., Kohlbacher, J. (2009) Housing and segregation of migrants - Case study: Vienna, Austria, European Foundation for the Improvement of Living and Working Conditions, Dublin.
Granato, M., Ulrich, J. G. (2009) Junge Menschen mit Migrationshintergrund auf dem Weg in eine berufliche Ausbildung Integrationspotenzial des Ausbildungssystems? In: Lassnigg, L., Babel, H., Gruber, E., Markowitsch, J. (Hrsg.), Öffnung von Arbeitsmärkten und Bildungssystemen. Beiträge zur Berufsbildungsforschung. Studienverlag, Innsbruck, S.40-56.
Green, A. E. (2011) Impact of economic downturn and migration: a discussion paper commissioned from the Regeneration and Economic Development Analysis Expert Panel. http://webarchive.nationalarchives.gov.uk/20120919132719/http://www.communities.gov.uk/documents/corporate/pdf/1854800.pdf (download am 3.8.2017).
Huber, P., Horvath, Th., Bock-Schappelwein, J. (2017) Österreich als Zuwanderungsland. WIFO-Monographie, Wien.
Kohlbacher, J., Reeger, U. (2003) Die Wohnsituation von AusländerInnen in Österreich. In: Fassmann, H., Stacher, I. (Hrsg.), Österreichischer Migrations- und Integrationsbericht: de-

mographische Entwicklungen, sozioökonomische Strukturen, rechtliche Rahmenbedingungen. Klagenfurt, S. 87-108.

Ku, L., Jewers, M. (2013) Health Care for Immigrant Families: Current Policies an Issues. Migration Policy Institute, Washington DC.

Lassnigg, L. (2011) Research-based policy proposals for the improvement of school-to-work-transition, with special reference to immigrants. In: Biffl, G., Dimmel, N. (Hrsg), Migrationsmanagement. Grundzüge des Management von Migration und Integration. Omninum Verlag, S. 301-320.

Longhi, S., Rokicka, M. (2012) European immigrants in the UK before and after the 2004 enlargement: is there a change in immigrant self-selection? ISER Working Paper Series 22.

McDonald, J. T., Kennedy, S. (2004) Insights into the 'healthy immigrant effect': health status and health service use of immigrants to Canada. Social science & medicine, 59(8), S. 1613-1627.

Münz, R. (2007) Migration, labor markets, and integration of migrants: An overview for Europe. No. 3-6. HWWI policy paper.

OECD – EU (2015) Indicators of Immigrant Integration 2015: Settling In. OECD Publishing, Paris.

Reichel, D. (2011) Staatsbürgerschaft und Integration – Die Bedeutung der Einbürgerung für MigrantInnen, VS Verlag, Wiesbaden.

Sprung, A. (2011) Weiterbildung in der Migrationsgesellschaft. In: Biffl, G., Dimmel, N. (Hrsg), Migrationsmanagement. Grundzüge des Management von Migration und Integration. Omninum Verlag, S. 265-274.

Stamm, M., Burger, K., Brandenberg, K., Edelmann, D., Holzinger-Neulinger, M., Mayr, K., Müller, C., Nedrini, L., Wetzel, M. (2011) Integrationsförderung im Frühbereich. Was frühkindliche Bildung, Betreuung und Erziehung (FBBE) benötigt, damit sie dem Anspruch an Integration gerecht werden kann. ZeFF, Universitäres Zentrum für frühkindliche Bildung, Fribourg.

Stanciole, A. E., Huber, M. (2009) Access to health care for migrants, ethnic minorities, and asylum seekers in Europe! Policy Brief, European Centre, S. 1-8.

Tamesberger, D., Bacher, J. (2014) NEET youth in Austria: a typology including socio-demography, labour market behavior and permanence. Journal of Youth Studies Vol. 17, No. 9, S. 1239-1259.

Van Den Boogaart E., Emmer, P.C. (1986) Colonialism and migration: an overview. In: Emmer P.C. (eds) Colonialism and Migration; Indentured Labour Before and After Slavery. Comparative Studies in Overseas History, vol 7. Springer, Dordrecht, S 3-15.

Längsschnittanalyse der Erwerbsverläufe der Migrationskohorten 2010, 2011 und 2012

Stephan Marik-Lebeck, Josef Kytir

Zusammenfassung

Migration und Integration sind zu zentralen politischen gesellschaftlichen Themen geworden. Damit steigt der Bedarf an zuverlässigen Informationen über die sozioökonomischen Charakteristika der zugewanderten Bevölkerung im Zeitverlauf. Die Einführung statistischer Register in vielen Bereichen der öffentlichen Verwaltung und ihre statistische Nutzung eröffnen dazu zahlreiche Auswertungsmöglichkeiten. Denn die Verknüpfung von verschiedenen Registern ermöglicht es mit vergleichsweise geringem Aufwand, Informationen zu erhalten, welche zuvor nur durch maßgeschneiderte Befragungen erhoben werden konnten.

Die vorliegende Studie analysiert drei Kohorten von Personen, die in den Jahren 2010, 2011 oder 2012 erstmals nach Österreich zugezogen sind. Diese Jahre wurden ausgewählt, um die Auswirkungen der Einführung der vollen Arbeitnehmerfreizügigkeit für die 2004 beigetretenen EU-Staaten abzubilden. Für diese Kohorten wurden einerseits die Meldeepisoden ausgewertet, um die Aufenthaltsdauer zu analysieren. Andererseits erfolgte eine Verknüpfung mit den registerbasierten Erwerbsverläufen (basierend auf sozialversicherungspflichtigen Beschäftigungsverhältnissen) zur Darstellung des Verlaufs der Arbeitsmarktintegration in Österreich.

Die Auswertungen zeigen, dass ein erheblicher Teil der Zugewanderten Österreich innerhalb kurzer Zeiträume wiederum verlässt, so dass nach fünf Jahren nur noch weniger als die Hälfte der ursprünglichen Kohorte in Österreich gemeldet ist. Die Verbliebenen erreichen nach fünf Jahren ähnliche Erwerbstätigenquoten wie die Gesamtheit der in Österreich lebenden ausländischen Staatsangehörigen, wobei die Erwerbsintegration bei EU-Bürgerinnen und Bürgern schneller vonstattengeht als bei Drittstaatsangehörigen. Die Unterschiede liegen wesentlich im Niveau der Erwerbsbeteiligung von Frauen begründet, sind zum Teil aber auch der Dauer von Asylverfahren (mit einem de-facto Arbeitsverbot) geschuldet.

Einleitung

Zuwanderung ist in den letzten Jahrzehnten zu einem zentralen gesellschaftlichen und politischen Thema geworden. Der Arbeitsmarkt bzw. die Rolle und Funktion von zugwanderten Personen für den Arbeitsmarkt stehen dabei immer wieder im Mittelpunkt des Interesses. So ist das Arbeitskräfteangebot in Österreich in den vergangenen zehn Jahren deutlich gestiegen, nämlich von 5,54 Mio. Personen (2006) auf 5,81 Mio. Personen (2016). Zuwanderung spielt bei dieser Entwicklung eine entscheidende Rolle. Denn einem (geringfügigen) Rückgang von im Inland geborenen Erwerbspersonen (-43.000) steht ein beträchtlicher Zuwachs von im Ausland geborenen Erwerbspersonen (+307.000) gegenüber. Der Anteil der labour force mit ausländischem Geburtsort stieg demnach von 16,9% (2006) auf 21,4% (2016).

Nicht zuletzt durch die gestiegene quantitative Bedeutung für den Arbeitsmarkt hat sich auch das wissenschaftliche Interesse an strukturellen Merkmalen der Zugewanderten stark erhöht. Insbesondere der sozio-ökonomische Status von Migranten und Migrantinnen und seine Veränderung im Zeitverlauf sind für die Integrationsdebatte zu zentralen Fragen geworden, messen sie doch letztlich den „Erfolg" von Zugewanderten im Zielland. Dabei stehen vor allem Fragen der Arbeitsmarktintegration, aber auch des Bildungsstandes von Migranten und Migrantinnen im Vordergrund.

Vor diesem Hintergrund ermöglicht der umfassende Aufbau von Registern zur Unterstützung der öffentlichen Verwaltung gleichsam als statistisches Nebenprodukt die systematische Erfassung einer Vielzahl von personenbezogenen Merkmalen. Deren systematische Verknüpfung (unter Wahrung des Datenschutzes mit einem eindeutigen Pseudonym, das in allen statistischen Registern geführt wird) bietet die Möglichkeit, Informationen statistisch auszuwerten, welche bislang nur durch maßgeschneiderte Befragungen verfügbar waren.

Methodik

Die meisten statistischen Register in Österreich wurden in Vorbereitung der Registerzählung 2011 eingerichtet. Bis auf wenige Ausnahmen handelt es sich dabei um Spiegeldatenbanken von administrativen Registern, deren Informationen für statistische Zwecke systematisiert, historisiert und harmonisiert wurden. Jede Analyse personenbezogener Charakteristika der Zugewanderten baut in Österreich auf Informationen aus dem Zentralen Melderegister (ZMR) bzw. dessen bevölkerungsstatistischem Spiegelregister, dem POPREG auf. Hier sind für alle mit Hauptwohnsitz in Österreich gemeldeten Personen die wesentlichen Strukturmerkmale erfasst, wie Geburtsdatum (Alter), Geburtsland, Geschlecht, Staatsangehörigkeit und Wohnort in Österreich. Für die Arbeitsmarkteinbindung sind die sogenannten registerbasierten Erwerbsverläufe (REV) die zentrale Datenquelle,

	2006	2011	2016
Insgesamt	**5.543**	**5.626**	**5.808**
Österreich	4.608	4.625	4.565
Nicht-Österreich	935	1.001	1.242
EU/EWR	343	374	502
EU vor 2004	143	172	212
EU ab 2004	200	201	290
Drittstaaten	592	627	740

Tabelle 1: Zahl der in Österreich lebenden Erwerbspersonen nach Geburtsland 2006 bis 2016 (absolut in 1.000)

Quelle: Statistik Austria, Mikrozensus-Arbeitskräfteerhebung; Jahresdurchschnitt.

welche auf Informationen des Hauptverbandes der Sozialversicherungsträger sowie des Arbeitsmarktservice beruhen. Diese sind ab dem Berichtsjahr 2009 verfügbar.

Im Hinblick auf die Zielsetzung einer Analyse der Integrationsverläufe von Migranten und Migrantinnen erschien eine längsschnittliche Analyse der in einem bestimmten Jahr nach Österreich Zugewanderten am zielführendsten. Ein Blick in die Migrationsstatistik zeigt für die Jahre ab 2010 eine starke Zunahme der Zuwanderung aus dem Ausland nach Österreich. Dies ist vor allem im Kontext der schrittweise bis 2011 aufgehobenen Zugangsbeschränkungen zum Arbeitsmarkt für die 2004 beigetretenen EU-Staaten zu sehen. Daher schien ein Vergleich der Arbeitsmarkteinbindung von Personen sinnvoll, welche in den Jahren 2010, 2011 und 2012 nach Österreich zuwanderten. In einem ersten Schritt waren somit die Migrationskohorten der genannten drei Jahre zu definieren. Im Hinblick auf die unverzerrte Messung des Integrationsverlaufs erschien es ratsam, nur jene Personen auszuwählen, welche in den drei genannten Jahren *erstmals* nach Österreich zuwanderten und sich somit erst in Österreich etablieren mussten. Grundlage für die Auswahl war die Wanderungsstatistik, welche seit 2002 auf der Basis der An- und Abmeldungen von Hauptwohnsitzen in Österreich im Zentralen Melderegister (ZMR) erstellt wird. Für die erstmaligen Zuzüge der Jahre 2010, 2011 und 2012 waren somit alle Personen auszuwählen, welche im Zentralen Melderegister erstmals[1] in einem der drei Jahre aufscheinen. Auszuschließen waren danach alle Anmeldungen, die sich auf Geburten bezogen. Die so ermittelte Zahl der erstmalig Zugezogenen stellt eine Teilmenge aller Zuzüge in den betrachteten Jahren dar. Im Unterschied zur Grundgesamtheit, die sich auf Fälle bezieht, handelt es sich dabei um eine personenbezogene Teilmenge, welche durch individuelle bereichsspezifische Personenkennzeichen definiert wird und über diese auch mit anderen Datenbeständen verknüpfbar ist.

---

[1] Korrekterweise erstmals seit 2002. Die Zahl der Personen, welche bereits vor 2002 eine aufrechte Meldung in Österreich hatten und in den Jahren 2010-2012 wiederum nach Österreich zogen, dürfte bei ausländischen Staatsangehörigen verschwindend gering sein. Bei Österreichischen Staatsangehörigen spielt diese Gruppe etwa bei Rückkehrern aus dem Ausland (insbesondere Ruhestandswanderung) eine wesentlich größere Rolle. Sie ist aber nicht Gegenstand der vorliegenden Analyse.

Für die so definierten Migrationskohorten 2010, 2011 und 2012 wurde sodann ein längsschnittlicher Datenauszug aus dem POPREG erstellt, welcher alle Meldeepisoden (Abfolgen von Wohnsitzan- und -abmeldungen im ZMR innerhalb Österreichs sowie nach dem Ausland) der erstmals in den drei betrachteten Jahren Zugezogenen bis zum Stichtag 1.1.2017 enthält. Enthalten sind zudem demographische Informationen zu Alter, Geschlecht sowie Staatsangehörigkeit der Zugewanderten. Um Verzerrungen durch allfällige Einbürgerungen zu minimieren, wurde die Staatsangehörigkeit zum Zeitpunkt des erstmaligen Zuzugs für den gesamten Analysezeitraum fortgeschrieben.

Die Analyse der Meldeepisoden lieferte zudem Informationen über die Aufenthaltsdauer in Österreich. Sie kann zukünftig im Hinblick auf das Auftreten zirkulärer Migrationsmuster sowie die Mobilität innerhalb Österreichs unter den Zugewanderten erweitert werden. Ebenso ließen sich durch einen Zeitvergleich auch allfällige Wechsel der Staatsangehörigkeit (Einbürgerungen) abbilden.

In einem zweiten Schritt wurden die Längsschnittdaten aus dem ZMR mit den sogenannten *Registerbasierten Erwerbsverläufen* verknüpft. Dabei handelt es sich um Längsschnittauswertungen, welche die Erwerbsbiographie von Personen lückenlos abbilden. Dabei wurden Registerinformationen des Hauptverbandes der Sozialversicherungsträger sowie des Arbeitsmarktservice über Versicherungsverhältnisse zusammengeführt und gemeinsam überschneidungsfrei gemacht. Jeder Person kann somit für den Zeitraum 1. Jänner 2009 bis derzeit 31. Dezember 2015 für jeden Tag ein eindeutiger Arbeitsmarktstatus entsprechend der Abgestimmten Erwerbsstatistik[2] zugeordnet werden. Für jede Person, die Teil der aus dem Zentralen Melderegister identifizierten Migrationskohorten der Jahre 2010, 2011 und 2012 war, wurde somit eine lückenlose Abfolge von Arbeitsmarktstatus für die Zeitspanne zwischen dem erstmaligen Zuzug nach Österreich und dem Jahresende 2015 ermittelt. Daraus ließen sich die Formen, das Ausmaß sowie die Dauer bis zur erfolgreichen Eingliederung in den österreichischen Arbeitsmarkt analysieren.

Eine Verknüpfung der im POPREG identifizierten Migrationskohorten mit dem Bildungsstandregister erbrachte dagegen keine statistisch belastbaren Ergebnisse. Hier wird deutlich, dass Bildung von den Zugewanderten überwiegend „mitgebracht" wird und nur eine Minderheit (weitere) Bildungsabschlüsse in Österreich erwirbt.

Die gewonnenen Ergebnisse stellen jedenfalls einen ersten Schritt in Richtung der Erstellung eines sozio-ökonomischen Profils der nach Österreich Zugewanderten dar.

---

[2] Für eine methodische Beschreibung des Projektes „Registerbasierte Erwerbsverläufe" siehe: http://www.statistik.at/wcm/idc/idcplg?IdcService=GET_PDF_FILE&RevisionSelectionMethod=LatestReleased&dDocName=110458.

Migrationskohorten 2010-2012
(erstmalig nach Österreich Zuziehende)

Die Zuwanderung nach Österreich erhöhte sich im Zeitraum von 2010 bis 2012 um gut ein Viertel von rund 113.000 auf 140.000. Davon zogen 2010 rund 78.000 Personen (69% aller Zuzüge) erstmals nach Österreich, während diese Zahl bis 2012 auf 103.000 Personen anstieg (73%). Blieb die Zuwanderung österreichischer Staatsangehöriger in diesem Zeitraum weitgehend unverändert, erhöhte sich der Zuzug von ausländischen Staatsangehörigen deutlich von rund 97.000 Fällen im Jahr 2010 auf 125.000 im Jahr 2012. Von diesen waren 2010 rund 75.000 erstmalige Zuwanderer, 2012 bereits 100.000.

	Zuzüge insgesamt			Erstmalige Zuzüge nach AT			Erstmalige Zuzüge nach AT in % aller Zuzüge		
	2010	2011	2012	2010	2011	2012	2010	2011	2012
Insgesamt	112.691	124.619	140.358	77.887	89.218	102.503	69%	72%	73%
Österreich	15.795	14.698	14.753	2.895	2.705	2.612	18%	18%	18%
Nicht-Österreich	96.896	109.921	125.605	74.992	86.513	99.891	77%	79%	80%
EU-Staaten vor 2004, EFTA	27.007	27.181	29.643	23.097	23.677	26.050	86%	87%	88%
Deutschland	17.966	17.410	17.774	15.248	15.134	15.492	85%	87%	87%
EU-Staaten ab 2004	33.351	42.688	49.543	24.552	32.701	38.938	74%	77%	79%
Ungarn	6.412	9.250	13.066	4.999	7.530	11.007	78%	81%	84%
Rumänien	11.344	12.907	13.362	8.444	9.682	9.931	74%	75%	74%
Drittstaatsangehörige	36.538	40.052	46.419	27.343	30.135	34.903	75%	75%	75%
Ehem. Jugoslawien (nicht-EU)	12.242	12.257	13.472	7.765	7.038	7.654	63%	57%	57%
Türkei	4.258	3.812	4.088	3.160	2.853	3.001	74%	75%	73%
Afghanistan	1.281	2.908	3.756	1.216	2.775	2.755	95%	95%	73%
Russland	2.205	2.643	3.438	1.729	2.458	3.340	78%	93%	97%
Afrikanische Staaten	3.135	3.685	3.808	2.295	2.167	2.805	73%	59%	74%

Tabelle 2: Zuwanderung und erstmalige Zuwanderung nach Österreich 2010-2012 nach Staatsangehörigkeit

Quelle: Statistik Austria, Wanderungsstatistik.

Zugewanderte ausländische Staatsangehörige verteilten sich nahezu gleichmäßig auf drei große Gruppen: Angehörige der EU-Staaten vor 2004 (vorwiegend aus Deutschland und Italien), Angehörige der EU-Beitrittsstaaten ab 2004 (überwiegend aus Ungarn, Rumänien, der Slowakei) und Drittstaatsangehörige. Innerhalb der letzteren Gruppe waren einerseits Zuzüge im Rahmen des Familiennachzugs aus dem ehem. Jugoslawien sowie der Türkei bedeutsam, andererseits Migration mit einem Fluchthintergrund aus der Russischen Föderation (vorwiegend Tschetschenen) und einigen anderen Staaten Westasiens (insbesondere Afghanistan).

Nahm die Zahl der Zugezogenen aus den EU-Staaten vor 2004 zwischen 2010 und 2012 nur um 10% zu, erhöhte sie sich deutlich bei den EU-Beitrittsstaaten ab 2004. Hier stieg die Zahl der Zuzüge von rund 33.000 im Jahr 2010 auf knapp 50.000 im Jahr 2012, eine Zunahme um 49%. Die Zahl der erstmaligen Migrationsbewegungen aus diesen Staaten stieg sogar noch etwas stärker (+58%), nämlich von 25.000 (2010) auf 39.000 (2012). Die Zuzüge aus Drittstaaten nahmen im Beobachtungszeitraum ebenso wie die Zahl der erstmalig Zugezogenen um 27%

zu. Der Anteil der erstmalig nach Österreich Zugezogenen war unter den Angehörigen der EU-Staaten vor 2004 mit über 86% deutlich höher als bei den beiden übrigen Gruppen. Dies dürfte durch den höheren Anteil von Bildungsmigrantinnen und -migranten aus Deutschland und Italien bedingt sein, welche überwiegend erstmals nach Österreich zuwandern.

Im Gegensatz dazu spielen zirkuläre Migrationsmuster unter den Angehörigen der EU-Staaten ab 2004 sowie dem ehem. Jugoslawien und der Türkei eine wesentlich bedeutendere Rolle (vgl. Marik-Lebeck 2012), was sich in niedrigeren Anteilen an erstmals Zugezogenen niederschlägt. Bei den übrigen Drittstaatsangehörigen ist der Anteil der erstmaligen Zuwanderer hingegen deutlich höher, in einigen Fällen bei bis zu 95%.

Alters- und Geschlechtsstruktur der Migrationskohorten 2010-2012

Rund 87% der erstmalig nach Österreich Zuziehenden in den Jahren 2010-2012 waren im Haupterwerbsalter zwischen 15 und 64 Jahren. Die Zuzüge konzentrierten sich jedoch sehr stark im jungen Erwachsenenalter: rund 30% gehörten der Altersgruppe 15-24 und weitere 38% der Altersgruppe 25-39 an. Insgesamt überwog der Zuzug von Männern geringfügig (51% bzw. 52% zwischen 15 und 64 Jahren), allerdings hatten Frauen höhere Anteile in den Altersgruppen zwischen 15 und 24 Jahren sowie ab 55.

		Zuzüge			erstmalige Zuzüge			Frauenanteil der erstmaligen Zuzüge		
		2010	2011	2012	2010	2011	2012	2010	2011	2012
Ausländische Staatsangehörige	Gesamt	96.896	86.513	99.891	74.992	86.513	99.891	49%	47%	47%
	0-14	10%	9%	10%	11%	12%	12%	48%	48%	49%
	15-64	90%	91%	90%	87%	86%	87%	48%	46%	46%
	15-24	27%	25%	30%	30%	30%	31%	52%	49%	49%
	25-39	39%	42%	37%	38%	39%	39%	46%	44%	44%
	40-54	16%	17%	15%	14%	14%	14%	47%	45%	44%
	55-64	5%	4%	5%	4%	4%	3%	54%	54%	52%
	65+	3%	2%	3%	2%	2%	2%	56%	54%	55%

Tabelle 3: Altersstruktur und Geschlechterverhältnis der erstmals nach Österreich zuziehenden ausländischen Staatsangehörigen 2010-2012

Quelle: Statistik Austria, Wanderungsstatistik.

Erstmalige Zuwanderer mit ausländischer Staatsangehörigkeit weisen in allen Altersklassen höhere Anteile auf als die Zugezogenen insgesamt, ausgenommen bei den 25 bis 54-Jährigen. Dies deutet im Umkehrschluss darauf hin, dass zirkuläre Migration vor allem in dieser Altersgruppe stattfindet. Dies gilt gleichermaßen für Angehörige der EU-Staaten vor und nach 2004 sowie für Drittstaatsangehörige.

Aufenthaltsdauer der Migrationskohorten 2010-2012

Eine längsschnittliche Auswertung der Meldeepisoden der Migrationskohorten 2010-2012 in der bevölkerungsstatistischen Datenbank POPREG ermöglichte Aussagen über die Aufenthaltsdauer der in diesen Jahren erstmals zugewanderten Personen. Demnach war fünf Jahre nach dem erstmaligen Zuzug nur noch knapp weniger als die Hälfte der Kohorte 2010 (45%) in Österreich gemeldet. Rund ein Drittel (31%) verließ Österreich binnen eines Jahres nach Zuzug, 18% sogar binnen sechs Monaten, weitere 13% nach einem Aufenthalt von sechs bis zwölf Monaten. Daran zeigt sich die bedeutende Rolle von saisonaler und temporärer Migration in Österreich, selbst wenn nur erstmals zugezogene Migrantinnen und Migranten betrachtet werden.

Weitere 10% der 2010 erstmals Zugezogenen verließen Österreich nach einem Aufenthalt von ein bis zwei Jahren, weitere 13% schließlich nach zwei bis unter fünf Jahren. In Summe ergab dies eine Reduktion um 55% in fünf Jahren. Die Migrationskohorte des Jahres 2011 verzeichnete mit 53% in fünf Jahren eine etwas geringere Reduktion. Für 2012 liegen zwar noch keine Informationen für eine fünfjährige Aufenthaltsdauer vor; der Verlauf in den ersten beiden Jahren gestaltet sich aber sehr ähnlich der beiden anderen Kohorten.

Bei näherer Betrachtung einzelner Staatsangehörigkeitsgruppen zeigt sich deutlich, dass die Aufhebung der Zugangsbeschränkungen zum österreichischen Arbeitsmarkt für die EU-Beitrittsstaaten 2004, welche endgültig am 1.5.2011 erfolgte, spürbare Auswirkungen auf die Aufenthaltsdauer von Migranten hatte. So umfasste die Migrationskohorte 2010 bei dieser Gruppe fünf Jahre später nur noch 39% ihrer ursprünglichen Größe, wogegen es bei der Kohorte 2011 noch 44% waren. Zudem war die 2011er Kohorte deutlich größer, so dass die Zahl der nach fünf Jahren in Österreich lebenden Zugewanderten des Jahres 2011 aus den EU-Beitrittsstaaten in Summe um 50% größer war als jene der 2010 Zugewanderten.

Auch bei den Drittstaatsangehörigen zeigten sich Veränderungen im Anteil der Daueraufenthalte (nach EU-Definition nach 5 Jahren) im Zeitverlauf. Machte die Zuwanderungskohorte 2010 nach fünf Jahren noch 47% ihrer ursprünglichen Größe aus, waren es bei der Kohorte 2011 mit 50% etwas mehr. Die Kohorte 2012 folgt im Verlauf der ersten beiden Jahre eher der Kohorte 2010. Eine weitere Untergliederung innerhalb dieser Gruppe zeigt, dass die Kohorten von Migrantinnen und Migranten aus dem ehem. Jugoslawien nach fünf Jahren relativ konstant etwa 45% ihrer Ursprungsgröße ausmachen. Bei türkischen Staatsangehörigen ergab sich dagegen zwischen den Kohorten 2010 und 2011 ein deutlicher Rückgang von 63% auf 56%.

Die größten Veränderungen im Anteil der Zugewanderten, die sich für mehr als fünf Jahre in Österreich aufhielten, gab es zwischen den Kohorten 2010-2012 jedoch bei jenen Staaten, aus denen Asylwanderungen überwiegen. Beispiele

		2010	2011	2012
ausländische Staatsangehörige	Erstmalige Zuzüge	74.992	86.513	99.891
	Aufenthaltsdauer <= 6 Monate	18%	17%	16%
	Aufenthaltsdauer 6 bis unter 12 Monate	13%	11%	15%
	Aufenthaltsdauer 1 bis unter 2 Jahre	10%	12%	10%
	Aufenthaltsdauer 2 bis unter 5 Jahre	13%	13%	k.A.
	Kohorte nach 5 Jahren	33.637	40.328	k.A.
	in % der erstmaligen Zuzüge	45%	47%	k.A.
EU-Staaten vor 2004, EFTA	Erstmalige Zuzüge	23.097	23.677	26.050
	Aufenthaltsdauer <= 6 Monate	14%	12%	13%
	Aufenthaltsdauer 6 bis unter 12 Monate	10%	9%	14%
	Aufenthaltsdauer 1 bis unter 2 Jahre	10%	13%	11%
	Aufenthaltsdauer 2 bis unter 5 Jahre	18%	18%	k.A.
	Kohorte nach 5 Jahren	11.162	11.152	k.A.
	in % der erstmaligen Zuzüge	48%	47%	k.A.
EU seit 2004	Erstmalige Zuzüge	24.552	32.701	38.938
	Aufenthaltsdauer <= 6 Monate	22%	20%	18%
	Aufenthaltsdauer 6 bis unter 12 Monate	16%	12%	17%
	Aufenthaltsdauer 1 bis unter 2 Jahre	11%	13%	11%
	Aufenthaltsdauer 2 bis unter 5 Jahre	12%	11%	k.A.
	Kohorte nach 5 Jahren	9.610	14.257	k.A.
	in % der erstmaligen Zuzüge	39%	44%	k.A.
Drittstaatsangehörige	Erstmalige Zuzüge	27.343	30.135	34.903
	Aufenthaltsdauer <= 6 Monate	19%	16%	17%
	Aufenthaltsdauer 6 bis unter 12 Monate	13%	11%	13%
	Aufenthaltsdauer 1 bis unter 2 Jahre	9%	11%	9%
	Aufenthaltsdauer 2 bis unter 5 Jahre	11%	12%	k.A.
	Kohorte nach 5 Jahren	12.865	14.919	k.A.
	in % der erstmaligen Zuzüge	47%	50%	k.A.

Tabelle 4: Entwicklung der Größe der Kohorten der 2010-2012 erstmals nach Österreich Zugezogenen im Zeitverlauf nach Staatsangehörigkeit

Quelle: Statistik Austria, Wanderungsstatistik.

dafür sind insbesondere Afghanistan und die Russische Föderation[3], welches die die beiden bedeutendsten Herkunftsländer von Asylantragstellern in Österreich im Zeitraum 2010-2012 waren. Im Vergleich zwischen den Kohorten ist kein klarer Trend erkennbar; vielmehr sind die Schwankungen zwischen den Jahren erheblich. So verringerte sich etwa der Anteil der permanenten Migranten mit afghanischer Staatsangehörigkeit zwischen den Kohorten 2010 und 2011 von 82% auf 53%, während er bei russischen Staatsangehörigen zugleich von 54% auf 77% anstieg. Eine mögliche Erklärung liegt in der durchschnittlichen Dauer von Asylverfahren in Österreich. Eine andere leitet sich aus dem Verhältnis von neu ankommenden Asylwerbern und dem Familiennachzug (als Funktion der Migration vergangener Jahre) ab.

Obwohl diese Faktoren zweifellos auch auf die Zuwanderung afrikanischer Staatsangehöriger nach Österreich zutreffen, waren die absoluten Kohortengrößen

---

[3] Deren Zuwanderung zum allergrößten Teil aus Asylmigration (vermutlich aus Tschetschenien) besteht, wie ein Vergleich der Zahl der Zuzüge russischer Staatsangehöriger insgesamt mit der Zahl im selben Jahr gestellten Asylanträge von russischen Staatsangehörigen belegt.

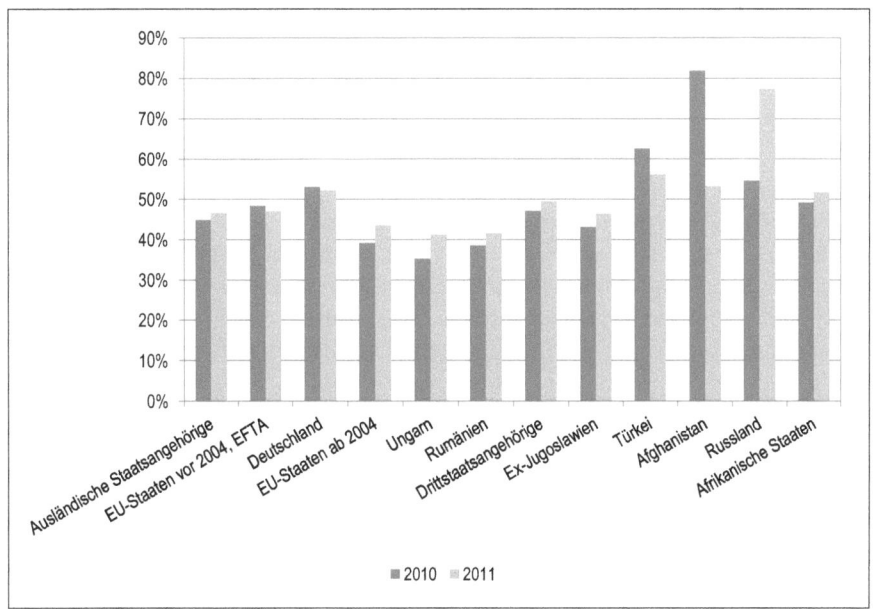

Abbildung 1: Anteil der 2010-2012 erstmals nach Österreich Zugewanderten mit einer Aufenthaltsdauer von mehr als fünf Jahren nach Staatsangehörigkeit

Quelle: Statistik Austria, Wanderungsstatistik.

sowie der Anteil der Personen mit einer Aufenthaltsdauer von mehr als fünf Jahren für den Zeitraum 2010-2012 weitgehend stabil. So dürfte der Familiennachzug für ägyptische und nigerianische Staatsangehörige, welche das Gros der Migration afrikanischer Staatsangehöriger nach Österreich ausmachen, eine wichtigere Rolle spielen als die Neuzuwanderung, was vor dem Hintergrund einer länger zurückliegenden initialen Migration nach Österreich durchaus plausibel erscheint.

Zusammenfassend lässt sich festhalten, dass die Zahl der nach Österreich Zugezogenen eines Jahres sich innerhalb von fünf Jahren etwas mehr als halbiert. Das bedeutet, dass ein wesentlicher Teil der Zuwanderung nach Österreich nicht permanent ist, sondern nur für begrenzte Zeit stattfindet und daher eher dem Typus von temporärer oder zirkulärer Migration zuzuordnen ist. Dies trifft insbesondere auf die Migration mit den Nachbarstaaten Österreichs zu.

Eingliederung in den Arbeitsmarkt und Erwerbsverläufe

Die Entwicklung der Zahl der Wegzüge innerhalb der Migrationskohorten sowie ihre zeitliche Lage sind zu einem wesentlichen Teil abhängig von den Möglichkeiten der Zugewanderten, sich auf dem österreichischen Arbeitsmarkt zu etablieren.

Daher beschäftigt sich der folgende Abschnitt mit der Arbeitsmarktintegration der Migrationskohorten 2010-2012. Bei der Betrachtung von Erwerbstätigenquoten bestimmter Kohorten ist allerdings immer auch die gesamtwirtschaftliche Situation bzw. das konjunkturelle Umfeld ab dem Zeitpunkt der Zuwanderung zu betrachten, welche einen bedeutenden Einfluss auf die Möglichkeiten ausüben, sich in Österreich auf dem Arbeitsmarkt zu etablieren.

Das breite Themenfeld der Arbeitsmarktintegration wird durch die Bestimmung von Erwerbstätigenquoten der 15- bis 64-jährigen Mitglieder der Migrationskohorten im Vergleich zur gesamten Bevölkerung gleicher Staatsangehörigkeit dargestellt. Nicht nachgegangen wird der Frage, warum die Erwerbstätigenquoten für ausländische Staatsangehörige in Österreich niedriger sind als für inländische. Dazu wird auf bestehende Literatur verwiesen, insbesondere auf die Studie von Bauer (2017), welche dies an Hand des Geburtslands umfassend darstellt. Auch die Unterscheidung der Erwerbsverhältnisse in Vollzeit-, Teilzeit- und geringfügige Beschäftigung würde den Rahmen dieser Studie sprengen und bleibt Folgeanalysen vorbehalten.

Die Ergebnisse der Registerbasierten Erwerbsverläufe beziehen sich auf die Jahre 2009 bis 2015. Daher sind nur für die Migrationskohorte 2010 Informationen über die Erwerbsbeteiligung fünf Jahre nach dem erstmaligen Zuzug verfügbar. Die Zeitreihen für die Migrationskohorten 2011 und 2012 sind dagegen entsprechend kürzer. Allerdings zeigten sich für die ersten beiden Jahre nach dem Zuzug zwischen den Migrationskohorten der Jahre 2010, 2011 und 2012 hinsichtlich der Erwerbsbeteiligung nur geringe Unterschiede. Verschiedene Muster von Teilgruppen innerhalb der Kohorte nach Alter, Geschlecht und Staatsangehörigkeit bestanden in ähnlichem Ausmaß für alle drei Zuzugsjahrgänge. Daher wurden bei der weiteren Analyse die kürzeren Zeitreihen der Kohorten 2011 und 2012 als Kontrollgruppe für 2010 verwendet, jedoch nicht eigenständig interpretiert.

Zu beachten ist weiters, dass der Erwerbsstatus der vorliegenden Studie auf Registerinformationen beruht und daher nur formale (nämlich sozialversicherungspflichtige) Arbeitsverhältnisse abbildet. Alle anderen Formen von Erwerbsarbeit dürften in der Befragung der Mikrozensus-Arbeitskräfteerhebung besser abgebildet sein.

Abbildung 2 zeigt die Erwerbstätigenquoten der Migrationskohorten 2010-2012 im Haupterwerbsalter zu verschiedenen Zeitpunkten nach dem erstmaligen Zuzug für die vier wichtigsten Gruppen ausländischer Staatsangehöriger im Vergleich mit den Erwerbstätigenquoten im Durchschnitt der Jahre 2011-2015 der österreichischen Staatsangehörigen sowie dem Bestand der betrachteten Gruppe ausländischer Staatsangehörigkeit insgesamt.

Die Erwerbstätigenquoten der österreichischen Staatsangehörigen im Haupterwerbsalter zwischen 15 und 64 Jahren lagen im Durchschnitt der Jahre 2011 bis 2015 insgesamt bei 72%. Ausländische Staatsangehörige zwischen 15 und 64 Jahren hatten im Durchschnitt der Jahre 2011-2015 insgesamt eine Erwerbstätigenquote von 57% (vgl. auch Wanek-Zajic 2016). Bei der Migrationskohorte 2010

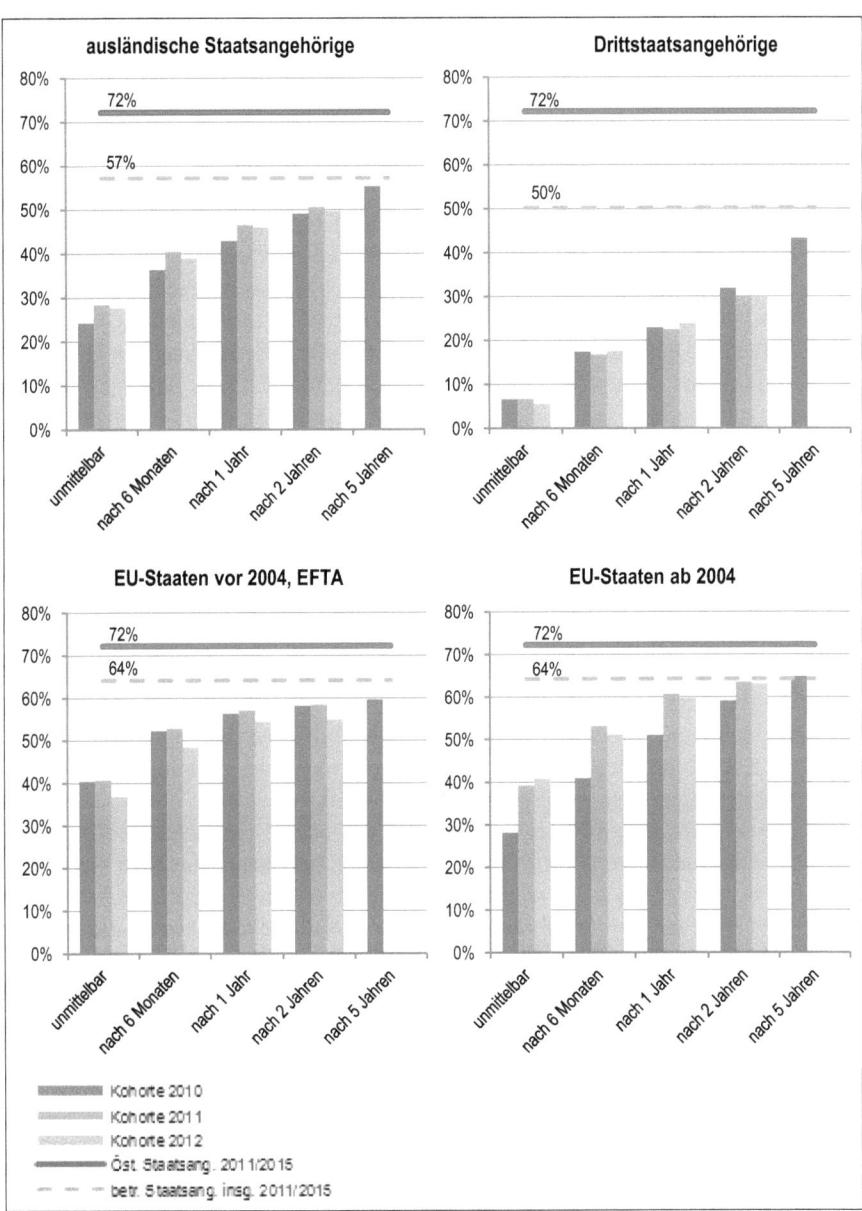

Abbildung 2: Erwerbstätigenquoten im Haupterwerbsalter (15-64 Jahre) der Migrationskohorten 2010-2012 zu verschiedenen Zeitpunkten nach dem Zuzug im Vergleich zu österreichischen Staatsangehörigen sowie der betrachteten Staatsangehörigkeit insgesamt im Durchschnitt 2011-2015

Quelle: Statistik Austria, Abgestimmte Erwerbsstatistik, Registerbasierte Erwerbsverläufe.

lag die Erwerbstätigenquote unmittelbar nach dem Zuzug bei 24% und stieg in Folge auf 36% nach sechs Monaten, 43% nach einem Jahr, 49% nach zwei Jahren sowie 55% nach fünf Jahren an. Für die Kohorten 2011 und 2012 waren die Anteile für den verfügbaren Zeitraum der ersten zwei Jahre etwas höher.

Angehörige der EU-Staaten vor 2004 hatten im Mittel der Jahre 2011-2015 insgesamt eine etwas höhere Erwerbstätigenquote von 64%, die aber dennoch unterhalb des Wertes der Österreicherinnen und Österreich blieb (72%). Etwa 40% der Kohorten 2010-2012 mit einer EU-Staatsangehörigkeit vor 2004 waren unmittelbar nach dem Zuzug erwerbstätig, 52% nach sechs Monaten und 59% nach fünf Jahren. Dabei fällt auf, dass die Kohorte 2012 etwas niedrigere Anteilswerte aufweist. Dies dürfte teilweise durch die größere Bedeutung von Bildungswanderungen aus Deutschland und Italien an österreichische Universitäten in dieser Kohorte bedingt sein, welche die Erwerbsbeteiligung etwas verringern.

Auch bei Angehörigen der EU-Beitrittsstaaten ab 2004 lag die Erwerbstätigenquote im Durchschnitt 2011-2015 bei 64% der Bevölkerung im Haupterwerbsalter. 28% der Kohorte 2010 trat unmittelbar mit dem Zuzug in die Erwerbstätigkeit ein, nach sechs Monaten waren 41% erwerbstätig, nach einem Jahr 51% und nach zwei Jahren 59%. Mit 65% lag die Erwerbstätigenquote dieser Kohorte nach fünf Jahren sogar leicht über dem Wert aller Personen gleicher Staatsangehörigkeit. Dies könnte in Zusammenhang mit einem höheren Anteil von jüngeren Personen in dieser Kohorte stehen. Bei den Kohorten 2011 und 2012 zeigt sich bei dieser Gruppe ein starker Unterschied zur Kohorte 2010, nämlich dahingehend, dass die Erwerbsbeteiligung nach kurzer Zeit bereits deutlich höher ist. Hier ist ein Effekt der am 1.5.2011 für diese Gruppe großteils aufgehobenen Zugangsbeschränkungen zum österreichischen Arbeitsmarkt naheliegend.

Die Erwerbstätigenquote der in Österreich lebenden Drittstaatsangehörigen im Haupterwerbsalter betrug im Durchschnitt der Jahre 2011 bis 2015 insgesamt 50%. Sie war damit erheblich niedriger als jene der österreichischen Staatsangehörigen (72%) und lag auch unter dem Durchschnitt der ausländischen Staatsangehörigen (57%). Nur 7% der Drittstaatsangehörigen in der Migrationskohorte 2010 traten unmittelbar mit dem Zuzug in den österreichischen Arbeitsmarkt ein. Dies ist im Wesentlichen auf zwei Faktoren zurückzuführen: Zum einen ist Asylzuwanderern eine formale Beschäftigung auf dem österreichischen Arbeitsmarkt bei laufendem Asylverfahren untersagt – und diese Gruppe macht einen großen Teil der zuwandernden Drittstaatsangehörigen aus. Zum anderen besteht die zweite große Gruppe der zuwandernden Drittstaatsangehörigen aus nachziehenden Familienangehörigen bereits in Österreich lebender Migrantinnen und Migranten und hat einen entsprechend geringeren Anreiz, unmittelbar auf dem Arbeitsmarkt tätig zu werden. Die Erwerbstätigenquote der Drittstaatsangehörigen in der Migrationskohorte 2010 erhöhte sich nach sechs Monaten auf 17%, nach einem Jahr auf 23%, nach zwei Jahren auf 30% und nach fünf Jahren auf 43%.

Weitere Auswertungen nach detaillierteren Staatsangehörigkeiten zeigen, dass die Erwerbstätigenquoten innerhalb von fünf Jahren nach dem erstmaligen Zuzug in vielen Fällen ein vergleichbares Niveau der ansässigen Bevölkerung gleicher

Staatsangehörigkeit erreicht. Betrug die Erwerbstätigenquote aller in Österreich lebenden ausländischen Staatsangehörigen im Haupterwerbsalter 57%, erreichte die Migrationskohorte 2010 innerhalb von fünf Jahren 55%.

Bei einigen der EU-Beitrittsstaaten ab 2004 waren die Erwerbstätigenquoten der Migrationskohorte 2010 sogar höher als für die Bevölkerung gleicher Staatsangehörigkeit insgesamt. Dies traf insbesondere auf Ungarn und Rumänien zu, deren Erwerbsbeteiligung bei der Migrationskohorte 2010 um 4 bis 5 Prozentpunkte über der Bevölkerung gleicher Staatsangehörigkeit lag. Dieser Unterschied wurde allerdings ausschließlich von Männern getragen, wogegen die Erwerbstätigenquoten bei Frauen knapp unter jenen der Bevölkerung gleicher Staatsangehörigkeit lagen.

Selbst in Österreich lebende EU-Staatsangehörige erreichten nicht das Niveau der Erwerbsbeteiligung von Österreichern (76%) und Österreicherinnen (68%). So lag die Erwerbstätigenquote für Männer aus den EU-Staaten vor 2004 bei 67% und für Frauen bei 61%. Die Migrationskohorte 2010 erreichte mit 65% nach fünf Jahren bei Männern einen vergleichbaren Wert wie die Gesamtbevölkerung. Die Frauenerwerbstätigenquote blieb dagegen mit 53% deutlich unter dem Durchschnitt.

Ähnliche Unterschiede zeigten sich auch bei Angehörigen der EU-Beitrittsstaaten ab 2004. Hier lag die Erwerbstätigenquote insgesamt bei 69% für Männer und 60% für Frauen. Die Migrationskohorte 2010 erzielte mit 72% bei Männern einen noch etwas höheren Wert, wogegen die Erwerbsbeteiligung bei Frauen mit 59% weitgehend dem Durchschnitt entsprach.

Innerhalb der Gruppe der Drittstaatsangehörigen zeigten sich große Unterschiede bei den Erwerbstätigenquoten. Diese waren in entscheidendem Ausmaß durch geschlechtsspezifische Unterschiede bedingt. Lag die Erwerbstätigenquote im Durchschnitt 2011-2015 für Männer bei dieser Gruppe insgesamt bei 57%, waren es für Frauen nur 43%. Die Migrationskohorte 2010 erreichte innerhalb von fünf Jahren nach dem erstmaligen Zuzug bei Männern mit 54% einen ähnlichen Wert, während die Erwerbsbeteiligung der Frauen mit 34% deutlich unterdurchschnittlich blieb.

Zum Teil sehr geringe Frauenerwerbstätigenquoten bedingten auch eine insgesamt deutlich niedrigere Erwerbstätigenquote bei Drittstaatsangehörigen als bei den ausländischen Staatsangehörigen insgesamt.

Angehörige der Nachfolgestaaten Jugoslawiens wiesen im Durchschnitt 2011-2015 insgesamt eine Erwerbstätigenquote von 59% auf. Die Migrationskohorte 2010 erreichte nach fünf Jahren eine Quote von 50%. Dabei stachen geschlechtsspezifische Unterschiede hervor: Betrug die Erwerbstätigenquote der Männer insgesamt 66% (und war damit vergleichbar mit den Quoten der EU-Staaten vor und nach 2004), lag die Erwerbsbeteiligung der Frauen mit 52% deutlich niedriger. Bei der Migrationskohorte 2010 bewegte sich die Erwerbstätigenquote der Männer nach fünf Jahren mit 61% bereits nahe am Durchschnitt der gesamten Gruppe gleicher Staatsangehörigkeit. Mit 39% bei den Frauen wurde allerdings ein wesentlich unterdurchschnittlicher Wert erzielt.

		Österr. Staatsang.	Ausländische Staatsang.	EU-Staaten vor 2004, EFTA	Deutschland	EU-Staaten ab 2004	Ungarn	Rumänien
Migrationskohorte 2010		-	55%	59%	61%	65%	71%	64%
Betrachtete Staatsangehörigkeitsgruppe insgesamt 2011/2015		72%	57%	64%	66%	64%	66%	60%
Männer	Migr.koh.2010	-	63%	65%	67%	72%	81%	71%
	Betr. Gruppe insg.	76%	62%	67%	68%	69%	72%	66%
Frauen	Migr.koh.2010	-	48%	53%	56%	59%	61%	58%
	Betr. Gruppe insg.	68%	52%	61%	63%	60%	62%	56%

		Österr. Staatsang.	Drittstaatsangehörige	Ex-Jugoslawien	Türkei	Russische Föderation	Afghanistan	Afrikan. Staaten
Migrationskohorte 2010		-	43%	50%	42%	33%	31%	37%
Betrachtete Staatsangehörigkeitsgruppe insgesamt 2011/2015		72%	50%	59%	50%	32%	22%	36%
Männer	Migr.koh.2010	-	54%	63%	61%	32%	40%	44%
	Betr. Gruppe insg.	76%	57%	66%	65%	33%	26%	42%
Frauen	Migr.koh.2010	-	34%	39%	22%	34%	8%	28%
	Betr. Gruppe insg.	68%	43%	52%	35%	31%	13%	29%

Tabelle 5: Erwerbstätigenquoten im Haupterwerbsalter (15-64 Jahre) der Migrationskohorte 2010 fünf Jahre nach dem Zuzug im Vergleich zur Gesamtbevölkerung gleicher Staatsangehörigkeit

Quelle: Statistik Austria, Registerbasierte Erwerbsverläufe.

Ähnliche Muster zeigten sich auch bei türkischen Staatsangehörigen, wobei als Spezifikum dieser Gruppe die Frauenerwerbstätigenquoten sowohl insgesamt (35%) als auch bei der Kohorte 2010 nach fünf Jahren (22%) nochmals erheblich niedriger waren. Ein Grund dafür dürfte in der Bedeutung des Familiennachzugs bei der Zuwanderung dieser beiden Gruppen liegen, wobei die Unterschiede im Niveau der weiblichen Erwerbsbeteiligung auch auf unterschiedlich stark ausgeprägte patriarchale Strukturen hindeuten.

Im Gegensatz dazu waren die Erwerbstätigenquoten der Migrationskohorte 2010 bei Staatsangehörigen mit einem vermutlichen Fluchthintergrund deutlich höher als bei der in Österreich lebenden Bevölkerung gleicher Staatsangehörigkeit. Dies zeigt sich am klarsten bei afghanischen Staatsangehörigen, deren Mitglieder der Migrationskohorte 2010 fünf Jahre nach dem Zuzug eine um 11 Prozentpunkte höhere Erwerbstätigenquote aufwiesen als die in Österreich lebenden Afghaninnen und Afghanen insgesamt. Das absolute Niveau der Erwerbsbeteiligung war mit 31% für die Kohorte 2010 allerdings immer noch sehr niedrig, wenn auch vermutlich zu einem großen Teil durch weiterhin laufende Asylverfahren bedingt. In geringerem Ausmaß galt Gleiches auch für Angehörige der Russischen Föderation (die zu einem Großteil aus Flüchtlingen aus Tschetschenien bestehen) sowie afrikanischer Staaten, wenngleich die Unterschiede zwischen der Kohorte 2010 und der Gesamtbevölkerung hier geringer ausfielen. Dies dürfte eine Folge eines geringeren Anteils erst nach 2010 ins Land gekommener Zugewanderter bei diesen Gruppen sein.

An den Erwerbstätigenquoten der Migrationskohorte 2010 innerhalb von fünf Jahren nach erstmaligem Zuzug zeigt sich deutlich, dass die Arbeitsmarktintegration für Frauen, insbesondere aus Drittstaaten, langsamer vor sich geht als jene von Männern. Dies mag zu einem Teil auch durch die größere Verbreitung des traditionellen männlichen Ernährermodells bedingt sein, aber auch möglicherweise durch die stärkere Einbindung von Frauen in nicht-formale Arbeitsmärkte.

Zusammenfassung und Ausblick

Die vorliegende Studie ergab drei wesentliche Ergebnisse:

1. Die Zahl der Zugezogenen, die für mehr als fünf Jahre in Österreich bleiben (und damit nach der Definition der europäischen Union „permanente" Zuwanderer sind), liegt bei etwas weniger als der Hälfte aller Zugezogenen eines Jahres. Das hat entscheidende Auswirkungen für alle politischen Überlegungen, welche auf Integration und eine demographische Stabilisierung durch Migration abzielen.
2. Die Erwerbsbeteiligung der Zugezogenen erreicht innerhalb von fünf Jahren nach erstmaligem Zuzug nach Österreich ein der jeweiligen Staatsangehörigkeitsgruppe vergleichbares Niveau. Die Arbeitsmarktintegration geht bei EU-Staatsangehörigen schneller von statten als bei Drittstaatsangehörigen (was nicht zuletzt auch durch rechtliche Hürden bedingt ist). Allerdings zeigen sich nach fünf Jahren bei Männern deutlich geringere Unterschiede als bei Frauen. Die stärkere Einbindung von Frauen unter den EU-Staatsangehörigen schlägt sich in höheren Erwerbstätigenquoten insgesamt nieder.
3. Die Arbeitsmarktintegration von Zugewanderten mit einem Fluchthintergrund dauert deutlich länger als bei allen anderen Gruppen. Dies ist in erster Linie durch Arbeitsverbote während laufender Asylverfahren bedingt, aber auch durch erheblich geringere Frauenerwerbstätigenquoten. Dieses Ergebnis deckt sich auch mit Studien aus anderen Ländern, insbesondere Schweden (Konle-Seidl 2016).

In der Knappheit des zur Verfügung stehenden Platzes können die Ergebnisse der vorliegenden Studie nur einen ersten Anknüpfungspunkt für weitere Analysen darstellen. Sie reihen sich jedenfalls in andere Studien zum Thema ein, welche allerdings auf eine Stock-Betrachtung abstellen (z.B. Bauer 2017). Der hier gewählte originäre Ansatz liegt in der Definition und Betrachtung von Kohorten, was über längere Zeiträume wesentliche Erkenntnisgewinne verspricht und damit auch dem vermehrten Bedarf der Politik nach spezifischer Information entgegenkommt.

Literatur

Bauer, Adelheid (2017), Labour market status and length of stay of migrants in Austria. Working paper presented at the DGINS conference in Budapest, 21 Sept 2017. http://www.ksh.hu/dgins2017/ papers/dgins2017_session3_at.pdf (abgerufen am 21.10.2017).

Konle-Seidl, Regina (2016), Arbeitsintegration von Flüchtlingen – Determinanten und Erfahrungen in europäischen Ländern. In: Wirtschaftspolitische Blätter Jg. 63, H.3, Wien, S.607-621.

Marik-Lebeck, Stephan (2012): Temporäre und zirkuläre Migration in Österreich – Eine statistische Darstellung anhand des bevölkerungsstatistischen Spiegelregisters POPREG (2002-2009). Background Paper für den Länderbericht „Temporäre und Zirkuläre Migration in Österreich" des Europäischen Migrationsnetzwerks. International Organisation for Migration, Wien, 28 S.

Wanek-Zajic, Barbara (2016), Registerbasierte Erwerbsverläufe: Konzepte, Methoden und Umsetzung. In Statistik Austria (Hg.) Schnellbericht Registerbasierte Statistiken Nr. 10.28. http://www.statistik.at/wcm/idc/idcplg?IdcService=GET_PDF_FILE&RevisionSelectionMethod=LatestReleased&dDocName=107462 (abgerufen am 23.10.2017).

Qualifikationen aus dem Ausland und die Schwierigkeit, sie adäquat in Beschäftigung zu bringen

August Gächter

Zusammenfassung

Um das Jahr 2000 herum erwähnte Gudrun Biffl verschiedentlich die zunehmende Bildung der ausländischen Staatsangehörigen, und dass sie am Arbeitsmarkt nicht die gebührende Chance erhalte (z.B. Biffl 2000, 2002). Erst eine ganze Weile später, nämlich als 2004 die Daten der Volkszählung 2001 verfügbar wurden, ließ sich zeigen, in welchem Maß sie Recht hatte.[1]

In diesem Kapitel wird skizziert, wie sich die Häufigkeit von Ausbildungen aus dem Ausland im Lauf der Jahrzehnte in Österreich entwickelt hat und wie diese Qualifikationen im Beschäftigungswesen genutzt werden, und zwar anhand von Daten der Volkszählungen, besonders auch jener von 2001, und ab 2004 des Mikrozensus. Zum einen sollen die Entwicklungen über Zeit beschrieben werden, zum anderen sollen aber auch Hypothesen entwickelt und zumindest in Ansätzen auf ihre Stichhaltigkeit überprüft werden, die die häufig unzulängliche Nutzung der Ausbildungen aus dem Ausland teils erklären könnten. Es finden sich deutliche Hinweise, dass auch wenn andere beschäftigungsrelevante Merkmale berücksichtigt werden dennoch die Herkunft der Ausbildung und selbst die Herkunft der Eltern ein Risikofaktor bleibt. Ebenso zeigt sich, dass Personen mit Ausbildung umso größere Schwierigkeiten haben, adäquat beschäftigt zu werden, je größer der Anteil der Bevölkerung mit der gleichen Herkunft ohne Ausbildung ist.

Einleitung: Zuzug mit Ausbildung

Ausbildung aus dem Ausland als Neuigkeit

Die Anwerbung seit 1961 hatte vor allem Arbeitskräfte und in der Folge Familienangehörige ohne Ausbildung nach Österreich gebracht. Das galt bei Jugoslawien kaum weniger als bei der Türkei. Der Anteil mit höchstens Pflichtschule an den

---

[1] Genauer müsste man sagen, für den Ankauf und damit zur eigenen Auswertung verfügbar wurden, denn die amtliche Statistik weist das Phänomen auch 2017 noch nicht aus und macht es durch die Art der Aufbereitung und durch nutzerfeindliche Beschränkungen nahezu unmöglich, es in den alten Volkszählungs- und den neuen Registerdaten ausfindig zu machen.

25-59 jährigen[2] Staatsangehörigen der Türkei hatte 1971 94% betragen, 1981 noch immer 92%, verringerte sich bis 1991 auf 86% und bis 2001 auf 84%. Das heißt, auch 2001 hatten noch sechs von sieben türkischen Staatsangehörigen zwischen 25 und 59 Jahren höchstens die Pflichtschule abgeschlossen. Die wesentliche Verringerung hatte sich bereits in den 1980er Jahren ereignet, lag also schon einige Zeit zurück, und sie war zu gering gewesen, um für das bloße Auge sichtbar zu werden (vgl. Abbildung 1).

Bei Staatsangehörigen aus Jugoslawien betrug 1971 der Anteil mit höchstens Pflichtschule an den 25-59 Jährigen 87%, 1981 fast unverändert 86%, 1991 aber nur mehr 74% und 2001 bei der Gesamtheit der Nachfolgestaaten 59% (vgl. Abbildung 1). Das heißt, auf die substanzielle Verringerung in den 1980er Jahren folgte eine noch etwas größere in den 1990er Jahren.

Bei den österreichischen Staatsangehörigen zwischen 25 und 59 Jahren war der Anteil mit höchstens Pflichtschulabschluss von 56% 1971 auf 43%, dann 30% und 2001 noch 21% gesunken. Im Gegenzug waren mittlere berufliche Ausbildungen ohne Matura zur dominanten Bildungsebene geworden. 2001 betrug ihr Anteil 56%. Davon waren die in Österreich lebenden Bürger mancher der jugoslawischen Nachfolgestaaten nicht sehr weit entfernt, denn Slowenien, Kroatien und Bosnien erreichten in dieser Hinsicht Anteile um die 40%, während Serbien nur auf 24% kam und die Türkei nur auf 11%. Besonders unter den Männern war die Nähe 2001 bereits relativ groß, denn den 62% bei den Männern mit österreichischer Staatsangehörigkeit standen bei Slowenien 47%, bei Kroatien 48% und bei Bosnien 49% gegenüber, bei Serbien aber nur 31% und bei der Türkei nur 15% (Zeitreihe Volkszählungen StatCube Abo 2017-09-25, eigene Auswertung, vgl. Abbildung 1). Aus den Ähnlichkeiten kann sich größere soziale Akzeptanz ergeben haben.

In den 2000er Jahren immer mehr Bildung

Ab 2004 stehen aus dem neu aufgesetzten Mikrozensus Daten über die berufliche Integration der eingewanderten Bevölkerung in Österreich zur Verfügung. Anders als die Volkszählungen enthielt der Mikrozensus ab 2004 stets die Frage nach dem Datum des Aufenthaltsbeginns in Österreich, sodass sich Zuzugskohorten unterscheiden lassen. Zudem lässt sich im Mikrozensus bestimmen, ob die Befragten ihren höchsten Bildungsabschluss vor oder nach Beginn des Aufenthalts in Österreich gemacht haben. Dadurch lässt sich sichtbar machen, dass alle jene im erwerbsfähigen Alter, die zwischen 1997 und 2005 von außerhalb der (späteren)

---

[2] Die Darstellung folgt in diesem Abschnitt der Konvention, ab 25 Jahren anzunehmen, die Ausbildungskarriere sei im Wesentlichen abgeschlossen. Es ist stets irreführend, nicht abgeschlossene Ausbildungsverläufe in Berichte über den Bildungsstand einer Bevölkerung einzubeziehen. Bei den Auswertungen aus dem Mikrozensus, die weiter unten folgen, bieten sich differenziertere Möglichkeiten, die dort auch genutzt werden.

Qualifikationen aus dem Ausland und die Schwierigkeit adäquater Beschäftigung 255

Abbildung 1 Anteil der 25-59-jährigen mit höchstens Pflichtschule bei den Volkszählungen nach Staatsangehörigkeit

Quelle: Statistik Austria, Zeitreihe Volkszählungen, eigene Berechnungen und Darstellung.

EU28 und EFTA zugezogen sind und in Österreich keine Ausbildung mehr abschlossen, zu etwa 55% einen Abschluss über der Pflichtschule mitbrachten. Das ist fast gleich, wie beim Zuzug 1986 bis 1996, wo dasselbe auf rund 53% zutrifft.

Seitdem haben diese Anteile weiter zugenommen. Der Zuzug ab 2006 aus Drittstaaten begann mit einem Anteil von 63% bei den Abschlüssen über der Pflichtschule und steht mittlerweile bei über 70%. Während aber jene, die um 1990 herum zuzogen, zu rund einem Drittel mittlere, berufliche Abschlüsse ohne Matura mitbrachten, trifft dasselbe auf nur mehr etwa ein Viertel jener zu, die um 2000 herum zuzogen, und auf nur mehr etwa ein Fünftel jener, die seit 2006 zuzogen sind. Mit anderen Worten, je später der Zuzug desto weniger mittlere, berufliche Bildung enthielt er und desto mehr verteilte er sich auf geringe Bildung einerseits und höhere Bildung andererseits. Das hängt auch mit Verschiebungen bei den Herkunftsländern zusammen, denn außerhalb Europas werden formale, berufliche Ausbildungen unterhalb des Hochschulniveaus nur selten in größerer Menge angeboten.

Bei der 1986 bis 1996 zugezogenen Bevölkerung im erwerbsfähigen Alter ist festzustellen, dass der Anteil mit mitgebrachten Abschlüssen über der Pflichtschule zwischen 2004 und 2016 allmählich von 54% auf 52% sank. Diese Verringerung spielte sich zur Gänze bei den Hochschulabschlüssen ab. Ihr Anteil sank von 8% auf 6%. Sie könnte ein Alterseffekt sein oder aber auch durch Abwanderung bedingt sein. Nachfolgende Zuzugskohorten brachten Verdoppelungen des Anteils mit Hochschulabschlüssen mit sich. Jene von 1997 bis 2005 hatte 2005 zu 13% Hochschulabschlüsse, 2016 noch zu 12%, und jene seit 2006 begann mit

22%, was bis 2016 auf 25% zunahm. Hochschulabschlüsse sind meist viel schwieriger und nur mit großem Aufwand in den Arbeitsmarkt zu transferieren.

Beschäftigung in Hilfs- bzw. Anlerntätigkeiten

Maße der inadäquaten Nutzung von Ausbildungen

Es gibt eine Reihe von Maßen, die man verwenden könnte, um die inadäquate Nutzung von Ausbildungen am Arbeitsmarkt sichtbar zu machen. Nahe liegend ist es, zunächst nur die Beschäftigten zu betrachten und den Anteil der unter ihrer Qualifikation Beschäftigten zu betrachten. Die OECD hat das verschiedentlich so gemacht und dabei internationale Klassifikationen der Ausbildungen (ISCED) und der Berufe (ISCO) verwendet, um sowohl die Berufe wie die Ausbildungen in drei Schichten zu teilen. (vgl. auch Biffl, Pfeffer und Skrivanek 2012, 3ff.) Im vorliegenden Fall wird eine simplere Einteilung gewählt, nämlich jeweils nur zwei Schichten. Bei den Berufen sind es einerseits Hilfs- und Anlerntätigkeiten und alle anderen, hier als Fachtätigkeiten bezeichnet, andererseits. Bei den Ausbildungen erfolgt die Unterscheidung in Abschlüsse bis maximal Pflichtschule, also neun Schulstufen, hier häufig als geringe Bildung bezeichnet, sowie alle anderen.

Die Erwartung ist, dass Beschäftigte mit geringer Bildung in der Regel in Hilfs- bzw. Anlerntätigkeiten beschäftigt sind, da für diese keine Ausbildung mit formalem Abschluss erforderlich ist, und dass Beschäftigte mit Ausbildung nach der Pflichtschule in der Regel in Fachtätigkeiten beschäftigt sind. Wenn Beschäftigte mit Ausbildung in Hilfs- bzw. Anlerntätigkeiten beschäftigt sind, wird das im Folgenden als Dequalifizierung bezeichnet. Das umfasst offensichtlich nicht die gesamte inadäquate Nutzung von Qualifikationen, denn, zum Beispiel, eine Ärztin, die als Krankenpflegerin beschäftigt ist, scheint dabei nicht als dequalifiziert auf, und ebenso wenig eine Architektin, die als technische Zeichnerin arbeitet.

Da es hier nicht um den internationalen Vergleich, sondern rein um Österreich geht, werden nicht die internationalen Klassifikationen eingesetzt, sondern die nationalen der Statistik Austria. Die nationalen Klassifikationen haben gegenüber der ISCO den Nachteil, dass selbständig Erwerbstätige nicht nach dem Qualifikationserfordernis der Tätigkeit eingeteilt werden können. Sie werden im Folgenden immer alle als adäquat beschäftigt eingestuft, obwohl das selbstverständlich nicht immer zutrifft. Man darf daher die unten berichteten Zahlen nicht als genaues Maß der Dequalifizierung betrachten, sehr wohl aber als Indikator des Ausmaßes und der Unterschiede, die es gibt.

Unter Umständen kann es informativ sein, statt nur die aktuell Beschäftigten alle jemals Beschäftigten in den Blick zu nehmen. Man sieht dann, wie die Erfahrung der Dequalifizierung in der Bevölkerung im Erwerbsalter verteilt ist. Eventuell erkennt man auch Unterschiede zwischen jenen, die aktuell in Beschäftigung sind, und jenen, die es nicht sind. Es kann dann je nach konkreter Fragestellung sinnvoll sein, bei den aktuell nicht Beschäftigten die Frist seit der letzten Erwerbstätigkeit einzuschränken oder es nicht zu tun.

In eine andere Richtung erweitert man den Blick, wenn er statt nur auf die Beschäftigten auf die Erwerbspersonen oder sogar auf die ganze Bevölkerung in erwerbsfähigem Alter gerichtet wird, und zwar weil man Beschäftigungslosigkeit als die ausgeprägteste Form der Dequalifizierung ansehen kann.

Die Beschäftigten im Jahr 2001

Bei entsprechender Auswertung hätte die Volkszählung 2001 gezeigt, dass das Risiko, trotz Ausbildung eine Beschäftigung als Hilfs- oder als angelernter Arbeiter bzw. Arbeiterin auszuüben, für Drittstaatsangehörige viel größer war als für österreichische oder EU15 Staatsangehörige, und dass es auch für Eingebürgerte erhöht war. Wobei sich durch die Beschränkung auf die Arbeiterinnen und Arbeiter das volle Ausmaß der Dequalifizierung nicht zeigen ließ. Angelernte Angestellte, die es besonders im Handel zahlreich gibt, sind hier nicht in den Hilfs- bzw. Anlerntätigkeiten enthalten. Geringfügig Beschäftigte sind in dieser Auswertung bei den Beschäftigten mit enthalten, Lehrlinge dagegen nicht.

- Von den in Österreich geborenen 15-59 jährigen[3], beschäftigten Frauen mit österreichischer Staatsangehörigkeit und mit Abschlüssen über der Pflichtschule waren 9,8% als Hilfs- oder Anlernarbeiterinnen beschäftigt
- von den entsprechenden im Ausland geborenen Frauen ohne österreichische oder EU15 Staatsangehörigkeit waren es 45,9%, das ist das 4,7-fache.
- Bei den Männern lagen die Anteile bei 10,4% bei jenen mit österreichischer und bei 40,1% bei jenen mit ausländischer Staatsangehörigkeit, das ist das 3,9-fache.
- Von den im Ausland geborenen österreichischen Staatsbürgerinnen betraf es 17,7%; von den entsprechenden Männern 16,7%, also das 1,8- bzw. 1,6-fache der jeweiligen in Österreich geborenen österreichischen Staatsangehörigen.

Die übrigen Beschäftigten mit einer über die Pflichtschule hinausgehenden Ausbildung waren in selbständiger Beschäftigung oder übten Beamten-, Vertragsbediensteten-, Angestellten- oder Facharbeitertätigkeiten aus. Diese Anteile lagen zwischen nur 54,1% (im Ausland geborene Frauen mit Drittstaatsangehörigkeit) und bis zu 91,9% (im Ausland geborene Männer mit EU-15 Staatsangehörigkeit) (vgl. Abbildung 2).

---

[3] Da hier nur Beschäftigte betrachtet werden, muss nicht, wie bei der Bildung, das untere Limit der Altersgruppe auf 25 gesetzt werden.

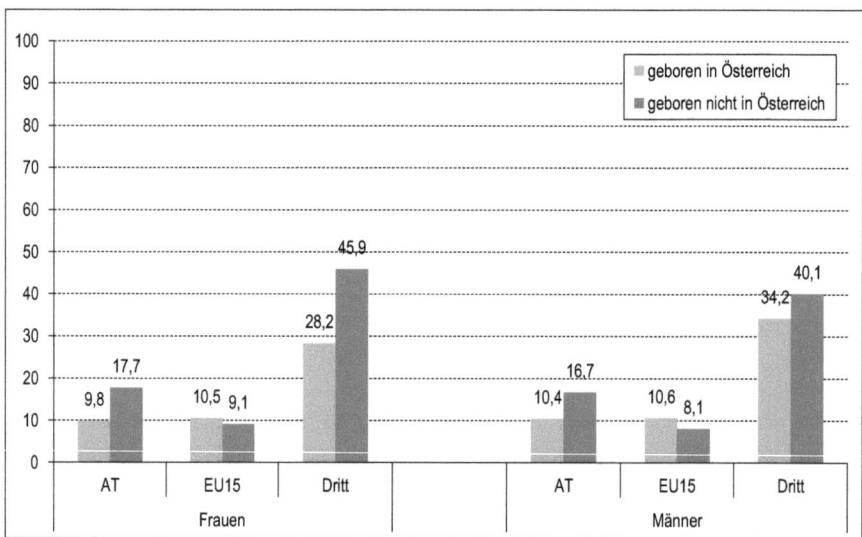

Abbildung 2 Anteil Hilfs- bzw. Anlernarbeiter*innen an den Beschäftigten mit mindestens Lehrabschluss, nach Geschlecht, Staatsangehörigkeit und Geburtsort (Volkszählung Mai 2001)

Quelle: Statistik Austria, eigene Berechnungen (projektbezogene Sonderauswertung 2005) und Darstellung.

Die Tendenz zur Dequalifizierung wäre aber nicht nur bei den Beschäftigten mit Abschlüssen über der Pflichtschule erkennbar gewesen, sondern auch schon bei denjenigen mit höchstens Pflichtschulabschluss. Während nämlich von den in Österreich geborenen Frauen mit österreichischer Staatsangehörigkeit und höchstens Pflichtschulabschluss, die zum Zeitpunkt der Volkszählung beschäftigt waren, nur 40% als Arbeiterinnen in Hilfs- oder Anlerntätigkeiten beschäftigt waren, traf dasselbe auf 71% der entsprechenden im Ausland geborenen Frauen ohne EU15-Bürgerschaft zu und auf 61% der im Ausland geborenen österreichischen Staatsbürgerinnen. Bei den Männern stand es 31% zu 64% zu 54%. Dass von den formal gering qualifizierten, im Inland geborenen Beschäftigten mit österreichischer Staatsangehörigkeit so niedrige Prozentsätze als Hilfs- oder Anlernkräfte in Arbeitsberufen beschäftigt sind, mag auf den ersten Blick überraschen. Teils liegt es daran, dass es auch im Angestellten- und im Beamtenbereich zahlreiche Tätigkeiten gibt oder damals noch gab, die zumindest beim Einstieg nur geringe formale Bildung verlangten. Teils liegt es auch daran, dass eingewanderte Beschäftigte kaum in den Genuss betrieblicher Höherqualifizierungen kamen (siehe dazu Biffl 2000, 2002).

Die jemals Beschäftigten

Ein überraschendes Muster tritt zutage, wenn man die aktuell Beschäftigten mit den aktuell nicht mehr Beschäftigten vergleicht und dabei zwischen in Österreich geborenen österreichischen Staatsangehörigen und im Ausland geborenen Drittstaatsangehörigen sowie nach Ausbildung und nach Qualifikationserfordernis der Tätigkeit unterscheidet. Es zeigt sich, dass 2001 ebenso wie in späteren Jahren unter den früher Beschäftigten der Anteil der trotz Ausbildung in Hilfs- oder Anlernarbeitertätigkeiten Beschäftigten geringer ist als unter den aktuell Beschäftigten, dass es aber eine Ausnahme gibt. Die Ausnahme sind die ausgebildeten Beschäftigten mit Geburt im Inland und österreichischer Staatsbürgerschaft. Bei ihnen ist unter den früher Beschäftigten der Anteil in Hilfs- oder Anlernarbeitertätigkeiten höher als unter den aktuell Beschäftigten. Das gilt bei beiden Geschlechtern. Wenn man das in der AKE nachvollzieht, bleibt das über die Jahre so erhalten. Mit anderen Worten, das Muster ist bei den im Ausland geborenen Drittstaatsangehörigen mit Ausbildung dasselbe wie bei den im Inland geborenen österreichischen Staatsangehörigen ohne Ausbildung, und zwar besonders bei den Frauen.

Mögliche Erklärungen gibt es dafür sicher nicht nur eine. Eine nähere Untersuchung der Situation der aktuell nicht mehr Beschäftigten könnte helfen, die plausibleren von den weniger plausiblen Möglichkeiten zu scheiden, muss an dieser Stelle aber unterbleiben.

Henke (2008) testete die Hypothese, dass Dequalifizierung mit kürzerem Verbleib im Beschäftigungsverhältnis verbunden sei. Der Hintergrund dazu war, dass er mit steigendem Alter geringere Dequalifizierungsraten der Beschäftigten vorfand, was ähnlich der Beobachtung ist, dass früher Beschäftigte höhere Dequalifizierungsraten haben als die aktuell Beschäftigten. Henke fand anhand der Daten der AKE von 2006 und einer dreischichtigen ISCED bzw. ISCO Klassifizierung, dass Bildung über den beruflichen Erfordernissen die Beschäftigungsdauer um 18 Monate verkürzte, nachdem er für Geschlecht, Alter, Bildungsebene, Geburtslandgruppen, Betriebsgröße, Wirtschaftsabschnitte Normalarbeitszeit, Verstädterungsgrad und Erfahrung kontrolliert hatte. 43% der Varianz konnten aufgeklärt werden. Die Regressionsanalyse scheint mit den ungewichteten Daten der AKE durchgeführt worden zu sein. Henkes Ergebnis lässt vermuten, die früher Beschäftigten seien häufiger dequalifiziert als die aktuell Beschäftigten, was in der Abbildung oben lediglich als Ausnahme erscheint, die nur bei den in Österreich geborenen Beschäftigten mit österreichischer Staatsangehörigkeit und Abschluss über der Pflichtschule auftritt. Das ist aber bei weitem die größte Gruppe der Beschäftigten, sodass sie das Ergebnis von Henkes Regressionsanalyse dominiert. Um der Unterschiedlichkeit der Muster zu entsprechen, müsste die Regressionsanalyse entweder für jede Gruppe einzeln durchgeführt werden oder es müssten Interaktionsterme zwischen Ausbildung, Geschlecht und Herkunft gesetzt werden, was aber beides bei manchen der Kontrollvariablen zu sehr kleinen Fallzahlen für die einzelne Ausprägung führen würde.

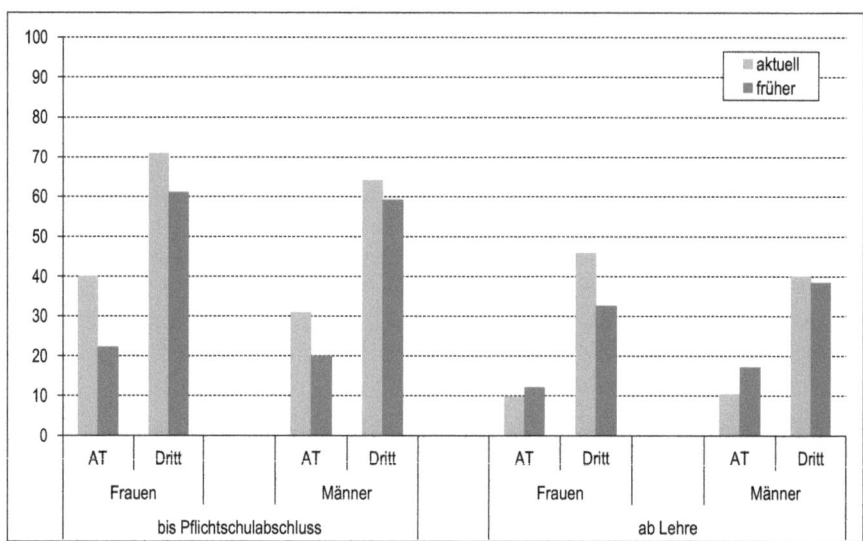

Abbildung 3 Anteil der Beschäftigten in Hilfsarbeit oder Anlernarbeit nach dem Zeitpunkt der Beschäftigung, Geschlecht, Geburtsland/Staatsangehörigkeit und Bildungsabschluss (Volkszählung 2001)

Quelle: Statistik Austria, eigene Berechnungen (projektbezogene Sonderauswertung 2005) und Darstellung.

Nach der Volkszählung 2001 keine großen Veränderungen

Wenn man die Volkszählungsergebnisse mit Hilfe des Mikrozensus ab 2004 fortschreibt und sich dabei auf zwei Bevölkerungsteile konzentriert, nämlich die im Inland Geborenen mit österreichischer Staatsangehörigkeit und die im Ausland Geborenen ohne EU15/EFTA Staatsangehörigkeit, dann sieht man bei den ersteren bis 2016 kaum eine Veränderung, weder beim einen Geschlecht noch beim anderen, obwohl, anders als bei der Volkszählung, zwischen den Geschlechtern ein Unterschied zu beobachten ist. Weniger Unterschied zwischen den Geschlechtern als bei der Volkszählung tritt dagegen nun bei der zweiten Gruppe auf. Sichtbar wird bei beiden Geschlechtern ein Trend zur Verringerung des Anteils in Hilfsarbeits- und Anlernarbeitstätigkeiten, der aus dem Bereich von 40% bis 45% in jenen von 35% bis 40% führt. Es ist allerdings noch ein sehr weiter Weg bis zu den etwa 10% der ersten Gruppe. Wenn die Verringerung weiterhin etwa 0,5 Prozentpunkte im Jahr betrüge, dauert es noch rund 50 Jahre.

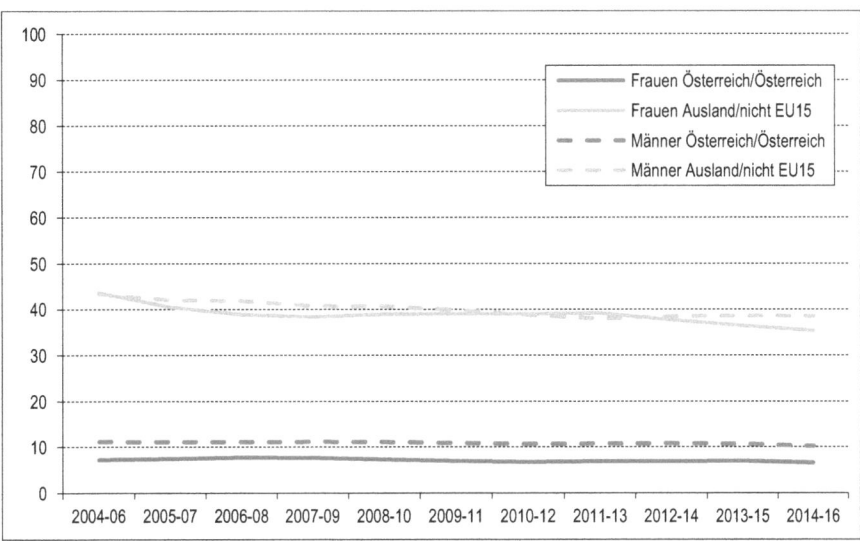

Abbildung 4 Anteil in Hilfs- bzw. Anlernarbeit an den Beschäftigten mit Abschlüssen über der Pflichtschule, nach Geschlecht und Geburtsort/Staatsangehörigkeit

Quelle: Statistik Austria, Mikrozensus 2004-2016, eigene Berechnungen und Darstellung.

Unterschiedliche Niveaus und unterschiedliche Verläufe der Beschäftigung in Hilfs- bzw. Anlerntätigkeiten

Es ist vielleicht sinnvoll, sich an dieser Stelle von den Vorgaben der Fragestellung und Datenaufbereitung der letzten Volkszählung zu verabschieden und auf das flexiblere und in die Gegenwart reichende Instrument des Mikrozensus zu wechseln. Für den vorliegenden Zweck hat der Mikrozensus den gewichtigen Vorteil einer eigenständigen Qualifikationsskala unabhängig davon, ob es sich um einen Arbeiter- oder einen Angestelltenberuf handelt. Unter 17 Kategorien können drei mit Gewissheit unterhalb der Ebene der Fachtätigkeit angesiedelt werden, nämlich die „Hilfstätigkeiten (manuell)", die „angelernten Tätigkeiten (manuell)" und die „Hilfstätigkeiten (nicht manuell)". Sie werden im Folgenden summarisch als „Hilfs- bzw. Anlerntätigkeiten" bezeichnet. Man kann spekulieren, dass vielleicht auch ein Teil der „mittleren Tätigkeiten (nicht manuell)", die den weitaus größten Brocken der Beschäftigung ausmachen, ebenfalls nur das Niveau einer Anlerntätigkeit hat, aber betrieblich durch eine höfliche Bezeichnung ein höheres Qualifikationsniveau suggeriert, aber aus diesen Spekulationen ließe sich nur mit exzessivem Aufwand eine belastbare Auskunft machen, und es geht hier, wie schon erwähnt, mehr um einen Indikator der Dequalifizierung als um ein exaktes Maß. Der zweite große Vorteil des Mikrozensus ist, dass sie seit 2004 stets sowohl die Frage nach dem Jahr, in dem der höchste Abschluss gemacht wurde, enthielt, als auch die Frage, wann der Aufenthalt in Österreich begonnen habe. Dadurch lässt sich zwar nicht perfekt, aber mit geringer Fehlerwahrscheinlichkeit – etwa 1% bis

1,5% – angeben, ob der höchste Abschluss in Österreich oder im Ausland gemacht wurde. Etwas größer, aber nicht viel größer ist der Fehler vermutlich, wenn man im nächsten Schritt schließt, der höchste Abschluss sei im Geburtsland gemacht worden.

Wenn im Folgenden von Beschäftigten die Rede ist, so stets ohne die unter 25 Jährigen, die zugleich in formaler Ausbildung sind. Das heißt, Lehrlinge, Schülerinnen und Schüler, Studierende und Präsenz- oder Zivildiener unter 25 Jahren sind weder bei den Beschäftigten noch den Beschäftigungslosen enthalten. Sie existieren im Folgenden nicht.

Um Stichprobenschwankungen zu glätten, werden die Ergebnisse in Form von gleitenden Dreijahresdurchschnitten präsentiert. Der erste Punkt einer Linie bezieht sich dabei auf den Zeitraum 2004-2006, der nächste auf den Zeitraum 2005-2007, der dritte auf 2006-2008 usw. bis 2014-2016.

Wendet man die Aufmerksamkeit zunächst den beschäftigten Frauen mit positiv abgeschlossenen Ausbildungen über der Pflichtschule zu, so werden je nach wahrscheinlichem Bildungsstaat sehr große Unterschiede in der Häufigkeit von Beschäftigung in Hilfs- bzw. Anlerntätigkeiten sichtbar, nämlich zwischen 12% und 82% (Abbildung 5a). Im Wesentlichen sind drei Gruppen von Bildungsstaaten zu erkennen. Sehr hohe Raten der Dequalifizierung von Ausbildungen finden sich bei Türkei, Serbien und Bosnien. Sie lagen zuletzt im Bereich zwischen 70% und 80%. Frappierend ist die unterschiedliche Entwicklung im Zeitverlauf, nämlich bei Türkei ansteigend, bei Serbien oszillierend, bei Bosnien fallend. Die zweite, mittlere Gruppe liegt zwischen 30% und 50% und besteht aus den sonstigen Drittstaaten sowie den seit 2004 der EU beigetretenen Staaten. Auch hier ist die Entwicklung über Zeit wieder unterschiedlich, nämlich flach bei EU und sinkend bei den sonstigen Drittstaaten, sodass der Abstand zwischen den beiden größer geworden ist. Die dritte Gruppe bilden die EU15/EFTA-Staaten und Österreich mit zuletzt noch 12% oder 13% und ganz allmählicher Verringerung. Insgesamt sind die Unterschiede zwischen 2004-2006 und 2014-2016 nur um wenige Prozentpunkte größer geworden.

Bei den Männern verhält sich die Sache im Prinzip ähnlich, aber bei vier der sieben Bildungsherkünfte ist das Niveau niedriger (Abbildung 5b). Das sind Türkei, Serbien-Montenegro-Kosovo-Mazedonien, Bosnien und die seit 2004 der EU beigetretenen Staaten. Bei ihnen ist die Häufigkeit von Hilfs- bzw. Anlerntätigkeiten trotz Abschlüssen über der Pflichtschule um 10 bis 20 Prozentpunkte geringer als bei den jeweiligen Frauen. Bei Serbien und Türkei war der Verlauf im Wesentlichen flach, bei Bosnien zeichnet sich seit etwa 2011 eine Verringerung ab, bei den sonstigen Drittstaaten gab es vor 2009 eine deutliche Verringerung, bei den EU15/EFTA Staaten um 2008 herum eine Steigerung, bei den seit 2004 der EU beigetretenen Staaten ab 2012 eine Steigerung und bei Österreich eine anhaltende allmähliche Verringerung.

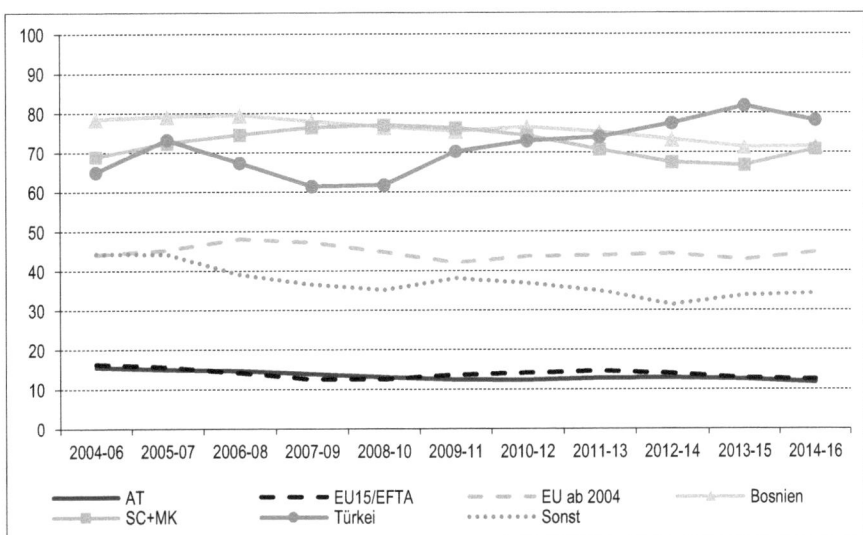

Abbildung 5a Frauen, Anteil in Hilfs- bzw. Anlerntätigkeiten, Abschluss über der Pflichtschule, nach dem Bildungsstaat, erwerbsfähiges Alter, ohne unter 25-jährige in Ausbildung

Quelle: Statistik Austria, Mikrozensus 2004-2016, eigene Berechnungen und Darstellung.

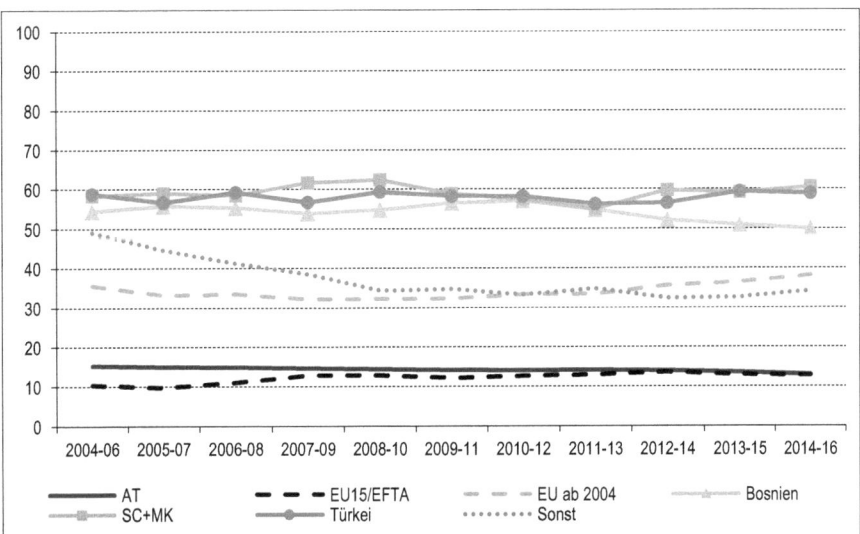

Abbildung 5b Männer, Anteil in Hilfs- bzw. Anlerntätigkeiten, Abschluss über der Pflichtschule, nach dem Bildungsstaat, erwerbsfähiges Alter, ohne unter 25-jährige in Ausbildung

Quelle: Statistik Austria, Mikrozensus 2004-2016, eigene Berechnungen und Darstellung.

Verringerungen – das darf man nicht übersehen – können bei Betrachtung nur der Beschäftigten auch dadurch zustande kommen, dass Beschäftigte in Hilfs- und Anlerntätigkeiten die Jobs verlieren oder aufgeben, während die Fachkräfte sie behalten. Das ist der wesentliche konzeptuelle Nachteil des nur auf die Beschäftigten bezogenen Indikators.

Eine Aufschlüsselung nach Bundesländern würde große Unterschiede zeigen, deren Ursachen noch nicht geklärt sind. Unterschiedliche Wirtschaftsstrukturen sind als Erklärung nur begrenzt plausibel. Pendeldistanzen könnten eine Rolle spielen ebenso wie die Vermittlungspraktiken des örtlichen AMS.

Obwohl der Anteil sinkt, haben die meisten Beschäftigten, die trotz Abschluss über der Pflichtschule eine Hilfs- bzw. Anlerntätigkeiten ausüben, ihre Ausbildung in Österreich abgeschlossen. Bei den Frauen ging er seit 2004 von 78% auf 68%, bei den Männern von 80% auf 73% zurück.

Mehr geringe Bildung, folglich mehr Dequalifizierung der Ausgebildeten?

Es gibt deutliche Anzeichen, dass bei den Frauen ein höherer Dequalifizierungsanteil der Beschäftigten mit einem höheren Bevölkerungsanteil an gering Gebildeten aus demselben Bildungsstaat einhergeht. Korreliert man die sieben in der Abbildung als rechte Endpunkte der Linien dargestellten Dequalifizierungsraten des Jahrdritts 2014-2016 mit den sieben zeitgleichen Anteilen der gering Gebildeten an den Frauen im Erwerbsalter, so ergibt sich ein Korrelationskoeffizient von r=0,86. Diese Korrelation besteht in jedem der Dreijahresintervalle von 2004-2006 bis 2014-2016 im Bereich zwischen r=0,77 und r=0,89. Der Koeffizient schwankt, mit den niedrigsten Werten um 2008-2009 herum, wobei möglicherweise die Konjunktur eine Rolle spielt, aber ein Anstieg über den Zeitraum lässt sich nicht mit Sicherheit nachweisen.

Der Befund hält im Wesentlichen auch bei den Männern, aber die Korrelationskoeffizienten liegen nur zwischen 0,73 und 0,83. Seltsamerweise verlaufen sie über die Jahre annähernd spiegelbildlich zu jenen bei den Frauen. Selbst für einzelne Bundesländer, etwa Wien, lässt ich der Befund nachweisen, und zwar auch dann, wenn man den Bildungsstaat Österreich in sieben Kategorien je nach dem Geburtsland der Eltern zerlegt.

Man kann diesen Befund in entgegen gesetzte Richtungen interpretieren. Er könnte ein Hinweis sein, dass die geringe Häufigkeit von Ausbildungen in einer Gruppe, den Ausgebildeten in derselben Gruppe zum Nachteil wird, einesteils vielleicht, weil demselben Land, das so viele Unausgebildete hervorbringt, nicht zugetraut wird, auch gute Ausbildungen anbieten zu können, anderenteils, weil dadurch die Idee einfach nicht nahe liegend ist, in dieser Herkunftsgruppe überhaupt Personen mit Ausbildung zu vermuten. Diese Rationalisierungen werden in der ökonomischen Literatur seit gut 45 Jahren als „statistische Diskriminierung" bezeichnet (vgl. Phelps 1973).

Ungenutzte Qualifikationen

Speziell bei den Frauen ist es sinnvoll, nicht nur die Beschäftigung zu analysieren, sondern die Beschäftigungslosen mit in das Bild hereinzuholen. Erst dann sieht man das volle Ausmaß, zu dem Ausbildungen, in die Lebenszeit sowie private und öffentliche Gelder investiert wurden, nicht genutzt werden können. Beim Bildungsstaat Türkei bewegt sich der Anteil ungenutzter Qualifikationen im Bereich um 90%, bei Serbien und Bosnien zuletzt um 80%, bei den sonstigen Drittstaaten und den seit 2004 der EU beigetretenen Staaten zwischen 60% und 70%, bei den EU15/EFTA-Staaten in Richtung 30% sinkend und bei Österreich bereits unter 30% und sinkend. Die Spannweite der Werte ist seit der Dreijahresperiode 2004 bis 2006 von 51 auf 66 Prozentpunkte angewachsen.

Bei den Männern beträgt die Spannweite etwa 45 Prozentpunkte und hat sich nicht verändert. Die Rangfolge ist dieselbe wie bei den Frauen: Türkei und Serbien um die 70%, Bosnien zwischen 60% und 65%, sonstige Drittstaaten von über 60% auf 50% gesunken und wieder auf über 55% angestiegen, seit 2004 der EU beigetretene Staaten zwischen 45% und 50%, Österreich und EU15/EFTA-Staaten im Bereich von 15% bis 20%. Alle Anteile sind niedriger als bei den Frauen, besonders aber trifft das am oberen Ende der Verteilung zu.

Der Mikrozensus enthält seit 2008 Fragen nach dem Geburtsstaat von Mutter und Vater und macht es damit möglich, bei Personen mit in Österreich gemachtem höchstem Abschluss nach den Geburtsstaaten der Eltern zu unterscheiden. Diese Unterscheidung wird in den beiden folgenden Abbildungen dargestellt, in dem die eine bisherige Linie für Österreich ausdifferenziert wird nach Geburtsstaat der Eltern.

Im Vergleich zur Bevölkerung mit im Ausland erworbenen Abschlüssen findet man in der Gruppe der in Österreich erworbenen Abschlüsse dieselbe Reihung, allerdings auf einem niedrigeren Niveau der Dequalifizierung und bei kleineren Abständen sowie geringen Unterschieden zwischen den Geschlechtern. Veränderungen im Lauf der Zeit, die einen Trend in die eine oder andere Richtung konstituieren würden, sind nur beim elterlichen Herkunftsstaat Österreich zu erkennen, und zwar bei beiden Geschlechtern ein allmähliches, leichtes Sinken. Von den Frauen mit Abschluss über der Pflichtschule aus Österreich und mindestens einem Elternteil aus der Türkei (aber keinem aus den sonstigen Drittstaaten) sind um die 45% herum in Hilfs- bzw. Anlerntätigkeiten beschäftigt, von den entsprechenden Männern 40% bis 45%. Bei Serbien sind es bei den Frauen 35% bis 40%, bei den Männern um die 40% mit einem möglicherweise leicht steigenden Trend. Bosnien bewegt sich bei den Frauen ebenfalls im Bereich von 35% bis 40%, bei den Männern um 37% herum. Die sonstigen Drittstaaten bewegen sich bei beiden Geschlechtern um 35% herum, die seit 2004 der EU beigetretenen Staaten zwischen 30% und 35%, Österreich zwischen 25% und 30%, die EU15/EFTA-Staaten um 25% herum.

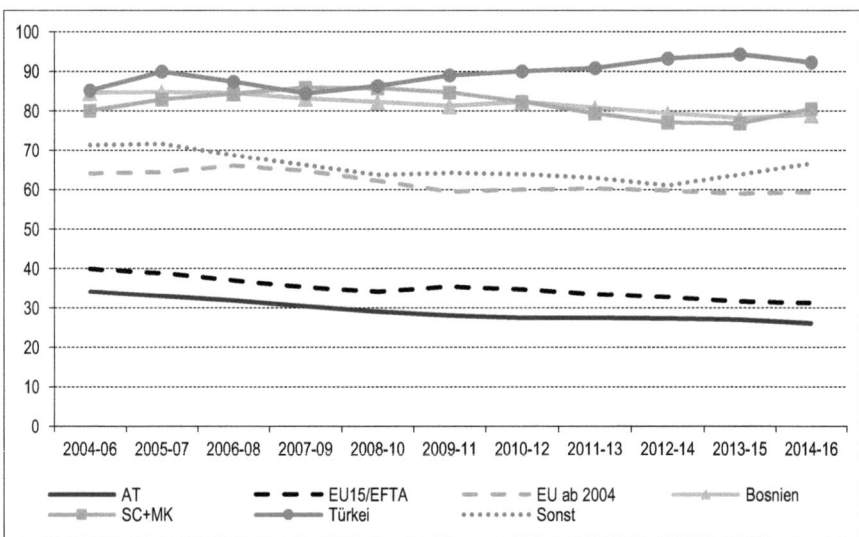

Abbildung 6a Frauen, Anteil nicht erwerbstätig oder in Hilfs- bzw. Anlerntätigkeiten, Abschluss über der Pflichtschule, nach dem Bildungsstaat, erwerbsfähiges Alter, ohne unter 25-jährige in Ausbildung

Quelle: Statistik Austria, Mikrozensus 2004-2016, eigene Berechnungen und Darstellung.

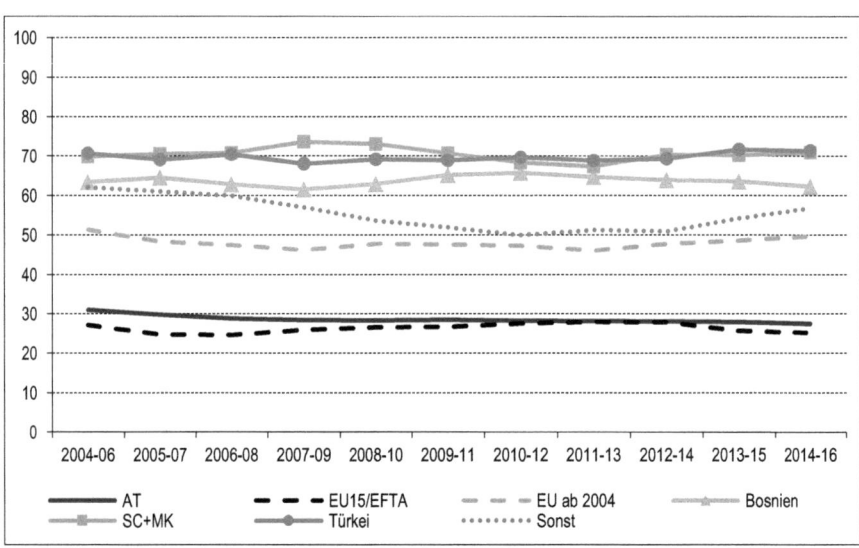

Abbildung 6b Männer, Anteil nicht erwerbstätig oder in Hilfs- bzw. Anlerntätigkeiten, Abschluss über der Pflichtschule, nach dem Bildungsstaat, erwerbsfähiges Alter, ohne unter 25-jährige in Ausbildung

Quelle: Statistik Austria, Mikrozensus 2004-2016, eigene Berechnungen und Darstellung.

So viel der Blick auf die Nichtnutzung von Ausbildungen, wie sie in den vier vorangehenden Abbildungen dokumentiert wurde, enthüllt, soviel verschleiert er auch. So ist nicht erkennbar, ob es sich bei der Nichtnutzung im jeweiligen Fall eher um Beschäftigung unter der Qualifikation oder um Beschäftigungslosigkeit handelt. Da wird man sich eventuell einen dramatischen Unterschied zwischen den Geschlechtern erwarten, aber dem ist gar nicht so. Bei den Frauen wie den Männern mit Ausbildung aus dem Ausland entstanden im Lauf der letzten zehn Jahre zwei Ländergruppen. In der einen Gruppe sind jeweils etwa 40% der Nichtnutzung durch Beschäftigung unter der Qualifikation und 60% durch Beschäftigungslosigkeit begründet, in der anderen Gruppe ist das Verhältnis genau umgekehrt. Die beiden Gruppen setzen sich folgendermaßen zusammen:

- Bei den Frauen mit Ausbildung im Ausland befinden sich jene mit den Staatsangehörigkeiten Österreich, EU15/EFTA, Türkei und sonstige Drittstaaten in der 40:60 Gruppe, also überwiegend Beschäftigungslosigkeit, und EU seit 2004, Bosnien und Serbien in der 60:40 Gruppe.
- Die Männer unterscheiden sich nur dadurch, dass die Türkei nicht zur 40:60, sondern zur 60:40 Gruppe gehört (überwiegend Beschäftigung unter der Qualifikation).
- Bei den Frauen mit Ausbildung aus Österreich gibt es nur ein Land in der 60:40 Gruppe, also mit überwiegend Beschäftigung unter der Qualifikation, nämlich Bosnien, wobei die anderen sechs eher eine 30:70 Gruppe darstellen.
- Bei den Männern mit Ausbildung aus Österreich gehört neben Bosnien auch die Türkei zur 60:40 Gruppe.

Wie bereits erwähnt, waren diese erstaunlichen Regelmäßigkeiten vor fünf oder zehn Jahren noch nicht so klar, aber gegenwärtig springen sie ins Auge. Unklar ist, ob darin eine zeitliche Zufälligkeit zu sehen ist, die in fünf Jahren verschwunden sein wird, oder ob man sich Gedanken über ihr Entstehen machen soll.

Erklärungsbedarf

Regressionsanalysen bestätigen, dass
Abschlüsse aus dem Ausland dequalifizierungsgefährdet sind

Es ist hier nicht Raum, um auf die Modellierung von Beschäftigung unter dem Ausbildungsniveau ausführlich einzugehen. Es sei nur berichtet, dass sie möglich ist, wobei die Erfolge über die Jahre recht unterschiedlich waren.

Henke (2008) führte in einer logistischen Regression Beschäftigung unter im Vergleich zu Beschäftigung auf dem Ausbildungsniveau zurück auf Geschlecht, Alter, Bildungsabschluss, Geburtslandgruppen, Betriebsgröße, Wirtschaftsabschnitte, Normalarbeitszeit, Urbanitätsgrad, studierend sowie weiblich ab 55 Jahre und fand, dass Geburt in einem EU15 Staat kein erkennbar größeres Risiko der

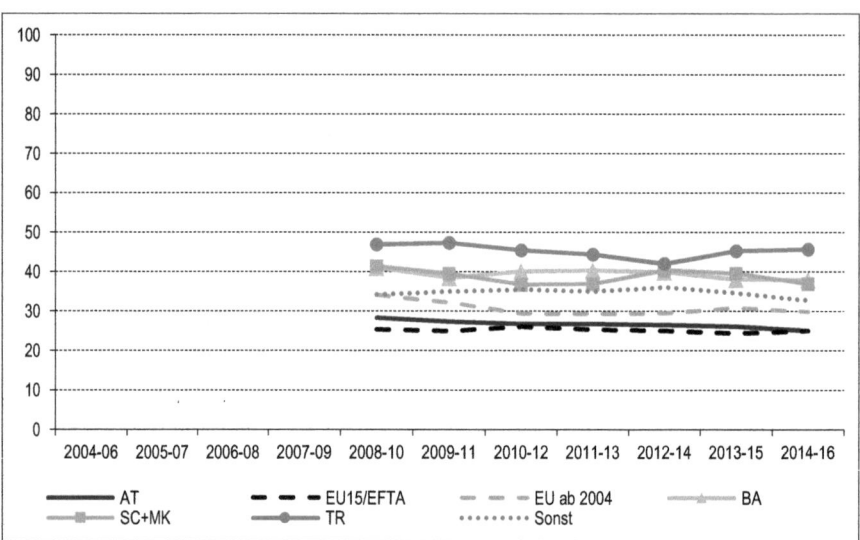

Abbildung 6c Frauen, Anteil nicht erwerbstätig oder in Hilfs- bzw. Anlerntätigkeiten, Abschluss über der Pflichtschule, erwerbsfähiges Alter, Bildungsabschluss aus Österreich, nach dem Geburtsstaat der Eltern, ohne unter 25-jährige in Ausbildung

Quelle: Statistik Austria, Mikrozensus 2004-2016, eigene Berechnungen und Darstellung.

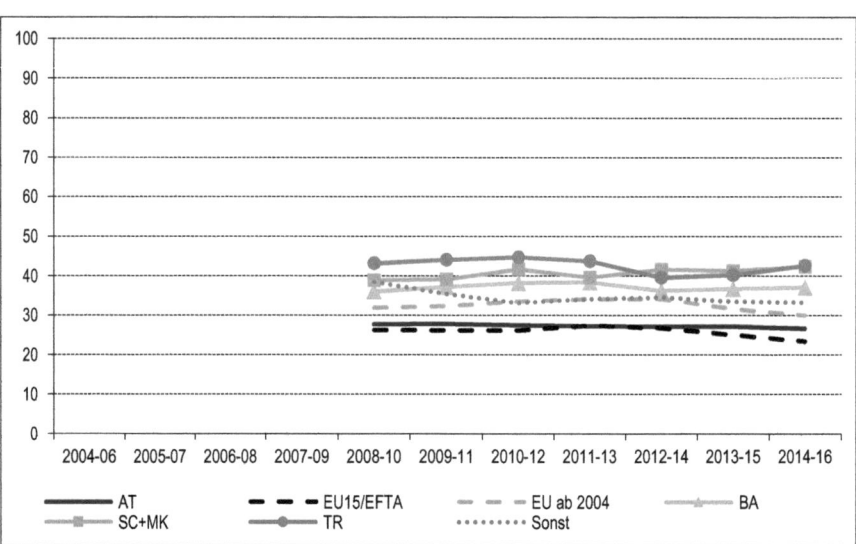

Abbildung 6d Männer, Anteil nicht erwerbstätig oder in Hilfs- bzw. Anlerntätigkeiten, Abschluss über der Pflichtschule, erwerbsfähiges Alter, Bildungsabschluss in Österreich, nach dem Geburtsstaat der Eltern, ohne unter 25-jährige in Ausbildung, ohne Präsenz- und Zivildiener

Quelle: Statistik Austria, Mikrozensus 2004-2016, eigene Berechnungen und Darstellung.

Beschäftigung unter dem Ausbildungsniveau mit sich brachte als Geburt in Österreich, während das Risiko bei Geburt in den 2004 der EU beigetretenen Staaten deutlich erhöht war und zwar in fast gleichem Maß wie bei Geburt außerhalb der EU. Dass der Wirtschaftsabschnitt einbezogen wurde, kommt den kollektivvertraglich geprägten Gewohnheiten der Sozialpartner entgegen, unterstellt aber, dass alle die gleiche Chance hätten, in jeder beliebigen Branche beschäftigt zu werden, was doch berechtigten Zweifeln unterliegt (vgl. Biffl 2002), weil die Lohnniveaus nicht gleich sind. Es ist kein Zufall, dass in der Energieversorgung kaum Einwanderer zu finden sind. Henke erzielte ein Pseudo-R-Quadrat nach Nagelkerke von 0,24.

Meine eigenen Versuche mit multinominalen logistischen Regressionen anhand des bei Wiedenhofer-Galik und Fasching (2015) näher beschriebenen Mikrozensus-Sondermoduls 2014 setzten Beschäftigung in Hilfs- bzw. Anlerntätigkeiten in Kontrast zu anderer Beschäftigung, zu Beschäftigungssuche bzw. Beschäftigungswilligkeit und zu beruflicher Inaktivität. Unter 25 Jährige in Ausbildung waren ausgeschlossen und ebenso die Bevölkerung außerhalb des Erwerbsalters. In den Regressionsmodellen wurden die folgenden erklärenden Variablen berücksichtigt: Ausbildungsniveau, selbst eingeschätzte Deutschkenntnisse, die Interaktion zwischen den beiden, Fachrichtung des höchsten Abschlusses (sieben Kategorien), Anerkennungsstatus der Ausbildung (Abschluss in Österreich & Eltern aus Österreich, Abschluss in Österreich & Eltern von außerhalb EU/EFTA, Abschluss aus dem Ausland und anerkannt, Abschluss aus dem Ausland und nicht anerkannt), Staatsbürgerschaft, wichtigster Grund der Einreise in Kombination mit dem Zeitpunkt der Einreise, Ausbildungsniveau der Eltern, Alter, Vorhandensein eines Partners oder einer Partnerin im Haushalt, Bildungsstaat des Partners bzw. der Partnerin, bei Frauen das Vorhandensein von Kindern (unter 3 Jahren, zwischen 3 und 5 Jahren, zwischen 6 und 14 Jahren), summierte wöchentliche Arbeitszeit des Haushalts, wohnrechtliche Situation, Quadratmeter pro Kopf und Quartals des Jahres. Damit entsteht ein differenziertes Bild, in dem nicht nur die Herkunft der Ausbildung und ihr Niveau eine wichtige Rolle spielen, sondern auch die Deutschkenntnisse.

In aller Kürze lässt sich bei den Frauen sagen, dass Abschlüsse aus dem Ausland, aber auch aus dem Inland mit einem höheren Risiko einhergehen, auf Jobsuche zu sein, wenn die Eltern aus Drittstaaten sind. Bei der Frage von qualifizierter Beschäftigung statt Hilfs- bzw. Anlerntätigkeit ist ein anerkannter Abschluss aus dem Ausland günstiger als ein nicht anerkannter, der ist aber seinerseits günstiger als einer aus dem Inland mit Eltern aus Drittstaaten.

Ebenfalls bei den Frauen gilt, dass je höher die Ausbildung desto günstiger wirken sich verbesserte Deutschkenntnisse auf die Wahrscheinlichkeit einer Beschäftigung in qualifizierten Tätigkeiten aus. Bei geringer Bildung nimmt mit besseren Deutschkenntnissen vor allem das Risiko ab, nicht in Beschäftigung zu sein, es bleibt aber auch bei (quasi-)muttersprachlichen Deutschkenntnissen hoch. Bei mittlerer, beruflicher Ausbildung wirken sich die Deutschkenntnisse dagegen nicht stark auf die Beschäftigungswahrscheinlichkeit aus, sondern vielmehr innerhalb der Beschäftigungslosigkeit auf die Häufigkeit von Beschäftigungssuche statt Inaktivität und innerhalb der Beschäftigung auf die Häufigkeit von qualifizierter statt Hilfs- bzw. Anlerntätigkeit. Mit höherer Bildung verringern bessere Deutschkenntnisse zunächst das Risiko, auf Beschäftigungssuche statt beschäftigt zu sein. Sobald die Deutschkenntnisse nicht mehr nur gering sind, sinkt die berufliche Inaktivität auf ein niedriges Niveau. Mit steigenden Deutschkenntnissen nimmt zunächst die Beschäftigung auf beiden Qualifikationsniveaus zu. Bei (quasi-) muttersprachlichen Deutschkenntnissen kommt aber Beschäftigung in Hilfs- bzw. Anlerntätigkeiten nur mehr in geringem Ausmaß vor; es konzentriert sich fast alles auf entweder qualifizierte Beschäftigung oder Beschäftigungssuche.

Bei den Männern gilt, dass nach Kontrolle der oben aufgezählten Einflüsse die Arbeitsmarktaktivität, der Beschäftigungserfolg und die Häufigkeit von qualifizierter Beschäftigung im Vergleich zu den Männern mit Abschluss und Eltern aus dem Inland stets nachweislich erhöht oder nicht nachweislich verringert ist. Bessere Deutschkenntnisse gehen auf allen Ausbildungsebenen mit einem größeren Anteil von qualifizierter Beschäftigung an den Beschäftigten einher, besonders bei höherer Bildung und (quasi-)muttersprachlichen Deutschkenntnissen. Bei geringer und mittlerer, beruflicher Ausbildung spielen die Deutschkenntnisse für die Häufigkeit von Beschäftigungslosigkeit keine Rolle und auch nicht für die Häufigkeit von Inaktivität bzw. von Beschäftigungssuche, sondern nur für die Häufigkeit von qualifizierter im Vergleich zu unqualifizierter Beschäftigung. Bei höherer Bildung ist das anders. Mit durchschnittlichen statt nur geringen Deutschkenntnissen ist die Wahrscheinlichkeit der Beschäftigungslosigkeit viel kleiner und jene der Beschäftigung in Hilfs- bzw. Anlerntätigkeiten viel größer. Bei fortgeschrittenen statt durchschnittlichen Deutschkenntnissen kehrt sich das wieder um und bei (quasi-)muttersprachlichen Deutschkenntnissen verstärkt sich die Umkehrung. Wie bei den Frauen mit höherer Bildung und (quasi-)muttersprachlichen Deutschkenntnissen, sind dann qualifizierte Beschäftigung und Beschäftigungssuche verbreitet.

Interviews im Zuge der Evaluierung der im Jahr 2013 eingeführten „Anlaufstellen für Personen mit im Ausland erworbenen Qualifikationen" (AST) zeigten, dass die Betroffenen selbst Deutsch immer wieder als wichtiger für adäquate Beschäftigung empfinden als die formale Anerkennung ihres im Ausland gemachten Abschlusses (Danzer, Lechner und Wetzel 2016, 47).

Die in den vorangehenden Absätzen getroffenen Formulierungen laden zwar mitunter dazu ein, sich die Deutschkenntnisse als Ursache des Arbeitsmarktstatus zu denken. Davor sei aber gewarnt. Es handelt sich um selbst eingeschätzte Deutschkenntnisse. Damit ist nicht auszuschließen, dass Befragte, weil es ihnen am Arbeitsmarkt relativ gut geht, ihre Deutschkenntnisse entsprechend besser einschätzen als Befragte mit weniger befriedigendem Erfolg im Beschäftigungswesen, die sich die Situation damit erklären, ihre Deutschkenntnisse seien nicht ausreichend.

Die beschriebenen Versuche erbrachten bei den Frauen ein Pseudo-R-Quadrat nach Nagelkerke von 0,50 und bei den Männern von 0,55 bzw. nach Cox & Snell von 0,45 und 0,49. Die Regressionen wurden mit den bevölkerungsgewichteten

Daten durchgeführt, der Standardfehler wurde auf die ungewichtete Zahl der Befragten korrigiert. Bundesländer oder andere regionale Merkmale konnten aufgrund der Fallzahlen nicht einbezogen werden. Den regionalen und anderen Kontextmerkmalen muss bei einer auf Maßnahmen orientierten Forschung aber Bedeutung zukommen.

Spät einsetzendes Problembewusstsein

Das Thema der adäquaten Bildungsverwertung am Arbeitsmarkt hat in Österreich lange keine Rolle gespielt, auch nicht in Bezug auf die im Inland ausgebildete Bevölkerung, wenn man berücksichtigt, dass die Beziehung zwischen Beruf und Ausbildung nie zum Auswertungsprogramm der Volkszählungen gehörte und selbst die Auswertung der Ausbildungen an sich stets rudimentär blieb. Das kann der schon erwähnten Bildungsmonokultur geschuldet gewesen sein. Ein Problembewusstsein entstand erst Mitte der 2000er Jahre, vermittelt vielleicht zum Teil durch die Vorbereitungen für das einschlägige, von Eurostat beschlossene Ad-Hoc-Modul 2008 der Arbeitskräfteerhebung. Im Zuge dessen zeigte Henke (2008) mit Daten des Mikrozensus, dass die Häufigkeit von Beschäftigung unter dem Qualifikationsniveau in Österreich zwischen 1996 und 2006 merklich zugenommen hatte und zwar besonders zwischen 2001 und 2006 (Henke 2008, 819), und dass Geburt außerhalb der EU15 das Risiko dramatisch steigert, gleich ob in den Beitrittsstaaten 2004 geboren oder in Drittstaaten (Henke 2008, 822). Die OECD hob 2011 hervor, dass in Österreich *„der Anteil von MigrantInnen, die einer Beschäftigung nachgehen, die unter ihrem eigentlich erreichten Qualifikationsniveau liegt, einer der höchsten in der OECD"* ist (Krause/Liebig 2011). Das hohe Risiko, bei der Einreise nach Österreich all seiner Qualifikationen beraubt zu werden, macht die Einreise für Personen mit Ausbildung nur dann attraktiv, wenn sie andere als beruflichen Ambitionen haben. Zeitgleich wurde das Staatssekretariat für Integration eingerichtet. Studien in Deutschland (Englmann und Müller 2007) und in Österreich (Bichl 2011; Biffl, Pfeffer und Skrivanek 2012; Girlasu und Zitz 2012, 2013) machten das Thema plastisch. Da der OECD Bericht im Auftrag des BMASK entstand, erreichte die Thematik auch die Gremien der Sozialpartnerschaft. In der Folge wurden Migrantinnen und Migranten zu einer weiteren speziellen Zielgruppe des AMS erklärt und die Mitarbeiterinnen und Mitarbeiter angewiesen, Ausbildungen aus dem Ausland so zu erfassen, wie sie ihnen angegeben werden. Die praktische Umsetzung dieser Anweisung in den Regionalstellen ging allerdings nur sehr zögerlich voran. In dem Zusammenhang wurde auch mit den Vorarbeiten für die Schaffung der AST zu Jahresbeginn 2013 begonnen. Die AST sind aber nur Beratungsstellen. Sie sollen als Schmiermittel im System fungieren, was am System als solchem nichts ändert.

Es gibt etwa 200 Berufe, in denen die Anerkennung – oder alternativ der Erwerb – der Berufsberechtigung zwingend ist. Das ist aber nur ein kleiner Teil der Berufe und Dequalifizierung ist offensichtlich nicht auf sie beschränkt. In allen anderen Fällen liegt die Anerkennung bei den Beraterinnen und Beratern des AMS und bei den Betriebsleitungen. Sie sehen offenbar bislang keine hinreichenden Gründe, im Ausland erworbene Qualifikationen für in Österreich anwendbar zu halten. Wie anhand des Zusammenhangs zwischen der Häufigkeit von geringer Bildung in einer Gruppe und dem Dequalifizierungsrisiko gezeigt, fließen in die Beurteilung der Qualifikationen Sachverhalte ein, die nichts mit ihnen zu tun haben. Der Zusammenhang mit den Deutschkenntnissen wiederum muss als Indiz gelten, dass sie häufig als Indikator der Qualifikation hergenommen werden, in etwa nach dem Motto, „wer nicht Deutsch kann, kann auch nichts anderes können." Zwar ist es unbestritten, dass es Tätigkeiten gibt, für die eine Juristin gute Deutschkenntnisse braucht, aber nicht für alle Tätigkeiten, die sie ausüben könnte. Das gilt ebenso für die medizinischen Professionen usw. Den Deutschbedarf der Tätigkeiten zu bestimmen, könnte ohne weiteres dem Markt überlassen bleiben und sollte daher nicht Teil der Anerkennungsverfahren sein.

Literatur

Bichl, Norbert (2011) Österreich: Anerkennung von aus dem Ausland mitgebrachten Qualifikationen, Manuskript (Wien).
Biffl, Gudrun (2000) Zuwanderung und Segmentierung des österreichischen Arbeitsmarktes. Ein Beitrag zur Insider-Outsider-Diskussion. In: Husa, Karl / Parnreiter, Christof /Stacher, Irene (Hrsg.) Internationale Migration. Die globale Herausforderung des 21. Jahrhunderts? Reihe Historische Sozialkunde 17/Intenationale Entwicklung, (Brandes & Apsel/Südwind, Wien), 207-227.
Biffl, Gudrun (2002) Ausländische Arbeitskräfte auf dem österreichischen Arbeitsmarkt. In: WIFO-Monatsberichte 8/2002, 537-550.
Biffl, Gudrun / Pfeffer, Thomas / Skrivanek, Isabella (2012) Anerkennung ausländischer Qualifikationen und informeller Kompetenzen in Österreich. Studie im Auftrag des Bundesministeriums für Inneres. (Schriftenreihe Migration und Globalisierung, Krems).
Biffl, Gudrun / Pfeffer, Thomas / Skrivanek, Isabella (2016) Zugänge und Verfahren zur Anerkennung von im Ausland erworbenen Qualifikationen und Kompetenzen. In: Österreichischer Integrationsfonds (Hrsg.) Anerkennung von im Ausland erworbenen Qualifikationen in Österreich - eine theoretische und empirische Auseinandersetzung. (ÖIF-Forschungsbericht, Wien), 47-66.
Danzer, Lisa / Lechner, Ferdinand / Wetzel, Petra (2016) Evaluierung der Anlaufstellen für Personen mit ausländischen Qualifikationen; (L&R Sozialforschung, Wien).
Englmann, Bettina / Müller, Martina (2007) Brain Waste. Die Anerkennung von ausländischen Qualifikationen in Deutschland; (Tür an Tür, Augsburg).
Girlasu, Mioara / Zitz, Edith (2012) Erhebung der Ist-Situation im Bereich „Anerkennung von im Ausland erworbenen Berufsqualifikationen in der Steiermark"; Anerkannt! Projekt zur Anerkennung von im Ausland erworbenen Berufsqualifikationen; inspire thinking.
Girlasu, Mioara / Zitz, Edith (2013) Aktualisierte Erhebung der Ist-Situation im Bereich „Anerkennung von im Ausland erworbenen Berufsqualifikationen in der Steiermark"; Anerkannt! Projekt zur Anerkennung von im Ausland erworbenen Berufsqualifikationen; inspire thinking.
Henke, Justus (2008) Beschäftigung und Qualifikation. Über- und Unterqualifikation in Österreich. In: Statistische Nachrichten 63(9), 816-826.
Krause, Karolin / Liebig, Thomas (2011) The labour market integration of immigrants and their children in Austria, OECD Social, Employment and Migration Working Papers No. 127, Directorate for Employment, Labour and Social Affairs (OECD Publishing, Paris).

Phelps, Edmund S. (1972) The Statistical Theory of Racism and Sexism. In: The American Economic Review, 62(4), 659-661.

Stadler, Bettina / Wiedenhofer-Galik, Beatrix (2011) Dequalifizierung von Migrantinnen und Migranten am österreichischen Arbeitsmarkt. In: Statistische Nachrichten 66(5) 383-399.

Wiedenhofer-Galik, Beatrix / Fasching, Melitta (2015) Arbeitsmarktsituation von Migrantinnen und Migranten in Österreich. Modul der Arbeitskräfteerhebung 2014. (Statistik Austria, Wien).

Teil 5:
Migration und Bildung

Wer zu spät kommt? Zuwanderung als ‚blinder Fleck' in der österreichischen Bildungspolitik

Lorenz Lassnigg, Mario Steiner

Zusammenfassung

Im vorliegenden Beitrag werden die Fragen der Zuwanderung in den breiteren und längerfristigen Kontext der Bildungspolitik gestellt. Die Grundmuster im Föderalismus sind nicht gut geeignet, mit den Verteilungsproblemen zwischen den Ländern und zwischen Stadt und Land umzugehen, die wiederum eng mit der Konzentration der Zuwanderung zusammenhängen. Es gibt wesentliche Datenmängel zu zentralen Aspekten der Förderung (z.B. außerordentliche SchülerInnen, Deutschförderung). Die Hauptthese besteht darin, dass von den direkt in diesem Politikfeld engagierten AkteurInnen seit Jahrzehnten eine integrative Ausrichtung verfolgt wird, die jedoch vor dem Hintergrund der allgemeinen politischen Verdrängung der Fragen der Zuwanderung nicht den nötigen Nachdruck bekommen hat. Dadurch hat sich ein Klima der Unsicherheit aufgebaut, das im politischen Tageskampf ausgenützt wird. Die Dynamik der Zuwanderung, die regionale und schulische Konzentration und die Kompetenzunterschiede sowie Unterschiede im frühen Schulabbruch werden näher analysiert.

Einleitung

Mit der aktuellen politischen ‚Flüchtlingskrise' sind heftige politische Auseinandersetzungen um bildungspolitische Fragen hochgekocht, die sich insbesondere auf Aspekte der Sprachpolitik (‚Deutsch zuerst') und der Religion (‚politischer Islam') konzentrieren. Damit sind Auseinandersetzungen in das offene Licht der Politik getreten, die bereits seit langem ‚unterirdisch' geführt werden. Mit der Einrichtung des ‚Integrations-Staatssekretariats' ist die Bildungspolitik stärker in den Vordergrund getreten, einerseits mit der Betonung ihrer Wichtigkeit in diesem Zusammenhang, andererseits aber auch mit mehr oder weniger offener Kritik an der bisherigen Praxis im Schulwesen. Dabei wurden mehrere Dimensionen vermischt, nämlich (1) die Frage nach ausreichenden Interventionen mit (2) Fragen der inhaltlichen Ausrichtung der Politik (Mehrsprachigkeit und Kosmopolitismus versus deutsche Einsprachigkeit und christlich-nationaler Patriotismus), und (3) dem Missbrauch dieser Thematik für parteipolitische und persönliche Profilierung.

Der vorliegende Beitrag versucht den bildungspolitischen Umgang mit der Zuwanderung längerfristig nachzuzeichnen und einige spezifischere Probleme in diesem Zusammenhang herauszuarbeiten. Es erscheint insbesondere wichtig, zwischen der inhaltlichen Ausrichtung und dem politischen Nachdruck in diesem Politikfeld zu unterscheiden. Die Forschungsfrage besteht vor allem darin, den Aspekt der Zuwanderung im Kontext der allgemeineren Strukturen und Praktiken der österreichischen Bildungspolitik zu betrachten. Die Hauptthese besagt, dass von den direkt in diesem Politikfeld engagierten AkteurInnen im Kern eine integrative Ausrichtung verfolgt wurde, diese jedoch in den vorhandenen bildungspolitischen Strukturen und Praktiken vor dem Hintergrund der allgemeinen politischen Verdrängung der Fragen der Zuwanderung nicht den nötigen Nachdruck bekommen hat. Dadurch haben sich verschiedenste Unsicherheiten im Zusammenhang mit den Herausforderungen und Auswirkungen der Zuwanderung im Schul- und Bildungswesen aufgebaut, die im politischen Tageskampf ausgenützt werden, um ein Klima der Überforderung aufzubauen und in einer Sündenbock-Rhetorik die Zuwandererkinder für die Probleme verantwortlich zu machen. Eine Politik der Mehrsprachigkeit wird als nicht funktionsfähig dargestellt, und ‚deutschpatriotische' Einsprachigkeit bis in die Pausengespräche als einzige ‚realistische' Ausrichtung propagiert.

Im Folgenden wird zuerst eine Kontextualisierung der Behandlung der Zuwanderung in einer breiteren Konzeptualisierung der österreichischen Bildungspolitik versucht, anschließend werden einige Aspekte anhand empirischer Anhaltspunkte näher illustriert, erstens die regional-lokale Konzentration der Zuwanderung, zweitens Vielfalt vs. Normierung und Exklusion in die Sonderpädagogik, drittens Unterschiede bei Schulabbruch und Übergang, fünftens internationale Vergleiche zur Kompetenzentwicklung – als ein wichtiges Thema zieht sich durch alle Aspekte ein Mangel an zureichender Informations- und Datenbasis.

Zuwanderung in den längerfristigen bildungspolitischen Grundmustern

‚Endemically insufficient improvement' als Grundproblem im politisierten Föderalismus Österreichs

Im durchregulierten österreichischen Bildungswesen ist offensichtlich ein Phänomen, das mit Vielfalt und Abweichung von der Norm zu tun hat, schwer zu ‚managen'. Erschwerend kommt hinzu, dass sich die Zuwanderung nicht gleich verteilt, sondern in bestimmten Regionen konzentriert, wobei sich diese Konzentration im Falle der Metropole Wien noch einmal mit den traditionellen föderalistischen Konfliktlinien (rotes) Wien vs. (schwarze) Bundesländer überschneidet[1]

---

[1] ‚Wiener Skandale' kommen in dieser Konstellation jedem recht und werden weidlich ausgeschlachtet, während umgekehrt Wien wiederum möglichst problembelastete Auffälligkeiten vermeiden muss (‚Wien ist anders' gilt nur in positiver Richtung), um nicht in diese Skanda-

(und die Konzentration in den städtischen Regionen innerhalb der Bundesländer auch aufgrund ‚regionaler Blindheiten' des politischen Föderalismus viel weniger wahrgenommen wird). Die Politik ist gegenüber der Vielfalt in doppelter Weise ‚flach', erstens auf ein durchschnittliches Bundesgebiet hin zugeschnitten (im Zentralismus), zweitens auf durchschnittliche Bundesländer hin ausgerichtet (im Föderalismus); die lokalen Einheiten (Städte, Gemeinden, ev. Bezirke), wo die Vielfalt zum Tragen kommt, haben nicht das entsprechende Gewicht, um mit dieser wirklich umzugehen.

Im Schulwesen kommt dazu, dass der Bund im Pflichtschulwesen keine wirklichen Durchgriffsmöglichkeiten hat und die Länder die Konfliktlinien gegenüber dem Bund im Föderalismus ausspielen, aber in ihrem Inneren keine nachvollziehbaren und transparenten Strategien verfolgen. Der Bund kann politische Vorschläge und Strategien entwickeln und in Form von ‚Rundschreiben' vorschlagen, es fehlt aber letztlich die Handhabe, diese wirklich umzusetzen. Dies führt zu einer speziellen politischen Konstellation, die man als ‚*law of endemically insufficient improvement*' (Lassnigg und Vogtenhuber 2015) bezeichnen kann. D.h. es gibt zu allen oder den meisten Problemen politische Vorschläge und oft auch Regulierungen oder designierte Maßnahmen, die jedoch jeweils unzureichend für eine Problemlösung sind und in ihrer Summe überdies zu einer unüberschaubaren Fülle an Politiken und Strategien führen (die eher als lästig denn als zielführend gesehen werden).

Zum Umgang mit Zuwanderung wurde seit den 1970ern in Versuchsform ein Förderinstrumentarium im Schulwesen entwickelt, das Anfang der 1990er in das Regulationssystem übernommen wurde (von Schulpflicht- und Lehrplanregelungen, über die Deutschförderung und den ‚muttersprachlichen Unterricht' bis zur Interkulturalität als Unterrichtsprinzip). Dieses wurde in den 2000ern in verschiedenen Aspekten – immer politisch umstritten – weiter ausgebaut (Widmung von Planstellen, Kindergartenjahre, Sprachfeststellungen, etc.). Da die Umsetzung dieser Regelungen in hohem Maße den AkteurInnen überlassen wird, bieten sie Gelegenheiten für Engagierte, aber die meisten BeobachterInnen gehen davon aus, dass es hier bedeutende Lücken gibt.

Verspätete Reaktion

Diese skizzierte Konstellation soll im Folgenden am bildungspolitischen Umgang mit der Zuwanderung illustriert werden, wobei gerade das Phänomen der ‚verspäteten Reaktion' von besonderer Bedeutung ist. Im Hinblick auf die Bildungspolitik sind hier zwei Aspekte hervorzuheben, warum diese verspätete Reaktion besonders fatal erscheint. Offensichtlich sind Integration und Inklusion umso leichter, je kleiner die betroffenen ‚Massen' sind (gleichzeitig erscheinen – entgegenwirkend – die Normierungen umso selbstverständlicher, je weniger Vielfalt oder Abweichung es gibt); dies gilt speziell bei Kindern und Jugendlichen, wo die integrati-

---

lisierungs-Falle zu gehen. Gleichzeitig ‚verschenkt' Wien viele seiner Potentiale an das umliegende Niederösterreich, ohne dass dies entsprechend geachtet wird.

ven Vorgänge auf der Mikroebene, und damit die Zahl und Konstellation der Kontakte zwischen Kindern verschiedener Gruppen, sehr wichtig sind. Ein Beispiel: Wenn 80% nicht Deutsch sprechen, so ist die Zahl der potentiell möglichen Kontakte mit deutsch-sprachigen Kindern offensichtlich schon aus Gründen der Kombinatorik viel kleiner, als wenn es 20% sind (was manchmal als Obergrenze für selbstläufiges informelles Sprachenlernen gesehen wird). Die Illustration zur zeitlichen Dynamik im nächsten Abschnitt zeigt, dass gute 10 bis 15 Jahre Zeit vorhanden war, bevor sich die populistischen und fremdenfeindlichen Kräfte wirklich formiert haben; und es hat auch bereits früh Kräfte gegeben, die auf ‚Handlungsbedarf' hingewiesen haben – diese Auseinandersetzungen nachzuzeichnen wäre eine reizvolle Aufgabe für die Policy-Forschung.

Der zweite Aspekt besteht in der (heute) allenthalben betonten hohen Bedeutung von Bildung ‚für Alles', auch für Integration und Inklusion.[2] In der Tat kann man phantasieren, dass durch eine rechtzeitige adäquate Bildungspolitik möglicherweise vieles abgefangen werden hätte können; die politischen Kräfte und Strukturen waren aber offensichtlich nicht in der Lage, diese Potentiale der Bildungspolitik zu erkennen, solange sie noch *vergleichsweise leicht* wirksam werden hätten können. Dieses Phänomen, dass vom Bildungswesen eine vorausschauende Aktivität erwartet wird, dieses de facto aber im Allgemeinen verspätet reagiert, wurde bereits von Karl Marx (1845/1888) in der dritten seiner ‚Feuerbach-Thesen' damit angesprochen, dass eben *„der Erzieher selbst erzogen werden muß"*, was entsprechende Komplikationen und Zeitverzögerungen mit sich bringt (Wer erzieht die ErzieherInnen? Welchen Vorlauf braucht es dazu?). In der Illustration zur zeitlichen Dynamik der Zuwanderung (siehe unten Abbildung 1) sieht man die vergleichsweise moderate Entwicklung von den 1960ern bis in die 1980er. Diese hätte Gelegenheit zum Aufbau entsprechender Kompetenzen und institutioneller Vorkehrungen geboten, um die ‚Absorptions-Kapazität' für die spätere Steigerung der Anforderungen zu schaffen. Dem stand jedoch die politische Erwartung des temporären Verbleibs und der Rückwanderung entgegen. Dementsprechend wurde ein Rahmen für den ‚muttersprachlichen Unterricht' aufgebaut, der seit dem Ende der 1990er auch gut dokumentiert ist, während für die Deutsch-Förderung zwar in Form des maximalen Stundenrahmens und der Allokation von Dienstposten regulatorische Vorkehrungen getroffen wurden, deren Umsetzung jedoch nicht öffentlich dokumentiert ist.[3] Gerade in der LehrerInnenbildung (der ‚Erziehung der Er-

---

[2] Dieser wichtige Punkt von realistischen versus überzogenen Erwartungen in die Bildungspolitik geht heute gewissermaßen gegen den Zeitgeist und kann hier nicht näher behandelt werden. Colin Crouch hat mit seinen MitarbeiterInnen in einer europäischen Studie die neoliberale Verdrängung anderer Politikprioritäten durch die Hypostasierung der Bildungspolitik herausgearbeitet (Crouch/Finegold/Sako 1999); in den USA wurde diese Hypostasierung unter dem Begriff der ‚Education Gospel' analysiert (Grubb/Lazerson 2004; siehe Lassnigg 2012 für eine nähere Auseinandersetzung, v.a. Hintergrundbericht Kap. 2.3)

[3] Die regulatorische Basis für diese Maßnahmen sind der Status der außerordentlichen SchülerInnen und die Schulreife-Bestimmungen, die die Kenntnis der (deutschen) Unterrichtssprache umfassen, und in der gegenwärtigen Reform durch die Verpflichtung der Eltern, für diese Kenntnis zu sorgen, erweitert wurden. Dies geht Vertretern der FPÖ nicht weit genug, die im

zieher') hat es besonders lange gedauert, bis mit der aktuell im Gange befindlichen Reform der PädagogInnenbildung stärkere Vorkehrungen für Inklusion und Mehrsprachigkeit getroffen wurden.

**Illustration zur zeitlichen Dynamik:
Zuwanderung und Schulwesen**

Abbildung 1 gibt einen Überblick über die zeitliche Dynamik der Zuwanderung seit den 1960ern. Im oberen Teil werden die expansiven und restriktiven Perioden der Zuwanderung und der Fluchtbewegungen in stilisierter Weise auf das Schulwesen projiziert (siehe dazu die ausführliche Darstellung in Lassnigg 2017a). Dabei wird von einer stilisierten Kerngruppe von 25-30-jährigen ZuwanderInnen der ersten Generation ausgegangen, die nach fünf Jahren schulpflichtige Kinder hat (2. Generation), welche sich kohortenmäßig durch die kalendarische und gleichzeitig tagespolitische Zeit schieben; wenn die 2. Generation 25-30 Jahre alt wird, wiederholt sich dieser Prozess. Damit kann man stilisiert sehen, wie sich die Zuwanderungsdynamik in Schule und Bildungspolitik abbildet.

Wenn man die 25-30-jährigen ZuwanderInnen durch die kalendarische und politische Zeit laufen lässt (die 25-30-Jährigen der frühen 1960er sind am Ende der Periode bereits 75-80 Jahre alt) und die Reproduktions-Dynamik einfügt, so wird sichtbar, dass sich die erste Welle der Anwerbung von ‚GastarbeiterInnen' vor allem zwischen den 1970ern und den 1990ern auf das Schulwesen auswirkt. An den Einbürgerungen sieht man, dass trotz der konzipierten Rückwanderung ein Teil geblieben ist. Ab den späten 1980ern – zeitgleich mit der Wendung der FPÖ zum Rechtspopulismus – werden die Enkel der 1. Generation für das Schulwesen wirksam, die sich dann ab der Mitte der 1990er mit der 2. Generation aus der Flucht aus Ex-Jugoslawien überschneiden. Wieder 10 Jahre später wirkt sich die Osterweiterung, gefolgt von der Flucht aus Afghanistan aus, so dass sich in den 2000ern drei verschiedene Gruppen von ZuwanderInnen kombinieren.

Im unteren Teil von Abbildung 1 werden die quantitativen Informationen zur Zuwanderung seit den 1960ern in Fünf-Jahresperioden in Form der Zahl der Einbürgerungen, der Nettozuwanderung von AusländerInnen und zum Vergleich auch der Asylanträge seit 1999 dargestellt. Man sieht, dass die Größenordnung der Einbürgerungen als Grundlage für die zweite Generation seit den 1960ern sukzessive steigt, ab den 1990ern verstärkt, gefolgt von einem Rückgang in den 2000ern. Die Netto-Zuwanderung als Differenz zwischen Ein- und Auswanderung als dynamischer Wert schwankt stärker nach der Expansions-Restriktions-Dynamik und steigt bereits mit der Flucht-Periode aus Ex-Jugoslawien vor dem Höhepunkt 2015 deutlich an. In dieser Darstellung ist die Verweildauer nicht sichtbar, die jedoch das tatsächliche Ausmaß stark bestimmt. Die Summe aus Einbürgerung und Nettozuwanderung gibt eine Art Maximalwert an, indem ein längerer Verbleib der

---

Sinne ihres Deutsch-Patriotischen Kurses für die Schule den Deutsch-Unterricht ausgliedern und Deutsch als Pausensprache „allgemein verankern" wollen (Der Standard 24.9.2017).

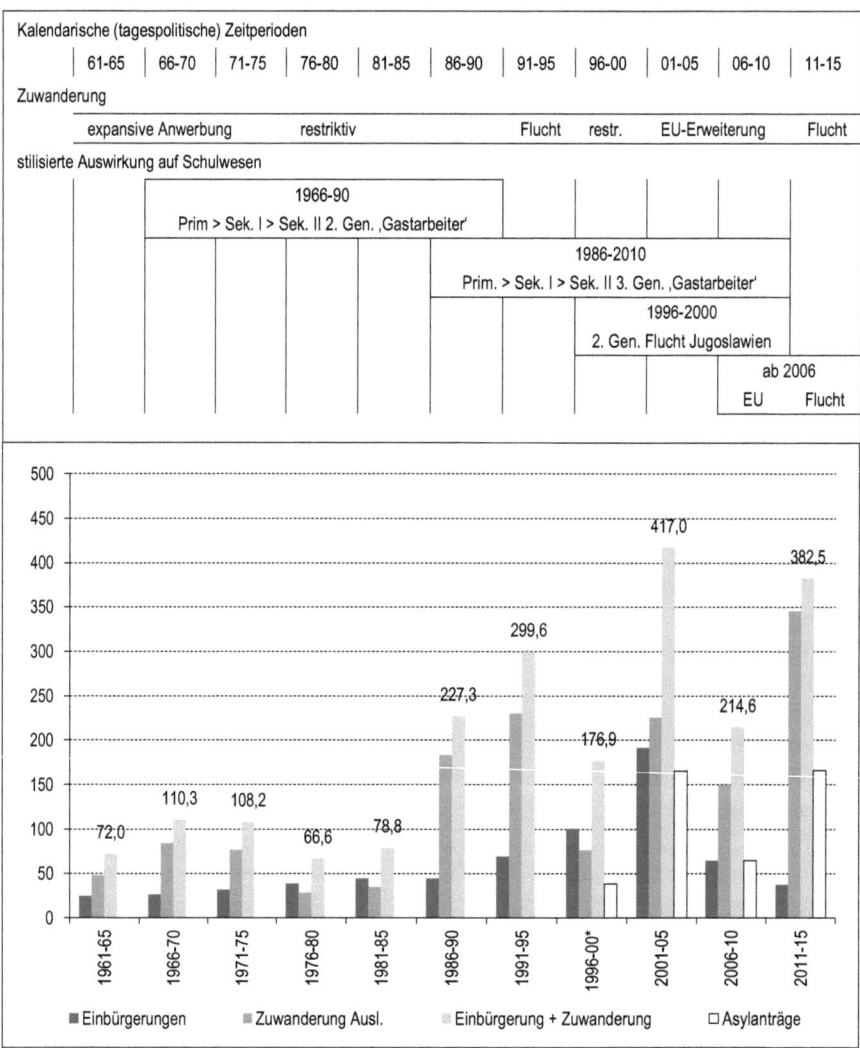

Abbildung 1 Zuwanderung und Schulwesen, zeitliche Dynamik.(oben) und quantitative Auswirkungen (unten)

Quelle: Statistik Austria (Zuwanderung), BMI (Asylstatistik)und Herzog-Punzenberger/Schnell 2014 (Zuwanderungsphasen), eigene Berechnung und Darstellung.
Stäbe geben die Einbürgerung (Staatsbürgerschaft), die Nettozuwanderung, und die Summe dieser beiden Größen als fiktives maximales Ausmaß an; zum Vergleich wird auch die Zahl der Asylanträge dargestellt, *in der ersten Periode sind für Asylanträge nur die Jahre 1999-2000 verfügbar.

ZuwanderInnen angenommen wird (de facto reduzieren die Einbürgerungen diesen Wert, da diese nach einer gewissen Verbleibsdauer stattfinden, dies ist aber für die illustrative Darstellung unerheblich).

Der politische Umgang mit dieser Entwicklung lässt sich nicht ohne weiteres rekonstruieren, da in entscheidenden Aspekten die Informationen zur Umsetzung fehlen. Nähere Analysen gibt es erst ab der Mitte der 2000er Jahre, also im Gefolge der verstärkten Einbürgerungen nach der Flüchtlingswelle aus Ex-Jugoslawien (Abbildung 1), viereinhalb Jahrzehnte nach dem Beginn der Anwerbung von ‚GastarbeiterInnen'.[4] Beginnend in den 1970ern wurden über zwei Jahrzehnte Maßnahmen in Form von Schulversuchen entwickelt (1971 Förderkurse Deutsch, ab 1975 Unterricht in der Erstsprache, ab 1990 Seiteneinsteigerkurse), die zu Beginn der 1990er ins Regelschulwesen übernommen wurden, ohne jedoch definitive Verpflichtungen zu schaffen. Mit den Leistungsunterschieden zwischen den ZuwanderInnen und den Einheimischen in der PISA-Erhebung werden die bestehenden Strategien und Maßnahmen in Frage gestellt. Es besteht Einigkeit, dass ihre Quantität und Qualität nicht ausreicht, gleichzeitig treten neben den Fragen der Sprachenbildung auch die vorschulische Erziehung bzw. Bildung (Kindergartenjahre) und die fast völlig fehlende LehrerInnenbildung für Mehrsprachigkeit in den Vordergrund (vgl. MiMe-Policy Brief Nr.2).

Empirische Befunde zu zentralen Aspekten der Zuwanderung

Regional-lokale Konzentration der Zuwanderung und Schwächen der Informationsbasis und Maßnahmenkonzentration

An anderer Stelle wurden die Probleme der Stadt-Land-Unterschiede in der österreichischen Bildungspolitik dargelegt: Verdrängung der städtischen Problemlagen und umgekehrte Schwerpunktsetzung der Förderung der ländlichen Gebiete während in der internationalen Forschung die Probleme der ‚Urban Education' und der Metropolenbildung im Vordergrund stehen (Lassnigg 2017b). Die vorhandene Politikstruktur verbindet die Stadt-Land-Unterschiede einerseits mit dem Wien-Bundesländer-Gegensatz und verdeckt durch die starke Betonung der Länder-Ebene im Föderalismus die Unterschiede innerhalb der Länder.[5]

Tatsächlich scheint sich im Hinblick auf die Konzentration der Zuwanderung der aggregierte Unterschied Wien-Bundesländer innerhalb der Länder zwischen den städtischen Agglomerationen und den ländlichen Gebieten zu reproduzieren. Die letzteren Unterschiede sind jedoch in der statistischen Berichterstattung meist nicht sichtbar, die nur bis zu Länder-Unterschieden differenziert. Wenn man für

---

[4] Wichtige Quellen sind Rechnungshof 2013, Herzog-Punzenberger und Schnell 2012, Biffl und Skrivanek 2011, Herzog-Punzenberger und Unterwurzacher 2009, OECD 2009, BMUKK/BMWF 2008; siehe auch Abschlussarbeiten aus jüngerer Zeit Scharinger 2013, Pepelnik 2011.

[5] Versuche, die starken Unterschiede der Schulstrukturen und -ausgaben zwischen den Bundesländern auf systematische Muster zurückzuführen, haben (bisher) keine klaren Ergebnisse gebracht. Es hat eher den Anschein, dass hier politische Vorlieben, Netzwerke und Machtkonstellationen eine größere Rolle spielen als sachlich-systematische Faktoren. (NBB 2015 Bd. 1; Lassnigg, Bruneforth und Vogtenhuber (2016))

die verschiedenen Indikatoren für Zuwanderung die aggregierten Durchschnittswerte nimmt, so liegen diese in der Größenordnung von 20%, spiegeln aber nicht die Realität, da diese Anteile in den Ballungsgebieten im Schulwesen bei 60-80% liegen. Innerhalb der Schulen konzentrieren sich diese noch einmal (siehe Tabelle 1 und 2).

Aufgrund der Schwächen und langsamen Entwicklung der statistischen Erfassung sind diese Informationen jedoch erst seit kurzer Zeit verfügbar. Noch bis vor wenigen Jahren haben sich die Diskussionen im Forschungsbereich aufgrund dieser Mängel nicht auf die empirische Situation bezogen, sondern auf die Frage, welche Indikatoren (z.B. Staatsbürgerschaft oder erlernte/gesprochene Sprache, Erste und Zweite Generation) notwendig sind und sinnvoll verwendet werden können.[6] In der Zeit, in der die Zuwanderung gewachsen ist und sich aufgebaut hat, bestand daher eine große Kluft zwischen den verfügbaren Informationen und den Erfahrungen auf der Praxisebene. Die eingangs skizzierte Verdrängung der Thematik hat auch noch zusätzlich einem näheren Hinschauen entgegengewirkt. Aus dieser Interaktion von Information und Praxis entsteht bei derart emergenten Phänomenen das Paradox, dass die Informationen mit der Problemlage wachsen und man gute Informationen erst im Laufe der Zeit hat, wenn den gewachsenen Herausforderungen viel schwerer entgegengewirkt werden kann.

Erschwerend kommt die etablierte Logik der Politik hinzu, die durch zwei Komponenten gekennzeichnet ist, erstens die Dominanz der Finanzierung gegenüber anderen Aspekten, und zweitens die Art, wie die Verteilung der Mittel geregelt ist, die (1) die verschiedenen Bereiche des Schulwesens willkürlich voneinander trennt, (2) im Pflichtschulwesen unflexibel politische Aufteilungen zwischen den Ländern vornimmt, (3) innerhalb der Länder keine transparenten Regeln der Mittelverteilung vorsieht. Obwohl in den letzten Jahren gewisse allgemeine Regeln der Bindung der Mittelverteilung an die SchülerInnenzahlen etabliert wurden, bestehen v.a. im Pflichtschulwesen sehr große Unterschiede zwischen den Bundesländern in den Finanzindikatoren, die kaum systematische Muster aufweisen und die auf dem Hintergrund der Regelungen eigentlich unerklärlich sind (Lassnigg et al. 2016).

---

[6] Noch heute greift der Integrationsfonds in seinen statistischen Dokumentationen noch sehr stark auf die Staatsbürgerschaft als Merkmal zurück, die im Schulwesen aber nur etwa die Hälfte der Zuwanderung erfasst (z.B. OEIF 2015); auch der Rechnungshof kritisiert in seinen Empfehlungen die Verwendung unterschiedlicher Kategorisierungen (Rechnungshof 2013, S. 321).

	Regionale Konzentration Anteil der SchülerInnen ndA, die in dbG lebt an allen SchülerInnen nicht deutscher Alltagssprache (ndA) nach Bundesländern (jeweils alle SchülerInnen ndA in ÖST bzw. LAND=100%)	Schulische Konzentration Anteil der SchülerInnen ndA an allen SchülerInnen in dicht besiedelten Gebieten (dbG) nach Bundesländern (jeweils alle SchülerInnen in dbG in ÖST bzw. LAND=100%)
W	100%	56%
V	0%	-
ÖST	56%	51%
S	49%	47%
O	26%	48%
T	29%	35%
N	0%	-
St	51%	39%
B	0%	-
K	31%	23%

Tabelle 1 Regionale und schulische Konzentration der PrimarschülerInnen in dicht besiedelten Gebieten nach Bundesländern (2013/14)

Quelle: NBB 2015 Bd.1, Abb.B2.a1, eigene Berechnung.
Bundesländer geordnet nach dem Gesamtanteil an SchülerInnen nicht deutscher Alltagssprache; Lesebeispiel: 56% aller VolksschülerInnen nicht deutscher Alltagssprache (ndA) in Österreich sind in dicht besiedelten Gebieten situiert (1.Spalte) und 51% aller SchülerInnen in dicht besiedelten Gebieten (dbG) in Österreich sprechen eine nicht deutsche Alltagssprache (2. Spalte); in drei Bundesländern (V, N, B) gibt es keine dicht besiedelten Gebiete in der verwendeten sehr differenzierten europäischen Klassifikation.

Seit längerem wird davon ausgegangen, dass die insgesamt rückläufige einheimische Geburtenentwicklung durch die Zuwanderung kompensiert wird. Zudem ist hier seit langem ein qualitativer Unterschied zwischen Wien und den anderen Bundesländern bekannt, indem nur Wien eine steigende Entwicklung für die SchülerInnenpopulation aufweist (siehe dazu die demografischen Indikatoren in den Nationalen Bildungsberichten). Auswertungen für die Volksschule, wo die Population mit den SchülerInnenzahlen mehr oder weniger übereinstimmt, zeigen, dass die Entwicklung der Ausgaben gegenüber der demografischen Entwicklung nicht sensitiv ist. Die Bundesländer mit demographisch sinkenden SchülerInnenzahlen bekommen eine ‚demografische Dividende' in Form von steigenden Ausgaben pro SchülerIn, während Wien mit steigenden oder stagnierenden SchülerInnenzahlen im Wesentlichen stabile Ausgaben verzeichnet, also relativ verliert. Wenn man die Zuwanderung berücksichtigt, die im Prinzip zusätzliche Mittel erfordert und in Wien deutlich höher ist, so verliert Wien doppelt. Die Auswertungen des Rechnungshofes (2013) zeigen jedoch, dass diese Mehrbelastung in Wien durch die Förderausgaben teilweise kompensiert wird.

Die Tabellen 1 und 2 zeigen die Konzentration der Zuwanderung nach differenzierten regionalen Einheiten und auch innerhalb der Schulen. Es ist offensichtlich, dass sich die Zuwanderung in den Städten und Agglomerationen konzentriert. Dies schafft Anforderungen, die zum österreichischen Verteilungsprinzip der Förderung des ländlichen Schulwesens gegenläufig sind. In dieser Frage überschneiden sich die Bedarfe mit dem Prinzip der ‚Economies of Scale', demzufolge

	% der SchülerInnen mit nicht deutscher Alltagssprache in Klassen mit...			Spaltenprozent
	...75% oder mehr SchülerInnen nicht deutscher Alltagssprache	...50-75% SchülerInnen nicht deutscher Alltagssprache	...50% oder mehr SchülerInnen nicht deutscher Alltagsspr. (=Summe Sp 1+2)	Verteilung der SchülerInnen nicht deutscher Alltagssprache auf Schultypen
PRIMARSCHULE gesamt	29%	24%	53%	57,0
Vorschulstufen	47%	35%	82%	3,9
Volksschulen	28%	23%	51%	51,0
Sonderschulen	25%	21%	46%	0,6
Sonstige, statutO	75%	17%	92%	1,5
SEKUNDARSTUFE I gesamt	26%	23%	49%	43,0
AHS-Unterstufe	13%	19%	32%	5,4
Hauptschulen	35%	22%	57%	15,9
Neue MittelschulenB	27%	27%	54%	19,3
Sonderschulen	26%	27%	53%	1.0
Sonstige, statutO	70%	70%	92%	1,4
PRIMAR und SEKUNDAR I	28%	24%	52%	100,0

Tabelle 2 Innerschulische Konzentration der SchülerInnen mit nicht deutscher Alltagssprache in Klassen nach Schultyp bzw. Schulstufe (2013/14)

Quelle: NBB 2015 Bd.1, Abb.B2.d, eigene Berechnung und Darstellung.
in Spalten 1-3 Reihenprozente: jeweils alle SchülerInnen nicht deutscher Alltagssprache in Schultypen=100%; Spalte 4 gibt den Anteil der jeweiligen Kategorien an allen SchülerInnen der Primarstufe und der Sekundarstufe 1

größere (schulische) Einheiten kostengünstiger sind. Zur Erhaltung des ländlichen Schulwesens, die während der gesamten Zweiten Republik ein wesentliches Prinzip der Politik war, sind aufgrund der Ausdünnung der Strukturen zusätzliche Mittel erforderlich. Andererseits konzentrieren sich in den Städten sowohl der Wohlstand als auch die soziale Benachteiligung, was durch die schlechten Bedingungen, unter denen die ZuwanderInnen oft leben und arbeiten, noch verstärkt wird. In der Stadt gibt es daher gegenläufige Faktoren, erstens die Einsparungen durch Economies of Scale, zweitens zusätzlichen Bedarf aufgrund von Benachteiligungen und besonderen Bedürfnissen. Dieser zweite Faktor war in Österreich bis vor kurzem Tabu, Forderungen nach zusätzlichen Mitteln werden immer pauschal erhoben (das bedeutet de facto, dass bei zusätzlichen Mitteln für Benachteiligte immer auch die Bevorzugten mitpartizipieren, was im Sinne einer breit akzeptierten Wohlfahrtpolitik durchaus bis zu einem gewissen Grad Sinn machen kann). Erst die Diskussionen um eine soziale Indexierung haben diese Frage auf die politische Agenda gehoben. Im Fall Österreichs muss aber auch berücksichtigt werden, dass bisher die Mittelverteilung offensichtlich nicht treffsicher ist, indem höhere Mittel nicht mit höheren Leistungen einhergehen (Lassnigg et al. 2016).

Vielfalt vs. Normierung und Exklusion in die Sonderpädagogik: Zuwanderung als ‚Politikum'

In der bildungspolitischen Debatte wird häufig auf die positiven Seiten der differenzierten Strukturen hingewiesen und das Bild von gleichförmigen ‚Eintöpfen' als Schreckgespenst an die Wand gemalt. Dabei wird aber vergessen, dass mit der differenzierten Struktur eine Homogenisierung der Einheiten stattfindet, die bei einigermaßen breiten Einheiten ein System von nebeneinander liegenden Eintöpfen konstituiert, deren Nachteil in der Tendenz zu starren, sich selbst perpetuierenden Normierungen besteht. Was in diese Normierungen nicht passt, wird ausgeschlossen oder ausgesondert. Das diesbezügliche Ventil war lange Zeit die Sonderschule, die in sich einen grundsätzlichen unauflöslichen Widerspruch enthält: auf der einen Seite kann sie sich im Inneren um ihre SchülerInnen sehr bemühen, und tut dies tatsächlich, auf der anderen Seite ist sie von außen als ‚unzureichend' stigmatisiert, was diese Bemühungen dann in den Auswirkungen wieder zu Nichte macht. Hier stellen sich die Fragen der Inklusion, die eigentlich einen demokratischen Inhalt haben, d.h. es geht im Bereich der Pflichtschulbildung zuerst um die gemeinsame Erfahrung und in zweiter Linie um die technologische Effizienz. Damit ist auch der Konflikt um positionale Vorteile ‚besserer' gegenüber ‚schlechterer' Schulen eröffnet, der hier nicht weiter vertieft werden kann.

Im Hinblick auf die Zuwanderung ist dieser Konflikt insofern relevant, als damit eben besondere Bedingungen verbunden sind (Sprache, Gewohnheiten, Benachteiligungen etc.), die – je nach Hintergrund unterschiedlich – eher als unvorteilhaft denn als vorteilhaft wahrgenommen werden, und damit in die positionalen Kämpfe hineingezogen werden: Die ‚fremden' Kinder und Jugendlichen brauchen Aufmerksamkeit und diese wird ‚unseren' Kindern ‚weggenommen' – als Konsequenz ‚schicken wir sie woanders hin, Nachsatz: wo sie ohnehin besser aufgehoben sind'. Im Effekt kommt zur Stigmatisierung aufgrund der ‚Fremdheit' die Stigmatisierung durch die Sonderschule dazu.

In die Struktur dieser Konfliktlinien, die bis zu einem gewissen Grad auch der politischen Lagerbildung entsprechen, passen genau die sich überschneidenden ‚Deutsch'- und ‚Anpassungs'-Debatten: Damit ZuwanderInnen im regulären Schulwesen teilnehmen können, müssen sie sich zuerst ‚integrieren', d.h. in Sprache und Gewohnheiten der Norm anpassen. Diese simple Normierungsposition wurde politisch von außen (seitens der Zuwanderungspolitik, vom Innenministerium bzw. v.a. auch dem ‚Integrations'-Staatssekretariat) der Bildungs- und Schulpolitik entgegengestellt, deren Strategie der graduellen Integration auf Basis von informellen Lern- und Austauschprozessen unter den SchülerInnen in hohem Maß nicht sachlich diskutiert, sondern als ‚Untätigkeit' oder ‚Versagen' diskreditiert wird (wobei auch noch zusätzlich die Konfliktlinie Wien-Bundesländer aktiviert wird).

In der Tat überschneiden sich hier politische und strategische Fragen einer sinnvollen und demokratischen Vorgangsweise mit den Fragen der technischen Umsetzung und vor allem auch ausreichender Ressourcen, wobei es nicht nur um die notwendigen finanziellen Ressourcen, sondern auch um die erforderlichen Kompetenzen und die dafür notwendigen theoretischen und sachlichen Voraussetzungen geht. Ein Ansatz kann durchaus im Prinzip sinnvoll und demokratisch sein, aber hinsichtlich der Ressourcen wie auch der Kompetenzen unzureichend umgesetzt werden. Heidi Schrodt (2014) arbeitet hier mehrere wichtige Aspekte heraus. Erstens strukturell, indem die Teilung der Unterstufe in den Städten gleichsam automatisch zu einer Konzentration der ZuwanderInnen im ‚niedrigeren' Schultyp führt und auch die ‚Pipeline' hierhin beeinflusst, sodass damit automatisch auch die Kontaktmöglichkeiten kanalisiert werden. Zweitens im Hinblick auf die Schulkultur, indem die ZuwanderInnen institutionell und personell Unterstützung brauchen, auch durch Lehr- und Unterstützungspersonen aus ihrem mehrsprachigen Umkreis. Drittens im Umgang der einheimischen Lehrpersonen und der Verwaltung mit den ZuwanderInnen, der eine Balance von Unterstützung und Leistungserwartungen erfordert (hier wird für Wien gezeigt, dass anscheinend in hohem Maße die Senkung der Leistungserwartungen als falsch verstandene ‚Förderung' eingesetzt wurde) (Schrodt 2014, S. 94-111).

Der Ansatz war über lange Jahre, ZuwanderInnen der ersten Generation als ‚außerordentliche SchülerInnen' aufzunehmen, was v.a. hinsichtlich der Beurteilung einen Unterschied macht: Wenn sie die Voraussetzungen für den regulären Unterricht erfüllen, werden sie in ordentliche SchülerInnen umgewandelt. Um diesen Prozess des Aufholens zu unterstützen, sind zusätzliche Förderungen vorgesehen. Dieses Modell ist integrativ und inklusiv, setzt aber vor allem voraus, dass die informellen Mechanismen der graduellen Enkulturation und des Sprachenlernens funktionieren, was auf den interkulturellen Kontaktmöglichkeiten beruht. Diese Kontaktmöglichkeiten mit den einheimischen Kindern und Jugendlichen beruhen auf der Gruppenzusammensetzung, und sie sinken mit steigendem Anteil der ZuwanderInnen. Hier ist die Konzentration ein zentraler Faktor, da die Kontaktmöglichkeiten mit den Deutsch sprechenden Kindern und Jugendlichen bei einer großen Mehrheit von nicht Deutsch sprechenden Kindern und Jugendlichen nur noch gering sind, was die informellen Prozesse stark schwächt. Förderungen sind ein zweiter Faktor, in diesem Modell vom Konzept her subsidiär, gewinnen aber mit der Konzentration von ZuwanderInnen an Gewicht.

Hier scheint eine grundlegende Lücke in der österreichischen Praxis zu bestehen, die jedoch empirisch nicht wirklich geschlossen werden kann, da die wesentlichen Informationen dafür nicht öffentlich zugänglich sind. Während der ‚muttersprachliche' Unterricht seit 1998 gut dokumentiert ist und eine etablierte Infrastruktur umfasst (BMB 2017),[7] gibt es über die Förderung des Lernens der deut-

---

[7] Auf der Web-Seite ‚Schule mehrsprachig' (http://www.schule-mehrsprachig.at/index.php?id=61) gibt es zu diesem Thema auch weitere ausführliche Informationen, die Auswertung zum muttersprachlichen Unterricht zeigen einen von 23% auf 16% gesunkenen Anteil an mehrsprachlichen SchülerInnen, die am muttersprachlichen Unterricht teilnehmen, im Durchschnitt der erfassten Jahre ist etwa jede 6. Schule involviert, ca. 350 Lehrpersonen halten je ca. 18 Wochen-Stunden, auf eine Lehrpersonen kommen 80 SchülerInnen, die Stunden pro teilnehmenden SchülerInnen betragen ca. 0,22 (wenn man durchschnittliche Gruppen von 5

schen Bildungssprache nur sehr punktuell Informationen. Ein Gutachten des Rechnungshofes (2013) umfasst für die Periode 2006-2011 Angaben für wichtige Parameter, wie etwa die Zahl der außerordentlichen SchülerInnen sowie die für Deutsch-Förderung vorgesehenen und abgerufenen Planstellen. Die Botschaft aus diesen Informationen ist widersprüchlich, da einerseits österreichweit weniger als 80% der Planstellen abgerufen wurden (in Wien waren es fast 95%), aber andererseits die durchgeführten Unterrichtsaktivitäten eher gering waren, in der Größenordnung der Ressourcen wurde für Deutschförderung etwas mehr verausgabt als für den ‚muttersprachlichen' Unterricht (umgelegt auf die außerordentlichen SchülerInnen 0,35 Wochen-Stunden österreichweit bzw. 0,45 in Wien (siehe Näheres in Lassnigg 2017a).[8] Da der Bedarf nicht klar ist, sind diese Werte schwer einzuschätzen.

Seit den 2000ern, auch im Gefolge der vergleichsweise schlechten PISA-Ergebnisse, haben die Fragen des Sprachenlernens und der Sprachendiagnostik stark an Aufmerksamkeit gewonnen. Dabei geht es auch um die Kompetenzen der einheimischen deutschsprechenden SchülerInnen und insbesondere der LehrerInnen. In den Kinderbetreuungseinrichtungen hat die Sprachstandserhebung 2008 ergeben, dass immerhin 24.100 deutschsprachige Kinder (10%) eine Sprachförderung benötigen gegenüber 59.000 mit anderer Erstsprache (58%), zusammen etwa ein Viertel aller Kinder; in 28,7% der Einrichtungen werden Förder-Maßnahmen durchgeführt (OEIF 2015, S.3). Analysen des Leseunterrichts zeigen, dass die RisikoschülerInnen von der Volksschule (PIRLS-Erhebung) zum Ende der Pflichtschule sich von ca. 15% auf etwas unter 30% beinahe verdoppeln, was mit unzureichender Methodologie im Unterricht erklärt wird (Schabmann et al. 2012). Die Risikogruppe im Lesen besteht in der 4. Klasse der Volksschule zu 63% aus Kindern mit deutscher Alltagssprache und zu 37% mit anderer Alltagssprache (in absoluten Zahlen wären das in der 4. Schulstufe der Volksschule etwa 8.200 Kinder mit deutscher Alltagssprache und 4.800 mit anderer Alltagssprache, hochgerechnet auf 4 Jahre mehr als 30.000 zu knapp 20.000, also ziemlich abweichende Zahlen von der Sprachstandserhebung). Salchegger und Herzog-Punzenberger (2017) haben in einer vergleichenden Analyse der PISA-Werte im Zeitverlauf gezeigt, dass sich zwischen 2000 und 2012 die Werte der SchülerInnen ohne Migrationshintergrund (wie auch der Gesamtdurchschnitt) nicht verändert haben, die Werte der ZuwanderInnen sich jedoch um ca. 50 Punkte *verbessert* haben, wodurch die letzteren immer noch um 50 Punkte niedriger liegen. Der Unterschied hat sich jedoch etwa halbiert. Offensichtlich kann man nicht die ZuwanderInnen

---

unterstellt, so wäre das ca. 1 Stunde, wenn man Gruppen von 10 unterstellt, so wären es 2 Stunden pro SchülerIn und Woche; auf alle mehrsprachigen SchülerInnen umgelegt, wären es ca. 0,04 Stunden).

[8] Wenn man aus diesen Angaben Jahres-Stunden hochrechnet, so kommt man im Durchschnitt auf 14 Jahresstunden pro ao. SchülerIn (18 in Wien), bei durchschnittlichen Gruppengrößen von 5 würde dies 70 bzw. 90 Unterrichts-Stunden, bei Gruppengrößen von 10 würden sich 140 bzw. 180 Stunden errechnen, an denen ein Kind teilnimmt.

für die Leistungsprobleme im Schulwesen verantwortlich machen, was jedoch in der Politik häufig geschieht.

Berücksichtigt man den Aspekt der Kompetenzen im Umgang mit der Zuwanderung, so kommt den Lehrpersonen eine Schlüsselstellung zu, die eng mit der ‚Sprachpolitik' zusammenhängt. Hier sind bisher wenig Voraussetzungen gegeben, ZuwanderInnen sind im Lehr- und Unterstützungspersonal als potentielle Brücke in die Institution sehr wenig vertreten (siehe dazu Schrodt 2014, Kapitel 7), auch die Kompetenzen des einheimischen Lehrpersonals im Umgang mit Diversität und Inklusion sowie Fremdsprachigkeit sind offensichtlich wenig entwickelt (Ataç und Lageder 2009). Grundsätzliche politische Fragen des Umganges mit Zuwanderung beziehen sich auf die Akzeptanz von Diversität, wobei den Kompetenzen und der Positionierung der Lehrpersonen wesentliche Bedeutung zukommt (Reich 2013; siehe auch die Schulbeispiele bei Schrodt 2014, Kapitel 6).

Schulabbruch und Migrationshintergrund: bemerkenswerte regionale Muster

Verminderung von frühem Bildungsabbruch und Förderung des Überganges in Beschäftigung oder in weitere Bildungslaufbahnen sind zentrale bildungspolitische Ziele im nationalen wie auch im Europäischen Rahmen. Der Anteil früher AbbrecherInnen soll entsprechend der EU2020-Strategie bis zum Ende des Jahrzehnts europaweit unter 10% sinken. In Österreich wurde dieses Ziel nach den offiziellen Berechnungen mit einem Anteil von 7,3% (2015) bereits erreicht. Mit dem ‚Bildungsbezogenen Erwerbskarrierenmonitoring' steht nun eine alternative und verlässliche Datenbasis zur Berechnung des Anteils früher AbbrecherInnen auf Grundlage von Verwaltungsdaten und einer Vollerhebung zur Verfügung. Auf dieser Basis errechnet sich (bezogen auf das Jahr 2012) ein höherer Anteil von 12,3%.

Es ist seit langem bekannt, dass Migrationshintergrund einen der stärksten Risikofaktoren für frühen Abbruch darstellt (z.B. NBB 2015 Bd.1, S. 135). Neuere Analysen zur statistischen Erklärung frühen Schulabbruchs auf individueller, schulischer und strukturell-systemischer Ebene zeigen auch, dass eine differenzierte Betrachtung sowohl nach Herkunftsregionen als auch nach Generationen nötig ist (Steiner/Pessl/Bruneforth 2016). So liegt das Abbruchs-Risiko für die 1. Generation aus Drittstaaten beim Vierfachen, für die 2. Generation aus Drittstaaten beim Zweieinhalbfachen und auch für die 1. Generation aus EU/EWR-Staaten immer noch beim Doppelten der Jugendlichen ohne Migrationshintergrund (ebd., S.198). Der Anteil an SchülerInnen mit nicht deutscher Alltagssprache erhöht auch am stärksten die schulspezifische Abbruchquote, gefolgt u.a. von den selektierenden und ausgrenzenden Merkmalen des Besuchs der Vorschule und der Zahl der Sonderschulen im Bezirk (ebd. S. 202). Auf Schulebene erhöht das Ausmaß an Zuwanderung (gemessen durch den Anteil der SchülerInnen mit Migrationshintergrund: beide Elternteile im Ausland außer Deutschland geboren) das Abbruchrisiko stärker als der soziale Hintergrund oder das Niveau der Mathematikleistungen;

dies gilt sowohl österreichweit als auch besonders ausgeprägt in den Bundesländern Niederösterreich, Kärnten, Wien und Salzburg (ebd. S.192-194).

Die neue Datenbasis erlaubt erstmals auch, den Anteil für politische Bezirke zu berechnen. Dabei kommt eine große Spanne von frühen AbbrecherInnen zwischen 5% im Bezirk Zwettl (NÖ) bis 26% in Wien-Favoriten zum Vorschein. Eine ähnliche Streuung findet sich auch in anderen Bundesländern, etwa in Oberösterreich mit einer Spanne von 6% in Urfahr-Umgebung bis 21% in Wels-Stadt, oder in Salzburg mit 7% im Bezirk Tamsweg und 17% in Salzburg-Stadt. Früher Ausbildungsabbruch ist ein stark städtisches Phänomen, hohe Werte zeigen sich nicht nur in den Landeshaupt- oder Großstädten, sondern auch in vielen Städten mittlerer Größe wie eben in Wels, Steyr oder Wiener Neustadt. Eine bemerkenswert positive Ausnahme bildet Graz als zweitgrößte Stadt Österreichs mit einem Anteil von 12%, leicht unter dem österreichischen Durchschnitt.

Berücksichtigt man den Migrationshintergrund, verändert sich jedoch die regionale Verteilung grundlegend. Trotz aller Unterschiede in der Qualifikationsstruktur von zugewanderten Personen, die es zu beachten gilt, dreht sich das Stadt-Land-Verhältnis beim frühen Bildungsabbruch um: Das Abbruch-Risiko ist für Jugendliche mit Migrationshintergrund am Land deutlich höher als in der Stadt, auch hier bei großer Streuung, zwischen 19% in Wien-Neubau und 49% im Bezirk Baden (NÖ). Könnte man diesen Unterschied noch mit speziellen Merkmalen, wie dem hohen Qualifikationsniveau in Wien-Neubau oder dem Erstaufnahmezentrum für AsylwerberInnen im Bezirk Baden erklären, so zeigen sich doch konsistente Muster. Imst (Tirol) liegt mit 47% deutlich über Wien-Donaustadt mit 27%, und es liegen 17 von 23 Wiener Bezirken und Städte wie Villach, Klagenfurt, Graz, Salzburg und St. Pölten unter dem österreichischen Durchschnitt. Zugleich liegen viele eher ländliche oder klein- bis mittelstädtische Bezirke wie Schwaz, Schärding, Kirchdorf/Krems, Feldbach oder Bruck/Leitha (um nur exemplarisch einige zu nennen) mehr oder weniger deutlich über dem Durchschnitt.

Abbruchquoten bis über 25% in einzelnen politischen Bezirken und von annähernd 50% bei Jugendlichen mit Migrationshintergrund in einzelnen Regionen sind als Alarmsignal zu werten. Es fragt sich, wovon der Anteil früher AbbrecherInnen in einem Bezirk abhängt. Steiner/Pessl/Bruneforth (2016) zeigen, dass die selektiven Strukturen des österreichischen Bildungssystems ihren Beitrag leisten. Ein Beispiel dafür ist die strukturell vorgegebene Möglichkeit der Abschiebung von Schülern und Schülerinnen von einer Schulform in die nächst niedrigere anstatt sich selbst vor Ort um die Herausforderung kümmern zu müssen. Aber auch die Selektionspraktiken der handelnden (Schul-)Akteure sind von großer Bedeutung. So trägt beispielsweise die Zusammensetzung von Schulklassen nach Herkunft zum hohen Ausmaß des frühen Bildungsabbruchs in einem Bezirk bei. Dabei wird beispielsweise die Praxis, Kinder und Jugendliche mit Migrationshintergrund in eine Klasse und jene ohne Migrationshintergrund in eine andere Klasse zu geben, je nach Bezirk sehr unterschiedlich intensiv praktiziert, und abhängig vom Ausmaß dieser Praxis steigt bzw. sinkt der Anteil früher AbbrecherInnen im jeweiligen Bezirk (siehe zur Segregation und ihren Effekten auch Biedermann et al. 2016). Eine Rolle könnte auch das große Gewicht der betrieblichen Lehre am Land spielen, die für ZuwanderInnen eher schwerer zugänglich ist.

Internationale Vergleiche zur Kompetenzentwicklung: Kontextbedingung, Auswahl und Erwachsenenbildung

Ein wichtiger Kontextfaktor für das Schulwesen sind die Kompetenzen der Elterngenerationen der ZuwanderInnen, da sich diese – vor allem in einer Halbtagsschule – auf die Ressourcen für das Lernen und die Bildungskarrieren der Kinder und Jugendlichen stark auswirken. Laut OECD (2015) gibt es vergleichende Anhaltspunkte für den Bildungsstand der Eltern v.a. aus den PISA-Erhebungen (siehe auch Lassnigg 2017a). Im Durchschnitt der PISA-Teilnehmer-Länder haben 2003 bis 2012 ca. 60% der Eltern der 15-Jährigen mit Migrationshintergrund den gleichen Bildungsstand wie die einheimische Bevölkerung, in Österreich lag dieser Anteil bereits 2003 um etwa 10 Prozentpunkte niedriger und hat sich bis 2012 weiter auf nur etwas über 40% verringert. Es gab nur in wenigen Ländern einen derartigen Rückgang und 2012 haben lediglich drei Länder (USA, Mexiko, Griechenland) einen geringeren Anteil an Zuwanderer-Eltern mit gleichem Bildungsstand wie einheimische Eltern. Entsprechend lag der Anteil an niedrig gebildeten Müttern in Österreich 2003 mit etwas unter 50% um 10 Prozentpunkte über dem internationalen Durchschnitt, dieser Anteil hat sich bis 2012 jedoch verringert und liegt im Vergleich etwa am Durchschnitt bei einem Drittel. In der Periodisierung der Zuwanderung hat in dieser Periode v.a. der Zuzug aus EU-Ländern zugenommen.

Die international vergleichende Erhebung und Analyse der Kompetenzen der erwachsenen Bevölkerung in PIAAC[9] ermöglicht auch einen Vergleich der Kompetenzen von ZuwanderInnen mit denen der einheimischen Bevölkerung in den verschiedenen Ländern. Abbildung 2 und Tabelle 3 zeigen Befunde zur Kompetenzentwicklung über die verschiedenen Altersgruppen in Abhängigkeit vom Ausmaß der Zuwanderung im internationalen Vergleich (Lassnigg und Vogtenhuber 2014).

Die Abbildung 2 zeigt für den Bereich der ‚Literacy' (Lesen bis höhere literale Kompetenzen; im Bereich ‚Numeracy', Rechnen und mathematische Kompetenzen, ergibt sich ein ähnliches Muster), dass – entgegen verbreiteten Meinungen im österreichischen Diskurs – in der mittleren Altersgruppe über die Länder hinweg ein tendenziell positiver Zusammenhang zwischen dem Ausmaß an Zuwanderung und dem Kompetenzniveau besteht, dass das Kompetenzniveau aber in allen Ländern unter dem der Gesamt-Bevölkerung liegt (die Spanne liegt zwischen 95% in Kanada und nur etwas über 75% in Finnland). Der Abstand der ZuwanderInnen

---

[9] PIAAC, populär auch ‚PISA für Erwachsene', ist das Acronym für ‚Programme for the International Assessment of Adult Competencies', siehe OECD, Survey of Adult Skills http://www.oecd.org/skills/piaac/

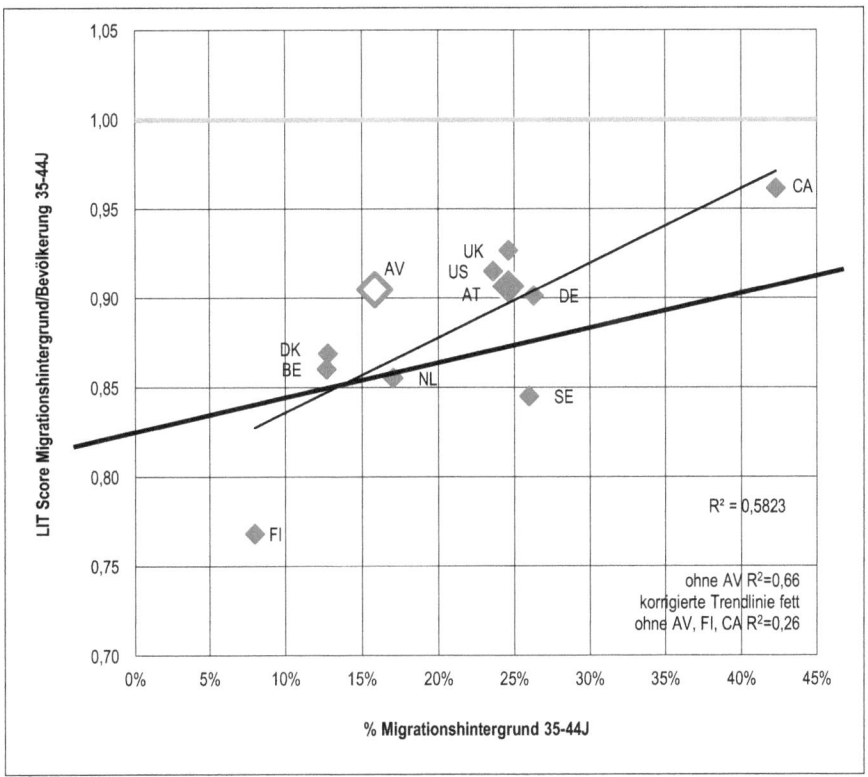

Abbildung 2 ‚Literacy': Relatives Kompetenzniveau der ZuwanderInnen in der mittleren Altersgruppe (35-44-Jährige) im Vergleich zum Ausmaß der Zuwanderung in ausgewählten Ländern

Quelle: OECD-PIAAC, eigene Berechnung und Darstellung (siehe auch ‚Numeracy': http://www.equi.at/material/grafik-web.pdf).
vertikal: Kompetenzniveau=Index des PIAAC-Scores der ZuwanderInnen/Score Bevölkerung; horizontal: Anteil der ZuwanderInnen in gleichaltriger Bevölkerung; AV=Ländermittel; Länderauswahl zum Vergleich von liberalem (CA=Kanada, US=USA, UK=Verein. Königreich), Nordischem (DK=Dänemark, FIN=Finnland, SE=Schweden) und Kontinentalem Regulationsregime (AT hervorgehoben=Österreich, DE=Deutschland, BE=Belgien, NL=Niederlande), die korrigierte Trendlinie (fett) wurde zur Kontrolle ohne die beiden ‚Ausreißer' Kanada und Finnland berechnet.

Alter	% mit Migrationshintergrund nach Altersgruppen			LITERACY Index Kompetenzniveau MigrantInnen/Bev.			NUMERACY Index Kompetenzniveau MigrantInnen/Bev.		
	55 plus	35-44	bis 24	55 plus	35-44	bis 24	55 plus	35-44	bis 24
INT-av	11% <	16% >	12%	0,94 >	0,90 <	0,92	0,94 >	0,90 <	0,92
CND	32% <	42% >	33%	0,95 <	0,96 <	0,98	0,95 <	0,97 <	0,98
US	12% <	24% >	21%	0,84 <	0,92 <	0,97	0,83 <	0,92 <	0,97
UK	11% <	25% >	20%	0,91 <	0,93 <	0,95	0,87 <	0,90 <	0,93
SE	16% <	26% >	21%	0,88 >	0,85 <	0,86	0,88 >	0,84 <	0,86
NL	12% <	17% >	16%	0,88 >	0,86 <	0,93	0,85 >	0,83 <	0,93
DK	7% <	13% <	16%	0,87 =	0,87 <	0,92	0,89 >	0,88 <	0,91
FIN	2% <	8% >	5%	0,91 >	0,77 <	0,81	0,88 >	0,76 <	0,82
DE	24% <	26% >	20%	0,96 >	0,90 =	0,90	0,96 >	0,90 =	0,90
AT	16% <	25% >	19%	0,92 >	0,91 >	0,90	0,91 >	0,90 >	0,89
BE	6% <	13% >	11%	0,90 >	0,86 =	0,86	0,91 >	0,86 >	0,85

Tabelle 3 Kompetenzen von MigrantInnen im Vergleich zur Bevölkerung nach Altersgruppen und Ausmaß der Zuwanderung in den Altersgruppen in ausgewählten Ländern

Quelle: OECD-PIAAC, eigene Berechnung und Darstellung (siehe auch die grafische Darstellung unter: http://www.equi.at/material/grafik-web.pdf).
Kompetenzniveau=Index des PIAAC-Scores der ZuwanderInnen/Score Bevölkerung jeweils in den einzelnen Altersgruppen; Ausmaß der Zuwanderung=Anteil der ZuwanderInnen in gleichaltriger Bevölkerung, Länderauswahl und Kennungen siehe Abbildung 2; INT-av ist der internationale Durchschnitt aller Länder, die an PIAAC beteiligt waren.

zur Bevölkerung ist in Österreich vergleichsweise gering ausgeprägt, in ‚Literacy' liegt Österreich etwa beim internationalen Durchschnitt in einer Gruppe mit dem Vereinigten Königreich, den USA und sehr nahe bei Deutschland (das Kompetenzniveau der ZuwanderInnen liegt bei 90% der Bevölkerung; der Wert in ‚Numeracy' liegt ebenfalls etwa beim internationalen Durchschnitt, sehr knapp bei Deutschland, hinter Kanada und USA)

Tabelle 3 zeigt im ersten Abschnitt den Anteil der ZuwanderInnen in drei Altersgruppen und in den beiden weiteren Abschnitten für ‚Literacy' und ‚Numeracy' die Kompetenzniveaus der jüngeren, mittleren und älteren ZuwanderInnen im Vergleich zur Gesamt-Bevölkerung in Österreich und in den ausgewählten Ländern. Es treten drei unterschiedliche Muster auf, die auch im Zeitverlauf der Zuwanderung von den früher zugewanderten Älteren zu den Jüngeren hin interpretiert werden können.

Erstens zeigt sich im Durchschnitt der PIAAC-Länder in beiden Kompetenzbereichen von den Älteren (55+Jahre) zu den Mittleren ein Rückgang der Kompetenzen bei steigendem Anteil von ZuwanderInnen, und dann wieder ein Anstieg der Kompetenzen zu den Jüngeren (<25 Jahre) bei sinkendem Anteil. Dieses Durchschnitts-Muster reproduziert sich in den Nordischen Ländern und den Niederlanden. In den drei liberalen Ländern (Kanada, USA und UK) zeigt sich im Prinzip die gleiche Dynamik beim Ausmaß der Zuwanderung, aber ein zweites Muster mit durchgängig steigenden Kompetenzen von den Älteren zu den Jüngeren. Österreich zeigt mit Deutschland und in ‚Numeracy' auch in Belgien ein drittes gegenteiliges Muster sinkender oder gleichbleibender Kompetenzen bei ähnlicher Dynamik des Ausmaßes der Migration.

Die Unterscheidung der Altersgruppen ermöglicht einen Bezug zur Periodisierung der Zuwanderung in Österreich. In der älteren Gruppe ist die 1. Generation aus den 1960ern und 1970ern vertreten, in der mittleren Altersgruppe überschneiden sich die 2. Generation aus der ersten Welle und die neuen ZuwanderInnen aus Ex-Jugoslawien und der EU-Erweiterung, in der jüngsten Gruppe schließlich kombinieren sich drei unterschiedliche Gruppen, die 3. Generation aus der ersten Zuwanderungswelle, die 2. Generation aus der Fluchtzuwanderung aus Ex-Jugoslawien und die erste Generation aus der EU-Erweiterung. Österreich zeigt zwar auf den ersten Blick kein vorteilhaftes Entwicklungsmuster, indem die Jüngeren keine positive Entwicklung der Kompetenzen zeigen, jedoch liegt das relative Kompetenzniveau der ZuwanderInnen beim Durchschnitt – die vier Länder Österreich, Deutschland, UK und USA liegen sehr nahe zusammen – und auch die Kompetenzunterschiede zwischen den Altersgruppen sind gering.

Fazit und Ausblick

Dieser Beitrag hat versucht, die Entwicklung des bildungspolitischen Umgangs mit der Zuwanderung in eine breitere Interpretation der österreichischen Bildungspolitik einzubauen. Wichtige Faktoren, die die Schwäche der Politik in diesem Bereich erklären können, ergeben sich – neben den grundlegenden ideologischen Differenzen zwischen Mehrsprachigkeit und Kosmopolitismus einerseits und dem rechtspopulistischen ‚Patriotismus' der deutschen Einsprachigkeit andererseits – aus dem Föderalismus und den damit zusammenhängenden politischen Konfliktpositionen zwischen Wien und den Bundesländern sowie zwischen Stadt und Land. Lücken in den Beobachtungs- und Informationssystemen ergeben sich teilweise aus diesen Strukturen.

Die langfristige Betrachtung hat gezeigt, dass sich die Zuwanderung über mehrere Jahrzehnte seit den 1960ern zunächst langsam aufgebaut und sich dann ab den späten 1980ern verstärkt hat. Anfang der 1990er wurden die legistischen Instrumentarien eingesetzt, es hat jedoch viel zu lange gedauert, bis ein breiterer sachlicher Diskurs über den engen Kreis an ExpertInnen hinaus in der Mitte der 2000er begonnen hat. Erst der Nationale Bildungsbericht 2012 hat die Themen der Mehrsprachigkeit und Zuwanderung als Querschnittsthema proklamiert.

Populistische politische Strömungen haben sich in den 1980ern das Thema der Zuwanderung zunutze gemacht, und begonnen, Konflikte – die sich teilweise aus der Vernachlässigung und Verdrängung des Themas ergeben – zu schüren und zu verstärken, was eine gedeihliche Lösung weiter erschwert. Durch die Flüchtlingswelle hat sich gewissermaßen ein ‚Schock' für dieses Thema zu einem Zeitpunkt ergeben, als die langfristigen integrativen Ansätze und Strategien breitere Aufmerksamkeit erzielt haben und verstärkt wurden. Die schwache Informationsbasis aufgrund der flexiblen und dezentralen Umsetzung der Maßnahmen ermöglicht zudem verschiedenste politische Skandalisierungen von zweifellos vorhandenen Problemen und Defiziten.

Im EU-MIPEX (2015) Monitoring schneidet die österreichische Bildungspolitik nicht sehr gut ab, aber dieses beruht auf sehr groben Indikatoren, die schwer eindeutig zu beantworten sind. Die OECD-Analyse (2015) für die 2000er-Jahre ergibt im internationalen Vergleich hohe Herausforderungen und bei allen Unterschieden und Defiziten im Vergleich zu den teilweise ‚katastrophalen' Diskursen eine moderate Performance. Auch die Kompetenzen von Erwachsenen ergeben ein gemischtes Bild.

Mangelnde deutsche Sprachkenntnisse von ZuwanderInnen haben in den politischen Auseinandersetzungen teilweise eine ‚Sündenbock-Rolle' bekommen, obwohl dies durch Forschungsergebnisse zumindest stark relativiert wird. Da die Konflikte politisch geschürt werden, und dabei der Normierungszwang in den Vordergrund rückt, werden die Lehrpersonen in diese Konflikte unweigerlich hineingezogen und die unterschiedlichen politischen und gesellschaftlichen Positionierungen spiegeln sich in der LehrerInnenschaft. Die Notwendigkeit der Auseinandersetzung mit den grundlegenden Fragen kosmopolitischer und patriotischer Zugänge (Gutmann 2009, v.a. im Epilog S. 309-316) zu Migration, Interkulturalität und Mehrsprachigkeit (Herzog-Punzenberger und Unterwurzacher 2009) stellt sich auch für die Lehrpersonen in ihrer Rolle als BürgerInnen. De facto besteht aktuell die ‚tragische' Situation, dass eben die lange Zeit nicht ausreichend zur Etablierung sinnvoller integrativer und inklusiver Praktiken genutzt wurde und nun die Normierungspolitik aus politischem Kalkül von außen seitens der für ‚Integrationspolitik' verantwortlichen Instanzen die latenten Konflikte im Schulwesen verstärkt.

Mit den Erkenntnissen zu den regionalen Unterschieden beim Schulabbruch muss auch die Selektivitätsdiskussion vertieft werden. Institutionelle Lösungen wie die Gesamtschule oder die Sonderschulen reichen nicht aus, daher muss auch die praktische Anwendung formaler Regelungen beachtet werden. Obwohl die zugrundeliegenden Normen in ganz Österreich formal gleich sind, werden diese offensichtlich sehr unterschiedlich angewendet. Die angesprochene Normierung wird auch unterlaufen. Der Glaube, im Schulwesen würde überall (zumindest annähernd) nach gleichen Kriterien vorgegangen, wird beispielsweise auf Basis der regional stark differierenden Zahlen zur Überrepräsentation von SchülerInnen mit nicht deutscher Umgangssprache in Sonderschulen, die beispielsweise in Wien „nur" 20% aber in Tirol 90% beträgt, eines Besseren belehrt. Eine Systemreform wird also für eine Veränderung nicht ausreichen, vielmehr ist es ebenso sehr notwendig, bei den handelnden Akteuren ein Bewusstsein dafür zu schaffen, welche weitreichenden und lebensbeeinflussenden Konsequenzen mit Selektionsentscheidungen für die betroffenen Jugendlichen verbunden sind. Ob die vermeintlich mit einer homogeneren SchülerInnenstruktur einhergehenden Vorteile im Unterricht die Konsequenzen rechtfertigen, sollte bei dieser Bewusstseinsbildung nicht ausgespart bleiben.

Literatur

Ataç, Ilker/ Lageder, Miriam (2009) Welche Gegenwart, welche Zukunft? Keine/eine/doppelte Integration? Eine qualitative Paneluntersuchung zum Verlauf von Einstellungen und Erwartungen in Bezug auf Familie, Bildung und Beruf bei Wiener Schülerinnen und Schülern mit Migrationshintergrund (Forschungsbericht). Wien: Universität http://homepage.univie.ac.at/ilker.atac/LAF.pdf

Biedermann, Horst/ Weber, Christoph/ Herzog-Punzenberger, Barbara/ Nagel, Arvid (2016) Auf die Mitschüler/innen kommt es an? Schulische Segregation – Effekte der Schul- und Klassenzusammensetzung in der Primarstufe und der Sekundarstufe I in NBB 2015 Bd.2, S.133-173 https://www.bifie.at/wp-content/uploads/2017/05/NBB_2015_Band2_Kapitel_4.pdf

Biffl, Gudrun/ Skrivanek, Isabella (2011) Schule-Migration-Gender. Endbericht. Krems: DUK https://www.donau-uni.ac.at/imperia/md/content/department/migrationglobalisierung/forschung/schule_migration_gender_bmukk-duk.pdf

Biffl, Gudrun/ Skrivanek, Isabella/ Berger, Johannes/ Hofer, Helmut/ Schuh, Ulrich/ Strohner, Ludwig (2010) Potentielle Auswirkungen einer Änderung der österreichischen Migrationspolitik in Richtung qualifizierte Zuwanderung auf das mittel- bis langfristige Wirtschaftswachstum. Forschungsbericht DUK/IHS https://www.wko.at/site/Migration/wko-duk-ihs-gesamtbericht-migrationspolitik.pdf

BMB (2017) Der muttersprachliche Unterricht in Österreich. Statistische Auswertung für das Schuljahr 2015/16. Informationsblätter zum Thema Migration und Schule Nr. 5/2016-17 http://www.schule-mehrsprachig.at/fileadmin/schule_mehrsprachig/redaktion/hintergrundinfo/info5-15-16.pdf

BMUKK/BMWF, Hg. (2008) Sprach- und Sprachunterrichtspolitik in Österreich: Ist-Stand und Schwerpunkte. Länderbericht an den Europarat, Language Education Policy Profiles (LEPP). Wien https://www.coe.int/T/DG4/Linguistic/Source/Austria_CountryReport_final_DE.pdf ; siehe auch editierte reduzierte Fassung http://www.oesz.at/download/publikationen/Themenreihe_4.pdf

Crouch, Colin/ Finegold, David/ Sako, Mari (1999) Are Skills the Answer? The Political Economy of Skill Creation in Advanced Industrial Countries. Oxford: Oxford UP.

de Cillia, Rudolf (2007) Sprachförderung, in Fassmann, Heinz, Hg. 2. Österreichischer Migrations- und Integrationsbericht 2001-2006. Klagenfurt/Celovec: Drava, 251-256 https://erwachsenenbildung.at/downloads/themen/PDF_DeCilla.pdf

Der Standard, 24.9.2017 FPÖ-Politiker Krauss: "Kurz ist nur ein aalglatter Karrierist". Interview P. Mayr http://derstandard.at/2000064663317/FPOe-Politiker-Krauss-Kurz-ist-nur-ein-aalglatter-Karrierist

Grubb, W. Norton/ Lazerson, Marvin (2004) The Education Gospel. The Economic Power of Schooling. Cambridge, MA.: Harvard UP.

Gutmann, Amy (1999) Democratic education. With a new preface and epilogue. Princeton: Princeton University Press https://erwachsenenbildung.at/magazin/16-28/15_lassnigg.pdf

Herzog-Punzenberger, Barbara/ Schnell, Philipp (2012) Die Situation mehrsprachiger Schüler/innen im österreichischen Schulsystem – Problemlagen, Rahmenbedingungen und internationaler Vergleich, in NBB 2012, 229-267 https://www.bmb.gv.at/schulen/sb/nbb_2012_b02_gesamt_23883.pdf?5te6pz

Herzog-Punzenberger, Barbara/ Schnell, Philipp (2014) Austria in Stevens, Peter/Dworkin, Gary (Hg.) The Palgrave Handbook on Race and Ethnic Inequalities in Education. Houndmills: Palgrave MacMillan

Herzog-Punzenberger, Barbara/ Unterwurzacher, Anne (2009) Migration – Interkulturalität – Mehrsprachigkeit. Erste Befunde für das österreichische Bildungswesen, in NBB 2009 Bd.2, 161-182 https://www.bmb.gv.at/schulen/sb/nbb_band2_17992.pdf?61ecac

Lassnigg, Lorenz (2017a) Annex: Migration und Schule in Österreich 2000er Jahre, ein quantitativ-vergleichendes Bild auf Basis von OECD 2015, September 2017, im Internet http://www.equi.at/material/annex-migra.pdf

Lassnigg, Lorenz (2017b) Urban Education in Austria: 'Repression' of the Topic and a 'Reversed' Political Agenda, in: Pink, William T.; Noblit, George W. (eds.), Second International Handbook of Urban Education, 2017, Springer, Cham, Switzerland, pp. 1307-1333 http://www.equi.at/dateien/urban-education-hp.pdf

Lassnigg, Lorenz (2012) Die berufliche Erstausbildung zwischen Wettbewerbsfähigkeit, sozialen Ansprüchen und Lifelong Learning – eine Policy Analyse, in NBB 2012 Bd.2, S. 313-354 Hintergrundbericht http://www.equi.at/dateien/nbb-hintergrund.pdf.

Lassnigg, Lorenz/ Vogtenhuber, Stefan (2015) Challenges in Austrian educational governance revisited. Re-thinking the basic structures, IHS Sociological Series 107 http://www.ihs.ac.at/fileadmin/public/soziologie/pdf/rs107.pdf

Lassnigg, Lorenz/ Bruneforth, Michael/ Vogtenhuber, Stefan (2016) Ein pragmatischer Zugang zu einer Policy-Analyse: Bildungsfinanzierung als Governance-Problem in Österreich, in NBB 2015 Bd.2, S. 305-351 https://www.bifie.at/wp-content/uploads/2017/05/NBB_2015_Band2_Kapitel_8.pdf

Lassnigg, Lorenz/ Vogtenhuber, Stefan (2014) Das österreichische Modell der Formation von Kompetenzen im Vergleich, in: Statistik Austria (Hrsg.), Schlüsselkompetenzen von Erwachsenen – Vertiefende Analysen der PIAAC-Erhebung 2011/12, Statistik Austria, Wien, S. 49-79. Siehe auch den ausführlichen Hintergrundbericht http://www.equi.at/dateien/IHS-PIAAC.pdf

Marx, Karl (1845/1888) Thesen über Feuerbach. Im Internet http://www.mlwerke.de/me/me03/me03_005.htm (1845); http://www.mlwerke.de/me/me03/me03_533.htm (1888)

MiMe (Migration und Mehrsprachigkeit) - Policy Brief Nr. 02 (2016) Die Vielfalt der Familiensprachen. JKU Abteilung für Bildungsforschung und AK Wien, Bildungspolitik http://paedpsych.jku.at/index.php/mimepol2/

MIPEX (2015) Austria, conclusions and recommendations. Im Internet http://www.mipex.eu/austria; siehe auch http://www.mipex.eu/key-findings

OECD (2009) Country Background Report for Austria. OECD Thematic Review on Migrant Education. Paris: OECD http://www.oecd.org/austria/42485003.pdf

OECD (2015) Immigrant Students at School: Easing the Journey towards Integration. Paris: OECD Publishing. http://dx.doi.org/10.1787/9789264249509-en

OEIF (2015) Fact Sheet 18 Migration und Bildung https://integrationsfonds.at/news/detail/article/fact-sheet-18-migration-und-bildung/

Pepelnik, Maria Sarah (2011) Sprachförderung an österreichischen Schulen. Diplomarbeit, Allgemeine und Angewandte Sprachwissenschaft, Univ.Wien.

Rechnungshof (2013) Schüler mit Migrationshintergrund, Antworten des Schulsystems. Bericht des Rechnungshofes, Bund 2013/6, 247-324 http://www.rechnungshof.gv.at/fileadmin/downloads/2013/berichte/teilberichte/bund/Bund_2013_06/Bund_2013_06_4.pdf

Reich, Hans H. (2013) Pädagogische Herausforderungen aus Migration und Umgang mit Migration, in Lassnigg, Lorenz/Laimer, Andrea/Markowitsch, Jörg, Hg., Zukunft der Berufsbildung. Herausforderungen und internationale Lösungsansätze, IHS-Forschungsbericht, Dokumentation der IHS-3s-BMUKK-Veranstaltung 7.12.2012, Wien: IHS, 69-87 http://www.equi.at/dateien/ZukunftBerufsbildung-Fin.pdf

Salchegger, Silvia/ Herzog-Punzenberger, Barbara (2017) Lesekompetenz und sozioökonomischer Status von Jugendlichen mit Migrationshintergrund: Entwicklungen seit dem Jahr 2000 in Österreich, der Schweiz und Deutschland. In Zeitschrift für Bildungsforschung 7(1), 79–100 DOI 10.1007/s35834-016-0172-1, siehe auch S.32 http://www.equi.at/material/annex-migra.pdf

Schabmann, Alfred/ Landerl, Karin/ Bruneforth, Michael/ Schmidt, Barbara Maria (2012) Lesekompetenz, Leseunterricht und Leseförderung im österreichischen Schulsystem. Analysen zur pädagogischenFörderung der Lesekompetenz, in NBB 2012 Bd 2, S.17-69 https://www.bifie.at/wp-content/uploads/2017/05/NBB2012_Band2_Kapitel01_20121217.pdf

Scharinger, Ursula (2013) Förderung von Deutsch als Zweitsprache durch generatives Schreiben auf Basis einer Sprachstandsdiagnose nach USB DaZ in Ö im morphologisch syntaktischen Bereich. Masterarbeit. Deutsch als Fremd- und Zweitsprache. Universität Wien.

Schrodt, Heidi (2014) Sehr gut oder nicht genügend?. Schule und Migration in Österreich. Wien: Molden https://cms.falter.at/falter/rezensionen/buecher/?issue_id=546&item_id=9783854853275

Steiner, Mario/ Pessl, Gabriele/ Bruneforth, Michael (2016) Früher Bildungsabbruch - Neue Erkenntnisse zu Ausmaß und Ursachen, in NBB 2015 Bd.2, S. 175-220 http://www.equi.at/dateien/NBB_2015_Band2_Kapitel_5.pdf

Reziproke Lerneffekte:
Einsichten aus einem europäischen Projekt der Erwachsenenbildung mit ethnischen Minderheiten und MigrantInnen

Gülay Ateş, Christoph Reinprecht

Zusammenfassung

Lernen und das Schaffen von Lernsettings schließt, aus der Perspektive der Interaktionstheorie betrachtet, eine Begegnung der gegenseitigen Annäherung, der gegenseitigen Öffnung, des beiderseitigen Austausches und Verweilens ein. Eine Öffnung und Annäherung an „neue" Lerngruppen kann wechselseitige intendierte und nicht-intendierte Lern- und Reflexionsarbeit auslösen. In Übereinstimmung mit dem ursprünglichen Auftrag von Volkshochschulen boten im Rahmen eines EU (Grundtvig) geförderten Projekts fünf ausgewählte Einrichtungen der Erwachsenbildung in fünf Ländern der europäischen Union Kurse zur Persönlichkeits- und Allgemeinbildung für Angehörige migrantischer und ethnischer Minderheiten an. Die Ergebnisse der wissenschaftlichen Begleitforschung bildeten unter anderem die Grundlage für kontext- und zielgruppengerechte Kursangebote und Lernansätze. Aus der Analyse der quantitativen und qualitativen Erhebung lassen sich zugleich Voraussetzungen und Rahmenbedingungen von (Erwachsenen-) Bildungsangeboten für nicht traditionelle TeilnehmerInnengruppen ableiten. Während aufgezeigt werden kann, dass niederschwellige und lebensnahe Lerninhalte sowohl Lernende als auch Lehrende in ihren Aktivitäten stärken und bereichern können, unterstreichen die Ergebnisse den großen Handlungsbedarf seitens der Kursanbieter hinsichtlich vertrauensbildendender Maßnahmen sowie der Adaption der Lernziele und Lernzwecke an die Gegebenheiten und Lernwelten der „neuen" Zielgruppen.

Förderung des lebenslanges Lernen als Ziel von Erwachsenenbildungseinrichtungen

Volkshochschuleinrichtungen hatten ursprünglich den Auftrag, Bildungsungleichheiten zwischen den Gesellschaftsmitgliedern zu verringern. Die Bildungsangebote sollten *„die Erwachsenen dazu befähigen (...), ihre Lebenswelt zu verstehen, politische Zusammenhänge zu beurteilen, berufliche und gesellschaftliche Aufgaben erfüllen zu können sowie übergeordnet persönliche Kompetenzen weiterzu-*

entwickeln" (Mandl et al. 2004). Ziel war es, Personen mit fehlenden Grundqualifikationen und bildungsferne Randgruppen zu integrieren und ihnen eine nachhaltige gesellschaftliche Teilhabe zu ermöglichen.

Analysen von Kursteilnehmenden (vgl. etwa Reinprecht 2003) zeichnen für die Gegenwart ein etwas differenzierteres Bild ab. Sind es doch insbesondere Mittelschichtsangehörige, die im Zuge der Persönlichkeitsweiterbildung oder Freizeitgestaltung Kurse in Anspruch nehmen. Die Aneignung von (neuen) Techniken zum Pflegen von Hobbies (Malen, Bildhauerei, Sport etc.) oder Kultur (Sprach- und Wissenskurse) entfaltet ihren Nutzen im Privaten einer spezifischen bildungsschichtzugehörigen Gruppe.

Der Benachteiligung von großen Bevölkerungsanteilen bei der Fort- und Weiterbildung im Erwachsenenalter Rechnung tragend, wurde auf europäischer Ebene mit dem Grundtvig Förderprogramm auf politischer Ebene eine Initiative zum Perspektivenwechsel gesetzt. Angeregt durch diese Maßnahme hat sich, so Alheit (2009), ein Diskursambiente entwickelt, das Programmen und Angeboten von Erwachsenenbildungseinrichtungen einen zentralen Stellenwert in der Vermittlung von anschlussfähigem Wissen beimisst. Einerseits wurden zunehmend die Lernenden in den Fokus der Programme gerückt und anderseits die Förderung von Programmen für schwer erreichbare und marginalisierte Gruppen als vorrangig gesetzt (Rothe 2009). In Verbindung mit neuen Lernansätzen in der Erwachsenenbildung wird die strukturelle Koppelung zunehmend thematisiert. Dies hat zur Folge, dass institutionell unterstützende Lernansätze an einer *„Stärkung und Aktivierung eigener Ressourcen"* (Ateş und Reinprecht 2015) interessiert sind.

Die folgenden Ausführungen fußen auf Einsichten einer sozialwissenschaftlichen Begleitforschung des Grundtvig-Projekts Enter[1], das im Sinne der migrationssoziologischen Perspektive die stimulierenden Bildungs- und Lernprozesse, die im Zuge der Arbeitsmigration in Gang gebracht werden, zum Gegenstand hatte. Eine der forschungsleitenden Fragen lautete: Was passiert, wenn strukturiert organisierte Bildungseinrichtungen auf nicht institutionell geförderte individualbiographische Lernende stoßen? Neben dem Auftrag einer Potentialanalyse bestand das Ziel der Begleitforschung auch in der Förderung von Bewusstseins- und Reflexionsarbeit mit Hilfe von wissenschaftlichen Erhebungsmethoden, so dass gegensei-

---

[1] Das von Einrichtungen der Erwachsenenbildung in fünf europäischen Ländern initiierte Projekt und vom Grundtvig Lifelong Learning Programm geförderte Projekt ENTER wurde vom Institut der Soziologie der Universität Wien sozialwissenschaftlich begleitet (Reinprecht und Ates 2010). Das Akronym ENTER (Adult Educational Development for Migrants and Ethnic Minorities) steht für die Ansprüche emanzipatorischer Bildungsarbeit: Niederschwelligkeit, Aktivierung, Zielgruppenorientierung (vgl. Volkshochschule Tirol/ Verein Multikulturell 2009). Ausgangspunkt bildete zum einen die These, dass Bildungsarbeit für die gesellschaftliche Partizipation im Allgemeinen wie auch für eine aktive und subjektiv als erfolgreich wahrgenommene Lebensführung im Speziellen einen essentiellen Beitrag zu leisten vermag, zum anderen die auf Vorgängerstudien beruhende Diagnose, dass der Zugang zu den Einrichtungen der Erwachsenenbildung durch erhebliche Barrieren erschwert ist (für Österreich bzw. Wien vgl. Reinprecht und Pohn-Weidinger 2005). Gudrun Biffl begleitete dieses Projekt als Expertin und Evaluatorin (vgl. Biffl 2009).

tige Annäherungen, Veränderungsfähigkeiten und Wirksamkeit auf beiden Seiten, der Lernenden und Erwachsenenbildungseinrichtungen, herausgearbeitet werden konnten (u.a. Bönsch 1991, S.161). Den Erwachsenenbildungseinrichtungen kam in diesem Projekt nicht zuletzt deshalb eine Schlüsselrolle zu, da sie in früheren Zeiten Institutionen waren mit einem Angebot an zukunftsweisenden gesellschaftlichen Lernfeldern, verbunden mit dem Ziel, Erwachsenen über den Erwerb von Bildungsinhalten und Qualifikationen hinaus eine gesellschaftliche und dabei stets auch klassen- und generationsübergreifende Teilhabe zu ermöglichen.

Biographizität als Ansatz für Lernprozesse im Erwachsenenalter

Migration und lebenslanges Lernen werden selten mit der ersten Generation ArbeitsmigrantInnen in Verbindung gebracht. Dabei wird durch die Wanderung über Landesgrenzen hinweg eine Öffnung in mehrfacher Hinsicht begünstigt. Eine Öffnung findet sowohl auf institutioneller und organisatorischer Ebene bei Einrichtungen der (Erwachsenen-)Bildungsarbeit als auch auf individueller Ebene statt. Neben den nicht-institutionellen informellen Lernerfolgen kommen bildungspolitische Programme zum Tragen.

Während lange Zeit kompensatorische Bildungsangebote dominierten, welche die Angehörigen der ersten Generation ArbeitsmigrantInnen (und deren Nachfahren) primär als Träger von Bildungsdefiziten wahrnehmen (siehe dazu u.a. Reinprecht und Pohn-Weidinger 2015), rücken heute vermehrt auch andere Lernsettings und Lerninhalte in den Vordergrund, die Fertigkeiten, Qualifikationen und (auch informelle sowie non-formale Lern-)Erfahrungen anerkennen. Die Implementierung von verpflichtenden Integrationskursen mit Sprachbildungs- und Landeskundeprogrammen bedeutet demgegenüber neuerlich eine Stärkung der kompensatorischen Ausrichtung und unterstreicht damit die sozialisierende und disziplinierende Funktion von Erwachsenenbildung.

Wenn der Wert und die Funktion von Bildung aus der Perspektive der Befähigungsdimension betrachtet werden, rücken die Dimensionen der Lebensqualität und die Erfüllung von Autonomieansprüchen sowie eine reflexive Steuerung des Handelns in den Mittelpunkt von Bildungsangeboten. Dieser Perspektivenwechsel eröffnet den Raum für einen diskursiven Lernprozess von Lehrenden und Lernenden. Sie begünstigen eine produktive und differenzierte Betrachtung bzw. Auseinandersetzung von Bildungsunterschieden, was wiederum in dynamische und unkonventionelle Lernangebote münden kann (vgl. Ateş und Reinprecht 2015).

Wenn Erwachsenenbildungsanbieter und Lehrende die Kursplanungen, -inhalte und -gestaltung an die Lebenswelten der Lernenden anzupassen vermögen, rückt der Blick auf das Prozessgeschehnis, weshalb die Lerngruppendynamik und dynamische Lehrverfahren bei der Planungs- und Verfahrensebene berücksichtigt werden (Tietgens 1991). In solchen Lernmodulen finden Transaktionen zwischen Lehrenden und Lernenden statt und werden aktiv gefördert. Demnach nehmen bei

„transaktionalen Lernmodellen" fachspezifische bzw. inhaltliche Lernziele eine untergeordnete Rolle ein. Knowles, Holton und Swanson (2005, S. 72) schreiben in diesem Zusammenhang:

„(...) adults have a readiness to learn those things that they need to know in order to cope effectively with real-life situations; adults are life-centered in their orientation to learning; and adults are more responsive to internal motivators than external motivators."

Das Projekt Enter -
Adult Educational Needs of Migrants and Ethnic Minorities

Methode, Design und Stichprobe

Nach Knowles, Holton und Swanson (2005, S.3) funktionieren Erwachsenenbildungskonzepte am besten, wenn sie sich in der Praxis an der Einzigartigkeit der Lernenden und der Lernsituation orientieren *(„when it is adapted to fit the uniqueness of the learners and the learning situation")*. Erwachsenenbildung aus der Perspektive von Lernenden zielt darauf ab, Wissensbedarf (1), Selbstkonzept, Vorerfahrungen (3), Lernbereitschaft (4), Lernorientierung (5) und Lernmotivation (6) zu erfassen.

Genau diese Punkte mittels Fragebögen einzufangen und auf die Kursangebote zu übertragen, war unter anderem einer der ersten Schritte in der Umsetzung des Enter-Projekts. Generelles Projektziel war es, in fünf europäischen Ländern Lernende aus verschiedenen migrantischen und ethnischen Minderheiten zu erreichen und für neu entwickelte Kursangebote zu gewinnen, um deren Teilhabe in der Gesellschaft zu stärken. Demzufolge wurde in den Jahren 2008-2009 in Kooperation mit der Projektleitung und den fünf Projektpartnern[2] in einer ersten Phase der Begleitforschung ein standardisierter Fragebogen entwickelt, mit dessen Hilfe eine Reihe von projektrelevanten Themen wie Bildungsbedürfnisse und Bildungsmotivation, Interesse und Teilnahme an Erwachsenenbildungsmaßnahmen, informelle Aktivitäten und alltagsbezogene Ressourcen sowie die Einstellung zu verschiedenen Lebensbereichen erhoben wurde[3]. Nach Ermittlung der Ressourcen und Inte-

---

[2] Deutschland: IEIE – International Education Information Exchange e.V., Stuttgart. Frankreich: Elele – Migrations et Cultures de Turquie, Paris. Österreich: Volkshochschule Tirol, Innsbruck. Rumänien: ANUP – Asociaţia Naţională a Universităţilor Populare, Bucharest. Slowakei: ANNWIN – Centrum na podporu a rozvoj ľudského potenciálu, Bratislava.

[3] Befragt wurden, entsprechend dem Projektdesign, Personen mit einem türkisch-sprachigen, bosnischen oder Roma Hintergrund im Alter von 40 bis 60 Jahren. Insgesamt wurden 289 Personen mittels des quantitativen Fragebogens befragt, 69 Interviews wurden in Österreich (Innsbruck), jeweils 59 in Frankreich (Paris) und in der Slowakei (Bratislava), 57 in Deutschland (Stuttgart) und 45 in Rumänien (Bukarest) durchgeführt.

ressen wurden in jedem Land zwei Erwachsenbildungskurse[4] ausgearbeitet und angeboten. Die eigens hierfür entwickelten Module wurden in einer zweiten Runde mittels qualitativer Fragebögen für Lernende, Lehrende und Organisationen evaluiert.

Einsichten aus der Befragung

Motive und Interessen der Beteiligung an Angeboten der Erwachsenenbildung

In Bezug auf die Motivation, an einer Weiter- oder Fortbildung teilzunehmen, unterscheiden die Antwortkategorien zwischen sozialen und beruflichen Gründen sowie Neugier, wobei das Antwortverhalten unter den Befragten zwischen den Ländern kaum divergiert. Unter den Befragten in Österreich und Deutschland dominieren eher berufliche Gründe (62% und 40%), gefolgt von Neugier (40% resp. 30%) und sozialen Gründen (34% resp. 26%). In Frankreich wurden die beruflichen (35%) und sozialen Gründe (34%) gleich oft genannt, Neugierde spielt bei 26% der Befragten eine Rolle. Unter den Befragten in der Slowakei sind alle drei Antwortmöglichkeiten mit einem guten Drittel besetzt, in Rumänien würde ein Großteil der Befragten aus beruflichen Gründen, gefolgt von Neugierde sowie zuletzt aus sozialen Gründen an solchen Kursen teilnehmen. In Bezug auf aktuelle und vergangene Partizipation an Fort- und Weiterbildungskursen zeigen sich die in Frankreich interviewten Personen am aktivsten (24% resp. 36%). Nahezu drei Viertel der Befragten teilen mit, auch an nicht berufsbezogenen Kursen interessiert zu sein. 15 von 20 Befragten, die in den letzten zwei Jahren an einem Kurs teilgenommen haben, antworten, dass es sich hierbei um einen Sprachkurs gehandelt habe.

Auf die Frage, zu welchen praktischen Fähigkeiten die Befragten gerne einen Kurs besuchen möchten, gaben in Österreich 71% der Befragten einen Sprachkurs, 74% Computer, Internet und Emailkurs an. In Frankreich verkündeten 91% Interesse an einem Sprachkurs, 76% an Lesen und Schreiben und 70% an einem Kurs zum Erwerb von Fähigkeiten im Umgang mit Computer, Internet und E-Mails. In der Slowakei interessierten sich 56% der RespondentInnen für einen Computer-, Internet- und E-Mailkurs, gefolgt von Kochen, Krankenbetreuung und Pflege. In Rumänien gab es keine große Interessensbekundung in Hinblick auf die abgefragten Tätigkeiten.

---

[4] Deutschland: Photographie und Nordic Walking Kurse. Frankreich: Computer/Internet und Schauspiel Kurse. Österreich: Malen und Gymnastik Kurse. Rumänien: Computer/Internet und Blumengesteck Kurse. Slowakei: Persönlichkeitsentwicklung/Kommunikation und Gesundheit, Nahrung und Kochen Kurse.

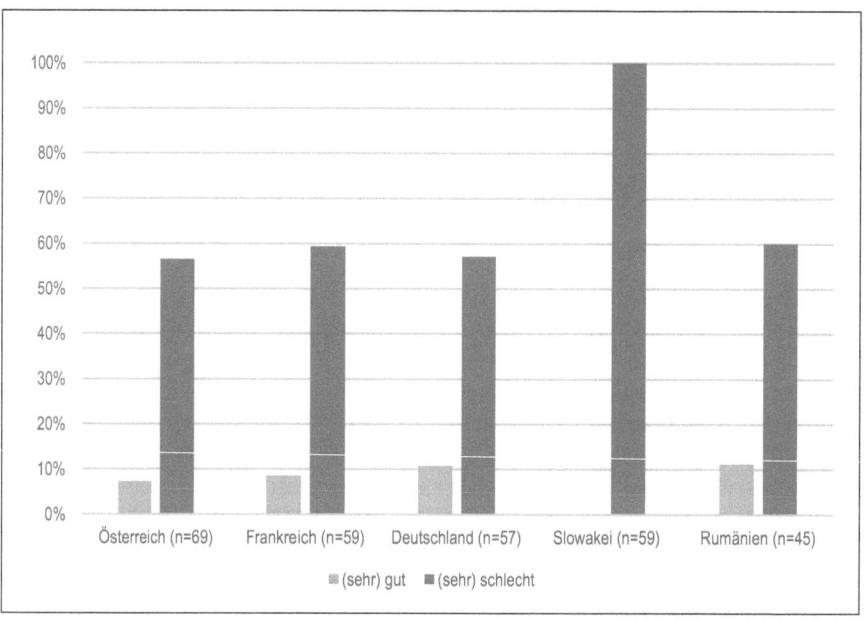

Abbildung 1 Informiertheitsgrad über Bildungsangebote aufgeschlüsselt nach Ländern.
Quelle: Eigene Daten, eigene Darstellung.

Erhebliche Informationsdefizite

Informationsdefizite bilden, den Befragungsergebnissen zufolge, die größte Barriere im Zugang zu Bildungsangeboten. In Bezug auf die Frage, wie gut sich die Personen über das Angebot an Erwachsenenbildungskursen informiert fühlen, teilen in der Slowakei ausnahmslos alle Befragten mit, sich (sehr) schlecht informiert zu fühlen. In Rumänien und Frankreich trifft dies auf jeweils 60% der Befragten zu, in Deutschland auf 58% und in Österreich auf 57%.

Der ungenügende oder überhaupt fehlende Zugang zu Information korrespondiert mit dem Eindruck vieler Befragter, von der gesellschaftlichen Teilhabe ausgeschlossen zu sein. Für keinen anderen Lebensbereich zeigen die Ergebnisse eine so starke Diskrepanz zwischen Wichtigkeit und Zufriedenheit.

Die Bedeutung der lebensweltlichen Einbettung von Bildungsangeboten

Die intrinsische Motivation und damit einhergehend das Interesse, Gelerntes über den Kurs hinaus anzuwenden und sich auch Zeit zu nehmen, war insbesondere bei jenen Teilnehmenden geweckt, die eine Verbindung mit ihren eigenen Bedürfnissen und Alltagsaktivitäten herstellen konnten. So sind mittleres Interesse bis hin zu Desinteresse in Österreich von Malkursteilnehmenden und bei Photographie-Kursen in Deutschland geäußert worden. Dahingegen gab es hohe Zufriedenheit und damit einhergehendes Interesse in den Sport und Gymnastikkursen (Deutschland und Österreich) und in den Computer und Internet Einführungskursen (Frankreich und Rumänien). Bei letzteren machten sich insbesondere die Autonomiebestrebungen der älteren Generationen bemerkbar. So waren Äußerungen wie folgende keine Seltenheit[5]:

„Ich möchte mit dem Sportkurs meine Kondition verbessern; Selbstvertrauen finden um mich richtig ausdrücken zu können; in der Gesellschaft zeigen, dass es mich gibt; Freundschaft und Kommunikation mit anderen Menschen [knüpfen Anm. d. A.] (...).
(Zitat einer Kursteilnehmerin in Österreich)

"The experience, that one can still learn something and it is good"
(Zitat eines Kursteilnehmers in Deutschland)

"This course opened to me a whole world"
(Zitat eines Kursteilnehmers in Rumänien)

"From now one I do not ask my nephew to show me at the computer how to find information."
(Zitat einer Kursteilnehmerin in Rumänien)

Künstlerische Aktivitäten mit einem starken Alltagsbezug, wie in Frankreich mittels Schauspielunterricht, boten die Gelegenheit einer reflexiven Auseinandersetzung mit dem eigenen Körper, der gesprochenen Sprache und das Wirken auf andere (z.B. bei Behördengängen). Insbesondere kopftuchtragende Frauen, die der französischen Sprache nicht ganz mächtig waren, wurden in Bezug auf das eigene Wirken hin geschult. In Rumänien wurde das Alltagsgeschäft (Blumenverkaufen) der Roma verbunden mit einem Floristikkurs, der als berufliche Weiterbildungsmaßnahme gesehen werden kann. Das Lernen von Arrangements, Ästhetik und Stil stand somit im großen Zusammenhang mit der Arbeitswelt und der Lebenskontexte der Zielgruppe in Rumänien und führte zu einer großen Zufriedenheit mit den Kursen. Obwohl in der Slowakei zuerst klassische Computer und Internetkurse im Interesse der Wissensvermittlung standen, wurden im Zuge dieses Projektes und den Ergebnissen der ersten Erhebungswelle zwei Kurse zur Bewältigung von Alltagsproblemen angeboten. Hierzu zählten die Kurse zur Persönlichkeitsentwicklung bzw. Kommunikation und Gesundheit, Nahrung und Kochen.

Tagesstrukturelle Passung der Bildungsangebote

Ein interessantes Resultat zeigt sich in Hinblick auf die Frage nach der Tagesstruktur und den darin eingebetteten Aktivitäten. Wenig erstaunlich kontrastiert der eher gleichförmige Tagesablauf von Personen mit Vollzeiterwerbsarbeit im Vergleich zu jenem von Personen mit einer eher durchbrochenen Tagesstruktur und ohne kontinuierliche Erwerbstätigkeit. In diesem Zusammenhang spiegeln die

---

[5] Die Interviews wurden in der jeweiligen Landessprache geführt und anschließend ins Englische übersetzt.

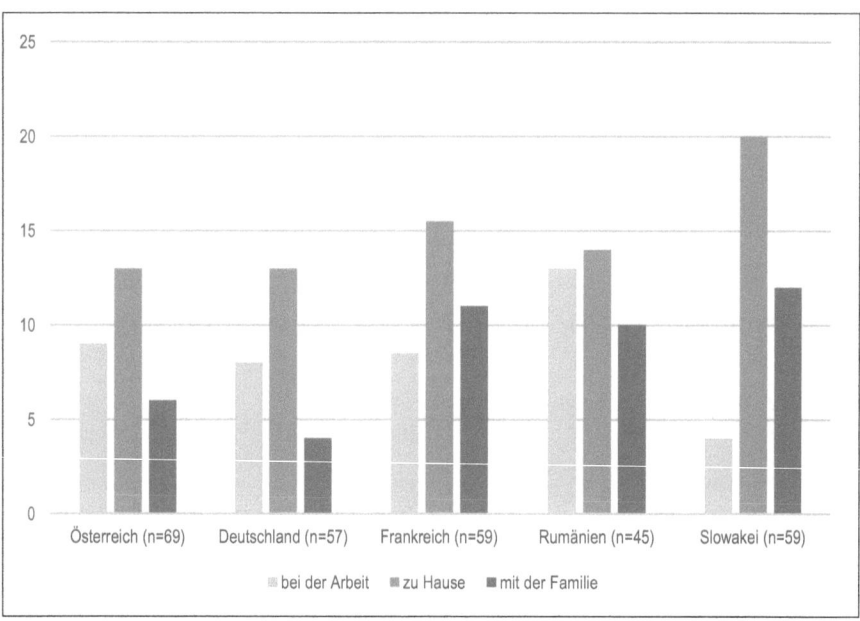

Abbildung 2 Ausgewählte Aspekte der Tagesstruktur, Aktivitäten und Aufenthaltsort aufgeschlüsselt nach Ländern (Medianstunden).

Quelle: Eigene Daten, eigene Darstellung.

Ergebnisse der Befragung eindrücklich die vom Sozial- und professionellem Status beeinflusste Einbettung der Erwerbsarbeit in den Gesamtzusammenhang des Alltagslebens wider. Zeit als frei verfügbare Ressource zur Vereinbarkeit von Bildungsinteressen, Familienzeit und Arbeit wurde in allen Ländern im Zuge der qualitativen Erhebungsphase als notwendige Ressource angeführt.

Bei der Gestaltung der Kursangebote wurde deshalb versucht, die Tagesstrukturen und damit einhergehende Verfügbarkeit von (Frei-)Zeit, aber auch Aufenthaltsorte und, sofern möglich, familiäre Verpflichtungen zu berücksichtigen. So etwa wurden in Deutschland die eigens für Frauen konzipierten „Nordic Walking" Kurse auf den Vormittag verlegt, wenn die Kinder in der Schule oder im Kindergarten waren. Zusätzlich konnte eine Kinderbetreuung während der Kurszeiten angeboten werden, so dass eine institutionelle, räumliche und zeitliche Teilhabe gewährleistet werden konnte.

> *"The course still works indoors with a constant team of seven Turkish women and some additional three or four who attend on a less regular base due to family obligation. Our participants found it more suitable to have the course in the morning when older children are at school. For the younger children we offer a baby-care service which allows the women to attend the course and to know that their little ones are well taken care of."*
>
> (Zitat aus dem Organisationsteam in Deutschland)

Örtliche Nähe und Erreichbarkeit

Nicht nur die Tagesstruktur, auch die örtliche Erreichbarkeit bildet eine immer wieder genannte Voraussetzung für die Inspruchnahme von Bildungsangeboten. Dies bezieht sich etwa auf die Frage des Transports zum und vom Veranstaltungsort:

> *„This includes sometimes also to pick up an old 65 years old Turkish lady from home and bring her to the course."*
> (Zitat aus dem Organisationsteam in Österreich)

In der Slowakei wiederum wurde anhand der Rückmeldungen rasch ersichtlich, dass Bildungsangebote von der Roma Gemeinschaft am besten angenommen werden und funktionieren, wenn sie die Lebenswelten der Teilnehmenden berücksichtigen und „wohnortsnah" stattfinden. Niederschwelligkeit bedeutete hier, dass die Kurse in den Wohnquartieren der Roma Community und den dort befindlichen Gemeinschaftsräumen durchgeführt wurden.

> *„The low threshold approach was very useful, it would be plenty of obstacles for them to come for the course e.g. to other place. The necessity to invite them each time was something special, as if they would not trust that we would really come again to spend the time with them, so we had to come and say we are here and you are invited, this would not be possible if it is on other place. There is big barrier between Roma and the community workers (...). "*
> (Zitat aus dem Organisationsteam in der Slowakei)

Während die einen die Gelegenheit nutzten, in neue Räume und andere Welten eintauchen zu können, brauchten andere Gruppen wiederum die gewohnte Umgebung, um Vertrauen zu den Anbietern und Lehrenden fassen zu können.

Erfolgsfaktoren: Alltagsrelevanz, Vertrauensbildung und Reziprozität

In nahezu allen Ländern wurde das Aufbauen von Vertrauen als zentrale Voraussetzung für Erfolg thematisiert. In den Vertrauensaufbau zu investieren, wurde nicht zuletzt im Zusammenhang mit den von vielen TeilnehmerInnen geteilten Ausschlusserfahrungen in der Majoritätsgesellschaft als notwendig erachtet. Auf dieser Grundlage konnten Kurse auch über die Projektlaufzeit hinaus weitergeführt werden, entwickelte sich also Nachhaltigkeit.

> *"The good news are: the women will continue with the course even after the end of the official piloting phase. We found AOK Stuttgart, Germany's National Health Service, as sponsor. They have been providing the Nordic Walking instructor so far for the piloting (Silke, a qualified Nordic Walking, health and nutrition instructor and expert) and Silke will continue the work with the Turkish women now after the Easter break. Thus, our course will become part of AOK's mainstream adult education provision in Germany."*
> (Zitat aus dem Organisationsteam in Deutschland)

"The piloting in Innsbruck is a huge success, because we have now more interested people in our courses and a lot of them asking for new courses like swimming too. Therefore, we'll run a second turn of courses and try to evaluate them too." (Zitat aus dem Organisationsteam in Österreich)

Vertrauensbildung gelingt auf der Grundlage von Reziprozität, was voraussetzt, dass die Teilhabe an Bildungsangeboten weder ausschließlich durch Marktprinzipien (Kosten) noch durch administrative Zwänge (Pflicht) begründet ist. Reziprozität (beruhend auf den Prinzipien von Gabe und Gabentausch) erfüllt eine zentrale gesellschaftliche Funktion in Hinblick auf die Begründung und Schaffung von sozialen Anerkennungsverhältnissen, wobei diese im Kontext der (Erwachsenen-)Bildungsarbeit in spezifischer Weise institutionell gerahmt ist (Caille 2008). In der Literatur werden Freiwilligkeit, Empathie und positive Reziprozität als Grundlage für die Schaffung von Solidarität (als Anerkennungsverhältnis) angesehen (vgl. Honneth 1992). Wildt und Wildt (2017) bezeichnen Gabentausch als „test of humanity": „als Probe und Ausdruck der Humanität des jeweiligen Gegenüber („Sie sind wie ich/wie wir")". Der aktuelle Kontext, der nicht nur durch eine wachsende soziale und kulturelle Heterogenität der Lernenden und Lehrenden, sondern auch durch eine programmatische „Verlagerung von Lehre zu Lernen" (ebenda) gekennzeichnet ist, unterstreicht diesen Bedeutungswandel von Bildung als performativen Prozess (Wulf & Zirfas 2006). Das Enter-Projekt schuf einen Rahmen für einen in diesem Sinn gegenseitigen Lernprozess. Für die Lehrenden implizierte dies die Erkenntnis einer hohen Motivation und eines ausgeprägten Lernwillens seitens der teilnehmenden Angehörigen migrantischer und ethnischer Minderheiten.

"I learnt that older migrants have a need to learn and are willing to learn." (Zitat einer Lehrenden in Deutschland)

"I learnt, that the women are interested in sportive activities. The women are willed to learn" (Zitat einer Lehrenden in Deutschland)

"I have learned they are very warm and grateful people. There is a general impression that Roma are not grateful for the help. My experience was opposite. It was about mutual giving and receiving. It was part of the meta skills we were able to develop as team of trainers." (Zitat einer Lehrenden in der Slowakei)

„*I have learned there is absolute shortness in any services for this group of people, no willingness to develop some and really systematically solve their situation.*" (Zitat einer Lehrenden in der Slowakei)

Zusammenfassung und Fazit

Migration als biographischer Einschnitt und Wandel, als Erfahrungszusammenhang von Kontinuität von früh Angeeignetem *und* Bruch mit Gewohntem, als

Loslassen und Einlassen auf Neues, folglich als ein Prozess der Aktivierung von individueller bildungsbiografischer Lernfähigkeit (im Sinne des informalen, non-formalen[6] oder impliziten Lernens) war der Ansatzpunkt des Enter-Projekts. Auf Grundlage einer Erhebung bildungsbezogener Motive, Interessen und Bedürfnisse wurden kontext- und zielgruppengerechte Kursangebote und Lernansätze entwickelt und umgesetzt. Die Analysen der qualitativen Erhebung nach Abschluss der Kurse verweisen auf wichtige Voraussetzungen und Rahmenbedingungen der (Erwachsenen-) Bildungsarbeit im Kontext von Migration und ethnischer Minderheiten. Auf folgende Aspekte soll zusammenfassend noch einmal hingewiesen werden:

- Lerninhalte bedürfen einer lebensweltlichen Relevanz
- Niederschwelligkeit bezieht nicht nur materielle Aspekte ein (Erschwinglichkeit), sondern auch eine zeitliche (Anpassung an die Tagesstruktur) und räumliche Dimension (Erreichbarkeit; Nähe zum Wohnort)
- Es fehlt an zugänglicher Information; Informationen erreichen jedoch nur sozial eingebettet ihr Ziel
- Lernen beruht auf einer Vertrauensbeziehung, dieses aufzubauen ist insbesondere aufgrund der vielfach negativen Erfahrungen mit Einrichtungen der Dominanzgesellschaft essentiell
- Lernen beruht wesentlich auf Reziprozität (Gabe und Gabentausch) und sollte unter dem Gesichtspunkt von Bildung als performativer Prozess gestaltet werden.

Neben diesen Aspekten wurde in allen beobachteten Lernkontexten zurückgemeldet, dass in der inhaltlichen und organisationalen Planung und Gestaltung ausreichend Zeit und Raum für das Einbringen und den Austausch von persönlichen Belangen und privaten Problemen zu berücksichtigen sind. Im Vergleich zu herkömmlichen Bildungsteilnehmenden, vor allem jenen aus der bildungsaffinen Mittelschicht, kommen in den Lernkontexten und -gruppen zahlreiche aktuelle und akute Themen, oftmals von tiefer existentieller und emotionaler Bedeutung, auf, die den Lernprozess nachhaltig beeinflussen können und seitens der Lehrenden spezielle Kompetenzen erfordern. Dazu gehören neben Empathie und Situationsflexibilität vor allem auch ein weites Spektrum an Wissen über die Kontexte und Lebenslage der TeilnehmerInnen. So eröffnete sich im Zuge des Fotokurses mit bosnischen Teilnehmenden ein Einblick in familiäre Migrationsabläufe, die mit einer ethnografisch-psychologisch geschulten Heranführung (biographischer Ansatz, oral history, Traumabewältigungsstrategien) an die Aufarbeitung von Familiengeschichten einhergingen. In der Slowakei wurde den Lehrenden schnell bewusst, dass Themenkomplexe wie Traumata, psychische Probleme oder auch Menschenrechtsverletzungen und Präventionsmaßnahmen hinsichtlich (physischer) Gewalterfahrungen ein Schulungsdesiderat darstellen. Die entscheidende

---

[6] Genauere Definitionen zur Unterscheidung siehe Kommission der Europäischen Gemeinschaften 2000: Memorandum über Lebenslanges Lernen, SEK (2000) 1832, Brüssel

Herausforderung für die involvierten Lehrenden (wie auch für die Lernenden) bestand darin, sich auf eine positive Reziprozität mit den Teilnehmenden einzulassen, damit sich auf diese Weise ein Kurs zugleich als ein Raum für die Schaffung und Stärkung von Anerkennungsverhältnissen konstituieren kann.

Die Projektevaluation hat, in Übereinstimmung mit Diduck et al. (2013, S. 8), positive Effekte auf die Ich-Stärkung der Kursteilnehmenden zu Tage gebracht. Sehr positiv wurden die Kurse vor allem dann wahrgenommen, wenn sie offen waren für das Einbringen und den Austausch von Erfahrungshorizonte und Lebenswirklichkeiten; dann förderten und begünstigten sie in besonderen Maße *"the understanding of ourselves, others, and the social norms of the community or society in which we live"* (Cranton 2002, S. 64).

Schließlich bewirkte das aktive Herantreten an ethnische Minderheiten und MigrantInnen bei den beteiligten Bildungsanbietern und Lehrenden eine Reflexion eigener Normierungen und Wahrnehmungsmuster. Dies stimulierte die Auseinandersetzung mit eigenen Vorurteilen und Befangenheiten (Newman 2012, S. 51) und setzte auf diese Weise Prozesse normativen Lernens in Gang (Baird, Plummer, Haug, and Huitema 2014).

Literatur

Alheit, P. (2009). "Diskurspolitik": Lebenslanges Lernen als postmodernes Machtspiel?. In Alheit, P. & Felden, H. von (Hg.), Lebenslanges Lernen und erziehungswissenschaftliche Biographieforschung. Konzepte und Forschung im europäischen Diskurs. Wiesbaden, 77-88.

Ates, G. & Reinprecht, C. (2015). Migration als Bildungsprozess. In: Faschingeder, G. & Kolland, F. (Hg.), Bildung und ungleiche Entwicklung. Globale Konvergenzen und Divergenzen in der Bildungswelt. Wien, new academic press, 175-187

Baird, J.; Plummer, R.; Haug, C. & Huitema, D. (2014). Learning effects of interactive decision-making processes for climate change adaptation. *Global Environmental Change, 27*, 51-63.

Biffl, G. (2009). ENTER – Adult Educational Development for Migrant and Ethnic Minorities. Project report, funded by the European Commission as part of the Grundtvig Lifelong Learning Programme. Monograph Series Migration and Development, Krems (Edition Donau-Universität Krems).

Bönsch, M. (1991). Adressatenorientierte Didaktik - entwickelt primaer als Planungs-und Beratungsdidaktik, sekundaer als Vermittlungsdidaktik. In Tietgens, H. (Hg.). Didaktische Dimensionen der Erwachsenenbildung. Studienbibliothek für Erwachsenenbildung Bd. 2. Frankfurt, Main: Pädagogische Arbeitsstelle, Didaktische Dimensionen der Erwachsenenbildung, 158-167.

Caille, A. (2008). Anthropologie der Gabe. Frankfurt/M: Suhrkamp.

Cranton, P. (2002). Teaching for transformation. New Directions for Adult and Continuing Education, 93, 63-71.

Diduck, A. P., Pratap, D., Sinclair, A. J., & Deane, S. (2013). Perceptions of impacts, public participation, and learning in the planning, assessment and mitigation of two hydroelectric projects in Uttarakhand, India. Land Use Policy, 33, 170-182.

Honneth, A. (1992). Kampf um Anerkennung. Frankfurt a. M.

Knowles, M., Holton, E., & Swanson, R. (2005). The adult learner: The definitive classic in adult education and human resource development. Elsevier, (6th ed.).

Mandl, Heinz ; Kopp, Birgitta ; Dvorak, Susanne. (2004). Aktuelle theoretische Ansätze und empirische Befunde im Bereich der Lehr-Lern-Forschung. Deutsches Institut für Erwachsenenbildung, Bonn, https://www.die-bonn.de/esprid/dokumente/doc-2004/mandl04_01.pdf.

Newman, M. (2010). Calling Transformative Learning Into Question. Some Mutinous Thoughts. Adult Education Quarterly 62(1), 36 – 55.

Reinprecht, C. (2003). Merkmale und Sicherung der Programmqualität im Angebot der Wiener Volkshochschulen. Unveröffentlichter Forschungsbericht. Wien: Institut für Soziologie.

Reinprecht, C. & Pohn-Weidinger, A (2005). Migrantinnen und Migranten in Wiener Einrichtungen der Erwachsenenbildung. Unveröffentlichter Forschungsbericht.Wien: Institut für Soziologie.

Rothe, Daniela. (2009). Lebenslanges Lernen als Regierungsprogramm: Der deutsche bildungspolitische Diskurs in gouvernementalitätstheoretischer Perspektive. In Alheit, P. & Felden, H. von (Hg.), Lebenslanges Lernen und erziehungswissenschaftliche Biographieforschung. Konzepte und Forschung im europäischen Diskurs. Wiesbaden, 89-110.

Wildt, B. & Wildt, J. (2017). Gabentausch als Paradigma für Bildungsprozesse? International Dialogues in Education: Past and Present. IDE-Online Journal, Vol. 4(1).

Wulf, Ch. & Zirfas, J. (2006). Bildung als performativer Prozess - ein neuer Fokus erziehungswissenschaftlicher Forschung. In Fatke, R. & Merkens, H.(Hg.), Bildung über die Lebenszeit, Wiesbaden: Verlag für Sozialwissenschaften, 291-301

Young people's participation in the globalised world

Manfred Zentner

Abstract

Participation of young people today happens in the frame defined by globalisation and digitalisation and thus needs new forms of education and training. Youth today is growing up in a mediated society: The omnipresence of information, its pervasive accessibility as well as the active involvement of users in the creation, dissemination and provision of content are the main distinctive features of a digital era. In comparison with only the recent past, not only information from institutions is mediated but also interpersonal contact is. This new form of involvement and contact between people and institutions transformed the ways of participation both in everyday social life and in democracy. Furthermore, globalisation – driven by migration as well as by digital transnational media – has altered the way how people feel interconnected with issues on the local level and around the globe: social surrounding and the feeling of belonging become more and more location-independent and thus interest in participation is not limited to the local surrounding. This article focuses on the challenges of media pedagogy to enable youth (political) participation in a digitalised world in the framework of globalisation.

Introduction

Young people are often labelled as "digital natives" since they are born in a time when the access to the world wide web is available to the majority of young people – at least in the European Union and in most countries of the so-called West and global North – and thus they are believed to know how to participate fully in the digitalised world. But in reality, it is not equally easy for all youth to participate fully in society – not only due to a lack of technical and economic accessibility but rather due to a deficiency of competences. Participation in a digitalised world requires competences and digital literacy as well as knowledge about the framework of the digitalised world, regarding the offers for participating and shaping the offline "reality" by using online methods.

Education is the most important means to integration in society for young people; knowledge is key to success, skills are needed to enter the labour market and almost every profession needs certain accreditation of training or experience and lifelong learning is a must for everyone.

But education in the digitalised world needs new skills for both educators and learners – among others there is handling new digital instruments, knowing how to deal with personal data and more enhanced forms of media literacy. On the one hand schooling has to react on new developments in technology and thus competences beside reading, writing and calculating seem to become important. Education must integrate and adapt the traditional cultural techniques into digital literacy that enables a responsible and reflective use of digitalised media. On the other hand, new forms of participation and involvement are opened by digital media and this has to be reflected in political education in formal and non-formal settings.

Growing up in a digitalised world

The so called Millennials, those young people born after 2000, experience digital media and especially the offers of the world-wide web in a more elaborate way than any generation before.

Simplified, it can be stated that those born before 1975 had to learn to use mobile phones only in their late adolescence and experienced the world-wide web as an additional information provider and as a supplementary means for exchange. On the other hand, people born between 1975 and 1995, often labelled as Generation Y, understood the internet already naturally as an always accessible home for media as well as instrument for communication and also for consumption.

At the turn of the century the internet became an implicit channel for information, communication and exchange: the traditional one-to-one communication of personal communication merged with the one-to-many communication of mass media and allowed direct response from the users to the information provider – visible for all other users. User feedback and customer rating became important elements of a developing participating culture. Information was checked and commented by many and with the foundation of Wikipedia in 2001 the era of user generated content was definitively started.

And with the development of tablets and smartphones and the convergence of technical gadgets on the one hand and the creation of online social network platforms and thus the direct involvement of the users in content creation on the other hand digital media became a truly new form of information provision: Now every user can co-create information always and everywhere.

While in the early days of the internet news groups (which would soon develop into special interest forums) allowed exchange between people with similar interests to communicate and exchange first-hand experience, blogs enabled a new form of citizen journalism which reached its first peak with the establishment of microblogging services like Twitter.

Social media – especially online social networks like myspace and later on facebook – allow presenting oneself and staying in contact with far more people than in former times. This lead to new forms of connectivity between people: instead of strict bonds like existing in traditional socio-economic and socio-cultural groups, weak ties determine inter-personal relationships, which – at least in theory – can be designed and moderated by every individual.

With these developments the internet became not only a storage for information of any kind, and a medium for communication and exchange of people, but a virtual place for being and the various platforms of social communities became literally extended living rooms – all in all, the internet developed into a place for living.

Soon research approaches focused on different aspects of involvement in social media, especially of young people – on identity formation, on social and institutional privacy as well as data protection, on violence and mobbing, or on socially affected differences of access and use. Research on self-presentation in online settings show, that young people do not invent different identities for their online presence but do improve their images to their benefits (e.g. Davies 2014). These researches focused on the transfer of established and elaborate sociological concepts, like the dichotomy of individual and group (Weber 1980 [1922]), individuation (Giddens 1991) or self-representation (Goffman 1959), on the virtual space. Recent research (e.g. Trnka-Kwiecinski, Zentner 2016) opposes the duality of virtual online and real offline communities, but points out the mutual influence of these spheres.

The network society (Castells 1996 & 2009) as a result of individualised group integration with weaker ties on the one hand and the technological development towards easy world-wide connectivity on the other hand leads to parallel structures of power and to new mechanisms of control and new opportunities of liberation for people.

Young people today are living simultaneously in networks, in hierarchical settings and traditional environments, so they have access to far more information than former youth generations but on the other hand are also challenged to a higher degree to judge existing information and adapt it to their individual living circumstances. Therefore, education and training have to focus on the newly developed mediated structures of a digitalised society.

Is education in a digitalised world different from education in analogue times? Ongoing discussions on education and pedagogy focus on various topics. Regarding the formal education system, the main discussion focuses on the utilisation of education, on education outcomes and on employability. Another key question deals with the content of education (both in the formal system as well as in non-formal and informal settings), which is connected to the sense and meaningfulness of education. A more systemic approach highlights the roles of providers and receivers of education, when it is not obvious any longer that the young are learning from the old, but still youth stays the main target group of education. So the questions can be summarised: what should young people learn, for what reason and who can teach it? But are these questions different nowadays than in the past? No, but the answers might differ. Most noticeable maybe the widening of the target group and the inversion of direction of teaching and learning between the generations: Not only children and young people are the audience of education, but offers for life-long learning, adult education and special training for elderly people are necessary and commonly taken for granted.

Education is seen as the main instrument to prevent and tackle poverty, social exclusion and discrimination, especially by reaching out to disadvantaged groups, and thus fostering upwards social convergence. Education plays an important role in promoting inclusion and equality, it should build up mutual respect and builds up the foundation for active citizenship. Furthermore, education is regarded the main means to successfully enter the labour market in a highly competitive economy. These high expectations on the value of educations are expressed on political level of the European Union in the "Draft 2015 Joint Report of the Council and the Commission on the implementation of the Strategic framework for European cooperation in education and training" (European Commission 2015 b).

But the question remains what education to these ends has to look like? Data of the Education and Training Monitor 2015 (European Commission 2015 c) point out that the various (formal) education systems in European countries face several challenges, like a high rate of early school leavers without finishing secondary education, but also quite a high percentage of pupils score poorly in reading, science and mathematics as international tests show. In this report the main challenges of education are highlighted: the rate of early school leavers (described as the share of 18 to 24 year-olds having attained ISCED level 0-2 and not receiving any formal or non-formal education or training in the four weeks preceding the survey) is EU-wide still above 10%, which was set as the target for Europe in 2020. The data show also big differences between the various groups of pupils and differences between the Member States. Male youth show a higher average of early school leavers (12.7%) compared to female youth (9.5%) and foreign-born youth score half as good as native born (10.3% vs. 20.1%), indicating inability of the education systems in the EU Member states to level out social inequalities. The differences between the countries are also challenging since the rate of early school leaving is above 20% in countries like Spain or Malta and low as approx. 5% in Poland or Slovenia. Data for foreign born youth are somehow unreliable since they are not available in the same data collection method for all states. But we can find in some education systems less variation between those labelled as foreign born and the natives than in others: in Ireland the rate for foreign born early school leavers is lower than for natives, whereas in Slovenia it is three times as high.

Another challenge for the education systems is the still existing underachievement in reading, writing and mathematics. Also the OECD's PISA studies (Programme for International Student Assessment) shows inequalities between male and female, foreign and native born as well as the strong impact of the socio economic background on performance in reading, mathematics and science.

Furthermore, we currently are facing rather a skill based approach to education than a knowledge based concept, focusing, eventually more on the usability of knowledge: and this usability should be employability. But already in the 1990ies a dilemma was pointed out when Ferchhoff described formal education as necessary but not sufficient: One needs to finish formal education at least at secondary level, thus gaining a "good" education, to have chances to enter the labour market successfully, but a "good" education does not guarantee such successful entry (Ferchhoff 1993). Therefore, young people have not only to complete a good – secondary or even a higher – education path, but they also have to finish it with good grades, if they want to have smooth transition from school to work. But back in the 1990ies in Ferchhoff's analysis it was not even addressed which kind of schooling was finished – only if any certification leads to labour market chances –, thus the usability of the content of curricula was not questioned.

In the EU guidelines for the employment policies Member States are asked to improve the effectiveness and efficiency of the education systems to raise the skill level of the workforce, allowing it to better anticipate and meet the rapidly changing needs of dynamic labour markets in an increasingly digital economy. And consequently, the recently published draft joint report ET2020 highlights six new priority areas reflecting the expectations on quality education – with a clear focus on usability in the labour market thus on employability:

1. Relevant and high-quality skills and competences, focusing on learning outcomes, for employability, innovation and active citizenship
2. Inclusive education, equality, non-discrimination and promotion of civic competences
3. Open and innovative education and training, including by fully embracing the digital era:
4. Strong support for educators
5. Transparency and recognition of skills and qualifications to facilitate learning and labour mobility
6. Sustainable investment, performance and efficiency of education and training systems

Especially the third area focuses on the importance of ICT mentioning the promotion of the use of ICT as a driver for systemic change to increase quality and relevance of education at all levels and fostering the availability and quality of open and digital educational resources. So here ICT is understood as a tool and as instrument for education.

But also in other areas the importance of ICT is highlighted: In the first area the reduction of low achievement in mathematics, literacy science and digital literacy is a main issue as well as developing and strengthening of transversal skills and competences in particular digital entrepreneur and linguistic competences. Enhancing of critical thinking as well as of cyber and media literacy is an issue in the second area, training of digital competences of educators is crucial in the fourth area. In these areas the competences essential for using digital technologies are pointed up, but not only for pupils and students but also for educators and teachers.

All in all, the importance of digital literacy in contemporary debate on education is beyond dispute.

Special challenges of pedagogy in a digitalised world

The EU Youth Report 2012 highlighted the still ongoing increase of daily computer and internet use among young people (EU Youth Report 2012, 260). Referring to a Eurostat household survey the daily internet use rose from below 50% in 2006 to above 80% in 2011 among all EU-youth, aged 16 to 24.

The report also points to the fact that young people's confidence in their computer skills grows with their (formal) educational level, since among those lower education (i.e. with maximum secondary lower level education) show that only about 45% think "their computer or internet skills would be sufficient, if they were to look for a job or change job within a year", whereas more than 85% of young people having finished tertiary education agree to this statement. Furthermore, the report shows that "learning by doing" is perceived by the youth as the main way of acquiring ICT skills, formal education and social contacts (friends and relatives) follow after.

Differences according to levels of education exist furthermore regarding the awareness of risks of internet use: In EU average one third of the youth aged 16 to 24 with high education is concerned about the abuse of personal information sent on the internet, compared to less than a quarter of those with low education level. Similar is the concern regarding financial loss as a result of receiving "phishing" mails. This is a clear indication that more ICT training and education is needed in all levels of education and also non-formal approaches should be intensified (and their results have to be recognised).

Other challenges for any education – from upbringing in the family to formal schooling and non-formal trainings – come with the progress in technology and the growing accessibility of new technical and digital gadgets. The commonplace use of mobile devices leads to diversified access to media and information which again increases the need of media pedagogy to enable people to find and evaluate information.

The developments in technology ask for more skills beyond the basic cultural skills of reading, writing and calculating; thus, digital skills and media literacy are main elements of current curricula in formal and non-formal education.

The definitions of digital literacy reach "from simply being technology fluent to the ability to apply information literacy skills (e.g., locating, extracting organizing, managing, presenting and evaluating information) in digital environments to broader, more complex conceptual frameworks that encompass a wide variety of skills, understandings, norms and practices (Meyers et al. 2013). Current definitions of digital literacy combine important elements like ability to find and evaluate information in digital resources, but also to create and share information online in user-generated platforms. It emphasises critical thinking to judge and interpret underlying ideologies and also to understand the needs of addressed audiences. Another perspective interprets digital literacy as the general capability for living, learning and working in the digital society. Meyers et al. ask for a holistic perspective that combines skills, mental models and practices and point out that this concept of digital literacy should also involve a reflexive understanding of oneself in relation to technologies and networked structures (Meyers et al. 2013).

A digital literate person is not only a critical consumer of information but also a technically skilled creator of information and on one's responsibility reflecting active participant in the digitalised world. Therefore, digital literacy includes – beside the traditional media literacy – also all ways of providing information in digital media: conscious presentation of personal information in the internet, generating of any content in the internet, leaving traces when using online services and more. (This element of media pedagogy in a digitalised world reacts on the risks of use of digital media, like possible abuse of personal information)

Jenkins (2006) identified a number of new skills beyond the traditional competences of reading, writing and calculating that have to be mastered in order to be a full member of a participatory culture. A participatory culture is described as a culture with relatively low barriers to artistic expression and civic engagement, and in which its participants believe their contributions matter – and this description holds in a high degree for the modern Web 2.0. The skills that Jenkins recognised include:

1. play (experiment with one's surroundings as a form of problem-solving);
2. performance (adopt alternative identities for the purpose of improvisation and discovery);
3. simulation (interpret and construct dynamic models of real-world processes);
4. appropriation (meaningfully sample and remix media content);
5. multitasking (scan one's environment and shift focus as needed to salient details);
6. distributed cognition interact meaningfully with tools that expand mental capacities);
7. collective intelligence (pool knowledge and compare notes with others toward a common goal);
8. judgment (evaluate the reliability and credibility of different information sources);
9. transmedia navigation (follow the flow of stories and information across multiple modalities);
10. networking (search for, synthesize, and disseminate information); and
11. negotiation (travel across diverse communities, discerning and respecting multiple perspectives, and grasping and following alternative norms).

Jenkins also points out the need of political and pedagogical intervention beside the ongoing self-socialisation of youth in popular culture by highlighting three main reasons and hence affirms the role of education to promote equality and mutual respect also as a foundation of active citizenship:

- The Participation Gap — the unequal access to the opportunities, experiences, skills, and knowledge that will prepare youth for full participation in the world of tomorrow.
- The Transparency Problem — the challenges young people face in learning to see clearly the ways that media shape perceptions of the world.
- The Ethics Challenge — the breakdown of traditional forms of professional training and socialisation that might prepare young people for their increasingly public roles as media makers and community participants. (Jenkins 2006, 3)

Consequently, education in a digitalised world will not only have to provide digital literacy by informing young people about e.g. the hidden messages in media or the way media shape "realities", and making them aware of their own role in co-creating these "realities".

One can argue that this does not imply that digital literacy is a new skill but, in reality, is applying skills already essential in education before to new settings. The main difference between "old-school" media pedagogy and its application in digital world can be seen in the ethical dimension of information co-production. The awareness of the personal responsibility of every single digital media user in creating the own world and interacting with other people's opinions and thus consequently influencing and co-creating society is a main element of active participation. Thus, not only the use of digital technology but digital literacy can and should be perceived as an important element of cultural capital.

Integrating digital technology in teaching and learning

Digital resources and media are not only topics of education; they become more and more important as instruments of teaching. Elements of e-learning find access to formal education in schools as well as in tertiary education: flipped classroom, self-study using digital media, blended learning or game-based learning are used by many teachers as means to activate their pupils and students by using more "modern" techniques.

Various trend researches like the NMC Horizon report focus on possible and expected future developments of implementing new technologies in teaching and information. In this report the new Media Consortium (a consortium driven by IT companies like Apple, Adobe or Oracle together with academic partner institutions) various new developments are predicted to be very influential in the next years for education worldwide. For example, MakerSpace-Labs (workshops focusing on experiencing, knowledge sharing and peer-learning on programming, hacking or implementing of ICT) will become important not only in self-organised and non-formal settings but is seen to be integrated in formal education for promoting and fostering creativity and problem-solving skills. BYOD (bring your own device) refers to the trend that people are bringing their own devices (laptops, tablets, smartphones) to the work- and study environments and use these for work. This trend asks for the opportunity to connect to the school's, university's or company's network and get access not only to the internet but to the internal servers. This asks for new IT security solutions. (NMC 2015)

But also new forms of communication in and via social communities can be used in keeping contact and enabling exchange between educators and learners in the education system. An implementation of services like What'sApp or snapchat in education and in communication between teachers and students allows also to work on digital literacy by doing.

In the informal setting remote learning offers are of high importance since they allow access to information beyond the formal education setting. Here, for example, blended learning (the mixture between instructor-lead and self-study sessions) is expected to gain more importance than pure online learning since it enables more exchange between students and educators.

MOOCs (Massive Open Online Courses) run by universities or by (commercial) training centres enable people to attend courses and even gain certificates in other countries. MOOCs were in their beginning also seen as an instrument for promoting equal changes and inclusion by reaching out to disadvantaged people since most of these courses are free to attend (only certificates are fee-based). The challenge for compensating educational inequality with offers like MOOCs is to keep the users active in the courses. It seems that people with lower education and with less experience in attendance of education are less likely to stay in these courses. MOOCs run by big universities are also seen as a threat to the tertiary education system in smaller countries, where these courses in some subjects offered by top ranked universities might even replace existing offers from smaller universities to some extent.

The development towards a stronger integration of digital technology in teaching and learning is an indicator for the dissemination of digital technology in everyday life around the world. Furthermore, this can be observed in the non-formal sector as well as in youth work and in youth services. Already for a long time, youth centres had to be equipped with computers to access the internet, currently they should rather provide W-Lan access points so the kids can connect their own devices (BYOD) or should think of remote offers (live-streaming of parties, or even online youth centres). And youth information centres need to have online services as well.

Does youth participation need knowledge or competences – or both?

Beside the integration of digital media into the education system as issues on the one hand or as instruments for teaching and learning on the other hand the questions of relation of education and (political) participation arises.

Reflected political participation has various prerequisites, among which are the competence of political analysis and judgement, the competence of methods, and the competence of political decision making and acting. For acquiring these competences for example in political education (in or out of school) basic political knowledge is a precondition.

Thus, any form of active participation in the democratic system, be it in as voter or otherwise active citizen, has knowledge and competences as preconditions. For the process of rational decision-making access to information is an essential prerequisite as well as the ability of judging the relevance, accuracy and objectivity versus ideological bias of any information. Citizen participation should be – ideally – based on a comprehensible aggregation of all available opinions and their reflective and rational combination to a valid opinion.

Currently a debate on the opportunities for active political (online) participation fostered by digital media – especially the Web 2.0 – concentrates on three aspects: on the one hand the opportunities for the users to create information and get involved in opinion making processes in online social media and on the restricted access to various essential information on the other hand. The third field of debate is focussing on the important role of globalisation per se for political participation – it will be discussed later in the text.

Regarding the topic of user-generated information in the Web 2.0 the debate focuses on the prerequisites and the limitations of such participation. As basic condition for active political participation in a digitalised world factual knowledge on existing opportunities of online participation is essential, thus people should have to know about opportunities of online voting, participating in online consultations, using of online open data and more. Furthermore, performance as well as language skills are required, as are creativity and other basics for getting involved in the participatory culture. Thus, digital literacy is seen as a prerequisite of (online) participation in a digitalised world. Concerning the limitations of the existing systems in the digitalised world the superficial involvement in political debates (e.g. clicktivism) as well as the lack of consequences of "virtual" online participation in "reality", and thus the claimed dualism between online offers and real world, are topic of research and debate.

But digital media also open new forms of direct contact with policy makers and political active people and enabled virtually everybody to react publicly on developments and ongoing debate in both specific online platforms as well as in unspecified social networks. Violence and hate speech in form of personal offence as well as general defamation of political dissidents became a phenomenon of political activism. This lead also to an increased vulnerability of politically active people. So-called "online shit storms" as reactions to certain political developments can be seen as examples here. Consequently, not only certain politicians may become victims of insults and even threats but the seemingly anonymous online discussion gets ever more heated and leads to extreme contrasts and an apparently divided society.

This is also reflected in the second stream of discussion which highlights the problems and limits of selection of information from a seemingly infinite pool. Here are two different approaches of reduction of complexity problematized. The first can be seen in the personalisation of information by the users themselves when using RSS feeds, twitter or special selection of news which reduces the sources of information and eventually can lead to separated publics with totally different information. The second approach to a restriction are the filter systems of the information providers like google or facebook. In the case of facebook an algorithm based on various criteria like affinity, or time decay decides on the selection of information and status messages in the personal stream and thus invites to react more on messages and information that "seem" to be more interesting to the user than others and thus reinforcing the affinity. Also google will provide different search results depending on previous search history, or the place and time of the search. These forms of pre-selected information by a filter bubble was analysed and discussed in detail by Pariser (2011).

Both cases of information restriction – individual decisions or automated algorithms – might lead to the loss of relevant "alternative" information that should be included in the decision making process of active participation. It furthermore creates the impression that the own opinion and the personal attitudes are generally accepted in society since alternative or opposing views are far less represented in the "information bubble". This eventually allows extreme online expression of opinions since no or only few negative reactions will be triggered in a community that shares similar opinions; and this is why shit storms are made possible. Critics argue that with reduction of information a rational decision making process lacks the prerequisite of having all relevant information.

Dörre and Bukow (2014) argue that these forms of information reduction are not new phenomena that exist exclusively in digital media; the reinforcement of personal opinion can be found in any personal social network (offline as well as online) and the filter and algorithms are not abolishing any information. But in the end, discussing and problematizing these shortcomings of information selection with digital media should be one element of digital literacy education and of media pedagogy.

But more and more political educators use digital media especially online networks like facebook or twitter but also online gaming or programming of apps as methods for knowledge transfer, fostering responsible behaviour or promoting equality. Even hacking a webpage can be a successful tool for political education.

But when arguing about education for youth participation in democratic societies one has also must have a focus on the recent developments in political participation at a whole. Elections with small and still decreasing voter turnouts in Europe on the one hand coincide with powerful demonstrations in many countries around the world and with personal politics, implying that people just live their life following personal ideological value systems but don't get active in the democratic area on the other hand. Thus, discussions regarding the role of participation in general and of elections in particular become important. Is participation in the democratic system more than a show-off, is participation in elections the main idea of participation? By etymology participation roots in the Latin "participare" which itself is a combination of the noun "pars" and the verb "capere"; therefore, it means to take a part, but the translation is either sharing or to be part of or to attend something. So, it could be concluded, that participation is a reaction to an invitation to be active part in something.

In political sense it implies that someone is being involved in political decision making. And therefore, it was for a long time perceived as the engagement of citizens in the political system – as voters, delegates, representatives, activists, protesters or even dissidents. Thus also non-confirming forms to change the (political or societal) system are (sometimes) understood as participation. Nevertheless, the definition of participation is the result of a given power relation in the society. This bears the risk that participation becomes nothing more than tokenism, when the "establishment" is the only instance for determining any form of participation.

How can involvement in (post-) modern societies be described and who holds the power to define if it counts as participation? We observe new forms of (political) engagement like "clicktivism" in social media or self-created information in the internet – is this participation in the sense of those in power?

Political participation in the globalised world

Following Castells, the social structure of the network society is created around networks activated by microelectronics-based digitally processed information and communication technologies (Castells, 2009) enabling it to become a global society – and thus the network society model of the globalised world. Furthermore, the description of societies as networks allows new power relations parallel to existing power relations in states – and sometimes completely independent of states: Power in networks is defined as the ability to include or exclude nodes of a given network.

New forms of participation that are not any longer connected to states, municipalities, regions, or other political entities, but inside of networks running cross and through these entities gain importance. Thus, participation is not any more restricted to formal existing and traditional political formations, but through various networks political commitment in different parts of the world, from local to global level, becomes possible. And networks allow targeted involvement following the personal interests.

Globalisation, understood not only as an economic topic, but as a cultural phenomenon indicating the establishment of inter- and multi-cultural societies inside and beyond the nation states, allows new and independent but interlocked options of participation in local and global structures at the same time. This increased mutual influence of cultures is driven – among other – by migration and by digitalised media fostering network societies – and has a major impact on culture of participation: Digitalised media enable users to get independent information from all over the world fitting their interests and ideologies. This lead to the formation of various inter- and trans-national networks of persons connected across the continents by their interest in political, economic, scientific, ecological or cultural interests. And topics and developments around the world that were seemingly of minor importance for locals in the past suddenly can become the main drivers for political or social commitment both for long distance or in the local surrounding: petitions against fast food companies to protect the rain forest, boycotts of sport equipment brads to promote fair working conditions but also demonstrations in front of the national government to highlight the need of environment protection in another continent. Participation in a globalised world does not end at national borders and digital media makes it easily possible.

Migration leads to interaction between members of different cultures and to a form of trans-cultural mutual interference of cultures –of the culture(s) of origin and of the culture(s) the host country. Migrants have to adapt to new languages, to (maybe) unexperienced values and they see new forms of communication, interaction, traditions and behaviour. On the other hand, migrants bring their own culture into the host society often in the first steps represented by food, music and interpersonal behaviour. Thus, a mutual influence of cultures happens – where the dominant host culture normally changes less than the migrant must assimilate. Integration in a host society is often described as this process of inter-cultural dialogue and mutual interference. But integration is also described as the ability and interest to participate fully in society – in the whole sense of being a part of the society and influencing its development.

Regarding the integration of migrants – and their descendants –in a host society Esser (2001) points to the social integration, where he presents a progressive scheme of "Kulturierung", "Platzierung", "Interaktion" and "Identifikation". Here Kulturation refers to the acquisition or adoption of cultural techniques, necessary for any participation (this includes language skills, understanding of norms and attitudes) enabling situation related behaviour. The social achievement refers to Platzierung, thus taking a certain place in society. Interaction follows when intercultural contact and exchanges happens regularly – beyond the mandatory exchange in the formal system (education, labour market). The last phase refers to the identification with the values and attitudes of the host society. This scheme is valid for any member of society independent of migrant background or not.

Another sociological model of integration differentiates between structural functional and culturally identifying integration, where cultural and identification integration can only happen after the structural-functional integration is given (Löffler 2011). The structural functional integration focuses strongly on performance, on the outer affiliation of persons and systems in the social structure. To speak of entire integration in the sense of culturally identifying an awareness of community, of belonging, an emotional bond must be given. Following Löffler, complete integration is a combination of external or outer affiliation and internal setting.

Political participation, or more broadly participation in the democratic life of a society, depends thus not only on the legal rights, but also – and maybe foremost – on feelings of belonging and of opportunities to influence the development.

Different feelings of belonging for bigger groups of people from migration background do lead to different wishes of participation in various settings:

1. in the host country on local, regional and national level as citizen (and thus participants in elections) or at least recognised inhabitant, but also
2. in the former home country of the family of the person, since the connection is not broken, as well as
3. in the cultural community of migrants in the host country but also transnational
4. in the network of migrants from that country in the diaspora all over the world.

For youth with migrant background these four opportunities for participation form an additional challenge. The second-generation youth often has no legal right (due to lacking citizenship) to politically participate as citizen but on the other hand has no interest or information to participate in the home country of the parents. But in both societies and cultures opportunities as well as expectations regarding their involvement and participation exist: young migrants can integrate in the host country and thus bring their voices in alternatives ways and having their say – but until they get the citizenship – only to a certain extent. On the other hand, migrant culture organisations invite youth to participate and examine the own roots and try to uphold traditions also in host countries. Furthermore, trans-national networks even in the own broader families show young migrants the magnitude of diaspora. Finally, in many cases the young person is still (also) citizen of the home countries of the parents – and could get involved there. The complexity of these opportunities for participation – with often complete different methods – and its consequences for training and education needs further research[1].

Thus, migration and globalisation change the framework of participation and digitalised media enable people around the world to get involved in the topics that are most important for them. But these forms of participation need further improvement of education both of media education and of political education to allow people to understand not only the mutual interference of politics worldwide as well as the connection with economy, religions, or culture, but also new power relations in networks and the basics of digital literacy.

Consequently, education in a digitalised world has to provide equal opportunities and one of its main objectives is to enable social upwards mobility by creating accessibility to digital content for everyone and at the same time empower young people to fully participate in society. To gain this an elaborate concept of digital literacy – covering media literacy as well as performative skills – has to be part of the curriculum in formal education already in lower levels, to enable young people

---

[1] This is also part of a recent research project "Gender in a Changing Society" in Austria, Serbia, Croatia and Bosnia and Hercegovina in which young people in Austria coming from migrant families from the three Western Balkan States.

to gain the necessary competences to participate in democratic live in a digitalised world.

Furthermore, educators have to integrate digital media as a matter of fact in their teaching – be it in formal or non-formal settings. This implies that educators are not just presenting information with digital media and invite pupils and students to deliver their work via e-mail, but it means to consequently use digital media as means for the involvement of students in the education by using learning platforms as well as approaches of blended learning. But it also implies that new forms of communication, exchange and information provision, which are common for youth could and should be used in the education system for critically reflecting on the challenges and limits of digital communication but also for accessing new information not (yet) covered in school books.

A systematic and reflected use of digital media in formal and non-formal education will enable young people to critically reflect on the chances and shortcomings of digital media for participation in a digitalised world.

References

Bennett, Andy; Robards, Brand (eds.) (2014): Mediated Youth Cultures. The Internet, Belonging and New Cultural Configurations, Palgrave Macmillan, New York
Biermann Ralf; Fromme, Johannes; Verständig, Dan (eds.) (2014): Partizipative Medienkulturen. Positionen und Untersuchungen zu veränderten Formen öffentlicher Teilhabe. Springer, Wiesbaden
Castells, Manuel (1996): The Information Age: Economy, Society, and Culture, Volume 1: The Rise of the Network Society, Blackwell Publishers, Oxford / Malden MA
Castells, Manuel (2009): Communication power. Oxford University Press, Oxford / New York
Davies, Katie (2014): Youth Identities in a Digital Age: The Anchoring Role of Friends in Young People's Approaches to Online Identity Expression, in: Bennet, A.; Robards, B: 2014
Dörre, Jakob; Bukow Gerhard (2014): Die Grenzen geteilten Handelns und neuer partizipativer Demokratieformen; in: Biermann et.al., 89-112
Esser, Hartmut (2001): Integration und ethnische Schichtung, Arbeitspapiere – Mannheimer Zentrum für Europäische Sozialforschung, Nr. 40
European Commission (2012): EU Youth Report 2012, Brussels
European Commission (2015 a): Proposal for a Council decision on guidelines for the employment policies of the Member States (COM (2015) 98 final)
European Commission (2015 b): Communication from the Commission to the European Parliament, the Council, the European Economic and Social Committee and the Committee of regions: Draft 2015 Joint Report of the Council and the Commission on the implementation of the Strategic framework for European cooperation in education and training (ET2020): New priorities for European cooperation in education and training. {SWD(2015) 161 final}
European Commission (2015 c): Education and Training Monitor 2015, Luxembourg
Ferchoff, Wilfried (1993): Jugend an der Wende vom 20. zum 21. Jahrhundert. Lebensformen und Lebensstile, Leske + Budrich, Opladen
Giddens, Anthony (1991): Modernity and Self-Identity. Self and Society in Late Modern Age, Polity Press, Cambridge (UK)
Goffman, Erving (1959): The Presentation of Self in Everyday Life, Anchor Books, New York
Jenkins, Henry (2006): Confronting the Challenges of Participatory Culture: Media Education for the 21st Century, An occasional paper on digital media and learning, MacArthur Founda-

tion, (download: https://www.macfound.org/press/publications/white-paper-confronting-the-challenges-of-participatory-culture-media-education-for-the-21st-century-by-henry-jenkins/)

Löffler, Bernhard (2011): Integration in Deutschland. Zwischen Assimilation und Multikulturalismus, Oldenburg Verlag, München

Meyers, Eric M., Erickson, Ingrid & Small, Ruth V. (2013): Digital literacy and informal learning environments: an introduction, Learning, Media and Technology, 38:4, 355-367.

Mihailidis, Paul and Thevenin, Benjamin (2013): Media Literacy as a Core Competency for Engaged Citizenship and Participatory Democracy, American Behavioural Scientist, 57(11)1611-1622.

New Media Consortium (NMC) (2015): Horizon Report (download http://www.nmc.org/nmc-horizon/; 4.9.2015)

Pariser, Eli (2011): The Filter Bubble. What the Internet is hiding from us, Penguin Books, Johannesburg

Skoric, Marko; Kwan, Grace (2011): Do Facebook and Video Games promote Political Participation among Youth, JeDEM 3(1) 70-79, 2011.

Trnka-Kwiecinski, Aga; Zentner, Manfred (2016): Vom Suchen und Finden und (Nicht)Gefunden Werden Wollen 2.0 – Über Generationsübergreifende Migrationserfahrungen. In: Friesinger, Günther, Schoßböck, Judith, Ballhausen, Thomas (Hg.) (2016) Digital Migration. Konstruktion – Strategien – Bewegungen, Wien: edition monochrom.

Weber, Max, Winckelmann Johannes (Hg.) (1980 [1922]): Wirtschaft und Gesellschaft. Grundriß der verstehenden Soziologie, Mohr, Tübingen

Teil 6:
Migration und soziale Ungleichheit

Armut und Ausgrenzung von Migrant/inn/en in Österreich: Aktuelle Situation und Entwicklungen zwischen 2010 und 2016

Karin Heitzmann

Zusammenfassung

In diesem Beitrag soll ein Überblick über die Armuts- und Ausgrenzungsgefährdung von Migrant/inn/en in Österreich gegeben werden. Ziel ist es einerseits, die aktuelle Situation abzubilden und Veränderungen zwischen 2010 und 2016 zu skizzieren. Andererseits sollen durch einen Vergleich mit der nicht-migrantischen Bevölkerung Ursachenzusammenhänge abgeleitet werden, welche erklären, warum Migrant/inn/en in Österreich im Hinblick auf ihre Armuts- und Ausgrenzungslage gegenüber nicht-migrantischen Bewohner/inne/n benachteiligt sind. In diesem Sinne fokussiert der Beitrag auf eine sehr spezifische Benachteiligung von Migrant/inn/en in Österreich – im Gegensatz zum thematisch weit umfangreicheren Oeuvre von Frau Universitätsprofessorin Dr.[in] Gudrun Biffl, der dieser Artikel gewidmet ist und deren Arbeiten zu Standard(nachschlage)werken im Hinblick auf die Thematiken der Migration und Integration in Österreich geworden sind (vgl. z.B. Biffl 2016; Biffl und Dimmel 2001; Biffl und Dimmel 2016).

Einleitung

Um die Ziele des vorliegenden Beitrags zu erreichen, ist er folgendermaßen aufgebaut: Im nächsten Kapitel werden zunächst die wesentlichsten in dieser Arbeit verwendeten Begriffe (Armut, Ausgrenzung, Migrant/inn/en) definiert. Zudem wird ein Vergleich der aktuellen Armuts- und Ausgrenzungslage zwischen Migrant/inn/en und Nicht-Migrant/inn/en vorgenommen. Im darauf folgenden Kapitel wird die Entwicklung der Armut und Ausgrenzung von Migrant/inn/en in Österreich zwischen 2010 und 2016 illustriert und mit der Dynamik bei der nicht-migrantischen Bevölkerung verglichen[1]. In einem weiteren Kapitel werden Hinweise zu den Ursachen für die – und so viel sei schon vorweggenommen – doch deutlich höhere Ausgrenzungs- und Armutsgefährdung von Migrant/inn/en in Österreich geliefert. Im Fazit werden die wichtigsten Ergebnisse des Beitrags zusammengefasst und die Notwendigkeit argumentiert, aufgrund der benachteili-

---

[1] Vgl. zur Entwicklung von 2004 bis 2010 Gächter (2014) bzw. zur Entwicklung zwischen 2004 und 2009 Wiesböck (2011), die für diesen Zeitraum auch eine Trend- und Strukturanalyse durchgeführt hat.

gen Lebenslagen von Personen mit Migrationshintergrund sozialpolitisch vor allem auch in sie zu investieren.

Sofern nicht anders angegeben, stammen die in den folgenden Kapiteln verwendeten Daten zur Armut und Ausgrenzung von Migrant/inn/en aus den Tabellenbänden zu den österreichischen Auswertungen des EU-SILC[2] (Statistik Austria 2015a, 2015b, 2015c, 2015d, 2016, 2017a, 2017b).

Armut und Ausgrenzung von Migrant/inn/en in Österreich

Ziel dieses Kapitels ist es zunächst, die wesentlichsten in diesem Beitrag verwendeten Begriffe zu definieren. Daran anschließend wird die Armut und Ausgrenzung von Migrant/inn/en in Österreich dargestellt. Dabei werden diese Benachteiligungen erstens für unterschiedliche Gruppen von Migrant/inn/en aufgezeigt und zweitens ein Vergleich zwischen der migrantischen und der nicht-migrantischen Bevölkerung gezogen.

Armut, Ausgrenzung, Migrant/inn/en: Begriffsbestimmungen

In diesem Beitrag wird für die Erfassung von Armut und Ausgrenzung jener Indikator herangezogen, welcher vom Europäischen Statistischen Zentralamt (Eurostat) für die Überprüfung des entsprechenden Europa-2020-Ziels Verwendung findet[3]. Um als armuts- oder ausgrenzungsgefährdet zu gelten, müssen Haushalte eine von drei Bedingungen erfüllen. Sie müssen (i) entweder armutsgefährdet sein, oder (ii) in einem Haushalt leben, in dem keine oder eine sehr niedrige Erwerbsintensität vorliegt, oder (iii) in Haushalten mit erheblicher materieller Deprivation leben. Bedingung (i) beschreibt eine Armutsgefährdung, Bedingung (ii) und (iii) eine Ausgrenzungsgefährdung. Sie können einzeln oder in unterschiedlichen Kombinationen auf Haushalte zutreffen. In Abhängigkeit davon gilt ein Haushalt dann als armuts- und/oder ausgrenzungsgefährdet. Dieser Armuts- oder Ausgrenzungsindikator wird in Österreich seit etlichen Jahren von der österreichischen Statistik verwendet. Er ist darüber hinaus öffentlich und politisch akzeptiert, etwa durch seine Verwendung in den österreichischen Sozialberichten (z.B. Bundesministerium für Arbeit, Soziales und Konsumentenschutz 2017). In Summe waren in Österreich im Jahr 2016 18% oder 1,54 Millionen Personen von zumindest einer der drei Benachteiligungen betroffen. Sechs Jahre zuvor, im Jahr 2010 belief sich die Quote noch auf 19% (1,57 Millionen Personen). Österreich

---

[2] EU-SILC steht für "European Community Statistics on Income and Living Conditions". In einer jährlichen repräsentativen Erhebung werden die wesentlichsten Informationen zu Einkommen, Armut und Lebensbedingungen erfasst und ausgewertet. Die Informationen aus dieser Datenquelle, die nicht nur durch Befragungen, sondern auch durch Administrativdaten gespeist wird, werden auch für die Europa-2020-Informationen auf Ebene der Europäischen Union herangezogen.

[3] http://ec.europa.eu/social/BlobServlet?docId=10421&langId=en

hat sich verpflichtet, zwischen 2008 und 2020 die Anzahl der von Armut oder Ausgrenzung betroffenen Menschen um 235.000 zu reduzieren (Bundeskanzleramt o.J.). Bis einschließlich 2016 wurde eine Reduktion um 157.000 Personen erzielt[4].

Im Folgenden wird genauer dargestellt, wie die drei Subindikatoren gemessen werden. Als *armutsgefährdet* (synonym zur Armutsgefährdung wird in diesem Beitrag auch der Begriff *Armut* verwendet) gelten alle Personen, die in einem Haushalt mit einem äquivalisierten Haushaltseinkommen unterhalb eines festgelegten Schwellenwertes leben. Die Festlegung auf diese Eurostat-Definition von Armut bedeutet dreierlei: erstens wird Armut unter alleiniger Berücksichtigung von Einkommen bestimmt. Inwiefern mit diesen Einkommen auch ein Auskommen erzielt werden kann, wird nicht weiter berücksichtigt. Mit anderen Worten: Ausgaben von Haushalten bleiben bei der Berechnung der Armutsgefährdung unberücksichtigt. Um ein Beispiel zu nennen: € 1000 sind in jedem Haushalt gleich viel Wert, unabhängig davon, ob damit eine teure oder billige Miete bezahlt werden muss oder – im kreditfreien Eigenheim – keine Mietzahlung anfällt. Zweitens wird Armut nach den Usancen der Eurostat-Definition als Haushaltsphänomen definiert. Das bedeutet einerseits, dass alle Einkommen[5] innerhalb eines Haushalts zusammengefasst werden und andererseits, dass in einem Haushalt entweder alle Haushaltsmitglieder armutsgefährdet sind oder eben nicht: Ungleichverteilungen der Einkommen innerhalb eines Haushalts bleiben damit unberücksichtigt. Die Berechnung der Armutsgefährdung basiert, drittens, auf einem relativen Armutskonzept. Die Armutsschwelle, die darüber entscheidet, ob das verfügbare Haushaltseinkommen den Haushalt zu einem armen oder einem nichtarmen Haushalt „macht", wird einerseits länderspezifisch und andererseits zeitabhängig berechnet. Mit anderen Worten: die Armutsschwelle bezieht sich jeweils auf das gegenwärtige Einkommensniveau des Landes, für das sie berechnet wird. Daraus folgt nicht nur, dass Armutsschwellen zwischen Ländern divergieren, sondern auch, dass sich die Armutsschwelle innerhalb eines Landes von Jahr zu Jahr verändern kann. Damit soll sichergestellt werden, dass Armut in Relation zum aktuellen Lebensstandard in einer bestimmten Region bemessen wird.

Nun aber zur verwendeten Eurostat-Armutsdefinition: ein Haushalt gilt dann als armutsgefährdet, wenn sein Einkommen unterhalb eines bestimmten Schwellenwerts liegt. Bei diesem Schwellenwert handelt es sich um 60% des Medians der äquivalisierten Haushaltseinkommen eines Landes in einem bestimmten Jahr. Berechnet für einen Einpersonenhaushalt belief sich dieser Schwellenwert in Österreich für das Jahr 2016 auf € 14.217; ein Zwölftel davon entspricht einer monatlichen Armutsschwelle von € 1185. Haushalte von mehreren Personen werden äquivalisiert, um sie miteinander vergleichbar zu machen. Dabei wird unterstellt, dass das Einkommen in einem Einpersonenhaushalt denselben Lebensstandard

---

[4] https://tinyurl.com/armut-soziale-eingliederung
[5] Das relevante Einkommen ist dabei das im Haushalt verfügbare Einkommen. Dazu zählen alle Nettoerwerbseinkommen, aber auch soziale und private Transferzahlungen an den Haushalt, abzüglich bezahlter Steuern und an andere Haushalte überwiesene private Transfers.

nach sich zieht, wie das Eineinhalbfache dieses Einkommens in einem Zweipersonenhaushalt. Der Gewichtungsfaktor pro weiterem Erwachsenem in einem Haushalt beträgt damit 0,5. Für jedes Kind (unter 14 Jahren) wird ein Gewichtungsfaktor von 0,3 berücksichtigt. Um ein Beispiel zu nennen: € 1000 in einem Einpersonenhaushalt ziehen denselben materiellen Lebensstandard nach sich, wie € 1500 in einem Zweipersonenhaushalt oder € 1800 in einem Haushalt von zwei Erwachsenen und einem Kind. Mit Hilfe dieser Gewichtungsfaktoren wird dann ein (fiktives) Pro-Kopf-Äquivalenzeinkommen berechnet. Für die oben zitierte Familie mit zwei Erwachsenen und einem Kind bedeutet dies, dass ein verfügbares Haushaltseinkommen von € 1800 einem gewichteten Pro-Kopf Äquivalenzeinkommen von € 1000 entspricht (€ 1800 dividiert durch den Gewichtungsfaktor 1,8).

Basierend auf der Eurostat-Armutsdefinition betrug die entsprechende Quote in Österreich im Jahr 2016 14%. Damit waren etwa 1,21 Millionen Menschen in diesem Land armutsgefährdet. Im Vergleich zu 2010 bedeutet dies eine relative Abnahme des Armutsrisikos (von 15 auf 14%), aber eine stabile Anzahl an Armutsgefährdeten (die sich in beiden Jahren auf etwa 1,21 Millionen Menschen beläuft).

Zu *Haushalten mit keiner oder nur einer sehr niedrigen Erwerbsintensität* zählen all jene Haushaltsmitglieder, in denen die erwachsenen Personen (im Alter zwischen 18 und 59 Jahren[6]) in Summe weniger als 20% ihrer maximal möglichen Erwerbszeit ausschöpfen. Dabei wird unterstellt, dass jede/r Erwachsene ganzjährig Vollzeit (40 Stunden) arbeiten könnte. Bei einem Einpersonenhaushalt führt damit eine ganzjährige Erwerbstätigkeit von maximal sieben Wochenstunden dazu, zu dieser Risikogruppe zu gehören: Acht Wochenstunden entsprechen, bei einem unterstellten Maximum von 40 Stunden, bereits einer 20-prozentigen Erwerbsintensität, die damit nicht mehr als „sehr niedrig" definiert wird. Im Jahr 2016 lebten 8% der österreichischen Bevölkerung, oder knapp 530.000 Personen, in Haushalten, die keine bzw. nur eine sehr niedrige Erwerbsintensität aufwiesen. Zwischen dem Jahr 2010 und 2016 variierte diese Quote zwischen 8 und 9% bzw. zwischen knapp 500.000 und 600.000 Personen.

Zur Operationalisierung des Indikators „*erhebliche materielle Deprivation*" wird im Rahmen der EU-SILC Erhebung ein Haushaltsmitglied befragt, ob es für den Haushalt finanziell möglich ist (i) regelmäßige Zahlungen (Miete, Betriebskosten etc.) rechtzeitig zu begleichen, (ii) unerwartete Ausgaben bis zu einer Höhe von € 1160 zu finanzieren[7], (iii) die Wohnung angemessen warm zu halten, (iv) jeden zweiten Tag Fleisch, Fisch oder eine entsprechende vegetarische Speise zu essen, (v) einmal im Jahr auf Urlaub zu fahren, (vi) einen PKW, (vii) eine Waschmaschine, (viii) ein Fernsehgerät, oder (ix) ein Telefon oder Handy zu besitzen. Antwortet das Haushaltsmitglied mindestens vier Mal mit „nein", dann gilt dieser Haushalt als erheblich materiell depriviert. Wohlgemerkt werden die

---

[6] Dieser Indikator umfasst daher auch nur Haushalte mit Personen zwischen 0 und 59 Jahren.
[7] Dieser Betrag wird regelmäßig angepasst. Im Jahr 2010 wurde beispielsweise nach Ausgaben bis zu einer Höhe von € 950 gefragt.

Haushalte nicht danach gefragt, ob sie diese Güter besitzen bzw. diese Bedürfnisse befriedigen, sondern ob sie sich dies finanziell überhaupt leisten könnten. Im Jahr 2016 litten 3% der österreichischen Haushalte bzw. knapp 260.000 Personen unter erheblicher materieller Deprivation. Im Jahr 2010 betrug diese Quote noch 4%, die Anzahl der betroffenen Personen belief sich damals auf etwa 350.000.

Nachdem nun geklärt ist, wie Armut und Ausgrenzung in diesem Beitrag definiert werden, wird im Folgenden erläutert, welche Begriffsabgrenzung für „Migrant/inn/en" vorgenommen worden ist.

In diesem Beitrag werden *Migrant/inn/en* – basierend auf der Verfügbarkeit entsprechender Daten zu ihrer Armutsgefährdung – auf Basis ihrer individuellen Staatsbürgerschaft von Nicht-Migrant/inn/en abgegrenzt. In der weiteren Darstellung werden dabei unterschiedliche Gruppen von Migrant/inn/en und Nicht-Migrant/inn/en berücksichtigt. Es wird nicht nur zwischen Personen mit österreichischer Staatsbürgerschaft und Personen ohne österreichische Staatsbürgerschaft unterschieden. Bei den Personen mit österreichischer Staatsbürgerschaft (die im Folgenden auch als „Österreicher/innen" oder „Nicht-Migrant/inn/en" tituliert werden) kann zudem danach differenziert werden, ob die Person eingebürgert worden ist (wobei aufgrund der vorliegenden Daten lediglich Einbürgerungen aus Nicht-EU oder EFTA-Staaten berücksichtigt werden können). Bei den Personen, die über keine österreichische Staatsbürgerschaft verfügen (und die in diesem Beitrag auch als „Nicht-Österreicher/innen" oder als „Migrant/inn/en" bezeichnet werden), wird zwischen jenen unterschieden, die eine EU- oder EFTA-Staatsbürgerschaft haben, und jenen, die eine andere Staatsbürgerschaft aufweisen. Letztere werden in diesem Text auch als Drittstaatsangehörige bezeichnet. Im Hinblick auf die Darstellung der Armutsgefährdung, die über das Haushaltseinkommen bestimmt wird, ist eine Abgrenzung von Nicht-Migrant/inn/en und Migrant/inn/en nach einem individuellen Merkmal (ihrer Staatsbürgerschaft) nicht unproblematisch. Denn Migrant/inn/en können mit Nicht-Migrant/inn/en zusammenleben. Ihre Armut und Ausgrenzung wird dann auf Basis des gemeinsamen Haushaltseinkommens bzw. auf Basis gemeinsamer Haushaltscharakteristika bemessen – was zu einer verzerrten Einschätzung der Armutsgefährdung von Migrant/inn/en und Nicht-Migrant/inn/en führen könnte (vgl. dazu auch Gächter 2014, S. 280).

Für das Jahr 2016 weist die EU-SILC Statistik zu Einkommen, Armut und Lebensbedingungen insgesamt 8,590 Millionen Personen für Österreich aus. Im Vergleich dazu ist die tatsächliche Anzahl der in Österreich lebenden Menschen höher: mit Stichtag 1.1.2016 wird diese Anzahl von der Statistik Austria mit 8,700 Millionen Personen angegeben[8]. Diese Diskrepanz lässt sich dadurch erklären, dass in der (gewichteten) EU-SILC Statistik lediglich Personen in Privathaushalten berücksichtigt sind. Menschen in Anstaltshaushalten oder Heimen sind von der Erhebung ausgeschlossen. Von den in der EU-SILC Statistik berücksichtigten 8,590 Millionen Personen besaßen 7,343 Millionen oder etwa 85% die österreichi-

---

[8] https://tinyurl.com/staatsangehoerigkeit-geburt

sche Staatsbürgerschaft. Rund 299.000 Personen (das sind etwa 4% der Österreicher/innen) waren eingebürgert. Die Anzahl der Nicht-Österreicher/innen wird für das Jahr 2016 mit 1,247 Millionen (oder knapp 15%) ausgewiesen. 579.000 verfügten über die Staatsbürgerschaft eines EU- oder EFTA-Landes, 669.000 waren Drittstaatsangehörige.

Tabelle 1 zeigt abschließend eine Übersicht über die in diesem Beitrag verwendeten Indikatoren, inkl. Kennzahlen für Österreich im Jahr 2016.

Österreich 2016	in 1000	in %
Gesamtbevölkerung in Privathaushalten (nach EU-SILC)	8590	100%
Armuts- oder Ausgrenzungsgefährdung	1542	18%
Armutsgefährdung	1208	14%
Keine/sehr niedrige Erwerbsintensität	528	8%
Erhebliche materielle Deprivation	257	3%
Österreichische Staatsbürger/innen	7343	85%
davon eingebürgert	299	3%
Nicht-österreichische Staatsbürger/innen	1247	15%
davon EU/EFTA	579	7%
davon sonstiges Ausland	669	8%

Tabelle 1 Kennzahlen zu den im Beitrag verwendeten Indikatoren zur Armut, Ausgrenzung und zu Migrant/inn/en und Nicht-Migrant/inn/en, Österreich 2016

Quelle: Statistik Austria 2017b: Tabelle 5.4a, S. 80-81, eigene Darstellung

**Armut und Ausgrenzung von
Migrant/inn/en und Nicht-Migrant/inn/en in Österreich**

Im Rahmen einer Analyse der Armuts- und Ausgrenzungsgefährdung von Österreicher/inne/n und Nicht-Österreicher/inne/n zeigt sich eine deutliche Benachteiligung der zweiten Gruppe. Im Jahr 2016 betrug die Armuts- oder Ausgrenzungsquote der Österreicher/innen (nach dem Europa-2020-Indikator) 13%. Jene der Nicht-Österreicher/innen belief sich auf 44%. Innerhalb der Gruppe der Österreicher/innen sind jene, die eingebürgert worden sind, stärker von Armut oder Ausgrenzung betroffen: Ihre Quote betrug 22%. Bei den Nicht-Österreicher/inne/n besteht ein deutlicher Unterschied zwischen Personen mit einer EU- oder EFTA-Staatsbürgerschaft (36%) und Drittstaatsangehörigen (51%). Der Unterschied zwischen den Armuts- oder Ausgrenzungsraten von Österreicher/inne/n und Nicht-Österreicher/inne/n zeigt sich bei Kindern zwischen 0 und 15 Jahren besonders drastisch: Kinder mit österreichischer Staatsbürgerschaft wiesen 2016 eine Quote von 14% auf. Bei Kindern mit nicht-österreichischer Staatsbürgerschaft beläuft sich der Anteil auf 52%. Die hohe Kinderarmuts- oder -ausgrenzungsquote im Jahr 2016, die für ganz Österreich mit 21% ausgewiesen wird, ist somit vor allem auf die benachteiligte Situation von Kindern mit Migrationshintergrund zurückzuführen.

Wie oben dargelegt, setzt sich der Armuts- oder Ausgrenzungsindikator aus drei Subindikatoren zusammen. Ergebnisse zu diesen drei Indikatoren werden im Folgenden für Österreich und das Jahr 2016 angeführt. Im Hinblick auf die *Armutsgefährdung* zeigt sich die unterschiedliche Betroffenheit von Österreicher/inne/n und Nicht-Österreicher/inne/n besonders deutlich. Die gesamtösterreichische Quote von 14% setzt sich einerseits aus einer Gefährdung in Höhe von 10% bei den Österreicher/inne/n und andererseits aus einer Gefährdung von 40% bei den Nicht-Österreicher/inne/n zusammen: die Wahrscheinlichkeit von Migrant/inn/en zur Gruppe der armutsgefährdeten Menschen in Österreich zu gehören, ist damit viermal höher als von Nicht-Migrant/inn/en. Einmal mehr zeigt sich innerhalb der Gruppe der Österreicher/innen eine höhere Gefährdung von Personen, die eingebürgert worden sind (16%). Und bei den Migrant/inn/en besteht eine deutlich höhere Gefährdung von Drittstaatsangehörigen (46%) gegenüber Personen mit einer EU-oder EFTA-Staatsbürgerschaft (32%). Eine noch ausgeprägtere Distanz zwischen Bürger/inne/n mit österreichischer und nicht-österreichischer Staatsbürgerschaft zeigt sich zudem, wenn lediglich die Gefährdung der Kinder zwischen 0 und 15 Jahren betrachtet wird. Die österreichweit geltende Gefährdungsrate von 17% setzt sich aus einer deutlich niedrigeren Gefährdungsrate der Kinder mit österreichischer Staatsbürgerschaft (11%) und einer deutlich höheren Rate von Kindern mit nicht-österreichischer Staatsbürgerschaft (50%) zusammen: jedes zweite Kind mit nicht-österreichischer Staatsbürgerschaft lebt damit in Österreich in einem armutsgefährdeten Haushalt.

Auch im Hinblick auf den zweiten Subindikator zur Ermittlung des österreichischen Armuts- oder Ausgrenzungsrisikos, dem Vorliegen *keiner oder einer nur sehr niedrigen Erwerbsintensität*, zeigt sich eine Diskrepanz zwischen Personen mit österreichischer und nicht-österreichischer Staatsbürgerschaft. Erstere weisen eine Quote von 6% auf, zweitere eine Quote von 16%. Das entsprechende Risiko von Migrant/inn/en ist damit knapp dreimal höher als jenes von Nicht-Migrant/inn/en. Auffallend sind wieder die großen Diskrepanzen innerhalb der Gruppe der Nicht-Österreicher/innen: lediglich 6% der Personen mit einer EU- oder EFTA-Staatsbürgerschaft weisen keine oder nur eine sehr geringe Erwerbsintensität auf. Damit ist ihr Risiko identisch mit jenem der Österreicher/innen. Im Vergleich dazu beträgt der Anteil bei den Drittstaatsangehörigen 24%. Damit ist es für sie viermal wahrscheinlicher in einem Haushalt mit sehr niedriger Erwerbsintensität zu wohnen als für Österreicher/innen oder EU- bzw. EFTA-Staatsbürger/innen.

Wie schon oben festgestellt, weist nur ein kleiner Prozentsatz der österreichischen Wohnbevölkerung Probleme im Hinblick auf das Bestehen einer *erheblichen materiellen Deprivation* auf – dem dritten Subindikator zur Berechnung der österreichischen Armuts- oder Ausgrenzungsgefährdung. 2016 waren lediglich 3% der Bevölkerung in Privathaushalten betroffen. Bei einem Vergleich der Österreicher/innen und der Nicht-Österreicher/innen zeigt sich allerdings einmal mehr ein eklatanter Unterschied zwischen den beiden Gruppen, wenngleich sich das Risiko auf einem geringeren absoluten Niveau befindet: Für die Österreicher/innen beläuft sich die entsprechende Deprivationsrate auf lediglich 2%, bei den Nicht-Österreicher/innen ist sie mit 10% aber immerhin fünfmal höher. Auch bei diesem Indikator besteht ein deutlicher Unterschied zwischen EU- oder EFTA-Staatsbürger/inne/n (5%) im Vergleich zu Angehörigen aus Drittstaaten (14%).

Erwähnenswert ist in diesem Zusammenhang auch der relativ hohe Anteil erheblicher materieller Deprivation unter den eingebürgerten Österreicher/inne/n: 2016 waren 7% von ihnen materiell depriviert und damit ein höherer Anteil als verglichen mit EU- oder EFTA-Staatsbürger/inne/n, die in Österreich leben.

Entwicklung der Armut und Ausgrenzung von Migrant/inn/en in Österreich zwischen 2010 bis 2016

Nach diesem Überblick über den *status quo* der Armuts- und Ausgrenzungslage von Migrant/inn/en in Österreich soll in diesem Kapitel aufgezeigt werden, wie diese Entwicklung seit 2010 verlaufen ist – wieder im Vergleich mit Nicht-Migrant/inn/en. Dazu gilt zunächst festzuhalten, dass die Anzahl der im EU-SILC definierten „Österreicher/innen" im Zeitverlauf relativ konstant geblieben ist, die Anzahl der „Nicht-Österreicher/innen" allerdings (mit einem Plus von etwa 340.000 Personen) deutlich zugenommen hat. Innerhalb der Gruppe der Nicht-Österreicher/innen ist die Zunahme unter den Personen mit einer EU-oder EFTA Staatsbürgerschaft mit etwa 233.000 Personen übrigens deutlich höher ausgefallen als im Vergleich zu Drittstaatsangehörigen (+108.000 Personen)[9].

Im Folgenden wird die Entwicklung der Armut und Ausgrenzung vor allem im Hinblick auf zwei Gruppen durchgeführt: Österreicher/innen und Nicht-Österreicher/innen. Es zeigt sich zunächst, dass die Entwicklung des Armuts- oder Ausgrenzungsrisikos in Österreich zu einer Verbesserung der Lage bei den Österreicher/inne/n geführt hat. Ihr Risiko ist von 16% im Jahr 2010 auf 13% im Jahr 2016 gesunken. Parallel dazu hat sich die Lage der Nicht-Österreicher/innen nach einer kurzfristigen Erholung (2010: 41%, 2012: 35%) verschlechtert (2016: 44%). Zusammengefasst bedeutet dies, dass sich der Risikoabstand zwischen Österreicher/inne/n und Nicht-Österreicher/inne/n im Hinblick auf ihre Armuts- oder Ausgrenzungsgefährdung im Zeitverlauf erhöht hat. War das Armuts- oder Ausgrenzungsrisiko im Jahr 2010 bei den Nicht-Österreicher/inne/n noch um 25 Prozentpunkte höher als im Vergleich zu den Österreicher/inne/n, so beträgt dieser Abstand mittlerweile 31 Prozentpunkte.

Wie oben bereits ausgeführt worden ist, setzt sich die Armuts- oder Ausgrenzungsgefährdung in Österreich aus drei Indikatoren zusammen. Auf die Entwicklungen dieser drei Indikatoren zwischen 2010 und 2016 wird im Folgenden nacheinander eingegangen. Bezogen auf die Gruppe der Österreicher/innen wird deutlich, dass ihr *Armutsrisiko* im 7-Jahresvergleich abgenommen hat. Betrug es im Jahr 2010 noch 12%, beläuft es sich im Jahr 2016 auf 10%. Besonders drastisch

---

[9] Ab der EU-SILC Erhebung von 2014 werden Bürger/innen mit kroatischer Staatsbürgerschaft als EU-Staatsbürger/innen gefasst, bis einschließlich 2013 zählten sie zur Gruppe der Drittstaaten. Dies hat auch Konsequenzen für die Gruppe der eingebürgerten Österreicher/innen, bei der vormalige Bürger/innen eines EU- oder EFTA-Staates nicht inkludiert sind – auch bei dieser Gruppe kommt es zu einem Zeitreihenbruch zwischen 2013 und 2014.

zeigt sich eine Reduktion der Armutsgefährdung übrigens bei der Gruppe der eingebürgerten Österreicher/innen: deren Armutsgefährdung reduzierte sich von 29% im Jahr 2010 auf 16% im Jahr 2016, und damit um fast die Hälfte. Bei den Nicht-Österreicher/inne/n ist ein gegenläufiger Trend zu beobachten: Ihr Armutsrisiko reduzierte sich zunächst von 36% im Jahr 2010 auf 31% im Jahr 2012. Danach kam es allerdings zu einem stetigen Anstieg ihrer Armutsgefährdungsquote, der im Jahr 2016 mit 40% seinen (vorläufigen?) Höhepunkt erreichte. Bei den Nicht-Österreicher/innen unterscheidet sich der Armutsverlauf, je nachdem ob EU- oder EFTA-Bürger/innen oder Staatsbürger/innen von Drittstaaten untersucht werden. Bei der ersten Gruppe blieb die Armutsgefährdung im Verlauf der beobachteten Jahre zwischen 2010 und 2016 mit 32 bzw. 33% relativ stabil. Bei der zweiten Gruppe ist dagegen ein deutlicher Anstieg der Armutsgefährdung von 37% im Jahr 2010 auf 46% im Jahr 2016 zu beobachten. Zwar reduzierte sich ihr Armutsrisiko zunächst zwischen 2010 und 2012 auf 28% (2012), allerdings nur, um darauf hin wieder kräftig anzusteigen. Für den Vergleich zwischen 2010 und 2016 bedeuten diese Entwicklungen in Summe, dass der Abstand zwischen den Nicht-Österreicher/inne/n und den Österreicher/inne/n im Hinblick auf ihr Armutsrisiko zugenommen hat. Belief sich die Differenz im Jahr 2010 noch auf 24 Prozentpunkte, so stieg sie bis zum Jahr 2016 auf 30 Prozentpunkte an. Obwohl die gesamtösterreichische Armutsquote zwischen 2010 und 2016 um einen Prozentpunkt abgenommen hat (von 15 auf 14%), spiegelt sich diese Reduktion damit weder relativ noch absolut in der Gruppe der Nicht-Österreicher/innen wider. Mit anderen Worten: die österreichische Armutsquote ist gesunken, *obwohl* sie bei der Gruppe der Nicht-Österreicher/innen drastisch zugenommen hat.

Eine derartige Auseinanderentwicklung zeigt sich auch, wenn lediglich Informationen zur Kinderarmut in Österreich betrachtet werden: zwischen 2011 und 2016 reduzierte sich die Kinderarmutsquote in Österreich von 19% auf 17%. Die Reduktion zeigt sich bei den Österreicher/inne/n überdeutlich, durch eine Abnahme ihrer Gefährdungsrate von 15 auf 11%. Bei den nicht-österreichischen Kindern ist demgegenüber ein gegenläufiger Trend zu beobachten: dort verringerte sich zwischen 2011 und 2013 die Kinderarmutsquote zwar zunächst von 46 auf 38%, allerdings nur, um bis 2015 auf das Niveau von 50% zu klettern und seither dort zu verharren. Kinder in Migrant/inn/enhaushalten sind aktuell somit stärker von Armutsgefährdung betroffen als noch vor 6 Jahren. Weil benachteiligte Lebenslagen von Erwachsenen an ihre Kinder in Österreich zu einem großen Teil vererbt werden (vgl. z.B. Altzinger et al. 2013), ist dies auch nicht weiter verwunderlich: eine Zunahme der Armutsrate bei den Erwachsenen führt zwangsläufig zu einer Zunahme der Armutsrate bei den Kindern, sofern dem nicht politisch entgegengewirkt wird.

Die zwei weiteren Indikatoren, die bei der Armuts- oder Ausgrenzungsgefährdung berücksichtigt werden, sind das Vorhandensein keiner oder nur einer sehr niedrigen Erwerbsintensität im Haushalt sowie das Vorliegen einer erheblichen materiellen Deprivation. Auch im Hinblick auf diese beiden Indikatoren schnitten Nicht-Österreicher/innen in diesem Land 2016 deutlich schlechter ab als Österreicher/innen. Wie veränderten sich ihre Gefährdungsquoten zwischen 2010 und 2016? Bezogen auf den Indikator *keine oder eine sehr geringe Erwerbsintensität* schwankte die Betroffenheit bei den Österreicher/inne/n zwischen 7 und 8% und erreichte im Jahr 2016 ein Ausmaß von 6%. Bei den Nicht-Österreicher/inne/n können ebenso Schwankungen im Zeitverlauf beobachtet werden. In Summe kam es allerdings zwischen 2010 und 2016 zu einer Zunahme der Betroffenheit von 10 auf 16%. Im Vergleich mit den Entwicklungen bei den Nicht-Migrant/inn/en bedeutet dies einmal mehr, dass der Unterschied in der Risikobetroffenheit zwischen den beiden Gruppen im Zeitverlauf größer geworden ist. Tatsächlich betrug der Risikoabstand zwischen den beiden Gruppen im Jahr 2010 lediglich 3 Prozentpunkte, im Jahr 2016 aber bereits 10 Prozentpunkte.

Mitglieder, die in Haushalten leben, die unter einer *erheblichen materiellen Deprivation* leiden, findet man unter der Bevölkerung mit österreichischer Staatsbürgerschaft im 7-jährigen Beobachtungszeitraum eher wenig: zwischen 2010 und 2016 schrumpfte ihr Anteil sogar um einen Prozentpunkt von 3 auf 2%. Auch bei der Bevölkerung mit nicht-österreichischer Staatsbürgerschaft kam es bei diesem Indikator – im Gegensatz zu den beiden anderen Indikatoren zur Armuts- oder Ausgrenzungsgefährdung – zu einer Reduktion der Benachteiligung. Zwischen 2010 und 2016 verringerte sich der Anteil jener, die depriviert sind, von 13% auf 10%. Damit ist der Indikator der erheblichen materiellen Deprivation auch der einzige der bislang betrachteten Indikatoren, bei dem sich der Risikoabstand zwischen der österreichischen und der nicht-österreichischen Bevölkerung im 7-Jahresvergleich verringert hat: von 10 Prozentpunkten im Jahr 2010 auf 8 Prozentpunkte im Jahr 2016.

Abbildung 1 skizziert zusammenfassend die unterschiedlichen Entwicklungen im Hinblick auf die Armuts- und Ausgrenzungsgefährdung sowie der drei Subindikatoren zwischen 2010 und 2016 bei den Österreicher/inne/n und den Nicht-Österreicher/inne/n.

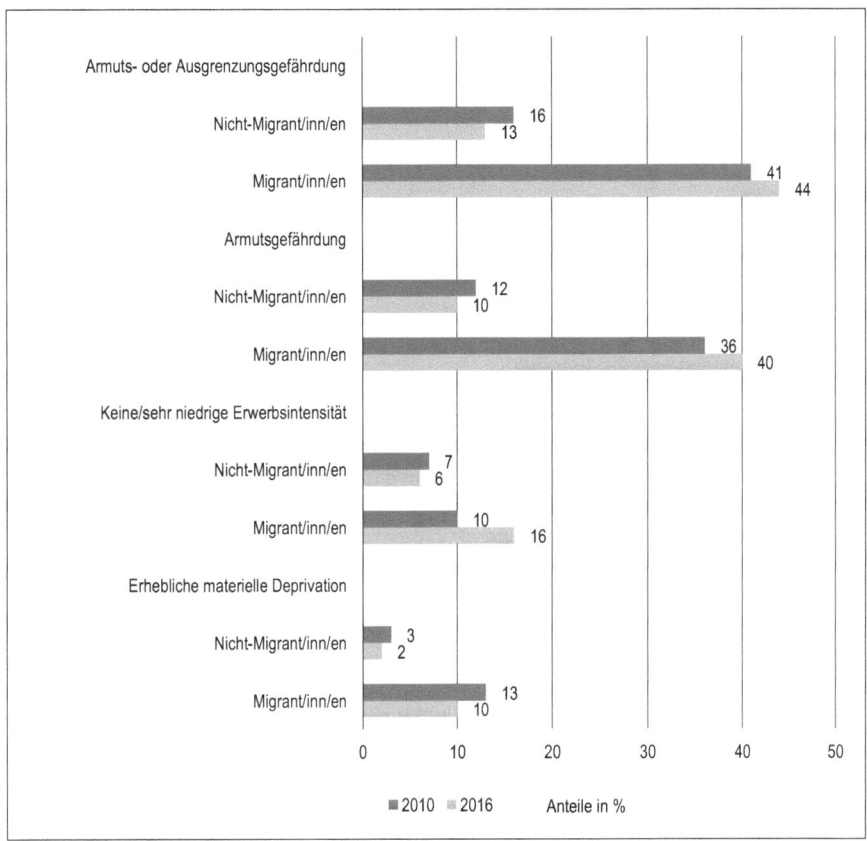

Abbildung 1 Entwicklung der Armuts- oder Ausgrenzungsgefährdung bei Migrant/inn/en und Nicht-Migrant/inn/en, Österreich 2010 und 2016

Quelle: Statistik Austria 2017b: Tabelle 5.4a; Statistik Austria 2016: Tabelle 5.4a, eigene Darstellung

Ursachen für die höhere Armuts- und Ausgrenzungsgefährdung von Migrant/inn/en in Österreich

In der Regel werden ein hohes Armuts- oder Ausgrenzungsrisiko durch verschiedene Ursachenzusammenhänge erklärt, die sich im Groben auf drei Stränge reduzieren lassen (Heitzmann 2017, S. 42ff.). Erstens zeigt sich, dass eine möglichst Vollzeit-Erwerbstätigkeit der Erwachsenen in einem Haushalt maßgeblich zur Reduktion ihres Armuts- und Ausgrenzungsrisikos beiträgt. Dieser Zusammenhang galt etwa ausnahmslos für alle Mitgliedsstaaten der Europäischen Union: 2014 war die Armutsgefährdung dieser Haushalte in allen EU-Mitgliedstaaten geringer als im Bevölkerungsschnitt. Auch der umgekehrte Zusammenhang ließ sich nachweisen: Personen in Haushalten, in denen die Erwerbsintensität unter 45% lag, hatten alle eine höhere Armutsgefährdungsrate als im Vergleich zum Bevölkerungsschnitt (Heitzmann 2017, S. 43). Zweitens macht es einen Unterschied, wie die Haushalte der Menschen zusammengesetzt sind. So zeigte sich in allen Ländern der Europäischen Union einerseits eine höhere Armutsgefährdung von alleinerziehenden Haushalten im Gegensatz zur Durchschnittsbevölkerung und – mit Ausnahme von nur zwei Mitgliedsstaaten – eine überproportionale Armutsgefährdung von Großfamilien (mit mehr als drei Kindern). Der dritte Ursachenzusammenhang, welcher die überproportionale Betroffenheit mancher Gruppen im Zusammenhang mit Armut und Ausgrenzung erklärt, ist zentraler Inhalt dieses Beitrags: die Herkunft. Mit Ausnahme einiger osteuropäischer Staaten weisen Migrant/inn/en innerhalb der EU eine in der Regel deutlich höhere Armutsgefährdung auf als die nicht-migrantische Bevölkerung.

In diesem Beitrag wurde bereits auf die eklatanten Unterschiede in der Armuts- und Ausgrenzungsgefährdungslage von österreichischen und nicht-österreichischen Bewohner/inne/n eingegangen. Durch die Darstellung der Ergebnisse zum Indikator „keine oder sehr geringe Erwerbsintensität" wurde auch schon die Bedeutung der bezahlten Erwerbsarbeit als wichtiger Präventionsfaktor gegen Armut skizziert. Doch es ist nicht nur die Erwerbsintensität im Haushalt von Relevanz, sondern generell die Qualität der Erwerbsarbeit, die sich nicht zuletzt in der Höhe des Erwerbseinkommens widerspiegelt. Dazu muss zunächst festgehalten werden, dass laut EU-SILC Statistik im Jahr 2016 für 67% der Personen mit österreichischer Staatsbürgerschaft das Einkommen aus selbständiger oder unselbständiger Arbeit das Haupteinkommen im Haushalt ausmacht (Statistik Austria 2017b, Tabelle 1.7a). Bei den eingebürgerten Österreicher/inne/n beläuft sich der entsprechende Anteil sogar auf 81%. Aber auch in den Haushalten der Nicht-Österreicher/innen ist mit 73% das Erwerbseinkommen die Haupteinkommensquelle ihres Haushalts. Das gilt vor allem für EU- und EFTA-Bürger/innen mit 82%. Aber auch Drittstaatsangehörige weisen mit 65% eine ähnlich hohe Quote wie die Österreicher/innen auf. Betrachtet man demgegenüber das monatliche Erwerbseinkommen der aktuell unselbständig erwerbstätigen Personen im Alter zwischen 20 und 64 Jahren, dann zeigt sich ein deutlicher Unterschied im Medianeinkommen: Österreicher/innen bezogen laut EU-SILC Statistik im Median ein Bruttomonatsgehalt von € 2400 (waren sie eingebürgert, dann belief sich ihr Bruttoerwerbseinkommen auf € 2007). Nicht-Österreicher/innen erhielten im Median ein monatliches Bruttogehalt von € 1900 (Statistik Austria 2017b, Tabelle 9.3). Diese Diskrepanz lässt sich unter anderem damit erklären, dass ausländische Mitbürger/innen deutlich häufiger einer Niedriglohnbeschäftigung nachgehen (16%) als Österreicher/innen (7%). Nicht-Österreicher/innen sind selbst bei hohem Arbeitsvolumen (mehr als 34 Stunden pro Woche) deutlich häufiger niedriglohnbeschäftigt (12%) als Österreicher/innen (4%).

Ein Grund für ihre schlechtere Positionierung am Arbeitsmarkt und die daraus folgenden geringeren Erwerbseinkommen ist das im Durchschnitt niedrigere Bildungsniveau der Nicht-Österreicher/innen. Beispielsweise wiesen nach der EU-

SILC Statistik im Jahr 2016 etwa 19% der österreichischen Staatsbürger/innen über 16 Jahre die Pflichtschule als höchste abgeschlossene Ausbildung aus. Bei Haushalten von Nicht-Österreicher/inne/n waren dies 31%. Auch bei diesem Indikator zeigen sich deutliche Unterschiede innerhalb der Gruppen der Österreicher/innen und der Nicht-Österreicher/innen: So liegt der Anteil der eingebürgerten Österreicher/innen mit maximal Pflichtschulabschluss sogar bei 33%. Demgegenüber haben EU- oder EFTA-Staatsbürger/innen mit 13% den geringsten Anteil an Personen mit lediglich einem Pflichtschulabschluss. Anders verhält es sich bei Drittstaatsangehörigen: knapp die Hälfte (47%) wies als höchsten Bildungsabschluss die Pflichtschule auf und hat damit auch die geringsten Chancen, am österreichischen Arbeitsmarkt zu reüssieren und hohe Gehälter zu verdienen.

Weil auch die Haushaltszusammensetzung einen wichtigen Einfluss auf das Armuts- und Ausgrenzungsrisiko in Österreich hat, wird diese im Folgenden zwischen Österreicher/inne/n und Nicht-Österreicher/inne/n verglichen (Statistik Austria 2017b, Tabelle 10.2a und 10.2b). Im Gegensatz zu den bisherigen Darstellungen – und aufgrund der Betrachtung eines Haushaltszusammenhangs – wird dafür eine andere Abgrenzung von Migrant/inn/en vorgenommen als bisher. Zum einen werden im Folgenden Haushalte berücksichtigt, in denen zumindest ein Haushaltsmitglied über die Staatsbürgerschaft eines Drittstaats verfügt („Haushalte mit Drittstaatsmitglied"), zum anderen Haushalte, in denen zumindest eine Person eingebürgert worden ist, die vormals die Staatsbürgerschaft eines Drittstaates besessen hat („Haushalte mit eingebürgertem Mitglied"). In Haushalten mit einem Drittstaatsmitglied lebten laut EU-SILC Statistik im Jahr 2016 immerhin 1,002 Millionen Personen, in Haushalten mit einem eingebürgerten Mitglied immerhin noch 356.000 Personen. Im Vergleich mit der Anzahl der Drittstaatsangehörigen und der eingebürgerten Österreicher/innen in den vorigen Kapiteln, die auf Basis individueller Staatsbürgerschaften berechnet wurde, ist die Anzahl der Personen, die in den beiden jetzt untersuchten Haushaltstypen leben, deutlich höher. dies untermauert, dass in diesen Haushaltstypen auch Menschen mit österreichischer, EU- oder EFTA-Staatsbürgerschaft zusammen leben.

Zunächst lässt sich festhalten, dass im österreichischen Durchschnittshaushalt ein höherer Altersschnitt erzielt wird als in Haushalten mit einem Drittstaatsangehörigen oder einem eingebürgerten Mitglied. Das zeigt sich etwa daran, dass 19% der österreichischen Durchschnittsbevölkerung in Haushalten mit Pensionseinkommen leben. Das gilt aber nur für 3% der Personen in Haushalten mit einem Drittstaatsmitglied und für 6% in Haushalten mit einem eingebürgerten Mitglied. Demgegenüber leben 76% der Personen in Haushalten mit einem Drittstaatsmitglied (64% mit einem eingebürgerten Mitglied) in Haushalten, in denen auch Kinder leben – im Gegensatz zu 46% im österreichischen Durchschnitt. Wie oben angeführt, zeigt sich bei Einelternhaushalten aber bei auch Haushalten mit mindestens drei Kindern europaweit eine überproportionale Armutsgefährdung. Im Vergleich zur österreichischen Bevölkerung leben weniger Personen in Haushalten mit einem Drittstaatsangehörigen in einem Einelternhaushalt (8% versus 5%), aber deutlich mehr in Haushalten mit mindestens drei Kindern (19% versus 34%).

Drittstaatsangehörige wohnen somit sehr häufig mit mindestens vier weiteren Personen zusammen. Die Wohnungsgröße dürfte mit dieser Bewohner/innenanzahl nicht mithalten, leiden doch 36% der Personen in Haushalten mit einem Drittstaatsangehörigen unter Überbelag (im Gegensatz zum österreichischen Durchschnittswert von 7%).

Angehörige von Haushalten mit einer eingebürgerten Personen weisen einen höheren Anteil von Alleinerziehenden auf (10%), aber einen der österreichischen Durchschnittsbevölkerung ähnlichen Anteil an Großfamilien mit mindestens drei Kindern (20%): nichtsdestotrotz klagen 16% über Überbelag. Tatsächlich weisen Personen in Haushalten von Eingebürgerten und Drittstaatsangehörigen eine schlechtere Wohnqualität als der österreichische Durchschnitt auf (z.B. in Hinsicht auf Feuchtigkeit, Schimmel, dunkle Räume etc.). Unterschiede gibt es aber auch im Hinblick auf das Rechtsverhältnis zur Wohnung (z.B. leben sie häufiger in Miete und weniger häufig im Eigentum als im Vergleich zu Österreicher/innen) oder auf die Wohnregion: So leben etwa 42% der Personen, die in einem Haushalt mit einem Drittstaatsangehörigen wohnen, in Wien. Ein ähnlich hoher Wert – und tatsächlich ein deutlich höherer als im Schnitt der österreichischen Bevölkerung (21%) – zeigt sich auch bei Personen, die mit eingebürgerten Österreicher/inne/n zusammenleben (37%).

Fazit

Im vorliegenden Beitrag wurde die Armut und Ausgrenzung von Migrant/inn/en in Österreich skizziert. Dazu wurden insbesondere drei Subindikatoren betrachtet: die Armutsgefährdung, das Vorliegen keiner oder nur einer sehr niedrigen Erwerbsintensität und das Vorhandensein einer erheblichen materiellen Deprivation. Als Migrant/inn/en wurden Personen definiert, die eine nicht-österreichische Staatsbürgerschaft besitzen.

Bei der empirischen Analyse zeigte sich einerseits eine gegenwärtig deutlich höhere Armuts- und Ausgrenzungsgefährdung dieser Bevölkerungsgruppe im Gegensatz zu Nicht-Migrant/inn/en. Auch Personen mit österreichischer Staatsbürgerschaft aber migrantischem Hintergrund wiesen eine höhere Gefährdung auf. Andererseits wurde auch die Entwicklung der letzten Jahre beobachtet und insbesondere ein Vergleich mit dem Jahr 2010 angestellt. Mit Ausnahme der erheblichen materiellen Deprivation hat sich dabei gezeigt, dass die Unterschiede in der Gefährdung zwischen den Österreicher/inne/n und den Nicht-Österreicher/inne/n im Zeitverlauf zugenommen haben. Dieser Trend erschwert es dem österreichischen Wohlfahrtsstaat nicht nur, das Europa-2020-Ziel zur Reduktion der Armuts- und Ausgrenzungsquote zu erreichen. Die empirische Evidenz deutet zudem darauf hin, dass sich die Lebenschancen der österreichischen und der nicht-österreichischen Bevölkerung in diesem Land auseinander entwickelt haben. Eine Umkehrung dieses Trends ist – mit Ausnahme des Indikators zur erheblichen materiellen Deprivation – aktuell nicht sichtbar. Besonders drastisch – und im

Hinblick auf zukünftige Lebenschancen auch besonders besorgniserregend – zeigt sich dies an der Entwicklung der Kinderarmut.

Der österreichische Wohlfahrtsstaat ist seit Jahren unter Druck: ökonomische Entwicklungen (z.B. geringes Wirtschaftswachstum, hohe Arbeitslosigkeit), soziale Entwicklungen (z.B. Veränderungen in Familienstrukturen, wie etwa weniger stabile Partnerschaften), vor allem aber demographische Entwicklungen (z.B. steigende Lebenserwartung, abnehmende Fertilitätsquoten) führen unter Berücksichtigung der hohen Staatsschulden und des damit verbundenen geringen Gestaltungsspielraums für sozialpolitische Maßnahmen zu einem engen finanziellen Korsett und dem Druck, Sozialausgaben zu reduzieren (Österle und Heitzmann 2016). Umso wichtiger ist es, den Bürger/inne/n Österreichs die Möglichkeit zu geben, sich aus eigener Kraft ökonomisch absichern zu können. Dies gelingt allerdings nur dann, wenn Chancengleichheit garantiert werden kann. Wie gezeigt wurde, ist diese Chancengleichheit in vielen Bereichen im Vergleich von Migrant/inn/en und Nicht-Migrant/inn/en nicht gegeben. Darüber hinaus haben sich die Lebenslagen der Nicht-Österreicher/innen, im Hinblick auf die Indikatoren zur Armutsgefährdung und zur Erwerbsintensität, im Vergleich zu den Österreicher/inne/n in den letzten Jahren absolut und relativ sogar noch verschlechtert. Dies erfordert höhere Investitionen vor allem in das Humankapital von Migrant/inn/en (und eingebürgerten Österreicher/inne/n) – vornehmlich in deren Kinder. Studien haben gezeigt, dass in Österreich insbesondere der Bildungsstatus von den Eltern an die Kinder vererbt wird (Altzinger et al. 2013). Eine gute Ausbildung ist aber Grundlage für den Einstieg in eine qualitativ hochwertige Beschäftigung. Und eine hochwertige Beschäftigung führt zu einem höheren Einkommen, das wiederum die Einkommensarmut des einzelnen, aber – mittels Durchbrechung der Armutsvererbung – auch das Risiko der Kinder reduziert, von Einkommensarmut aktuell oder in Zukunft betroffen zu sein. Gerade aufgrund der oben beschriebenen demographischen Herausforderungen ist es notwendig, der Bevölkerung mit Migrationshintergrund eine gleichberechtigte Teilhabe am österreichischen Lebensstandard zu ermöglichen. Das ist nicht nur aus humanen Gründen erstrebenswert und aus menschenrechtlicher Sicht notwendig, sondern vor allem auch aus ökonomischen und sozialpolitischen Überlegungen sinnvoll (Biffl 2016). Im aufgeheizten Diskurs rund um die im Jahr 2015 stattgefundene „Flüchtlingskrise" gilt es damit vor allem die Chancen der Zuwanderung aufzuzeigen und nicht (nur) die unbestritten schwierigen Herausforderungen ins Zentrum der Debatten zu stellen.

Literatur

Altzinger, Wilfried / Lamei, Nadja / Rumplmaier, Bernhard / Schneebaum, Alyssa (2013) Intergenerationelle soziale Mobilität in Österreich. In: Statistische Nachrichten 2013(1), 48-62.

Biffl, Gudrun (2016) Auf dem Weg zu einer nachhaltigen Migrationspolitik. In: Wirtschaftspolitische Blätter 2016(3), 579-594.

Biffl, Gudrun / Dimmel, Nikolaus (Hrsg.) (2011) Migrationsmanagement, Band 1: Grundzüge des Managements von Migration und Integration (omninum, Bad Vöslau).

Biffl, Gudrun / Dimmel, Nikolaus (Hrsg.) (2016) Migrationsmanagement, Band 2: Wohnen im Zusammenwirken mit Migration und Integration (omninum, Bad Vöslau).

Bundeskanzleramt (o.J.) Reformprogramm Österreich 2015 (Bundeskanzleramt, Wien).

Bundesministerium für Arbeit, Soziales und Konsumentenschutz (2017) Sozialbericht: Sozialpolitische Entwicklungen und Maßnahmen 2015-2016. Sozialpolitische Analysen (BMASK, Wien).

Gächter, August (2014) Migration und Armut. In: Dimmel, Nikolaus / Schenk, Martin / Stelzer-Orthofer, Christine (Hrsg.) Handbuch Armut in Österreich (Studienverlag, Innsbruck, Wien, Bozen) 280-288.

Heitzmann, Karin (2017) Poverty Prevention: Towards good reform quality, but not equally addressed for all. In: Bertelsmann Stiftung (Hrsg.) Social Policy in the EU - Reform Barometer 2016: Social Inclusion Monitor Europe (Bertelsmann Stiftung, Gütersloh) 42-60.

Österle, August / Heitzmann, Karin (2016) Reforming the Austrian Welfare System: Facing demographic and economic challenges in a federal welfare state. In: Schubert, Klaus / de Villota, Paloma / Kuhlmann, Johanna (Hrsg.) Challenges to European Welfare Systems (New York, Springer) 11-35.

Statistik Austria (2015a) Einkommen, Armut und Lebensbedingungen: Tabellenband EU-SILC 2011 VWD (Rev. 4 vom 19.11.2015) (Statistik Austria, Wien).

Statistik Austria (2015b) Einkommen, Armut und Lebensbedingungen: Tabellenband EU-SILC 2012 (Rev. 3 vom 20.03.2015) (Statistik Austria, Wien).

Statistik Austria (2015c) Einkommen, Armut und Lebensbedingungen: Tabellenband EU-SILC 2013 (Rev. 4 vom 13.08.2015) (Statistik Austria, Wien).

Statistik Austria (2015d) Einkommen, Armut und Lebensbedingungen: Tabellenband EU-SILC 2014 (Rev. 4 vom 19.11.2015) (Statistik Austria, Wien).

Statistik Austria (2016) Einkommen, Armut und Lebensbedingungen: Tabellenband EU-SILC 2010 VWD (Rev. 4 vom 22.07.2016) (Statistik Austria, Wien).

Statistik Austria (2017a) Einkommen, Armut und Lebensbedingungen: Tabellenband EU-SILC 2015 (Rev. 1 vom 16.05.2017) (Statistik Austria, Wien).

Statistik Austria (2017b) Einkommen, Armut und Lebensbedingungen: Tabellenband EU-SILC 2016 (Statistik Austria, Wien).

Wiesböck, Laura (2011) Migration - Exklusion - Armut. Trend- und Strukturanalysen zur Ausgrenzung von MigrantInnen in Österreich. In: Verwiebe, Roland (Hrsg.) Armut in Österreich: Bestandsausnahme, Trends, Risikogruppen (Braumüller, Wien) 209-231.

Migration als Prüfstein des sozialinvestiven Wohlfahrtsstaats

Thomas Leoni

Zusammenfassung

Internationale Migration stellt den Wohlfahrtsstaat vor große Herausforderungen. Um diese Herausforderungen zu bewältigen, bedarf es einer stärkeren Ausrichtung auf präventive, sozialinvestive Eingriffe und auf langfristige Ziele. Bei der Gestaltung des sozialpolitischen Instrumentariums ist eine Lebenslaufperspektive notwendig, um gezielt auf Zusammenhänge und Übergänge zwischen Lebensphasen einzugehen. Zentrale Hebel einer solchen sozialinvestiven Ausrichtung des Wohlfahrtsstaats sind Investitionen in Bildung und Humankapital, Unterstützung bei der Aktivierung und Integration am Arbeitsmarkt in allen Lebenslagen, sowie die Förderung von Chancengerechtigkeit bereits in frühen Lebensphasen. Im Laufe der Jahrzehnte hat Österreich vor allem in Bezug auf die berufliche und gesellschaftliche Eingliederung von Migrant/inn/en und ihrer Nachkommen große Defizite aufgebaut. Versäumnisse auf politischer Ebene haben sich mit unterschiedlichen Einwanderungswellen und stets neuen Herausforderungen überlagert. In der jüngsten Vergangenheit fand in der österreichischen Migrationspolitik eine Stärkung der integrationspolitischen Dimension statt, die auch von Entwicklungen auf EU-Ebene gefördert wurde. Die Integration von Migrant/inn/en wird aber auch in der absehbaren Zukunft ein schwieriger Prüfstein für die sozialinvestive Weiterentwicklung des Wohlfahrtsstaats bleiben.

Einleitung

Der tiefgreifende wirtschaftliche und gesellschaftliche Wandel der letzten Jahrzehnte brachte in Österreich und den anderen europäischen Ländern neue Herausforderungen für den Wohlfahrtsstaat, veränderte aber auch das Verständnis seiner Rolle und Funktionen. Das Sozialsystem wird nach wie vor in erster Linie mit der Absicherung gegen Erwerbs- und Lebensrisiken wie Krankheit, Arbeitslosigkeit und Armut assoziiert. Ausgehend vom sozialwissenschaftlichen Diskurs ist in den vergangenen Jahren mit dem Konzept des „investiven Sozialstaats" bzw. „sozialinvestiven Wohlfahrtsstaats" aber zunehmend ein Verständnis in den Vordergrund gerückt, das den Wohlfahrtsstaat nicht auf seine Absicherungs- und Schutzfunktion beschränkt (Esping-Andersen et al. 2002; Morel et al. 2012).

Der Wohlfahrtsstaat soll demnach vermehrt präventiv wirken, d.h. die Eintrittswahrscheinlichkeit von negativen Ereignissen wie Arbeitslosigkeit, Arbeitsunfähigkeit und Armut minimieren. Der Sozialstaat wird darüber hinaus als eine Produktivkraft verstanden, die auch einen maßgeblichen Beitrag zur Innovationskraft und internationalen Wettbewerbsfähigkeit wissensbasierter Volkswirtschaften leisten kann. Investitionen in Bildung und Humankapital, Unterstützung bei der Aktivierung und Integration am Arbeitsmarkt, Maßnahmen, um Menschen bereits in frühen Lebensphasen zu fördern und Chancengerechtigkeit herzustellen: Das sind die zentralen Hebel, mit denen der Wohlfahrtsstaat in wirtschaftlich hoch entwickelten, sozial und kulturell stark ausdifferenzierten und in einem globalen Verflechtungsgefüge stehenden Gesellschaften gleichzeitig soziale Teilhabe, ökonomischen Erfolg und fiskalische Nachhaltigkeit gewährleisten soll.

Obwohl in der Forschung und auch auf Policy-Ebene die Diskussion und Analyse einer sozialinvestiven Ausrichtung des Wohlfahrtsstaats bereits fortgeschritten ist[1], wurde bisher der Zusammenhang zwischen sozialinvestivem Wohlfahrtsstaat und Migration kaum thematisiert.[2] Der vorliegende Beitrag will in einem ersten Schritt aufzeigen, inwiefern der im sozialpolitischen Diskurs vollzogene Perspektivenwechsel für Migrationspolitik von Relevanz ist. In einem zweiten Schritt wird der Frage nachgegangen, inwieweit auf nationaler bzw. europäischer Ebene das Verständnis und die bisherige Umsetzung von Migrationspolitik mit den Grundgedanken eines sozialinvestiven Wohlfahrtsstaats konsistent sind.

Vorab ist anzumerken, dass Migrationspolitik ein sehr breites Spektrum an Handlungsfeldern abdeckt und unterschiedlich abgegrenzt werden kann. Sie erstreckt sich von Grenzschutz, Aufenthalts- und Einreisebestimmungen, über die Regelung der Rechte und Pflichten von Ausländer/inne/n im Inland bis hin zu einem weitläufigen Feld an Maßnahmen zur beruflichen und gesellschaftlichen Integration. Stjernø (2017) unterscheidet vereinfachend zwischen einer Kontroll- und einer Integrationsfunktion der Migrationspolitik. Auch Migration selbst ist ein vielschichtiges, heterogenes Phänomen. Wichtige Unterscheidungsmerkmale in Bezug auf Einwanderungsformen sind die Zeitlichkeit (dauerhafte Niederlassung, zeitlich begrenzter Aufenthalt, Pendeltätigkeit usw.), der vorwiegende Beweggrund (Beschäftigungsaufnahme, Familiennachzug, Flucht, Ausbildung, usw.) und die Charakteristika der Migrant/inn/en selbst (Herkunftsland, Alter, Qualifikation, usw.).

Im vorliegenden Beitrag stehen die integrationspolitische Komponente der Migrationspolitik und längerfristige (dauerhafte) Migrationsformen im Vordergrund. Das hängt einerseits damit zusammen, dass der Aktionsradius des Wohlfahrtsstaats viel stärker die Integrations- als die Kontrollfunktion der Migrationspolitik betrifft. Aber auch damit, dass in einer österreichischen Perspektive v.a. aufgrund der Personenfreizügigkeit in der EU die fremdenrechtliche Steuerung der Migrationsströme einen relativ geringen Handlungsspielraum aufweist (Biffl et al. 2016).

---

[1] Für einen umfassenden Überblick siehe Hemerijck (2017).
[2] Eine Ausnahme ist Stjernø (2017).

Die Kernkonzepte des sozialinvestiven Wohlfahrtsstaats

Die Idee des Sozialstaats als Produktivkraft ist zum Teil eine Reaktion auf die (reduktive) Wahrnehmung des Wohlfahrtsstaats als reinen Kostenfaktor. Während sich in dieser (neoliberalen) Sicht ökonomische Effizienz und soziale Gerechtigkeit in einem unüberwindbaren Zielkonflikt befinden, hebt die sozialinvestive Perspektive Handlungsfelder und Maßnahmen hervor, die, vor allem in einer Betrachtung über die Zeit, nicht zwangsläufig eine Zielgröße der anderen opfern. Gleichzeitig sind die analytischen Konzepte und handlungspolitischen Lösungsansätze der sozialinvestiven Perspektive als Antwort auf die wirtschaftlichen und sozialen Herausforderungen der Post-Industrialisierung und der damit einhergehenden Entstehung von „neuen sozialen Risiken" entwickelt worden.[3] Zu den Veränderungen, die seit den 1970er-Jahren neue gesellschaftliche Risikostrukturen nach sich gezogen haben, zählen der stets neue Qualifikationen erfordernde technologische Wandel, das Aufbrechen traditioneller Beschäftigungsformen, die Intensivierung des internationalen Wettbewerbs und der Anstieg der Ungleichheit. Hinzu kommen die Alterung der Bevölkerung, die Zunahme der internationalen Migration und das Aufbrechen traditioneller Familienstrukturen. Der Sozialstaat sieht sich daher mit einer Reihe von neuen Herausforderungen konfrontiert - bei gleichzeitig stark eingeengtem budgetärem Spielraum.[4]

Die Anerkennung der wirtschaftspolitischen Bedeutung des Wohlfahrtsstaats und die Verfolgung von Effizienzzielen mittels sozialstaatlicher Eingriffe ist für sich genommen nichts Neues.[5] Neu am sozialinvestiven Ansatz ist das Bestreben, einen konsistenten konzeptuellen Rahmen zu schaffen und diesen mit entsprechenden Maßnahmen zu füllen, um die unterschiedlichen Zielsetzungen des Wohlfahrtsstaats im Kontext neuer sozialer und wirtschaftlicher Herausforderungen zu verorten. Anstatt sich auf spezifische Risikotypologien zu konzentrieren und Personen, die von entsprechenden negativen Ereignissen betroffen sind, zu kompensieren, soll das Sozialsystem verstärkt präventiv eingreifen, um das Auftreten dieser Ereignisse zu vermeiden oder ihre Auswirkungen zu minimieren.

Vor allem drei Erkenntnisse sind kennzeichnend für die sozialinvestive Perspektive auf den Wohlfahrtsstaat. Erstens die zentrale Bedeutung von Humankapital, sowohl für das individuelle Wohlergehen als auch für die gesamtwirtschaftli-

---

[3] Der Begriff „neue soziale Risiken" geht unter anderem auf Arbeiten von Peter Taylor-Gooby (2004) und Giuliano Bonoli (2006) zurück. Typische Beispiele für neue soziale Risiken sind Probleme der Arbeitsmarktintegration aufgrund fehlender bzw. veralteter Qualifikationen, Armutsgefährdung trotz Erwerbstätigkeit, Unvereinbarkeit von Familien- und Erwerbsleben sowie unzureichende soziale Absicherung aufgrund von atypischer Beschäftigung (Eppel und Leoni 2011).

[4] Paul Pierson (1998) prägte dazu den Begriff der „permanent austerity".

[5] So wurde beispielsweise bereits in den Nachkriegsjahrzehnten in Schweden die aktive Arbeitsmarktpolitik auch mit Blick auf die konjunkturstabilisierenden Auswirkungen entwickelt. Wichtige Teile des Sozialsystems, wie die Kranken-, Arbeitslosen- und Pensionsversicherung dienen nicht nur der Absicherung, sondern auch der Korrektur von Marktversagen (siehe dazu z.B. Barr 2012).

che Entwicklung. Diese Erkenntnis stützt sich unter anderem auf die in den 1980er-Jahren entwickelte endogene Wachstumstheorie, die in Bildung sowie im Erwerb von Fertigkeiten und Kompetenzen die wichtigste Triebkraft wirtschaftlicher Entwicklung sieht. Ein zweiter Schwerpunkt betrifft die zentrale Rolle des Arbeitsmarkts und der Erwerbstätigkeit als Anker für soziale Teilhabe und Prävention gegen soziale Risiken. Um seine präventive Funktion ausbauen zu können, muss der Wohlfahrtsstaat demnach eine breite Palette an Programmen und Politikfeldern aktivieren, mit dem Ziel, Humankapitalbildung und Beschäftigung zu fördern: Angefangen im Bildungs- und Weiterbildungsbereich, in der aktiven Arbeitsmarktpolitik, aber auch im Bereich der Maßnahmen zur Erleichterung der Vereinbarkeit von Familie und Beruf sowie zur Unterstützung der Beschäftigung bei gesundheitlichen Beeinträchtigungen.

Die dritte und wohl wichtigste Erkenntnis bezieht sich auf den analytischen Rahmen zur Identifikation von sozialen Risiken und zur Gestaltung von Maßnahmen. Statt einer Querschnittsperspektive, in der spezifische Bedürfnisse und Risiken einzeln (d.h. unabhängig von früheren und späteren Ereignissen) betrachtet und entsprechende Maßnahmen dazu entworfen werden, betont der sozialinvestive Ansatz die Bedeutung einer Längsschnittbetrachtung, d.h. einer Lebenslaufperspektive, in der die Interdependenzen zwischen den einzelnen Lebensphasen im Vordergrund stehen (Abbildung 1). Diese Lebenslaufperspektive ist essentiell, um Verbindungen zwischen Risiken in unterschiedlichen Lebensphasen erkennen, verstärkt auf kumulative Benachteiligungsprozesse eingehen und langfristige Ziele verfolgen zu können. Forschungsergebnisse aus den Sozialwissenschaften, den kognitiven Wissenschaften und anderen Disziplinen belegen den starken Einfluss der frühen Lebensphasen auf die spätere Entwicklung. Aufgrund ihres Potenzials für hohen langfristigen Nutzen räumt der sozialinvestive Ansatz implizit einer Politik, die frühzeitig im Lebensverlauf eingreift, eine hohe Priorität ein. Es besteht zudem ein wachsender Konsens darüber, dass eine hohe gesellschaftliche Ungleichheit nicht nur ethische Probleme aufwirft und den sozialen Zusammenhalt gefährdet, sondern auch auf gesamtwirtschaftlicher Ebene schädlich ist, weil sie soziale Mobilität verringert und die Bildungschancen von Menschen aus benachteiligten Haushalten beeinträchtigt (siehe z.B. OECD 2015). Ungleichheit und Humankapitalbildung sind somit eng miteinander verflochten, weshalb soziale Investitionen in frühe Lebensphasen sowohl normativ wünschenswert als auch notwendig sind, um Benachteiligung entgegenzuwirken und die Erwerbschancen im späteren Leben zu fördern.

Darüber hinaus leitet sich aus der Lebenslaufbetrachtung ein verstärktes Augenmerk auf die Übergänge zwischen Lebensphasen ab, die in den individuellen Biographien kritische Momente mit potentiell langfristigen negativen Folgen darstellen. Beispiele dafür sind der Übergang von Ausbildung zum Arbeitsmarkt, abwechselnde Phasen von Erwerbsarbeit und Kinderbetreuung sowie die Wiedereingliederung am Arbeitsmarkt nach einer schweren Erkrankung. Die Anzahl der

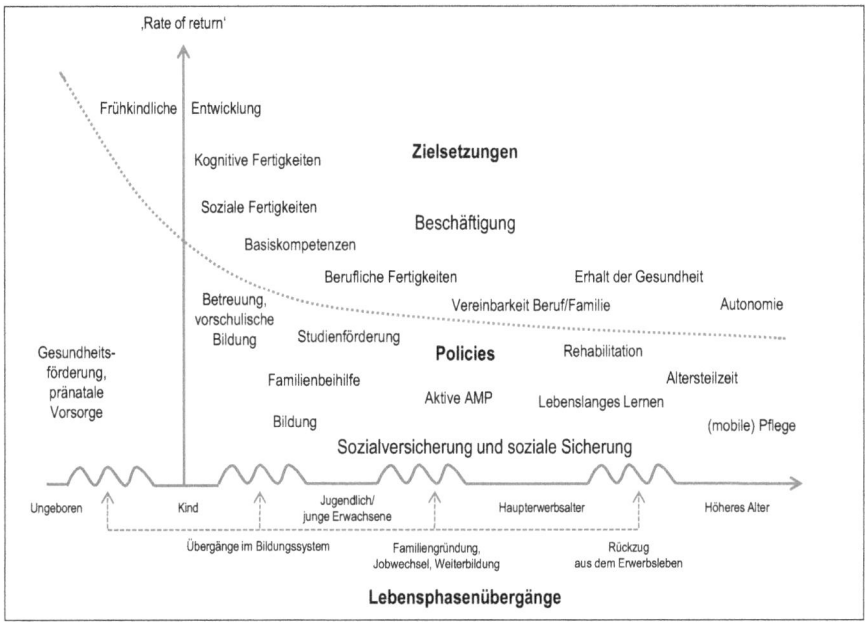

Abbildung 1 Lebenslaufperspektive auf soziale Investitionen
Quelle: Eigene Darstellung auf Basis von Kvist (2014).

Übergänge, die die Menschen im Laufe ihres Lebens meistern müssen, ist gestiegen. Jobwechsel sind viel häufiger geworden, die Verschränkung zwischen Erwerbs- und familiärer Betreuungstätigkeit hat sich vergrößert, die Halbwertszeit von Wissen hat sich verkürzt und somit die Notwendigkeit von Phasen der Weiterbildung und beruflichen Umorientierung erhöht. Die individuellen Biographien sind „flüssiger" und die Erwerbsbiographien länger geworden, weshalb Einzelpersonen ein höheres Maß an Flexibilität und Anpassungsfähigkeit benötigen als in der Vergangenheit.

Der Fokus auf Prävention und den investiven Charakter bestimmter Leistungen und sozialstaatlicher Interventionen darf allerdings nicht darüber hinwegtäuschen, dass „passive" Sozialleistungen und die Absicherung gegen „alte" Risiken nach wie vor eine zentrale Rolle spielen. Prävention und Aktivierung können konventionelle Einkommensabsicherung nicht ersetzen. Eine effektive wohlfahrtsstaatliche Strategie bedarf eines positiven Kreislaufs, wodurch sozialer Schutz und soziale Investitionen sich gegenseitig verstärken (Esping-Andersen et al. 2002; Vandenbroucke und Vleminckx 2011). Vereinfachend gesprochen ruht das sozialinvestive Wohlfahrtskonzept auf drei Säulen. Die erste ist Bildung und Humankapitalbildung als Voraussetzung für den Erfolg in der ökonomischen Sphäre und als Basis für das Wohlbefinden. Die zweite ist die Unterstützung der Beschäftigung und der Arbeitsmarktintegration, mit Erwerbstätigkeit als Kardinalpunkt der wirtschaftlichen Unabhängigkeit. Die dritte Säule entspricht der "traditionellen" Dimension der Wohlfahrtsstaatstätigkeit, die dem sozialen Schutz und der Umverteilung gewidmet ist. Eine von Hemerijck (2015) vorgeschlagene Konzeptualisierung unterscheidet in diesem Zusammenhang zwischen „flows" (Aktivierungs- und Arbeitsmarktübergänge), „stocks" (Humankapital) und „buffers" (Sicherheitsnetze für Sozialschutz).

Der sozialinvestive Blick auf die Migrations- und Integrationspolitik

Österreich weist seit Jahren einen wachsenden Anteil der Personen mit Migrationshintergrund an der Gesamtbevölkerung auf. 2016 waren rund 22% der in Österreich lebenden Bevölkerung Zuwanderer/inne/n der ersten oder zweiten Generation.[6] Gleichzeitig haben sich die Migrationsströme über die Zeit stark verändert; durch die Überlagerung unterschiedlicher Einwanderungswellen ist der Kreis der Personen mit Migrationshintergrund ein sehr heterogener und durch unterschiedlichste Voraussetzungen und Bedürfnisse gekennzeichnet. Nicht nur die Zahl der eingewanderten Personen und ihrer Nachkommen hat sich erhöht, sondern auch ihre kulturelle und sprachliche Diversität (Biffl et al. 2016).

Internationale Migration ist somit ein Grund dafür, dass unsere Gesellschaft vielfältiger geworden ist, aber auch dafür, dass deren Komplexität und Ausdifferenzierung zugenommen haben. Soziale Risiken sind auch in Zusammenhang mit Ein- und Auswanderung heterogener sowie diffuser geworden und daher grundsätzlich schwerer abzusichern. Migrant/inn/en gehören oftmals zu den vulnerablen Gruppen, die in zentralen Bereichen wie Bildung und Arbeitsmarkt besonders stark von neuen sozialen Risiken betroffen sind. Gleichzeitig liegt auf der Hand, dass die Gestaltung von Migration und vor allem die wirtschaftliche, soziale und politische Integration der Zugewanderten eines langfristigen Zeithorizonts bedürfen. Sowohl die Zielsetzungen als auch die analytischen Instrumente der sozialinvestiven Perspektive sind daher für die Migrationspolitik und vor allem für ihre integrationspolitische Dimension relevant.

Für jene Gruppen, die als Erwachsene im Zuge von Familiennachzug oder Asylsuche ins Land kommen, bildet der Arbeitsmarkt die wichtigste Quelle für gesellschaftliche Integration und individuelle Einkommenssicherung. Aber auch jene Gruppen, die zum Zweck einer Beschäftigungsaufnahme nach Österreich gekommen sind, stehen vor besonderen Herausforderungen am Arbeitsmarkt. Ausländische Arbeitskräfte sind etwa überproportional oft von instabiler Beschäftigung betroffen und verzeichneten in den vergangenen Jahren nur sehr geringe Lohnzuwächse (Eppel, Leoni und Mahringer, 2017). Noch problematischer ist die Arbeitsmarktsituation von Arbeitnehmer/inne/n aus früheren Einwanderungswellen, die sich in den letzten Jahren, wahrscheinlich auch aufgrund von Verdrängungseffekten im Zuge der Arbeitsmarktöffnung, deutlich verschlechterte. So

---

[6] Daten von Statistik Austria, berechnet auf Basis der Mikrozensus-Arbeitskräfteerhebung.

erhöhte sich die Arbeitslosenquote der Personen mit türkischer Staatsbürgerschaft zwischen 2008 und 2016 von 10,6% auf rund 20%, jene der Personen aus dem ehemaligen Jugoslawien von 8,0% auf 14,1% (im gleichen Zeitraum veränderte sich die Arbeitslosenquote der österreichischen Staatsbürger/innen von 5,6% auf 8,0%).[7]

Dem Arbeitsmarkt vorgelagert und zunehmend mit diesem verschränkt sind die Bildungs- und Weiterbildungschancen. Auch in diesem Bereich konfrontiert Migration den Wohlfahrtsstaat mit spezifischen Herausforderungen. Kinder und Jugendliche, die entweder selbst eingewandert sind oder die zweite Migrantengeneration bilden, bedürfen in vielen Fällen einer gezielten Förderung und Unterstützung im Bildungssystem. Auch Erwachsene und Jugendliche, die bereits das Schulpflichtalter überschritten haben, brauchen oft unterstützende Maßnahmen in Bezug auf die Anerkennung und Verwertung von bestehenden Qualifikationen, den Anschluss zu weiterführender Bildung, aber auch in Bezug auf berufliche Weiterbildung und die laufende Anpassung an sich ändernde Arbeitsmarktanforderungen.

Insgesamt lassen sich für alle zentralen sozialinvestiven Handlungsfelder - wie Bildung, Förderung in frühen Lebensphasen, Aktivierung, Unterstützung bei Lebensphasenübergängen - spezifische Empfehlungen für die Zielgruppe der Personen mit Migrationshintergrund ableiten, darüber hinaus aber auch Erkenntnisse für andere wichtige Politikfelder der Migrations- und Integrationspolitik. Dazu gehören beispielsweise die Gesundheitspolitik (siehe Biffl und Altenburg 2012) und die Wohnpolitik (siehe z.B. Kohlbacher und Reeger 2007; Huber, Horvath und Bock-Schappelwein 2017), also Bereiche mit einem großen „investiven" Hebel zur Verfolgung längerfristiger Zielsetzungen. Besondere Bedeutung hat die sozialinvestive Perspektive bei der Definition von Rahmenbedingungen und Maßnahmen für Familien- und Fluchtmigration, weil diese Migrationsformen meist dauerhaft und die Betroffenen oft durch besonders ausgeprägte sozio-ökonomische, sprachliche und kulturelle Unterschiede gekennzeichnet sind. Grundsätzlich ist es aber bei allen unterschiedlichen Migrationsformen notwendig, eine langfristige Perspektive einzunehmen und das sozialstaatliche Instrumentarium mit Blick auf Prävention und Absicherung einzusetzen. Die nachfolgende Tabelle 1 soll exemplarisch verdeutlichen, wie die „Säulen" des sozialinvestiven Wohlfahrtsstaats (Bildung und Förderung von Humankapital; Aktivierung und Arbeitsmarktintegration; sozialer Schutz und soziale Teilhabe) mit unterschiedlichen Migrationsformen verschränkt werden können. Es handelt sich dabei um einen vereinfachten Abriss, der sich auf die dauerhafteren bzw. sozialpolitisch relevantesten Migrationsformen konzentriert. Dieses Raster könnte um weitere Migrationsformen (wie

---

[7] WIFO Berechnungen auf Basis von Daten des Arbeitsmarktservice und des Hauptverbands der österreichischen Sozialversicherungsträger.

	Arbeitsmigration (Erwachsene, zeitlich befristet, z.T. dauerhaft)	Familienmigration (alle Personengruppen, dauerhaft)	Fluchtmigration (alle Personengruppen, zeitlich befristet oder dauerhaft)
Bildung und Förderung von Humankapital	Allgemeine und berufliche Weiterbildung	Frühkindliche Betreuung und Entwicklung	
		Chancen im Bildungssystem, Basis- und weiterführende Bildung	
		Unterstützung bei Übergängen im Bildungssystem	
	Spracherwerb und Maßnahmen zur kulturellen Integration		
Aktivierung und Arbeitsmarktintegration	Aktivierende Arbeitsmarktpolitik	Arbeitsmarktzugang	Arbeitsmarktzugang (während Asylverfahren)
	Vermeidung von Lohn- und Sozialdumping	Anerkennung von formalen Qualifikationen	
		Maßnahmen zur Vereinbarkeit von Beruf und Familie	Beratung und Vermittlung
		Maßnahmen zur beruflichen Eingliederung	
Sozialer Schutz und soziale Teilhabe	Einbindung in Sozialversicherungssysteme		
	Einbürgerung (in Abhängigkeit von Zeitaspekt)	Einbürgerung	Einbürgerung (in Abhängigkeit von Zeitaspekt)
	Portabilität von Sozialleistungsansprüchen	Wohnpolitik	
	Bekämpfung von Diskriminierung, Anerkennung politischer Rechte		
	Soziale Sicherungsnetze		

Tabelle 1 Beispiel für die Zuordnung von Politikfeldern und Maßnahmen zu unterschiedlichen Migrationsformen in einer sozialinvestiven Perspektive

Quelle: Eigene Darstellung.

z.B. Bildungsmigration) ergänzt und nach weiteren Unterscheidungsmerkmalen des Migrationsphänomens (wie das Qualifikationsniveau der Eingewanderten) gegliedert werden. Darüber hinaus geht diese Darstellung nur auf die integrationspolitische Ebene ein. Auch die vorgelagerten Handlungsfelder, mit denen über Einreise- und Aufenthaltsbestimmungen die Migrationsströme gesteuert werden, können aber in einer sozialinvestiven Perspektive beleuchtet werden. Nachdem Österreich lange Zeit durch Arbeitsmigration im niedrig qualifizierten Bereich gekennzeichnet war, hat die Bestrebung, höher qualifizierte Einwanderungsgruppen anzuziehen, an Bedeutung gewonnen. Zwar sind die fremdenrechtlichen Instrumente, um Migration nach den Bedürfnissen des Arbeitsmarktes und der wirtschaftlichen Entwicklung auszurichten, beschränkt, dennoch gibt es – angefangen bei der Attraktivität des höheren Bildungssystems und der daran anknüpfenden Beschäftigungsmöglichkeiten - indirekt viele Schnittstellen, um gut qualifizierte Arbeitskräfte anzuziehen. Darüber hinaus spielen integrationspolitische Überlegungen, beispielsweise die Rahmenbedingungen für den Aufenthalt von Familienangehörigen, auch bei Instrumenten zur Anwerbung von qualifizierten Arbeitskräften wie der Rot-Weiss-Rot-Karte eine Rolle.

Vom Fremdarbeitermodell zum Einwanderungsland

Inwiefern sind die soeben beschriebenen Handlungsfelder und Prioritäten bereits im migrations- und integrationspolitischen Diskurs in Österreich verankert? Grundsätzlich fällt die Antwort auf diese Frage differenziert aus, je nachdem, welche Zeitperiode betrachtet wird.

Österreich hatte in den sechziger Jahren und bis hinein in die späten 1980er-Jahre keine eigenständige, umfassende Migrationspolitik, sondern ein durch Arbeitsmarktbedürfnisse bestimmtes Zuwanderungsmodell zur Abdeckung des (zeitlich befristeten) Bedarfs an Arbeitskräften. In dieser Phase der Gastarbeitermigration, die sich in den 1960er- und frühen 1970er-Jahren voll entfaltete, wurde versucht „das österreichische soziale Reproduktionsmodell so wenig wie möglich zu verändern" (Biffl 2011). Beschäftigungsbewilligungen wurden nicht den ausländischen Arbeitskräften, sondern den Unternehmen für einen bestimmten Arbeitsplatz gewährt. Eine Nichtverlängerung der Beschäftigungsbewilligung bedeutete für die betroffenen Gastarbeiter/innen meist den Verlust der Voraussetzungen für den weiteren Aufenthalt in Österreich. Die rechtlichen Rahmenbedingungen für die zugezogenen Ausländer/inne/n, vor allem in Bezug auf Beschäftigung und Arbeitsmarkt, änderten sich bis zu den späten 1980er-Jahren kaum. Um einen Befreiungsschein und somit einen freien Zugang zum Arbeitsmarkt zu erhalten, waren acht Jahre mit (fast) kontinuierlicher Beschäftigung notwendig.[8] Diese Regelung, die dem Schutz des Arbeitsmarkts dienen sollte, erschwerte die berufliche aber auch die soziale Eingliederung der Migrant/inn/en in erheblichem Maße, vor allem jene der nachgezogenen Familienmitglieder (Krause und Liebig 2011). Es war bisweilen leichter, eine Arbeitskraft neu anzuwerben, als bereits zugezogenen Familienangehörigen die Arbeitsaufnahme zu ermöglichen (Nowotny 2007).

Erst ab den späten 1980er-Jahren wurde ein gradueller Paradigmenwechsel vollzogen. Die 1988 und 1990 verabschiedeten Novellen des Ausländerbeschäftigungsgesetzes (AuslBG) enthielten eine bevorzugte Behandlung der längerfristig aufhältigen Ausländer/inne/n am österreichischen Arbeitsmarkt (Ende des „Rotationsmodells") und erste Integrationsmaßnahmen. Während das AuslBG in seiner ursprünglichen Fassung (1975) sehr stark dem Prinzip der temporären Arbeitsmigration verhaftet war, trugen die sukzessiven Änderungen der Tatsache Rechnung, dass aus den befristeten Arbeitsaufenthalten in vielen Fällen eine bleibende Niederlassung mit Familiennachzug und somit aus dem Gastarbeiterphänomen ein integraler Bestandteil der österreichischen Gesellschaft geworden war. Diese Anpassungen erfolgten aber nur reaktiv und trugen nur eingeschränkt zur Erleichterung der Integration bei (Nowotny 2007).

Die verspätete politische Reaktion auf die realen Verhältnisse in Österreich als Einwanderungsland überlagerte sich mit den wirtschaftlichen und geopolitischen Umbrüchen der frühen 1990er-Jahre, die eine starke Erhöhung des Wanderungs-

---

[8] Während der 1980er-Jahre hatten durchschnittlich nur etwa 15% der Ausländer/inne/n einen Befreiungsschein (Biffl 1990).

saldos nach sich zogen. Innerhalb von fünf Jahren, zwischen 1989 und 1994, kam es fast zu einer Verdopplung des Anteils der ausländischen Bevölkerung an der Wohnbevölkerung von 4,5% auf 8,4% (Biffl und Bock-Schappelwein 2013). Die starke Zuwanderung zog eine Reihe von Maßnahmen nach sich, vor allem zu deren Bremsung. Wichtige Instrumente waren Niederlassungsquoten und Quoten für den Arbeitsmarktzugang, mit dem Ziel, den Anteil der Ausländer/inne/n an den Beschäftigten mit 10% zu deckeln (Krause und Liebig 2011). Diese Maßnahmen erschwerten den Arbeitsmarktzugang der Personen, die im Rahmen von Familienzusammenführungen ins Land gekommen waren, wovon insbesondere Frauen betroffen waren. Familienzugehörige, die im Rahmen einer Niederlassungsquote eingewandert waren, erhielten bis 2005 erst nach fünf Jahren Aufenthalt Zugang zum Arbeitsmarkt. Zwar begründete das 1997 eingeführte „Integrationspaket" erstmalig einen formalen Rahmen für die Integration. Das Paket legte das Prinzip der „Integration vor neuer Einwanderung" fest und beschränkte den Eintritt neuer Migrant/inn/en durch Arbeits- und Familienmigration bei gleichzeitiger Verbesserung des Rechtsstatus von bereits länger ansässigen Migrant/inn/en. Als zentrale Komponente der Integration wurde der Spracherwerb festgeschrieben. Integration wurde aber nicht als horizontale Materie verankert, wichtige Handlungsfelder wie die Herstellung von Chancengerechtigkeit im Bildungsbereich waren ausgeklammert. Eingliederung und Teilhabe waren auch in anderen Bereichen mit erheblichen Hindernissen konfrontiert. Drittstaatsangehörige hatten beispielsweise bis 2005 kein passives Wahlrecht bei Betriebsrats- und Arbeiterkammerwahlen.[9]

Sowohl in der durch die Anwerbung der Gastarbeiter geprägten Phase als auch in der Periode nach dem Fall des Eisernen Vorhangs beinhaltete die österreichische Migrationspolitik weder ein langfristiges Konzept zur erfolgreichen Integration der zugewanderten Personen, noch eine ausreichend starke Fokussierung auf die Herstellung von Chancen und die Humankapitalentwicklung innerhalb dieser Bevölkerungsgruppe. Es fehlten somit sowohl die präventive Komponente als auch eine durch Lebenslaufperspektive geprägte Migrations- und Integrationspolitik. Zwar standen die Bedürfnisse des Arbeitsmarkts bei den politischen Weichenstellungen im Vordergrund, aber aus der Warte des kurzfristigen Bedarfs nach Arbeitskräften und nicht aus jener einer längerfristigen Aktivierung und Arbeitsmarktintegration der Ausländer/innen im erwerbsfähigen Alter. Auch die längerfristige Verschiebung in der Nachfrage nach Arbeitskräften, mit zunehmendem Bedeutungsgewinn höher qualifizierter Segmente, blieb weitgehend unberücksichtigt.

---

[9] Türkische Staatsangehörige hatten aufgrund des EG-Türkei-Assoziationsabkommens das passive Wahlrecht bei Arbeiterkammerwahlen.

Die neueren Entwicklungen

Der Zugang zur Gestaltung von Migration hat sich im vergangenen Jahrzehnt deutlich verschoben, insbesondere im Sinne einer Aufwertung der integrationspolitischen Dimension. Integrationspolitik war lange Zeit das „Stiefkind der österreichischen Politik", insbesondere in Bezug auf die Entwicklung bundesweiter Strukturen (Biffl und Faustmann 2013). Auf institutioneller Ebene änderte sich dieses Bild in den Jahren 2010/2011, mit der Verabschiedung des ersten nationalen Aktionsplans für Integration, der Ernennung eines Expertenrates und der Einrichtung des Staatssekretariats für Integration. Damit wurden auf Bundesebene die Voraussetzungen für eine koordinierte horizontale Integrationspolitik geschaffen. Der öffentliche Diskurs wurde vielschichtiger und bewusste Integrationsmaßnahmen, die bis dahin vor allem auf Ebene der Bundesländer und in teils sehr unterschiedlicher Form gesetzt worden waren, gewannen auch auf Bundesebene an Bedeutung (*ebenda*). Die für Integrationsförderung zur Verfügung stehenden Mittel wurden in den vergangenen Jahren deutlich aufgestockt.

Eine Reihe von konkreten Maßnahmen und Initiativen zeugt von einer verstärkten Ausrichtung auf langfristige Ziele und einer Fokussierung auf integrationspolitische Kernbereiche wie frühkindliche Förderung, Bildung und Arbeitsmarktaktivierung. Dabei waren nicht alle Neuerungen ausschließlich auf Personen mit Migrationshintergrund zugeschnitten, sondern adressierten diese als wichtige Zielgruppe im Rahmen breiterer Anpassungen. Das gilt z.B. für die Einführung des verpflichtenden letzten Kindergartenjahrs, die 2010 erfolgte, sowie für die Initiative Erwachsenenbildung, mit der seit 2012 grundlegende Bildungsabschlüsse für Erwachsene gefördert werden. Auch über das Arbeitsmarktservice (AMS) werden zahlreiche Maßnahmen angeboten, die nicht nur Personen mit Migrationshintergrund offen stehen, aber diese Zielgruppe stark ansprechen. Ein spezifischer Fokus wird auf Jugendliche und junge Erwachsene gelegt, beispielsweise durch Jugendcoaching oder Berufsorientierung an Schulen, aber auch durch Initiativen wie die über den Integrationsfonds organisierten Schulbesuche von Integrationsbotschafter/inne/n, welche als Rollenvorbilder fungieren. Auch in Bezug auf andere Zielgruppen wurden in den jüngsten Jahren relevante Änderungen eingeführt. Dazu zählen das 2016 in Kraft getretene neue Anerkennungs- und Bewertungsgesetz für im Ausland erworbene Qualifikationen, das eine Vereinfachung und Beschleunigung bei der Anerkennung für Migrant/inn/en und Flüchtlinge zum Ziel hat, sowie das verpflichtende Integrationsjahr für Flüchtlinge, das im Rahmen des Integrationspakets 2017 beschlossen wurde. Auch in Bezug auf den Arbeitsmarktzugang anderer Gruppen gab es Neuerungen, wie die Weiterentwicklung der 2011 eingeführten Rot-Weiß-Rot-Karte (R-W-R-Karte) und die Einführung der R-W-R-Karte Plus, mit der Familienangehörige von Personen mit R-W-R-Karte vom ersten Tag an Zugang zum Arbeitsmarkt erhalten.

Diese Verschiebung in der Schwerpunktsetzung kann zum Teil als Folge der in den 1990er-Jahren eingesetzten Bemühungen der EU gewertet werden, eine koordinierte und kohärente gemeinsame Migrationspolitik zu fördern. Mit den Verträgen von Maastricht (1993 in Kraft getreten) und von Amsterdam (1999) wurden die rechtlichen Rahmenbedingungen für eine gemeinsame Asyl- und Migrationspolitik gelegt und deren Agenden zu erheblichen Teilen in die erste Säule der „vergemeinschafteten" Politikbereiche überführt (Biffl et al. 2016). Der Vertrag von Nizza (2003) brachte Mitentscheidungsmöglichkeiten für das Europäische Parlament und etwa seit dem Jahr 2000 begann auch die Kommission, eine aktivere Rolle in der Gestaltung der Migrations- und Asylpolitik einzunehmen.

Von besonderer inhaltlicher Relevanz war auf europäischer Ebene die Formulierung von „Gemeinsamen Grundprinzipien" (GGP), die vom Rat der EU 2004 verabschiedet wurden (Kienl 2012). Die GGP umfassen elf Grundsätze, die bei der Entwicklung und Umsetzung von Integrationsmaßnahmen beachtet werden sollen. Integration wird als Querschnittsthematik definiert; unter anderem wird in den GGP die Notwendigkeit zum Erwerb von Grundkenntnissen „der Sprache, Geschichte und Institutionen der Aufnahmegesellschaft", festgeschrieben. Auch wird betont, dass im Bildungswesen Anstrengungen unternommen werden müssen, um Einwanderer und vor allem auch deren Nachkommen zu einer erfolgreicheren und aktiveren Teilhabe an der Gesellschaft zu befähigen. 2005 wurde von der EU-Kommission auch ein „Handbuch zur Integration" heraus gegeben. Mit dem Rahmenprogramm „Solidarität und Steuerung der Migrationsströme" (2007-13) wurden 2007 die finanziellen Gemeinschaftsinstrumente der EU entlang von vier Schwerpunkten erweitert.[10] Bedeutsam für die Ausrichtung der europäischen Migrations- und Asylpolitik war zudem der Europäische Pakt zu Einwanderung und Asyl von 2008. Der Pakt wies insgesamt eine restriktive Ausrichtung und einen Fokus auf irreguläre Einwanderung auf, aber er forderte auch die Mitgliedsstaaten dazu auf, ambitionierte Integrationsziele zu setzen.

In der Phase rund um die Wirtschafts- und Finanzkrise etablierte sich auch das Konzept der sozialen Investitionen auf europäischer Ebene (Stjernø 2017). 2013 verabschiedete die Kommission das „Sozialinvestitionspaket für Wachstum und Zusammenhalt", den bis dahin ambitioniertesten Versuch, die sozialpolitische Agenda in der EU weiter zu entwickeln und den Schwerpunkt weg von kurzfristigen Konsolidierungsmaßnahmen hin zu längerfristigen Zielsetzungen zu verschieben. Allerdings werden Migrant/inn/en im Sozialinvestitionspaket und auch in weiteren begleitenden Unterlagen nicht als eigene Zielgruppe definiert. Im Zuge der Flüchtlingswelle von 2015/16 wurden längerfristige Konzepte und Fragen der Integration vom Krisenmanagement und der politischen Diskussion um die Steuerung der Flüchtlingsströme verdrängt. Auch in Österreich war der öffentliche Diskurs zuletzt stark von kontroll- und sicherheitspolitischen Aspekten beherrscht, mit teils negativen Rückwirkungen auf der Policy-Ebene. Ein klares Beispiel für einen Rückschritt sind die unkoordinierte Handhabe und die Kürzungen bei der Bedarfsorientierten Mindestsicherung auf Bundesländerebene. Damit wurden die

---

[10] Das waren die Kontrolle und der Schutz der Außengrenzen, die Asylpolitik, die Integration von Drittstaatsangehörigen sowie die Bekämpfung der illegalen Immigration (Biffl et al. 2016).

früheren Bemühungen um eine Harmonisierung des sozialen Sicherheitsnetzes in Österreich zunichte gemacht. Gleichzeitig wurden wichtige, langfristige gesellschaftliche Ziele, wie der Schutz vulnerabler Bevölkerungsgruppen und die bundesweit koordinierte Handhabe von Fluchtmigration, auf dem Altar kurzfristiger politischer Überlegungen geopfert.

Ausblick

Zentrale Themen des sozialinvestiven Wohlfahrtsstaats, wie die Ausrichtung auf langfristige Ziele, der Fokus auf Aktivierung und Beschäftigung sowie die Priorisierung von Unterstützung in frühen Lebensphasen und bei Lebensabschnittsübergängen, sind für die Bewältigung der Herausforderungen in Zusammenhang mit Migration von großer Bedeutung. Sowohl auf nationaler wie auch auf europäischer Ebene ist eine Verschiebung im migrationspolitischen Diskurs beobachtbar, die mit den Kerngedanken dieses Wohlfahrtsstaatskonzeptes übereinstimmt. Die Spuren dieser inhaltlichen Verschiebung sind in Österreich auf institutioneller und inhaltlicher Ebene gut sichtbar. Vor allem in Bezug auf den integrationspolitischen Rahmen wies Österreich einen über Jahrzehnte aufgebauten Rückstand auf. Noch vor einigen Jahren hielten internationale Beobachter fest, dass Österreich in Bezug auf die integrationspolitischen Rahmenbedingungen hinter anderen OECD-Ländern herhinke (Krause und Liebig 2011). In einer neueren Bewertung kommt der Sachverständigenrat deutscher Stiftungen für Integration und Migration zu einer deutlich positiveren Einschätzung (Sachverständigenrat 2016).

Die langfristigen Folgen der migrationspolitischen Versäumnisse der Vergangenheit sind allerdings gut belegt. Frühere Studien zeigten, dass Drittstaatsangehörige und insbesondere Personen mit türkischem, nahöstlichem oder afrikanischem Migrationshintergrund viel höhere Arbeitslosenquoten und (vor allem bei Frauen) niedrigere Partizipationsquoten als die österreichische Bevölkerung aufwiesen (Biffl 2007). Diese Unterschiede im Erwerbserfolg spiegelten zum Teil die Ungleichheit in den Bildungsstrukturen der einzelnen Gruppen wider. Auch die Mitglieder der zweiten Generation von Migrant/inn/en aus der Türkei und dem ehemaligen Jugoslawien, den Anwerbeländern Österreichs, hatten keine Angleichung an die Bildungs- und Qualifikationsstrukturen der einheimischen Bevölkerung erreicht (Weiss und Unterwurzacher 2007). Der geringere Bildungserfolg der jüngeren Generationen mit Migrationshintergrund konnte zwar ebenfalls teilweise auf die soziale Schichtung der Elternhaushalte zurück geführt werden. Es zeigten sich aber auch Defizite, die nicht mit strukturellen Faktoren in der Zusammensetzung der Migration zusammen hingen. Gleichzeitig wiesen Jugendliche aus der zweiten Generation auch bei gleicher beruflicher Qualifikation gegenüber ihren österreichischen Altersgenossen Benachteiligungen auf: Etwa längere Übergangsdauern zwischen Bildungsabschluss und erstem Arbeitsplatz, höhere Arbeitslosigkeit und – was von zunehmender Bedeutung ist – eine deutlich geringere Partizipation an betrieblicher Fortbildung (Weiss und Unterwurzacher 2007).

Auch jüngere Studien, die sich zum Teil auf umfassendere und international vergleichbare Datengrundlagen stützen, zeichnen ein sehr ähnliches Bild (siehe z.B. Biffl und Faustmann 2013). Huber, Horvath und Bock-Schappelwein (2017)[11] belegen, dass Österreich in einem internationalen Vergleich in keiner der zentralen integrationspolitischen Dimensionen in der Ländergruppe mit den besten Ergebnissen liegt. Detaillierte Analysen weisen nach wie vor besonders im Bildungsbereich und bei der Chancengerechtigkeit große Defizite auf, sowohl für die im Ausland geborenen Jugendlichen als auch für die zweite Generation. Zwar verbessern sich vor allem die Indikatoren zur beruflichen Eingliederung der Migrant/inn/en im internationalen Vergleich, sobald die Struktur der Migration mitberücksichtigt und somit in erster Linie Vergleiche mit Ländern wie Belgien, Frankreich und Deutschland gezogen werden. Doch die Ausgangsschwierigkeiten aufgrund der strukturellen Merkmale der eingewanderten Personengruppen überlagerten sich mit fehlenden Rahmenbedingungen und Kompensationsmechanismen, die diesen strukturellen Faktoren entgegenwirken hätten können. In Österreich sind demnach besondere Anstrengungen in der Entwicklung einer konsistenten, auf langfristige Ziele orientierten Migrations- und Integrationspolitik notwendig. Die Gestaltung von Migration ist ein wichtiger Prüfstein für die Weiterentwicklung und sozialinvestive Ausrichtung des Wohlfahrtsstaats. In den vergangenen Jahren wurden zahlreiche Schritte gesetzt, um die migrationspolitischen Defizite aus der Vergangenheit zu kompensieren. Wie auch die Entwicklungen in Zusammenhang mit der jüngsten Flüchtlingswelle zeigen, sind die österreichische Gesellschaft und Politik aber nach wie vor mit enormen Herausforderungen konfrontiert.

Gudrun Biffl hat einen wichtigen Teil ihres Schaffens als Wissenschafterin dem Migrationsphänomen gewidmet und die Erfahrungen aus unterschiedlichen Einwanderungswellen, im deutschsprachigen Raum aber auch international, tiefgründig aufgearbeitet und untersucht. Sie hat damit wesentlich dazu beigetragen, dass heute ein besseres Verständnis der empirischen Sachlage und der Wirkungszusammenhänge, sowie damit einhergehend ein Maßnahmeninstrumentarium vorliegen, um die gegenwärtigen und zukünftigen migrationspolitischen Herausforderungen besser zu bewältigen als in der Vergangenheit. Es liegt an den politischen Entscheidungsträger/inne/n, bei allen Schwierigkeiten und trotz der großen Komplexität der Materie, Migrationspolitik entsprechend zu gestalten, und an den Bürger/inne/n, diese auch mitzutragen.

Literatur

Barr, N. (2012) Economics of the Welfare State. (University Press, Oxford).
Biffl, G. (1990) SOPEMI Report on Labour Migration – Austria 1989/90. (Vienna: WIFO).

---

[11] Siehe dazu auch den Beitrag von Huber, Horvath und Bock-Schappelwein im vorliegenden Band.

Biffl, G. (2007) Erwerbstätigkeit und Arbeitslosigkeit: die Bedeutung von Einbürgerung, Herkunftsregion und Religionszugehörigkeit. In: Heinz Fassmann (Hrsg.), 2. Österreichischer Migrations- und Integrationsbericht. (Drava Verlag: Klagenfurt/Celovec), S. 265-282.

Biffl, G. (2011) Entwicklung der Migrationen in Österreich aus historischer Perspektive. In Gudrun Biffl und Nikolaus Dimmel (Hrsg.) Grundzüge des Managements von Migration und Integration. Band 1: S 33-50. (Omninum Verlag, Bad Vöslau).

Biffl, G., Berger, J., Graf, N., Pfeffer, T., Schuh, U., Skrivanek, I., Strohner, L. (2016) Österreichische Migrationspolitik: Vision und Entwicklung eines Migrations-Monitoring-Systems. Donau-Universität Krems, Schriftenreihe Migration und Globalisierung.

Biffl, G., Altenburg, F. (Hrsg.) (2012) Migration and Health in Nowhereland. Access of undocumented migrants to work and health care in Europe. (Omninum: Bad Vöslau).

Biffl, G., Bock-Schappelwein, J (2013) Zur Niederlassung von Ausländerinnen und Ausländern in Österreich. (WIFO-Monographie, Wien).

Biffl, G., Faustmann, A. (2013) Österreichische Integrationspolitik im EU Vergleich. Zur Aussagekraft von MIPEX. Donau-Universität Krems, Schriftenreihe Migration und Globalisierung.

Bonoli, G. (2006) New social risks and the politics of post-industrial social policies. In: Armingeon, K./Ders. (Hrsg.): The Politics of Post-Industrial Welfare States. London-New York, S. 3–26.

Eppel, R., Leoni, T. (2011) Neue soziale Risiken für Kinder – ein europäischer Vergleich. In: Blaha, B./Kapeller, J. (Hrsg.), Solidarität. Beiträge für eine gerechte Gesellschaft. (Wien).

Eppel, R., Leoni, T., Mahringer, H. (2017) Österreich 2025 – Segmentierung des Arbeitsmarktes und schwache Lohnentwicklung in Österreich.WIFO-Monatsberichte, 90(5), S. 425-439.

Esping-Andersen, G., Gallie, D., Hemerijck, A., Myles, J. (Hrsg.) (2002) Why We Need a New Welfare State. (Oxford: University Press).

Hemerijck, A. (2015) The quiet paradigm revolution of social investment. In: Social Politics, 22(2), S. 242-256.

Hemerijck, A. (Hrsg.) (2017) The Uses of Social Investment. (Oxford University Press: Oxford).

Huber, P., Horvath, T., Bock-Schappelwein, J. (2017) Österreich als Zuwanderungsland. (WIFO-Monographie, Wien).

Kienl, M. (2012) Integrationspolitik im Rahmen der Europäischen Union. Die Zusammenarbeit der EU-Mitgliedstaaten bei der Integration von Migranten. SIAK-Journal – Zeitschrift für Polizeiwissenschaft und polizeiliche Praxis (2), S. 17-29.

Kohlbacher, J., Reeger, U. (2007) Wohnverhältnisse und Segregation. In: Heinz Fassmann (Hrsg.), 2. Österreichischer Migrations- und Integrationsbericht. (Drava Verlag: Klagenfurt/Celovec), S. 305-333.

Krause, K., Liebig, T. (2011) The Labour Market Integration of Immigrants and their Children in Austria. OECD Social, Employment and Migration Working Papers, No. 127, OECD Publishing.

Kvist, Jon (2014) A framework for social investment strategies: Integrating generational, life course and gender perspectives in the EU social investment strategy. In: Comparative European Politics, 14, 1-19.

Morel, N., Palier, B., Palme, J. (Hrsg.) (2012) Towards a Social Investment Welfare State? Ideas, policies and challenges. (Policy Press: Chicago).

Nowotny, I. (2007) Das Ausländerbeschäftigungsgesetz: Die Regelung des Zugangs von Ausländer/inne/n zum österreichischen Arbeitsmarkt. In: Fassmann, H. (Hrsg.), 2. Österreichischer Migrations- und Integrationsbericht. (Drava Verlag: Klagenfurt/Celovec), S. 47-82.

OECD (2015), In It Together: Why Less Inequality Benefits All. (OECD Publishing, Paris).

Pierson, P. (1998) Irresistible forces, immovable objects: Postindustrial welfare states confront permanent austerity. In: Journal of European Public Policy, 5, 4: S. 539–60.

Sachverständigenrat deutscher Stiftungen für Integration und Migration (2016), Fünf Jahre Integrationspolitik in Österreich. (Berlin).

Stjernø, S. (2017) Social investment as a means of integrating immigrants in Europe. In: James Midgley, Espen Dahl, Amy Conley Wright (eds.), Social Investment and Social Welfare. International and Critical Perspectives. (Edward Elgar: Cheltenham), S.196-214.

Taylor-Gooby, P. (Hrsg.) (2004) New Risks, New Welfare. The transformation of the European welfare state. (New York).

Vandenbroucke, F., Vleminckx, K. (2011) Disappointing poverty trends: is the social investment state to blame? In: Journal of European Social Policy, 21(5), S.450-471.

Weiss, H., Unterwurzacher, A. (2007) Soziale Mobilität durch Bildung? Bildungsbeteiligung von Migrant/inn/en. In: Heinz Fassmann (Hrsg.), 2. Österreichischer Migrations- und Integrationsbericht, (Drava Verlag: Klagenfurt/Celovec), S. 227-241.

Bedingungsloses Grundeinkommen und Globalisierung

Hedwig Lutz, Christine Mayrhuber

> *„Die größte Schwierigkeit der Welt besteht nicht darin, Leute zu bewegen, neue Ideen anzunehmen, sondern alte zu vergessen."*
> John Maynard Keynes

Zusammenfassung

Die ökonomischen, politischen und kulturellen Globalisierungstendenzen sowie die Auswirkungen der Digitalisierung und Automatisierung kommen nicht Allen gleichermaßen zugute. Sie vergrößern Einkommensungleichheiten und fördern Unsicherheiten über die zukünftigen Erwerbseinkommenserzielungschancen aufgrund von Veränderungen der Leistungserstellungsprozesse. Dies trifft auf Schwellenländer ebenso zu wie auf entwickelte Industrienationen. So setzte die Entwicklung des EU-Binnenmarktes als Player in einer globalisierten Wirtschaft auf einer ökonomischen und sozialen Absicherung breiter Bevölkerungsschichten auf. Die wirtschaftlichen Erfolge hoben jedoch nicht alle Bevölkerungsgruppen gleichermaßen auf ein höheres Wohlfahrtsniveau, sondern koppeln einige davon ab. Wohlfahrtsstaatliche soziale Absicherung gewinnt vor diesem Hintergrund an Bedeutung, verliert aber an Akzeptanz. Dazu tragen unter anderem zunehmende Kosten, Intransparenzen, vermeintliche und tatsächliche Ineffizienzen, sowie die Einschätzung der mangelnden Fairness bzw. Gerechtigkeit der existierenden Systeme bei. Das Bedingungslose Grundeinkommen (BGE) wird immer häufiger als Antwort auf diese Herausforderungen gesehen. Ob und inwieweit das BGE als Lösung vielschichtiger ökonomischer Fragen geeignet ist, soll im vorliegenden Beitrag erörtert werden.

Einleitung

Nach einer Ära wirtschaftlicher Prosperität und sozialer Inklusion stehen seit der Jahrtausendwende bzw. seit der Finanz- und Wirtschaftskrise, die 2008 einsetzte, die gewachsenen nationalen Sozialsysteme am europäischen Binnenmarkt verstärkt unter Finanzierung- und Legitimierungsdruck. Vor allem einkommenszentrierte Sicherungsmechanismen verlieren auf zunehmend segmentierten Arbeitsmärkten und durch die anhaltend hohe Arbeitslosigkeit ihre nationalstaatliche Kohäsionsfunktion. Das Bedingungslose Grundeinkommen (BGE) stellt eine Abkehr der erwerbseinkommenszentrierten Wohlfahrtsstaatsarchitektur dar. Ob und inwieweit sich das Bedingungslose Grundeinkommen als ein Instrument zur Lösung der sozialen Frage in Europa eignet, ist nachfolgend erörtert. Es wird gezeigt, dass sowohl die Konzepte als auch die damit verbundenen Erwartungen vielschichtig und hoch, die empirischen Evidenzen der Wirkungsweisen aber gering sind. Der Beitrag argumentiert die Notwendigkeit eines gesamteuropäischen Sozialdiskurses zur sozialen Fundierung des Binnenmarktes, da der gegenwärtige nationalstaatlich geführte Diskurs zum Bedingungslosen Grundeinkommen im europäischen Wirtschafts- und Währungsraum zu kurz greift.

Eckpunkte eines Bedingungslosen Grundeinkommens

Das Bedingungslose Grundeinkommen (BGE) ist ein individueller Anspruch auf eine finanzielle Zuwendung in definierter Höhe für jede und jeden. Der monetäre Transfer ist weder an eine Bedürftigkeit noch an eine Bereitschaft zu arbeiten, zu lernen, zu betreuen, weder an ein Alter[1] oder eine Staatsbürgerschaft[2] geknüpft.

Die ProponentInnen in der Schweiz, allen voran Prätorius (2010), formulierten es so: *„Unabhängig davon, wie er/sie sich ins Durcheinander aus Konsum, Care, Produktion, Innovation, Freizeit, Muße etc. einbringt, garantieren wir uns gegenseitig ein Bedingungsloses Grundeinkommen."*[3] Im Gegensatz dazu steht der ökonomische Zugang „There is no such thing as a free lunch" (TINSTAAFL), mit dem der herrschende Leistungsgedanke unsers Wirtschaftssystems ausgedrückt ist.

Diese Bedingungslosigkeit stellt eine grundlegende Unterscheidung zu den vorhandenen Grundsicherungsmodellen (bedarfsorientierte Grundsicherung, in-work-benefits, family tax credit et al.) dar. Die Bedingungslosigkeit stellt das gegenwärtige Leistungsbewertungs- und Entlohnungssystem in Frage. Darin liegt aus progressiver Sicht der neue Ansatz im Sozialstaatsdiskurs. Ein weiteres Unterscheidungsmerkmal ist, dass Modelle der BGE meist nicht als Ergänzung, sondern als Ersatz für das gesamte Sozialsystem gedacht sind. In diesen Fällen ist das BGE immer mit einem strukturellen Umbau der gegebenen Institutionenlandschaft verbunden.

Die nachfolgend kurz skizzierten Modelle würden vielschichtige soziale und gesellschaftliche Ungleichheiten beheben (Appel 2010, Prätorius 2010, Rätz und Krampertz 2011, Gubitzer und Heintel 2012) und die intransparenten Strukturen in der derzeitigen Sozialstaatlichkeit überwinden. Auch budgetpolitische Probleme und Fehlanreize sozialer Sicherungselemente könnten verbessert werden (Hohenleitner und Straubhaar 2007). Hatte der Diskurs zum BGE in den 1980er Jahre noch emanzipatorischen Charakter, ist es jetzt der Reformbedarf der gegebenen Sozialstaatlichkeit, neue Maßnahmen der Armutsbekämpfung, Vereinfachung der Sozialsysteme, Reduktion der negativen Arbeitsanreize etc., die den Diskurs be-

---

[1] Die meisten Modelle sehen eine geringere Höhe für Kinder vor.
[2] Anknüpfungspunkt ist ein gültiger Aufenthaltstitel oder ein Hauptwohnsitz.
[3] Ina Prätorius, Theologin und engagiert in der Schweizer Grundeinkommensbewegung.

fördern. Dieser kurze Abriss und die zwei nachfolgend skizzierten Zugänge zeigen, in welchem Spektrum die Modelle[4] zum BGE liegen und wie unterschiedlich die gesellschafts- und wirtschaftspolitischen Zielsetzungen jeweils sind.

Potential des BGE aus progressiver Sicht

Als Einkommen ohne Vorleistungen und ohne Bedürftigkeit stellt das BGE aus feministischer Sicht eine Überwindung und Abkehr vom gegenwärtigen (Leistungs-)Prinzip dar. Die klassische Ökonomie betrachtet Knappheiten als den Hauptantrieb jeglichen Wirtschaftens. Tatsächlich leben wir in Europa aber in einer Überflussgesellschaft mit ungleicher Verteilung. Erwerbsarbeit ist – aus feministischer Perspektive – der zentrale Reproduktionsmechanismus von Macht im herrschenden patriarchalen System (Michalitsch 2007). Geld ohne Gegenleistung würde sowohl den Wert der Erwerbs- aber auch der Reproduktionsarbeit relativieren. *„Wenn das Grundeinkommen wegen seiner Bedingungslosigkeit nichts entgeltet, setzt es jede Form von Leistung als Bewertungsmaßstab für ein Recht auf Einkommen außer Kraft."* (Appel 2010, S. 50). Darin liegt von den BefürworterInnen des BGE das gesellschaftliche Transformationspotential (Haug 2003, Blaschke et al. 2010).

Aus soziologischer Sicht wird das BGE als Ausweg aus den sozialen Verwerfungen gesehen. Prekäre Erwerbs- und Einkommensverhältnisse sind mittlerweile eine generalisierte Erfahrung der Moderne (Reinprecht 2008). Gegenwärtig kann durch Jobverlust oder Jobwechsel die finanzielle Eigenständigkeit jederzeit verloren gehen. Erwerbsarbeit ist auch für aktiv Erwerbstätige aufgrund der zunehmenden Einkommensunsicherheiten nicht mehr emanzipativ. Es entstehen neue individualisierte Abhängigkeitsverhältnisse (beispielsweis Solo-Selbständige mit nur einem Auftraggeber). Mit dem BGE ist die Erwerbsarbeit vom Einkommen entkoppelt, das entspricht der längst eingetretenen Entkopplung von menschlicher Arbeitsleistung und produzierten Werten (ebenda). Kreisky et al. (2011) zeigen, dass die kapitalistische Marktökonomie autoritäre politische und kulturelle Systeme formt, Asozialität organisiert und antipolitische Versionen von Politik fördert. Geldleistungen ohne (Erwerbsarbeits-)Gegenleistung wäre ein Gegenmodell.

Modell „Emanzipatorisches Grundeinkommen"

„Die Linke" in Deutschland entwickelte ein Grundsicherungsmodell, das sowohl den sozialen Ausgleich, eine starke Umverteilung als auch eine freie Arbeits- und Lebensplanung umfasst. BGE dienst als Instrument zur Ermächtigung der Bevölkerung. Die Höhe des Grundeinkommens orientiert sich am Volkseinkommen, die Hälfte wird als Grundeinkommen ausbezahlt[5]. Versicherungstransfers werden nicht ersetzt, sondern in eine solidarische Bürgerversicherung überführt. Die Fi-

---

[4] Ein Überblick über Modelle in Europa findet sich bei Schneider und Dreer (2017)
[5] In Österreich liegt das Volkseinkommen pro Kopf bei 1.000€ im Monat. Derzeit liegen die monetären Transfers in Österreich bei durchschnittlich 650€ im Monat.

nanzierung erfolgt durch eine Grundeinkommensabgabe sowie weitreichende Steuererhöhungen bei hohen Einkommen und Vermögen. Zudem sollen in diesem Modell präventive Sozialpolitik und Investitionen in Bildung und soziale Infrastruktur forciert werden. Auf dem Weg starker staatlicher Regulierungen soll gesellschaftliche Teilhabe unterstützt werden.

Potential des BGE aus konservativer Sicht

Liberale ÖkonomInnen entwickelten in den 1940er Jahren Modelle[6] zur Verbesserung der Einkommenslagen der arbeitenden Bevölkerung. Die Empfehlungen des Beveridge-Reports (1942) sahen staatliche Anreize für Individuen vor, die durch ein „national minimum" stärker dem Arbeitsmarkt zur Verfügung stehen sollten. Friedman (2002) argumentierte eine finanzielle Grenze, ab der Steuern vom Einkommen zu zahlen sind, unter der Grenze soll ein Transfer (Negativsteuer) alle existierenden Wohlfahrtsleistungen ersetzen. Das Sicherungselement in Form einer negativen Einkommensteuer steht hier in enger Verbindung mit dem Erwerbseinkommen, auch hier kommt der Begriff Grundeinkommen zur Anwendung. Aus konservativer Sicht werden sozialstaatliche Mechanismen als zu komplex und zu intransparent bezeichnet, ein BGE könnte die vielschichtigen Sicherungselemente ablösen und die Arbeitsanreize stärken helfen (Hohenleitner und Straubhaar 2007). Ein anderes Modell, ein *„Aktivbürgergeld"*, schlägt Atkinson (2011) vor: Hier sollen ausschließlich sozial nützliche Tätigkeiten gefördert werden.

Modell „Solidarisches Bürgergeld"

Dieses Modell wurde in Deutschland mit dem Ziel einer Senkung der Lohnnebenkosten und einer Arbeitsmarktflexibilisierung vom Ökonomen Thomas Straubhaar und dem CDU-Politiker Dieter Althaus entwickelt. Ausgehend von der älter werdenden Bevölkerung und einer drohenden Massenarbeitslosigkeit argumentieren sie ein Bedingungsloses Existenzminimum für alle EinwohnerInnen. Die Höhe im Vorschlag aus dem Jahr 2006 betrug für Erwachsene monatlich 600 € und für Kinder 300 €, jeweils ergänzt durch eine Gesundheitsgutschrift in der Krankenversicherung im Ausmaß von 200 €. Gleichzeitig werden alle anderen Sozialleistungen abgeschafft und auch die Flächentarifverträge und die Mindestlöhne aufgehoben. Das Finanzierungskonzept sieht eine Einkommenssteuer von 50 Prozent für NettoempfängerInnen und 25 Prozent für NettozahlerInnen vor[7]. Steuern auf Einkommen über der Transfergrenze werden direkt mit der Zahlung des Bürgergeldes verrechnet. Es handelt sich um ein Modell der „negativen Einkommenssteuer". Das Modell ist durch die Abschaffung aller anderen Sozialtransfers kostenneutral (Opielka und Strengmann-Kuhn 2006).

---

[6] Beispielweise Juliet Rhys-Williams (Mitglied der Beveridge Kommission), 1943 in Großbritannien.
[7] Die Transfergrenze entsprach im Erstvorschlag 1.600 €.

Die zwei skizzierten theoretischen Modelle – „Emanzipatorisches Grundeinkommen" und „Solidarisches Bürgergeld" – wurden aufgrund lokaler Problemlagen entwickelt. Tatsächlich sind in der europäischen Wirtschafts- und Währungsunion lokale Antworten für europäische Strukturdefizite für die Zukunft nicht ausreichend, das bestätigen auch neue Analysen des IMF (2017) und von UNCTAD (2017).

Vergangene sozialpolitische Entwicklungen in Europa

Die erfolgreiche europäische Wirtschaft hob nicht alle Bevölkerungsgruppen gleichermaßen auf ein höheres Wohlfahrtsniveau. Die Markteinkommen werden wieder ungleicher, das soziale Gefälle steigt. Insgesamt stand bis in die 1970er Jahre die Inklusion breiter Bevölkerungsschichten in die Systeme der sozialen Sicherheit im Vordergrund. Ab dem Zeitpunkt, wo die Erwerbsbevölkerung maßgeblich sozial abgesichert war (1970er Jahre), konnte der EU-Binnenmarkt weiterentwickelt werden. Soziale Sicherheit sieht Leibfried (2013) als Grundlage für eine breite Akzeptanz der Öffnung der nationalen Märkte. Die europäischen Wohlfahrtsstaaten bildeten und bilden damit die Grundlage der wirtschaftlichen Neuausrichtung in Europa.

Die anfängliche Annahme, dass der EU-Binnenmarkt, also der freie Verkehr von Waren, Kapital, Dienstleistungen und Personen, ohne Auswirkungen auf die nationalen Sozialsysteme bleibt, erweist sich mittlerweile als nicht richtig. Leibfried und Pierson beschrieben 1998 – noch vor den wirtschaftlichen Einbrüchen der 2000er Jahre – den steigenden sozialen Druck, der mit der Vollendung des Binnenmarktes einhergeht: Die Orientierung an der Wettbewerbsfähigkeit führt zu einem nationalen Druck auf die Löhne und damit auf die Finanzierungsbasis der einkommens- und erwerbszentrierten Sicherungssysteme. Der freie Kapitalverkehr forcierte die Finanzwirtschaftsorientierung zulasten der Realwirtschaft (Schulmeister 2013). Die Freizügigkeit der ArbeitnehmerInnen entzieht der nationalen Sozialpolitik die Autonomie über ihre Sozialsysteme.

Gleichzeitig veränderte sich die wohlfahrtsstaatliche Ausrichtung in Form einer Abkehr von einer langfristigen Gemeinwohlorientierung mit sozialen Grundrechten, Daseinsvorsorge und Umverteilung. Nach Mätzke (2011) manifestiert sich der sozialpolitische Paradigmenwechsel darin, dass Individuen bzw. ihr Verhalten unmittelbare Adressaten staatlicher Anreizpolitik geworden sind. „Workfare" bedeutet eine stärkere Verbindung von sozialen Rechten wie der Bezug von Transferleistungen an bestimmte Verhaltensweisen und Handlungen der Individuen (Koch et al. 2005, Sesselmeier und Somaggio 2009, Eichhorst et al. 2016, European Commission 2014). Aktivierung, Eigenverantwortung und Autonomie der Individuen sind die Schlüsselkategorien in den wohlfahrtsstaatlichen Veränderungen in der jüngeren Vergangenheit (Obinger 2015, Lessenich 2012, Leitner et al. 2013). Diese Neuausrichtung steht auch von feministisch-progressiver Seite unter

Kritik (Klatzer und Schlager 2011). Die Bedingungslosigkeit des Grundeinkommens stellt diese Grundausrichtung prinzipiell in Frage.

What's 'Binnenmarkt' got to do with it?

Am europäischen Binnenmarkt bzw. in einer kleinen offenen Volkswirtschaft wie Österreich gibt es starke Außenhandelsverflechtungen. Die Exportwirtschaft steht (zumindest) in einem europäischen Wettbewerb, der sich stark an den Arbeitskosten orientiert (Leoni 2017). Seit der Krise 2008 zeigt sich keine Konvergenz des Wohlstandsniveaus in den Ländern und Regionen. Die Konsequenzen von Globalisierung, Digitalisierung und Automatisierung sind regional unterschiedlich ausgeprägt. Arbeitsplätze, besonders in Routine-Tätigkeitsbereichen, gehen verloren, Ersatz-Arbeitsplätze dafür sind bisher nicht ersichtlich (Peneder et al. 2017, Bock-Schappelwein und Huemer 2017).

Soziale Fragen können im Binnenmarkt und in der Währungsunion nicht mehr nur mit nationalstaatlichen Maßnahmen beantwortet werden. Aber es gibt auf EU-Ebene keine direkten Kompetenzen, sozialpolitische Gegenmaßnahmen zu ergreifen, Leibfried und Pierson (1998) sprechen in diesem Zusammenhang von einem „*hohlen Kern*" (S. 87). Der Vorschlag einer europäischen Arbeitslosenversicherung des EU-Sozialkommissar László Andor im Jahr 2014 fand keine Unterstützung durch die Nationalstaaten[8]. Auch die neue „*Europäische Säule der sozialen Rechte*" (Europäische Kommission 2017) fokussiert nationale und nicht europäische arbeitsmarkt- und sozialpolitische Instrumente (Mayrhuber 2017).

Die steigende (Einkommens-)Ungleichheit, die hohe Arbeitslosigkeit etc. schränken die Möglichkeiten der eigenständigen Absicherung über die Erwerbsarbeit ein, Mindestsicherungselemente gewinnen vor diesem Hintergrund an Bedeutung, verlieren aber in der Bevölkerung an Akzeptanz. Der Binnenmarkt auf der einen Seite und die kleinräumige[9] kompensatorische Sozialpolitik auf der anderen Seite führt zu zunehmenden sozialen Spannungen. Die negativen Folgen zeigen sich an der wachsenden sozialen und ökonomischen Exklusion großer Bevölkerungsgruppen (Statistik Austria 2017). Vor diesem Hintergrund gewinnen Fragen nach grundsätzlichen materiellen Mindeststandards – jenseits der Erwerbsarbeit – in Form von Bedingungslosen Einkommenskomponenten an Bedeutung.

In der Wirtschafts- und Währungsunion wirken Veränderungen im nationalen Sicherungssystem eines Landes über die Grenzen hinaus. So zeigen Giulietti und Wahba (2012) für 16 europäische Staaten (u.a. auch Österreich), dass die Generosität der wohlfahrtsstaatlichen Leistungen vor allem Geringqualifizierte in ihrer EU-Binnenmigrationsentscheidung beeinflusst[10]. Gibt es ein Regime der kontrollierten Zuwanderung, migrieren eher höher Qualifizierte (Razin und Wahba 2012). Österreich hat keine kontrollierte Zuwanderung aus der EU und ist ein klassisches

---

[8] Der Vorschlag hat in der Juncker-Kommission keine Priorität mehr.
[9] In Österreich haben wir auf Bundesländerebene neun unterschiedliche Regulierungen der bedarfsorientierten Mindestsicherung.
[10] Sie bestätigen die „Welfare Magnet Hypothesis".

Zielland für Arbeitsmigration (Huber et al. 2017). Ein BGE würde die Migration nach Österreich jedenfalls verändern. Die Auswirkungen einer Einführung nur in Österreich hängen von der konkreten Ausgestaltung ab, könnte aber die Immigration aus den ärmeren Mitgliedsstaaten nach Österreich tendenziell erhöhen.

Die Abfederung von Konjunktureinbrüchen ist in einer Währungsunion nicht mehr durch Währungsabwertungen möglich. Auch daraus leitet sich die Notwendigkeit transnationaler Sicherungsnetze ab. Die 2014 vorgeschlagene – aus Steuermitteln finanzierte – europäische Arbeitslosenversicherung hätte gemäß DIW (2014) eine deutliche Stabilisierung der wirtschaftlichen Entwicklung nach sich gezogen.

Durch den Binnenmarkt sind die Gesellschaften in den Mitgliedsstaaten miteinander verbunden und von den sozialen Standards, Möglichkeiten und Einschränkungen beeinflusst. Soziale Innovationen – zu denen Modelle des BGE gezählt werden können – sollen daher nicht auf Regionen oder Nationalstaaten beschränkt bleiben, sondern EU-weit systematisch gefördert werden (Andersson et al. 2016).

Ökonomische Effekte eines Bedingungslosen Grundeinkommens

Da die Absicherung über Erwerbsarbeit im Sozialstaat mit bismarckscher Prägung löchrig geworden ist (Stichwort „New Social Risks"), braucht es in Zeiten der Globalisierung und Digitalisierung, die sich u.a. in steigender Erwerbsarbeitslosigkeit zeigen, ein neues Sicherungsmodell. Nachdem das Produktionsproblem gelöst ist, muss das Verteilungsproblem gelöst werden (Keynes 1930), das BGE könnte ein mögliches Instrument dafür sein.

Die Diskurse zum BGE und auch die empirische Literatur dazu bleiben im nationalstaatlichen Rahmen verhaftet, obwohl sich globalisierungsbedingt aus wirtschafts-, verteilungs- und demokratiepolitischen Entwicklungen die Notwendigkeit einer stärkeren Transferorientierung in Europa zeigt.

Empirische Evidenz

Die möglichen Wirkungsweisen unterschiedlicher BGE-Modelle auf Wirtschaft (Binnen- und Außenwirtschaft) und Gesellschaft bzw. einzelne Gruppen können nur annäherungsweise quantifiziert werden. Die Einschränkungen ergeben sich einerseits aus der Tatsache, dass die diskutierten Modelle höchst verschieden konzipiert sind: Sie unterscheiden sich in Höhe, Finanzierung, Einbettung in das Gesamtsystem (Ergänzung/Ablöse) etc. Andererseits sind die Ergebnisse vorhandener Evaluierungen auf der Grundlage von theoretischen Modellen von den getroffenen (Verhaltens-)Annahmen getrieben. Effekte alternativer Politikmaßnahmen auf der Grundlage gegenwärtiger (makro-)ökonometrischer Modelle können die neuen Rahmenbedingungen, unter denen Individuen, Betriebe, Institutionen ihre Entscheidungen treffen, nicht beobachten (Lucas-Kritik) und quantifizieren. Diesem strukturellen Mangel wird in neueren Forschungen mit Feldexperimenten begegnet: Zur Erforschung möglicher individueller Verhaltensänderungen beziehen beispielsweise seit Jahresanfang 2017 2.000 zufällig ausgewählte arbeitslose Menschen in Finnland monatlich 560 € als Bedingungsloses Grundeinkommen (bei einem allgemeinen Existenzminimum von 1.000 €), befristet auf zwei Jahre. Die ersten Ergebnisse zeigen keine Veränderung in der Arbeitsbereitschaft (Jonas 2017).

Fraglich ist, ob aus dem Experiment auf allgemeine Verhaltensänderungen durch die Einführung eines BGE rückgeschlossen werden kann. Wenn alle einen Grundeinkommensanspruch –nicht nur einige wenige auf eine bestimmte Zeit – haben, verändern sich die Erwerbs- und Einkommensverhältnisse, die Preisrelationen etc. strukturell, damit sind Verhaltensänderungen der Unternehmen und der Personen wahrscheinlich. Diese Veränderungen treten in Experimenten von wenigen Grundeinkommensbeziehenden nicht auf, sind aber für die Beurteilung der Zielerreichung essenziell.

Von den wenigen vorhandenen Arbeiten zur Quantifizierung möglicher Wirkungsweisen, die mit der Einführungen eines BGE in Verbindung stehen, sind nachfolgend einige Aspekte festgehalten. Wiederrum gibt es ausschließlich (wenige) Analysen zu den Auswirkungen innerhalb der Nationalstaaten.

Beschäftigungswirkung

Der Einfluss des Bedingungslosen Grundeinkommens auf Erwerbstätigkeit und Löhne wird im traditionellen ökonomischen Ansatz über die Arbeitsangebotselastizitäten (Einkommens- und Substitutionseffekt) untersucht. Diese (Verhaltens-) Effekte hängen sowohl vom individuellen Einkommen als auch vom Steuersystem (Individual- versus Haushaltsbesteuerung, Höhe der Grenz-, Durchschnittssteuerbelastung etc.) und vom Haushaltskontext ab.

Ergebnisse aus mikroökonomischen Arbeitsangebotselastizitätsstudien auf der Grundlage des Steuer- und Abgabensystems zeigen die hohe Bandbreite der Arbeitsangebotsreaktionen auf (Meghir und Phillips 2010, Keane 2010). Insgesamt haben Männer eine geringere Arbeitsangebotselastizität als Frauen, alleinerziehende Mütter haben die höchste Partizipationselastizität. Schratzenstaller und Dellinger (2017) zeigen, dass durch den ausbezahlten „Tax Credit" bei einer Erwerbstätigkeit von 16 Wochenstunden in Großbritannien die Beschäftigungsquote von Alleinerzieherinnen um 5% steigt. Frauen in der Rolle als Zweitverdienerinnen hingegen reduzieren ihr Arbeitsangebot, wenn die Obergrenze für die Auszahlung überschritten wird. Hieraus kann vermutet werden, dass ein BGE zu einem tendenziellen Arbeitsmarktrückzug von Menschen mit geringer Arbeitsmarktintegration führen wird, wovon Frauen stärker als Männer betroffen sein würden.

Empirische Befunde ergeben somit eine große Bandbreite von Arbeitsangebotsreaktionen entlang unterschiedlicher Bevölkerungsgruppen. Die Gesamtwirkung eines BGE auf das Arbeitskräfteangebot lässt sich a priori nicht quantifizieren.

Mit einem Grundeinkommen sollten die Lohnkosten reduzierbar sein, eine Verbilligung des Produktionsfaktors Arbeit würde zu einer steigenden Arbeitsnachfrage führen. In jenen Wirtschaftsbereichen mit Arbeitskräfteüberangebot könnte darüber hinaus auch das Lohnniveau weiter sinken. Weniger attraktive Arbeitsplätze im Niedriglohnsegment wiederum müssen unter Umständen höher entlohnt werden, weil das entsprechende Arbeitsangebot sinkt. Die Wirkung eines BGE ist jedenfalls von der konkreten Ausgestaltung abhängig, vor allem mit der Frage, wie die Lohnkosten vom BGE beeinflusst werden. Damit kann auch die Arbeitsnachfragereaktion a priori nicht quantifiziert werden.

Wirkung auf die Lohnhöhe

Unter der Annahme, dass Löhne individuell ausverhandelt werden, hängt die Verhandlungsmacht der ArbeitnehmerInnen von Alternativen ab. Diese Alternativen können das Arbeitslosengeld etc. oder das BGE sein. Haywood (2014) argumentiert, dass durch ein BGE die Verhandlungsposition der ArbeitnehmerInnen geschwächt wird, da ArbeitgeberInnen das BGE als impliziten Lohnbestandteil wahrnehmen würden: Insgesamt könnte sowohl das Lohnniveau als auch die geleisteten Arbeitsstunden in einer Volkswirtschaft sinken. Haywood (2014, S. 3) erwartet aber auch eine sinkende Arbeitslosigkeit, da sich Arbeitslose mit schlechten Arbeitsmarktperspektiven und Personen mit gesundheitlichen Beeinträchtigungen ganz aus dem Arbeitsmarkt zurückziehen würden.

Fehlende Analysen zu ökonomischen Wirkungen

Das bisher Gezeigte macht deutlich, dass für die Modelle des BGE zum gegenwärtigen Zeitpunkt kaum ökonomische Bewertungen vorliegen. Wichtige Fragen sind nur punktuell behandelt und immer nur auf nationalstaatlicher Ebene. Die Wirkungen auf die europäischen Migrationsströme sind von den BefürworterInnen wie GegnerInnen des BGE weder angedacht noch konkretisiert.

Rückwirkungen auf das Preisniveau, auf das gesamtwirtschaftliche Arbeitsvolumen und dessen Aufteilung, auf die Arbeitsbeziehungen (Lohnverhandlungssysteme) und das institutionelle Sozialstaatsgefüge etc. sind ebenso wenig untersucht wie die gesamtwirtschaftlichen Finanzierungsmöglichkeiten. Mögliche Effekte sind jedenfalls von der Ausformulierung der jeweiligen Grundeinkommensmodelle abhängig. Studien zeigen jedoch die armutsreduzierende Wirkung von gezielten bedarfsunabhängigen Transfers an Kinder (Levy et al. 2013).

Chancen und Gefahren eines nationalen BGE in einer europäischen Wirtschaft

Eine abschließende Beurteilung des Bedingungslosen Grundeinkommens als taugliches Instrument zur Sicherung der Wohlfahrt für alle in einer globalisierten Welt muss an dieser Stelle offen bleiben. Die Erwartungen an das BGE als Lösungsansatz der dargestellten vielschichtigen Veränderungen im sozialstaatlichen Gefüge sind sehr hoch. Sowohl die Analysen zum Status quo der Schwachstellen und Problemlagen in den europäischen Sozialstaaten unterscheiden sich maßgeblich voneinander, als auch die Zielstellungen in welche Richtung Reformen gehen sollten.

Abschließend sind daher ohne Anspruch auf Vollständigkeit die Chancen und Gefahren eines BGE festgehalten, die dieses Instrument am globalisierten Produktions- und Arbeitsmarkt und weiterhin nationalstaatlichen Sicherungssystemen haben könnte.

Chancen

- Die Diskussion um das BGE dreht sich im Wesentlichen um die Ausgestaltung eines Basiseinkommens für erwerbsfähige Menschen und die damit verbundenen Implikationen sowie Anpassungsprozesse für Individuen, Wirtschaft und Gesellschaft. Als erster Schritt könnte das Bedingungslose Grundeinkommen jedoch jene weiten Teile der Bevölkerung adressieren, von denen gesellschaftlich keine wirtschaftliche Leistung verlangt wird (etwa Kinder und Jugendliche oder Erwerbsunfähige und Alte).
- Die Zunahme von digitalisierten Arbeitsverhältnissen am globalen Arbeitsmarkt (Beispiel Cloudworker) führt in Österreich zu einer Zunahme der Neuen Selbständigen (Bock-Schappelwein und Mayrhuber 2017). Geringe Einkommensniveaus, unregelmäßige Einkommenszuflüsse, regelmäßige Erwerbsunterbrechungen etc. bedeuten im einkommenszentrierten Alterssicherungssystem eine höhere Wahrscheinlichkeit, von Altersarmut betroffen zu sein. Mittel- und langfristig könnte mit einem BGE im Alter der möglichen Altersarmut begegnet werden. Schon derzeit garantiert das Instrument der Ausgleichszulage und die Mindestsicherung eine (bedarfsgeprüfte) Mindestpension. Eine Bedingungslose Mindestpension würde die ökonomische Eigenständigkeit der Frauen, die den überwiegenden Teil der unbezahlten Versorgungsarbeit leisten, verbessern.
- Die gewachsenen nationalen Systeme der sozialen Sicherheit und die Steuersysteme haben teilweise einen hohen Komplexitätsgrad erreicht. Sowohl die Wahrnehmung der Möglichkeiten für die Menschen als auch die Zielstellungen der einzelnen Instrumente bergen die Gefahr von ungewollten Effekten. Ein BGE könnte weniger komplex und intransparent ausgestaltet werden. Armutsfallen können durch die Überführung der unterschiedlichen Modellkomponenten in ein BGE vermieden werden.

Gefahren

- Die Modelle zum BGE sind derzeit im nationalstaatlichen Rahmen verhaftet, sie stellen dadurch keine adäquaten Ansätze zum Umgang mit wachsenden ökonomischen Ungleichheiten in Europa dar.

- Eine flächendeckende Einführung eines BGE verändert die nationale Arbeitsangebot- und Arbeitsnachfrage, die absoluten und relativen Preise etc. Ein BGE in einer kleinen offenen Volkswirtschaft würde darüber hinaus auch den Exportsektor und Migrationsströme berühren. Eine Veränderung in der Wettbewerbsposition hätte nicht nur Rückwirkungen auf die Akzeptanz, sondern unter Umständen auch auf die nationale Wertschöpfung.
- Die Finanzierung eines BGE hat ebenfalls Auswirkungen auf das Arbeitsangebot, die Arbeitsnachfrage und die relativen Preise. Es bedarf einer beschäftigungsfördernden und aus der Verteilungsperspektive gerechten Finanzierungsstruktur. Schon gegenwärtig existieren diese Zielkonflikte, diese werden durch ein BGE vermutlich weiter an Bedeutung gewinnen.
- In der derzeitigen Arbeitsgesellschaft hängen sozialer Status, Lebenszufriedenheit bis hin zum Selbstwertgefühl an der Berufstätigkeit bzw. an dem damit verbunden Einkommen. Werden Personen im Erwerbsalter hinkünftig durch ein Grundeinkommen materiell abgesichert, braucht es dennoch Strukturen und Instrumente, um die soziale Integration – die dann nicht mehr über den Erwerbsarbeitsmarkt läuft – zu forcieren. Es bestünde sonst die Gefahr, dass sich durch das BGE Tendenzen zu Parallelgesellschaften, etwa von schlecht Qualifizierten und Erwerbslosen, verstärken.
- An der ungleichen Verteilung von Vermögen und Wohlstand würde ein BGE wenig ändern, die ungleiche (Vermögens-)Ausstattung würde nicht adressiert sein. Insgesamt wird mit dem BGE die Auswirkung der ökonomischen Ungleichheiten reduziert, die Ursachen der Ungleichheiten bleiben aber aufrecht. Dementsprechend bedarf es weiterhin, im Sinne einer inklusiven Gesellschaft, der Herstellung größerer Chancengleichheit und der Wahrung der gesellschaftlichen Akzeptanz des Systems sowohl ergänzender finanzieller Leistungen für besonderen Bedarf (etwa bei Behinderungen oder Wohnproblemen) und insbesondere öffentlich finanzierter Sachleistungen.
- In den Konzepten zum BGE fehlen die Übergangswege vom gegenwärtigen System der sozialen Sicherung in das neue System des BGE. Die Abkehr von einkommenszentrierten Sicherungssystem hin zum BGE sollte eine Schlechterstellung bei höheren Erwerbseinkommen vermeiden, um die Akzeptanz einer Veränderung nicht zu untergraben.

Noch kann das Bedingungslose Grundeinkommen als Utopie bezeichnet werden. Am Diskurs darüber und den vorhandenen Modellen zeigt sich allerdings die Notwendigkeit einer Neuausrichtung der sozialen Sicherungsmechanismen in einer globalisierten Wirtschaft und einem europäischen Arbeitsmarkt. Dieser Diskurs muss im Sinne der sozialen Nachhaltigkeit unseres Wirtschaftssystems jedenfalls weiter intensiviert werden.

Literatur

Andersson, L., Antti, A., Buhr, D., Fink, Ph., Stöber, N. (2016) Innovationsstrategien in Zeiten der Digitalisierung: Ein Vergleich der Innovationspolitik in Finnland, Schweden und Deutschland, Berlin, Friedrich-Ebert-Stiftung, 2016.

Appel, M. (2010) Bedingungslosigkeit politisieren. In: Blaschke, R., Praetorius, I., Schrupp, A., (Hg.), Das Bedingungslose Grundeinkommen, Feministische und postpatriarchale Perspektiven, Ulrike Helmer-Verlag, Sulzbach, 2010, 46-63.

Atkinson, A. B. (2011) Basic Income: Ethics, Statistics and Economics. Überarbeitete Version einer Rede die auf dem Workshop „Basic Income and Income Redistribution" an der Universität Luxembourg gehalten wurde, April 2011. http://www.nuff.ox.ac.uk/users/atkinson/ Basic _Income%20Luxembourg%20April%202011.pdf

Blaschke, R., Praetorius, I., Schrupp, A., (Hg.) (2010), Das Bedingungslose Grundeinkommen, Feministische und postpatriarchale Perspektiven, Ulrike Helmer-Verlag, Sulzbach, 2010.

Bock-Schappelwein, J., Huemer, U. (2017) Österreich 2025 – Die Rolle ausreichender Basiskompetenzen in einer digitalisierten Arbeitswelt. WIFO-Monatsberichte, 2017, 90(2), S.131-140

Bock-Schappelwein, J., Mayrhuber, Ch., (2017) Dimensionen und Rahmenbedingungen plattformbasierter Arbeit in Österreich und Europa. WIFO-Monographie, im Erscheinen.

DIW (2014) Eine Arbeitslosenversicherung für den Euroraum als automatischer Stabilisator – Grenzen und Möglichkeiten. Berlin, 2014.

Eichhorst, W., Marx, P., Wehner, C. (2016) Labor Market Reforms in Europe: Towards More Flexicure Labor Markets?, IZA DP No. 9863, April 2016

Europäische Kommission (2017) Zur Einführung einer Säule sozialer Rechte. COM(2017) 250 final, https://ec.europa.eu/transparency/regdoc/rep/1/2017/DE/COM-2017-250-F1-DE-MAIN-PART-1.PDF

European Commission (2014) A Decade of Labour Market Reforms in the EU: Insights from the LABREF database, Economic and Financial Affairs, Economic Papers 522. Bruxelles, July 2014.

Friedman, M., (2002) Capitalism and Freedom: Fortieth Anniversary Edition. University of Chicago Press, 2002, ISBN 0-226-26421-1, S. 192–194.

Giulietti, C., Wahba, J. (2012) Welfare Migration, IZA DP No. 6450, 2012.

Gubitzer, L, Heintel, P., (2012) Koppeln oder Entkoppeln: Grundsicherung versus Grundeinkommen. iff texte - Band 4, Alternative Ökonomie, 37-43.

Haug, F., (2003) „Schaffen wir einen neuen Menschentyp": von Henry Ford zu Peter Hartz. In: Das Argument Jg. 45 (2003), H. 4/5 S. 606-617 ISSN 0004-1157.

Haywood, L. (2014) Unconditional Basic Income: An Economic Perspective. DIW Round up, 33/2014.

Hohenleitner, I., Straubhaar, Th. (2007) Bedingungsloses Grundeinkommen und Solidarisches Bürgergelt – mehr als sozialutopische Konzepte. HWWI, 2007.

Huber, P., Horvath, Th., Bock-Schappelwein, J. (2017) Österreich 2025 – Österreich als Zuwanderungsland. WIFO-Monatsberichte, 2017, 90(7), S.581-588.

IMF (2017) Fiscal Monitor: Tackling Inequality, Washington D.C., http://www.imf.org/en/ Publications/FM/Issues/2017/10/05/fiscal-monitor-october-2017

Jonas, U. (2017) Finnland testet das bedingungslose Grundeinkommen - und widerlegt das wichtigste Argument der Kritiker, 2017. In: http://www.huffingtonpost.de/2017/06/ 23/finn land-testet-seit-5-monate-bedingungsloses-grundeinkommen-sozialsystem-skandinavien_n_17 257998.html

Keane, M.P. (2010) Labor Supply and Taxes: A Survey. Sydney, 2010.

Keynes, J. M. (1930) The Economic Possibilities of Our Grandchildren. In: Nation and Athenaeum, October; reprinted in Essays in Persuasion (1963), New York: W. W. Norton.

Klatzer, E., Schlager, Ch. (2011) EU macroeconomic governance and gender orders: the case of Austria. In: Young, B. et al. (eds.): Questioning Financial Governance from a Feminist Perspective, Routledge, London and New York, 2011.
Koch, S., Stephan, G., Walwei, U. (2005) Workfare: Möglichkeiten und Grenzen. IAB-Discussion Paper 17/2005.
Kreisky, E., Löffler, M., Zegler, S., (2011) (Hg.) Staatsfiktionen. Denkbilder moderner Staatlichkeit. Wien, 2011.
Leibfried, St. (2013) Europa am Scheideweg: Wege aus der Depression. In: Soziale Sicherheit, 2013, (4), S. 180-185.
Leibfried, St., Pierson, P. (1998) Halbsouveräne Wohlfahrtsstaaten: Der Sozialstaat in der europäischen Mehrebenen-Politik. In: Leibfried, St., Pierson, P. (Hg.) Standort Europa: Europäische Sozialpolitik.
Leitner, S.; Klammer, U.; Leiber, S. (2013) Leben im transformierten Sozialstaat (TransSoz): Zielgruppenspezifische Reformwirkungen und Alltagspraxen. Antrag auf Förderung einer Forschungskooperation zwischen der Universität Duisburg-Essen sowie den Fachhochschulen Düsseldorf und Köln, http://transsoz.web.th-koeln.de/wp/wp-content/uploads/2013/08/vorhabensbeschreibung.pdf [15.10.16].
Leoni, Th. (2017) Entwicklung und Struktur der Arbeitskosten und der Lohnstückkosten 2000 bis 2015. Ein kommentierter Datenüberblick. WIFO-Monographien, 2017.
Lessenich, S. (2012) Theorien des Sozialstaats. Hamburg: Junius.
Levy, H., Manos, M., Sutherland, H., (2013) Towards a European Union Child Basic Income? Within and between country effects. In: International Journal of Microsimulation, International Microsimulation Association, 1(6), 2013, 63-85.
Mätzke, M. (2011) Staatsbürger als Wirtschaftssubjekte und als demografische Ressource, Die Ziele staatlicher Akteure in der Sozialpolitik. In: Leviathan, 2011, 39(3), S. 385-406.
Mayrhuber, Ch. (2017) Die neue „Europäische Säule der sozialen Rechte". In: ATTAC (Hg.), Europa neu denken, Wien, 2017.
Meghir, C., Phillips, D. (2010) Labour Supply and Taxes. In: Mirrlees, J., Adam, S., Besley, T., Blundell, R., Bond, S., Chote, R., Gammie, M., Johnson, P., Myles, G., Poterba, J. (Hrsg.), Dimensions of Tax Design. The Mirrlees Review, Oxford, 2010, S. 202-274.
Michalitsch, G. (2007) Grundeinkommen. Bedingungslose Befreiung oder bewusste Befriedung?, In: kulturrisse, 3/2007, 3-7.
Obinger, H. (2015) Österreichs Sozialstaat im internationalen Vergleich. In: Austrian Journal of Political Science.
Opielka, M., Strengmann-Kuhn, W. (2006) Das Solidarische Bürgergeld, Finanz- und sozialpolitische Analyse eines Reformkonzepts. Oktober, 2006.
Peneder, M., Bock-Schappelwein, J., Firgo, M., Fritz, O., Streicher, G. (2017) Ökonomische Effekte der Digitalisierung in Österreich. In: WIFO-Monatsberichte, 2017, 90(3), S.177-192
Prätorius, I (2010). Ökonomie der Geburtlichkeit: Wer das bedingungslose Grundeinkommen will, muss Wirtschaft vom menschlichen Anfang her denken. In: Blaschke, R., Prätorius, I., Schrupp, A., (Hg.), Das Bedingungslose Grundeinkommen, Feministische und postpatriarchale Perspektiven, 2010, 31-46.
Rätz, W., Krampertz, H. (2011) Bedingungsloses Grundeinkommen– woher, wozu und wohin? 2011.
Razin, A., Wahba, J. (2012) Welfare Magnet Hypotheis, Fiscal Burden and Immigraion Skill Selektivity, Norface Migration Discussion Paper No. 2012/36.
Reinprecht, Ch., (2008) Prekarisierung und die Re-Feudalisierung sozialer Ungleichheit. In: Kurswechsel, 1/2008, 13-23.
Schneider, F., Dreer, E. (2017) Grundeinkommen in Österreich? Linz, 2017.
Schratzenstaller, M., Dellinger, F. (2017) Genderdifferenzierte Lenkungswirkungen des Abgabesystems. WIFO-Monographien, 2017.

Schulmeister, St. (2013) Realkapitalismus und Finanzkapitalismus – zwei „Spielanordnungen" und zwei Phasen des „langen Zyklus". In: Kromphardt, J. (Hg.), Weiterentwicklung der Keynes'schen Theorie und empirische Analysen, Schriften der Keynes-Gesellschaft, Marburg, 7.

Sesselmeier, W., Somaggio, G., (2009) Arbeitsmarktpolitik im wohlfahrtsstaatlichen Vergleich. In: Bothfeld, S., Sesselmeier, W., Bogedan, C. (Hrsg.): Arbeitsmarktpolitik in der sozialen Marktwirtschaft - Vom Arbeitsförderungsgesetz zu Sozialgesetzbuch II und III, Wiesbaden 2009, S. 21-48

Statistik Austria (2017) Einkommen, Armut und Lebensbedingungen, Tabellenband, EU-SILC 2016, Wien 2007.

UNCTAD (2017) Trade and Development Report. Beyond Austerity: Towards a Global New Deal, New York/Genf, 2017, http://unctad.org/en/pages/PublicationWebflyer.aspx?publicationid=1852

Polarisierungstendenzen in Österreich?
Ergebnisse einer latenten Klassenanalyse der Einstellungen zur Immigration

Johann Bacher[1]

> „Ein erster Ansatzpunkt der Analyse fremdenfeindlicher Orientierung ist aus dieser Perspektive die Lösung der Verteilungsfragen. Das ist etwas, was wir in den 1960er- und 1970er-Jahren viel diskutiert haben, in den 1980er- und 1990er-Jahren aber oft vergessen haben. Verteilungsfragen, Zugang zur Arbeit, zu Wohnen, zu Sozialleistungen, all das sind meines Erachtens wichtige Themen, die zu beachten sind, wenn man will, dass Fremde nicht für die veränderte wirtschaftliche und soziale Lage verantwortlich gemacht werden."
> (Biffl 2010, S. 13)

Zusammenfassung

Der Beitrag greift die bei der letzten Bundespräsidentenwahl feststellbaren Polarisierungstendenzen in der österreichischen Wählerschaft auf und untersucht mit Hilfe einer latenten Klassenanalyse die Frage, ob und wie stark diese Polarisierungstendenzen bereits vorab in der österreichischen Bevölkerung latent vorhanden waren, wie dies theoretisch zu vermuten ist. Empirische Re-Analysen des Europäischen Sozialen Surveys zeigen, dass bereits 2001 Polarisierungstendenzen hinsichtlich der Einstellung zu Immigration latent vorhanden waren, die sich sozialstrukturell gut verorten lassen. Darauf aufbauend werden Überlegungen angestellt, wie diese Polarisierungstendenzen abgeschwächt werden können.

Einleitung

Die letzte Bundespräsidentenwahl in Österreich hat eine deutliche Polarisierung erkennen lassen. Mit dem späteren Präsidenten Alexander Van der Bellen stand ein weltoffener, Europa und Menschenrechte befürwortender Kandidat dem europakritischen, national orientierten Kandidaten Norbert Hofer gegenüber. Ein zentrales Polarisierungsfeld bilden neben Europa die Einstellungen zur Immigration. Soziodemographisch verlief die Konfliktlinie u.a. entlang einem Stadt-Land-

---

[1] Ich möchte mich an dieser Stelle sehr herzlich bei Isabella Skrivanek für die Rückmeldungen zum vorliegenden Beitrag bedanken, die zur inhaltlichen Schärfung beigetragen haben. Verbleibende Ungenauigkeiten gehen auf das Konto des Autors.

Gefälle. In den meisten Städten konnte Van der Bellen eine Mehrheit erzielen, in ländlichen Gebieten gewann Norbert Hofer, wobei auch innerhalb der Kommunen und in den Städten Polarisierungen bestanden.

In 55,6% der Gemeinden mit mehr als 10.000 Wahlberechtigten erzielte Van der Bellen beim 2. Wahlgang im Mai 2016, dessen Ergebnisse später vom Verfassungsgerichtshof aufgehoben wurden, mehr als 50%, wobei der Stimmenanteil in 13,3% dieser Gemeinden über 60% lag. Umgekehrt ist in 48,3% der Gemeinden mit bis zu einschließlich 3.000 Wahlberechtigten ein Stimmenanteil für Van der Bellen von unter 40% bzw. für Hofer von über 60% zu beobachten. Insgesamt hat Hofer in 83,1% der Gemeinden mit bis zu 3.000 Wahlberechtigten eine Mehrheit erzielt. Bei der Wiederholung des 2. Wahlgangs im Dezember ist in allen Gemeindegrößenklassen ein Zugewinn von Van der Bellen beobachtbar, da sich der Ausgang der BREXIT-Abstimmung und jener der USA-Wahl und die darauf folgende Ernüchterung zugunsten Van der Bellen auswirkten. Bei der Wiederholung konnte Van der Bellen in 71,8% der Gemeinden mit mehr als 10.000 Wahlberechtigten eine Mehrheit erzielen, in 28,3% einen Stimmenanteil von mehr als 60%. Umgekehrt reduzierte sich in Gemeinden mit weniger als 3.000 Wahlberechtigten der Anteil, wo Hofer mehr als 60% erreichte, auf 30,4%.

Gemeinden mit ... Wahlberechtigten	n=	Stimmenanteile von Van der Bellen					
		bis unter 40%	40% bis unter 45%	45% bis unter 50%	50% bis unter 55%	55% bis unter 60%	60% und mehr
		Zweiter aufgehobener Wahlgang im Mai 2015					
bis einschließlich 3.000	1.722	48,3%	19,1%	15,7%	9,2%	4,2%	3,5%
3.001 bis einschließlich 5.000	206	36,4%	18,0%	20,4%	13,6%	7,3%	4,4%
5.001 bis einschließlich 10.000	127	19,7%	26,8%	18,9%	16,5%	13,4%	4,7%
10.001 und mehr	45	6,7%	15,6%	22,2%	26,7%	15,6%	13,3%
Gesamt	2.100	44,5%	19,4%	16,5%	10,5%	5,3%	3,9%
		Wiederholung des Zweiten Wahlgangs im Dezember 2016					
bis einschließlich 3.000	1.720	30,4%	20,3%	19,5%	15,7%	7,5%	6,6%
3.001 bis einschließlich 5.000	208	22,6%	17,3%	21,6%	16,8%	13,0%	8,7%
5.001 bis einschließlich 10.000	126	9,5%	19,0%	27,8%	14,3%	16,7%	12,7%
10.001 und mehr	46	4,3%	8,7%	15,2%	32,6%	10,9%	28,3%
Gesamt	2.100	27,8%	19,7%	20,1%	16,1%	8,7%	7,6%

Tabelle 1 Wahlergebnisse bei der Präsidentenwahl (Ergebnisse des 2. Wahlgangs vom 22.5.2016 und der Wiederholung des 2. Wahlgangs vom 4.12.2016)

Quelle: BMI 2016a, 2016b, Eigene Berechnungen; ungewichtete Ergebnisse, d.h. jede Gemeinde ging unabhängig von der Größe als ein Fall in die Analyse ein.

In dem Beitrag soll der Frage nachgegangen werden, ob die beobachtbaren Polarisierungen durch die Wahl erzeugt oder bereits länger auf einer latenten Ebene von Einstellungen und Werthaltungen vorhanden waren und die Wahlauseinandersetzungen zu einer Manifestation bzw. Verstärkung führten. Der Beitrag konzentriert sich dabei auf Einstellungen zur Immigration, einem der Themenfelder, wo sich inhaltliche Polarisierungen deutlich zeigten und zu dem die zu Ehrende federführend geforscht hat. Nach einem – allerdings nur kursorischen – Blick in die Literatur (Abschnitt 2) untersucht er am Beispiel des European Social Surveys, ob sich in Österreich Polarisierungstendenzen in den Einstellungen zur Immigration empirisch auffinden lassen und durch welche Faktoren sie bedingt sind (Abschnitt 3). Sich daraus ergebende Schlussfolgerungen diskutiert Abschnitt 4.

Theoretische Vorüberlegungen

Theoretisch und auf Basis der vorhandenen Literatur ist es sehr unwahrscheinlich, dass die Polarisierungen erst durch die Wahlauseinandersetzungen ausgelöst wurden. Studien zur Fremden- und Ausländerfeindlichkeit, also zu Phänomenen mit einem engen Bezug zu Fragen der Zuwanderungen, weisen durchgehend einen starken Einfluss der schulischen Bildung aus (Rosar 2001; Fuchs 2003; Rippl 2003). Es ist daher anzunehmen, dass die entsprechenden Einstellungen in der Kinder- und Jugendphase erworben sind, wobei Eltern und Freunden als nahen Bezugspersonen ein besonderer Einfluss bei der Entstehung von Einstellungen zukommt (Bacher 2001a). Fremdenfeindliche Einstellungen werden – wie in einer Studie zu BerufsschülerInnen in Nürnberg gezeigt werden konnte – im engen Nahumfeld durch Familie und Freunde geprägt (ebenda).

Von Relevanz ist aber auch die aktuelle Lebenssituation. Fremdenfeindliche und rechtspopulistische Einstellungen stehen im Zusammenhang mit aktuellen Deprivationserfahrungen, wie z.B. Arbeitslosigkeit (Bacher 2001b), sowie mit Erfahrungen mangelnder Anerkennung (Anhut / Heitmeyer 2009; Kaletta 2008), z.B. durch prekäre Beschäftigung. Diese Erfahrungen können dann zu fremdenfeindlichen Einstellungen führen, wenn der Politik (oder anderen Institutionen) keine Problemlösungen gelingen und in der Folge politische Unzufriedenheit entsteht, die sich in einer Zuwendung zu nationalistischen und rechtspopulistischen Parteien und Ideen widerspiegelt, sofern entsprechende (nationalistische und rechtspopulistische) Interpretationsangebote bestehen. Eine verstärkende Wirkung kommt dabei – wie in der frühen Sozialisation – der direkten Kommunikation und Interaktionen mit VertreterInnen der entsprechenden politischen Parteien und mit Freunden/Bekannten zu, wobei soziale Medien in den letzten Jahren gänzlich neue Möglichkeiten eröffnet haben (z.B. Helbich 2016; Boulianne 2015; Bond u.a. 2012). Durch soziale Medien kann eine große Zahl erreicht werden und sie ermöglichen eine Homogenisierung der Kommunikation unter Gleichgesinnten. Die Relevanz der Kommunikation im (virtuellen) Freundeskreis konnte beispielsweise in einem umfangreichen und viel beachteten Experiment mit ca. 61 Millionen TeilnehmerInnen, das während der Kongresswahlen 2010 in den USA vorgenommen wurde, nachgewiesen werden (Bond u.a. 2012). Neben dem Einfluss der bloßen Informationsübermittlung wurde ein wesentlich stärkerer Effekt auf das Wahlverhalten festgestellt, wenn die Befragten die Informationen innerhalb ihres eigenen persönlichen Netzwerks kommentierten und weiterverbreiteten. Die Studie bestätigt somit den bereits von Lazarsfeld u.a. (1969) in ihrer richtungsweisenden Studie über das Wahlverhalten ermittelten Befund, dass für die Wirkung von Wahlwerbung eine Verstärkung durch direkte Kommunikation und

Interaktion erforderlich ist. Insgesamt erscheint damit folgendes Modell zur Erklärung der beobachtbaren Polarisierungen in der letzten Bundespräsidentenwahl plausibel:

- Es bestanden bereits vorher auf einer latenten Ebene Polarisierungen im Hinblick auf Einstellungen zu MigrantInnen und zur Immigration in der österreichischen Bevölkerung.
- Die Polarisierungen auf der latenten Ebene sind die Folge unterschiedlicher Sozialisationserfahrungen in der Kindheit und Jugend[2], unterschiedlicher Betroffenheit von Deprivation und mangelnder Anerkennung in der aktuellen Lebenssituation sowie vorhandener nationalistischer und rechtspopulistischer Interpretationsangebote auf Seite der Politik und der Öffentlichkeit. Wichtig sind für den Erwerb der Einstellungen direkte Kommunikationen und Interaktionen.
- Durch die Wahlauseinandersetzungen manifestierten und verstärkten sich diese. Wahlergebnisse hängen aber auch von situativen Faktoren ab, wie der Unterschied zwischen der aufgehobenen Stichwahl der Bundespräsidentenwahl und ihrer Wiederholung verdeutlicht (siehe oben), sodass vom Wahlverhalten nicht automatisch auf entsprechende Einstellungen geschlossen werden kann.

Das notwendige Zusammentreffen von in der Bevölkerung vorhandenen Einstellungen einerseits und von politischer Propaganda andererseits für die Entstehung von totalitären Tendenzen heben Horkheimer und Adorno in einem 1952 veröffentlichten Aufsatz (Horkheimer / Adorno 1972) hervor. Die Autoren halten fest:

„Die Gewalt solcher massenfeindlichen Massenbewegungen rührt von mächtigen politischen und wirtschaftlichen Interessen her, und ihre Anhänger, die sich nicht um sonst Gefolgschaft nennen, sind keineswegs ihre bestimmenden Träger. Dennoch bedürfen die Nutznießer jener Bewegungen in der modernen Massengesellschaft der Massen." (Horkheimer / Adorno 1972, S. 83)

Ähnlich äußert sich Hobsbawn (1991) in seiner Studie zur Entstehung von Nationen und des Nationalismus, wobei es seiner Ansicht nach sowohl Konstellationen geben kann, in denen die Wirkung der Einstellungen der Bevölkerung stärker ist, also auch solche, in denen der Nationalismus von oben durch (politische) Eliten erzeugt wird.

Für die Plausibilität der Annahme der Existenz von vorhandenen latenten Einstellungen und Polarisierungstendenzen in Österreich lässt sich des Weiteren anführen, dass Fremde und Ausländer in den letzten Jahrzehnten Gegenstand politi-

---

[2] Eine besonders prägendere Wirkung von Familie und Gleichaltrigen in der Kindheit und Jugend kann dann vermutet werden, wenn sich die Einstellungen auf soziale Werte beziehen. Charakteristisch für Werte ist, dass sie sich auf zentrale Vorstellungen beziehen, wie der Mensch, sein Verhältnis zur Natur und Gesellschaft und die menschliche Gesellschaft sein sollte (Schwartz 1992). Werte sind Kennzeichen der Kultur einer Gesellschaft, die in der Kindheit und Jugend an die nachfolgende Generation vermittelt werden. Die von einer Person geteilten Werte werden als Wertorientierungen bezeichnet. Sie werden als relativ stabil betrachtet.

scher Auseinandersetzungen waren. Erinnert sei hier an das von Jörg Haider 1992 initiierte Anti-Ausländer-Volksbegehren „Österreich zuerst", das von 416.531 Menschen unterstützt wurde[3], sowie die von der Zivilgesellschaft als Lichtermeer bezeichnete Gegendemonstration mit 200.000 bis 300.000 TeilnehmerInnen[4]. Als weiteres Beispiel zu nennen sind die wöchentlichen Donnerstagdemonstrationen zwischen 2000 und 2002 gegen die von Schüssel geführte ÖVP-FPÖ-Regierung.[5] Es lässt sich schwer argumentieren, dass jedes Mal die zugrundeliegenden Einstellungen neu erzeugt und dann wieder vergessen wurden.

Zu den Folgen von Polarisierungen liegen in der Soziologie abhängig von der eingenommenen theoretischen Position unterschiedliche Einschätzungen vor (Bacher 1995). Die Einschätzung möglicher Folgen ist davon abhängig, ob die Polarisierung nur in einem Themenbereich (z.B. der Zuwanderung) gegeben ist oder alle relevanten gesellschaftspolitischen Themenbereiche betrifft. Ein weiterer Faktor ist, wie zentral der entsprechende Themenbereich ist. Bezüglich der Bewertung von Immigration kann angenommen werden, dass es sich derzeit um einen zentralen Themenbereich handelt, sodass Konsequenzen auf politischer, ökonomischer und sozialer Ebene nicht ausgeschlossen werden können. Sie sind auf politischer Ebene auch seit 2015/16 in Form von Grenzkontrollen, Kürzungen im Sozialbereich (Stichwort: Bedarfsorientierte Mindestsicherung) und einer restriktiveren Handhabung von Asyl und Zuwanderung beobachtbar. Unschwer lässt sich vermuten, dass das Thema der Sicherheit in Politik und Gesellschaft an Relevanz gewinnen wird. Ob es in der Summe Problemlösungen geben wird, die für alle produktiv sind und zu einer Vermehrung der Lebenschancen führen, hängt – wenn wir die zu Unrecht in Vergessenheit geratene Konflikttheorie von Dahrendorf (1959, 1994) aufgreifen – davon ab, ob ein Dialog zwischen den Gruppen gelingt und ein Grund- oder zumindest Verfahrenskonsens erzielt werden kann. Dieser Konsens ist schwieriger zu erreichen, je stärker die Polarisierung ist, aber nicht unmöglich.

Inwiefern die bisher angenommenen Polarisierungstendenzen empirisch in repräsentativen Bevölkerungsumfragen auffindbar sind, wird nachfolgend untersucht.

---

[3] Siehe https://de.wikipedia.org/wiki/%C3%96sterreich_zuerst (26.7.2017) sowie http://www.bmi.gv.at/cms/BMI_wahlen/volksbegehren/Alle_Volksbegehren.aspx
[4] Siehe https://de.wikipedia.org/wiki/Lichtermeer (26.7.2017)
[5] Siehe https://de.wikipedia.org/wiki/Donnerstagsdemonstrationen (26.7.2017)

Empirische Evidenz

Datenbasis

Als Datenbasis für die nachfolgenden Analysen wird der European Social Survey (ESS) verwendet. Der ESS[6] ist ein seit 2001 durchgeführtes Umfrageprogramm. Die erste Erhebungswelle fand 2002/2003 statt. Im Jahr 2014/15 wurde die siebte Welle realisiert. Sie wurde vor dem Sommer 2015 und damit vor der Flüchtlingsbewegung abgeschlossen. Allerdings war das Flüchtlingsthema auch bereits während des Erhebungszeitraums präsent (siehe dazu später). Ziel des ESS ist die regelmäßige Erfassung von Einstellungen und Verhaltensweisen mittels repräsentativer nationaler Umfragen in Europa. Verwendet wird immer ein Standardprogramm von Fragen, bei jeder Welle kommen Spezialfragen hinzu. Die Umfragen müssen besondere Qualitätsansprüche erfüllen. An dem Programm beteiligten sich bisher insgesamt 32 Länder, Österreich nahm an den ersten drei Wellen und an der siebten Welle teil.

In der ersten und siebten Welle wurden Spezialfragen zur Migration gestellt. Erfasst wurden u.a. Items, die sich allgemein auf die Zuwanderung beziehen, Items zur Einschätzung möglicher positiver oder negativer Effekte von Zuwanderung sowie Items zu erforderlichen Qualifikationen, die MigrantInnen mitbringen sollen. Die nachfolgende Analyse stützt sich auf die allgemeinen Einstellungsfragen zur Immigration sowie auf die Beurteilung möglicher Effekte von Zuwanderung (siehe Tabelle 2).[7] Die Items wurden auf den Zahlenbereich von -3 bis +3 reskaliert. Der Skalenwert -3 repräsentiert – abhängig von der Formulierung des Items – eine starke Ablehnung bzw. Zustimmung, der Skalenwert 0 eine mittlere/neutrale Position und der Skalenwert +3 eine starke Zustimmung bzw. Ablehnung. Im Durchschnitt – mit Ausnahme der Einschätzung der Kriminalität – liegt sowohl 2003 als auch 2014/15 eine neutrale Bewertung der Aussagen zu Zuwanderung vor. Lediglich im Bereich der Einschätzung der Kriminalität zeigt sich eine leichte Zustimmung zur Aussage, dass Zuwanderung zu einer Zunahme von Kriminalitätsproblemen führt. Zwischen 2003 und 2014/15 ist eine sehr schwache Tendenz in Richtung einer negativeren Beurteilung der Immigration beobachtbar. Die Veränderungen sind in vier der sechs Fälle auch statistisch signifikant (p<0,05), numerisch aber nur klein.

---

[6] Siehe http://www.europeansocialsurvey.org/ (26.7.2017)
[7] Die Fragen nach den erforderlichen Qualifikationen setzen voraus, dass Zuwanderungen erwünscht sind, und wurden daher nicht einbezogen.

Variable	Name[a)]	Bedeutung von -3	Bedeutung von +3	ESS1 2003[b)]	ESS7 2014/15[c)]	Differenz	Fehler-niveau p
		Allgemeine Einstellungen					
eimpcnt	Zulassen/Nicht-Zulassen von Zuwanderern aus armen Ländern Europas	vielen erlauben	keinem erlauben	0,191	0,022	-0,170	0,002
gvrfgap	Der Staat sollte großzügig sein in der Beurteilung der Asylanträge dieser Menschen.	stimme voll zu	stimme überhaupt nicht zu	0,282	-0,062	-0,344	0,000
pplstrd	Es ist besser für ein Land, wenn fast alle die gleichen Bräuche und Traditionen haben	stimme voll zu	stimme überhaupt nicht zu	-0,123	-0,117	0,006	0,908
		Einschätzung von möglichen Effekten von Zuwanderung					
imbleco	Steuern und Sozialsystem: Zuwanderer holen mehr heraus oder zahlen mehr ein	nehmen generell mehr heraus	zahlen generell mehr ein	-0,343	-0,631	-0,289	0,000
imtcjob	Zuwanderer nehmen den österreichischen Arbeitern die Jobs weg oder schaffen neue Jobs	nehmen Jobs weg	schaffen neue Jobs	-0,152	-0,202	-0,050	0,225
imwbcrm	Durch Zuwanderer Österreichs nehmen Probleme mit der Kriminalität zu oder ab	Kriminalitätsprobleme nehmen zu	Kriminalitätsprobleme nehmen ab	-1,017	-1,186	-0,169	0,000

[a)] *Genauer Wortlaut kann entnommen werden:* http://www.europeansocialsurvey.org/data/ country.html?c=austria
[b)] *n=2081-2217*
[c)] *n=1691-1771*

Tabelle 2 Analysierte Items zur Immigration im ESS (Welle1 und Welle 7)

Quelle: European Social Survey[8], ESS1 und ESS7, Österreichteil, eigene Berechnungen, gewichtet mit pspwght

Messung von Polarisierungstendenzen

Für die Auswertung ist eine Operationalisierung von Polarisierungstendenzen erforderlich. Zur Entwicklung einer operationalen Definition lassen sich Diskussionen zu Polarisierungstendenzen dahingehend zusammenfassen, dass eine Polarisierung dann angenommen werden kann, wenn sich zwei Gruppen mit konträren Einstellungen gegenüberstehen (Bedingung 1), die in sich homogen (Bedingung 2) und etwa gleich groß (Bedingung 3) sind. Auf der Grundlage dieser Überlegungen lässt sich ein Polarisierungsindex definieren, wobei aus Gründen der Einfachheit der Darstellung zunächst angenommen wird, dass die Polarisierung anhand nur einer Variablen X erfasst wird und sich zwei Gruppen 1 und 2 gegenüberstehen. Unter diesen vereinfachenden Annahmen, die allerdings die Allgemeinheit des Index nicht beeinträchtigen, ist der Index wie folgt definiert:

$$P_X = \left(\frac{p_1 \cdot p_2}{0,25}\right)^\alpha \cdot \frac{|\bar{x}_1 - \bar{x}_2|^\beta}{\left(s_{w(1,2)}\right)^\gamma}$$

Der Index trägt der Bedingung 1 von zwei Gruppen mit konträren Einstellungen dadurch Rechnung, dass er die Differenz der Mittelwerte $|\bar{x}_1 - \bar{x}_2|$ der beiden Gruppen 1 und 2 in der untersuchten Variablen X in die Berechnung einbezieht. Je

---

[8] http://www.europeansocialsurvey.org

größer die Differenz ist, desto höhere Werte nimmt ceteris paribus der Index an. Die Bedingung 2 wird dadurch berücksichtigt, dass in die Berechnung die Streuung innerhalb der beiden Gruppen $s_{w(1,2)}$ und damit die interne Heterogenität einfließt. Eine größere Streuung führt – ceteris paribus – zu kleineren Indexwerten. Die Größe der beiden Gruppen (Bedingung 3) schließlich wird durch den Faktor $p_1 \cdot p_2$ erfasst. Sind die Anteilswerte gleich 0,5, also beide Gruppen gleich groß und keine weiteren Gruppen vorhanden, ergibt sich ein Wert von 1,0, andernfalls Werte kleiner 1,0.

Die Gewichtungsparameter α, β, γ messen den drei Bedingungen ein unterschiedliches Gewicht bei. Wird z.B. $\alpha = 0$ gesetzt, wird die Bedingung 3 als unbedeutend betrachtet. Die Größe der sich gegenüberstehenden Gruppen ist irrelevant. Erste Erfahrungswerte, die der Autor mit dem Index gesammelt hat, sprechen dafür, für α einen Wert von 1/3, 1/4 oder einen noch kleineren Wert zu wählen, da bei größeren Werten, z.B. für $\alpha = 1/2$ oder $\alpha = 1$, den Anteilswerten der beiden Gruppen ein zu großes Gewicht zukommt. Für die nachfolgenden Analysen wurde ein Wert von 1/3 gewählt. Die beiden anderen Gewichtungsparameter wurden gleich 1 gesetzt.

Da der Index nur latente Polarsierungen erfasst, wenn Einstellungen untersucht werden, soll bei der Ergebnisinterpretation von Polarisierungstendenzen gesprochen werden. Modellrechnungen für unterschiedliche Konstellationen (siehe Anhang A) legen nahe, dass Werte zwischen 1,2 und 1,8 eine schwache Polarisierungstendenz anzeigen, Werte zwischen 1,8 und 2,4 eine mittlere und Werte ab 2,4 eine starke. Bei einer schwachen Polarisierungstendenz ist die Gesamtverteilung noch eingipfelig und mesokurtisch, bei einer mittleren Polarisierungstendenz ergibt sich ebenfalls noch eine eingipfelige, aber bereits platykurtische Verteilung. Ab einem Wert von 2,4 sind bereits in der Gesamtverteilung zwei Gipfel gut zu beobachten (siehe Abbildungen A1 bis A3 im Anhang).

Die Berechnung des Polarisierungsindex setzt voraus, dass in den Daten latente Gruppen aufgefunden werden, die zunächst unbekannt sind. Dafür eignet sich die latente Klassenanalyse (Bacher, Pöge und Wenzig 2010). Sie untersucht, ob die Antworten der Befragten auf die zur Klassifikation verwendeten Variablen durch K latente Klassen (Gruppen) dargestellt werden können. Zwei Zugänge zur Ermittlung der latenten Klassen für den Polarisierungsindex sind denkbar. Es werden konfirmatorisch zwei latente Klassen vorgegeben und für die berechneten beiden latenten Klassen wird der Polarisierungsindex berechnet. Alternativ kann explorativ ermittelt werden, wie viele latente Klassen den Daten überhaupt zugrunde liegen. In den ermittelten Klassen werden – sofern die Zahl größer 2 ist – jene zwei Klassen mit der größten Distanz zueinander bestimmt. Für sie wird der Polarisierungsindex berechnet. Nachfolgend werden beide Ansätze verwendet. Die Analyse latenter Klassen wurde mit dem Computerprogramm LatentGOLD (Bacher, Pöge und Wenzig 2010, S. 398-426; Vermunt und Magidson 2005) durchgeführt. Die Klassifikationsvariablen wurden als ordinal skaliert definiert.

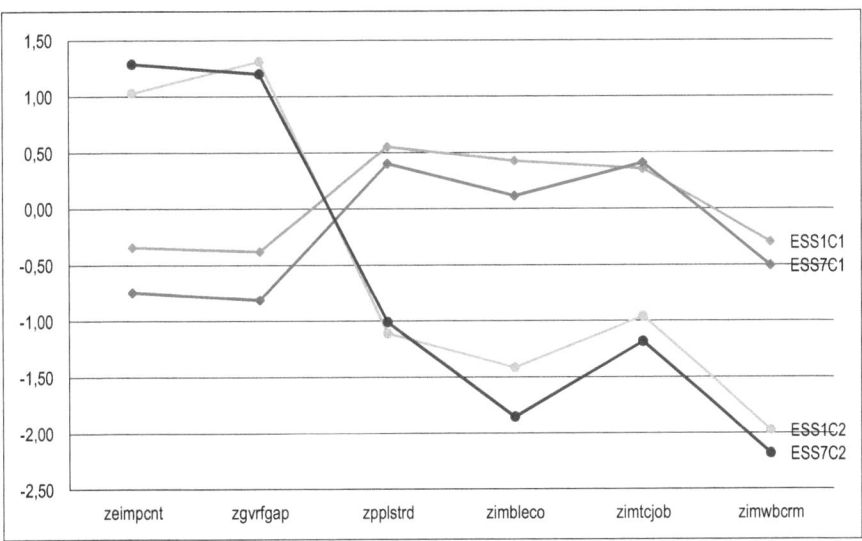

Abbildung 1 Ergebnisse der konfirmatorischen Analyse für die Berechnung des Polarisierungsindex

Quelle: European Social Survey, Österreichteil, eigene Berechnungen, gewichtet mit pspwght

Erkennbare Polarisierungen?

Abbildung 1 führt die bei der konfirmatorischen latenten Klassenanalyse ermittelten Zwei-Klassenlösungen an. Die mit ESS1C1 und ESS7C1 gekennzeichneten Cluster sind Personen mit einer positiven Haltung zur Zuwanderung in den beiden Wellen. Die Cluster ESS1C2 und ESS7C2 repräsentieren die Personen mit einer ablehnenden Haltung. Vergleicht man die beiden Wellen (ESS1 steht für die erste Welle im Jahr 2002/03 und ESS7 für die siebte Welle im Jahr 2014/15), so fällt auf, dass innerhalb der BefürworterInnen von Immigrationen die beiden ersten Items, die sich auf die Zuwanderung aus armen Ländern Europas und auf die Beurteilung der Asylverfahren beziehen, positiver befürwortet werden als 2003[9]. Umgekehrt wird die Aussage, dass Zuwanderer mehr in das Steuer- und Sozialsystem einzahlen, als sie herausholen, etwas weniger positiv eingeschätzt.

Auch bei den GegnerInnen ist in vier der sechs Items eine etwas ablehnendere Einstellung zu beobachten. In der Summe führt dies dazu, dass die durchschnittliche Distanz der Mittelwerte je Item der beiden Gruppen auf der verwendeten siebenstufigen Skala von -3 bis +3 von 1,59 Skaleneinheiten auf 1,78 zunimmt. Die Streuung innerhalb der Cluster und die Anteilswerte der beiden Cluster bleiben in etwa gleich. Durch die Zunahme der Distanz hat sich die Polarisierungstendenz etwas verstärkt. Die Indexwerte liegen mit 1,24 für 2003 und 1,42 für 2014/15 innerhalb der Grenzen einer schwachen Polarisierung. Zu beachten ist hier, dass bei der Ableitung der Schwellenwerte zur Interpretation des Polarisie-

---

[9] Ein negativerer Wert drückt eine größere Zustimmung aus.

rungsindex (siehe oben) von messfehlerfreien Werten ausgegangen wurde. Das tatsächliche Ausmaß der Polarisierung wird daher vermutlich unterschätzt. Unter der Annahme, dass die Streuung in den Daten zu 30% durch Messfehler bedingt ist (ein für Surveys durchaus realistischer Wert), resultieren höhere Polarisierungstendenzen. Für 2014/15 nähert sich der korrigierte Wert von 1,70 dem Schwellenwert einer mittleren Polarisierung von 1,80 an.

Klassenlösung	Polarisierungstendenz unter der Annahme keiner Messfehler		Polarisierungstendenz unter der Annahme eines Messfehleranteils von 30%	
	ESS1 (2003)	ESS7 (2014/15)	ESS1 (2003)	ESS7 (2014/15)
2-Klassenlösung	1,24	1,42	1,48	1,70
3-Klassenlösung	1,30	1,53	1,55	1,83
4-Klassenlösung	1,04	1,26	1,24	1,51

Tabelle 3 Polarisierungstendenzen in Österreich 2003 und 2014/15

Quelle: European Social Survey, Österreichteil, eigene Berechnungen, gewichtet mit pspwght

Die berechnete Zwei-Klassenlösung ist auch formal gerechtfertigt, die erklärten Varianzen sind aber gering. Empirisch geeignet zur Darstellung der Daten ist für die erste Welle des ESS noch eine 3-Klassenlösung, für die zweite Welle noch zusätzlich eine 4-Klassenlösung. Bei der 3-Klassenlösung gibt es eine neutrale mittlere Gruppe und eine Gruppe von BefürworterInnen und GegnerInnen. Bei der 4-Klassenlösung spaltet sich die mittlere Gruppe auf in eine Gruppe der gemäßigten BefürworterInnen und in eine der gemäßigten GegnerInnen. Bei allen Klassenlösungen zeigt sich eine leichte Zunahme der Polarisierungstendenzen zwischen den beiden Befragungszeitpunkten (siehe Tabelle 3).

Sozio-Demographie und weitere Einflussfaktoren

In einem nächsten Analyseschritt wurde die 3-Klassenlösung weiter analysiert. Es wurde der Frage nachgegangen, welcher Zusammenhang zwischen soziodemographischen Variablen und der Zugehörigkeit zur Gruppe der BefürworterInnen von Immigration oder zur Gruppe der GegnerInnen von Immigration besteht. In Übereinstimmung mit der Literatur (siehe oben) zeigt sich, dass BefürworterInnen häufiger eine höhere Bildung haben, jünger sind, in Städten leben und Eltern mit höherer Bildung haben. Sie gehören auch häufiger der Gruppe der Nicht-Erwerbstätigen an. Es handelt sich bei dieser Gruppe – unter Berücksichtigung des Alterseffekts – vermutlich um jüngere Personen, die sich noch im Bildungssystem befinden. Umgekehrt gehören Ältere, Personen mit geringer Bildung sowie Personen mit Eltern mit geringerer Bildung weniger häufig der Gruppe der BefürworterInnen an. Das Geschlecht ist irrelevant für die Tatsache, ob jemand zur Gruppe der BefürworterInnen gehört oder nicht. Die dargestellten Befunde gelten für beide Wellen. Für die zweite Befragungswelle selbst wird ein signifikanter Einfluss ermittelt, der besagt, dass – ceteris paribus – 2014/15 die Gruppe der BefürworterInnen kleiner geworden ist.

Unabhängige Variablen	BefürworterInnen			GegnerInnen		
	Regressions-koeffizient	Fehlerniveau p	Exp(B)	Regressions-koeffizient	Fehlerniveau p	Exp(B)
Finanzielle Spannungen	-0,044	0,435	0,957	0,274	0,000	1,316
Weiblich (1=ja, 0=nein)	-0,005	0,946	0,995	-0,076	0,500	0,927
Verheiratet (1=ja, 0=nein)	0,109	0,220	1,115	0,021	0,862	1,021
Bildung des Befragten[a]						
gering (Pflichtschulabschl.)	-0,212	0,041	0,809	0,315	0,014	1,371
hoch (Hochulabschluss)	0,770	0,000	2,161	-0,798	0,000	0,450
Bildung der Eltern[b]						
gering (Pflichtschulabschl.)	-0,209	0,024	0,812	0,112	0,354	1,119
hoch (Hochulabschluss)	0,665	0,000	1,944	-0,205	0,455	0,815
Erwerbstatus Befragter[c]						
arbeitslos	0,178	0,379	1,195	0,574	0,026	1,775
nicht erwerbstätig	0,190	0,046	1,209	-0,144	0,299	0,866
Alter[d]						
17 bis 34 Jahre	0,396	0,000	1,485	-0,117	0,417	0,890
65 Jahre und älter	-0,493	0,000	0,611	0,163	0,329	1,177
Städtischer Wohnort (1=ja, 0=nein)	0,543	0,000	1,720	-0,192	0,121	0,825
2. Welle (ESS7;1=ja, 0=nein)	-0,317	0,000	0,728	0,031	0,787	1,031
Konstante	-0,837	0,000	0,433	-1,676	0,000	0,187
Nagelkerkes R-Quadrat		0,129			0,060	

[a] Referenzkategorie = mittlere Bildung,
[b] Referenzkategorie = mittlere Bildung,
[c] Referenzkategorie = erwerbstätig,
[d] Referenzkategorie = 35 bis 64 Jahre

Tabelle 4 Befürwortung und Ablehnung von Immigration in Abhängigkeit von soziodemographischen Merkmalen

Quelle: European Social Survey, Österreichteil, eigene Berechnungen, gewichtet mit pspwght, Ergebnisse einer logistischen Regression.

Im Vergleich zu den BefürworterInnen zeigt sich, dass die Gruppe der Ablehnenden stärker durch die aktuelle Lebenssituation geprägt wird. Liegen Arbeitslosigkeit und/oder finanzielle Spannungen der Art vor, dass die Befragten mit dem gegenwärtigen Haushaltseinkommen nur schwer bzw. sehr schwer zurechtkommen, so erhöht dies die Wahrscheinlichkeit der Zugehörigkeit zur Gruppe der GegnerInnen. Von Relevanz ist des Weiteren die eigene Bildung, nicht aber jene der Eltern. Keine Bedeutung haben der Wohnort, das Geschlecht und der Zeitpunkt der Befragung.

Für die Ableitung von Handlungsempfehlungen wurde eine weitere Analyse durchgeführt, in der zusätzlich das Vertrauen in die Politik und in die politische Strukturen (Demokratie)[10], das politische Interesse und das Vertrauen in die Mitmenschen (soziales Vertrauen)[11] einbezogen werden. Die Ergebnisse sind überzeugend: wenn es gelänge, das Vertrauen in die Politik und die politischen Strukturen

---

[10] Summenindex aus folgenden drei Items: Vertrauen in PolitikerInnen, Vertrauen in politische Parteien, Vertrauen in das Parlament
[11] Summenindex aus folgenden drei Items: Die meisten Menschen verhalten sich fair. Die meisten Menschen sind hilfsbereit. Den meisten Menschen kann getraut werden.

	BefürworterInnen			GegnerInnen		
Unabhängige Variablen	Regressions-koeffizient	Fehlerniveau p	Exp(B)	Regressions-koeffizient	Fehlerniveau p	Exp(B)
Finanzielle Spannungen	0,098	0,105	1,103	0,13	0,110	1,139
Weiblich (1=ja, 0=nein)	0,108	0,201	1,114	-0,171	0,157	0,843
Verheiratet (1=ja, 0=nein)	-0,012	0,895	0,988	0,151	0,235	1,163
Bildung des Befragten[a]						
gering (Pflichtschulabschl.)	-0,058	0,597	0,944	0,236	0,087	1,266
hoch (Hochulabschluss)	0,613	0,000	1,847	-0,646	0,005	0,524
Bildung der Eltern[b]						
gering (Pflichtschulabschl.)	-0,240	0,013	0,787	0,165	0,197	1,179
hoch (Hochulabschluss)	0,528	0,000	1,695	-0,164	0,567	0,849
Erwerbstatus Befragter[c]						
arbeitslos	0,285	0,184	1,33	0,512	0,059	1,669
nicht erwerbstätig	0,137	0,169	1,147	-0,125	0,391	0,882
Alter[d]						
17 bis 34 Jahre	0,405	0,000	1,499	-0,014	0,926	0,986
65 Jahre und älter	-0,557	0,000	0,573	0,235	0,181	1,265
Städtischer Wohnort (1=ja, 0=nein)	0,562	0,000	1,753	-0,26	0,047	0,771
2. Welle (ESS7;1=ja, 0=nein)	-0,240	0,006	0,787	-0,069	0,572	0,933
Vertrauen in Politik und politische Strukturen	0,149	0,000	1,16	-0,223	0,000	0,800
Politisches Interesse	0,321	0,000	1,379	-0,085	0,219	0,919
Vertrauen in die Mitmenschen	0,205	0,000	1,228	-0,205	0,000	0,815
Konstante	-2,095	0,000	0,123	0,103	0,759	1,108
Nagelkerkes R-Quadrat		0,222			0,167	

[a] Referenzkategorie = mittlere Bildung,
[b] Referenzkategorie = mittlere Bildung,
[c] Referenzkategorie = erwerbstätig,
[d] Referenzkategorie = 35 bis 64 Jahre

Tabelle 5 Befürwortung und Ablehnung von Immigration in Abhängigkeit von soziodemographischen und weiteren Merkmalen

Quelle: European Social Survey, Österreichteil, eigene Berechnungen, gewichtet mit pspwght, Ergebnisse einer logistischen Regression.

sowie das Vertrauen in die Mitmenschen zu erhöhen, dann könnten die negativen Auswirkungen von Arbeitslosigkeit und finanziellen Spannungen auf Polarisierungstendenzen kompensiert werden. Dies ist daraus ersichtlich, dass den finanziellen Spannungen und der Arbeitslosigkeit keine signifikante Wirkung mehr zukommt, wenn diese beiden Variablen in die Analyse einbezogen werden.

Österreich ein Sonderfall?

Tabelle 6 gibt Auskunft, ob in Österreich die Polarisierungstendenzen im Vergleich zu anderen europäischen Ländern besonders stark, besonders schwach oder in etwa gleich hoch sind. Untersucht wurden nur die 2-Klassenanalysen. Für die erste Welle ergibt sich ein gemischtes Bild. Frankreich, Deutschland und Großbritannien haben vergleichbare Werte, geringere Werte haben Belgien, Schweiz, Dänemark und Niederlande. Bei der zweiten Welle im Jahr 2014/15 resultiert ein anderes Bild. Die Situation in Österreich ist nur mehr mit Großbritannien vergleichbar. Alle anderen Länder haben geringere Indexwerte und damit eine geringere Polarisierungstendenz.

Über die Ursachen lassen sich hier nur Vermutungen anstellen. Da Österreich die wirtschaftlichen Auswirkungen der Finanzkrise 2007/2008 besser überstanden hat als die meisten anderen Länder (OECD 2011), scheidet eine schlechtere Wirtschaftslage aus. Von Bedeutung könnte sein, dass die registrierte Arbeitslosigkeit – allerdings von einem niedrigen Wert ausgehend – von etwa 7% im Jahr 2003 auf über 9% im Jahr 2015 gestiegen ist (WKO 2017). Von Relevanz dürfte die Tatsache sein, dass viele Wahlauseinandersetzungen zwischen 2003 und 2014 um das Ausländerthema geführt wurden, sodass latent vorhandene Differenzen verstärkt wurden. Laut einer von SORA/ISA (2013) im Auftrag des ORF durchgeführten Wahlanalyse zur Nationalratswahl 2013 nannten beispielsweise die Befragten auf die Frage, welche Themen sie im Wahlkampf am stärksten diskutierten, Integration und Zuwanderung an vierter Stelle. Das Thema lag mit 37% Nennungen gleichauf mit Wirtschaft und Pensionen und nur knapp hinter Arbeitsplätzen (38%) und Steuern (39%). An erster Stelle mit deutlicherem Vorsprung rangierte mit 43% als Thema Bildung und Schule. Medial war das Thema der Integration vor allem gegen Ende des untersuchten Zeitraums von 2001 bis 2014/2015 immer wieder präsent. So wurde z.B. als Folge der Präsentation des Integrationsberichts 2014 die Einrichtung von Sonderklassen für Kinder von MigrantInnen mit schlechten Deutschkenntnissen diskutiert (Ettinger 2014). Berichtet wurde aber auch über eine Verbesserung des Integrationsklimas (Die Presse 2014), was auf das Vorhandensein von Unsicherheiten sowie von unterschiedlichen Meinungen und Einschätzungen hinweist.

Auch das Thema Flucht und Asyl war in der politischen Auseinandersetzung und in der medialen Berichterstattung während der siebten Welle des ESS 2014/2015 präsent. So leitete z.B. HEUTE am 25. Februar 2015 einen Bericht über ein Treffen der Landeshauptleute mit der Überschrift „Asylgipfel: Mehr Tempo im Kampf gegen Missbrauch" (Heute 2015) ein.

Land	Polarisierungstendenz unter der Annahme keiner Messfehler		Polarisierungstendenz unter der Annahme eines Messfehleranteils von 30%	
	ESS1 (2003)	ESS7 (2014/15)	ESS1 (2003)	ESS7 (2014/15)
AT Österreich	1,24	1,42	1,48	1,70
BE Belgien	1,16	1,21	1,39	1,45
CH Schweiz	1,16	1,11	1,39	1,33
DE Deutschland	1,28	1,21	1,53	1,45
DK Dänemark	1,00	1,24	1,20	1,48
NL Niederlande	1,11	1,14	1,33	1,36
FR Frankreich	1,20	1,10	1,43	1,31
UK Großbritannien	1,28	1,35	1,53	1,61

Tabelle 6 Polarisierungstendenzen in ausgewählten europäischen Ländern

Quelle: European Social Survey, eigene Berechnungen, Länder gewichtet mit pspwght.

Schlussfolgerungen

Ausgehend von den letzten Wahlen zum Bundespräsidenten wurde der Frage nachgegangen, ob in Österreich bereits seit der Jahrtausendwende latente Polarisierungstendenzen bezüglich der Einstellung zur Immigration empirisch beobachtbar sind. Dafür wurde eine Re-Analyse des European Social Survey vorgenommen. Die Ergebnisse lassen sich dahingehend zusammenfassen, dass schwache Polarisierungstendenzen auf der Ebene der Einstellungen zur Immigration bereits 2003 auffindbar sind. 2014/15 ist eine Zunahme zu beobachten.

Untersucht man die Gruppe der BefürworterInnen und der GegnerInnen von Zuwanderung sozio-demographisch, so zeigt sich in Übereinstimmung mit der Literatur, dass die BefürworterInnen häufiger aus höheren Bildungsschichten kommen, jünger sind und in Städten leben. GegnerInnen bringen eine geringere Bildung mit, leben häufiger unter angespannten finanziellen Verhältnissen und sind öfters von Arbeitslosigkeit betroffen. Weiterführende Analysen zeigen, dass die negativen Auswirkungen von finanziellen Spannungen und Arbeitslosigkeit durch politisches und soziales Vertrauen abgefedert werden können.

Aus den Analysen lässt sich zunächst ableiten, dass durch eine Bekämpfung von Arbeitslosigkeit und durch die Gewährleistung eines ausreichenden Einkommens negative Einstellungen zur Immigration und damit auch Polarisierungstendenzen abgeschwächt werden könnten, da die Gruppe der GegnerInnen kleiner werden würde bzw. ihre Mittelwerte weniger extrem ausfallen würden. Es geht also um die „Lösung von Verteilungsfragen", worauf Biffl (2010) in dem einleitenden Zitat des Beitrags zutreffend hingewiesen hat. Zur Gewährleistung eines ausreichenden Einkommens können unterschiedliche Maßnahmen beitragen, wie z.B. ein Mindestlohn, ausreichende Transferzahlungen, ein Grundeinkommen und/oder Miet- und Preisregulierungen sowie die Bereitstellung günstiger öffentlicher Infrastruktur (z.B. im Bereich des öffentlichen Verkehrs).

Darüber hinaus könnte einer Polarisierung entgegengewirkt werden, wenn es gelänge, das politische und soziale Vertrauen in der Gruppe der von Arbeitslosigkeit und prekärer finanzieller Situation Betroffenen zu erhöhen. Zum Aufbau des sozialen Vertrauens, das eine wesentliche Komponente des Sozialkapitals ist, können auch Kommunen oder Stadtteile beitragen (Kindler et al 2015, European Commission o.J.), indem sie z.B. Begegnungsräume schaffen und Projekte zur Reduktion von Vorurteilen initiieren. Entsprechend der Kontakthypothese von Allport (1979, S. 281) müssten diese Projekte folgende Bedingungen erfüllen: Sie müssten erstens ein gemeinsames Ziel haben, zweitens Kontakte/Zusammenarbeit auf drittens Augenhöhe ermöglichen und viertens von einer anerkannten Institution oder Autorität (z.B. dem/die BürgermeisterIn) unterstützt werden. Durch die Unterstützung des Bürgermeisters/der Bürgermeisterin oder anderer politisch Verantwortlicher könnte auch das politische Vertrauen erhöht werden. Allerdings ist fraglich, ob mit diesen Maßnahmen auf Kommunal- oder Stadtteilebene ohne entsprechende sozial- und arbeitsmarktpolitische Maßnahmen auf nationaler Ebene, wie sie im vorausgehenden Absatz angedeutet wurden, eine Erhöhung des politischen Vertrauens gelingt.

Insgesamt lag 2014/15 auf der Ebene der Einstellungen in der Bevölkerung – entgegen dem Bild, das sich heute medial ergibt – noch eine günstige Ausgangssituation für politische Maßnahmen vor, da nur schwache Polarisierungstendenzen beobachtbar waren und von zwei verfeindet gegenüberstehenden, relativ großen Gruppen nicht gesprochen werden konnte. Allerdings hat zwischen 2003 und 2014/15 die Polarisierungstendenz in Österreich stärker zugenommen als in anderen europäischen Ländern, was Anlass für Maßnahmen sein sollte, um eine weitere Verstärkung zu vermeiden. Die dargestellten Maßnahmen könnten auch dazu beitragen, in Österreich wieder ein positiveres Integrationsklima zu schaffen, da sie negative Bewertungen von Migration abschwächen würden.

Literatur

Allport, Gordon (1979 [1954]) The Nature of Prejudice. Perseus Book: Massachusetts.
Anhut, Reimund / Heitmeyer, Wilhelm (2009) Desintegration, Anerkennungsbilanzen und die Rolle sozialer Vergleichsprozesse für unterschiedliche Verarbeitungsmuster. In: Preyer, Gerhard (Hrsg.) Neuer Mensch und kollektive Identität in der Kommunikationsgesellschaft. (Verlag für Sozialwissenschaften: Wiesbaden), 212-236.
Bacher, Johann (1995): Latenter Wertedissens oder -konsens in Österreich. Ergebnisse einer Sekundäranalyse des sozialen Surveys Österreichs 1993. In: SWS-Rundschau (35 Jg.), 175-200.
Bacher, Johann (2001a) In welchen Lebensbereichen lernen Jugendliche Ausländerfeindlichkeit? Ergebnisse einer Befragung bei Berufsschülern. In: Kölner Zeitschrift für Soziologie und Sozialpsychologie (53. Jg.), 334-349.
Bacher, Johann (2001b) Macht Arbeitslosigkeit rechtsextrem? In: Zempel, Jeanette / Bacher, Johann /Moser, Klaus (Hrsg.) Erwerbslosigkeit. Ursachen, Auswirkungen und Interventionen (Opladen: Leske+Budrich), 171-186.
Bacher, Johann / Pöge, Andreas / Wenzig, Knut (2010) Clusteranalyse. Anwendungsorientierte Einführung in Klassifikationsverfahren, 3. Auflage (Oldenbourg, München).
Biffl, Gudrun (2010) Rationale und irrationale Aspekte der Integrationsdebatte. In: Biffl, Gudrun (Hrsg.) Migration und Integration - Dialog zwischen Politik, Wissenschaft und Praxis (Band 1): Beiträge zu Bildung, Arbeitsmarkt, Asyl, Menschenhandel, Gender und Religion (Bad Vöslau: Omnium), 5-14.
BMI (Hrsg.) (2016a) *Wahlen - Bundespräsidentenwahl - 2016*, verfügbar unter: http://www. bmi.gv.at/cms/BMI_wahlen/bundespraes/bpw_2016/Ergebnis_2WG.aspx (24.7.2017).
BMI (Hrsg.) (2016b) *Wahlen - Bundespräsidentenwahl - 2016*, verfügbar unter: http://www. bmi.gv.at/cms/BMI_wahlen/bundespraes/bpw_2016/Ergebnis_2WG_WH.aspx (24.7.2017)
Boulianne, Shelley (2015) Social media use and participation: a meta-analysis of current research. In: Information, Communication & Society (18), 524-538
Bond, Robert. M. u.a. (2012) A 61-million-person experiment in social influence and political mobilization. In: Nature (489), 295-298.
Dahrendorf, Ralf (1959) Soziale Klassen und Klassenkonflikt in der industriellen Gesellschaft. (Ferdinand Enke: Stuttgart).
Dahrendorf, Ralf (1994) Der moderne soziale Konflikt (dtv Wissenschaft: Stuttgart).

Die Presse (2014) Jeder fünfte Österreicher hat Migrationshintergrund. In: *Die Presse*, 28. Juli 2014, verfügbar unter: http://diepresse.com/home/innenpolitik/3845670/Integration_Klima-in-Oesterreich-verbessert-sich.

Ettinger, Karl (2014) ‚Integration: Sonderförderung in Sprachklassen'. In: *Die Presse*, 25. Juli 2014, verfügbar unter: http://diepresse.com/home/bildung/schule/3844662/Integration_Sonderfoerderung-in-Sprachklassen.

European Commission (Eds.) (o.J.) Examining Social Capital as a Means of Enhancing the Integration of Immigrants. Final Report. Verfügbar unter: http://www.cjd-nord.de/fileadmin/assets/eutin/Downloads/Publikationen/Social_Capital__Final_Report.pdf

Fuchs, Marek (2003) Rechtsextremismus von Jugendlichen. In: Kölner Zeitschrift für Soziologie und Sozialpsychologie (55. Jg.), 654-678.

Helbich, Stephan (2016) The effect of the internet on voting behavior. (IZA World of Labor (294): Germany)

Heute (2015) ‚Asylgipfel: Mehr Tempo im Kampf gegen Missbrauch'. In: *Heute*, 25. Februar 2016, verfügbar unter: http://www.heute.at/politik/news/story/Asylgipfel--Mehr-Tempo-im-Kampf-gegen-Missbrauch-14703223.

Hobsbawm, Eric, J. (1991) Nationen und Nationalismus. Mythos und Realität seit 1780 (Campus Verlag: Frankfurt a.M./New York).

Horkheimer, Max / Adorno, Theodor (1972 [1952]) Vorurteil und Charakter. Ein Bericht. In: Horkheimer, Max (Hrsg.) Gesellschaft im Übergang (Athenäum Fischer Taschenbuch Verlag: Frankfurt a. M.), 82-92.

Lazarsfeld, Paul Felix / Berelson, Bernard / Gaudet, Hazel (1969) Wahlen und Wähler: Soziologie des Wahlverhaltens (Luchterhand: Neuwied u.a.).

Kaletta, Barbara (2008) Anerkennung oder Abwertung. Über die Verarbeitung sozialer Desintegration. (Verlag für Sozialwissenschaften: Wiesbaden).

Kindler, Marta / Ratcheva, Vessalina / Piechowska, Maria (2015) Social Networks, Social Capital and Migrant Integration at Local Level. Verfügbar unter: http://www.birmingham.ac.uk/Documents/college-social-sciences/social-policy/iris/2015/working-paper-series/IRiS-WP-6-2015.pdf

OECD (Hrsg.) (2011) OECD Economic Surveys. Austria (OECD: Paris).

Rippl, Susanne (2003) Zur Erklärung negativer Einstellungen zur Zuwanderung. In: Kölner Zeitschrift für Soziologie und Sozialpsychologie (55. Jg.), 231-252.

Rosar, Ulrich (2001) Ethnozentrismus in Deutschland. (Westdeutscher Verlag: Wiesbaden).

Schwartz, Shalom H. (1992) Universals in the content and structure of values: theoretical advances and empirical tests in 20 countries. In: Advances in Experimental Social Psychology (25), 1-65.

SORA/ISA (2013) Wahlanalyse Nationalratswahl 2013. Verfügbar unter: http://strategieanalysen.at/wp-content/uploads/bg/isa_sora_wahlanalyse_nrw_2013.pdf

Vermunt, Jeroen K. / Magidson, Jay (2005) Latent Gold 4.0 User's Guide. (Belmont: Statistical Innovation).

WKO (Hg.) (2017) Arbeitslosenquote. Verfügbar unter: https://www.wko.at/service/zahlen-daten-fakten/langzeitreihen.html.

Anhang: Modellrechnung zur Ableitung von Schwellenwerten zur Interpretation des Polaritätsindex

Konstellation	Merkmale	Gruppe 1	Gruppe 2	Berechnungs-größen	Werte	Polarisierungs-tendenz
A: Keine Polarisierung, beide Gruppen haben denselben Mittelwert.	Mittelwerte	0	0	Differenz	0,000	keine
	Standardabw.	1	1	Streuung innerhalb	1,000	
	Anteilswerte	0,5	0,5	Skalierungsfaktor	1,000	
				Polarisierungsindex	**0,000**	
B: Die Differenz der Mittelwerte der beiden Gruppen beträgt 1,2 Skaleneinheit. Der maximale Unterschied wäre 6. Es gibt zwei gleichgroße Gruppen.	Mittelwerte	-0,6	0,6	Differenz	1,200	**schwach,** eingipflige, mesokurtische Gesamtverteilung siehe Abb. A1
	Standardabw.	1	1	Streuung innerhalb	1,000	
	Anteilswerte	0,5	0,5	Skalierungsfaktor	1,000	
				Polarisierungsindex	**1,200**	
C: Die Differenz der Mittelwerte der beiden Gruppen beträgt 1,8 Skaleneinheiten. Der maximale Unterschied wäre 6. Es gibt zwei gleichgroße Gruppen.	Mittelwerte	-0,9	0,9	Differenz	1,800	**mittel,** eingipflige, platykurtische Gesamtverteilung siehe Abb. A2
	Standardabw.	1	1	Streuung innerhalb	1,000	
	Anteilswerte	0,5	0,5	Skalierungsfaktor	1,000	
				Polarisierungsindex	**1,800**	
D: Die Differenz der Mittelwerte der beiden Gruppen beträgt 2,4 Skalenwerten. Der maximale Unterschied wäre 6. Es gibt zwei gleichgroße Gruppen.	Mittelwerte	-1,2	1,2	Differenz		**stark,** zweigipflige Gesamtverteilung siehe Abb. A3
	Standardabw.	1	1	Streuung innerhalb		
	Anteilswerte	0,5	0,5	Skalierungsfaktor		
				Polarisierungsindex	**2,400**	

Tabelle A1 Modellrechnungen für den Polarisierungsindex zur Ableitung von Interpretationsschwellen

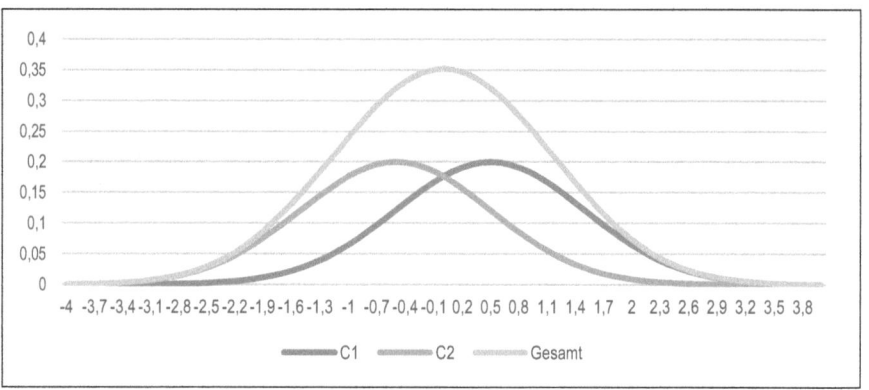

Abbildung A1 Zwei Gruppen C1 und C2 mit schwacher Polarisierungstendenz (Index=1,2)

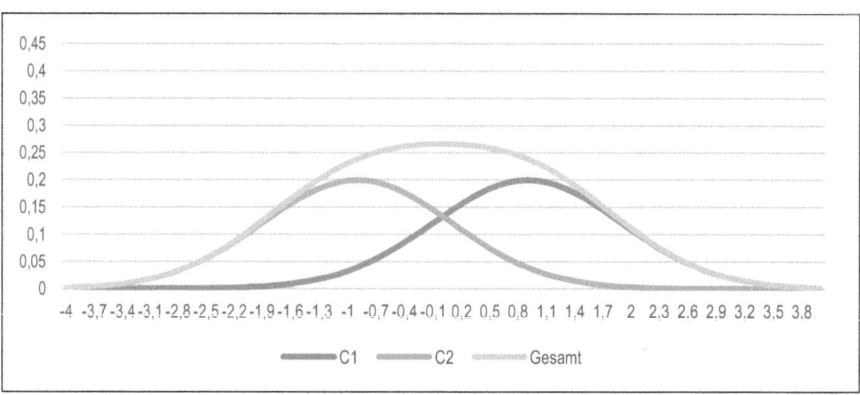

Abbildung A2 Zwei Gruppen C1 und C2 mit mittlerer Polarisierungstendenz (Index=1,8)

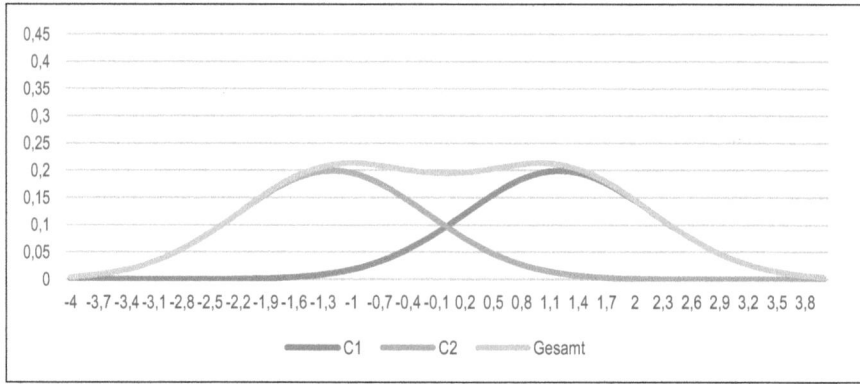

Abbildung A3 Zwei Gruppen C1 und C2 mit starker Polarisierungstendenz (Index=2,4)

Sozialraum, Wohnen und Migration

Tania Berger

Zusammenfassung

Aspekte der Diversität in der Wohnpolitik berühren in erster Linie die Frage, wie einkommensschwache Familien mit Migrationshintergrund mit leistbarem Wohnraum versorgt werden können.

Dieser Beitrag geht zudem der Frage nach, wie Segregation von ethnischen Gruppen in räumlichen abgegrenzten Wohnbereichen entsteht. (Lokal)Politik und mediale Öffentlichkeit vermitteln oftmals Befürchtungen, wonach die Konzentration von MigrantInnen in bestimmten Quartieren deren Kontakte mit der Mehrheitsgesellschaft behindere und dadurch die Übernahme von Verhaltensweisen und Kulturtechniken wie z.B. Sprachfähigkeit, und in Konsequenz: Integration, erschwere.

Daher wird hier untersucht, ob die Umsetzung eines von vor diesem Hintergrund oftmals angestrebten Ideals einer ethisch und sozial durchmischten Wohnbevölkerung demgegenüber die Integration von ZuwanderInnen in eine Aufnahmegesellschaft befördern kann. In diesem Kontext wird auch die Bedeutung von Nachbarschaft in zunehmend diversen Wohnquartieren beleuchtet.

Weiter wird gezeigt, welche (interkulturellen) Konfliktfelder sich oft in Wohnhausanlagen schon fast zwangsläufig aus dem Zusammenleben von Menschen mit unterschiedlichen Lebensstilen ergeben.

Es gehört zu den vielen Verdiensten Gudrun Biffls, dieses Konfliktpotential und die große Bedeutung des Themas Wohnen im Kontext von Migration und Integration klar erkannt zu haben. Der Fachbereich „Sozialraum und Migration" ihres Departments hat sich daher in den vergangenen Jahren in Forschung und Lehre intensiv mit eben diesem Thema auseinandergesetzt und dabei auch Lösungswege aufgezeigt, über die sich diesen Konflikten begegnen lässt. Der vorliegende Beitrag schöpft aus den Ergebnissen dieser Arbeiten.

Einleitung

Artikel 25 der Allgemeinen Menschenrechtserklärung der Vereinten Nationen von 1948 hält fest: *„Jeder hat das Recht auf einen Lebensstandard, der seine und seiner Familie Gesundheit und Wohl gewährleistet, einschließlich Nahrung, Kleidung, Wohnung, ärztliche Versorgung und notwendige soziale Leistungen, ... "*

Ganz ausdrücklich ist dieses Menschenrecht auf Wohnen ein unteilbares und daher nicht von einer bestimmten Staatsbürgerschaft abhängig zu machen. Dennoch ist die tagtägliche Lebensrealität gerade von MigrantInnen in vielen Ländern der Europäischen Union und auch in Österreich vielfach von der Schwierigkeit geprägt in ungeeignetem, zu kleinem oder zu teurem Wohnraum ein Auslangen finden zu müssen.

Stellt sich also die Frage nach Aspekten der Diversität und Wohnpolitik, so geht es in erster Linie um die Frage, wie insbesondere soziale schwache Haushalte – denn zu diesen zählen Familien mit Migrationshintergrund immer noch überproportional häufig – mit leistbarem Wohnraum versorgt werden können.

Schließlich belegen amtliche Statistiken in diesem Zusammenhang folgende Wirkzusammenhänge ganz deutlich: Menschen mit Migrationshintergrund weisen in Österreich im Bundesschnitt einen niedrigeren höchsten Bildungsabschluss auf als die Gesamtbevölkerung und insbesondere auch als Menschen ohne Migrationshintergrund (Abbildung 1). Da ArbeitnehmerInnen mit niedrigem Bildungsstand in der Regel auch weniger verdienen als solche mit höherem Bildungsstand, verfügen Menschen mit Migrationshintergrund also oft über vergleichsweise geringere (Haushalts)einkommen als die Durchschnittsbevölkerung (Abbildung 2) und sind daher überproportional häufig arm oder armutsgefährdet (Abbildung 3). Es steht dieser Personengruppe in absoluten Zahlen damit auch weniger Budget für monatliche Wohnausgaben zur Verfügung als nicht armen Personen.

Leistbar wird Wohnraum für die Betroffenen in der Regel durch Beschränkung auf kleine Wohnungen. Die untersuchte Bevölkerungsgruppe wohnt beengter, indem jedem Haushaltsmitglied proportional weniger Wohnraum zur Verfügung steht als im Gesamtbevölkerungsschnitt (Abbildung 4).

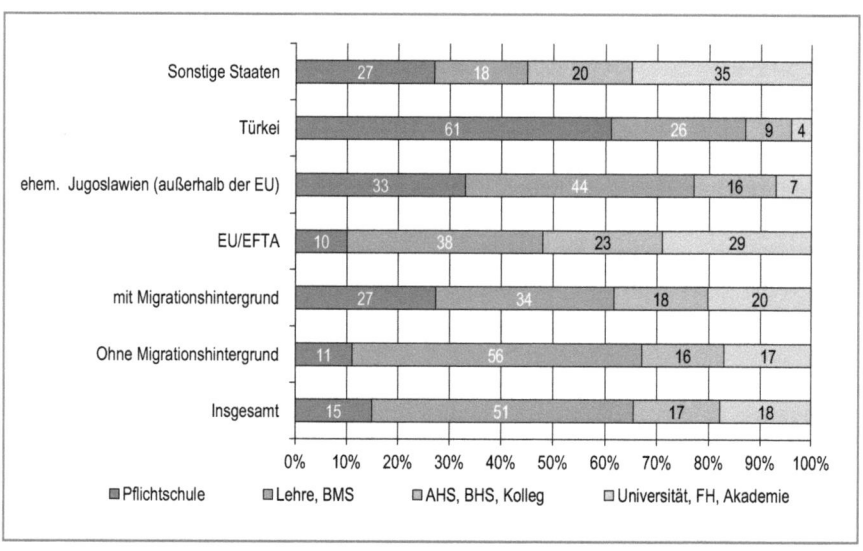

Abbildung 1 Bildungsstand der 15 bis 64 Jährigen 2016 nach Migrationshintergrund

Quelle: Statistik Austria.

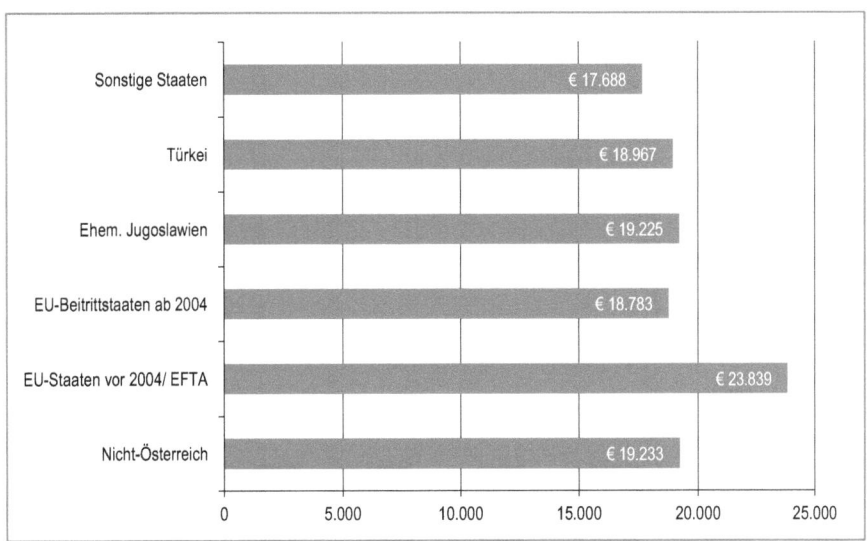

Abbildung 2 Netto-Jahreseinkommen[1] 2015 nach Staatsangehörigkeit

Quelle: Statistik Austria, Lohnsteuerdaten – Sozialstatistische Auswertung. Ohne Lehrlinge.

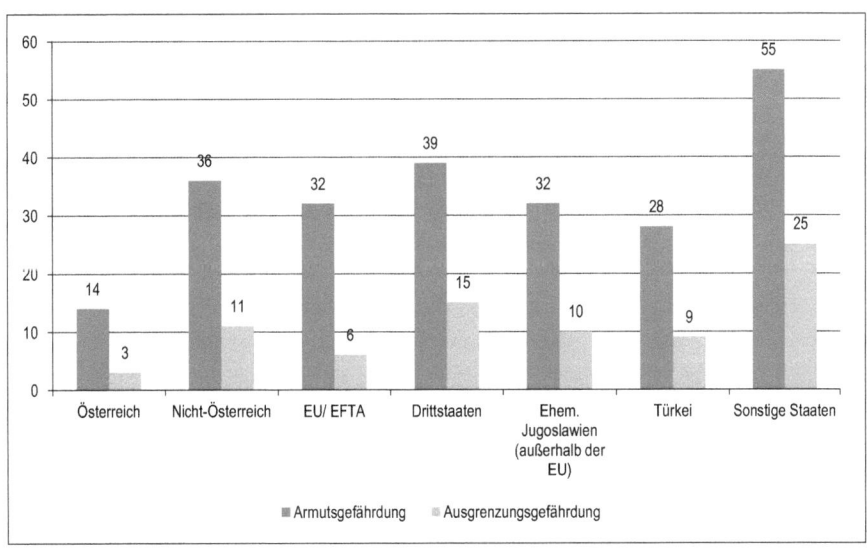

Abbildung 3 (Mehrfache) Armuts- und Ausgrenzungsgefährdung 2015 nach Geburtsland

Quelle: Statistik Austria, EU-SILC (Querschnittsfiles) – Ergebnisse beruhen auf einem Dreijahresdurchschnitt 2014 – 2015 – 2016 für Personen über 15 Jahren.

---

[1] Median des Netto-Jahreseinkommens der ganzjährig unselbstständig Erwerbstätigen

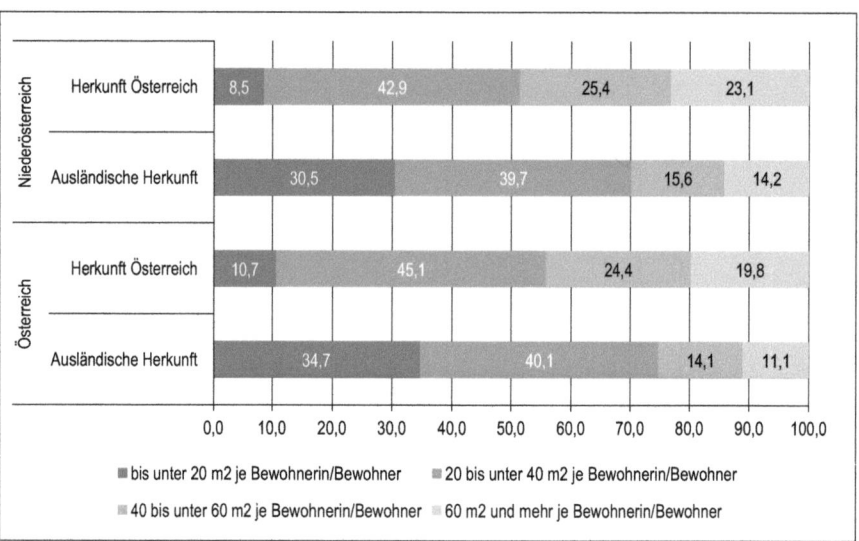

Abbildung 4 Wohnfläche je BewohnerIn in m² nach Herkunft in Österreich und Niederösterreich 2011

Quelle: Statistik Austria, Registerzählung 2011, DUK-Darstellung

Vor diesem Hintergrund untersucht der vorliegende Beitrag, wie die Segregation von ethnischen Gruppen in räumlichen abgegrenzten Wohnbereichen entstehen kann.

(Lokal)Politik und mediale Öffentlichkeit vermitteln oftmals das Ideal einer (sozial) durchmischten Wohnbevölkerung, das die Integration von ZuwanderInnen in eine Aufnahmegesellschaft befördern könne. Diese Annahme wird wissenschaftlich als „Kontakthypothese" untersucht. Doch bewirkt das Wohnen von MigrantInnen in gemischten Quartieren tatsächlich deren vermehrte Kontakte mit der Mehrheitsgesellschaft und dadurch die Übernahme von Verhaltensweisen und Kulturtechniken wie z.B. Sprachfähigkeit, und in Konsequenz: Integration? Der Kontakthypothese entgegenstehend behauptet die in der Literatur ebenfalls zu findende „Konflikthypothese" deren genaues Gegenteil: Die enge räumliche Nachbarschaft von Menschen mit unterschiedlichen Lebensweisen biete eine Vielzahl von Reibungsflächen und Konfliktmöglichkeiten.

In diesem Kontext wird auch die Bedeutung von Nachbarschaft in zunehmend diversen Wohnquartieren beleuchtet. Weiters wird gezeigt, welche generellen (interkulturellen) Konfliktfelder sich oft in Wohnhausanlagen schon fast zwangsläufig ergeben. Abschließend werden Lösungswege aufgezeigt, über die sich genau diesen Konflikten begegnen lässt.

Zugang von Menschen mit Migrationshintergrund zum Wohnungsmarkt

Migrantinnen mit niedrigem Bildungsniveau und entsprechend niedrigen Verdienstmöglichkeiten können sich meist nur schwer am frei finanzierten Wohnungsmarkt mit Wohnraum versorgen. Auch Mietwohnungen gemeinnütziger Wohnbaugenossenschaften sind für diese Menschen vielfach zu teuer. Gemeindewohnungen stehen oft nicht bedarfsdeckend zur Verfügung, zudem sind Menschen mit Migrationshintergrund z.T. vom Zugang zu diesen Wohnungen ausgeschlossen. Hierzu bestehen auf Gemeindeebne unterschiedliche Vorgaben, die Anforderungen an Mindestaufenthaltsdauer und/ oder Staatsbürgerschaft enthalten können. Damit verbleiben private Mietwohnungen mit niedrigem Qualitätsstandard oft als einzige Wohnoption, insbesondere für neu Zugezogene. Nicht selten werden aber gerade im privaten Mietwohnsektor auch vielfältige Diskriminierungen von Menschen mit Migrationshintergrund beobachtet (Berger et al. 2014: S. 51).

Ein überproportional hoher Anteil sozioökonomisch schwacher Personengruppen lebt daher vielfach lokal konzentriert in privaten Mietwohnungen von geringer Qualität – dies geschieht oft weniger aufgrund des Wunsches der Betroffenen nach Wohnen in Nachbarschaft mit Menschen des gleichen ethnischen oder sozialen Hintergrundes, sondern folgt vielmehr den Strukturen des Wohnungsmarkts und dem Diktat von (nicht vorhandenen) Fördermöglichkeiten. Verstärkt werden können derartige räumliche Segregationstendenzen zudem durch das Abwandern der autochthonen Bevölkerung aus den betroffenen Wohngebieten, wenn sich die Ortsansässigen am „hohen AusländerInnenanteil" im Viertel stoßen (Berger et al. 2014: S. 42).

Sind Wohnquartiere mit migrantisch geprägter Wohnbevölkerung darüber hinaus schlecht durch den öffentlichen Verkehr erschlossen, so bedingt dies in der Folge für die BewohnerInnen auch Einschränkungen in ihrer tagtäglichen Mobilität und trägt zur Minderung von Arbeitsmarkt- und Bildungschancen der Betroffenen bei.

Diese Problemfelder des Wohnungsmarktes haben auch Auswirkungen auf die unmittelbare Lebenssituation vor Ort: so zeigt sich, dass Personen mit Migrationshintergrund im Schnitt weniger Wohnraum zur Verfügung steht als dem Durchschnitt der ÖsterreicherInnen (Berger et al. 2014: S. 21, siehe auch: Abbildung). Knappe Haushaltsbudgets bedingen zudem, dass mehr Menschen auf engerem Raum zusammenleben. Angesichts der engen und zum Teil prekären Wohnverhältnisse ärmerer migrantischer Bevölkerungsgruppen ist es nachvollziehbar, dass gerade diese BewohnerInnen zur Bewältigung ihres Alltags stärker auf die Nutzung von halböffentlichen und öffentlichen Räumen im unmittelbaren Wohnumfeld angewiesen sind.

Ethnische Mischung von Wohnbevölkerung

Beckhoven und Kempen (2005) sehen insbesondere Wohnviertel mit homogener Bevölkerung, in denen sich also die meisten BewohnerInnen in ähnlicher sozio-ökonomischer Lage befinden, als unproblematisch; Konflikte würden dagegen vermehrt auftreten, wenn die Bewohnerschaft große Heterogenität aufweist.

Bestehen große kulturelle Unterschiede, ist auch eine Heterogenität von Normen, Moral und Werten zu erwarten. Das Schädigen des Anderen zum eigenen Vorteil wird in einem solchen Umfeld als wahrscheinlich erachtet, Vertrauen schwindet. Damit kann ethnischer Mix das soziale Vertrauen im Viertel tatsächlich reduzieren. Für das Wohnen vieler unterschiedlicher Ethnien im gleichen Gebiet fanden Gundelach und Freitag (2014) zu erwartende Unsicherheit auch zwischen diesen unterschiedlichen Gruppen.

Gemäß der Ähnlichkeitstheorie bevorzugen Menschen das Bekannte; Gefühle der Bedrohung können auf Angst vor dem Verlust der eigenen Identität beruhen. Demnach bilden BewohnerInnen Vertrauen entsprechend ihrem Status in Relation zu anderen in der Gemeinschaft aus. Auch die Homogenitätshypothese geht davon aus, dass Menschen in einem homogenen Kontext wahrscheinlicher gemeinsamer Normen eher darin übereinstimmen, was sie als angemessen erachten. Regeln werden als allgemein gültig angesehen, es besteht keine Unsicherheit in sozialer Interaktion. Damit kann sich Vertrauen ausbilden (Öberg 2011).

Weiters sind Aspekte der kulturellen Identität wie etwa die ethnische Zugehörigkeit, gemeinsame Werte und Alter wichtige Einflussfaktoren, ebenso wie die vorherrschenden Rechtsverhältnisse – Miete oder Eigentum - und die Art, wie BewohnerInnen an eine Wohnung im Viertel gelangen: werden sie beispielsweise, wie das etwa im stark residual geprägten Sozialwohnbau Großbritanniens der Fall ist, vom Wohnungs- bzw. Sozialamt zugewiesen, so beeinflusst dies ihre Bindung ans Viertel anders, als wenn sie ihre Wohngegend selbst und bewusst gewählt haben (Morrison 2003).

Morrison (2003) beobachtet weiter, dass Identität tatsächlich stärker auf Alter und Ethnizität zu beruhen scheint als auf Klassenzugehörigkeit; Die Gemeinsamkeit der Erfahrung von schwierigen Lebensumständen wirkt zwischen unterschiedlichen Gruppen demnach nicht verbindend. Als Beispiel führt Morrison häufige Konflikte zwischen Kindern und Jugendlichen mit Migrationshintergrund einerseits und alteingesessenen BewohnerInnen aus der Aufnahmegesellschaft andererseits an: Altersunterschied und Generationskonflikt sowie ethnische Unterschiede wiegen hierbei schwerer als ein ähnlicher sozialer Status.

Darüber hinaus bestimmen auch sozio-ökonomische Variablen wie Einkommen, Arbeitsplatzposition und Ausbildung die Bereitschaft und das eigene Vermögen, sich lokal einzubringen, Kontakte zu knüpfen und zu pflegen. Die ethnische Zugehörigkeit, v.a. in Verbindung mit niedrigem Einkommen, ist eine wichtige Variable (Beckhoven und Kempen 2005).

Soziale Mischung von Wohnbevölkerung

Stellt sich also die Frage nach Aspekten der Diversität und Wohnpolitik, so geht es in erster Linie um die Frage, wie insbesondere soziale schwache Haushalte – denn zu diesen zählen Familien mit Migrationshintergrund immer noch überproportional häufig – mit leistbarem Wohnraum versorgt werden können (s.o.).

Auch wird im vorliegenden Beitrag darauf eingegangen, inwieweit das Ideal einer (sozial) durchmischten Wohnbevölkerung die Integration von ZuwanderInnen in eine Aufnahmegesellschaft befördern kann und wie Segregation von ethnischen Gruppen in räumlichen abgegrenzten Bereichen entsteht. In diesem Kontext wird auch die Bedeutung von Nachbarschaft in zunehmend diversen Wohnquartieren beleuchtet.

Weiters wird gezeigt, welche generellen (und oft kulturell überformten) Konfliktfelder sich oft in Wohnhausanlagen schon fast zwangsläufig ergeben. Abschließend werden Lösungswege aufgezeigt, über die sich genau diesen Konflikten begegnen lässt. Demnach ist die Status – Homogenität mit diesen anderswo wohnenden Personen zum Aufbau persönlicher Beziehungen wichtiger als die räumliche Nähe zu den im gleichen Haus oder Viertel wohnenden NachbarInnen (Münch 2010).

Auch Hogg (2004, zitiert in: Guest 2008) weist darauf hin, dass die Kontakthypothese nur Gültigkeit haben könne, wenn ein offizielles und institutionelles Klima Integration stark unterstützt und gleichzeitig der Austausch in der sozial und ethnisch gemischten Nachbarschaft zwischen Gruppen von gleichem Status erfolgt.

Der Kontakthypothese entgegenstehend behauptet die in der Literatur ebenfalls zu findende Konflikthypothese deren genaues Gegenteil: Die enge räumliche Nachbarschaft von Menschen mit unterschiedlichen Lebensweisen biete eine Vielzahl von Reibungsflächen und Konfliktmöglichkeiten.

Schon bei Bourdieu (1991: 31) findet sich die Aussage: *„Tatsächlich steht einem nichts ferner und ist weniger tolerierbar als Menschen, die sozial fernstehen, aber mit denen man in räumlichen Kontakt kommt."*

In Summe besteht in der Fachliteratur jedoch wenig Konsistenz und wenig definitive Aussagen werden darüber gemacht, welche Ergebnisse residentielle Segregation sowohl hinsichtlich sozio-ökonomischer Faktoren als auch in Bezug auf die Integration von ZuwanderInnen zeitigen kann. Musterd (2008b) findet allerdings einen bescheidenen Konsens darüber, dass das Zusammenwohnen mit schlecht ausgebildeten oder arbeitslosen Individuen die ökonomischen Aussichten von MigrantInnen beeinträchtigt.

Beobachtet werden kann dagegen, dass das soziale Netz, in dem sich Menschen befinden, ihre Meinung über sozialen Mix stark beeinflusst: So bevorzugen Menschen, die in gemischten Vierteln leben und über starke soziale Verbindungen in ihrer Wohnumgebung verfügen, genau diese soziale Durchmischung. Menschen mit starken sozialen Verbindungen in homogenen Vierteln bevorzugen dagegen homogene Viertel. Menschen mit starken sozialen Netzwerken im Wohnumfeld sind also auch gemischten Vierteln gegenüber positiv eingestellt, wenn sie sich dort eingebunden fühlen. Wenn Menschen dagegen negative Meinungen über ihre sozial durchmischte Nachbarschaft haben, stehen sie dem sozialem Mix ablehnend gegenüber, v.a. wenn sie HausbesitzerInnen sind und Angst um den Wertverlust ihrer Immobilie durch ein schlechter werdendes Image ihres Wohngebietes haben (Musterd 2008a).

Neue Bedeutungen von Nachbarschaft

Wir leben heute allerdings nicht nur in einer zusehends ethnisch diverseren, sondern auch individualisierten Gesellschaft, in der viele Individuen von Abhängigkeitsverhältnissen frei sind, die die Entwicklung Einzelner in vergangenen Jahrhunderten oft stark einschränkten. Gleichzeitig aber müssen wir nun neue Formen des Zusammenlebens finden, für die es vielfach noch keine Vorlagen gibt. Die Neudefinition dessen, was unter „Nachbarschaft" zu verstehen ist, wird damit zur gesellschaftlichen Aufgabe.

Nachbarschaft ist als Begriff auch heute durchaus positiv besetzt und wird vielfach gewünscht. Aber: Diese Nachbarschaft soll möglichst unverbindlich sein, zu nichts verpflichten und nicht zu viel Zeit in Anspruch nehmen

Im Allgemeinen versteht die wissenschaftliche Fachliteratur Nachbarschaft als eine Sammlung von überlappenden Netzwerken (Beckhoven et al. 2005). Oft wird beobachtet, dass lokale Netzwerke an Bedeutung verlieren zugunsten von weit über lokale Grenzen hinausreichenden Netzwerken (Bridge et al. 2004). Insbesondere in urbaneren Umgebungen mit tendenziell kleineren Haushalten sei festzustellen, dass viele StädterInnen (insbesondere, wenn sie keinen unterprivilegierten, marginalisierten Gruppen angehören) stark außenorientiert sind (Wirth, 1938) und zusehends neue, räumlich diffusere Netzwerke aufbauen (Beckhoven et al. 2005).

Dennoch bleiben auch im städtischen Umfeld Nachbarschaften durchaus wichtig, aber sie spielen eine spezielle Rolle im Leben der Menschen und existieren parallel zu verstärkten, außernachbarschaftlichen Verbindungen. Gerade für die Freizeit vieler Menschen sei ihr jeweiliges zuhause von Bedeutung – es wird zu einem Statement für ihre Identität, dafür „wer wir sind".

Zahlreiche AutorInnen verweisen denn auch auf die enge Beziehung, die zwischen zivilem Engagement in vielen verschiedenen Formen und demokratischer Teilnahme besteht: engagierte Gemeinschaften produzieren demnach kohäsive Gesellschaften aktiver BürgerInnen; auch scheinen in derart aktiven Gemeinschaften eher Veränderungen möglich in Richtung verbesserter Bildung und Gesundheit, reduzierter Armut, Arbeitslosigkeit, Kriminalität und Drogenkonsum (Putnam 1993).

Dennoch ist „sozialer Zusammenhalt" nicht notwendigerweise ausschließlich positiv konnotiert; So können soziale Bindungen nach innen wie nach außen ausschließend wirken - stark in sich vernetzte Gruppen haben unter Umständen kaum Kontakte außerhalb der eigenen Community - interner Zusammenhalt existiert hier auf Kosten externer Beziehungen, gleichzeitig haben Andersartige es schwer, sich in derartige Gruppen einzufügen. Treffen mehrere solcher auf sich bezogenen Gruppen aufeinander, können zwischen ihnen starke Konflikte auftreten (Beckhoven et al. 2005).

Nachbarschaftseffekte sind auch stark von der jeweiligen Lebensphase abhängig, in der sich die betrachteten Bevölkerungsgruppen gerade befinden: so ist das Wohnumfeld für Kleinkinder, deren wichtigste Bezugspersonen die Eltern darstellen, deutlich weniger prägend als für Kinder und Jugendliche, die sich stärker an Gleichaltrigen (der Umgebung) zu orientieren beginnen oder für Erwachsene, denen soziale Netze wichtige Unterstützung im Alltag oder bei der Arbeitssuche bieten können. Es erweist sich jedoch als schwierig, Nachbarschaftseffekte klar von denen der jeweiligen Familienumstände (Haushaltseinkommen, Bildungslevel etc.) zu trennen. (Ellen und Turner 1997).

Kinder und Jugendliche in der Wohnumgebung

Wichtig bleibt Nachbarschaft insgesamt vor allem für jene Gruppen, die – aus unterschiedlichen Gründen – viel Zeit in der eigenen Wohngegend verbringen: etwa Kinder, Alte, Behinderte. Beckhoven et al. (2005) stellen aber auch fest, dass die lokale Arena für ArbeiterInnen mehr Bedeutung habe als für Angestellte - für Angehörige der Mittelklasse stellt sie nur eine unter mehreren Sphären dar, in denen diese sich bewegt.

Wird Nachbarschaft im eigenen Wohnviertel von den BewohnerInnen als sicherer Hafen erlebt, so kann sozialer Zusammenhalt – wechselseitiges, internes Verpflichtet sein – entstehen. Beckhoven und Kempen (2005) machen zahlreiche Faktoren aus, von denen eine derartige soziale Kohäsion abhängig ist: Sind in einem Haushalt beispielsweise Kinder vorhanden, besteht meist eine erhöhte Bereitschaft zu sozialen Kontakten im Viertel, etwa im Bereich von Kindergärten und Schule. Kinderlose, junge Paare und Studierende sind dagegen oft weniger am eigenen Viertel interessiert – nicht zuletzt deswegen, weil sie häufig nur für vergleichsweise kurze Dauer vor Ort wohnen.

Im Umfeld dieser Wohnquartiere sehen sich Kindergärten und Schulen mit Konzentrationen von Kindern konfrontiert, deren Umgangssprache nicht Deutsch ist. Die hohen Konzentrationen sind nicht nur die Folge der Wohnsegregation sondern auch der Tendenz deutschsprachiger Eltern, ihre Kinder in oft weiter entfernte Kindergärten und Schulen zu geben, die vor allem von Kindern mit deutscher Umgangssprache besucht werden. Für die SchülerInnen mit nicht deutscher Umgangssprache vermindern sich dadurch die Chancen und auch die Motivation, mit gleichaltrigen Kindern mit deutscher Muttersprache zu lernen, zu sprechen und zu spielen

Die ansonsten allgemein als wünschenswert angesehene soziale Kohäsion wird von Erwachsenen bei Jugendgruppen oft als antisozial wahrgenommen (Forrest und Kearns 2001). An solchen Gruppen lässt sich nämlich die nach innen wie nach außen ausschließende Wirkung starken sozialen Zusammenhalts beobachten: Deren interner Zusammenhalt existiert unter Umständen auf Kosten externer Beziehungen, gleichzeitig haben Andersartige Schwierigkeiten, sich in derartige Gruppen einzufügen. Treffen sie auf andere, können starke Konflikte auftreten.

Konfliktfelder im Alltag

Gerade BewohnerInnen von Mehrgeschossigen Wohngebäuden und großen Wohnanlagen sind tagtäglich auf zahlreiche Infrastruktureinrichtungen angewiesen, die von vielen anderen Personen genutzt werden, wie etwa Lifte, Stiegen, Müllabfuhr usw. Diese gemeinsame Benutzung verlangt von den BewohnerInnen ein Mindestmaß an Anpassungsfähigkeit, was als wiederkehrende Toleranzübung verstanden werden kann (Power 1997). So wird, vielfach unbemerkt, gelegentlich mit beträchtlicher Friktion, auf diesem lokalen Level im Alltag Bürgerschaft erlernt, getestet, geübt (Wolman 1995).

Insbesondere Kinder und Jugendliche mit Migrationshintergrund nutzen aufgrund ihrer beengten Wohnsituation verstärkt Spielmöglichkeiten im Freien in der unmittelbaren Wohnumgebung. Dies wiederum führt vielfach zu Klagen anderer BewohnerInnen über Lärmbelästigung. Vor allem in Wohngebieten mit alternder autochthoner Bevölkerung werden so klassische Generationskonflikte zwischen ruhebedürftigen Senioren und Kindern und Jugendlichen mit entsprechendem Bewegungsdrang zusätzlich mit stereotypen Vorurteilen über ethnisch-kulturelle Verhaltensmuster überfrachtet und damit belastet.

Generell sind Klagen über Lärmbelästigung der häufigste Konfliktgrund in vielen Wohnanlagen (vgl. Cser in Berger et al. 2013: S. 41-45). Diese Problematik ist sehr häufig mit dem Fehlen adäquater Spiel- und Freizeitmöglichkeiten vor allem für größere Kinder und Jugendliche verbunden. Hinzu kommt, dass gerade in größeren Wohn(neu)baugebieten, die zu unterschiedlichen Zeitpunkten von unterschiedlichen Bauträgern errichtet wurden bzw. werden, oft eine übergeordnete Koordination zur Schaffung von wohnungsnahen Freizeit- und Bewegungsmöglichkeiten fehlt.

Ein weiteres, häufiges Konfliktfeld im unmittelbaren Wohnumfeld stellen Verschmutzung und Müll(trennung) dar. Ebenso wie Lärm ist auch dieser Themenkreis dazu geeignet, durch entsprechend aufbereitete Information, Kommunikation und Konfliktmediation individuell und kleinräumig bearbeitet und einer Lösung zugeführt zu werden. Sinnvoll erscheinen daher übergreifende Strukturen, die derartige punktuelle Hilfestellungen anbieten.

Förderung von belasteten Quartieren

Durchaus nicht jede Nachbarschaft benötigt Unterstützung, in den meisten Wohnquartieren ist sie nicht erforderlich. In Siedlungen jedoch, die aufgrund der unausgewogenen Zusammensetzung der BewohnerInnenschaft – etwa dem Vorhandensein eines überproportional großen Anteils an wirtschaftlich schwachen, marginalisierten Haushalten – als „belastet" bezeichnet werden muss, ist Förderung durch ein aktives Quartiersmanagement nötig. Gerade in Gebäuden, die vorwiegend durch Zuweisung übers Sozialamt belegt werden, besteht vielfach eine unfreiwillige Nachbarschaft, die durch geringe Ressourcen, aber hohes Konfliktpotential gekennzeichnet ist. Hier sind Aktivierungs-, Beschäftigungs- und Beratungsangebote vor Ort gefragt.

Auch stellt sich natürlich die Frage, inwieweit auch die bauliche Ausformung von Wohngebäude und –umgebung ein nachbarschaftliches Miteinander unterstützen und fördern kann? Nähe kann zwar gebaut werden, soziale Beziehung aber nicht! Nachbarschaft durch Bauweise schaffen zu wollen ist langfristig meist nicht erfolgreich. Es können Räume für Begegnung angeboten werden, ob sie aber angenommen werden, hängt von sehr vielen, sehr individuellen Faktoren vor Ort ab – und stark von den dort handelnden Personen.

Im Rahmen mehrerer Forschungsarbeiten[2] des Fachbereichs „Sozialraum und Migration" im Department für Migration und Globalisierung der Donau-Universität Krems kristallisierten sich immerhin Beratung, Konfliktmanagement sowie Quartiersarbeit als wirkungsvolle Methoden und Instrumente heraus, um das Zusammenleben im Wohnumfeld tolerant und möglichst konfliktfrei zu gestalten und neue Formen der Nachbarschaft in einer zunehmend diversen Gesellschaft zu erarbeiten und zu gestalten. Anstoß zur bzw. Verbesserung der Kommunikation unter NachbarInnen stellt das zentrale Ziel all dieser Interventionen dar – schließlich eröffnet eine vorhande Gesprächsbasis mit den NachbarInnen auch die Chance über auftretenden Konflikte reden und Lösungen aushandeln zu können (Berger et al. 2014: S.108 ff).

Nachbarschaft sollte also nicht als eine Art Wundermittel gegen soziale Isolation und Konflikte überfordert werden. Erzwingen lässt sie sich nämlich nicht, fördern aber schon!

Literatur

Beckhoven, Ellen; Bolt, Gideon; Kempen, Ronald van (29 June - 2 July, 2005): Theories of neighbourhood change and neighbourhood decline. Their significance for post-WW II large housing estates. Paper for the ENHR-conference "Housing in Europe: New Challenges and Innovations in Tomorrow's Cities. European Network for Housing Research (ENHR). Reykjavik, 29 June - 2 July, 2005.

---

[2] Siehe dazu folgende Endberichte: https://www.donau-uni.ac.at/de/department/migration globalisierung/forschung/sozialraumanalyse/index.php; https://www.donau-uni.ac.at/imperia/md/content/department/migrationglobalisierung/forschung/endbericht_wohnen-und-zusammenleben.pdf; https://www.donau-uni.ac.at/de/department/migrationglobalisierung/forschung/id/23221/index.php (letzter Zugriff: 26.10.2017)

Beckhoven, Ellen van; Kempen, Roland van (2006): Toward more social cohesion in large Post-Second World War housing estates? A case study in Utrecht, the Netherlands. In: Housing Studies 21, July 2006 (4), S. 477–500.

Berger, Tania; Czerny, Margarete; Faustmann, Anna; Perl, Christian (2014): Sozialraumanalyse: Konzepte und Empfehlungen zur Umsetzung von Integration in Niederösterreich. Endbericht. Donau Universität Krems. Krems. Online verfügbar unter http://www.donau-uni.ac.at/imperia/md/content/department/migrationglobalisierung/forschung/schriftenreihe/sozialraumanalyse-2014.pdf, zuletzt geprüft am 25.08.2015.

Bourdieu, Pierre (1991): Physischer, sozialer und angeeigneter physischer Raum. In: Martin Wentz (Hg.): Stadt-Räume. Frankfurt/ New York: Campus Verlag, S. 25–34.

Bridge, G., Forrest, R. and Holland, E. (2004) Neighbouring: A Review of the Evidence. Centre for Neighbourhood Research

Cole, Ian; Goodchild, Barry (2001): Social Mix and the 'Balanced Community' in British housing policy – a tale of two epochs. In: GeoJournal 51, 2001, S. 351–360.

Ellen, Ingrid Gould; Turner, Margery Austin (1997): Does Neighborhood Matter? Assessing Recent Evidence. In: Housing Policy Debate 8, 1997 (4), S. 833–865.

Forrest, Ray; Kearns, Ade (2001): Social cohesion, soocial capital and the neighbourhood. In: Urban Studies 38, 2001 (12), S. 2125–2143.

Guest, Avery M.; Charis, e. Kubrin; Cover, Jane K. (2008): Heterogeneity and Harmony: Neighbouring relationships among whites in ethnically diverse neighbourhoods in Seattle. In: Urban Studies 45, 2008 (3), S. 501–526.

Gundelach, Birte; Freitag, Markus (2014): Neighbourhood diversity and social trust. an empirical analysis of interethnic contact and group-specific effects. In: Urban Studies 51, 2014 (6), S. 1236–1256.

Hogg, Michael A.; Abrams, Dominic; Otten, Sabine; Hinkle, Steve (2004): The Social Identity Perspective. In: Small Group Research 35, 2004 (3), S. 246–276.

Ludwig, Jens (1997): Information and inner city educational attainme. In: Economics of Education Review 18, 1999, S. 17–30.

Morrison, Nicola (2003): Neighbourhoods and social cohesion. Experiences from Europe. In: International Planning Studies 8, 2003 (2), S. 115–138.

Münch, Sybille (2010): Integration durch Wohnungspolitik?: Zum Umgang mit ethnischer Segregation im europäischen Vergleich; VS Verlag für Sozialwissenschaften; Auflage: 2010 (14. September 2010)

Musterd, Sako (2008a): Residents' views on social mix: social mix, social networks and sitmatisation in post-war housing estates in Europe 45, 2008 (4), S. 897–925.

Musterd, Sako; Andersson, Roger; Galster, George; Kauppinen, Timo M. (2008b): Are immigrants' earnings influenced by the characteristics of their neighbours? In: Environment and Planning 40, 2008, S. 785–805.

Power, Anne (1997): Estates on the Edge. The Social Consequences of Mass Housing in Northern Europe. London: Palgrave Macmillan UK.

Öberg, Perola; Oskarsson, Sven; Svensson, Torsten (2011): Similarity vs. homogeneity. contextual effects in explaining trust. In: European Political Science Review 3, 2011 (3), S. 345–369.

Putnam, Robert D.; Leonardi, Robert; Nanetti, Raffaella Y. (1993): Making Democracy Work: Civic Traditions in Modern Italy. Princton, New Jersey: Princton University Press.

Statistik Austria (2011): Bevölkerungsvorausschätzung 2011-2050 sowie Modellrechnung bis 2075 für Niederösterreich (Hauptszenario). Schnellbericht 8.2,Wien.

Wirth, Louis (1938): Urbanism as a way of life. In: The American Journal of Sociology XLIV, 1938 (1), S. 1–24.

Wolman, Harold (1995): Local government institutions and democratic governance. In: David Judge, Gerry Stoker und Harold Wolman (Hg.): Theories of urban politics. London: Sage.

Teil 7:
Inter- und transdisziplinäre Beiträge zur Migrationsforschung

Agriculture-dominated Societies, Climate Change and Migration: a Case for Transdisciplinarity

Gerald Steiner

Abstract

The capability of societal systems to adapt and innovate is crucial for ensuring their viability and resilience, especially in the context of disturbances, which could originate either from within the system or from its environment. In general, migration can be conceived as one specific dimension of a multifaceted system- and transition-mechanism. Climate change, e.g., can be a driving force of migration, particularly within agriculture-dominated societies. The underlying argument is that for dealing with such complex, coupled human-environment systems, a transdisciplinary approach as a specific form of science-society collaboration has the potential to help to better understand these systems and their future transition path and to develop interventions, e.g., innovations, which are aimed to increase their resilience and – ultimately – their sustainable development.

Introduction

Knowledge without understanding is a misguided missile.
(Ackoff and Rovin, 2005: 15)

Complex societal challenges

Migration is not per se a complex challenge, instead it may be understood as a phenomenon, which ranges from linear and *continuous* developments to non-linear and *disruptive developments*. On the one hand, in an increasingly interrelated world, *mobility of labor and capital* (Biffl, 2012; Sassen, 2001) is essential for the functioning of various societal systems. Hence, migration can be conceived as part of a multifaceted system mechanism, which characterizes any societal transition. The development of the United States and Europe for example would not have been possible without immigrants; further, both will depend on within- and between-mobility of labor between them as well as regarding third countries, in terms of their future development. On the other hand, *system disturbances* such as war, climate change, hunger, resource scarcity, and health crises challenge societal systems regarding their *capabilities to adapt and innovate*. However, innovation might not only be a key mechanism in coping with disturbances, but it may itself be a disturbance. E.g., in agriculture-dominated societies, digitalization might positively affect productivity (e.g., based on automated irrigation- and production systems), but it may also release labor force and, consequently, prompt workers to migrate to different regions within a country or even to move abroad. Current examples of system disturbances include the ongoing migration- and refugee movements to Europe (as the first mass influx of migrants/refugees to the European Union from outside its region), but also climate change induced migration. They demonstrate that not only persecution for gender, religion, conflict, and war, but also *climate change can be a driving force of migration* (e.g., increased sea levels, decreasing agricultural opportunities).

The example of *agriculture-dominated societies* also demonstrates the increasing complexity of the magnitude of change, which – with more than one interfering event co-occurring (e.g., technological impact of digitalization and climate change) – becomes increasingly difficult to predict along its future transition path. Simultaneously, since migration into urban areas is often a result of these agricultural developments, the societal development of *rural and urban areas* is affected as well.

Hence, the *understanding of coupling mechanisms* between human systems (e.g., agricultural society and labor migration) and environment systems (e.g., technological basis and ecosystems services), such as expressed in Scholz's theory of coupled human-environment systems (Scholz, 2011), is essential for the development of appropriate interventions, which strive to enhance the *resilience* of a given societal system in accordance to potential internal or external *vulnerabilities*. For innovation developments, which contribute to a more resilient society, system understanding is a prerequisite and – as a consequence – *vulnerabilities might become a source of innovation*.

Characterization of complex problems

Extending on the above described case of agriculture-dominated societies, it becomes obvious that the development of such *multilayered societal systems* in the light of *migration, technological developments, climate change, and innovation* (see Section 'Complex societal challenges' above) is an example of a real-world problem of complex nature. I.e. *complex problems* "are multifaceted, ill-defined, nonlinear, with innumerable sets of highly interdependent subsystems and elements, and they reveal dynamically changing development patterns over time" (Steiner, 2014, p. 8) (see also, e.g., Ackoff and Rovin, 2005; Meadows and Wright, 2008, pp. 181–182; Scholz and Tietje, 2002, p. 34; Steiner, 2013, p. 18; Sterman, 2000, pp. 3–39). The *adaptive capacities* of a complex system enable it to adapt dynamically and in nonlinear ways, which lead to unique *emerging properties* that distinguish it from other systems (e.g., Katz, 2006).

In the *case of agricultural production*, the introduction of new technologies might be considered positive or negative for the labor situation, depending on the overall system's capabilities to adapt. E.g., smart irrigation systems, appropriate fertilization strategies accompanied by reforestation, which is aimed to prevent soil erosion, together with training programs for workers to acquire the competences needed to understand the holistic agricultural system (as a coupled multi-layered system), to monitor and analyze it, and to derive proper intervention scenarios, may lead to positive economic, ecological, and social effect in parallel. By contrast, one-dimensional cause-effect thinking may lead to unintended economic, ecological, or social effects.

If a societal system strives towards *sustainable development* (regarding economic, ecological, and social dimensions), it is striving towards a dynamic and not a fixed state: "Sustainable development is a proactive, ongoing inquiry (...) on system-limit management in the framework of intra- and intergenerational justice (...)" (Scholz, 2017), whereby, social norms and values affect the inquiry regarding sustainable transitioning. The *understanding* of complex systems such as agriculture-dominated societies *in the context of societal resilience and sustainable development* goes beyond comprehending the current state, but it starts with the past and is – via the current state as an interface – related to potential future transition states. Hence, the complex system itself as well as its boundaries, how it functions and malfunctions, how it is interrelated with its environment, and how it transforms over time need to be thoroughly understood. However, these complex challenges most usually cannot be dealt with by individuals only, nor by a single discipline. In addition, expert knowledge beyond that of academia and including other experts from society cannot be neglected either.

Transdisciplinarity as a means of dealing with complex real-world challenges

Complex migration challenges such as described above call for specific forms of *science-society collaboration*, which provide "science-based, state-of-the-art, socially accepted options of solutions which acknowledge uncertainties and the incompleteness of different forms of epistemics" (Scholz and Steiner, 2015a). The integration of different epistemics from science and practice, i.e. Mode 2 transdisciplinarity, seems to be a key for a potentially sustainable societal transition (a comprehensive outline of the historical development of transdisciplinarity is outlined by Scholz and Steiner, 2015a). By contrast, *Mode 1 transdisciplinarity* "aspires to develop a meta-structure that allows for a more realistic description of material-biophysical and socio-cultural, epistemic structures, which are currently dealt with separately in a myriad of disciplines in the natural and social sciences, engineering, health sciences, and the humanities" (Scholz and Steiner, 2015a, p. 537). To sum it up, whereas Mode 1 transdisciplinarity by integrating epistemic structures of different disciplines (i.e. interdisciplinarity) helps to overcome disciplinary boundaries, Mode 2 transdisciplinarity is supplementing disciplinarity and interdisciplinarity by a multi-stakeholder discourse. Mode 2 transdisciplinarity "is conceived as a *facilitated process of mutual learning between science and society* that relates a targeted multidisciplinary or interdisciplinary research process and a multi-stakeholder discourse for *developing socially robust orientations* about a specific real-world issue" (Scholz and Steiner, 2015a, p. 531).

Transdisciplinary processes contribute to multidimensional knowledge integration by applying various transdisciplinary methods. They are meant to enable capacity building among all participants based on an equal footing throughout the whole process, i.e. problem definition and -representation, development of strategies for transforming the problem by *system innovations* (as combined form of technological and social innovations) at various levels of the coupled human-environment system. In an ideal form of transdisciplinarity, *co-leadership* between science leader(s) and practice leader(s) is realized within the whole project (i.e. within every subproject). *Accepting the "otherness of the other"* (including the differences in epistemics and modes of causation between science and practice) is fundamental for *mutual learning*, which is needed when dealing with complex real-world problems that are of societal relevance. In practice, transdisciplinary projects and processes will meet various forms of constraints and obstacles, which need to be dealt with (an comprehensive overview of obstacles within the transdisciplinary process based on the analysis of 41 mid- and large-scale transdisciplinary studies is provided by Scholz and Steiner, 2015b).

Within the transdisciplinary process, four forms of knowing and knowledge-integration are distinguished (Scholz, 2011; Scholz and Steiner, 2015a; Scholz and Tietje, 2002): (1) *Experience* as direct *experiential knowledge* (i.e. sensation- and perception-based) is of holistic nature and includes unconscious knowledge dimensions (experimental system knowledge is a particular strength of practice experts); (2) *Understanding* based on experiences as well as on empathy enables comprehending the complexity of multilayered coupled human-environment system; (3) *Conceptualizing* means relating of constituents of thought and single concepts, which also becomes the basis for a collaborative creative effort to generate innovations; (4) *Explaining* implies that past, present, and future cause and impact relationships can be sufficiently understood, which is also a prerequisite for evaluating the resilient capacities and sustainable potential of various development scenarios.

Within the transdisciplinary process, the multidimensional knowledge integration relates to five dimensions, i.e. modes of thought (i.e. intuitive and analytical thinking), (inter-)disciplinary (related to humanities, natural and social sciences), perspectives/interests, systems, and cultures (including religions).

Exemplified by the case of smallholder farmers in Kenya (Njoroge et al., 2015), the application of a transdisciplinary process led to a better understanding of the agriculture-dominated societal system (i.e. coupled human-environment system) by initiating a mutual learning process between science and society (including farmers) and the development of more sufficient management strategies for the agricultural system (e.g., from an agro-economic perspective, the transdisciplinary project design led to a yield increase of 54 %). Further, these developments followed a sustainability orientation, which encompasses economic, ecological, and social dimensions. In more detail, the transdisciplinary process encompassed: "(1) farmers' participation in a transdisciplinary process including extension officers and local scientists to construct farm-specific fertilization strategies based on (2) farm-specific soil testing and (3) the construction of cooperative strategies for purchasing fertilizers involving farmers, traders, and financial institutions in a timely manner" (Njoroge et al., 2015, p. 601). As stated above, a transdisciplinary process design can enhance a holistic understanding of the agricultural system (as a coupled multilayered system) and may lead to simultaneous positive economic, ecological, and social effects, which also affects labor migration mechanisms.

Transdisciplinarity at Danube University Krems and Outlook

Transdisciplinarity has become more than a philosophy at Danube University Krems in Austria. It is increasingly characterizing educational and research activities as such. In the following, four selected examples of a broad variety of transdisciplinary initiatives at Danube University Krems are introduced:

(1) Danube University Krems commits itself to being a 'transdisciplinary university', which follows the principles of transdisciplinarity as described above. As such, she was the first university that included a transdisciplinarity focus in her core strategy and with implications on both teaching as well as on research.
(2) Based on its focus on postgraduate education, Danube University Krems as Public University for Continuing Education provides a specific environment for educational programs, which emphasize applied real-world topics of relevance for students who are themselves professionals in a broad variety of societal fields (e.g., most recently as part of a teaching program on digital governance).
(3) Danube University Krems and particularly the Faculty of Business and Globalization is hosting a PhD program in migration studies, which is widely based on transdisciplinary principles. Further transdisciplinary PhD programs are in the process of development.
(4) Currently, three transdisciplinary research platforms exist: 1) the 'Transdisciplinarity Laboratory Sustainable Digital Environments' (SDE TdLab), 2) the 'Transdisciplinarity Laboratory Sustainable Mineral Resources' (SMR TdLab), and 3) the 'GovLabAustria'. Additional transdisciplinary initiatives such as in the field of democracy will follow.

With examples as outlined above, migration research in general and in particular at Danube University Krems is equipped with a state-of-the art basis for doing transdisciplinary teaching and research. Science-society based approaches such as offered by transdisciplinarity provide new possibilities for research and teaching, which aims to make a difference with respect to the societal relevant challenges we are facing today.

References

Ackoff, R.L., Rovin, S., 2005. Beating the system: using creativity to outsmart bureaucracies, 1st ed. ed. Berrett-Koehler, San Francisco, CA.

Biffl, Gudrun, 2012. Turkey and Europe: The role of migration and trade in economic development. Migr. Lett. 9, 47–63.

Katz, J.S., 2006. Indicators for complex innovation systems. Res. Policy 35, 893–909. doi:10.1016/j.respol.2006.03.007

Meadows, D.H., Wright, D., 2008. Thinking in systems: a primer. Chelsea Green Pub, White River Junction, Vt.

Njoroge, R., Birech, R., Arusey, C., Korir, M., Mutisya, C., Scholz, R.W., 2015. Transdisciplinary processes of developing, applying, and evaluating a method for improving smallholder farmers' access to (phosphorus) fertilizers: the SMAP method. Sustain. Sci. 10, 601–619. doi:10.1007/s11625-015-0333-5

Sassen, S., 2001. The mobility of labor and capital: a study in international investment and labor flow, Transferred to digital printing. ed. Cambridge Univ. Press, Cambridge.

Scholz, R., 2017. The Normative Dimension in Transdisciplinarity, Transition Management, and Transformation Sciences: New Roles of Science and Universities in Sustainable Transitioning. Sustainability 9, 991. doi:10.3390/su9060991

Scholz, R.W., 2011. Environmental literacy in science and society: from knowledge to decisions. Cambridge University Press, Cambridge et al.

Scholz, R.W., Steiner, G., 2015a. The real type and ideal type of transdisciplinary processes: part I—theoretical foundations. Sustain. Sci. 10, 527–544. doi:10.1007/s11625-015-0326-4

Scholz, R.W., Steiner, G., 2015b. The real type and ideal type of transdisciplinary processes: part II—what constraints and obstacles do we meet in practice? Sustain. Sci. 10, 653–671. doi:10.1007/s11625-015-0327-3

Scholz, R.W., Tietje, O., 2002. Embedded case study methods: integrating quantitative and qualitative knowledge. Sage Publications, Thousand Oaks, Calif.

Steiner, G., 2014. Problem discovery as a collaborative, creative, and method-guided search for the "real problems" as raw diamonds of innovation. Working Paper 2014-0003, Weatherhead Center for International Affairs, Harvard University, Boston.

Steiner, G., 2013. Competences for complex real-world problems: toward an integrative framework. Weather. Cent. Int. Aff. Harv. Univ. Boston.

Sterman, J., 2000. Business dynamics: systems thinking and modeling for a complex world. Irwin/McGraw-Hill, Boston.

Impact of Information and Communication Technologies and their Application to Challenges of Migration

Peter Parycek, Margarita Fourer, Shefali Virkar, Dino Pitoski,
Gabriela Viale Pereira, Thomas J. Lampoltshammer

Abstract

Migration is a powerful phenomenon, impacting on virtually all aspects of society. Therefore, it inherits a high grade of complexity and associated set of challenges, such as socio-economic and cultural integration, as well as the broader challenge of data collection, sharing and analysis. Information and Communication Technology (ICT) as integrated part of today's digital society therefore touches upon these areas frequently. Thus, this paper investigates the impact of ICT on challenges of migration and sheds light on current initiatives and potential solutions towards resolving some of the arising issues of regular migration.

Introduction

Migration is a powerful phenomenon, impacting on virtually all aspects of society. While the proportion of migrants compared to the global population is very small at 3.3% (United Nations International Migration Report 2015), migration itself greatly influences and is influenced by the wider processes of political, economic, cultural, and technological change. At every level - from municipal to federal – governments dedicate resources, policies, finances and election campaigns to the issue of migration.

Simultaneously, information and communication technologies (ICT) have a crucial role in societal progress (Majchrzak, Markus and Wareham 2016). The application of digital technologies in sectors such as governments, non-governmental organizations and organic social movements has the potential to improve participation, transparency and accountability (Majchrzak, Markus and Wareham 2012). The digital society also challenges and raises societal problems like the digital divide, unemployment, increasing economic disparity, instability of financial markets, as well as the need to deliver quality public services and renew the legitimacy of public policy-making, including relevant policies, from humanitarian assistance, to development cooperation, to migration (Walsham and Sahay 2006, Majchrzak, Markus and Wareham 2012, European Commission 2017).

While both fields of migration and ICT are broad and evolving, they are inherently interlinked. ICT both facilitates regular and irregular migration, and creates the means to enforce the borders against irregular arrival while improving and fast-tracking the experience of regular arrivals (Hamel 2009, pp. 15-16). While not by any means a comprehensive account of the interaction of ICT and migration, the work at hand strives to identify some of the developments of ICT and highlight their potential to address a few of the challenges faced in international regular migration.

After the introduction, the chapter will begin with sections presenting both the general challenges of migration (2) and the development of ICT (3). The fourth section will focus on the role of ICT in addressing the challenge of border control (4). The following three sections will elaborate on the impact of ICT on economic growth and how that can be utilised to address the challenges of economic integration (5); the impact of ICT on social capital and community development and its effect on the challenge of cultural integration (6); as well as ICT's impact on good governance and the delivery of public services and how these factors can improve the provision of reliable, timely and accurate data collection, sharing and analysis on migration (7).

Challenges of Migration

Regular migration poses its own set of challenges, including the areas of border control, both socio-economic and cultural integration as well as the broader challenge of data collection, sharing and analysis. Due to the complexity of issues associated with migration, it is important to clarify that when discussing global migration, unless otherwise specified, the figures and resulting policy considerations in this chapter refer to international regular rather than internal or irregular migration.

Border Control

While battling irregular migration has increasingly been on the agenda of governments, the refugee crisis of 2015 has kicked off an escalation of efforts with the European government resorting to various measures to secure and protect their borders. The so-called migration crisis hit its peak during summer of 2015, with the highest number of people seeking to enter the European Union (EU) to find shelter and protection due to disaster events or war situations in their home countries. This has created tensions among the EU states, not least of all within one of the overarching issues, being the task of harmonisation of policies, processes, and technologies over all EU member states, which is already a complex endeavour as, e.g., only 22 out of 28 EU member states fully implement the Schengen Acquis, yet have to find common ground with the remaining six member states (Lehton and Aalto 2017).

To add to the complexity of the border control challenges, the flow of regular migration is continuously increasing, with high transit rates of individuals in and out of the European Union, expected to reach up to 900 million by the year 2025 – with around 300 million being third country nationals (European Commission 2016). This situation poses a set of challenges for existing border control policies, processes, and technologies.

Integration

Recent terrorist attacks in London Paris and Brussels by second generation migrants have raised concerns regarding the failure of integration policies in Europe. Together with border control, integration is now seen as one of the biggest challenges of migration. In fact, it has been shown that *"improving the outcomes for immigrants will significantly contribute to achieving the Europe 2020 Strategy's overall goals"* (Huddleston et. al. 2013, p. 13). The EU Common Basic Principles defines integration as *"a dynamic, two-way process of mutual accommodation by all immigrants and residents of Member States"* that also involves *"the receiving society, which should create the opportunities for the immigrants' full economic, social, cultural, and political participation."* (Council of European Union 2004, Annex).

The difficulty of designing, implementing and assessing the success of integration policies at the legal/political, socio-economic and cultural levels (CSES and CoR 2013, p. 13) is further exacerbated by the wide range of countries, development levels and education that exists between migrant populations in any particular state. Even while taking differences into account, the EU migrant unemployment rate was higher than that of other OECD countries (OECD and EU 2015, p. 11). Challenges also arise from the perspective of cultural integration, specifically, a lasting perception of discrimination by the second-generation migrants, especially in Austria, Belgium, the Netherlands and the United Kingdom (OECD and EU 2015, p. 218).

Data on migration

For efficient governance, both in ordinary and times of crises, it is essential to have readily available, reliable information. In that sense, appropriate collection of and access to accurate, consistent and timely data is of great concern (Laczko 2015, p. 1). In fact, building up the capacity of developing states to *"increase significantly the availability of high-quality, timely and reliable data disaggregated by income, gender, age, race, ethnicity,* migratory status, *disability, geographic location and other characteristics relevant in national contexts"* is target 17.18 of the Sustainable Development Goals (UNGA 2015, emphasis added). Nonetheless, migration-related data suffers a myriad of challenges at every stage of collection, sharing and analysis.

Despite recent attempts to standardise collection procedures, varying methods are used by different actors to collect data on migratory movements (Laczko 2015, pp. 5-6). Different countries have differing standards. For example, the United Kingdom is one of the last countries in Europe to collect its migration data utilising the flawed collection of International Passenger Surveys of incoming and outgoing flights, which has been shown not to represent actual in- and out-bound movement of persons accurately (Warrell et. al. 2016). In the majority of countries, migration data collection is spread across a number of agencies and departments (Laczko 2015, p. 7). One of the flaws of this system, in addition to data being collected according to different disaggregation categories, can be seen in the inconsistency between the figures on emigration and immigration (United Nations Department of Economic and Social Affairs Population Division 2016, p. 10).

There are also challenges at the analysis level, due to the lack of funding, capacity and expertise of a large number of states in being unable to undertake meaningful analysis of the collected data (Laczko 2015, p.5). Analysis is naturally affected by the challenges of collection, and results in many outcomes of analysis being presented as estimates. Additional problems arise from the varying and inconsistent definitions, of even the basic terms - who is a migrant, and what is migration - as well as types of migration, geographical areas and other crucial terms. For example, Germany no longer considered anyone who has obtained citizenship as a migrant, while a large number of other countries count as migrants, those that are foreign-born, irrespective of citizenship status (Connor 2013).

As can be seen by the above brief introduction, the challenges of migration are many and varied. They are not, however, insurmountable. The development of ICT, discussed in the section below, and its ability to foster a more robust and responsive provision of administration and services through E-Governance, can be used to improve the experience of the migrants themselves and the host community in which they reside.

Impact of Information and Communication Technologies

Over the last few decades, unprecedented advances in telecommunications technology have, in collapsing vast differences of space and time, made it possible for people around the world to think, work, share, and interact in previously inconceivable ways (Virkar 2015). These so-called new information and communication technologies or ICT have ushered humanity into a highly interconnected world; one in which action is not and cannot be limited by physical boundaries, and where constrained physical spaces have been gradually replaced by a virtual 'cyberspace' that is not subject to traditional rules, hierarchies, or power relations. Popular and academic literature has long been telling us that we live data-driven societies poised, in the midst of the 'Information Age', where both information and technology have become 'symbol(s) of political potency and economic prosperity' (Martin 1998, p. 1).

It is not surprising therefore, that advances in ICT have been, and still are, regarded by many as the impetus behind radical socio-economic and political changes (Virkar 2015). Three fundamental technical reasons set ICT apart from earlier technological counterparts (Gage 2014, p. 4). The first is the *plummeting cost of smart devices*, wherein as a consequence more people are able to access and utilise communications hardware and software. The second is the *expansion of access to the network*, or a growth in the interconnectedness of people and devices giving rise to innovation and efficiency. The third is the *emergence of powerful human-computer interfaces*, allowing for ease-of-use and plug-and-play.

ICT possess many basic characteristics that enable them to play a significant role in the development process. These are *increased and faster access to knowledge* through the gathering and processing of large quantities of data; *increased efficiency and precision* through streamlining workflows and organisational processes, *overcoming geographies* such as physical and temporal boundaries, and *openness* to people and organisations without constraints on number or physical proximity (Virkar 2015, pp. 239-240).

In considering these characteristics of information and communication technologies, questions need to be further asked about their contribution to the creation of economic, social and political capital. In a broad sense, therefore, the significance of ICT may be examined more closely under the broad headings of their *impact on economic growth*, their *impact on social capital and community development*; and their *impact on good governance and the delivery of public services*.

Prior to embarking on the abovementioned categories together with their potential impact on the challenges of migration, it is important to identify the point at which the development of ICT in the area of E-Governance directly meets that of migration. Specifically, the area of border controls.

Smart border control:
The use of ICT in the area of migration policy

One observation that can be made considering the development of migration policies within recent years is that they, like many other government processes, more and more extensively utilise ICT. However, this trend is not only perceived positively, as it is not only seen as an enabler for harmonization as a critical aspect in the context of border security, but also as an economically-related problem. As technology is an inherent and compulsory part of border security, a rapidly-growing market within the European Union for security and surveillance technology has emerged, which is currently under intense discussion between scholars, activists, and journalists, whether this development, the included actors, and the entire ecosystem are ethically and politically acceptable (Baird 2017).

Yet, along the argumentation of Broeders & Hempshire (2013), the core movement of digital transformation in the context of border control is towards the implementation of domestic politics of immigration. It is the logical consequence of governments to adopt technology to ensure fulfilment of their responsibilities of securing national borders as well as to not only control migration flows but also to provide the required capabilities to also support individuals in the process of entering and leaving a member state. In this regard, current technology is providing the basis for efficient and effective E-Governance (Prins et al. 2011) in the context of migration.

This section is focused on the currently on-going EU research initiatives and projects in the area of border security, in particular, the development and application of smart border control. The main representative in this regard can be found in Automated Border Control (ABC) gates, which are nowadays present throughout numerous airports within the European Union. The main goal behind the installation of these ABC gates is to increase the overall speed at the airport security checkpoints, while at the same time also to increase security by reducing false rejections and to extend automation of the control in general – border control based on a self-service technology (Labati et al. 2015).

The project BODEGA (Proactive Enhancement of Human Performance in Border Control)[1] for example focusses on the increase of efficiency regarding border security, while preserving a high level of traveller satisfaction. In particular, the project investigates changes within the traveller process through border controls via the introduction of ICT-based smart border technologies, such as automated gates and biometric-based self-service control systems. The project therewith tackles an open point of technologies development in the area of border control. BODEGA targets four main stakeholder groups: The first group is represented by *Core Operational stakeholders*, as these are responsible for the operationalization of all relevant tasks associated to border control activities within the EU. The second group is present via *Policy stakeholders*, setting the basis for the border control activities, based on the issued regulations and legal requirements. The third group is comprised out of *Technical stakeholders*, who are working on the task of designing suitable systems for enabling the establishment of automated and ICT-enhanced boarder control systems, as well as to provide ways of integration of legacy systems and existing processes. The final group of stakeholders includes *Societal stakeholders*, who are actually affected by the work of all before-mentioned groups. Examples of these individuals are travellers, industry partners, or – basically – civil society as a whole.

While there is an increasing quality and coverage regarding security checkpoints in, for instance, airports, there still exists a variety of challenges and issues regarding the security of land and seaport checkpoints due to the inherit complexity of migratory movements. The project EFFicient Integrated SECurity Checkpoints (EFFISEC)[2] therefore strives for the provision of high-security equipment in the area of border control, for example, identification and luggage control – especially in vehicles – on both maritime and land-based checkpoints. This ena-

---

[1] http://bodega-project.eu.
[2] http://www.effisec.reading.ac.uk/about.htm.

bles agents at the borders to improve the flow of individuals and vehicles, while still being able to conduct in-depth inspection in an efficient, effective and also ergonomically-improved way – an aspect that is often neglected but strongly influences on-site working conditions. In particular, EFFISEC will push development in four main technical areas, namely, identity check, detection of illicit substances, video surveillance and secured communications.

Based on the lessons learned so far, harmonization of existing technologies and processes is key to achieving a sustainable environment regarding border security, especially in the areas of electronic passports, biometrics, the technical and functional design of gates as such, together with the interfaces for the acting border agents. The ABC4EU[3] project therefore tackles the open challenge of harmonization of e-passports, with a special focus on individuals from third countries. The project strives to integrate new technologies in the field of anti-spoofing, including biometric facial markers and fingerprints, as well as the possibility to fuse this information with the addition of biometric features. In addition to the improved e-passport, the project seeks to develop mobile handheld solutions of identity control for application scenarios such as trains and buses. The Intelligent Portable Control System (iBorderCtrl) project[4] also pushes towards this direction, yet with a special focus on land border crossing points such as roads, walkways, or train stations.

Developments in the area of border control – irrespective of whether it is implemented to stop irregular arrivals, facilitate a smoother experience for regular migrants, or enhance the data collection capabilities of governments – are intrinsically linked to advances in ICT. Other areas impacted by the growing availability, sophistication and use of ICT, such as economic growth, social capital and community development, and good governance and delivery of public services, are discussed in the following section, together with their applicability in fostering socio-economic and cultural integration as well as improved collection, sharing and analysis of migration data.

Impact of ICT on Economic Growth

Economic data and anecdotal evidence suggest that the economic growth and development of countries worldwide are increasingly being influenced by the availability of telecommunications hardware and informatics infrastructure, and that the economic benefits that ICT can bring to national economies are manifold (Andrianaivo and Kpodar 2011, Vu 2011, Katz 2009). The deployment of ICT within constituent firms across a national economy can result in increases of productivity and demand, of employment, of foreign direct investment flows, of supply chain management, and of improved financial service coverage.

---

[3] http://abc4eu.com/project/.
[4] http://www.iborderctrl.eu/.

Widespread use of technology is seen to level the economic playing-field, as large firms lose one of their key innate privileges – the unrestricted access to raw materials, human resources, and resource rich markets worldwide (Virkar 2015). In their study of the impact of ICT on the international business-to-business marketing activities of small- and medium-sized enterprises (SMEs) in Norway and Denmark, Moen et al. (2008) discovered that these enterprises used technology predominantly for market information search and to develop long-term relationships with customers. In both cases, the use of ICT appeared to reduce entry barriers for SMEs through enabling access to information and the development of knowledge (Moen et. al. 2008).

ICT also directly influence employment; both by creating new jobs and by acting as a tool that empowers workers to manipulate data and innovate (Raja et. al. 2013, Datta and Agarwal 2004). Telecommunications infrastructure generates employment across a wide range of sectors and within a variety of professions by aiding in the creation and maintenance of networks of communication (Andrianaivo and Kpodar 2011). Employment, according to Andrianaivo and Kpodar (2011), is also generated through the use of ICT to establish new retailing networks. Further, when taken as tools, ICT empower workers by making labour markets *"more transparent, innovative, and inclusive"* (Raja et. al. 2013, p. 9).

Application to socio-economic integration

Migration is often promoted as a contributing factor to a country's economic growth, especially over the long term (OECD 2014). This is at times conflated with two of the key indicators of socio-economic integration, namely education and employment. This is particularly so as a larger proportion of migrants in the EU are un- or underemployment in the short to medium term. A 2015 report by the OECD and EU has identified that, while a larger proportion of third country nationals (18% compared to 4% of host-country nationals) were under-educated, the migrants with a low level of education faced similar levels of unemployment as the host-country nationals at a comparable education level.

This equivalency is not seen in migrants who had attained higher education qualifications. Highly educated migrants who are least likely to find employment are those who attained their diplomas overseas. While migrants improve their chances of employment by attaining their diplomas in the host country, they are still less likely than their host-country counterparts to find employment or, alternatively, are more likely to be employed in positions requiring lower qualifications (OECD and EU 2015, p. 301).

There are a number of areas where ICT can play a role in improving the socio-economic integration of migrants. For instance, vocational courses have been shown to be instrumental in improving the chances of employment of migrants (OECD and EU 2015, p. 25). These can be in ICT itself or as a way to bridge overseas education and experience with that of the host country. The benefits of

ICT for businesses also translate to migrants, who often start small businesses as an alternative to obtain traditional employment (OECD and EU 2015, p. 118).

Another concern of socio-economic integration is that due to the un- and underemployment of migrants, they are liable to remain in situations of poverty and low socio-economic positions (OECD and EU 2015, p. 161). While ICT can mostly benefit the economic integration of migrants and as a consequence, the economic growth of the host country, it also has the potential of keep migrants from rising to a higher standard of living. This is due to the ease with which remittances are now able to be sent back to the country of origin. While the economy of remittances is beneficial to the migrant's family as well as country of origin, the ease with which, thanks to the developments of ICT, remittances can now be demanded and sent, has meant that migrants are often unable to retain money earnt in order to raise their own standard of living (Hamel 2009, p. 22).

The economic growth of a country, together with the socio-economic integration of migrants, can be facilitated through the developments in ICT and their ability to foster the participation and improved efficiency of individuals and small businesses as well as the development of trade between the country of origin and host nation.

Impact of ICT on Social Capital and Community Development

Information and Communication Technologies have given new powers and new responsibilities to those actors who are fast becoming central to the new electronically networked civil society (Virkar 2015). More specifically, ICT may be used by individuals, governments, and non-profit organisations to tackle social exclusion, a phenomenon defined as *"...a process of marginalisation, whereby citizens do not fully participate, have little access to decision making, and feel unable to take control over decisions affecting their lives"* (Ala-Mutka et al. 2009, p. 97).

The idea of social exclusion, together with the role played by ICT in its alleviation, may be explored from the perspective of individuals and groups in society, and the deployment of ICT to generate social capital. Ala-Mutka et al. (2009) contend that some social groups are more at risk of becoming socially excluded than others; including immigrants and ethnic minorities, disabled and elderly people, women, disadvantaged youth, and people living in poorer areas. Whilst there is general consensus that the use of ICT will have a significant impact on the building of social capital and the development of networks within a society (Norris 2003), there remains considerable disagreement about whether technology will exacerbate isolation through the replacement of face-to-face interactions or foster community building through the creation of channels of communication between people (Ibid., p. 2).

Norris (2003) examines the dual theoretical proposition that increased ICT use is altogether positive for a society, and will contribute to both the *widening* and *deepening* of the experience of community through the building and maintenance of social capital. Evidence from her study on the impact of technology on post-industrial societies suggests that ICT use enables the multiplication of human interactions and information exchange, leading to the establishment and maintenance of social relationships between social groups that already share commonalities and the formation of new ties across diverse social actors creating new channels of interaction (Ibid., p. 6).

Increased technology use also has the potential to mitigate social exclusion by supporting the activities of civil society organisations (or CSOs – charities, non-governmental organisations (NGOs), voluntary groups, citizens associations) involved in catering to the daily life and social needs of marginalised groups (United Nations, 2010). In particular, ICT as tools can be used by CSOs to create awareness about their work, to disseminate and share knowledge widely and rapidly, to improve the collection and management of financial resources, to broaden volunteer participation across borders, and to enhance their transparency and responsiveness (Ibid., pp. 1-2).

Aside from the question of social inclusion, the societal impact of ICT use may be felt in different sectors of the national economy concerned primarily with social development and the promotion of social welfare (Virkar 2015). In education, ICT can be adapted to support the activities of students, educators, and educational institutions in a number of different ways (Punie et.al. 2006); ranging from their use as tools to support traditional teaching methods to their deployment in fully ICT-enabled courses that involve the extensive use of digital tools, platforms and applications (Ibid., p. 9). Punie et al. (2006) argue that while ICT use generally has a positive impact on teaching and learning at both school and university level, the expectation that ICT could in some way revolutionise the education sector has not been fully realised.

Application to cultural integration

Unlike socio-economic and legal/political integration, which can be measured through employment and levels of education or voter participation, cultural integration is difficult to quantify. It is often assessed through surveys questioning a person's perception of discrimination as well as the host-communities' perception of the benefits of immigration (OECD/EU 2015, p. 224).

Nonetheless, ICT developments and their impact on social capital community and development can be used by governments and/or CSOs to facilitate better cultural integration by migrants and acceptance by the host-community (CSES and CoR, 2013, p. 97). This is already being attempted at the CSO level through the facilitation of cultural exchanges through the sharing of food.[5] Social connection can also be achieved through ICT by connecting to same-group social media groups or to groups hosted and participated in by host community nationals.

As mentioned above, ICT's use in educational settings benefits not only socio-economic inclusion through vocational training but also social capital through

---

[5] For example, http://refugeeswelcometodinner.com/.

language training and participation (OECD and EU 2015, p. 22). It is important to take into account that the diversity of migration brings with it a diversity of ICT literacy, often linked to the level of development of the country of origin (Hamel 2009, pp. 4-9). Additionally, it has been shown that even where access and use of the Internet is near universal, there remains a gap in usage between youth of low income families, compared to their middle to high income counterparts. The latter are more likely to use the internet for educational, news and research purposes, while the former have been found to use the online time for social media and online gaming (Hutt 2016). This divide is relevant to note, considering that migrants are more likely to remain in situations of poverty despite being employed.

Taking the above into account, cultural integration can be facilitated through better use of ICT and improved programs by CSOs and governments in the provision not only of education in the use communication technologies, but of beneficial use of those technologies.

Impact of ICT on
Good Governance and the Delivery of Public Services

The notion of 'good governance' has become, in recent years, an important criterion to determine a country's credibility and respect on the international stage (Virkar 2011). Worldwide enthusiasm for ICT, and recognition of the role that these new technologies, platforms, and applications can play in the attainment of institutional efficiency, public transparency and robust democratic accountability, has prompted their widespread adaption and adoption within public institutions. New possibilities for innovating governance have been created and are demanded on the one hand by the increasing complexity of public issues and on the other hand by the growth in data, computational power and social media (Janssen and Wimmer 2015, Wang, Medaglia and Zheng 2017). These new possibilities include for instance improving government services, automated process in non-stop government, and decision support systems for policy-making. This trend is known as E-Governance, defined as "*...the use of ICT by government, civil society and political institutions to engage citizens through dialogue to promote greater participation of citizens in the process of institutional governance*" (Bhatnagar 2003, p. 1).

Broadly speaking, therefore, the new information and communications technologies have the potential to improve institutions and processes of governance. Their increased integration and use might have a significant positive impact in three distinct ways:

Firstly, ICT help *enhance decision-making and the administration of the public good* (Virkar 2015, Michel 2005). Known in scholarly and practitioner circles as *e-Administration*, the application of technology to internal workflow processes within public institutions positively impacts the adopting organisation by streamlining internal processes, reducing administrative costs, speeding up the day-to-day processing of information, and increasing transparency and accountability.

Secondly, ICT *improve the provision of public services to citizens* via multiple electronic interfaces (Virkar 2015, Giritli Nygren 2009). Referred to as *eServices*, such initiatives involve the delivery of public utilities such as water, electricity, and sanitation, and help speed up the allocation of permits and the dispensation of complaints. Projects are further often benchmarked along the dimensions of quality, convenience, and cost. Among the emerging digital technologies that have been adopted in governments' innovative applications are artificial intelligence, smart things, and machine learning (Panetta 2006). Machine learning, for instance, has been applied to improve government services in many ways. Some applications of Chatbots can be used in government to optimize customer service provided by government employees or to facilitate collective intelligence, increasing the possibilities for citizens to engage and interact with data (Turban et al. 2018).

Automated decision-making has also been implemented in government, representing one of the main applications of collaborative governance. Viale Pereira et al. (2017) identified that information sharing and cooperation are the main elements in framing the use of ICT to enable collaborative governance along with participation and engagement practices in decision making. The Automatic Family Allowances (ALF) without Application[6] is a successful no-stop-shop government solution for parents to get family allowances for new-born children automatically. Launched in 2015, this solution has already received several international awards and supports about 80,000 families per year. The solution aims at saving hours for Austrian citizens and reducing the time and cost for the Austrian public administration. This case illustrates how smart governance can be applied by sharing databases among government agencies.

Thirdly, the proliferation and use of ICT in political processes can also *bring a government closer to its people*, altering the relationship between public sectors actors, private sector organisations, third sector bodies, and individual citizens (Virkar 2015, Jayashree and Marthandan, 2010). Falling under the umbrella of *eSociety*, these initiatives focus on allowing for popular access to decision-making and facilitating communication on three levels – citizen to citizen, citizen to government, and government to business.

Application to collection, sharing and analysis of data on migration

There are a number of ways in which E-Governance is helping to address the challenges of migration and, in particular, the management of data, through its collection, sharing and analysis.

For instance, to date, there is a small, but growing number of databases on migration, set up by the UN, OSCE, the World Bank and Eurostat. The IOM and the Economist Intelligence Unit (EIU) are also scheduled to release their Global Migration Data Portal,[7] which has been touted as the *"one-stop-shop ... for migration information, data ... and analysis"* (Laczko 2015, p. 12). However, the success of

---

[6] https://english.bmf.gv.at/e-government/projects/alf.html.
[7] https://gmdac.iom.int/global-migration-data-portal.

global migration databases depends on the information provided to them primarily by governments and organisations such as the United Nations High Commissioner for Refugees (UNHCR). While steps are being taken to standardise the collected data, and have at minimum aggregation according to age, sex, origin and destination (Laczko 2015, p. 5), it is the progress of ICT and E-Governance that encompasses user participation and shared databases, that has the potential to make migration data accurate, consistent and timely.

Decision support systems for policy-making include the use of techniques such as scenario simulation, visualization and mega-modelling. Open data and social media have been also recognized in literature by its great potential for government to, among other things, promote democratization of public policy making (Höchtl, Parycek and Schöllhammer 2016; Höchtl, Schossböck, Lampoltshammer and Parycek 2017). An example of decision support tools is the SmartGov project, which aims to create simulation of real world scenarios by exploiting the potential of social media feedback and open data to support smart cities decision making (Goraczek et al. 2016).

An example of multi-benefit partnership between E-Governance and data management can be seen with the implementation of the Finish government's distribution of a pre-paid mastercard (or debit card) to asylum seekers and refugees. Using distributed ledger technology (otherwise termed blockchain technology that has been successfully utilised by bitcoin), the method overcomes a number of challenges. Primarily, the use of the card is a textbook example of E-Governance through the provision of improved administration and services. Additionally, the use of the card and its associated technology allows asylum seekers and refugees to re-establish their identities, which then allows for their faster integration into the labour market. This is especially so, as the card permits for deposits not only by the Finish government but also by potential employers (Orcutt 2017).

This technology has the potential for broader application, especially as it fosters faster integration into the banking system. A version of this technology and its implementation can be of benefit to migrants in general, who are often excluded from banking services (OECD and EU 2015, p. 161). In fact, the system is being looked at for implementation across the European Parliament (European Parliament, Committee on Economic and Monetary Affairs 2017) and by the United Nations (Irrera 2017), targeting not only asylum seekers and refugees and their faster integration into the labour market, but also people of developing countries. The ability of the card to help establish a financial identity can be seen as a step forward towards improved chances of regular migration.

Finally, the card also addresses a number of issues of data management. Primarily, it overcomes one of the key challenges of data collection, being the sharing of information between the private sector and government departments. This is due to the fact that implementation of the reception allowance card is a result of a partnership between the Finish government and a private company that designed the system (Ibid.).

Conclusions

The development of information and communication technologies has impacted significantly on all areas of life. These areas have broadly been defined as economic growth, social capital and community development, and good governance and the delivery of public services (or E-Governance). Interlinked with these broad areas is the role of ICT as not only the driver of migration but also the facilitator of governments' migration management policies.

Due to the contentious nature of migration and the emerging tensions as a result of the 2015 migration crisis of irregularly arriving asylum seekers, refugees and migrants, together with the expansion of EU member states, countries in the European Union face a myriad of challenges. A few of these challenges have been identified in this chapter for discussion. Namely, these are border control, socio-economic integration, cultural integration and data management through the accurate, consistent and timely collection, sharing and analysis of data.

While the impact of ICT on the broader areas of economic growth, social capital and E-Governance can only be discussed in generality before narrowing down their application to the challenges of migration, the interaction of ICT and border control implementation by governments can only be discussed as a single topic. In particular, while it must be acknowledged that the primary use of border controls is stopping irregular arrivals, advances in and implementation of technologies and smart border controls such as BODEGA, EFFISEC and ABC4EU, also work toward automating and enhancing the border experiences of regular migration.

With regard to the impact of ICT on economic growth, it has been shown that it facilitates efficiency and productivity in employment, greater entrance and competition opportunities in small businesses through improved access to information, as well as facilitation of exchange of goods and services. The impact of ICT on economic growth is directly applicable to the issues of migration and in particular to the challenge of socio-economic integration. This is particularly so as migration has been shown to benefit the economic growth of the host nation in the long term.

Nonetheless, more can be done to assist migrant populations to integrate into the labour market, where they are currently un- or underemployed. Those particularly affected are migrants with a higher education, whose qualifications are not transferrable or recognized in the host country. Language and vocational courses have been shown to make a marked difference towards increasing labour participation of highly educated migrants.

It is also important to note that while it has been shown that ICT can bring benefits to the economic growth of a country (and, reciprocally, the country of origin), it can also perpetuate continuing poverty of migrants through the sending of remittances to maintain and assist their family in the country of origin.

The impact of ICT on social capital and community development has also been profound, with increased potential to tackle social exclusion as well as bring civil society organisations and their efforts to the forefront of the social consciousness. This is particularly applicable to the cultural integration of migrants, through cultural exchange programs with host-country nationals. The use of ICT itself by migrants, although varied depending on the economic development of the country of origin, needs to be addressed through education. This is particularly so as many migrants remain in poverty situations despite being employed. It has been shown that low socio-economic status has an effect on the manner in which ICT is used. It is therefore necessary not only to provide programs that educate in the use of ICT but in a more beneficial use of ICT.

Finally, the impact on E-Governance has been particularly pronounced, with a myriad of applications, from streamlining processes, to machine learning and automated decision-making. More sophisticated developments in data processing through scenario simulation and mega-modelling is facilitating the improvement of the collection, sharing and analysis of migration data that in turn informs relevant policy decisions that are also applicable to migration.

An example of E-Governance in action that also improves the collection, sharing and analysis of data has been seen in the implementation by the Finish government of a pre-paid mastercard for receipt of financial benefits and, where applicable, wages at refugee reception centres. The card, using distributed ledger technology, creates a financial identity for the refugee and accelerates their entry into the labour market and banking system. This technology has applications beyond the receipt of refugee allowances, with potential benefits for migrants that lag behind host-country nationals in their participation in the banking system. The technology also allows for data sharing between the private company implementing the cards and permits the government to analyse the data for improved provision of services.

It is therefore clear that the connection between the impacts of ICT and their application to the challenges of migration is of great interest and in need of further research and development.

References

Ala-Mutka, Kirsti / Broster, David / Cachia, Romina / Centeno, Clara / Feijoo, Claudio / Haché, Alexandra / Kluzer, Stefano / Lindmark, Stefano / Lusoli, Wainer / Misuraca, Gianluca / Pascu, Corina / Punie, Yves and Valverde, José A. (2009) The Impact of Social Computing on the EU Information Society and Economy. (European Commission Institute for Prospective Technological Studies, Scientific and Technical Reports).

Andrianaivo, Mihasonirina / Kpodar, Kangni R. (2011) ICT, Financial Inclusion, and Growth: Evidence from African Countries. (IMF Working Paper WP/11/73, International Monetary Fund).

Baird, Theodore (2017) Interest groups and strategic constructivism: business actors and border security policies in the European Union. In: Journal of Ethnic and Migration Studies, 1-19.

Bhatnagar, Subhash (2003) Transparency and Corruption: Does E-Government Help? Draft paper for the compilation of the Commonwealth Human Rights Initiative 2003 Report 'Open Sesame: looking for the Right to Information in the Commonwealth'.

Broeders, Dennis / Hampshire, James (2013) Dreaming of seamless borders: ICTs and the pre-emptive governance of mobility in Europe. In: Journal of Ethnic and Migration Studies 39(8), 1201-1218.

Centre for Strategy and Evaluation Services (CSES) / Committee of the Regions (CoR) (2013) Study on Practices of Integration of Third-Country Nationals at Local and Regional Level in the European Union.

Connor, Phillip (2013) 5 challenges to estimating global migration. In: Pew Research Center, 25 October 2013.

Datta, Anusua / Agarwal, Sumit, S (2004) Telecommunications and economic growth: a panel data approach. In: Applied Economics 36(15), 1649-1654.

European Commission (2016) Horizon 2020: 13. Europe in a changing world – inclusive, innovative and reflective Societies. Work Programme 2016-2017 (European Commission Decision C (2017)2468 of 24 April 2017).

European Commission (2016) Proposal for a regulation of the European parliament and of the council establishing an entry/exit system (EES) to register entry and exit data and refusal of entry data of third country nationals crossing the external borders of the member states of the European union and determining the conditions for access to the EES for law enforcement purposes and amending regulation (EC) No 767/2008 and regulation (EU) No 1077/2011 (European Commission, Brussels).

European Parliament, Committee on Economic and Monetary Affairs, 'Budget Amendments', (European Parliament, 2017/2044, 29 August 2017)

Giritli Nygren, Katarina (2009) e-Governmentality: on Electronic Administration in Local Government. In: Electronic Journal of e- Government 7(1), 55 – 64.

Goraczek, Malgorzata / Pereira, Gabriela Viale / Falco, Enzo / Kleinhans, Reinout / Parycek, Peter (2016) Using Fuzzy Cognitive Maps as Decision Support Tool for Smart Cities. In: CeDEM Asia, 81.

Hamel, Jean-Yves (2009) Information and Communication Technologies and Migration, (United Nations Development Programme Human Development Reports Research Paper, 2009/39 August 2009).

Höchtl, Johann / Parycek, Peter / Schöllhammer, Ralph (2016) Big data in the policy cycle: Policy decision making in the digital era. In: Journal of Organizational Computing and Electronic Commerce 26(1-2), 147-169.

Höchtl, Johann / Schossböck, Judith / Lampoltshammer, Thomas J. / Parycek, Peter (2017) The Citizen Scientist in the ePolicy Cycle. In: Government 3.0 - Next Generation Government Technology Infrastructure and Services (Springer International Publishing), 37-62.

Hutt, Rosamond (2016) Rich and poor teenagers use the web differently – here's what this is doing to inequality. In: World Economic Forum, 27 July 2016.

Irrera, Anna (2017) Accenture, Microsoft team up on blockchain-based digital ID network. In: Reuters, 19 June 2017.

Janssen, Marijn / Wimmer, Maria A. (2015) Introduction to Policy-Making in the Digital Age. In: Policy Practice and Digital Science (Springer International Publishing), 1-14.

Jayashree, Sreenivasan / Marthandan, Govindan (2010) Government to E-Government to E-Society. In: Journal of Applied Sciences(Faisalabad) 10(19), 2205-2210.

Katz, Raul L. (2009). The economic and social impact of telecommunications output. In: Intereconomics 44(1), 41-48.

Labati, Ruggero Donida / Genovese, Angelo / Munoz, Enrique / Piuri, Vincenzo / Scotti, Fabio / Sforza, Gianluca (2015, September) Advanced design of automated border control gates: biometric system techniques and research trends. In: In Systems Engineering (ISSE), 412-419 (2015 IEEE International Symposium on)

Laczko, Frank (2015) Improving Data on International Migration and Development: Towards a Global Action Plan?. Discussion Paper (IOM Global Migration Data Analysis Centre).

Lehtonen, Pinja /Aalto, Pami (2017) Smart and secure borders through automated border control systems in the EU? The views of political stakeholders in the Member States. In: European Security, 1-19.

Majchrzak, Ann / Markus, M. Lynne / Wareham, Jonathan (2016) Designing for Digital Transformation: Lessons for Information Systems Research from the Study of ICT and Societal Challenges. In: MIS Quarterly 40(2), 267-277.

Majchrzak, Ann / Markus, M. Lynne / Wareham, Jonathan D. (2012) ICT and societal challenges. In: MISQ special issue call for papers.

Martin, William J. (1998) The Information Society. (Aslib Press, London).

Michel, Helene (2005) e-Administration, e-Government, e-Governance and the Learning City: A typology of Citizenship management using ICTs. In: Electronic Journal of e-Government 3(4), 213-218.

Moen, Øystein / Koed Madsen, Tage / Aspelund, Arild (2008) The importance of the internet in international business-to-business markets. In: International Marketing Review 25(5), 487-503.

Norris, Pippa (2003) Social Capital and ICTs: Widening or Reinforcing Social Networks? Paper presented at the International Forum on Social Capital for Economic Revival held by the Economic and Social Research Institute (Cabinet Office, Japan in Tokyo, 24-25 March 2003).

OECD (2014 May) Is migration good for the economy? In: Migration Policy Debates.

OECD (2015) Emerging issues: The Internet of Things. In: OECD Digital Economy Outlook (OECD Publishing, Paris).

Orcutt, Mike (2017) How Blockchain Is Kickstarting the Financial Lives of Refugees: Finland's digital money system for asylum seekers shows what blockchain technology can offer the unbanked. In: MIT Financial Review, 5 September 2017.

Panetta, Kasey (2016) Gartner's Top 10 Strategic Technology Trends for 2017. In: Gartner, 18 October 2016.

Prins, Corien / Broeders, Dennis / Griffioen, Henk / Keizer, Anne-Greet / Keymolen, Esther (2011) iGovernment. (Amsterdam University Press).

Punie, Yves / Zinnbauer, Dieter / Cabrera, Marcelino (2006 October) A Review of the Impact of ICT on Learning. In: JRC Technical Notes, Working Paper prepared for the European Commission DG EAC.

Raja, Siddhartha / Imaizumi, Saori / Kelly, Tim / Narimatsu, Junko / Paradi-Guilford, Cecilia (2013) Connecting to Work: How information and communication technologies could help expand employment opportunities. (Report – ICT Sector Unit, The World Bank).

Turban, Efraim / Outland, Jon / King, David / Lee, Jae Kyu / Liang, Ting-Peng / Turban Deborrah C. (2018) Innovative EC Systems: From E-Government to E-Learning, E-Health, Sharing Economy, and P2P Commerce. In: Electronic Commerce (Springer Texts in Business and Economics, Springer, Cham).

UN (2010) Why are ICTs important for Civil Society Organizations? In: Position Paper [full citation not available]. Available at: http://www.un.org/esa/socdev/ngo/docs/2010/directory/ictcso.pdf (Accessed on: 17th October 2017).

UN Department of Economic and Social Affairs (2016) Cooperation on Migration Statistics in the UNECE region, Presented at the Inter-regional workshop on collecting and using migration-related data for development: Cooperation and exchange in the European-African corridor (Population Division, Rome, Italy, 30 November - 2 December 2016).

UN Department of Economic and Social Affairs (2017 March) Handbook on Measuring International Migration through Population Censuses. (Statistics Division).

UN Department of Economic and Social Development (2016) Inter-regional workshop on collecting and using migration-related data for development: Cooperation and exchange in the European-African corridor. (Population Division, Rome, Italy, 30 November - 2 December 2016).

UN General Assembly (2015) Transforming our world: the 2030 Agenda for Sustainable Development. (A/RES/70/1, 21 October 2015).

Viale Pereira, Gabriela / Cunha, Maria Alexandra / Lampoltshammer, Thomas J. / Parycek, Peter / Testa, Maurício Gregianin (2017) Increasing collaboration and participation in smart city governance: a cross-case analysis of smart city initiatives. In: Information Technology for Development, 1-28.

Virkar, Shefali (2011) Information and Communication Technologies in Administrative Reform for Development: Exploring the Case of Property Tax Systems in Karnataka, India. In: Steyn, Jacques and Fahey, S. (eds.) ICTs and Sustainable Solutions for Global Development: Theory, Practice, and the Digital Divide – Volume 2 (IGI Global Inc., Hershey, P.A, 127-149).

Virkar, Shefali (2015) The Politics of Access to Information: Exploring the Development of Software Platforms and Communications Hardware in the Digital Age. In: Zaman, Noor / Elhassan Seliaman, Mohamed / Fadzil Hassan, Mohd / Garcia Marquez, Fausto Pedro (eds.) Handbook of Research on Trends and Future Directions in Big Data and Web Intelligence (IGI Global Inc., Hershey, P.A., 233-265).

Vu, Khuong M. (2011) ICT as a source of economic growth in the information age: Empirical evidence from the 1996–2005 period. In: Telecommunications Policy 35(4), 357-372.

Walsham, Geoff / Sahay, Sundeep (2006) Research on information systems in developing countries: Current landscape and future prospects. Information Technology for Development, 12(1), 7-24.

Wang, Cancan / Medaglia, Rony / Zheng, Lei (2017) Towards a typology of adaptive governance in the digital government context: The role of decision-making and accountability. In: Government Information Quarterly.

Warrell, Helen / Smith, Alan / Fray, Keith (2016) Five reasons to question UK immigration figures: Main measure statisticians use was not designed for the job. In: Financial Review, 30 November 2016.

‚Jemand hat Migrationshintergrund' oder ‚Jemand hat *einen* Migrationshintergrund'? Eine zuschreibungskritisch-linguistische Reflexion

İnci Dirim

Zusammenfassung

Die gesellschaftliche Ausdifferenzierung von rechtlichen und symbolischen Zugehörigkeiten spiegelt sich in Bezeichnungsversuchen bzw. in einem Ringen um Bedeutung in der Bezeichnung von Menschen wider, da jede Bezeichnung auch eine symbolische Zuweisung der Bezeichneten an einen mehr oder weniger privilegierten Ort bedeutet. Bezeichnungen drücken in einem politisch umkämpften Feld auch Haltungen darüber aus, an welchen Ort die Bezeichneten gehören sollten. Im Zusammenhang mit Migration ist die Bezeichnung ‚Xy hat einen Migrationshintergrund' breit etabliert. Allerdings kann man in den letzten Jahren immer häufiger hören oder lesen, dass die Akkusativmarkierung ‚einen' zugunsten des Null-Artikels aufgegeben wird. Die vorliegende Kurzreflexion beschäftigt sich mit der Frage, welchen symbolischen Unterschied es macht, wenn die eine oder andere dieser Bezeichnungen gewählt wird.

Einleitung

„Beinahe ein Fünftel aller in Österreich lebenden Menschen (rund 1,5 Millionen, 17,8%) sowie beinahe jedes vierte Volksschulkind (23,2%) haben Migrationshintergrund" (ORF, o.J.) kann in einer Online-Information des Österreichischen Rundfunks (ORF) zum ‚Österreichischen Integrationspreis' gelesen werden. Die Medien-Servicestelle ‚Neue ÖsterreicherInnen' titelt auf ihrer Homepage: *„In Wien hat jede/r zweite Migrationshintergrund"* (Medienservicestelle 2014).

Nach meiner Beobachtung wird in letzter Zeit häufig anstelle des Ausdrucks ‚einen Migrationshintergrund haben' der Ausdruck ‚Migrationshintergrund haben' verwendet, wie es in den obigen Zitaten der Fall ist. Die beiden Zitate entstammen Internetseiten, in denen wichtige Informationen zu verschiedenen Migrationsphänomenen in Österreich bereitgestellt werden. In den Medien ORF und Medienservicestelle, aus denen die Beispiele stammen, werden, so meine Annahme, die Worte mit Bedacht gewählt – handelt es sich doch um sogenannte ‚Qualitätsmedien' und es geht in den Darstellungen darum, sachliche und konstruktive Informationen zu Themen rund um Migration zu liefern. Auch in diesen Medien wird die Ausdrucksweise einen ‚Migrationshintergrund haben' verwendet, wobei an keiner Stelle der Seiten dieser Medien und auch nicht in anderen Texten eine Erklärung dafür zu finden ist, warum aus dem Akkusativobjekt ‚einen Migrationshintergrund' ein Objekt mit Nullartikel ‚geworden' ist. Ziel des vorliegenden Beitrags ist es, zu eruieren, was der Bedeutungsunterschied zwischen beiden Formulierungen sein könnte und inwiefern es sich bei der neuen Bezeichnung um eine andere oder gar ‚bessere' als die alte handelt. Es geht nicht um eine Kritik der zitierten Medien – die diskutierte neue Ausdrucksweise findet sich in vielen anderen Texten – die Zitate dienen nur der empirischen Veranschaulichung. Die Analyse beider Formulierungen wird – nach einer Reflexion der Bezeichnung ‚Migrationshintergrund' – zunächst aus einer linguistischen Perspektive vorgenommen. Anschließend wird der analysierte Unterschied theoretisiert.

Zum Begriff ‚Migrationshintergrund'

Mit der Diskussion des Unterschieds zwischen den Bezeichnungen ‚einen Migrationshintergrund haben' und ‚Migrationshintergrund haben' soll nicht der Eindruck erweckt werden, dass einer der beiden Begriffe die ideale Bezeichnung für Menschen darstellt, die oder deren Vorfahren bzw. ein Teil derer nach Österreich bzw. in einen anderen Staat eingewandert sind, in dem Deutsch die (wichtigste) bzw. eine der Amtssprachen darstellt, und in denen diese Formulierungen verwendet werden. Der Begriff ‚Migrationshintergrund' ermöglicht zwar eine Bezeichnung, die zuweilen auch hilfreich sein mag. Zugleich drückt sich aber über den Begriff die Vorstellung einer ‚Halbzugehörigkeit' aus und er kann als verletzender Begriff verstanden werden, wie aus den folgenden Worten hervorgeht:

> *"Ein wenig später sprach man von Menschen mit Migrationshintergrund, um einen Namen für Menschen wie mich zu haben. (...) Das befanden dann auch Wissenschaftler, Politiker, Öffentlichkeitsmacher für politisch korrekt, und der Begriff blieb, bis er wie eine ansteckende Krankheit um sich griff, sich verbreitete wie ein Virus. (...) Aus verschiedenen Ländern, verschiedenen Kulturkreisen stammend, unterschiedliche Geschichten und Vergangenheiten mitbringend, unterschiedliche Wert- und Lebensvorstellungen, unterschiedliche Religionen und Bräuche, Sprachen erst recht, und der einzige gemeinsame Nenner: ach ja, der Migrationshintergrund! (...) Eine schöne Botschaft, die da mit diesem politisch korrekten Begriff versendet wird: Du bist hier geboren, du kennst – abgesehen von Urlaubserfahrungen – kein anderes Land, aber einer von uns bist du dennoch nicht. Nee, du hast da was. Was in deiner Biographie oder vielmehr der deiner Eltern. Einen Migrationshintergrund. Oder fällt jemandem spontan ein Satz ein, in dem Migrationshintergrund wie etwas Wünschenswertes, etwas Beneidenswertes klingt? [...] Ein Begriff, der auf eine so extreme Weise pauschalisiert, ist eine Erniedrigung. Was man daran sieht, dass ich*

noch nie jemanden mit Migrationshintergrund kennengelernt habe (Sie etwa?), der sich selbst so beschrieben hätte: ‚Hi, freut mich dich kennenzulernen! Ich bin Abdullah, ich habe einen Migrationshintergrund'" (Gorelik 2012, S. 33).

‚Harmlos' ist der Begriff ‚Migrationshintergrund' somit nicht, auch wenn er mit positiven Absichten verwendet wird. Marianne Krüger-Potratz weist mit Blick auf die gesellschaftliche Situation darauf hin, dass dieser Begriff eine Reaktion auf die *„zunehmende Ausdifferenzierung der Gruppe derjenigen darstellt, die in der Statistik unter ‚deutsch' firmieren"* (Krüger-Potratz 2009, S. 200). Das gilt etwa auch für den Begriff ‚Aussiedler'. Zugleich warnt sie vor dem Eindruck, dass mit dem Begriff ‚Migrationshintergrund' ein weniger stereotyper und ausgrenzender Sprachgebrauch oder gar eine solche Anschauung einhergeht:

„Aber es wäre eine Überbewertung, wenn man von einer veränderten Sprache und Begrifflichkeit in einzelnen Texten direkt auf ein verändertes Bewusstsein schließen würde. Generell und über die Zeit hinweg ist die Sprache der Presse und Politik quer durch die Lager zwar variantenreicher geworden, aber dies verhindert nicht, dass – insbesondere in Wahlkampfzeiten oder anlässlich politischer Krisen – auch mit dem neuen Vokabular die alten Stereotypen bedient werden" (a.a.O., S. 201).

Diese Annahme wird von Krüger-Potratz auch mit zahlreichen Zitaten aus Pressetexten belegt (a.a.O., S. 201).

Der Begriff ‚Migrationshintergrund' erscheint auf der einen Seite hilfreich, wenn es um die Erfassung systematischer Schlechterstellungen geht, auch wenn der Begriff unterschiedlich definiert wird und recht schwammig ist (vgl. Mecheril 2010). Das betrifft etwa die Schwächen der monolingualen Bildungssysteme im Hinblick auf den Umgang mit migrationsbedingter Pluralität, deren Diagnose u.a. über die Operationalisierung mit diesem Begriff einhergeht. Zudem eröffnet der Begriff die Möglichkeit der Differenzierung in verschiedenen Handlungsfeldern. Auf der anderen Seite werden mit ihm Menschen auf eine Herkunft, die Nicht-Zugehörigkeit markiert, festgelegt. Dirim und Mecheril machen zudem darauf aufmerksam, dass der Begriff Ausdruck einer binären Differenzordnung darstellt, die mit Oppositionen wie ‚Mann' und ‚Frau', ‚behindert' und ‚nicht behindert' operiert: *„Machtvoller Effekt binärer Ordnungen ist, dass ein enger Zwang zur Eindeutigkeit besteht, der zugleich solche Identitätspositionen abwertet, die sich der Eindeutigkeit entziehen"* (Dirim und Mecheril 2017, S. 42).

Analyse

Macht es einen Unterschied, wenn statt ‚einen Migrationshintergrund' das Attribut ‚Migrationshintergrund' verwendet wird? Die genaue Betrachtung seiner syntaktischen Struktur und deren semantischen Gehalts ermöglicht eine Annäherung an die symbolische Bedeutung des Unterschieds zwischen ‚Xy hat einen Migrationshintergrund' und ‚Xy hat Migrationshintergrund'.

Grundsätzlich lässt sich feststellen, dass mit beiden Äußerungen ein Besitzverhältnis angezeigt wird: jemand ‚hat' (einen) Migrationshintergrund und das Objekt ‚Migrationshintergrund', also der ‚Besitz' wird mit dem Akkusativartikel ‚einen' oder dem Nullartikel gekennzeichnet. Das Akkusativobjekt ermöglicht den Ausdruck eines nicht näher gekennzeichneten Besitzes, im Sinne von ‚irgendeinen' Migrationshintergrund. Soll dieser Hintergrund genauer gekennzeichnet werden, kommt der bestimmte Artikel im Akkusativ und ein dem Objekt nachgestelltes Attribut ins Spiel, z.B. ‚Xy hat den Migrationshintergrund Spanien'. Laut Duden drückt die Verwendung des Verbs ‚haben' allerdings nicht nur aus, dass jemand etwas ‚besitzt', sondern auch, *„dass etwas, ein bestimmter Sachverhalt o.Ä.* [für jemanden] *besteht, existiert"* (Duden online, o.J.). Diese Erklärung scheint mir das mit den beiden angeführten Konstruktionen Ausgedrückte treffend zu beschreiben.

Wird nun das Objekt ‚Migrationshintergrund' mit einem Nullartikel gekennzeichnet, kommt eine besondere Bedeutungskonnotation zu Stande: Nach den Regeln der Verwendung des ‚Null-Artikels' im Deutschen entsteht damit eine starre Zusammenfügung, also eine feste Wendung, ähnlich wie eine Redewendung (vgl. Hoffmann 2013, S. 137). Das heißt, dass der Unterschied zwischen dem Ausdruck ‚jemand hat einen Migrationshintergrund' und ‚jemand hat Migrationshintergrund' darin besteht, dass mit dem letzteren der beiden Ausdrücke ein Besitz benannt wird, mit dem man ‚verschmolzen' ist, den man nicht mehr loswird.

Fazit: Die Gefahr der Naturalisierung

Mit der Nullartikelmarkierung in dem Satz ‚Xy hat (einen) Migrationshintergrund' wird eine ‚Amalgamierung' zwischen einem Subjekt und dem sogenannten Migrationshintergrund erzeugt. Damit wird der Migrationshintergrund symbolisch naturalisiert. Das Wissen um den Umstand, dass er ein soziales Konstrukt, ‚eine Erfindung' ist, droht gänzlich in den Hintergrund zu geraten. Vielleicht ist die Ausdrucksweise ‚Xy hat Migrationshintergrund' aber auch gerade ein Ergebnis dessen, dass der Migrationshintergrund immer mehr normalisiert wird und nun die Naturalisierung ‚an der Reihe' ist. Beides, sowohl die Wahrscheinlichkeit, dass der Null-Artikel in der diskutierten Wendung das Ergebnis einer naturalisierenden Normalisierung sein könnte oder die Markierung des Beginns dieser Wahrnehmung, ist problematisch, weil damit Subjekte als mit dieser Konstruktion des ‚Hintergrunds' verschmolzen angesehen werden. Damit findet eine symbolische Fixierung an einer inferioren gesellschaftlichen Hierarchieebene statt. Dieser Fall zeigt, dass es dringend notwendig ist, immer wenn der Begriff ‚Migrationshintergrund' verwendet wird, zu überlegen und zu entscheiden, ob dies wirklich unerlässlich ist und ihn ggf. nicht zu verwenden. Außerdem stellt die identifizierte Problematik klar, dass es stets wichtig ist, Bezeichnungen für Menschen zu reflektieren, zu relativieren, zu erneuern, damit inferior markierende Bezeichnungspraxen reduziert werden.

Literatur

Dirim, İnci / Mecheril, Paul (2017) Heterogenitätsdiskurse. Einführung in eine machtkritische und kulturwissenschaftliche Perspektive. In: Dirim, İnci / Mecheril, Paul u.a.: Heterogenität, Sprache(n) und Bildung. (utb Stuttgart), 21-29.

Duden online (o.J.), haben. Abrufbar unter: http://www.duden.de/rechtschreibung/haben_besitzen_auf weisen_erhalten#Bedeutung1d

Gorelik, Lena (2012) "Sie können aber gut Deutsch!". Warum ich nicht mehr dankbar sein will, dass ich hier leben darf, und Toleranz nicht weiterhilft. (Pantheon, München).

Hoffmann, Ludger (2013) Deutsche Grammatik. Grundlagen für Lehrerausbildung, Schule, Deutsch als Zweitsprache und deutsch als Fremdsprache. (Erich Schmidt, Berlin).

Krüger-Potratz, Marianne (2005) Interkulturelle Bildung. Eine Einführung. (Waxmann, Münster).

Medienservicestelle (2014) Wien: Hälfte der Bevölkerung hat Migrationshintergrund. Abrufbar unter: http://medienservicestelle.at/migration_bewegt/2014/11/13/wien-haelfte-der-bevoelkerung-hat-migrationshintergrund/

ORF (o.J.) Österreichischer Integrationspreis. Abrufbar unter http://integrationspreis.orf.at/show_content.php?hid=8

Wenn die Hüllen fallen:
Ein Essay zum Verhältnis von
Geschlecht und Macht in Orient und Okzident

Aga Trnka-Kwiecinski

Der Körper dient mehr denn je als Projektionsfläche für Kultur. Die Massenmedien reduzieren Inhalte und Botschaften auf wenige Worte aber noch viel mehr auf Bilder. Somit ist es nicht verwunderlich, dass auch Wertediskussionen und gesellschaftliche Diskurse auf Körper projiziert werden und auf diesen verhandelt werden. Daher lohnt es sich, einen genaueren Blick auf Aspekte zu werfen, die genau das offenbaren: Frauenkörper unterliegen einer zunehmenden Sexualisierung und noch viel mehr einer Pornographisierung. Die Entscheidungsgewalt darüber, ob und welche Form von Enthüllung und Verhüllung des weiblichen Körpers gesellschaftlich akzeptabel und ideologisch, moralisch, religiös vertretbar ist, liegt meist nicht bei Frauen. Und letztlich führen durchaus unterschiedliche Entwicklungen in unterschiedlichen Gesellschaften zu ähnlichen Schlussfolgerungen – die Trends einer Refolklorisierung und das Machtmonopol männlich dominierter Diskurse mögen jeweils anders aussehen, aber letztlich ist ihnen allen mehr gemein als auf den ersten Blick sichtbar ist.

„Die Werte sind tot, es leben die Werte." So in etwa ließe sich die immer wieder aufbrandende Diskussion um abendländische Werte zusammenfassen. Je mehr man sie in Gefahr glaubt, desto lieber hält man an ihnen fest, auch wenn sie bisweilen fast völlig in Vergessenheit geraten sind. Kaum wähnt man eine Bedrohung von außen, gilt es sie zu schützen – und sei es mit seinem Leben. Und während aktuell in Österreich die Debatte um das Anti-Gesichtsverhüllungsgesetz, das mit 1. Oktober 2017 in Kraft getreten ist, eher skurrile Züge annimmt, weil maskierte Maskottchen (etwa das Parlamentsmaskottchen) und Frauen in Winterschals für öffentliche Aufregung gesorgt haben, steckt dahinter sehr viel mehr, als die Frage, wie viel Stoff ein Gesicht tatsächlich verhüllen soll. Die Frage der Verhüllung des weiblichen Körpers ist immer auch eine Frage der Machtverteilung. Wie viel Stoff akzeptabel ist, wird dabei meist von Männern entschieden. Dabei spannt sich der Bogen in der medialen Berichterstattung von Berichten über Frauen, die nicht im Burkini am Strand von Südfrankreich sitzen dürfen, (vgl. fin, ZEIT online 2016) bzw. gibt es im Volleyball-Sport eine Debatte darüber, wie knapp die Höschen der vorwiegend weiblichen Spielerinnen sein dürfen, (vgl. fivb 2004, S. 4 & 8) vermutlich damit noch alle Sponsorenlogos Platz darauf finden, und sie immer noch sexy genug anzuschauen sind. Doch diese Diskussion hat nicht erst 2017 begonnen.

Gesellschaftliche und historische Rahmenbedingungen

Mit dem Fall des Eisernen Vorhanges, so schien es, ist den westlichen Nationen über Nacht ein wichtiges Feindbild geradezu schlagartig abhanden gekommen. Der Kommunismus war unliebsame Geschichte, aber jedenfalls zunehmend Vergangenheit, und nach ein paar Jahren, in denen der Westen den Osten dabei beobachtete, wie er den Kapitalismus in Windeseile implementierte, und sogar einen regelrechten Turbokapitalismus kreierte, zeigte sich spätestens mit dem Attentat auf das US-amerikanische World Trade Center, dass mit einem Ereignis, das als 9/11 in die Geschichte einging, ein neues Kapitel aufgeschlagen wurde. Der neue Feind war zwar prinzipiell fern, aber er griff den Westen dort an, wo es am meisten schmerzte: Vor der eigenen Haustüre. Spätestens als am 11. September 2001 Selbstmordattentäter der Al-Quaida aus einem Anschlag mit mehreren Flugzeugen auf Ziele in den USA einen Akt größtmöglicher Symbolik gemacht haben, begann der so genannte „Krieg gegen den Terror". Aber eigentlich haben die westlichen Medien massiv dazu beigetragen, als die Bilder der herabstürzenden Türme und der in den Tod fallenden Menschen tagelang in Endlosschleifen die Fernsehsender der Welt dominierten, und damit die Symbolik des stürzenden Kapitalismus durch die Hand weniger Terroristen nachhaltig zementierten. So wie der Fall der Berliner Mauer das Symbol für den Fall des Eisernen Vorhangs wurde, kann der Einsturz der *„Ikone des selbstbewußten Kapitalismus"* (Emcke 2001) als Angriff auf die Gesellschaft sein, die auf den Kapitalismus ausgerichtet ist, hat somit mindestens genauso hochgradig symbolischen Charakter.

Seitdem steht der Westen in einem Kampf gegen einen schwer zu definierenden Osten, die Al-Quaida auf jeden Fall, den Islamischen Staat und alle ähnlich einzustufenden Interessensgemeinschaften und Ideologie-Lieferanten, gegen Staaten, die offen mit solchen sympathisieren, und gegen den Terror, der seitdem auch vor Europa nicht Halt macht. Anschläge in Paris, London, Nizza, Berlin haben in den letzten Jahren bewiesen, dass Außen- und Sicherheitspolitik definitiv keine nationale Angelegenheit mehr sind, und dass der Schauplatz von Kampf oder Terror näher in unser aller Wahrnehmungsfeld gerückt ist. Wenn dann Attentäter und Attentäterinnen immer wieder Menschen sind, die eigentlich europäische Pässe haben, Biographien und Lebensgeschichten haben, die eng mit dem Westen und hiesiger Zivilisation verbunden sind, dann wachsen das Erstaunen und die Erschütterung umso mehr, als unvorstellbar war, dass jemand, der unter Umständen gar mit christlichen, demokratischen Werten sozialisiert worden war, dazu fähig ist, scheinbar willkürlich Menschen zu töten, um der Idee des Islamismus zu dienen, oder schlichtweg Terror gegen den Westen zu sähen. Dabei sind zwei Aspekte bemerkenswert: Erstens die Annahme, es gäbe so etwas wie eine weitgehend homogene Version eines Westens (vgl. Kneissl 2007, S. 145), und zweitens, die Tatsache, dass jemand in einem Staat aufgewachsen ist, wäre gleichbedeutend damit, dass diese Person sich wohl automatisch mit den dort dominierenden Werten identifizieren würde. Wenn der erste Aspekt zwar einer intensiveren Auseinandersetzung bedürfe, so birgt der zweite Aspekt das weitaus größere Potential dafür, eine gesellschaftliche Spurensuche anzuregen. Denn die Erschütterung des Abendlandes mag immer wieder groß sein, wenn vor allem junge Menschen quasi aus der Mitte der Gesellschaft herausgerissen und für radikale Ideologien bzw. religiöse Konzepte angeworben werden. Jugendliche begeistern sich (plötzlich) beispielsweise für den Koran, vertreten angriffslustig Werte, die ihnen bisher vielleicht nicht bekannt aber meist auch nicht wichtig waren. Und hinter allem steckt die Hoffnung darauf, irgendeinen höheren, übergeordneten Sinn zu finden, im Dasein, im eigenen Leben, in der Gesamtheit der Existenz.

„Erfolgsgeschichte Integration" in Österreich

Dabei lohnt es sich zwei Dinge parallel im Auge zu behalten: Die Medien stilisierten mit dem Fall des Eisernen Vorhanges zunehmend das Feindbild aus dem Orient, und gleichzeitig versäumten die Gesellschaften der vergangenen Jahrzehnte, Menschen aus eben jenen Kulturräumen tatsächlich zu integrieren, noch viel mehr verabsäumte man generell weitgehend Migrantinnen und Migranten als Bestandteil der sich verändernden Gesellschaft zu sehen. Man duldete sie eher so lange, bis ein gewisser Gewöhnungseffekt auftrat, quittierte dies dann salopp mit der Einschätzung, dass hier Integration gelungen sei, forderte eigentlich von diesen Menschen, dass sie sich z.B. in Österreich assimilieren, um die maximal zu tolerieren, also zu ertragen. Von einer wirklichen Einbindung in die Gesellschaft kann nicht ernsthaft die Rede sein. Wer sich dem Prinzip der kapitalistischen Ideologie zu unterwerfen bereit war, durfte als Ausnahme und „Herzeige-Migrant" oder „Herzeige-Migrantin" als Neo-Österreicher bzw. Neo-Österreicherin einen Beitrag für die Gemeinschaft leisten, die anderen nahm man widerwillig in Kauf und kümmerte sich nicht weiter um sie. Leistung wurde zum Gradmesser dafür, ob jemand integriert war oder nicht. Auch wenn diese Einschätzung polemisch klingen mag, die Tatsache, dass eine Vielzahl von Migrationshintergründen und Muttersprachen, die nicht Deutsch sind, Schulen bald zu so genannten Brennpunktschulen machen, in denen Lehrkräfte zunehmend damit überfordert sein können, unterschiedlichste sprachliche und auch intellektuelle Niveaus in ihren Klassen auszubalancieren, ist nur ein Beleg dafür.
„Über ein Fünftel (22%) aller rund 1,13 Millionen Schüler/innen in Österreich hatte im Schuljahr 2014/15 eine andere Umgangssprache als Deutsch. Im Pflichtschulbereich – mit besonderem Schwerpunkt auf Wien – ist dieser Wert noch höher: Mehr als die Hälfte der Wiener Volksschüler/innen hatte eine nichtdeutsche Umgangssprache. Bei den Wiener Hauptschüler/innen lag dieser Wert mit über 70% noch höher." (Österreichischer Integrationsfonds 2017) Alleine diese Diversität stellt viele Lehrkräfte vor große Herausforderungen.

Während in den Jahren des großen wirtschaftlichen Aufschwunges in Österreich Gastarbeiter und Gastarbeiterinnen aus dem Osten (also aus dem slawischen Osten bzw. dem Balkan) in Österreich aufgenommen wurden, dachte man nicht daran, dass diese hier Fuß fassen würden, Familien gründen und nachholen würden, und eine Zukunft in Österreich aufbauen könnten. Doch für viele gab es nach 20 Erwerbsjahren keine Rückkehr mehr in ein Land, das im Laufe der Jahrzehnte fremd geworden war, weil auch dort die Zeit nicht stillgestanden ist. Der Krieg im ehemaligen Jugoslawien machte für etliche Familien selbst die Vorstellung, eines Tages irgendwohin zurückzukehren zunichte.

Refolklorisierung und Pornographisierung in Ost und West

In dieser Gesellschaft stellen sich die Menschen heute vielleicht sogar dieselben Fragen, aber sie kommen zu unterschiedlichen Antworten: Welchen Stellenwert habe ich in dieser Gesellschaft? Während Österreicher und Österreicherinnen hier selbstbewusst ihren Platz in der Mitte einnehmen, unterstreichen sie diesen Anspruch mit einer fortschreitenden Tendenz einer „Refolklorisierung", die an die Jahrhundertwende von 1900 erinnert. Damals wurde in den Wiener Gemeindebauten mehr Volkstanz betrieben, als je zuvor am Land. Sogar die Entstehung einiger Trachten geht auf das städtische Phänomen zurück und hat keinerlei historische Anbindung an Regionen oder Traditionen vom Land. Volkstümliche Feste wie die „Wiener Wiesn", Musikidole wie Andreas Gabalier, der selbsternannten „Volks Rock'n'Roller", die Renaissance des Dirndls und ländlich motivierter Kleidung sind nur einige aktuelle Indizien dafür.

Und so etabliert und anerkannt der Anblick von Frauen im Dirndl sein mag, so verstörend sei der Anblick von Frauen mit Verschleierung, und das ist insofern bemerkenswert, als die jeweilige Quelle der Empörung gar nicht so weit voneinander entfernt ist.

Das Dirndl in der heute bekannten Form, tailliert, mit Ausschnitt und den Busen der Frau betonend ist eigentlich eine „Erfindung" der Nationalsozialisten. Selbst der Begriff geht eigentlich von der bairisch-österreichischen Variante der Verkleinerungsform des Begriffes Dirne aus, einer Prostituierten, die als Bezeichnung euphemistisch erst auf Mägde im ländlichen Raum angewandt wurde, und später für junge Frauen niederen Standes gebraucht wurde. Die Betonung weiblicher Reize, sollte das Bild der Frau als „Gebärmaschine" natürlich im Dienste des Staates unterstreichen, und war daher nicht grundlos ein beliebtes Motiv nationalsozialistischer Propaganda bzw. nach dem Krieg Inbegriff eines verklärten und irregeleiteten Verständnisses von Weiblichkeit. (vgl. Egger 2008; vgl. Wallnöfer 2011) Das Dirndl ist somit von Nacktheit auch nicht mehr weit entfernt. Die Mode, die das Dirndl in den nächsten Jahrzehnten ablöste trennte sich bewusst von allem, was nach Folklore oder Land roch, und erst in den letzten Jahrzehnten zeigt sich, dass mit der Vergessenheit auf wieder eine Renaissance dieser modischen Trachtenelemente an Beliebtheit gewinnt. Heute erinnert sich freilich niemand an die braune Vergangenheit, und die Kritik an der Symbolik kann leicht ungehört bleiben, wenn man bedenkt, dass die Wiederentdeckung in eine Zeit der zunehmenden Pornographisierung des Frauenbildes in der Gesellschaft fällt. Wenn man also so möchte, dann ist die Idealisierung der Frau in einem sexuelle Reize unterstreichenden Dirndl ein Ausdruck fehlender Emanzipation. Und das Argument, dass diese Kleidung meist freiwillig und aus Überzeugung getragen wird, täuscht nicht darüber hinweg. Ähnlich ist der Schleier in islamischen Gesellschaften ein Ausdruck dessen, dass der weibliche Körper voller Verlockungen ist, denen schwer oder nicht zu wiederstehen ist, und daher bedarf er der Verhüllung. Diese wird ebenso häufig freiwillig von Frauen vorgenommen. Um Teil der Gemeinschaft zu sein, braucht es eine individuelle Akzeptanz einer Verschleierung, um gleichwertiges Mitglied einer Gruppe zu sein. *„Dass sich Menschen für ihre Handlungen gegenseitig zur Verantwortung ziehen, dass wir uns gegenseitig insoweit also einen ‚freien Willen' unterstellen, beruht nicht auf höherer Eingebung zu der Frage, ob die Welt determiniert ist oder nicht, sondern ist einzig und alleine das Ergebnis eines pragmatischen gesellschaftlichen Konsenses."* (Bauer 2013, S. 169) Unter dem Strich bleibt die Erkenntnis: Der weibliche Körper ist ein Körper einer schier unkontrollierbaren sexuellen Verfügbarkeit und die Frau hat angeblich die Entscheidungsgewalt darüber, ob sie offensiv (Dirndl) oder defensiv (Schleier) damit umgehen möchte. Den freien Willen der Frauen kann man aber keinesfalls vom gesamtgesellschaftlichen Kontext lösen, und dieser offenbart den freien Willen relativ schnell als Zugeständnis an Sozialisation, Kulturation und familiäres Umfeld. Ein Aufbegehren gegen gesellschaftliche Konventionen ist mit Widerstand und Hürden verbunden bzw. bringt eine Vielzahl von Sanktionen mit sich.

Spätestens seit dem Buch von Betty Mahmoody aus dem Jahr 1988 und dem gleichnamigen Film „Nicht ohne meine Tochter" (Vgl. imdb 2014) waren westliche Frauen dafür sensibilisiert worden, dass die islamische Kultur eine frauenfeindliche sei. Die Problematik einer Ehe zwischen einer Amerikanerin und einem Iraner, der seine Frau und die gemeinsame Tochter zunächst in seine Heimat auf Besuch mitnimmt, und beide nicht mehr in die USA zurückkehren lassen möchte, endet in einer spektakulären Flucht der Frau mit ihrer Tochter. Der weltweite Bestseller hat die auf einer wahren Geschichte basierende Erzählung als nachhaltige Prägung eines (Fremd-)Bildes einer islamischen Kultur etabliert. Für Generationen von Menschen stand fest, dass die Gesellschaft im Iran rückschrittlich, reaktionär und brutal sei, und die Vermutung lag nahe, dass dies nicht nur auf den Iran zuträfe. Entscheidend ist hierbei nicht, ob diese Annahmen gerechtfertigt oder auch bewiesen waren, sondern die Tatsache, dass es keine nennenswerten Gegendarstellungen gab. Dieses Bild reihte sich fast nahtlos an die Vorstellung des Abendlandes über das Morgenland, das weniger durch Fakten und Wissen als eher durch Mythen gekennzeichnet ist. Geschichten aus „1001 Nacht" sind genauso präsent wie das Gefühl einer prinzipiellen Überzeugung einer kulturellen Überlegenheit, die bereits im Mittelalter dokumentiert war, als die europäischen Kenntnisse im Bereich der Medizin den Heilkünsten aus dem fernen Osten unreflektiert vorangestellt wurden. Aus diesem Verständnis heraus wird auch die Stellung der Geschlechter immer noch von Stereotypien durchzogen, wobei selten eine Unterscheidung nach einzelnen Nationen bzw. nach Kulturen gemacht wird. Die Frau aus dem Morgenland ist seit Jahrhunderten im Haus oder im Harem verortet, womit auch immer eine latente sexuelle Konnotation verbunden ist. Die Frau, als ein stets für den Mann verfügbares sexualisiertes Wesen, weckt somit Phantasien einer legitimierten Unterdrückung. Dabei hat die Unterdrückung der Frau viele Gesichter. Und wenn sie in Österreich auch keinen Schleier trägt, so zeigt allein die Tatsache, dass Frauen bis in die späten 1970er Jahre in Österreich ohne schriftliche Erlaubnis ihrer Ehemänner oder Vormunde weder einen Arbeitsvertrag unterschreiben noch ein Konto eröffnen durften. Fortschritt oder Rückständigkeit haben somit unterschiedliche Erscheinungsformen und lassen sich sowohl im Orient als auch im Okzident finden. Dass die Diskussion und Bewertung nicht losgelöst vom historischen, zeitlichen und gesellschaftlichen Kontext erfolgen darf, zeigt auch die Einschätzung von Karin Kneissl: *„Führten wir eine Debatte über das Verhältnis zwischen Orient und Okzident im Jahre 1907 [...], so wären die Themen und die Atmosphäre völlig anders. Es stünden nicht die Angst des Westens vor Terror und täglicher Gewalt infolge der Kriege, die der Westen seit 2001 in die islamische Welt exportiert hat, im Vordergrund."* (Kneissl 2007, S. 15) Wo Bedrohungsszenarien fehlen, könnte intensiver Austausch stattfinden.

Der Schleier also ist einerseits das Instrument zur Verführung im erotisierten Schleiertanz, und wenn der Schleier fällt, dann ist dies ein Bruch mit der Tradition. Frauen, die Traditionen brechen, stellen sich dem bewährten Wertesystem entgegen. Egal ob es dazu der Entledigung eines Schleiers bedarf, oder aber die Verweigerung einer pornographisierten Stilisierung. Frauen pendeln sowohl im Osten als auch im Westen zwischen der uralten Dichotomie zwischen Heiliger oder Hure – und wer seine eigene Kultur verrät, sich den Konventionen entzieht, spricht damit sein Urteil über sich selbst. Egal, welchem Wertekatalog man Frauen sich unterwerfen mögen, wichtig ist, dass sie sich bestmöglich freiwillig unterwerfen.

Im Westen unterwerfen sich Frauen einem Frauenbild, das sich an Medienprodukten wie der TV-Serie „Sex and the City" oder an Bestsellern wie „50 Shades of Grey" (von E.L. James) orientiert, Frauen sind modebewusst, karrieregeil, verwirklichen sich selbst und stellen dafür auch mal die Familie oder Kinder hintan. Sexualität ist eine Waffe, kapitalistisch gesehen eine Währung, und Frauen bezahlen damit für ihre vermeintliche Freiheit. Und das macht aus Sexualität, die durchaus von Selbstbestimmung und Emanzipation getragen sein könnte, eigentlich schon Pornographisierung, weil sie stets einen imaginären oder gar realen Kunden bedient. *„Westliche Frauen hatten meiner Meinung nach eher allen Grund sich zu schämen. Wie konnte man sich als erwachsene Frau nur kleiden und benehmen wie eine Hure? Unverschleierte Frauen nahm ich nun als arme Opfer sexistischer Gesellschaftsverhältnisse wahr. Sie taten mir leid, weil sie sich Männern ‚anboten' und unterwarfen und darauf teilweise allen Ernstes auch noch stolz waren.*

Ich kam mir sehr klug und überlegen vor." (Anonyma 2010, In: Schwarzer 2010, S. 189) beschreibt eine deutsche Konvertitin ihre Eindrücke aus beiden Welten.

Die Debatte um die muslimischen Frauen, die – gemäß westlicher Wahrnehmung – unters Kopftuch geknechtet werden, oder gar unter eine Burka, die angeblich die Promiskuität westlicher Frauen bedenklich und gefährlich finden, und die sich bereitwillig einem starken Mann unterordnen, zeigen ein Bild doppelter Unterwerfung. In der Debatte ist relativ egal, wie viel der Schleier tatsächlich verhüllt, der hier zur Diskussion steht. Und de facto ist aus ideologischer Sicht schon wenig Unterschied zwischen Hidschab oder Burka – auch wenn das eine die Haare verhüllt und das Gesicht frei lässt und das andere die gesamte Person verdeckt. Jede Verschleierung kann im Selbstverständnis ein Ausdruck einer kulturellen und religiösen Überzeugung sein, aber auch das Symbol der Erniedrigung der Frau. Der Gruppendruck funktioniert allerdings nicht nur bei Frauen, die sich verschleiern sollen sondern findet sich als modisches Diktat bei Frauen, die sich einer ökonomisch motivierten Ideologie folgend einem Bündel an Vorbildern unterwerfen, um in der sozialen Hierarchie bestehen zu können. Politikerinnen müssen mediale und öffentliche Diskussionen ihrer Physiognomie sowie ihres Kleidungsstils ertragen, anstatt zu ihren politischen Positionen befragt zu werden. Angela Merkel interessierte als Kandidatin im Wahlkampf zunächst nicht mit ihrem Programm oder ihrem Intellekt sondern mit ihrer Frisur, ihrem Styling und ihrem so insgesamt unweiblichen Auftreten. Selbst wenn auf individueller Ebene die Entscheidungen von Frauen frei gefallen sind, Familie und Gesellschaft wirken sich ebenfalls stark darauf aus. Und so kann die Freiwilligkeit westlicher Frauen, ihr Äußeres beispielsweise durch Brustimplantate an ein kolportiertes Ideal optimiert anpassen zu müssen, durchaus mit der Freiwilligkeit östlicher Frauen verglichen werden, die ein Kopftuch anlegen oder gar zum Schleier greifen. Hier wie dort lauten die Erklärungen häufig, dass man das doch nur für sich selbst mache.

„Das verbreitete Unbehagen über den Islam, das sich an muslimischen Zuwanderern kristallisiert und wesentliche Impulse von islamistischen Terroranschlägen erfährt, äußert sich in Kampagnen. Dazu ist eine Ideologie, die Ressentiments bündelt und Feindbilder instrumentalisiert, unerlässlich. Sie wird von Demagogen unter Rückgriff auf historische Muster erzeugt. Elemente einer antiislamistischen Ideologie sind Verschwörungstheorien, die Gefühle der Bedrohung, Existenzängste und Identitätskrisen in der Mehrheitsgesellschaft aufnehmen und der Minderheit der Muslime Schuld zuweisen. Die Dämonisierung des Islam nutzt kulturrassistische Argumente, in denen sich Fremdenfeindlichkeit, traditionelle Deutungsmuster von fremd und eigen, völkisches Bewusstsein und Erklärungsbedarf für globale Entwicklungen mischen. Ziel der muslimfeindlichen Ideologie ist die Abwehr einer empfundenen Aggression, die im Schlagwort ‚Islamisierung Europas' Ausdruck findet und die Ausgrenzung der Minderheit beabsichtigt." (Benz 2012, S. 125)

Die Ambivalenz des Schleiers bzw. des Kopftuches ist die der Frau als hocherotisches Wesen, dem noch die Versprechungen von 1001 Nacht anhaften, die gleichzeitig ein konservatives Relikt einer religiös-ideologischen Zeit und Welt sind, als Ausdruck von Gefahr und Zurückgebliebenheit. Die Ambivalenz der Frau, die im Geiste der sexuellen Revolution ihren Körper zunächst befreit zur Schau stellt und dann ihn als erotisierte Ware an bietet, was einer Pornographisierung gleichkommt, und verdrängt damit den Gedanken der Selbstbestimmung zu Gunsten der Überzeugung, dass Frauen verfügbar sind. Somit ist die Verschleierung genauso wie die Zurschaustellung des weiblichen Körpers eigentlich Ausdruck eines gesellschaftlich geteilten Moralsystems. *„Moralsysteme sind [...] als Garantiesysteme für Zusammenhalt, Kooperation und gegenseitige Hilfeleistung entstanden. Paradoxerweise haben sie zugleich das Potential zur Erzeugung von Feindschaft und Gewalt. [...] Moralsysteme beschreiben die Regeln, nach denen größere Verbände von Menschen ihr Zusammenleben regeln. Sie sind Teil dessen, was man als ‚corporate identity', als das Identität stiftende Erkennungsmerkmal einer Organisation bezeichnet. Wer Lebensgewohnheiten miteinander teilt, miteinander Rituale und Feste feiert und gemeinsame Regeln des Zusammenlebens beachtet, befindet sich im unsichtbaren Geltungsbereich eines Moralsystems, auch wenn, wenn sich innerhalb dieser Zone nicht alle persönlich kennen. Moralsysteme markieren die Grenze zwischen dem eigenen Kulturkreis, dem ‚wir', und ‚denen', also jenen, die einer unbekannten Außenwelt zuzurechnen sind."* (Bauer 2013, S. 187)

Der Diskurs um das Moralsystem verschleierter oder pornographisierter Körper passiert aus einer androzentristischen Grundhaltung heraus. Und in beiden Themen zeigt sich durchaus ein komplementäres Bild von Frauen und Männern: Frauen sind sexuell unkontrollierte Wesen, und bedürfen daher entweder der Kontrolle des Schleiers oder aber des Ventils der pornographisierten (Selbst-)Darstellung. Das macht in dieser heteronormativen Sichtweise allerdings Männer zu triebgesteuerten, gierigen Wesen, die sich nicht zurückhalten können (und auch nicht müssen). Was sich über findet, ist die Unterstellung, weder Frauen noch Männer könnten reflektiert und überlegt, eigenverantwortlich handeln und sich auf einer Ebene gegenseitigen Respektes begegnen. Das macht Frauen und Männer zu Opfern, auch wenn in der Realität der Verlust für die Frau mit hierarchischen Hürden und Benachteiligungen verbunden ist, für Männer allerdings das Opferdasein aus einer Position der finanziellen und strukturellen Macht und Handlungsfähigkeit offenbar leichter zu verschmerzen ist.

Die Tradition eines „wissenschaftlichen Imperialismus" ist übrigens Teil des Problems und wird noch durch den Aspekt der Intersektionalität verstärkt: Wer Wissenschaft betrieben hat auch die Macht der Interpretation. Eine Dominanz des Westens, der gerne über Forschungsobjekte und –subjekte schreibt, anstatt mit ihnen zu forschen, zieht sich durch die Geschichte der Wissenschaft, Aristoteles, Charles Darwin, Bronisław Malinowski – sie alle haben ihre Weltsicht in ihre Erkenntnisse projiziert und damit unbewusst oder auch bewusst manipuliert. Aristoteles philosophierte über ein duales System, das Männlichkeit mit Aktivität und Weiblichkeit mit Passivität beschreibt, was bis heute hartnäckig in Diskursen erhalten geblieben ist. (Scherer 2009, S. 147) Darwin negierte die Tatsache, dass die viel friedliebenderen Bonobos dem Menschen am ähnlichsten waren, die streitbaren Menschenaffen passten besser zu einem Menschenbild, das mit Krieg konfrontiert war. (vgl. Taylor et.al. 2008, S. 205) Und Malinowski vertraute seinen Tagebüchern an, dass er seine Beobachtungen von Nativen Völkern durch Erfindungen bereicherte, die er aus Langeweile angestellt hatte. (vgl. Malinowski 1986)

Machtdiskurs zur weiblichen Verhüllung und Enthüllung

Wer darf sich ein Urteil über Schleier oder Nacktheit erlauben, und wie kann eine kulturelle Position ohne explizites Naheverhältnis sinnvoll dekonstruiert werden? Sollen Vorurteile, Stereotypien und etablierte Interpretationen überwunden werden, braucht es neue und vor allem viele Perspektiven. Der ewige Zwiespalt zwischen (glorifizierendem) Selbstbild und (kritikfreudigem) Fremdbild bringt Verzerrungen mit sich, denen das Potential fehlt, neue Antworten auf neu zu stellende Fragen zu bringen. Wenn also über verschleierte Frauen gesprochen wird, so kommen viele Gruppen zu Wort, am seltensten jedoch die verschleierten Frauen selbst. Dies ist nicht zu verwechseln mit der Binsenweisheit, nur Betroffene könnten etwas über den Aspekt ihrer Betroffenheit etwas aussagen. Das würde beispielsweise dazu führen, dass nur Menschen mit Migrationshintergrund über Migration sprechen könnten. Aber wenn diese Perspektive fehlt, dann verringert das die Problemlösungskapazität enorm. Eine solche Legitimierung sehen Berger und Luckmann als Prozess an, den sie als „sekundäre" Objektivation von Sinn bezeichnen. (Vgl. Berger / Luckmann 200017, S. 98f) *„Sie produziert neue Sinnhaftigkeit, die dazu dient, Bedeutungen, die ungleichartigen Institutionen schon anhaften, zu Sinnhaftigkeit zu integrieren. Die Funktion dieses Vorganges ist, ‚primäre' Objektivationen, die bereits institutionalisiert sind, objektiv zugänglich und subjektiv ersichtlich zu machen. Wenn wir Legitimation so definieren, ohne Ansehen der Motive, die einen Legitimierungsprozeß im einzelnen bewegen, so müssen wir hinzufügen, daß Integration dieser oder jener Art auch das übliche Motiv für die Legitimatoren ist."* (Berger / Luckmann 200017, S. 98f) Wenn davon auszugehen ist, dass nur diejenigen, die an einem Diskurs teilhaben, auch die Chance auf eine Legitimierung haben, so ist der Ausschluss von Frauen aus einer solchen Debatte entweder kurzsichtig oder die gezielte Verhinderung weiblicher politischer Handlungsfähigkeit.

Ist die Unterdrückung der Frau das Thema, dann ist dies im europäischen Kontext meist mit häuslicher Gewalt oder Benachteiligung, Diskriminierung am Arbeitsmarkt verknüpft, wohingegen Unterdrückung im Orient meist eng an den Islam geknüpft ist. Das schafft eine interessante Dichotomie zwischen einem vermeintlich politischen Westen im Gegensatz zu einem vermeintlich religiösen Osten. Der säkularisierte und aufgeklärte Okzident trotzt dem religiös fanatisierten Orient. *„Schlimmer als diese theologischen Probleme wog für mich allerdings die muslimische Wirklichkeit, die ich nonstop erlebte: Ablehnung und Hetze gegen die westliche Gesellschaft, unverhohlener Hass auf Juden, massive Unterdrückung* *von Frauen, Machoverhalten muslimischer Männer, Gewalt und Brutalität, Lügen"* (Anonyma 2010, In: Schwarzer 2010, S. 195) Die alltägliche Lebensrealität unzähliger Frauen in islamischen Staaten, die Gewalt, Unterdrückung und Diskriminierung mit sich bringt, soll hier keineswegs verharmlost werden, und eine tatsächliche Vergleichbarkeit mit Themen, die Frauen in Europa aktuell bewegen ist teilweise schwer möglich. Aber das Prinzip, das dahinter steht, weist eine ähnliche Funktionslogik auf, und das gilt es offenzulegen zu dekonstruieren.

"2004 gab ‚Women for Women International' eine landesweite Umfrage unter irakischen Frauen in Auftrag. Sie ergab: 94 Prozent aller Frauen sind für die gesetzliche Absicherung der Rechte für Frauen, 95 Prozent sprachen sich gegen eine Einschränkung der Bildungschancen aus, 84 Prozent fordern das Recht, über die endgültige Verfassung abzustimmen. 57 Prozent sind gegen eine Einschränkung der Berufstätigkeit von Frauen, 80 Prozent treten für unbeschränkte Beteiligung von Frauen an politischen Gremien ein. Die Realität sieht anders aus." (Weiss 2010, In: Schwarzer 2010, S. 293) Der Unterschied, ob man als Frau keinen Gebrauch von seinen rechtlich garantierten Möglichkeiten macht, oder ob es solche erst gar nicht gibt, ist enorm. Und die (massenmediale) Öffentlichkeit fokussiert nur allzu gerne die Debatte um die Verschleierung, die unglaublich nachhaltig vom eigentlichen Thema ablenkt. Wie die Spitze eines Eisberges steht das Kopftuch als Symbol für eine Welt, in der für den Westen viele Fragen unbeantwortet sind, wobei oft weder vermutet und schon gar nicht wahrgenommen wird, dass auch in Ländern, in denen vorwiegend traditionell verschleierte Frauen leben, ein Diskurs zum Thema stattfindet. Ein Beispiel von vielen ist die Initiative „My Stealthy freedom" (Vgl. Facebook 2014) hat Masih Alinejad auf Twitter sowie auf Facebook, die ganz massiv gegen das Kopftuch plädiert. Frauen posten Fotos von sich an unterschiedlichsten Orten dieser Welt – meist in der Öffentlichkeit aufgenommen – auf denen sie ihren traditionellen Schleier abgelegt haben und individuelle Freiheit inszenieren.

Die mittlerweile weltweit operierende Gruppe von Demonstrantinnen und Aktivistinnen rund um Femen machen deutlich, wie nahe Mittel und Gegenargument beieinander liegen. Femen steht für gefällig aussehende Frauen, nackte Oberkörper, traditionelle und ukrainisch-folkloristische Blumenkränze und stummen aber nicht stillen Protest gegen alles, was gerade an der Tagesordnung steht. Weibliche Brüste werden zum Blickfang und die politische Botschaft zum Begleitprodukt, das manchmal gar nicht bewusst wahrgenommen wird. Auf Transparenten oder gar auf den nackten Körper geschrieben verschwinden die Parolen und Botschaften auf den nackten Körpern, und die Symbole der ukrainischen Tracht, die den nackten Körper konterkarieren werden über die Grenzen der Ukraine hinaus zwar verwendet aber nicht verstanden. *„Scharf im Visier haben die Femen auch die Unterdrückung der Frauen in den islamistisch beherrschten Ländern. Für das Recht der Frauen in Saudi-Arabien, auch Autofahren zu dürfen, schlossen die Femen sich der internationalen Kampagne ‚Women2Drive' an. Sie demonstrierten mit nacktem Busen und schwarz verschleiertem Gesicht in Kiew. Slogan: ‚Autos für Frauen! Kamele für Männer!' Und aus Protest gegen das Todesurteil gegen*

Sakineh Mohammadi Ashtiani (die mit deutschen Journalistinnen/Journalisten gesprochen hatte und im letzten Augenblick begnadigt wurde) zogen die so - moralischen Schamlosen vor die iranische Botschaft in Kiew – und ersparten auch den bigotten Frömmlern den Anblick ihrer prächtigen Busen nicht." (N.N. In: Emma 2012) Weltweiten Problemen wie Menschenhandel und der Ausbeutung von Männern und Frauen begegnet auch Femen mit der universellen Sprache, die alle über die Massenmedien gelernt haben. *„In einem Land, in dem auf fast jedem Plakat ein nackter Busen zu sehen ist (um irgendetwas damit zu verkaufen), [...] kann frau diesen vielstrapazierten Busen vermutlich nur noch zur Waffe machen. Und das gilt ja nicht nur für die Ukraine, sondern für diese ganze sexistische Welt."* (N.N. 2012)

Die Verschleierung der Frau ist für manche ein Symbol für den Islam und für andere ist es ein religiöses Gebot und gelebte Glaubenspraxis. So oder so macht er Frauen gesellschaftlich unsichtbar, verbannt sie aus der Öffentlichkeit. Necla Kelek spricht sogar davon, dass dies eine geniale Doppelstrategie sei, die noch heute funktioniere. „Der Schleier trennt die Gläubigen von den Ungläubigen, die Reinen von den Lasterhaften, die Guten von den Bösen, die Öffentlichkeit – das Reich des Mannes – von dem ‚Haus' – das Reich der Frau." (Kelek 2006, S. 256) Allerdings, so Kelek, wieso sollte eine funktionierende Demokratie den Schleier als Schutz gegen sexuelle Gewalt akzeptieren, wenn es doch ausreichend Gesetze gäbe, die die Frauen eigentlich umfassend schützen sollten. „Und diese zwingen nicht das Opfer zur Freiheitseinschränkung, sondern den potentiellen Täter bei Androhung von Strafe zur Selbstbeherrschung. Heute aus dem Koran eine allgemeine religiöse Pflicht für das Kopftuch abzuleiten, ist nicht akzeptabel. [...] die Muslime sagen, der Koran ist nicht interpretierbar, er ist nicht historisierbar, er gilt Wort für Wort. Aber es käme doch auch niemand in den Sinn, Frauenraub, Frauentausch, Frauenkauf, Blutrache und das Halten von Sklavinnen als religiöse Pflichten zu akzeptieren, weil sie im Koran legitimiert sind. Das Kopftuch ist kein Zeichen des Glaubens," klagt Kelek (2006, S. 256) die Reduktion der Frau auf ihr Geschlecht an, die durch das Kopftuch passiere. Durch die permanente Ausgrenzung aus dem öffentlichen Raum sei in muslimischen Gemeinschaften die Trennungslinie zwischen Mann und Frau stärker herausgebildet worden, die religiöse Argumentation, wonach Frauen und Männer nicht gleichwertig wären, weil es der Frau von Natur aus an Vernunft fehle, stünde in direktem Widerspruch zu Artikel 3 des Grundgesetzes, und trotzdem würden die Deutschen das akzeptieren. (vgl. Kelek 2006, S. 256) Folgt man dieser Argumentation, dann ist der Schleier bzw. das Kopftuch ein Symbol für die Schwäche der deutschen Demokratie. Das wiederum macht aus dem Kopftuch weniger ein Symbol des Islam, sondern vielmehr ein Symbol für den schwachen Westen, der mit der Begründung der Religionsfreiheit und der politischen Korrektheit seine eigene Schwäche kaschiert. Damit verändert sich alles. Das scheinbare Entgegenkommen des Westens, also die Toleranz für verschleierte Frauen, wird plötzlich nicht mehr das Symbol für Weltoffenheit und religiösen Dialog, sondern es steht eigentlich für das Unvermögen, für seine eigenen Werte einzutreten. Vielleicht ist die Debatte daher so emotional aufgeladen, und das Ausmaß dessen, nicht nur die mediale Berichterstattung, sondern auch der wissenschaftliche und intellektuelle Diskurs und alle dazugehörigen Publikationen sind ein Indiz dafür, dass hier offenbar aneinander vorbeigeredet wird.

In der Entscheidung, sich kurz gesagt dem Wertekontext der Verschleierung bzw. dem Wertekontext des Dirndls zu verschreiben, erkennen allerdings gerade junge Menschen vielfach den Druck, dass eine erzwungene Wahl Probleme mit sich bringt: Wird man in ein Wertesystem gezwungen, manifestiert sich mitunter Protest, wird das Wertesystem von außen in Frage gestellt, dann wird es oft vehementer verteidigt als nötig. So gesehen wahren Generationen von Menschen mit Migrationshintergrund die Symbole und Ausdrücke ihrer Identität und Kultur mit hingebungsvoller Akribie, und je mehr dies in Frage gestellt wird, umso mehr werden sie diese zu legitimieren versuchen. So kann auch beobachtet werden, dass vor allem junge Menschen heute im Orient auf Symbole wie Schleier oder Kopftuch zurückgreifen, obwohl ihre Elterngeneration diese eigentlich bereits abgelegt hatte, also ist auch hier durchaus von einer Refolklorisierung die Rede. Wie schmal der Grat zwischen Religion und Folklore ist, hat bereits Józef Tischner thematisiert, der viele Ausdrücke von Religion eher als Folklore bezeichnet (vgl. Tischner 2008), die damit sehr wohl sinnstiftende Bedeutung haben, aber eben nicht religiös relevant sind. Interessant ist dies vor allem, wenn Gordon W. Allport mit seiner These über die Natur von Vorurteilen richtig lag: Kurz gesagt besagt diese, dass Stereotype und Vorurteile dort weniger werden, wo Macht weitgehend gleich verteilt ist, und dass sie dort vermehrt auftreten, wo es ein Ungleichgewicht von Macht gibt. (vgl. Allport 1963) Wenn also die Diskussion um das Kopftuch unter dem Gesichtspunkt der Machtverteilung innerhalb einer Gesellschaft gesehen wird, wobei diese durchaus von diversen Kulturen geprägt sein kann, dann liegt der Schluss nahe, dass die Vorurteile, die Konnotationen und auch die Argumentationen der jeweiligen Standpunkte in dieser Frage, auch Aufschluss darüber geben, dass die Machtverteilung zwischen den Parteien in einem Ungleichgewicht zu sehen ist.

Die westliche Frau, die in diesem Diskurs buchstäblich nichts mehr anhat, also die Frau, die von ihrem Körper getrennt wurde, und deren nackter pornographisierte Körper quasi als Referenz in den Medien präsent ist, die hat der verschleierten Frau aus dem Osten eigentlich nichts voraus. Nur weil mehr von ihr zu sehen ist, heißt dies nicht automatisch, dass sie auch wahrgenommen wird. Im Gegenteil, ihre ständige Präsenz und Verfügbarkeit verstärken den Eindruck, dass sie eine Ware ist über die der versierte – meist männliche – Konsument frei verfügen kann. Das Fallbeispiel der Ereignisse rund um die Silvesternacht 2015/16 macht es noch deutlicher. In jener Nacht kam es unter anderem in Köln zu massiven Übergriffen auf Frauen, bei denen wohl (teilweise sogar in Gruppen organisierte) Männer einschlägig image-vorbelasteter Herkunft Frauen im Tumult der Feierlichkeit belästigt haben. Tatsachen sexueller Belästigung sollen hier nicht in Frage gestellt werden, körperliche Übergriffe sind nicht akzeptabel, egal unter welchem Vorwand. Unabhängig von der Täterschaft ist die Integrität und Unversehrtheit des weiblichen – und übrigens auch des männlichen – Körpers nicht Gegenstand der Debatte und daher auch völlig berechtigterweise gesetzlich geschützt. Interessant an der Berichterstattung zu den Vorkommnissen war allerdings, dass Gewalt gegen Frauen und sexuelle Belästigung offenbar kontextabhängig verhandelt werden. In Österreich wurde erst mit der Sexualstrafrechtsreform 1989 geschlechtliche Nötigung und Vergewaltigung in der Ehe als strafbar eingestuft. Bis dahin durften Männer also über die Körper ihrer Ehefrauen im wahrsten Sinn des Wortes verfügen. Die medial stark vertretene Position, dass in Österreich und Deutschland Gleichberechtigung ein wichtiger Wert und eine etablierte Tradition wären steht der Tatsache gegenüber, dass Ende der 1970er Jahre die ersten Frauenhäuser in Österreich eröffnet wurden und erst 1997 das Betretungsverbot sowie die einstweilige Verfügung als Schutzmaßnahme im Rahmen des Bundesgesetzes zum Schutz vor Gewalt in der Familie geschaffen wurden. Dies sind Indizien dafür, dass Gewalt gegen Frauen in der österreichischen Gesellschaft tatsächlich real existierende Themen waren und nicht reine Fiktion. Bereits 2011 – also weit, bevor von irgendeiner Willkommenskultur die Rede war – gaben drei Viertel der Befragten Frauen im Alter zwischen 16 bis 60 Jahren an, Opfer sexueller Belästigung gewesen zu sein (74,3%), fast ein Drittel aller Frauen hat sexuelle Gewalt erfahren (29,5%). (vgl. Prävalenzstudie 2011, S. 76, 123) Welche Folgen das hat, ist ebenfalls dokumentiert: 99,1% der Betroffenen verbinden das Erleben sexueller Gewalt mit negativen psychischen oder körperlichen Folgen, und für 42,8% sind die Folgen aufgrund sexueller Gewalt langfristig. (vgl. Österreichisches Institut für Familienberatung 2017) Entsprechende Gewaltstatistiken zeigen auch häufig, dass Gewalt an Frauen meist vom Partner ausgeübt wird, und die meisten dokumentierten Fälle beziehen sich hierbei auf österreichische Staatsbürger und Staatsbürgerinnen. Die Behauptung, dass Gewalt gegen Frauen in Österreich eigentlich kein Thema sei, ist also offenbar falsch. Irgendwo zwischen Überdramatisierung und Trivialisierung werden die Diskussionen geführt, die dann plötzlich das unerwünschte „Begrapschen" des Gesäßes einer Person als „Prüfung ob die Frau Interesse hat" verstanden wissen wollen. (vgl. Schmidt 2015) Im Zuge mancher öffentlichen Diskussion wurde sogar die Reform des Sexualstrafrechts hinterfragt. Im gleichen Atemzug aber wird genau dieses Gesetz auch bemüht, wenn es darum geht „unsere Frauen" vor fremden Männern zu beschützen.

Fazit

Doppelmoral ist ein überaus interessantes Phänomen. Doch diese steht nicht so sehr im Zentrum der Diskussion wie die Definitionsversuche von überzogenem Feminismus und übereifrigem Fanatismus, wenn Frauen auf ihr Recht auf körperliche Unversehrtheit und Integrität pochen. Je nachdem, wer der potentielle Täter ist, verändert sich die Argumentation. Der Kontext entscheidet. Auf einem zünftigen Tanzfest gelten andere Regeln als auf dem Silvesterpfad, und noch viel mehr, der Grat zwischen „Anmache und Tuchfühlung" und zwischen „sexuellen Übergriffen" wird von einer meist männlichen Öffentlichkeit definiert. Man beachte dabei das Paradox doppelter Gewalt: Frauen werden Opfer von sexuellen Übergriffen, und dann werden sie nochmals Opfer einer aggressiven Argumentation, die darauf aufbaut, dass „unsere armen Frauen Opfer" sind. Wenn Opfer nicht für sich selbst sprechen können oder dürfen, werden sie nochmals zu Opfern. Viele Medien spiegelten die Angst „unserer Männer um unsere Frauen" wieder. Dabei bleibt Gewalt per se Gewalt und diese ist zu verurteilen. Die Dekonstruktion des Diskurses und ein Blick darauf, wer sich hinter dem gerne bemühten „Wir" und den davon abgegrenzten „Anderen" verbirgt, offenbart sehr viel über die Machtverteilung innerhalb und außerhalb von Gesellschaften. In der Realität entscheidet immer noch massiv der Kontext, aber auf der Metaebene ist die Debatte über Verschleierung oder Nacktheit eigentlich wie zwei Strophen desselben Liedes, das eigentlich niemand mehr singen möchte.

Literatur

Allport, Gordon: Pattern and Growth in Personality, Harcourt College Publishing, 1963.
Anonyma: Warum ich zum Islam übertrat...; In: Schwarzer, Alice (hg): Die grosse Verschleierung, Für Integration, gegen Islamismus; Kiepenheuer & Witsch, Köln 2010, S. 185-196.
Bauer, Joachim: Schmerzgrenze, Vom Ursprung alltäglicher und globaler Gewalt; Wilhelm Heyne Verlag, München 2013.
Benz, Wolfgang: Die Feinde aus dem Morgenland, Wie die Angst vor den Muslimen unsere Demokratie gefährdet; Verlag C.H. Beck, München 2012.
Berger, Peter L. / Luckmann, Thomas: Die gesellschaftliche Konstruktion der Wirklichkeit; Fischer Taschenbuch Verlag, Frankfurt am Main 200017.
Egger, Simone: Phänomen Wiesntracht: Identitätspraxen einer urbanen Gesellschaft, Dirndl und Lederhosen. München und das Oktoberfest, Band 2 von Münchner ethnographische Schriften, Herbert Utz Verlag, München 2008.
Emcke, Carolin / Hoyng, Hans / et. al.: „Wir werden zurückschlagen", 15.09.2001; Nr. 38/2001; Auf: http://www.spiegel.de/spiegel/print/d-20128547.html (letzter Zugriff: 6.11.2017)
Facebook: „My Stealthy freedom" (Vgl. https://www.facebook.com/StealthyFreedom (letzter Zugriff: 20.12.2014).
fin: Polizei geht gegen Burkini-Trägerinnen vor; In: ZEIT ONLINE, 24. August 2016; Auf: http://www.zeit.de/gesellschaft/zeitgeschehen/2016-08/frankreich-burkiniverbot-polizei-strand-nizza (letzter Abruf: 3.11.2017).
fivb Federation Internationale De Volleyball: Beach Volleyball Player's Uniforms Guidelines For Olympic Games; Auf: http://www.fivb.org/EN/BeachVolleyball/Rules/BVB%20Uniforms%20OG%202004.pdf (letzter Zugriff: 6.11.2017)
Frauenberatung 2017 http://frauenberatung.at/?page_id=423, Abruf: 10.10.2017)
Internet Movie Database: Nicht ohne meine Tochter: http://www.imdb.com/title/tt0102555/?ref_=fn_al_tt_1 (letzter Zugriff: 21.7.2014).
Kelek, Necla: 2006: *Die fremde Braut. Ein Bericht aus dem Inneren des türkischen Lebens in Deutschland.* Kiepenheuer & Witsch, Köln,
Kneissl, Karin: Die Gewaltspirale, Warum Orient und Okzident nicht miteinander können; Ecowin Verlag, Salzburg 2007.
Malinowski, Bronislaw: Ein Tagebuch im strikten Sinn des Wortes. Neuguinea 1914-1918, Schriften in vier Bänden, Syndikat Verlag, Frankfurt 1986

N.N.: Femen aller Länder, vereinigt euch!; In: Emma 1.1.2012; Auf: http://www.emma.de/artikel/femen-aller-laender-vereinigt-euch-265794 (letzter Zugriff: 1.8.2014).

Österreichischer Integrationsfonds: https://www.integrationsfonds.at/publikationen/zahlenfakten/migration-integration-schwerpunkt-kinder-und-jugend/ (letzter Zugriff: 31.10.2017).

Österreichischer Integrationsfonds: https://www.integrationsfonds.at/publikationen/zahlen-fakten/migration-integration-schwerpunkt-kinder-und-jugend/ Zugriff: 31.10.2017

Österreichisches Institut für Familienforschung an der Universität Wien (2011): Gewalt in der Familie und im nahen sozialen Umfeld. Österreichische Prävalenzstudie zur Gewalt an Frauen und Männern. Wien.; zit. n. Notruf. Beratung f. vergewaltigte Frauen und Mädchen Wien.: Daten und Fakten zu sexueller Gewalt. Stand 9/2014. S. 2. Auf: http://frauenberatung.at/wp-content/uploads/2014/10/Aktuelle_Version_DATENundFAKTEN-SexuelleGewalt...INFO_bis2013.pdf (Zugriff: 10.10.2017).

Scherer, Thorsten: Ein Bild von Welt: Glaubenssuche zwischen Physik und Metaphysik; Books on Demand 2009

Schmidt, Colette M.: Sexualstrafrecht bei "Im Zentrum": Herrenwitze zum Totlachen. 13.04.2015. Auf: http://derstandard.at/2000014242382/Herrenwitze-zum-TotlachenSexualstrafrecht-bei-Im-Zentrum, Zugriff: 27.2.2017.

Schwarzer, Alice (hg): Die grosse Verschleierung, Für Integration, gegen Islamismus; Kiepenheuer & Witsch, Köln 2010.

Taylor, Sue / Parker, Karin / Jaffe, Enstam: Darwin's Lgeacy: Scenarios in Human Evolution, Altamira Press, Lanham, New York, Toronto, Plymouth UK 2008

Tischner, Józef: Historia filozofii po góralsku, Znak, Kraków 2008.

Wallnöfer, Elisabeth: Geraubte Tradition. Wie die Nazis unsere Kultur verfälschten. Sankt Ulrich, Augsburg 2011.

Weiß, Anna: Iran 2010: Die Verzweifelten; In: Schwarzer, Alice (hg): Die grosse Verschleierung, Für Integration, gegen Islamismus; Kiepenheuer & Witsch, Köln 2010, S. 293-301.

Autorinnen und Autoren

Friedrich Altenburg studierte Geschichte, Publizistik und Kommunikationswissenschaft an der Paris-Lodron Universität Salzburg. Nach 20 Jahren operativer Arbeit in der internationalen Humanitären Hilfe und Entwicklungszusammenarbeit wechselte er 2011 an das Department Migration und Globalisierung der Donau-Universität Krems als wissenschaftlicher Mitarbeiter.

Gülay Ateş studierte Soziologie an den Universitäten in Heidelberg und Wien. Sie promovierte an der Universität Wien zum Thema „Transmission von Religion bei muslimischen Familien mit Migrationshintergrund". Sie ist wissenschaftliche Mitarbeiterin an der Klinik für Palliativmedizin am Universitätsklinikum Bonn und affiliierte Forscherin am Institut für Soziologie der Universität Wien.

Johann Bacher, Universitätsprofessor für Soziologie und Empirische Sozialforschung sowie Leiter der Abteilung für Empirische Sozialforschung des Instituts für Soziologie der Johannes Kepler Universität Linz. Arbeitsschwerpunkte: Methoden der empirischen Sozialforschung, Bildungsungleichheiten, Soziologie der Kindheit, Jugend und des abweichenden Verhaltens.

Rainer Bauböck ist Professor für soziale und politische Theorie am Europäischen Hochschulinstitut in Florenz und forscht zu den Themen Staatsbürgerschaft, Demokratietheorie, Migration, kulturelle Diversität, Nationalismus und Europäische Integration. Er ist Gründer und Kodirektor von GLOBALCIT, eines globalen online Observatariums zu Fragen der Staatsbürgerschaft und des Wahlrechts.

Johannes Berger ist Leiter des Forschungsbereichs Arbeitsmarkt und Soziale Sicherung bei EcoAustria und befasst sich mit ökonomischen Fragestellungen in diesem Forschungsbereich und im öffentlichen Sektor, u.a. unter Verwendung makroökonomischer Modelle. Davor war Johannes Berger mehrere Jahre am Institut für Höhere Studien tätig.

Tania Berger Ausgebildete Architektin und promovierte Bautechnikerin, leitet am Department für Migration und Globalisierung der Donau-Universität Krems das Zentrum für Europa und Globalisierung und den Fachbereich „Sozialraum und Migration", der sich auf nationaler Ebene mit Integration im Wohnen und Wohnumfeld befasst und im internationalen Kontext mit Urbansierungsprozessen und informellen Wohnlösungen für einkommensschwache Gruppen.

Daniela Bobeva is associate professor at the Bulgarian Academy of Sciences. She is teaching in three universities in the field of international economy and finance. She has a long experience in migration research with more than twenty publications and more than twenty years as a correspondent in the OECD international migration research network. Dr. Bobeva combines research and policy making experience as a Minister of Trade and Foreign Economic Co-operation (1997) and Deputy Prime Minister of Bulgaria (2013-2014).

Julia Bock-Schappelwein, Studium der Volkswirtschaft an der Universität Wien, seit 2004 als Referentin am Österreichischen Institut für Wirtschaftsforschung (WIFO) tätig. Ihre Arbeitsschwerpunkte umfassen arbeitsmarkt-, bildungs- und migrationsspezifische Fragestellungen. Aktuell arbeitet sie zu genderspezifischen Fragen sowie zu Digitalisierung und Arbeit.

Mathias Czaika ist Professor für Migration und Integration und Leiter des Departments für Migration und Globalisierung an der Donau-Universität Krems, sowie Research Associate am Department for International Development an der Universität Oxford. Er forscht zu internationalen Migrationsprozessen und der Rolle von Migrationspolitik.

İnci Dirim ist Übersetzerin, Deutschlehrerin, Germanistin, Linguistin und Erziehungswissenschaftlerin. Schulbesuch und Studium in Ankara und Bremen; Promotion 1997 am Fachbereich Erziehungswissenschaft der Universität Hamburg. 2004–2007 W1-Professorin für Schulpädagogik an der Leibniz Universität Hannover; 2007-2010 W2-Professorin für Erziehungswissenschaft an der Universität Hamburg. Seit März 2010 Professorin für Deutsch als Zweitsprache an der Philologisch-Kulturwissenschaftlichen Fakultät der Universität Wien.

Vedran Dzihic ist Senior Fellow am Österreichischen Institut für Internationale Politik (oiip) und Politologe an der Universität Wien. Darüber hinaus ist er non-resident Fellow am Center for Transatlantic Relations (CTR), SAIS, Johns Hopkins University, Washington D.C. Dzihic unterrichtet an der Universität Wien, im MA-Lehrgang „Balkan-Studies", sowie im „Vienna Master in Human Rights". Er ist Autor zahlreicher Buchpublikationen und Artikel in internationalen wissenschaftlichen Journalen und Medien.

Anna Faustmann studierte Soziologie an der Karl-Franzens-Universität Graz und der University of Wisconsin-Eau Claire. Sie ist seit 2009 wissenschaftliche Mitarbeiterin am Department für Migration und Globalisierung an der Donau-Universität Krems mit Forschungsschwerpunkten auf Migration und Integration im Kontext von Arbeitsmarkt-, Gesundheits- und Sozialsystemen.

Margarita Fourer is a PhD Candidate undertaking a double degree at the Danube University Krems and Maastricht University. Between 2015 and 2017, Margarita worked in relocation in Israel, which included Canadian sponsorship visas and family reunification to a number of EU countries, as well as in US resettlement in Kenya. Margarita's research interests are focused on durable solutions in refugee and migration law.

August Gächter, Studium der Soziologie. Seit 1989 mit Forschung zur Integration der aus dem Ausland zuziehenden Bevölkerung vor allem in das Beschäftigungs- und das Bildungswesen, aber auch in andere gesellschaftliche Bereiche befasst. Sozialraumanalysen und Indikatorenprojekte für große und kleine Städte und für Landesregierungen sowie Beratungstätigkeit für nationale und internationale Einrichtungen. Häufige Vortrags- und Referatstätigkeit. Von 1991 bis 2002 am Institut für Höhere Studien beschäftigt, seither am Zentrum für Soziale Innovation, beide in Wien. Vorstandsmitglied beim Beratungszentrum für MigrantInnen, Wien, Mitglied von Global Migration Policy Associates (GMPA).

Cengiz Günay ist Senior Fellow am Österreichischen Institut für Internationale Politik und Lektor an der Universität Wien (Institut für Politikwissenschaft und Institut für Internationale Entwicklung, Orientalistik). Zu seinen Forschungsschwerpunkten gehören: Islamismus, politische Reform und Demokratisierung sowie die Rolle von nicht-staatlichen Akteuren im Nahen Osten und der Türkei. Er ist Autor der Monographie „Die Geschichte der Türkei. Von den Anfängen der Moderne bis heute".

Friedrich Heckmann, Professor (em.) für Soziologie, Co-Leiter des europäischen forums für migrationsstudien (efms), Institut an der Universität Bamberg. Studium der Soziologie, Geschichte und Volkswirtschaftslehre in Münster, Kiel, Lawrence (USA) und Erlangen-Nürnberg. Arbeitsgebiete: Soziologie interethnischer Beziehungen und der Migration, Integration, Sozialstruktur Deutschlands, Sozialisationsforschung, soziologische Theorie. Politikberatung und gutachterliche Tätigkeit im Bereich Migration und Integration für Bundestag, Bundesregierung, Landesregierungen, EU Kommission, Kommunen, Verbände und gesellschaftliche Organisationen.

Karin Heitzmann ist habilitierte Sozioökonomin; Mitarbeiterin am Institut für Sozialpolitik (Department Sozioökonomie) und Leiterin des Forschungsinstituts Economics of Inequality (gemeinsam mit Wilfried Altzinger und Sigrid Stagl) an der WU Wien. Lehrt und forscht zu den Themen Sozialpolitik, Zukunft des Sozialstaats, Armut/Ausgrenzung.

Thomas Horvath, Studium der Volkswirtschaftslehre an der Universität Wien und anschließende Dissertation an der Universität Linz. Er ist seit 2010 als Referent am Österreichischen Institut für Wirtschaftsforschung tätig. Seine Arbeitsschwerpunkte bilden arbeitsmarkt- und migrationsspezifische Fragestellungen sowie die Evaluierung von Instrumenten der aktiven Arbeitsmarktpolitik.

Peter Huber studierte Volkswirtschaft an der Wirtschaftsuniversität Wien, am Institut für Höhere Studien sowie an der Universität Innsbruck. Seit 1998 arbeitet er als Referent am Österreichischen Institut für Wirtschaftsforschung: Dort beschäftigt er sich vor allem mit den Ursachen und Auswirkungen von Migration in Österreich und Europa.

Joe Isaac graduated at the University of Melbourne with degrees in Arts and Commerce in 1945 and later gained a PhD from the London School of Economics. He was Professor of Economics at Melbourne from 1962-1964 and at Monash from 1965-1973, whereupon he left academia to serve as the Deputy President of the Australian Conciliation and Arbitration Commission from 1974-1987. He then returned to academia as a Professorial Fellow in Melbourne's Department of Management. He has also held many other simultaneous appointments including memberships of the OECD's Expert Committee on Labour Market Flexibility in 1986. He has published many books and papers on industrial relations and wages policy.

Josef Kytir, Univ.-Doz. Dr., Studium der Geographie und Sozialgeschichte an der Universität Wien, langjähriger Mitarbeiter am Institut für Demographie der Österreichischen Akademie der Wissenschaften. 1996 Habilitation an der Grund- und Integrativwissenschaftlichen Fakultät der Universität Wien, Lektor am Institut für Geographie und am Institut für Soziologie der Universität Wien. Seit 2000 Mitarbeiter der Bundesanstalt Statistik Österreich, seit 2011 in der Funktion des Leiters der Direktion Bevölkerung. Zahlreiche Publikationen und Vorträge zu demographischen und sozialen Themen.

Thomas J. Lampoltshammer is Senior Scientist and research coordinator at the Center for E-Governance at the Department for E-Governance and Administration. He has a strong background in spatio-temporal analysis, semantics, data modelling, and visualisation. His current research projects focus on Strategic Information Management and Digital Transformation in inter- and transdisciplinary environments.

Lorenz Lassnigg, Senior Researcher am Institut für Höhere Studien in Wien, Forschungsgruppe equi: in_Equality in Education. Forschungsschwerpunkte: Governance, Lifelong Learning, Education and Social Progress.

Thomas Leoni, Studium an der Universität Bologna und der Johns Hopkins University, Dissertation an der Wirtschaftsuniversität Wien (WU). Seit 2005 wissenschaftlicher Mitarbeiter am WIFO. Forschungsschwerpunkte Arbeitsmarkt, Gestaltung des Wohlfahrtsstaats und Fragen der Gesundheit in der Arbeitswelt. Lehraufträge an der WU, der Universität Linz und der Donau-Universität Krems.

Hedwig Lutz ist Ökonomin und seit 1995 wissenschaftliche Mitarbeiterin im Forschungsbereich „Arbeitsmarkt, Einkommen und soziale Sicherheit" am Österreichischen Institut für Wirtschaftsforschung (WIFO). Zu ihren thematischen Schwerpunkten zählen die Bestimmungsgründe und die strukturelle Entwicklung von Erwerbstätigkeit und Arbeitslosigkeit, Gender-Fragen auf dem Arbeitsmarkt, aktive und passive Arbeitsmarktpolitiken sowie die Evaluierung der Wirkungen arbeitsmarkt-, familien- und sozialpolitischer Strategien auf die Erwerbsbeteiligung, die Beschäftigung und das Einkommen.

Stephan Marik-Lebeck, Studium der Geographie und Raumforschung in Wien und Rennes (Frankreich). Seit 2003 bei Statistik Austria, seit 2013 Leiter des Bereichs „Demographie, Gesundheit, Arbeitsmarkt". Er blickt auf eine fünfzehnjährige Tätigkeit im Bereich Migrations- und Integrationsstatistiken zurück, u.a. als Projektleiter für das Statistische Jahrbuch „migration&integration". Zahlreiche Veröffentlichungen zu den Themen Migration, Integration und Bevölkerung in Österreich.

Philip Martin is a professor at the University of California, Davis, chair of the UC Comparative Immigration & Integration Program, and editor of Rural Migration News. He has consulted on farm labor and migration issues with US and international organizations and has authored many books and articles on farm labor and migration.

Christine Mayrhuber, seit 1999 wissenschaftliche Mitarbeiterin im Forschungsbereich „Arbeitsmarkt, Einkommen und soziale Sicherheit" am Österreichischen Institut für Wirtschaftsforschung, WIFO. Ihre Forschungsschwerpunkte sind Gestaltung und Finanzierung des Wohlfahrtsstaates, Einkommensverteilung und Umverteilung unter besonderer Berücksichtigung des Gender-Aspekts. Langjähriges Mitglied der österreichischen Kommission zur langfristigen Pensionssicherung.

Peter Parycek is full Professor of E-Governance and Head of the Department for E-Governance and Administration at Danube University Krems. Since July 2017, he leads the Competence Centre Public IT at the Fraunhofer Institute for Open Communications Systems, which acts as think tank for the digital transformation of the public sector and is funded by the German Minsitry of Interiour. Prof. Parycek is the founder of the conference series CeDEM (International Conference for eDemocracy and Open Government) held in Austria and Asia and also responsible for the open access journal JeDEM (eJournal of eDemocracy and Open Government).

Bernhard Perchinig (Dr. phil, Universität Wien 1986), ist Senior Researcher am International Centre for Migration Policy Development (ICMPD) in Wien mit dem Schwerpunkt vergleichende Analyse von Migrationspolitiken und Migration und internationale Beziehungen. Er ist Faculty-Member am Department für Rechtswissenschaften und Internationale Beziehungen der Donau-Universität Krems und unterrichtet dort sowie am Salzburg College zum Thema Migration und Minderheiten. Beratungstätigkeit im Bereich Migrations- und Integrationsmanagement für regionale und nationale Regierungen und internationale Organisationen.

Thomas Pfeffer ist wissenschaftlicher Mitarbeiter am Department für Migration und Globalisierung. Als Soziologe mit Fokus auf Systemtheorie, Bildungs- und Organisationssoziologie beschäftigt er sich mit dem internationalen Transfer von Qualifikationen und Kompetenzen, mit institutionellen Formen des Umgangs mit Migration und Diversität und mit Anwendungen der Systemtheorie in der empirischen Migrationsforschung.

Dino Pitoski is a PhD candidate in the Migration Studies programme at Danube University Krems. He has a strong background in the area of maritime transport technology as well as in the domain of logistics. His PhD project observes migration from a complex networks perspective, relating the factors of migration identified in migration determinants theory with complex networks measures and models.

Christoph Reinprecht ist Professor für Soziologie an der Universität Wien. Er leitet das Masterstudium Europäische Studien an der Universität Wien und ist assoziierter Wissenschaftler am Centre de la Recherche sur l'Habitat in Paris. Zahlreiche Forschungsprojekte und Publikationen in den Bereichen Migration, Stadt, Wohnen, Ungleichheit, Politische Soziologie.

Martin Ruhs is Associate Professor of Political Economy at Oxford University. He is author of *The Price of Rights: Regulating International Labor Migration* (Princeton University Press, 2013) and Editor (together with Bridget Anderson) of *Who Needs Migrant Workers? Labour Shortages, Immigration, and Public Policies* (Oxford University Press, 2012).

Isabella Skrivanek ist wissenschaftliche Mitarbeiterin am Department Migration und Globalisierung der Donau-Universität Krems. Sie studierte Politikwissenschaft und Volkswirtschaftslehre an der Universität Wien und forscht zu Fragen der Migration und Integration mit Fokus auf den Arbeitsmarkt, Bildung und Qualifikationssysteme sowie Migrations- und Sozialpolitik.

Gerald Steiner received his Venia Legendi in "Systemic and Sustainability Management" in 2009 and is a Full Professor of Organizational Communication and Innovation, Head of the Department for Knowledge and Communication Management and Dean of the Faculty of Business and Globalization at Danube University Krems in Austria. He is a former Visiting Scholar and Schumpeter Professor at Harvard University's Weatherhead Center for International Affairs (WCFIA). Before, he was an Associate Professor of Systemic and Sustainability Management at the Institute of Systems Sciences, Innovation & Sustainability Research at the University of Graz.

Mario Steiner, Mag. Dr., Studium der Soziologie an der Universität Wien, Senior Researcher und Head of Research Group in Equality and Education am Institut für Höhere Studien Wien; Forschungsschwerpunkte zu „Social Progress" im Bildungsbereich, Bildungsarmut, benachteiligten Jugendlichen, Second Chance Education, sozialer Ungleichheit im Bildungssystem sowie Integration und Ausgrenzung vom Arbeitsmarkt.

Ludwig Strohner ist Leiter des Forschungsbereichs Öffentliche Finanzen bei EcoAustria und untersucht ökonomische Fragestellungen in diesem Bereich und am Arbeitsmarkt. Er war federführend an der Entwicklung mehrerer makroökonomischer Modelle beteiligt. Davor war Ludwig Strohner mehrere Jahre am Institut für Höhere Studien tätig.

Aga Trnka-Kwiecinski ist Publizistin- und Kommunikationswissenschafterin sowie Theater-, -Film- und Medienwissenschafterin. Seit 2012 ist sie wissenschaftliche Mitarbeiterin am Department Migration und Globalisierung, wo sie die Master-Studiengänge für Interkulturelle Kompetenzen sowie für Provokationspädagogik leitet. Thematische Schwerpunkte: Medienpädagogik, Sicherheit, Gender & Diversity, psychosoziale Aspekte in Kommunikation und Pädagogik.

Gabriela Viale Pereira is Senior Scientist at the Department for E-Governance and Administration at Danube University Krems in Austria and Visiting Post-doc at Fundação Getúlio Vargas (EAESP/FGV) in Brazil. Gabriela's research is focused on e-government, smart governance and the impacts of the digital transformation on governmental decisions and policy-making in a data-driven era.

Shefali Virkar is a postdoctoral Research Associate at the Department for E-Governance and Development at Danube University Krems. She is specialised in the theory and practice of electronic government, in particular, political, social, and economic implications of the new Information and Communications Technologies (ICT) and their impact on traditional forms of work and governance structures.

Ewald Walterskirchen, Dkfm. Dr., ist Emeritus Consultant am Österreichichen Institut für Wirtschaftsforschung. Er arbeitete 1970-2005 am WIFO, u.a. als Arbeitsmarktreferent, Koordinator des Fachbereichs Makroökonomie und Mitglied der Leitung. In den achtziger und neunziger Jahren war er wissenschaftlicher Koordinator der „International Commmission on Employment Issues in Europe". Er war Lektor an mehreren Hochschulen und publizierte vor allem auf den Gebieten Makroökonomie, Wirtschaftsprognose, europäische Wirtschaftspolitik und Arbeitsmarktforschung.

Manfred Zentner studierte Mathematik und Philosophie an der Universität Wien Er forscht zu Jugend und Jugendkultur seit 1997. Von 2001 bis 2013 arbeitete er am Institut für Jugendkulturforschung in Wien, seit 2013 ist er als Forscher am Department für Migration und Globalisierung der Donau-Universität Krems. Seine Forschungsschwerpunkte sind Jugendkulturen, Migration, Partizipation und Jugendpolitik. Zudem ist er Mitglied im Pool Europäischer JugendforscherInnen.

Gudrun Biffl:
Lebenslauf und Publikationen

Stationen einer wissenschaftlichen Karriere

1949 Geboren am 22.01.1949 in Vöcklabruck
1967 Matura mit Auszeichnung am Realgymnasium Erlgasse in Wien
1972 Magistra rer.soc.oec der Studienrichtung Handelswissenschaften an der Hochschule für Welthandel Wien, heute WU-Wien
1973 Postgraduale Ausbildung in Ökonomie am Institut für Höhere Studien (IHS) in Wien
1975 Doktorin der Philosophie (PhD) an der University of Newcastle/Tyne
Eintritt in das Wirtschaftsforschungsinstitut Österreich (WIFO) als Senior Researcher (bis 2009)
1977 Mitglied des Permanent Migration Observatory der Organisation für Wirtschaftliche Zusammenarbeit und Entwicklung (OECD) (bis heute)
1984 Researcher am Bureau of Labor Statistics in Washington, D.C.
1986 Forschungsaufenthalt am Labour Centre der London School of Economics
1991 Forschungsaufenthalt an der Curtin University of Technology und am Western Australian Labour Market Research Centre in Perth
1993 Habilitation an der Wirtschaftsuniversität Wien im Bereich der Arbeitsmarkttheorie und Arbeitsmarktpolitik
1998 Visiting Fellow and Professor an der University of Melbourne, Australien und der University of Christchurch, Neuseeland
2008 Berufung an die Donau-Universität Krems auf den Lehrstuhl für Migration, Integration und Sicherheit
Gründung des Departments für Migration und Globalisierung
2009 Mitglied des Expertenrats für Integration zunächst im Bundesministerium für Inneres (bis 2013), dann im Bundesministerium für Europa, Integration und Äußere Angelegenheiten (Bis heute)
Käthe Leichter Staatspreis für Frauenforschung, Geschlechterforschung und Gleichstellung in der Arbeitswelt
Goldenes Verdienstzeichen der Republik Österreich
2010 Ernennung zur Dekanin der Fakultät für Wirtschaft und Globalisierung an der Donau-Universität Krems (bis 2015)
2012 Liese Prokop-Frauenpreis in der Kategorie Wissenschaft
2015 Vorsitzende des Statistikrates der Statistik Austria
2017 Übergabe der Departmentleitung an Univ. Prof. Dr. Mathias Czaika
Kulturpreis des Landes Niederösterreich in der Kategorie Erwachsenenbildung
Gabriele-Possanner-Würdigungspreis für ihr Lebenswerk durch das Bundesministerium für Wissenschaft, Forschung und Wirtschaft

Publikationen

Gudrun Biffl blickt auf ein reiches Wirken als Autorin, Herausgeberin und Reviewerin zurück. Die wesentlichen Eckpunkte sind nachstehend dargestellt und sind zugleich nur ein Ausschnitt ihres breiten Wirkens in wissenschaftliche und gesellschaftliche Öffentlichkeiten hinein.

Gudrun Biffl als Herausgeberin und Mitglied von Editorial Boards

- Seit 1995 Editorial Board des „Journal of Contemporary Issues in Business and Government", Curtin University of Technology
- Seit 2004 Editorial-Board des "Journal of Immigrant and Refugee Studies", School of Social Welfare and Center for International Studies, University of Missouri – St. Louis
- Seit 2011 Herausgeberin der „Schriftenreihe zu Migration und Globalisierung" des Departments Migration und Globalisierung an der Donau-Universität Krems

Hinzu kommen Rezensionen und die Begutachtung von Artikeln im Journal of International Migration (Quarterly Review der International Organisation for Migration), im Journal of Economic Psychology (über verhaltenstheoretische Aspekte ökonomischer Prozesse), im Asia Pacific Journal of Economics and Business (Arbeitsmarkt, Migrationen und Entwicklungsökonomie), im Journal of Structural Change and Economic Dynamics, im Journal of Labour Market Research, im Journal of Feminist Economics und im Journal Migration Letters als eingetragene Gutachterin.

Monographien und Sammelbände

Biffl, Gudrun (1994): Theorie und Empirie des Arbeitsmarktes am Beispiel Österreich. Springer Verlag, Wien-New York.

Muhr, Rudolf/Biffl, Gudrun (Hg.) (2010): Sprache – Bildung – Bildungsstandards – Migration Verlag Peter Lang, Frankfurt/Main

Biffl, Gudrun (Hg.) (2010): Migration & Integration. Dialog zwischen Politik, Wissenschaft und Praxis. omninum, Bad Vöslau.

Biffl, Gudrun/Dimmel, Nikolaus (2011): Migrationsmanagement Band 1. Grundzüge des Managements von Migration und Integration. omninum, Bad Vöslau.

Biffl, Gudrun/Rössl, Lydia (Hg.) (2011): Migration & Integration 2. Dialog zwischen Politik, Wissenschaft und Praxis. omninum, Bad Vöslau.

Biffl, Gudrun/Rössl, Lydia (Hg.) (2012) Migration & Integration 3. Dialog zwischen Politik, Wissenschaft und Praxis. omninum, Bad Vöslau.

Biffl, Gudrun/Altenburg, Friedrich (Hg.) (2012): Migration and Health in Nowhereland. Access of Undocumented Migrants to Work and Health Care in Europe. omninum, Bad Vöslau.

Biffl, Gudrun/Berger, Tania/Czerny, Margarethe (Hg.) (2013): Wohnen und die regionale Dimension der Integration. Edition Donau-Universität Krems, Krems.

Biffl, Gudrun/Rössl, Lydia (Hg.) (2014): Migration & Integration 4. Dialog zwischen Politik, Wissenschaft und Praxis. Guthmann-Peterson, Wien.

Baatz, Ursula/Biffl, Gudrun. (2014): Die Krise und das Gute Leben. Tagungsband zum Symposion Dürnstein 2014. Edition Donau-Universität Krems, Krems.

Biffl, Gudrun/Pfeffer, Thomas/Trnka-Kwiecinski, Aga (2014): Joint efforts of police and health authorities to combat trafficking in human beings. Handbook for professionals at the interface of police & health authorities, NGO Payoke Antwerpen/Danube University Krems, Antwerpen und Krems.

Baatz, Ursula/Biffl, Gudrun (Hg.) (2015): Glücksbilder. Die Wirklichkeit der Utopien. Edition Donau-Universität Krems, Krems.

Biffl, Gudrun/Rössl, Lydia (Hg.) (2015): Suchtverhalten & Migration. Zur Praxis der Präventionsarbeit in Österreich. omninum, Bad Vöslau.

Biffl, Gudrun/Rössl, Lydia (Hg.) (2015): Migration & Integration 5. Dialog zwischen Politik, Wissenschaft und Praxis. omninum, Bad Vöslau.

Biffl, Gudrun/Stepan, Dorothea (Hg.) (2016): Europa und Demokratien im Wandel. Ausgewählte Beiträge zum Globalisierungsforum 2014-15. Reihe Europa und Globalisierung. Edition Donau-Universität Krems. Krems

Biffl, Gudrun/Dimmel, Nikolaus (2016): Migrationsmanagement Band 2. Wohnen im Zusammenwirken mit Migration und Integration. omninum, Bad Vöslau.

Baatz, Ursula/Biffl, Gudrun (2016): Vertrauen in unsicheren Zeiten. Optionen für die Zukunft. Tagungsband zum Symposion Dürnstein 2016. Edition Donau-Universität Krems. Krems.

Biffl, Gudrun/Rössl, Lydia (Hg.): (2017) Migration & Integration 6. Dialog zwischen Politik, Wissenschaft und Praxis. omninum, Bad Vöslau.

Buchbeiträge

Biffl, Gudrun (1984): Die Rolle des Arbeitsmarktes im Strukturwandel. In: Stephan Schulmeister (Koord.) Österreichische Strukturberichterstattung, Band IV, WIFO Gutachtenserie.

Biffl, Gudrun (1986): Der Strukturwandel der Ausländerbeschäftigung in Österreich. In: Wimmer, Hannes (Hg.): Ausländische Arbeitskräfte in Österreich. Campus, Frankfurt/New York.

Biffl, Gudrun (1987): Arbeitslosigkeit und Arbeitsmarktpolitik der Bauwirtschaft. In: Marin, Bernd (Hg.): Verfall und Erneuerung im Bauwesen. Internationale Publikationen, Wien.

Biffl, Gudrun (1989): Arbeitsmarktpolitik in Österreich. In: Abele, Hanns/Nowotny, Ewald/Schleicher, Stefan/Winckler Georg (Hg.): Handbuch der österreichischen Wirtschaftspolitik. Manz Verlag, Wien.

Biffl, Gudrun (1993): Gleichstellung von Mann und Frau. In: Enderle, Georges et al. (Hg.): Lexikon der Wirtschaftsethik. Herder, Wien.

Biffl, Gudrun (1993): Case Studies of the Role of Immigrants in Industry Restructuring. In: Stromback, Thorsten (Hg): Immigration and the Labour Market with Special Reference to Industry Restructuring in Western Australia. Bureau of Immigration Research, Melbourne.

Biffl, Gudrun (1994): Die Arbeitswelt der Frauen in Österreich: Erwerbs- und Hausarbeit. In: Good, David F./Grandner, Margarete/Maynes, Mary J (Hg.): Frauen in Österreich. Böhler Verlag, Wien.

Biffl, Gudrun (1995): Innovative Arbeitsmarktpolitik für Randgruppen. In: Schreckeneder, Rosian (Hg.): Arbeit im Modernisierungs-prozess. Kurswechsel Buch. Beigewurm, Wien.

Biffl, Gudrun (1995): Jugendliche - Berufsqualifikation und Arbeitsmarkt. In: Sieder, Reinhard et al. (Hg.): Österreich 1945-1995. Verlag für Gesellschaftskritik, Band 60, Wien.

Biffl, Gudrun (1995): Ökonomische Situation der Frauen in Österreich. In: Bundesministerium für Frauenangelegenheiten: Frauenbericht 1995. Bundeskanzleramt, Wien.

Biffl, Gudrun (1995): Wanderungsbewegungen und Integration. In: Pollan, Wolfgang (Koord.): Beschäftigungschancen und Integration. WIFO-Gutachtenserie, Wien.

Biffl, Gudrun (1995): "Innovative Labour Market Policies for Marginalised Workers", in Labour and the Process of Modernisation, Schreckeneder, Rosian (Hrsg.), Kurswechsel, Beigewum, Vienna.

Biffl, Gudrun (1996): Immigrant Labour Integration. In: Schmid/Günther et al. (Hg.): International Handbook of Labour Market, Policy and Evaluation. Wissenschaftszentrum Berlin, WTD, Berlin.

Biffl, Gudrun (1996): Österreicher/Innen in Australien. In: Horvath, Traude/Neyer Gerda (Hg.): Auswanderungen aus Österreich. Böhlau Verlag, Wien.

Biffl, Gudrun (1996): Makro-ökonomische Entwicklung: Wachstumseinbruch und Beschäftigungsrückgang. In: Talos, Emmerich/Falkner, Gerda (Hg.): EU - Mitglied Österreich - Gegenwart und Perspektiven: Eine Zwischenbilanz. Manz Verlag, Wien.

Biffl, Gudrun (1996): Schule - Wirtschaft – Frauen. In: Lassnigg, Lorenz/Paseka, Angelika (Hg.): Schule weiblich - Schule männlich: Zum Geschlechterverhältnis im Bildungswesen, , Studien zur Bildungsforschung und Bildungspolitik, Band 17, Studienverlag, Innsbruck-Wien.

Biffl, Gudrun (1996): Women and Work. In: Good, David F./Grandner, Margarete/Maynes, Mary J (Hg.): Austrian Women in the Nineteenth and Twentieth Centuries. Cross-Disciplinary Perspectives. Berghahn Books, Oxford.

Biffl, Gudrun (1997): Migration, Labour Market and Regional Integration: The role of the Education System. In: Bundeskanzleramt: Migration, Free Trade and Regional Integration in Central and Eastern Europe. Schriftenreihe Europa des Bundeskanzleramts, Verlag Österreich, Wien.

Biffl, Gudrun (1997): The Reproduction Paradigm. In: O'Hara, Philipp A. (Hg.): Ecyclopedia of Political Economy. Routledge, London.

Biffl, Gudrun (1998): Economic Consequences of Migration for National Economies. In: Stadt Wien: Migration and Sustainable Urban Development. Proceedings of the International Conference in Vienna 1998. Werkstattberichte Nr. 30 A, Wien..

Biffl, Gudrun (1999): Zukunft der Arbeit - Beschäftigungssituation für Jugendliche. In: Arbeitsgemeinschaft für wissenschaftliche Wirtschaftspolitik (Hg.): Europäische Beschäftigungspolitik in der Arbeitswelt 2000. Wien.

Biffl, Gudrun (1999): Der Arbeitsmarkt der Zukunft - Implikationen für die Sozialpartnerschaft. In: Tálos, Emmerich/Karlhofer, Ferdinand (Hg.): Zukunft der Sozialpartnerschaft. Veränderungsdynamik und Reformbedarf. Facultas, Wien.

Biffl, Gudrun (1999): Neuseeland - eine Erfolgsstory des Neo-Liberalismus? In: Schmee, Josef/Weissel, Erwin (Hg.): Armut des Habens. Wider den feigen Rückzug vor dem Neoliberalismus. Promedia, Wien.

Biffl, Gudrun (1999): Migration Policy - The Art of Drawing Conclusions from Insufficient Statistics. In: Matzka, Manfred/Wolfslehner Doris (Hg.): Europäische Migrationspolitik, Band 1, Beiträge zur Analyse der europäischen Zuwanderungspolitik und der internationalen Zusammenarbeit, Juridica Verlag, Wien.

Biffl, Gudrun (1999): Theoretische und empirische Grundlagen für eine koordinierte Beschäftigungspolitik in der EU. In: Piehl, Ernst/Timmann Hans-Jörg (Hg.) Der Europäische Beschäftigungspakt, Entstehungsprozess und Perspektiven. Nomos Verlag, Baden-Baden.

Biffl, Gudrun (1999): Theoretische und empirische Grundlagen für die koordinierte Europäische Beschäftigungspolitik. In: Platzer, Hans-Wolfgang (Hg.): Arbeitsmarkt- und Beschäftigungspolitik in der EU. Nationale und europäische Perspektiven. Nomos Verlag, Baden-Baden.

Biffl, Gudrun (1999): Hilde Behrend, Marianne A. Ferber, Elisabeth Maresch. In: Hagemann, Harald/Krohn, Claus-Dieter (Hg.): Biographisches Handbuch der deutschsprachigen wirtschaftswissenschaftlichen Emigration nach 1933. K.G. Saur, München.

Biffl, Gudrun (2000): Massenuniversität und Veränderungen im Beschäftigungssystem. In: Mitterauer, Lukas/Reiter Walter: (Hg.): Der Arbeitsmarkt für AkademikerInnen in Österreich. Entwicklungen, Probleme, Perspektiven. Wissenschaftsverlag, Wien.

Biffl, Gudrun (2000): Zuwanderung und Segmentierung des österreichischen Arbeitsmarktes. Ein Beitrag zur Insider-Outsider-Diskussion. In: Husa, Karl/Parnreiter, Christof/Stacher Irene (Hg.): Internationale Migration. Die globale Herausforderung des 21. Jahrhunderts? Reihe Historische Sozialkunde 17/ Internationale Entwicklung, Brandes & Apsel/Südwind, Wien.

Biffl, Gudrun (2000): Migration Policies in the Context of EU-Enlargement. In: OECD (Hg.): Migration Policies and EU Enlargement: The Case of Central and Eastern Europe. OECD, Paris.

Biffl, Gudrun (2000): Die Zeit ist reif für neue Theorien. Ein Nachwort. In: Krondorfer, Birge/Mostböck Carina (Hg.): Frauen und Ökonomie oder - Geld essen Kritik auf. Kritische Versuche feministischer Zumutungen. Pro Media Verlag, Wien.

Biffl, Gudrun (2000): Hilde Behrend. In: Dimand Robert W./Dimand, Mary A./Forget, Evelyn L. (Hg.): A Biographical Dictionary of Women Economists. Edwrad Elgar, Cheltenham, UK & Northampton, MA, USA.

Biffl, Gudrun (2000): Zukunft der Arbeit - Beschäftigungssituation für Jugendliche. In: Arbeitsgemeinschaft für wissenschaftliche Wirtschaftspolitik (Hg.): Europäische Beschäftigungspolitik in der Arbeitswelt 2000. Verlag des ÖGB, Wien.

Biffl, Gudrun (2002): Education Policy in Austria in the Context of Coordinated EU-Policy. In: Neisser Heinrich/Puntscher-Riekmann, Sonja (Hg.): Europäisierung der österreichischen Politik (Konsequenzen der EU-Mitgliedschaft). WUV-Universitätsverlag, Wien.

Biffl, Gudrun (2002): Arbeitsmarkt und Beschäftigungspolitik. Europäische Koordination als Antwort auf globalen wirtschaftlichen und gesellschaftlichen Umbruch. In: Neisser Heinrich/Puntscher-Riekmann, Sonja (Hg.): Europäisierung der österreichischen Politik (Konsequenzen der EU-Mitgliedschaft). WUV-Universitätsverlag, Wien.

Biffl, Gudrun (2003): Mobilitäts- und Verdrängungsprozesse auf dem österreichischen Arbeitsmarkt: Die Situation der unselbständig beschäftigten AusländerInnen. In: Fassmann, Heinz/ Stacher, Irene (Hg.): Österreichischer Migrations- und Integrationsbericht. Drava Verlag, Klagenfurt/Celovec.

Biffl, Gudrun/Bock-Schappelwein, Julia (2003): Soziale Mobilität durch Bildung? – Das Bildungsverhalten von MigrantInnen. In: Fassmann, Heinz/Stacher, Irene (Hg.): Österreichischer Migrations- und Integrationsbericht. Drava Verlag, Klagenfurt/Celovec.

Biffl, Gudrun (2004): Der Einfluss von Immigration auf Österreichs Wirtschaft. In: Nationaler Kontaktpunkt Österreich im Europäischen Migrationsnetzwerk (Hg.): Der Einfluss von Immigration auf die österreichische Gesellschaft. Österreichischer Beitrag im Rahmen der europaweiten Pilotstudie "The Impact of Immigration on Europe's Societies" IOM, Wien.

Biffl, Gudrun (2005): Jugend und Arbeit in Europa. In: Österreichisches Institut für Jugendforschung (Hg.): Die Jugend ist die Zukunft Europas – aber bitte noch nicht jetzt! Beiträge zum 1. Internationalen Symposium des Österreichischen Instituts für Jugendforschung am 3. 12. 2004 in Wien.

Biffl, Gudrun (2005): Reorganisation of Employees' Legal Protection. In Mazal, Wolfgang/Muranaka, Takashi (Hg.): Sozialer Schutz für atypisch Beschäftigte. Manzsche Verlags- und Universitätsbuchhandlung, Wien.

Biffl, Gudrun (2007): Age management – a coping strategy for employers: the case of the automotive industry. In: Sinigoj, Gabriele et al. (Hg.): Impact of Ageing – A common challenge of Europe and Asia. LIT Publishing international.

Biffl, Gudrun (2007): Erwerbstätigkeit und Arbeitslosigkeit: Die Bedeutung von Einbürgerung, Herkunftsregion und Religionszugehörigkeit. in Fassman, Heinz (Hg.) 2. Österreichischer Migrations- und Integrationsbericht 2001-2006. Drava Verlag, Klagenfurt/Celovec.

Biffl, Gudrun (2007): Sicherung von Grundbedürfnissen an der Schnittstelle zum Arbeitsmarkt. In: Tomandl, Theodor/Schrammel, Walter (Hg.): Sicherung von Grundbedürfnissen. Verlag Braumüller, Wien.

Biffl, Gudrun (2007): Soziales Europa – Grundrechte, Arbeit und Migration. In: Wirtschaftskammer (Hg.): Tagungsband „Europa am Scheideweg – Mehr oder Weniger Europa?. Wien,

Biffl, Gudrun (2008): Integration und Ökonomie. In: Leibetseder, Bettina/Weidenholzer, Josef (Hg.): Integration ist gestaltbar: Strategien erfolgreicher Integrationspolitik in Städten und Regionen. Sociologica Band 13, Braumüller Verlag, Wien.

Biffl, Gudrun (2008): Arbeitsmarktchancen für Jugendliche – Was ist in Österreich schief gelaufen? In: Poier, Klaus et al. (Hg.): Jugend und Soziale Gerechtigkeit. Schriftenreihe des Dr.-Karl-Kummer-Instituts Band 5, Graz.

Biffl, Gudrun (2008): Das Besoldungssystem der Pharmazeutischen Gehaltskasse und Wirkungsmechanismus In: 100 Jahre Gehaltskasse – 100 Jahre Zukunft, Festschrift 2008, Verlag Pharmazeutische Gehaltskasse in Österreich, Wien.

Biffl, Gudrun (2008): Bildung und Arbeitsmarkt aus ökonomischer Sicht. In: AK-NÖ (Hg.): Arbeitsmarkt ohne Schranken – Überwindet Bildung alle Grenzen? Tagungsband zur wissenschaftlichen Enquête des III. Dialogforum Hirschwang 2008.

Biffl, Gudrun (2008): Education and the Labour Market – Position of youth in Austria in comparison with the EU. In: Cesen, Tanja (Hg.): Proceedings of the conference and seminar "Youth Employment". Economski Institut Pravne Fakultete, Ljubljana.

Biffl, Gudrun (2009): Wahrnehmung einer – vermeintlichen – Bedrohung durch Zuwanderung und empirische Realität. In: Sir Peter Ustinov Institut (Hg.): Feindbild Zuwanderer: Vorurteile und deren Überwindung. Studienreihe Konfliktforschung Band 24. Braumüller Verlag, Wien.

Biffl, Gudrun (2009): Zur Rolle der Bildung für MigrantInnen in Österreich. In: Lassnigg, Lozenz et al. (Hg.): Öffnung von Arbeitsmärkten und Bildungssystemen. Beiträge zur Bildungsforschung. IBB-Forschung Band 6. Studien Verlag, Wien.

Biffl, Gudrun et al. (2009): Die Österreicher/-innen und der Wandel in der Arbeitswelt. In: Friesl Christian/ Polak, Regina/Hamachers-Zuber, Ursula (Hg.): Die Österreicher/-innen: Wertewandel 1990-2008. Czernin Verlag, Wien.

Biffl, Gudrun (2009): Wo Gleichstellungspolitik an ihre Grenzen stößt: Geschlechtersegregierte Arbeitsmärkte. In: Appelt, Erna (Hg): Gleichstellungspolitik in Österreich - eine kritische Bilanz. Studien Verlag, Innsbruck/Wien/Bozen.

Biffl, Gudrun (2010): Sprache und Bildung im Migrationskontext. In: Muhr, Rudolf/Biffl, Gudrun (Hg.): Sprache – Bildung – Bildungsstandards – Migration Verlag Peter Lang, Frankfurt/Main

Biffl, Gudrun (2010): Die ökonomische Situation der Frauen in Österreich. Teilbericht zum Frauenbericht 2010. In Bundeskanzleramt Österreich (Hg.): Frauenbericht 2010. BKA, Wien.

Biffl, Gudrun (2010): Workers rights and economic freedoms. In: Marterbauer, Markus/Mayerhuber; Christine (Hg.): Entwürfe für die Zukunft von Wirtschafts- und Sozialpolitik. LexisNexis ARD Orac, Wien.

Biffl, Gudrun (2010): Gibt es das bedarfsgerechte Zuwanderungsmodell? In: Bundesministerium für Inneres (Hg.): Asyl – Migration – Integration. Neuer Wissenschaftlicher Verlag, Wien, Graz.

Biffl, Gudrun (2010): Basisbildung. In: Rath, Otto (Hrg.): Zwischenbilanz – Die Basisbildung in Österreich in Theorie und Praxis. Verlag Isop Gmbh.

Biffl, Gudrun (2010): Kleinräumige Organisation der sozialen Dienste – Kinderbetreuung, Pflege, Weiterbildung. In: Bauer, Helfried/Pitlik, Hans/Schratzenstaller, Margit (Hg.): Demografischer Strukturwandel als Herausforderung für die öffentlichen Finanzen. Neuer Wissenschaftlicher Verlag, Wien, Graz.

Biffl, Gudrun (2010): Was bedeutet Armut in unserer Gesellschaft?. In: Sporschill, Georg (Hg.): Der Donauraum, Verlag Böhlau, Wien.

Biffl, Gudrun (2010): Integration auf dem Arbeitsmarkt in Wien. In: ÖIF (2010) Integration im Fokus. ÖIF, Wien.

Biffl, Gudrun (2010): Wirtschaftskrisen in der Vergangenheit und ihre Wirkungen auf MigrantInnen in Österreich. In: Oberlechner, Manfred/Hetfleisch, Gerhard (Hg.): Integration, Rassismen und Weltwirtschaftskrise. Verlag Braumüller, Wien.

Biffl, Gudrun (2010): Jugendliche MigrantInnen auf dem Tiroler Arbeitsmarkt. In: Oberlechner, Manfred/Hetfleisch, Gerhard (Hg.): Integration, Rassismen und Weltwirtschaftskrise. Verlag Braumüller, Wien.

Biffl, Gudrun (2010): Rationale und irrationale Aspekte der Integrationsdebatte. In: Biffl, Gudrun (Hg.): Migration & Integration. omninum, Bad Vöslau.

Biffl, Gudrun (2010): Wirtschaftskrisen in der Vergangenheit und ihre Wirkung. In: Biffl, Gudrun (Hg.): Migration & Integration. omninum, Bad Vöslau.

Biffl, Gudrun (2010): Gewerkschaften und Zuwanderung in Österreich. In: Biffl, Gudrun (Hg.): Migration & Integration. omninum, Bad Vöslau.

Biffl, Gudrun (2011): Die Rolle der Sprache in der Evaluationsforschung. In: Biffl, Gudrun/Rössl, Lydia (Hg.): Migration & Integration 2. omninum, Bad Vöslau.

Biffl, Gudrun (2011): Von der Generationenbilanz zu nationalen Transferkonten: Implikationen für die Politik. In: Biffl, Gudrun/Rössl, Lydia (Hg.): Migration & Integration 2. omninum, Bad Vöslau.

Biffl, Gudrun (2011): Bestimmungsfaktoren für Migrationen aus theoretischer Sicht der Ökonomie. In: Biffl, Gudrun/Dimmel, Nikolaus (Hg.): Migrationsmanagement Band 1. omninum, Bad Vöslau.

Biffl, Gudrun (2011): Entwicklung der Migrationen in Österreich aus historischer Perspektive. In: Biffl, Gudrun/Dimmel, Nikolaus (Hg.): Migrationsmanagement Band 1. omninum, Bad Vöslau.

Biffl, Gudrun (2011): Integration und Identitätsfindung. In: Biffl, Gudrun/Dimmel, Nikolaus (Hg.): Migrationsmanagement Band 1. omninum, Bad Vöslau.

Biffl, Gudrun (2011): Gewerkschaften und Zuwanderung in Österreich: MigrantInnen als neue Zielgruppe? In: Biffl, Gudrun/Dimmel, Nikolaus (Hg.): Migrationsmanagement Band 1. omninum, Bad Vöslau.

Biffl, Gudrun (2012): Migration in Europe and Undocumented Migrants. In: Biffl, Gudrun/Altenburg, Friedrich (Hg.): Migration and Health in Nowhereland - Access of Undocumented Migrants to Work and Health Care in Europe. omninum, Bad Vöslau.

Biffl, Gudrun (2012): Definitions and Methods of Estimation of Undocumented Migrants. In: Biffl, Gudrun/Altenburg, Friedrich (Hg.): Migration and Health in Nowhereland - Access of Undocumented Migrants to Work and Health Care in Europe. omninum, Bad Vöslau.

Biffl, Gudrun (2012): Sources of Irregularity: The Social Construction of Irregular Migration. In: Biffl, Gudrun/Altenburg, Friedrich (Hg.): Migration and Health in Nowhereland - Access of Undocumented Migrants to Work and Health Care in Europe. omninum, Bad Vöslau.

Biffl, Gudrun (2012): Access to Health Care in the European Union. In: Biffl, Gudrun/Altenburg, Friedrich (Hg.): Migration and Health in Nowhereland - Access of Undocumented Migrants to Work and Health Care in Europe. omninum, Bad Vöslau.

Altenburg, Friedrich/Biffl, Gudrun (2012): Good Practice Examples of Health Care Provision for UDMs. In: Biffl, Gudrun/Altenburg, Friedrich (Hg.): Migration and Health in Nowhereland - Access of Undocumented Migrants to Work and Health Care in Europe. omninum, Bad Vöslau.

Altenburg, Friedrich/Biffl, Gudrun (2012): The Voices of Undocumented Migrants. In: Biffl, Gudrun/Altenburg, Friedrich (Hg.): Migration and Health in Nowhereland - Access of Undocumented Migrants to Work and Health Care in Europe. omninum, Bad Vöslau.

Biffl, Gudrun/Pfeffer, Thomas (2013): Recognition of qualifications of citizens of another EU Member State. In: Staatssekretariat für Integration (Hg.): Europe on the move – Participation and Integration of EU-citizens. Wien.

Biffl, Gudrun/Bock-Schappelwein, Julia (2013): Zur Niederlassung von Ausländerinnen und Ausländern in Österreich. Expertise zur Niederlassungsverordnung 2014. In: BMI (Hg.): Expertisen zur Niederlassung von Ausländern in Österreich. BMI, Wien.

Biffl, Gudrun (2013): Regionale Konzentration von Personen mit Migrationshintergrund in Österreich: Zahlen, Daten, Fakten und Herausforderungen. In: Biffl, Gudrun/Berger, Tania/Czerny, Margarethe (Hg.): Wohnen und die regionale Dimension der Integration. Edition Donau-Universität Krems, Krems.

Biffl, Gudrun (2013): Country Case Study Austria. In: Urso, Guliana/Schuster, Anke (Hg.) Migration, Employment and Labour Market Integration Policies in the European Union International Organization for Migration, Regional Office for EU, EEA and NATO, Brussels.

Biffl, Gudrun (2014): The economic situation of women in the European Union. In: BMASK (Hg.): Old-age pensions for women. Entitlement and poverty avoidance. BMASK, Wien.

Biffl, Gudrun. (2014): Patchwork Identität und Suche nach Sinnfindung – Implikationen für das Bildungssystem. In: Gudrun Biffl/Lydia Rössl (Hg.): Migration & Integration 4. Guthmann-Peterson, Wien.

Biffl, Gudrun. (2014) Armut und die Frage der "Working Poor". In: Gudrun Biffl/Lydia Rössl (Hg.): Migration & Integration 4. Guthmann- Peterson, Wien.

Biffl, Gudrun/Jakopitsch, Bettina (2014): Angstfreies Wohnumfeld. Internationale Erfahrungen und Wien. In: Sir Peter Ustinov Institut (Hg.): Ressentiment und Konflikt. Vorurteile und Feindbilder im Wandel. Wochenschau Verlag, Wien.

Biffl, Gudrun. (2014): Schutz vor Diskriminierung in der Einwanderungsgesellschaft am Beispiel Arbeitsmarkt. In: Sir Peter Ustinov Institut, Ressentiment und Konflikt. Vorurteile und Feindbilder im Wandel. Wochenschau Verlag, Wien.

Biffl, Gudrun et al. (2014): Effizienz und Effektivität sozial- und wohlfahrtsstaaatlicher Transferleistungen. In: Dimmel, Nikolaus/Schrenk, Martin/Stelzer-Orthofer, Christine, Handbuch Armut in Österreich. StudienVerlag, Innsbruck, Wien, Bozen.

Biffl, Gudrun/Zentner, Manfred (2014): Soziale Netzwerke und ihr Einfluss auf Bildungs- und Berufsentscheidungen. In: Gudrun Biffl/Lydia Rössl (Hg.): Migration & Integration 5. omninum, Bad Vöslau.

Biffl, Gudrun (2014): Intra-EU Migration: Issues and Realities. In: Gudrun Biffl/Lydia Rössl (Hg.): Migration & Integration 5. omninum, Bad Vöslau.

Biffl, Gudrun. (2014) Universitärer Diskurs zum "Guten Leben". In: NÖ Forschungs- und Bildungsges.m.b.H und Donau-Universität Krems (H.g.): Die Krise und das Gute Leben: Edition Donau-Universität Krems, Krems.

Biffl, Gudrun (2014): Gute Arbeit auf globalisierten Arbeitsmärkten. In: NÖ Forschungs- und Bildungsges.m.b.H und Donau-Universität Krems (Hg.): Die Krise und das Gute Leben. Tagungsband zum Symposion Dürnstein: Edition Donau-Universität Krems, Krems.

Skrivanek, Isabella/Biffl Gudrun (2014): Sozio-ökonomische Situation der muslimischen Bevölkerung in Niederösterreich. In: Fürlinger, Ernst (Hg.): Muslimische Vielfalt in Niederösterreich. Edition Donau-Universität Krems, Krems.

Biffl, Gudrun (2015): Maschinen und ihre Rolle in der Neugestaltung der Arbeit und Gesellschaft.. In: NÖ Forschungs- und Bildungsges.m.b.H und Donau-Universität Krems (Hg.): Glücksbilder. Die Wirklichkeit der Utopien. Edition Donau-Universität Krems, Krems.

Biffl, Gudrun (2016): Verunsicherung durch Migration. In: NÖ Forschungs- und Bildungsges.m.b.H und Donau-Universität Krems (Hg.): Vertrauen in unsicheren Zeiten. Optionen für die Zukunft. Edition Donau-Universität Krems, Krems.

Biffl, Gudrun (2016): Wachstumschancen durch regionale Spezialisierung. In: Milford, Susan/Weber, Viktoria (Hg.): Der Donauraum. Möglichkeiten und Grenzen der EU-Strategie für den Donauraum. Böhlau, Wien Köln Weimar.

Biffl, Gudrun/Skrivanek, Isabella (2016): The Distinction Between Temporary Labour Migration and Posted Work in Austria: Labour Law Versus Trade Law. In: Howe Joanna/Owens, Rosemary (Hg.): Temporary Labour Migration in the Global Era. The Regulatory Challenges. Hart Publishing, Onati International Series in Law and Society. Bloomsbury, Oxford.

Biffl Gudrun (2016): Migration und die Vielfalt der Kulturen. In: Biffl Gudrun/Stepan Dorothea (Hg.) Europa und Demokratien im Wandel. Edition Donau-Universität Krems, 2016.

Biffl, Gudrun (2016): Urbanisierung und Landflucht: Zwei Gesichter eines Phänomens. In: Biffl, Gudrun/Dimmel, Nikolaus (Hg.): Migrationsmanagement 2. Wohnen im Zusammenwirken mit Migration und Integration. omninum, Bad Vöslau.

Biffl, Gudrun/Pfeffer, Thomas/Skrivanek, Isabella (2016): Zugänge und Verfahren zur Anerkennung von im Ausland erworbenen Qualifikationen und Kompetenzen. In: Kirilova, Sofia/Biffl, Gudrun et al. (Hg): Anerkennung von im Ausland erworbenen Qualifikationen in Österreich - eine theoretische und empirische Auseinandersetzung. ÖIF-Forschungsbericht, Österreichischer Integrationsfonds, Wien.

Biffl, Gudrun (2017): Migrationen und Entwicklungspolitik. In: Bayer, Kurt/Giner-Reichl, Irene (Hg.): Entwicklungspolitik 2030. Auf dem Weg zur Nachhaltigkeit. Manz'sche Verlags und Universitätsbuchhandlung GmbH, Wien, Budapest.

Biffl, Gudrun (forthcoming) Economics and Migration. In: Inglis, Christine (ed.) Sage Handbook of International Migration. Sage, New York.

Artikel in nationalen und internationalen begutachteten Journalen

Biffl, Gudrun (1978): Internationaler Vergleich der Arbeitslosenraten. Wirtschaftspolitische Blätter, 25(2).

Biffl, Gudrun (1979): Probleme der Saisonbereinigung am Beispiel der Arbeitslosigkeit in Österreich. Wirtschaftspolitische Blätter, 26(1).

Biffl, Gudrun (1980): Schwankung der Erwerbsbeteiligung im Konjunkturverlauf. Wirtschaftspolitische Blätter, 3/1980.

Biffl, Gudrun (1983): Jugendarbeitslosigkeit im Ausland und in Österreich das statistische Bild. Wirtschaftspolitische Blätter, 30(6).

Biffl, Gudrun (1985): Arbeitsmarktstatistik und Arbeitsmarktprognosen in den USA. Wirtschaftspolitische Blätter, 32(5).

Biffl, Gudrun (1985): Structural Shifts in the Employment of Foreign Workers in Austria. In: International Migration, Vol. XXIII(1): 45-72.

Biffl, Gudrun (1992): Bildung und Arbeitsmarkt", Wirtschaftspolitische Blätter, 40(2).

Biffl, Gudrun (1994): Eine nationale und eine internationale Arbeitslosenquote: Der Stein der Weisen? In: Österreichische Zeitschrift für Statistik und Informatik, 23(1), Wien.

Biffl, Gudrun (1996): Towards a Social Reproduction Model. In: Transfer, European Review of Labour and Research, Vol. 2(1):8-24.

Biffl, Gudrun (1996): Zur Wirtschaftslage: Der Arbeitsmarkt in Österreich - eine Herausforderung für Wirtschafts- und Arbeitsmarktpolitik. Wirtschaftspolitische Blätter, 43(1).

Biffl, Gudrun (1997): Der Arbeitsmarkt der Zukunft. Wirtschaftspolitische Blätter, 44(3-4).

Biffl, Gudrun (1998): Unemployment, Underemployment and Migration: A Challenge for Labour Market Policy in China. In: The Asia Pacific Journal of Economics and Business (APJEB), Vol. 2 (2).

Biffl, Gudrun (2000): Beschäftigungspolitik in Österreich vor dem Hintergrund einer Europäischen Beschäftigungspolitik. In: Österreichische Zeitschrift für Politikwissenschaft, 29(3):285-299.

Biffl, Gudrun (2000): Migracija i jejo rol b integracii zapatnou Ewropi (Migrationen und ihre Rolle in der europäischen Integration), Problemi, teorii i praktiki upravlenija (Theoretische und praktische Aspekte des Management), nr 4, Moskau (www.ptpu.ru).

Biffl, Gudrun (2001): Migration Policies and EU Enlargement. In: Intereconomics, Review of European Economic Policy, August 2001.

Biffl, Gudrun (2001): Coordination of Migration, Employment and Education policy in the EU-Labour market. In: The Journal of Contemporary Issues in Business and Government, Vol. 7 (2):47-60.

Biffl, Gudrun/Isaac, Joe (2002): Should Higher Education Students Pay Tuition Fees? In: European Journal of Education Vol. 37(4): 433-455.

Biffl, Gudrun (2004): Diversity of Welfare Systems in the EU: A Challenge to Policy Coordination. In: European Journal of Social Security, Volume 6/2.

Biffl, Gudrun/Isaac Koe (2005): Globalisation and Core Labour Standards: Compliance Problems with ILO Conventions 87 and 98. Comparing Australia and other English-Speaking Countries with EU Member States. In: The International Journal of Comparative Labour Law and Industrial Relations (IJCLLIR), Vol. 21 (3).

Biffl, Gudrun (2006): Towards a common migration policy: potential impact on the EU economy. In: Zeitschrift für Arbeitsmarktforschung/Journal of Labour Market Research, IAB-Nürnberg, ZAF 1/2006: 1-17.
Biffl, Gudrun (2006): The economic policy challenge of an ageing society: A comparison of Austria and Japan, Kyoto Journal of Law and Politics, Vol. 02(2):39-66.
Biffl, Gudrun (2006): Mehr Jobs und bessere Einkommenschancen für Frauen: Eine gesellschaftspolitische Herausforderung für Österreich. WISO 2/2006:89.
Biffl, Gudrun (2007): Weiterbildung und Lebensbegleitendes Lernen. Wirtschaft und Gesellschaft Nr. 102, Hrsg. Abteilung Wirtschaftswissenschaft und Statistik der Kammer für Arbeiter und Angestellte für Wien.
Biffl, Gudrun (2007): Erwachsenenbildung – Schlüssel für die Erhaltung der Wettbewerbsfähigkeit Österreichs. online-magazin erwachsenenbildung.at, Nr. 2/10/2007.
Biffl, Gudrun (2010): Arbeitsplatzsicherheit für Junge. In: Politicum 111, Verein für Politik und Zeitgeschichte, 2010
Biffl, Gudrun (2010): Der Weg zu Gender Mainstreaming führt über die Statistik. In Austrian Journal of Statistics Vol 39 2010, Bundesanstalt Statistik Österreich
Biffl, Gudrun (2012): Turkey and Europe: The role of migration and trade in economic development. Migration letters, volume 9, Number 1, January 2012, pp 47-63.
Biffl, Gudrun (2013): The role of migration in economic relations between Europe and Turkey. European review, Cambridge University Press, Volume 21 / Issue 03 / July 2013, pp 372-381
Biffl, Gudrun/Zentner, Manfred (2013): Jugend und ihre Lebenswelten. In: politicum 116 Jugend und Arbeitsmarkt, 34. Jahrgang: S. 13-18.
Biffl, Gudrun/Pfeffer, Thomas (2013): Recognition of Qualifications of Citizens of another EU Member State. In: FEANI News - The European Engineers Publication, Issue 11 June 2013: S. 19-26.
Biffl, Gudrun (2014): Case Study: Independent migration commissions in Europe: The case of Austria. In: Migration letters, volume 11 issue 1: S. 43-53.
Biffl, Gudrun (2014): Le travail, c'est permis. In: Alternatives Internationales, No. 62: S. 31-32.
Biffl, Gudrun (2016): Chancen und Risiken der Flüchtlingszuwanderung für die Wirtschaft. In: WISO - Wirtschafts- und Sozialpolitische Zeitschrift des ESW, 39(3): S. 107-122.
Biffl, Gudrun (2016): Auf dem Weg zu einer nachhaltigen Migrationspolitik. In: Wirtschaftspolitische Blätter 3/2016
Biffl, Gudrun (2016): Migration und Herausforderung von heute. Österreichische Zeitschrift für das Ärztliche Gutachten (DAG) Nr5/2016. Manz Verlag.
Biffl, Gudrun: (2017) Daten und Fakten zur Flüchtlingszuwanderung: Herausforderungen für das Erwachsenen-Bildungssystem und Erwerbssystem. In: Magazin erwachsenenbildung.at. Das Fachmedium für Forschung, Praxis und Diskurs. Ausgabe 31, 2017: 03-1 bis 03-14.

Studien und Forschungsberichte im Rahmen der Tätigkeit am Wirtschaftsforschungsinstitut Österreich (WIFO)

Biffl, Gudrun (1977): Der Einfluss der Konjunktur auf die Struktur der Arbeitslosigkeit in Österreich. WIFO-Monatsberichte, 1977, 50(2).
Biffl, Gudrun (1978): Der österreichische Arbeitsmarkt bis 1991. Revision der mittelfristigen Arbeits-marktprognose, WIFO-Monatsberichte, 1978, 51(2).
Biffl, Gudrun (1979): Die Entwicklung der Erwerbsbeteiligung unter veränderten Arbeitsmarktbedingungen. WIFO-Monatsberichte, 1979, 52(11).
Biffl, Gudrun (1980): Analyse der Bewegungen auf dem Arbeitsmarkt. WIFO-Monatsberichte, 1980, 53(11).
Biffl, Gudrun (1984): Der Strukturwandel der Ausländerbeschäftigung in Österreich. WIFO-Monatsberichte, 1984, 57(11-12).
Biffl, Gudrun (1985): Die Entwicklung der Ausländerbeschäftigung in den wichtigsten europäischen Industriestaaten. WIFO-Monatsberichte, 1985, 58(8).

Biffl, Gudrun (1985): Aspekte des Strukturwandels der Arbeitslosigkeit in Österreich. WIFO-Monatsberichte, 1985, 58(12).

Biffl, Gudrun (1986): Unterschiedliche Entwicklung der Arbeitslosigkeit in Österreich und in der BRD. WIFO-Monatsberichte, 1986, 59(4).

Biffl, Gudrun (1986): Auf dem Weg zu einer Arbeitskräftegesamtrechnung in Österreich. WIFO-Monatsberichte, 1986, 59(11).

Biffl, Gudrun (1986): Some Reasons for Low Unemployment in Austria, WIFO Working Papers, 1986, (19).

Biffl, Gudrun (1988): Der Wandel im Erwerbsverhalten in Österreich und im Ausland. WIFO-Monatsberichte, 1988, 61(1).

Biffl, Gudrun (1988): Entwicklung auf dem Arbeitsmarkt bis zum Jahr 2000. WIFO-Monatsberichte, 1988, 61(2).

Biffl, Gudrun (1988): Schwerpunkte der Arbeitsmarktpolitik in den achtziger Jahren. WIFO-Monatsberichte, 1988, 61(10).

Biffl, Gudrun (1989): Schwerpunkte der Arbeitsmarktentwicklung in den achtziger Jahren. WIFO-Monatsberichte, 1989, 62(3).

Biffl, Gudrun (1989): Der Haushaltssektor, Der volkswirtschaftliche Wert der unbezahlten Arbeit. WIFO-Monatsberichte, 1989, 62(9).

Biffl, Gudrun (1990): Konjunktur und Arbeitsmarkt was hat sich geändert? WIFO-Monatsberichte, 1990, 63(4)

Biffl, Gudrun (1990): Wandel der Ausländerpolitik als Folge der Öffnung Osteuropas. WIFO-Monatsberichte, 1990, 63(10).

Biffl, Gudrun (1991): Beschäftigung und Bildung im Wandel", WIFO-Monatsberichte, 1991, 64(6).

Biffl, Gudrun (1991): Betriebsinterne und externe Arbeitsmärkte in Österreich. WIFO-Monatsberichte, 1991, 64(7).

Biffl, Gudrun (1991): Women in Austria: Their Work in the Labour Market and in the Household, WIFO Working Papers, 1991, (42).

Biffl, Gudrun (1991): Employment of Foreign Workers in Austria, From the Sixties to the End of the Eighties, Special Report for the OECD, WIFO-Gutachtenserie.

Biffl, Gudrun (1992): Auswirkungen des Ausländerzustroms auf den Arbeitsmarkt. WIFO-Monatsberichte, 1992, 65(10).

Biffl, Gudrun (1993): Arbeitsvermittlung im internationalen Vergleich", WIFO-Monatsberichte, 1993, 66(9).

Biffl, Gudrun (1993): Restructuring of Some Western Australian Industries, WIFO Working Papers, 1993, (59).

Biffl, Gudrun (1994): Beschäftigungspolitische Empfehlungen der OECD und der EU aus österreichischer Sicht", WIFO-Monatsberichte, 1994, 67(9).

Biffl, Gudrun (1995): Jugendliche: Berufsqualifikation und Arbeitsmarkt, WIFO Working Papers, 1995, (74).

Biffl, Gudrun/Pollan Wolfgang (1995): The Austrian Labor Market. Analysis - Institutions Regulations – Policies. WIFO Working Papers, 1995, (75.

Biffl, Gudrun (1996): Entwicklung der Langzeitarbeitslosigkeit in Österreich und Maßnahmen zu ihrer Bekämpfung", WIFO-Monatsberichte, 1996, 69(1).

Biffl, Gudrun (1996): Ausbildung und Erwerbstätigkeit der Frauen in Österreich, WIFO Working Papers,1996, (87).

Biffl, Gudrun (1997): Erfassung der 'wahren' Arbeitslosigkeit in Österreich. WIFO-Monatsberichte, 1997, 70(1).

Biffl, Gudrun (1997): A National and an International Unemployment rate in Austria. WIFO, Austrian Economic Quarterly, 1997, 2(1).

Biffl, Gudrun (1997): Die Zuwanderung von Ausländern nach Österreich, Kosten-Nutzen-Überlegungen und Fragen der Sozialtransfers. WIFO-Monatsberichte, 1997, 70(9).

Biffl, Gudrun (1998): Unemployment, Underemployment and Migration A Challenge for Labour Market Policy in China. WIFO-Working Papers, 1998, (101).
Biffl, Gudrun (1998): Placement Activities in Austria Before and After Deregulation. WIFO Working Papers, 1998, (103).
Biffl, Gudrun (1998): Langfristige Prognose des Arbeitskräfteangebotes. Vorausschätzung 1996/2030 und Modellrechnung bis 2050 nach Bundesländern", WIFO-Monatsberichte, 1998, 71(6).
Biffl, Gudrun (1998): The Impact of Demographic Changes on Labour Supply in the EU. Austrian Economic Quarterly, 1998, 3(4).
Biffl, Gudrun (1999): Migrationen und ihre Rolle in der Integration Westeuropas. WIFO-Monatsberichte, 1999, 72(7).
Biffl, Gudrun (1999): Der Krankenstand in Österreich und sein Effekt auf das Arbeitsvolumen. WIFO Working Papers, 1999, (124).
Biffl, Gudrun (1999): Insider und Outsider, Inländer und Ausländer: Wo sind die Grenzen? WIFO Working Papers, 1999, (125).
Biffl, Gudrun (2000): Deregulation of Placement Services: The Case of Austria. Austrian Economic Quarterly, 2000, 5(1).
Biffl, Gudrun (2000): Der Arbeitsmarkt der Akademiker im Wandel: Implikationen für das Finanzierungssystem der Universitätsausbildung. WIFO-Monatsberichte, 2000, 73(2).
Biffl, Gudrun (2000): Die Entwicklung des Arbeitsvolumens und der Arbeitsproduktivität nach Branchen, WIFO Working Papers, 2000, (136).
Biffl, Gudrun (2001): Die Entwicklung des Arbeitsvolumens und der Arbeitsproduktivität nach Branchen, WIFO-Monatsberichte, 2001, 74(1).
Biffl, Gudrun (2001): The Development of Annual Working Hours and Labour Productivity by Industries, Austrian Economic Quarterly, 2001, 6(2).
Biffl, Gudrun (2001): Innovation and Employment in Europe in the 1990s. WIFO Working Papers, 2001, (169).
Biffl, Gudrun/Isaac Joe (2001): Should Higher Education Students pay Tuition Fees? WIFO Working Papers, 2001, (172).
Biffl, Gudrun (2002): Der Krankenstand als wichtiger Arbeitsmarktindikator. WIFO-Monatsberichte, 2002, 75(1).
Biffl, Gudrun (2002): Kosten und Nutzen des Bildungssystems im internationalen Vergleich. WIFO-Monatsberichte, 2002, 75(6).
Biffl, Gudrun (2002): Die Kosten des österreichischen Bildungssystems und der Wert der Ausbildung. WIFO-Monatsberichte, 2002, 75(6).
Biffl, Gudrun (2002): Der Bildungswandel in Österreich in den neunziger Jahren. WIFO-Monatsberichte, 2002, 75(6).
Biffl, Gudrun (2002): Ausländische Arbeitskräfte auf dem österreichischen Arbeitsmarkt. WIFO-Monatsberichte, 2002, 75(8).
Biffl, Gudrun/Isaac, Joe (2002): How Effective are the ILO's Labour Standards under Globalisation? WIFO Working Papers, 2002, (178).
Biffl, Gudrun (2002): Reorganisation of Employees' Legal Protection. Cause and Effect of Flexible Employment Relationships in the Labour Market. WIFO Working Papers, 2002, (189).
Biffl, Gudrun (2002): Labour Statistics Towards Enlargement. Labour Market Flexibility: The Role of the Informal Sector in the Context of EU Enlargement and the Need for a Systematic Statistical Base. WIFO Working Papers, 2002, (190).
Biffl, Gudrun (2002): Die Rolle zivilgesellschaftlicher Institutionen und des Gender Mainstreaming bei der Bekämpfung von sozial- und gesellschaftspolitischer Benachteiligung. WIFO Working Papers, 2002, (191).
Biffl, Gudrun (2003): Implikationen eines Freiwilligenheeres für den österreichischen Arbeitsmarkt. WIFO-Monatsberichte, 2002, 76(1).
Biffl, Gudrun (2003): The Household Labour Supply and the Labour Market of the Future. WIFO Working Papers, 2003, (193).

Biffl, Gudrun (2003): The Role of Migrants in the Production of Tradeables and Non-tradeables. The Case of Austria. WIFO Working Papers, 2003, (194).

Biffl, Gudrun (2003): Fördersysteme der Universitätsausbildung und Mobilität der Studierenden in Europa. WIFO-Monatsberichte, 2003, 76(6).

Biffl, Gudrun et al. (2003): Strukturpolitische Herausforderungen für das Waldviertel aus der EU-Erweiterung. WIFO-Monatsberichte, 2003, 76(8).

Biffl, Gudrun (2003): Socio-Economic Determinants of Health and Identification of Vulnerable Groups in the Context of Migration: The Case of Austria. WIFO Working Papers, 2003, (206.)

Biffl, Gudrun (2003): Diversity of Welfare Systems in the EU: A Challenge for Policy Coordination. WIFO Working Papers, 2003, (207).

Biffl, Gudrun (2003): Distribution of Household Income in Austria. WIFO Working Papers, 2003, (214).

Biffl, Gudrun (2004): Health and Employment Status. The Case of Austria. WIFO Working Papers, 2004, (219).

Biffl, Gudrun (2004): Increasing University Student Mobility: A European Policy Agenda. Austrian Economic Quarterly, 2004, 9(2).

Biffl, Gudrun (2005): The Socio-Economic Background of Health in Austria. With Special Emphasis on the Role of the Employment Status. Austrian Economic Quarterly, 2005 10(1).

Biffl, Gudrun (2005): Immigration: The Potential Impact on EU Society. WIFO Working Papers, 2005, (253)

Biffl, Gudrun (2005): Verschärfung der Arbeitsmarktprobleme von Randgruppen in Grenzregionen im Gefolge der Ostöffnung. Das Beispiel der Roma in Oberwart. WIFO-Monatsberichte, 2005, (78)2.

Biffl, Gudrun (2005): Sustaining Employment of Older Workers in an Ageing Society. WIFO Working Papers, 2005, (256).

Biffl, Gudrun (2006): Teilstudie 6: Bevölkerungsentwicklung und Migration, Teilstudie 16: Alternde Dienstleistungsgesellschaft, in: Aiginger Karl/Tichy, Gunther/Walterskirchen, Ewald (Projektleitung und Koordination): WIFO-Weißbuch: Mehr Beschäftigung durch Wachstum auf Basis von Innovation und Qualifikation, WIFO-Gutachtenserie, Wien.

Biffl, Gudrun (2006): Entwicklung des Arbeitskräfteangebotes in Österreich bis 2025. WIFO-Gutachtenserie, Wien.

Biffl, Gudrun (2006): Age Management – a Coping Strategy for Employers. The Case of the Automotive Industry. WIFO Working Papers 2006, (274).

Biffl, Gudrun (2006): Gender and the Labour Market: Comparing Austria and Japan. WIFO Working Papers 2006, (279).

Biffl, Gudrun et al. (2006): Auswirkungen der Übergangsregelungen im Bereich der Freizügigkeit und der Dienstleistungsfreiheit. WIFO-Studie im Auftrag des BMWA.

Biffl, Gudrun (2007): Auf dem Weg zu Gender Monitoring / Budgeting an der Akademie der Bildenden Künste in Wien. WIFO-Studie.

Biffl, Gudrun/Guger Alois/Leoni, Thomas (2007): Fehlzeitenreport 2007. WIFO-Monographie, Wien.

Biffl, Gudrun (2007): Sozialhilfe, Armut und Arbeitslosigkeit. WIFO- Monatsberichte, 2007, 80,(9).

Biffl, Gudrun (2008): Das Besoldungssystem der Pharmazeutischen Gehaltskasse und ihr Wirkungs-mechanismus, WIFO-Studie im Auftrag der Pharmazeutischen Gehaltskasse, Wien.

Biffl, Gudrun (2008): Auf dem Weg zu Gender Monitoring und Gender Budgeting an der Akademie der Bildenden Künste in Wien. WIFO-Monographie, 2008.

Biffl, Gudrun (2008): Verteilung der Haushaltseinkommen aus einer Gender Perspektive. WIFO-Monatsberichte, 2008, 81(10).

Biffl, Gudrun (2008): Bildung und Arbeitsmarkt aus ökonomischer Sicht. WIFO-Vorträge, 2008, (103).

Biffl, Gudrun (2008): The Promotion of Employment and Earning Opportunity of Women in Europe through Gender Mainstreaming. With Special Emphasis on Austria. WIFO Working Papers, 2008, (319).

Biffl, Gudrun (2008): Migrant Women and Youth: The Challenge of Labour Market Integration. WIFO Working Papers, 2008, (320).

Biffl, Gudrun (2008): Family Policy in Austria in Comparison: How to Reach Sustainability? WIFO Working Papers, 2008, (331).

Biffl, Gudrun/Leoni, Thomas (2008): Arbeitsbedingte Erkrankungen: Schätzung der gesamtwirtschaftlichen Kosten mit dem Schwerpunkt auf physischen Belastungen. WIFO-Monographie, Wien.

Biffl, Gudrun/Leoni, Thomas/Mayrhuber, Christine (2009): Arbeitsbelastungen, arbeitsbedingte Krankheiten und Invalidität. WIFO-Monographie, Wien.

Studien und Forschungsberichte im Rahmen der Schriftenreihe Migration und Globalisierung, Edition Donau-Universität Krems

Biffl, Gudrun (2009): ENTER – Adult Educational Development for Migrants and Ethnic Minorities. Project report, funded by the European Commission as part of the Grundtvig Lifelong Learning Programme. Monograph Series Migration and Globalization, Krems (Edition Donau-Universität Krems).

Biffl, Gudrun (2010): Impact of Migration on Employment in Austria and the role of integration policies (2000-2009). Draft-Report of the National Expert to the IOM Independent Network of Labour Migration & Integration Experts (LMIE-INET). Monograph Series Migration and Globalization, Krems (Edition Donau-Universität Krems).

Biffl, Gudrun/Aigner, Petra/Rössl, Lydia/Skrivanek, Isabella (2010): Vielfalt schätzen. Vielfalt nutzen! Analyse zu bestehenden Beratungs-/ Unterstützungs- und Projektangeboten in der Modellregion Linz/ Linz Land und Wels, und zu den bestehenden Arbeitsbeziehungen und Handlungsoptionen für die Integrationsarbeit in Oberösterreich. Studie im Auftrag von „Projekt Vielfalt schätzen. Vielfalt nutzen!". Schriftenreihe Migration und Globalisierung, Krems (Edition Donau-Universität Krems).

Biffl, Gudrun/Skrivanek, Isabella/Berger, Johannes/Hofer, Helmut/Schuh, Ulrich/Strohner, Ludwig (2011): Potentielle Auswirkungen einer Änderung der österreichischen Migrationspolitik in Richtung qualifizierte Zuwanderung auf das mittel- bis langfristige Wirtschaftswachstum. Studie im Auftrag der Wirtschaftskammer Österreich und der Industriellenvereinigung, durchgeführt vom Institut für Höhere Studien und vom Department für Migration und Globalisierung der Donau-Universität Krems. Schriftenreihe Migration und Globalisierung, Krems (Edition Donau-Universität Krems).

Biffl, Gudrun/Faustmann, Anna/Skrivanek, Isabella (2012): Frauen und die Wirtschaftskrise. Vernetzung sozialer Dienstleistungen als Antwort auf Konjunktur- und Strukturkrise in Wien. Studie im Auftrag der Arbeiterkammer Wien und des Österreichischen Gewerkschaftsbunds. Schriftenreihe Migration und Globalisierung (Edition Donau-Universität Krems).

Biffl, Gudrun (2011): Migration and Labour Integration in Austria. SOPEMI Report on Labour Migration Austria 2010-11. Report of the Austrian SOPEMI correspondent to the OECD. Monograph Series Migration and Globalisation, Krems (edition Donau-Universität Krems).

Biffl, Gudrun/Pfeffer, Thomas/Skrivanek, Isabella (2012): Anerkennung ausländischer Qualifikationen und informeller Kompetenzen in Österreich. Studie im Auftrag des Bundesministeriums für Inneres. Schriftenreihe Migration und Globalisierung, Krems (Edition Donau-Universität Krems).

Biffl, Gudrun/Faustmann, Anna/Rössl, Lydia/Skrivanek, Isabella (2012): STEPS_2 – begleitende Evaluierung. Schnittstelle Arbeitsmarkt. Studie im Auftrag der Steiermärkischen Landesregierung, der Stadt Graz und des AMS Steiermark. Schriftenreihe Migration und Globalisierung, Krems (Edition Donau-Universität Krems).

Biffl, Gudrun (2012): 2010-2011 Annual Monitoring Review on Migration, Employment and Labour Market Integration of Migrants and Research Question on Access to Labour Market Information - Austria. Report of the National Expert in Austria to the IOM Independent Network of Labour Migration & Integration Experts (LINET). Monograph Series Migration and Globalization, Krems (Edition Donau-Universität Krems).

Biffl, Gudrun (2012): Die Auswirkungen der Aussetzung der Wehrpflicht (Wehrersatzdienst-Zivildienst) auf den Arbeitsmarkt und die Organisation des Zivildienstes. Studie im Auftrag des Bundesministeriums für Landesverteidigung und Sport. Schriftenreihe Migration und Globalisierung, Krems (Edition Donau-Universität Krems).

Biffl, Gudrun (2012): Migration and Labour Integration in Austria. SOPEMI Report on Labour Migration Austria 2011-12. Report of the Austrian SOPEMI correspondent to the OECD. Monograph Series Migration and Globalisation, Krems (Edition Donau-Universität Krems).

Biffl, Gudrun/Pfeffer, Thomas/Skrivanek, Isabella (2012) Anerkennung ausländischer Qualifikationen und informeller Kompetenzen in Österreich. Studie im Auftrag des Bundesministeriums für Inneres. Schriftenreihe Migration und Globalisierung, Krems (Edition Donau-Universität Krems).

Biffl, Gudrun/Faustmann, Anna (2013): Österreichische Integrationspolitik im EU-Vergleich. Zur Aussagekraft von MIPEX. Studie im Auftrag des Bundesministeriums für Inneres. Schriftenreihe Migration und Globalisierung, Krems (Edition Donau-Universität Krems).

Biffl, Gudrun/ Pfeffer, Thomas/ Altenburg, Friedrich (2013): Diskriminierung in Rekrutierungsprozessen verstehen und überwinden. Studie finanziert von der Europäischen Kommission. Schriftenreihe Migration und Globalisierung, Krems (Edition Donau-Universität Krems).

Biffl, Gudrun (2013): Migration and Labour Integration in Austria. SOPEMI Report on Labour Migration Austria 2012-13. Report of the Austrian SOPEMI correspondent to the OECD. Monograph Series Migration and Globalisation, Krems (Edition Donau-Universität Krems).

Biffl, Gudrun, Schuh, Ulrich (2013) Machbarkeitsstudie zu einem Zuwanderungskonzept für Österreich. Erstellt von der Donau-Universität Krems in Kooperation mit EcoAustria - Institut für Wirtschaftsforschung, im Auftrag der Industriellenvereinigung. Schriftenreihe Migration und Globalisierung, Krems (Edition Donau-Universität Krems).

Biffl, Gudrun (2014) Migration and Labour Integration in Austria. SOPEMI Report on Labour Migration Austria 2013-14. Report of the Austrian SOPEMI correspondent to the OECD. Monograph Series Migration and Globalisation, Krems (Edition Donau-Universität Krems).

Biffl, Gudrun/Zentner, Manfred/Skrivanek, Isabella (2014) Der Einfluss sozialer Netzwerke auf die Bildungs- und Berufsentscheidungen von Jugendlichen mit Schwerpunkt auf Wien und Vorarlberg. Studie finanziert vom Bundesministerium für Europa, Integration und Äußeres und vom Bundesministerium für Familien und Jugend. Schriftenreihe Migration und Globalisierung, Krems (Edition Donau-Universität).

Biffl, Gudrun// Skrivanek, Isabella/ Berger, Johannes/ Schuh, Ulrich/ Strohner, Ludwig (2015) Volkswirtschaftliche Kosten-Nutzen-Kalkulation zur wirtschafts- und arbeitsmarktbezogenen Zu- und Rückwanderung in Oberösterreich. In: Donau-Universität Krems, Department für Migration und Globalisierung, Schriftenreihe Migration und Globalisierung, Edition Donau-Universität Krems, Krems.

Biffl, Gudrun/ Skrivanek, Isabella (2015) Jugendliche mit Migrationshintergrund in der Lehre. Strukturen, Barrieren, Potentiale. Studie finanziert von der Arbeiterkammer Wien. Studienreihe Migration und Globalisierung, Krems (Edition Donau-Universität Krems).

Biffl, Gudrun (2016): Migration and Labour Integration in Austria. SOPEMI Report on Labour Migration Austria 2014-15. Report of the Austrian SOPEMI correspondent to the OECD. Monograph Series Migration and Globalisation, Krems (Edition Donau-Universität Krems).

Biffl, Gudrun/ Berger, Johannes/ Graf, Nikolaus/ Pfeffer, Thomas/ Schuh, Ulrich/ Skrivanek, Isabella/ Strohner, Ludwig (2016): Österreichische Migrationspolitik: Vision und Entwicklung eines Migrations-Monitoring-Systems. Bericht des De-partments Migration und Globalisierung und von EcoAustria im Auftrag des Österreichischen Bundesministeriums für Inneres. Schriftenreihe Migration und Globalisierung, Krems (Edition Donau-Universität Krems).

Biffl, Gudrun/Berger Johannes/Graf, Nikolaus/Schuh, Ulrich/Strohner, Ludwig (2016): Ökonomische Analyse der Zuwanderung von Flüchtlingen nach Österreich. Studie im Auftrag der Wirtschaftskammer Österreich und des Bundesministeriums für Europa, Integration und Äußereres. Schriftenreihe Migration und Globalisierung, Krems (Edition Donau-Universität Krems).

Biffl, Gudrun (2016): Migration and Labour Integration in Austria. SOPEMI Report on Labour Migration, Austria 2015-16. Annual report, prepared by the Austrian correspondent of the Migration expert group (SOPEMI), OECD's reporting system on migration. Monograph Series Migration and Globalisation, Krems (Edition Donau-Universität Krems)

Biffl, Gudrun/Skrivanek, Isabella (2016): EMN FOCUSSED STUDY 2014. Admitting third country nationals for business purposes. Study commissioned by the European Migration Network. Monograph Series Migration and Globalisation, Krems (Edition Donau-Universität Krems).

Sonstige Studien und Forschungsberichte

Biffl, Gudrun (1985): Ausländische Arbeitskräfte in Österreich. In: Forschungsberichte aus Sozial- und Arbeitsmarktpolitik, BMfAS, Nr. 9.

Biffl, Gudrun (1985): Rechte der ausländischen Arbeitskräfte im In- und Ausland. In Forschungsberichte aus Sozial- und Arbeitsmarktpolitik, BMfAS, Nr. 9.

Biffl, Gudrun (1987): Verschiebungen der sektoralen, beruflichen und ausbildungsspezifischen Struktur der Arbeitskräfte in Österreich. In: Karl Aiginger (Koord.) Die internationale Wettbewerbs-fähigkeit Österreichs: Österreichische Strukturberichterstattung. Kernbericht 1986, Band III.

Biffl, Gudrun (1988): Arbeitsmarkt 2000, Vorausschau der Entwicklung am Arbeitsmarkt bis zum Jahr 2000, Forschungsbericht aus Sozial-und Arbeitsmarktpolitik, Nr. 21, BMfAS, Wien.

Biffl, Gudrun (1993): Employment Services: An International Perspective", Discussion Paper, 93/1, Western Australian Labour Market Research Centre, Curtin University of Technology, W.A.

Biffl, Gudrun (1994): Evaluierung von Instrumenten der experimentellen Arbeitsmarktpolitik, Gutachten für das BMfAS, WIFO-Gutachtenserie sowie AMS.

Biffl, Gudrun (1994): Migration and the Labour Market in Austria. In: Migration and Development, OECD, Paris.

Biffl, Gudrun (1997): Placement Activities in Austria before and after Deregulation. In: EU: Effects of Deregulation in Placement Activities in the EU.

Biffl, Gudrun (1999): Massenuniversität und Veränderungen im Beschäftigtensystem, Studie im Auftrag des Bundesministeriums für Wissenschaft und Verkehr.

Biffl, Gudrun (2001): Die österreichische Berufs- und Qualifikationslandschaft 2005, Analyse und Prognose vor dem Hintergrund der Entwicklung in den USA, AMS-Österreich.

Biffl, Gudrun (2002): Kosten-Nutzen-Analyse des Bildungssystems am Beispiel der Sekundarstufe II. Studie im Auftrag des Bundesministeriums für Bildung, Wissenschaft und Kultur.

Biffl, Gudrun (2002): Arbeitsmarktrelevante Effekte der Ausländerintegration in Österreich (Koordination), Studie im Auftrag des Bundesministeriums für Wirtschaft und Arbeit und des Bundesministeriums für Inneres.

Biffl, Gudrun (2003): Institutionelle Rahmenbedingungen an der Schnittstelle zwischen Arbeitsmarkt- und Sozialpolitik in der EU, Studie im Rahmen der EQUAL-Entwicklungspartnerschaft „Erweiterter Arbeitsmarkt – Integration durch Arbeit".

Biffl, Gudrun (2003): Entwicklung des Arbeitskräfteangebotes in Österreich bis 2025, WIFO-Gutachtenserie, Wien.

Biffl, Gudrun (2005): Ageing and Employment Policies: Austria. OECD, Paris.

Biffl, Gudrun (2005): Economic Conditions of Roma Women in Austria, in Economic Conditions of Roma Women in Europe, Report for the European Parliament, RMD 3 J 24/26, BIVS.

Biffl, Gudrun (2006): Bevölkerungsentwicklung und Migration, Teilstudie 6, und Alternde Dienstleistungsgesellschaft, Teilstudie 16. In: Aiginger, Kar/Tichy, Gunther,/Walterskirchen, Ewald (Projektleitung und Koordination): WIFO-Weißbuch: Mehr Beschäftigung durch Wachstum auf Basis von Innovation und Qualifikation, WIFO-Gutachtenserie, Wien.

Biffl, Gudrun (2006): Zur Qualität der Hochschulbildung und ihrer Messung. In: Qualitätssicherung im Hochschulbereich, Innovationen in der Hochschulbildung Nr.1, bm:bwk.

Biffl, Gudrun/Bock-Schappelwein, Julia/Leoni, Thomas (2006): Economic aspects of the condition of Roma Women", Berliner Institut für Verglei¬chende Sozialforschung (BIVS), Projectnumber: IP/C/FEMM/2005-09, Country Study Austria.

Biffl, Gudrun/Lassnigg, Lorenz (Koord.) (2007): Weiterbildung und Lebensbegleitendes Lernen: Vergleichende Analysen und Strategievorschläge für Österreich, Materialien zu Wirtschaft und Gesellschaft Nr. 102/2007.

Biffl, Gudrun (2007): Forschungsstandort Wien: Zur Rolle der Humanressourcen. Gutachten für die Stadt Wien (MA27), Wien.

Biffl, Gudrun et al. (2007): Evaluierung der Gleichstellung und Frauenförderung an österreichischen Universitäten. AQA (Österreichische Qualitäts-sicherungsagentur), Wien.

Biffl, Gudrun (2008): Migrant women and youth: the challenge of labour market integration, Thematic Review of the European Mutual Learning Programme Spring 2008.

Biffl, Gudrun (2008): Increasing labour supply by focusing on people at the margins of the labour market and youth, linked with the development of flexicurity policies, Synthesis Report Spring 2008 of the Mutual Learning Programme of the EC.

Biffl, Gudrun/Leoni, Thomas/Mayrhuber, Christine (2009): Arbeitsplatzbelastungen, arbeitsbedingte Krankheiten und Invalidität, Research Monograph, WIFO 2009

Biffl, Gudrun (2011): Deckung des Arbeitskräftebedarfs durch Migration in Österreich/Satisfying Labour Demand through Migration in Austria. Internationale Organisation für Migration Wien, Wien 2011

Biffl, Gudrun/Skrivanek, Isabella (2011): Schule-Migration-Gender. Studie des Departments Migration und Globalisierung der Donau Universität Krems im Auftrag des BMB.

Biffl, Gudrun/Faustmann, Anna et al. (2011): Psychische Belastungen der Arbeit und ihre Folgen.

Biffl, Gudrun et. al. (2011): Auswirkungen der Arbeitsmarktöffnung am 1. Mai auf den Wirtschafts- und Arbeitsstandort Österreich.

Biffl, Gudrun/Zentner, Manfred et al. (2016): Siebter Bericht zur Lage der Jugend in Österreich. Bundesministerium für Jugend und Familie (Hg.), Wien.